**Historical Dictionaries of Literature and the Arts**
**Jon Woronoff, Series Editor**

1. *Science Fiction Literature*, by Brian Stableford, 2004.
2. *Horror Literature*, by John Clute, 2004.

# Historical Dictionary of Science Fiction Literature

Brian Stableford

*Historical Dictionaries of Literature and the Arts, No. 1*

The Scarecrow Press, Inc.
Lanham, Maryland • Toronto • Oxford
2004

The Rowman & Littlefield Publishing Group, Inc.
4501 Forbes Boulevard, Suite 200, Lanham, Maryland 20706
www.scarecrowpress.com

PO Box 317
Oxford
OX2 9RU, UK



British Library Cataloguing in Publication Information Available

Library of Congress Cataloging-in-Publication Data

Stableford, Brian M.
Historical dictionary of science fiction literature / Brian Stableford.
p. cm. — (Historical dictionaries of literature and the arts ; no. 1)
Includes bibliographical references.
ISBN 0-8108-4938-0 (alk. paper)
1. Science fiction—Bio-bibliography—Dictionaries. I. Title. II. Series.
PN3433.4.S73 2004
809.3'762'03—dc22

2004002981

∞™ The paper used in this publication meets the minimum requirements of American National Standard for Information Sciences—Permanence of Paper for Printed Library Materials, ANSI/NISO Z39.48-1992.
Manufactured in the United States of America.

# Contents

# Foreword

It is a coincidence, but a felicitous one, that this *Historical Dictionary of Science Fiction Literature* should be the first volume in the new series on literature and the arts. Science fiction, also known as sci-fi or sf, is one of the most recent genres but it is also one of the most dynamic, growing out of isolated models in earlier centuries to become, over the latter half of the 20th century, a virtual industry with its specialized writers, its specialized publishers, its dedicated authors, and an amazingly faithful circle of fans. It is also a very vital sector, with many different types emerging and often combining, ranging from hard sf to soft sf, from Utopias to dystopias, with more than a smattering of horror, detective, war, and feminist titles. It even has pretensions that older genres cannot match, as authors try both to anticipate the future and to shape it. Although most of this is not "great" literature, a larger-than-usual share is at least gripping or amusing.

This volume covers all aspects of the genre and all types of works, from the very earliest days to the present, and it does not limit itself to the finer authors but includes hacks, who happen to proliferate in every genre although they are often easier to neglect elsewhere. It also takes a global view, certainly giving the United States its due, but not forgetting the significant roles of the United Kingdom, France, and other places. In the dictionary section, there are also entries on the more popular themes and literary practices, to say nothing of the magazines, fanzines, and publishers, without which this genre could never have achieved as much as it has, as fast as it has. The chronology shows just how fast this was. How much literature there actually is and how many studies exist on it can be gathered from the bibliography. The introduction, last but not least of the front matter, is essential to understanding what science fiction literature is all about.

Most of the books in this series will be written by academics. This volume was written by an academic who is a practitioner—or perhaps the other way around. At any rate, Brian Stableford is a part-time lecturer on creative writing at King Alfred's College, Winchester, U.K. He has also been a professional writer for nearly four decades, his writing consisting to a very large extent of sf novels and short stories as well as scholarly works and a how-to manual. Most relevant in this connection, he has also contributed numerous articles to periodicals and reference works. Now he has produced one of his own, which will certainly be welcome by sf fans who want to know who is who, who did what, and more generally what the literary context is. But it will also be very helpful for other readers and librarians, some rather new to the field, in answering questions they may already have and also giving them concise and informative answers to questions they have not yet formulated.

Jon Woronoff
Series Editor

# Acknowledgments

I thank all the authors who responded to my requests for biographical information, and the people who helped me track down their e-mail addresses, including David Pringle of *Interzone*, Ian Watson of the SFWA, and Tim Pratt of *Locus*. I am grateful to Michael M. Levy for reading the text with a critical eye, checking it for errors of fact and judgment.

# Acronyms and Abbreviations

| | |
|---|---|
| AI | A conventional contraction of artificial intelligence |
| aka | Also known as |
| APA | Amateur Press Association |
| BEM | A once-popular acronym signifying bug-eyed monster |
| BSFA | The British Science Fiction Association |
| Clute/ Nicholls *Encyclopedia* | *The Encyclopedia of Science Fiction* whose first edition was published in 1979 under Nicholls' by-line. It was considerably revised as well as updated for its second edition of 1992, jointly credited to John Clute and Peter Nicholls. |
| Con | A conventional contraction of *Convention* |
| ed | Edited by |
| ESP | A conventional contraction of extrasensory perception |
| ET | A popular contraction of extraterrestrial (as in SETI), more familiar in contexts where the full term is used as a noun than an adjective, when it becomes a synonym for alien |
| exp | Expanded version |
| fanzine | A conventional contraction of "fan magazine" |
| FAPA | The Fantasy Amateur Press Association |
| F&SF | The *Magazine of Fantasy and Science Fiction* |
| IAFA | The International Association for the Fantastic in the Arts |
| ICFA | The International Conference on the Fantastic in the Arts |
| ISFDB | The Internet Science Fiction Database |
| NASA | The North American Space Agency |

| | |
|---|---|
| NYRSF | The *New York Review of Science Fiction* |
| rev | Revised |
| RGP | *Rede Global Paraliterária* [Global Paraliterary Network]. See Spanish Science Fiction. |
| RPG | Role-playing game |
| SCI-FI | A contraction of "science fiction" |
| SETI | The Search for Extra-Terrestrial Intelligence |
| SF | The usual iconic abbreviation of "science fiction," whose initials are strategically redeployed in "speculative fiction" and "structural fabulation" |
| SFBC | The Science Fiction Book Club |
| SFF | The Science Fiction Foundation |
| SFOHA | The Science Fiction Oral History Association (see Lloyd Biggle) |
| SFPA | The Science Fiction Poetry Association (see Suzette Haden Elgin) |
| SFRA | The Science Fiction Research Association |
| SFWA | Originally the Science Fiction Writers of America, after 1992 the Science-Fiction and Fantasy Writers of America |
| stf | A relatively uncommon abbreviation of scientifiction |
| tr | Translated |
| TV | Television |
| UFO | An acronym signifying Unidentified Flying Object (see UFOlogy) |
| VR | Virtual reality |

# Chronology

**1726** Book 3 of Jonathan Swift's *Travels into Several Remote Nations of the World in Four Parts by Lemuel Gulliver* founds a fertile tradition of satirical antiscience fiction. (Earlier imaginary voyages, including numerous excursions to the moon, had paid relatively little attention to the exploits of scientists and the harvest of the scientific method.)

**1752** Voltaire's *Micromégas* employs extraterrestrial viewpoints in a definitive *conte philosophique*.

**1771** *L'an 2240* by Louis-Sebastien Mercier, the best-selling book of its era in France, offers the first image of a Utopian society situated in the future whose evolution has been enabled by technology. Luigi Galvani discovers the electrical activity of the nervous system, laying the imaginative groundwork for much sf.

**1775** James Watt and Matthew Boulton build the first modern steam engine. The American War of Independence begins.

**1778** The Comte du Buffon's *Époques de la nature* adds a new stimulus to evolutionary speculation. Friedrich Mesmer begins a new career in Paris.

**1783** The Montgolfier brothers' experiments with hot air balloons and Jouffroy d'Abbans's steamboat offer glimpses of a new era of transportation.

**1787** Charles Garnier's collection of *Voyages imaginaires, songes, visions, et romans cabalistiques* is launched; 36 volumes appear before its further extension is interrupted in 1789 by the French Revolution.

**1801** Robert Fulton constructs the first practical submarine in France before teaming up with Matthew Boulton and James Watt to build a steamboat.

**1808** John Dalton's *New System of Chemical Philosophy* popularizes his atomic theory.

**1814** George Stephenson builds an effective steam locomotive.

**1818** Mary Shelley's *Frankenstein* creates an important template for the sf thriller.

**1823** Charles Babbage begins constructing a calculating machine.

**1826** Mary Shelley's *The Last Man* imports science-fictional imagery into apocalyptic fantasy.

**1830** Humphry Davy's *Consolations in Travel: The Last Days of a Philosopher* broaches the notion of extraterrestrial reincarnation in bodies adapted for life in alien environments.

**1834** Félix Bodin's *Le roman d'avenir* discusses the potential scope of futuristic fiction.

**1836** Louis-Napoléon Geoffroy's *Napoleon apocryphe* introduces the alternative history subgenre. Samuel Morse builds his first telegraph.

**1840** Edgar Allan Poe's *Tales of the Grotesque and Arabesque* adds a new preface to "The Unparalleled Adventure of One Hans Pfaall" appealing (ironically) for "verisimilitude" in tales of lunar voyages.

**1846** Emil Souvestre's *Le monde tel qu'il sera* argues that technological progress might be injurious to the ideals of social progress.

**1848** Robert Hunt's *The Poetry of Science* popularizes the aesthetics of science. *The Communist Manifesto* is published. Poe's *Eureka* sets important precedents for cosmological fantasy.

**1851** William Wilson coins the term "science-fiction." The development of spectroscopy paves the way for wondrous astronomical revelations.

**1858** Fitz-James O'Brien's "The Diamond Lens" employs an optical instrument in a new kind of visionary fantasy.

**1859** Charles Darwin's *Origin of Species* lays the groundwork for new thought experiments in evolutionary philosophy.

**1861** Louis Pasteur revives the germ theory of disease.

**1862** Richard Gatling's machine gun offers significant insight into the shape of wars to come.

**1864** Jules Verne's *Voyage au centre de la terre* takes his *voyages extraordinaires* into the realms of sf. Camille Flammarion's *Les Mondes imaginaires et les mondes réels* provides the first historical study of interplanetary fiction.

**1866** Alfred Nobel invents dynamite.

**1868** Edward S. Ellis's *The Steam Man of the Prairies* adapts Vernian romance to the ideology of frontiersmanship and the medium of low-brow popular fiction. John Stuart Mill employs the term *dystopia*.

**1872** Flammarion's *Lumen* popularizes the notion of a universe filled with worlds inhabited by alien beings adapted to various physical environments.

**1878** Kurd Lasswitz's introduction to *Bilder aus der Zukunft* sets out a manifesto for modern speculative fiction.

**1879** Edward Page Mitchell's "The Ablest Man in the World" describes a cyborg with a computer for a brain.

**1880** Thomas Edison and J. W. Swan devise electric incandescent lamps, providing the means for a literal enlightenment of homes and cities.

**1882** Robert Duncan Milne's "Into the Sun" sets a precedent in catastrophist fantasy. Albert Robida begins his skeptical examination of *Le vingtième siècle*.

**1884** Edwin Abbott's *Flatland* champions the cause of lateral thinking.

**1885** Richard Jefferies's *After London* looks forward to a postindustrial pastoral golden age. Gottlieb Daimler invents the internal combustion engine.

**1886** C. H. Hinton's *Scientific Romances* helps to popularize a new generic term. Marie Corelli's *A Romance of Two Worlds* employs sf imagery to revitalize religious fantasy. Robert Louis Stevenson's *Strange Case of Dr. Jekyll and Mr. Hyde* mounts a significant psychological thought experiment. Richard Krafft-Ebing publishes *Psychopathia Sexualis*.

**1887** W. H. Hudson's *A Crystal Age* envisages an ecologically sophisticated mystical Utopia. Heinrich Hertz demonstrates the propagation of radio waves.

**1888** Edward Bellamy's *Looking Backward 2000–1887*, the best-selling book of its era in the United States, suggests that technological advancement will enhance the cause of evolutionary socialism. Walter Besant's *The Inner House* wonders whether human longevity might precipitate existential and cultural stagnation. Nikola Tesla invents an electric motor running on alternating current.

**1889** Mark Twain's *A Connecticut Yankee in King Arthur's Court* considers the social implications of rapid technological development.

**1890** Ignatius Donnelly's *Caesar's Column* argues that technological advancement will increase social divisions until it precipitates a ruinous revolution. William Morris's *News from Nowhere* suggests that the solution lies in the careful restraint of industrial technology.

**1893** George Griffith's *The Angel of the Revolution* popularizes future war fiction and lays the foundations for popular scientific romance.

**1894** Camille Flammarion's *La Fin du monde* juxtaposes anxieties about a catastrophic comet strike with speculations about the ultimate fate of the planet.

**1895** H. G. Wells's *The Time Machine* introduces a facilitating device to open up the past and future to speculative observation. Edgar Fawcett sets out a manifesto for "realistic romance" in the preface to *The Ghost of Guy Thyrle*. Wilhelm Röntgen's discovery of X rays and Guglielmo Marconi's invention of wireless telegraphy transform the spectrum of apparent technological potential.

**1896** Wells's *The Island of Doctor Moreau* introduces a new form of science-fictional allegory. Henri Becquerel's discovery of the radioactivity of uranium and Joseph J. Thomson's discovery of the electron offer further scope to technological speculation.

**1898** Wells's *The War of the Worlds* creates the most popular template of pulp sf. Ferdinand von Zeppelin builds an airship.

**1900** Max Planck develops quantum theory. Sigmund Freud publishes *The Interpretation of Dreams*.

**1901** M. P. Shiel's *The Purple Cloud* transfigures the Book of Job as an evolutionist parable. Wells's *The First Men in the Moon* introduces another useful facilitating device—antigravity—but takes it no further than the moon.

**1903** Anatole France's *Sur la pierre blanche* provides the first philosophical analysis of the utility of literary work in futuristic speculation.

**1904** G. K. Chesterton's *The Napoleon of Notting Hill* mocks the pretensions of futuristic fiction. Ernest Rutherford and Frederick Soddy produce a theory of radioactivity.

**1905** Wells offers a design for *A Modern Utopia*. Albert Einstein proposes the special theory of relativity.

**1909** E. M. Forster's "The Machine Stops" challenges the utility and sustainability of a Utopia of comforts based on mechanical production. Henry Ford markets the Model T.

**1911** Hugo Gernsback's "Ralph 124C41+" provides a paradigm example of "scientifiction." J. D. Beresford's *The Hampdenshire Wonder* attempts to anticipate the nature of humankind's descendant species.

**1912** Arthur Conan Doyle's *The Lost World*, Edgar Rice Burroughs's "Under the Moons of Mars" and George Allan England's "Darkness and Dawn" establish important templates for adventure sf. William Hope Hodgson's *The Night Land* offers an important exemplar of decadent far-futuristic fantasy.

**1913** Niels Bohr produces a model of the "planetary" atom.

**1914** **1–5 August:** The Great War begins, loudly advertised in Britain as a "war to end war."

**1916** *Outside the Earth* by Konstantin Tsiolkovsky pioneers the myth of the space age.

**1917** The February and October Revolutions in Russia secure the communist regime.

**1918** **11 November:** The Great War ends, having ruined Europe as the commercial and industrial heart of the civilized world, paving the way for American dominance of the 20th century. Wells's *The World Set Free* attempts to preserve optimism by proposing that the devastation wrought in the next war by atomic bombs might clear the way for saner social reconstruction. A. Merritt's "The Moon Pool" provides a significant exemplar for 20th-century escapist fantasy.

**1920** Edward Shanks's *The People of the Ruins* establishes the pattern of scientific romance's response to the lessons of the Great War.

**1921** Karel Čapek's "R.U.R." invents the word *robot*.

**1923** J. B. S. Haldane reads the paper published as *Daedalus; or, Science and the Future*, mapping out the potential of biotechnology and explaining why its progress will generate such horrified alarm. Wells anticipates *Men Like Gods*. *Weird Tales* begins publication and Hugo

Gernsback publishes an experimental scientifiction issue of *Science and Invention*.

**1924** *We* by Yegevny Zamyatin establishes the logical extreme of dystopian fiction. Stalin comes to power in Russia.

**1925** Adolf Hitler publishes the first volume of *Mein Kampf*.

**1926** The first issue of *Amazing Stories* appears, dated April.

**1927** Wilhelm Müller discovers that mutations can be induced in fruit flies by irradiation.

**1928** E. E. Smith's "The Skylark of Space" and Edmond Hamilton's "Crashing Suns" extend the scope of adventure sf into interstellar space. The first "soap opera" is broadcast.

**1929** Edwin Hubble determines that the universe is expanding. The U.S. stock market crashes. Hugo Gernsback founds the *Wonder* group of sf magazines. The comic strip *Buck Rogers in the 25th Century* carries sf to a mass audience for the first time, defining the genre's image within the arena of "popular culture."

**1930** Olaf Stapledon's *Last and First Men* takes futuristic fiction to a new extreme and introduces a new narrative voice into sf. *Astounding Stories of Super-Science* is launched. John Taine's *The Iron Star* pioneers mutational romance. The first sf fanzines appear.

**1931** John W. Campbell Jr.'s *Islands of Space* introduces the notion of hyperspace to sf. David Lasser's *The Conquest of Space* introduces the myth of the space age to the United States.

**1932** Aldous Huxley's *Brave New World* dramatizes the substance of Haldane's *Daedalus* and proves its case regarding horrified alarmism. Campbell's "The Last Evolution" sketches a future history in which humankind is replaced by sentient machines that subsequently evolve into beings of "pure energy."

**1933** C. L. Moore's "Shambleau" (1933) pioneers a new kind of "science-fantasy" hybridizing planetary romance with mythical fantasy.

**1934** Stanley G. Weinbaum's "A Martian Odyssey" imports a measure of ecological sophistication into pulp sf's representation of alien life. Campbell's "Twilight" imports Forsterian anxieties about technological dependence into pulp sf. Murray Leinster's "Sidewise in Time" imports alternative histories into pulp sf. Ernest Lawrence builds a cyclotron.

**1936** H. P. Lovecraft's "At the Mountains of Madness" introduces "cosmic horror" into pulp sf. The BBC begins television broadcasts from Alexandra Palace.

**1937** Stapledon's *Star Maker* extends the scope of visionary fantasy to embrace the entire spatial universe. Campbell becomes editor of *Astounding*.

**1938** Jack Williamson's "The Legion of Time" sets alternative histories at war for the privilege of existence. Action Comics and Superman establish superheroic adventures at the core of the comic book medium.

**1939** **3 September:** World War II—long anticipated and feared in scientific romance—begins in Europe. Campbell's *Unknown* provides an arena for the rapid evolution of chimerical fantasy. L. Sprague de Camp's "Lest Darkness Fall" sets the pattern for science-fictional timeslip (time-travel) romances and establishes the method of science-fictional alternative histories. The World SF Convention, the central institution of sf fandom, is founded as an annual event.

**1940** Robert A. Heinlein introduces a new realism and more sophisticated narrative methods to sf's depiction of future social problems. A. E. van Vogt's *Slan* creates a key template for sf's deployment of the superman.

**1941** **7 December:** A Japanese attack on Pearl Harbor brings the United States into World War II, transforming the ideological outlook and economic situation of pulp sf. The Manhattan Project is launched.

Isaac Asimov establishes key templates for pulp sf *contes philosophiques*.

**1942** Asimov's "Foundation" launches the series that established the future-historical pattern for much post–World War II sf. ENIAC, the first automatic computer, is constructed. The first V-2 rocket is launched.

**1944** Clifford Simak launches the City series, an exceedingly rare work of sf in which the meek inherit the Earth.

**1945** **6 August:** Hiroshima is destroyed by an atomic bomb, causing widespread elation in the U.S. sf community, where the event is seen as a prophecy fulfilled and a crucial justification of the genre's endeavors—which does not prevent the sf magazines from participating in a deluge of alarmist fiction anticipating a nuclear holocaust.

**1946** *The Best of Science Fiction*, edited by Groff Conklin, and *Adventures in Time and Space*, edited by Raymond Healy and J. Francis McComas, provide significant hardcover showcases for pulp sf.

**1947** The relaxation of paper rationing precipitates a boom in paperback sf in Britain, soon eclipsed by the flood of imported U.S. material. Williamson's "With Folded Hands" challenges the fundamental assumptions of Asimov's robotic *contes philosophiques*.

**1948** Arthur C. Clarke's "Against the Fall of Night" fuses the traditions of British scientific romance and American sf. The transistor is invented at Bell Telephone Laboratories.

**1949** George Orwell's *Nineteen Eighty-Four* establishes a new dystopian benchmark in futuristic political fantasy. *The Magazine of Fantasy & Science Fiction* is launched. The USSR begins atomic bomb tests.

**1950** Ray Bradbury's *The Martian Chronicles* provides a paradigm example of sf fabulation. The first issue of *Galaxy* appears. Dan Dare's debut in the *Eagle* introduces space-age sf to a generation of British boys.

**1951** Jack Williamson's *Dragon's Island* introduces the term "genetic engineering" into sf. The first commercially produced computer, UNIVAC 1, is acquired by the U.S. Census Bureau. Clarke's *Prelude to Space* extends the range of his propaganda for the space age.

**1952** **6 November:** The first hydrogen bomb is exploded at Eniwetok Atoll.

**1953** *The Space Merchants* by Frederik Pohl and C. M. Kornbluth establishes a new benchmark in satirical sf. Theodore Sturgeon's *More Than Human* sets the psi superman in a new moral context. Hal Clement's *Mission of Gravity* provides a paradigm example of hard-sf world-building. Reginald Bretnor's *Modern Science Fiction: Its Meaning and Its Future* attempts to analyze the genre's virtues and prospects.

**1954** Tom Godwin's "The Cold Equations" sharpens the cutting edge of the sf *conte cruel*.

**1955** "A Canticle for Leibowitz" launches Walter M. Miller's groundbreaking mosaic. Pierre Teilhard de Chardin's *The Phenomenon of Man* popularizes the idea of the Omega Point.

**1956** Alfred Bester's *The Stars My Destination* sets new standards for science-fictional transfiguration. Damon Knight inaugurates the annual Milford Science Fiction Writers' Workshop.

**1957** **4 October:** Sputnik I launched by USSR, rapidly followed (**3 November**) by the dog-carrying Sputnik II. Fred Hoyle's *The Black Cloud* initiates a new train of thought regarding the origins of life. Philip K. Dick's *Eye in the Sky* foregrounds his concern with the potential deceptiveness of the perceived world. P. Schuyler Miller is moved to coin the term "hard sf." Ayn Rand's *Atlas Shrugged* puts in libertarian capitalism's bid for the moral high ground.

**1958** **31 January:** The United States launches its own artificial satellite, Explorer I, rapidly followed (**17 March**) by the Vanguard I rocket. Ivan Yefremov's *Andromeda* assesses the space-age ambitions of Soviet communism.

**1959** **12 September:** Lunik II reaches the moon. Heinlein's *Starship Troopers* and Gordon R. Dickson's *Dorsai!* establish paradigm examples for military sf. Kurt Vonnegut's *The Sirens of Titan* sets a new benchmark for satirical *contes philosophiques*. Daniel Keyes's "Flowers for Algernon" does likewise for sentimental *contes philosophiques*.

**1960** J. G. Ballard's "The Voices of Time" begins an extensive exploration of inner space. James White pioneers pacifist space opera. Project Ozma, established by Frank Drake, begins the Search for Extraterrestrial Intelligence (SETI). *Astounding Science Fiction* becomes *Analog*.

**1961** **12 April:** Yuri Gagarin orbits the Earth in an artificial satellite. An Atlas computer is installed at Harwell to facilitate atomic research and weather forecasting. Anne McCaffrey's *The Ship Who Sang* adapts sf imagery to the modern allegory of love. James Gunn's *The Joy Makers* skeptically examines the notion that the ultimate goal of human endeavor is happiness. Heinlein's provocative messianic fantasy *Stranger in a Strange Land* strikes a chord with the emergent zeitgeist.

**1962** **10 July:** The communications satellite Telstar is launched. Rachel Carson's *Silent Spring* adds massive impetus to environmentalist anxiety. The notion of "paradigm shifts" set out in Thomas Kuhn's *The Structure of Scientific Revolutions* begins to change the way sf writers envisage the nature of future scientific evolution. Madeleine l'Engle's *A Wrinkle in Time* sparks a boom in children's soft sf.

**1963** Data recovered from probes of Mars and Venus confirm the utter inhospitability of their surface environments.

**1964** Michael Moorcock becomes editor of *New Worlds* and launches the British "new wave." IBM markets the 360 series of computers, equipped with integrated circuits.

**1965** Frank Herbert's *Dune* establishes a new benchmark in planetary romance. SFWA is founded. Soviet cosmonauts and U.S. astronauts walk in space for the first time.

**1966** Samuel R. Delany's *Babel-17* sets a new standard for sophisticated space opera; Bob Shaw's "Light of Other Days" provides a paradigm example of the *multum-in-parvo* approach to sf plot development.

**1967** *Dangerous Visions*, edited by Harlan Ellison, provides a showcase for the U.S. new wave. Robert Scholes's *The Fabulators* popularizes the notion of modern fantastic fiction as "fabulation."

**1968** Philip K. Dick's *Do Androids Dream of Electric Sheep?* and Stanislaw Lem's *Solaris* establish key examples of postmodern sf. Thomas M. Disch's *Camp Concentration* offers a new image of evolving superhumanity. An annual summer school workshop for sf writers is established at Clarion State College, Pennsylvania. *Locus* is founded. Garrett Hardin's "The Tragedy of the Commons" explains the logic of impending ecological crisis.

**1969** **20 July:** Neil Armstrong sets foot on the moon, proclaiming it a "great leap for mankind." Ursula K. le Guin's *The Left Hand of Darkness* demonstrates sf's utility in the exploration of sexual politics. Paul Ehrlich's "Ecocatastrophe" summarizes the potentially apocalyptic effects of overpopulation, environmental pollution, and dwindling resources.

**1970** Larry Niven's *Ringworld* pioneers megastructural sf.

**1971** The Science Fiction Foundation is established in the U.K. The Science Fiction Research Association is established in the United States. David Rorvik's *As Man Becomes Machine* popularizes cyborgs, anticipating a new era of man/machine "participant evolution." The first microprocessors are produced by Intel.

**1972** Robert Silverberg's *Dying Inside* brings speculative existentialist fantasy up to date. Pierre Versins's *Encyclopédie de l'Utopie et de la sf* provides a model for the Nicholls *Encyclopedia*. Donald A. Wollheim founds DAW Books.

**1973** *Science-Fiction Studies* is founded.

**1974** Le Guin's *The Dispossessed* establishes a new benchmark for Utopian speculation in sf. Joe Haldeman's *The Forever War* establishes important new precedents for military sf. Philip K. Dick experiences a series of "visions" whose implications color all his subsequent works.

**1975** Joanna Russ's *The Female Man* sets significant precedents for feminist sf.

**1976** Pamela Sargent's *Cloned Lives* investigates the intersection of biotechnology and existentialist fantasy. Samuel R. Delany's "ambiguous heterotopia" *Triton* takes the fictional analysis of future social possibilities to a new level of complexity. Marge Piercy's *Woman on the Edge of Time* takes feminist sf into the literary mainstream. Howard Waldrop pioneers the steampunk subgenre.

**1977** *Isaac Asimov's Science Fiction Magazine* is founded. Gerard K. O'Neill's *The High Frontier* provides a new blueprint for the early phases of the space age. Darko Suvin's *Metamorphoses of Science Fiction* introduces yet another new critical vocabulary.

**1978** Suzette Haden Elgin founds the Science Fiction Poetry Association.

**1979** The first edition of the *Encyclopedia of Science Fiction*, edited by Peter Nicholls and John Clute, provides sf scholarship with a central reference point. James Lovelock's *Gaia: A New Look at Life on Earth* popularizes the notion that the Earth's ecosphere operates as a highly integrated holistic system.

**1980** Gregory Benford's *Timescape* provides a rare depiction of life in a modern laboratory.

**1981** William Gibson's "Johnny Mnemonic" and Vernor Vinge's "True Names" begin the exploration of the cyberspatial frontier.

**1982** The International Association for the Fantastic in the Arts is formed.

**1983** The notion of a technological singularity is popularized in an article by Vernor Vinge. Baen Books is founded.

**1984** Gibson's *Neuromancer* provides the paradigm example of cyberpunk fiction.

**1985** Greg Bear's *Blood Music* and Bruce Sterling's *Schismatrix* demonstrate a new appreciation of the potential of biotechnology. Donna J. Haraway's "Cyborg Manifesto" adds new metaphorical significance to the term.

**1986** *Mirrorshades: The Cyberpunk Anthology*, edited by Bruce Sterling, popularizes the term. Lois McMaster Bujold begins a revival of military sf. Gardner Dozois becomes the most influential short fiction editor in the genre.

**1987** *Consider Phlebas* launches Iain Banks's series of space operas set in a new kind of galactic empire. James Gleick's *Chaos* popularizes a new kind of thinking about the nature and precariousness of order. K. Eric Drexler's *Engines of Creation* popularizes the notion of nanotechnology, the key sf motif of the new fin de siècle.

**1988** Peter Dickinson's *Eva* sets a new standard for the sophistication of children's sf. David Hartwell launches *The New York Review of Science Fiction*.

**1989** Dan Simmons's *Hyperion* begins a significant metaphysical sf series.

**1990** **1 October:** James Watson announces the commencement of the Human Genome Project, predicting 30 September 2005 as a completion date.

**1992** Kim Stanley Robinson's *Red Mars* refreshes an important venue for political fantasy.

**1993** Jeff Noon's *Vurt* surrealizes virtual experience.

**1994** Frank Tipler's *The Physics of Immortality* redefines the Omega Point and adds a vital new component to far-futuristic fantasy.

**1995** Ken MacLeod's *The Star Fraction* and Ian McDonald's *Chaga* set significant new precedents in near-futuristic political fantasy and metamorphic evolutionary fantasy.

**1996** Peter F. Hamilton's Night's Dawn trilogy is launched, blending hard space opera and horror-sf.

**1997** **February:** The birth is announced of Dolly, a sheep cloned by means of nuclear transfer technology, dramatically increasing controversial public interest in biotechnology. Greg Egan's cosmological extravaganza *Diaspora* and *conte philosophique* "Reasons to be Cheerful" take hard sf to new extremes. Michael Swanwick's *Jack Faust* reiterates and reinforces the argument of Bertrand Russell's *Icarus*.

**1998** Poul Anderson's *Starfarers* exemplifies the new standard applicable to hard sf versions of sophisticated space opera. Mike Resnick's *Kirinyaga* offers the subject matter of anthropological science an opportunity to fight the corrosions of the uncertainty principle.

**1999** Stephen Baxter's Manifold trilogy is launched, setting a precedent for the development of cosmological fantasy in the context of an aborted space age. Paul Levinson's *The Silk Code* pioneers the futuristic forensic science detective thriller.

**2000** The millennial year begins and ends without catastrophe. A "working draft" of the human genome is published, confirming that the 21st century is more likely to be an era of biological transformation than a significant phase of the space age. Ellen Datlow becomes fiction editor of the Sci-Fi Channel website SciFiction. Jamil Nasir's *Distance Haze* dramatizes an sf writer's struggle to reconcile incompatible worldviews.

**2001** Tony Daniel's *Metaplanetary* provides a paradigm example of space opera hybridized with far-futuristic fantasy. Ian R. McLeod's "New Light of the Drake Equation" provides a requiem for 20th-century sf's mythical future.

**2002** Kim Stanley Robinson's *The Years of Rice and Salt* wipes out Western civilization in a far-reaching alternative historical coup. Karl Schroeder's *Permanence* and John C. Wright's *The Golden Age* bring sf representations of the posthuman space age up to date.

**2003** Charles Stross's *Singularity Sky* and continuing Accelerando sequence define the current position of sf's cutting edge.

# Introduction

## THE PROBLEM OF DEFINITION

It is more difficult to provide a functional description of science fiction than for any other genre, whether "genre" is taken to mean "a collection of texts sharing particular thematic or formal characteristics" or "a collection of texts assembled under a particular label for marketing purposes." Most commercial genres are easily delineated by their themes—detective stories are stories about detectives solving crimes; westerns are stories about the "taming" of the western frontier by means of gunplay; romances are stories about women obtaining promises of commitment from potential life-partners—and have standardized plot formulas. Readers picking up books carrying these genre labels can be reasonably sure of what they are getting, and literary historians usually have no difficulty tracing the evolution of the commercial genres from similar texts that existed before the labels became commonplace. Science fiction, by contrast, has no obvious thematic core or fundamental plot formula; if it is "about science" at all, it is certainly not about it in the same way that crime fiction is about crime, or romantic fiction about love.

Although the term was first coined in 1851, science fiction—abbreviated hereafter as sf—did not obtain substantial currency until the 1930s, when it was attached as a label to a group of American pulp magazines. It entered popular usage ready-equipped with illustrative exemplars—Jules Verne, H. G. Wells, Edgar Allan Poe, and Edward Bellamy were those cited by Hugo Gernsback in his editorial in the first issue of the first sf magazine—but the writers in question were so various that there were as many differences as similarities between them, and the commercial genre was no sooner born than it began to spawn new subgenres in some profusion, rapidly increasing its nebulosity.

Almost as soon as sf was invented, controversies erupted as to which previously existing texts could legitimately be described as sf and which could not. Hugo Gernsback's account of the ambitions that the genre might legitimately entertain was soon challenged; every editor who entered the pulp sf arena imported different assumptions and priorities, and their conflict never seemed likely to produce a consensus. An orthodoxy of sorts was established in the 1940s by John W. Campbell Jr.—who not only promoted his own manifesto more assertively and more persuasively than any of his rivals but recruited as committed disciples many of the writers who were to become central figures of the commercial genre, most significantly Robert A. Heinlein and Isaac Asimov—but the effect it had on other sf editors was muted, and the orthodoxy soon began to generate its own dissenters and schismatics.

The central problem of "defining" sf was that its promoters sought to distinguish it from both aspects of what had hitherto seemed a simple dichotomy, between "realistic" or "naturalistic" texts on the one hand, and "fantastic" texts on the other. Although the world within a literary text is not bound by the laws of nature—anything can happen that the author can put into intelligible words—most worlds-within-texts pretend to be the actual world, or as close a simulation of it as can be contrived. Such texts routinely demand to be evaluated in terms of the accuracy of their representation, and their admirers routinely denigrate texts in which events occur that could not occur in the real world. The great majority of literary texts handed down from antiquity are, of course, fantastic, embodying supernatural aspects of myth or folklore and exploiting such narrative devices as fabulation, allegory, and satire, but devotees of literary "realism" throughout the 19th and early 20th centuries tended to regard such material as relics of obsolete beliefs, whose modern literary utility was limited to whimsical artifice, idle nostalgia, and deplorable indulgence.

This denigration of the fantastic may have been seriously mistaken, and the fact that resistance to it became stronger during the latter part of the 20th century was a significant force in the evolution of "literary fiction" as well as the spectrum of popular genres. Even so, any attempt to define sf as a genre must engage with two dimensions of difference: sf is clearly not mimetic, but it also resists categorization as a supernatural genre. The genre's early prophets—many of whom did aspire to be prophets of a new and perhaps finer kind—usually tried to define a third dimension of possibility, embracing a kind of "realism" that lay beyond the scope of mere mimesis. It is not obvious that this "non-mimetic realism" is an achievable ambition but, if it is, it certainly cannot be accomplished easily. Most of the texts that have been published under the sf label, or retrospectively recruited to the genre, fail so abjectly to achieve it that their pretences become ludicrous when subjected to logical analysis. Such failures have increased the ignominy in which sf is often held far beyond that which would have been attached to it had its promoters retained the unpretentious modesty of other non-mimetic genres, such as magical fantasy and supernatural horror fiction.

No substantial consensus has ever existed as to how sf might be succinctly defined, and many commentators on the genre have refused even to try. One of the tasks of this *Historical Dictionary of Science Fiction Literature* will, inevitably, be to identify the manner in which confusions surrounding the genre are reflected in its terminology, but some fundamental characterization must be attempted in order to determine the scope of the book. Given that sf is not about science in the way that crime fiction is about crime, it is necessary to ask how sf *is* concerned with science.

The most obvious way in which science is relevant to sf is that sf stories often deal with the technological products of science, especially with new technologies that are not yet invented but to which scientific theory lends plausibility: submarines and airships in the 19th century, atomic bombs and spaceships in the 20th. This is, however, merely one aspect of a more fundamental process, by which the literary method of sf attempts to mimic the scientific method. Sf writers often represent their endeavor as a matter of establishing hypotheses, extrapolating the logical consequences, and assessing the consequences of that extrapolation. Sf thus becomes a medium of literary "thought-experiments," which may take in inventions of a much broader kind than mechanical gadgets: alien life-forms shaped by the operation of natural selection in exotic environments; entities indicated as possibilities by theoretical physics, like antimatter and black holes; alternative histories that might have developed had crucial events worked out differently; and so on.

One corollary of this attempted imitation of scientific method is that sf stories require literary means of establishing a wide variety of quasi-experimental situations. Useful viewpoints cannot be established in the remote reaches of past and future time, or in the vast regions of space, without convenient means of conveyance. For this reason, sf requires an armory of "facilitating devices" that enable the thorough exploration of experimental scenarios. Because these facilitating devices (time machines, parallel worlds, galactic empires, and so on) are usually disguised as scientific notions or technological devices in order to conserve psychological plausibility, they are often seen as flagrant violations of the genre's ambition to remain within the bounds of rational plausibility; the politics of their deployment is complicated, especially where there is an overlap between useful facilitating devices and rationally plausible technologies, as in the case of spaceships.

The facilitating devices necessitated by sf's narrative method can easily be used in the construction of fantastic stories whose appeal to readers is essentially similar to those of other kinds of fantastic fiction. Many stories that use the imaginative apparatus of sf are, in consequence, seen by firm adherents to the genre's central dogma as being in some sense "fake," or at least "insignificant." Nor is this problem confined to facilitating devices; the rationally plausible notions whose extrapolation and assessment is often supposed to constitute the heart of the sf enterprise can also be used in a manner closely akin to the use of magical devices and unreal entities in other kinds of fantastic fiction. Such "illicit" uses undeniably comprise the vast majority of all the texts that carry the sf label, creating a curious situation in which the fiercest apologists for sf are required to assert that almost all of what passes for sf is not *really* sf at all, and that most of it is indefensible in terms of the genre's pretensions. To readers who admire at least some of that majority of texts and to writers whose interests lie there, this seems at best inconvenient and at worst absurd; to those who despise the entire genre, it may well seem hilariously comical.

## SCIENCE FICTION AND FANTASY

As the problems of defining and defending sf developed, becoming increasingly obvious in the 1940s as John Campbell and his disciples attempted to sophisticate and refine pulp magazine sf, it became clear that there were two principal strategic routes open to the genre's adherents. One the one hand, they could continue to insist that although much sf was "fake" or "insignificant," there was a precious residue of intellectually serious works that possessed a unique claim to literary importance quite distinct from the claims of mimetic fiction or apologies that might be constructed for other kinds of fantastic fiction—and that writers and editors should therefore work tirelessly to increase that minority. On the other hand, they could concede that sf was nothing more than a new aspect of fantastic fiction, while arguing that fantastic fiction in general had been unjustly denigrated by those determined to find virtue only in mimesis—and that sf, by employing a fresh vocabulary of ideas, could help to demonstrate the virtues of fantastic fiction to readers who no longer found the supernatural plausible.

The former strategy was, unsurprisingly, followed by John Campbell when he was called upon to describe and justify the form into which he was trying to mold the genre in the preface he contributed to one of its first showcase anthologies, *The Best of Science Fiction* (1946), edited by Groff Conklin. It was also followed by Robert Heinlein when he tried to relabel the genre "speculative fiction" in the essay that led off Lloyd Arthur Eshbach's groundbreaking symposium on sf writing, *Of Worlds Beyond* (1947), and by Isaac Asimov in the essay on "Social Science Fiction" he contributed to Reginald Bretnor's pioneering critical account of *Modern Science Fiction: Its Meaning and Its Future* (1953).

Campbell's essay argues that the best sf stories "are extrapolations of known science into future engineering." Although he also expresses sympathy for "philosophical stories" and is not averse to "adventure science fiction," he is anxious to stress that real sf is not like fantasy, whose writers and readers know that what they are sharing could not possibly happen. Heinlein is keen to stress that sf ought to be about "*human* problems" arising from technological innovation, and not mere gadgetry or futuristic costume drama. Asimov argues that the only "significant" fraction of sf is that which deals with "the impact of scientific advance upon human beings," differentiating this kind of fiction from "social fiction," which features hypothetical societies without any reference to technological determinism (a category to which he dismisses Utopias, satires, and the work of contemporary writers like Ray Bradbury) and also from "adventure science fiction" and "space opera." Bretnor, whose own essay on "The Future of Science Fiction" concludes *Modern Science Fiction* in a fervently polemical fashion, concurs with Asimov; he was subsequently to construct a dictionary definition of sf as "fiction based on rational speculation regarding the human experience of science and its resultant technologies"—a definition that works, as is only to be expected, far better as a prescription than a description.

The second strategy can be seen in juxtaposition with the first in Groff Conklin's own introduction to *The Best of Science Fiction*, which stresses sf's kinship with other "primary types" of "fantasy" and places it in parallel with "the utopia, the fairy tale [and] the supernatural story." In *Of Worlds Beyond*, Heinlein's essay stands in stark contrast with Jack Williamson's account of "The Logic of Fantasy," which casually accepts that sf "is more popular nowadays than fantasy of the supernatural type, because science has become the modern equivalent of magic." In *Modern Science Fiction*, L. Sprague de Camp's essay on "Imaginative Fiction and Creative Imagination" speaks of a "science-fictional wing" of "the genre of imaginative fiction," and goes on to analyze the construction of an item of fantastic fiction in terms that apply equally to all kinds of nonmimetic fiction.

These two argumentative strands remained parallel throughout the subsequent history of sf, lending an awkward elasticity to the meaning of the term "fantasy" when it was used in conjunction with "science fiction." Some readers and critics routinely spoke of sf and fantasy as if they were mutually contradictory terms, some as if they were adjacent territories in a larger field, and others as if sf were a subcategory of fantasy. The first group of users tended to use "fantasy" as a pejorative term, taking it for granted that those kinds of fiction that could not live up to the "realistic" standards of sf were innately inferior; Gregory Benford, borrowing an analogy used by Robert Frost to compare rhymed and free verse, once suggested that compared with writing sf, writing fantasy is "like playing tennis without the net." The third group of users, by contrast, attached no pejorative connotations to the word "fantasy," and took it for granted that sf stories can only make legitimate claims to literary virtue on exactly the same basis as other nonmimetic texts. The middle group compromised by avoiding the issue.

In practice, magazine editors—including John Campbell—always recognized that many, though not all, sf readers also had a strong affection for at least some other kinds of fantastic fiction. For some years, Campbell's sf magazine, *Astounding*, had a fantasy companion, *Unknown*, whose contents were mostly written and read by the same people. Sf's cult following—usually known as "fandom"—always embraced the supernatural fiction magazine *Weird Tales* as well as the sf pulps. *The Magazine of Fantasy & Science Fiction* boasted of its flexibility, and when "genre fantasy" became popular in the last quarter of the 20th century, bookshops and libraries automatically filed it on the same shelves as sf (although most continued to give "horror" a separate section). When Peter Nicholls and John Clute began compiling *The Encyclopedia of Science Fiction* in 1977, they had no idea that genre fantasy would take off so spectacularly that it would soon demand an encyclopedia of its own, and took it for granted that their volume ought to cover such subgenres as "sword and sorcery," heroic fantasy, and surreal fantasy (but not horror fiction, which Clute also excluded from *The Encyclopedia of Fantasy* he subsequently compiled with John Grant).

Although there is no obvious solution to the problem of how to distinguish "sf" and "fantasy," the compilation of a historical dictionary requires that a pragmatic decision be made as to how the terms will be deployed for the purposes of description, and that some kind of neutrality should be maintained. The usual compromise position—which represents "sf" and "fantasy" as different aspects of "imaginative fiction" while withholding judgment as to their precise relationship—is tempting, but its calculated avoidance of comparison would make it difficult to analyze the arguments concerned. The alternative neutral position is to argue that the apparent dichotomy between the two argumentative strategies mapped out by Campbell, Heinlein, and Asimov on the one hand, and Conklin, Williamson, and de Camp on the other, are not, in fact, mutually exclusive, and the fact that they seemed so in 1946–1953 was, in large measure, a historical accident. The subsequent history of sf has demonstrated that the relationship between sf and fantasy is much more complicated than was once thought. The "real sf" that makes a conscientious attempt to live up to the quasi-scientific ambitions of the genre—"hard sf," as it ultimately came to be labeled—remains dependent on "fantasizing" in several different ways, some of them unavoidable and others so convenient as to be irresistibly tempting.

Any attempt to analyze individual texts, or whole subgenres, readily reveals that boundaries between sf and other fantastic genres are not merely difficult to draw but are explicitly challenged and defied by large numbers of texts, in which aspects of sf and other fantastic genres are deliberately and purposively mingled. The calculated construction of genre-confusing works has been evident within the domain of labeled sf since its inception, but it became increasingly common as the genre evolved; in 1953 it could still be plausibly regarded as an interesting anomaly, but in 2003 it has to be regarded as a commonplace strategy intrinsic to the genre's methodology. Writers working outside the domain of labeled sf have, of course, always felt free to avoid and mock the boundaries imposed by commercial "branding," and that tendency too has increased markedly since 1953. So common is "genre-bending" as a contemporary literary strategy, in fact, that it is necessary to distinguish several different ways in which texts, and subgenres, may combine and confuse various kinds of fantastic fiction. Using "fantasy" as if it meant "not sf" would make it very difficult to do so.

The entitlement of texts to be labeled sf obviously depends on what can or cannot be called a science. Because there are numerous intellectual disciplines whose scientific credentials are dubious, the status of stories based in those sciences is bound to be ambiguous. Some such ambiguity attends many texts whose premises are derived from the human sciences, and all of those whose premises are derived from "fringe sciences" and "pseudosciences." The ambiguity of many imaginative motifs and devices has, inevitably, been seen as an opportunity by many writers, who have not only produced stories that attempt to resolve existing ambiguities but also stories that attempt to create new ones. For this reason, there has been a continual tendency within the sf genre to deal with the substance of myth and magic by providing "rational explanations" for all manner of rationally implausible motifs that figure in mythical, folkloristic, and magical fantasy, thus creating "hybrid" works whose sf and fantasy aspects are fused into what is intended to be a coherent whole. On the other hand, many writers have realized that there is a certain narrative energy to be derived from the juxtaposition and confrontation of mutually incompatible notions and motifs, and they have been content to combine them in a frankly "chimerical" manner rather than trying to reconcile them within the same ideative framework.

Furthermore, using "sf" as if it meant "not fantasy" would confuse sensible discussion of the manner in which many sf stories use rationally implausible notions as facilitating devices. It would, for instance, be ridiculous to argue that a text as fundamental to the sf genre as H. G. Wells's *The Time Machine* ought to be excluded therefrom because time travel is manifestly paradoxical, and equally ridiculous to argue that because it *is* sf, the time machine must be taken seriously as a rationally plausible hypothesis. The sensible course is surely to admit that *The Time Machine* is a work of fantasy, but one that employs the admittedly fantastic time machine as a facilitating device for speculations about the possible future evolution of life on Earth that are quintessentially science fictional.

The sum of these arguments favors the "stronger" compromise, which unhesitatingly accepts that sf is a kind of fantasy but also asserts that such classification does not weaken the case for asserting that some sf has unique virtues arising from its scrupulous mimicry of the scientific method. The usage of this book will, therefore, follow the examples of Conklin and Williamson in accepting "fantasy" as an umbrella term encompassing sf as well as other non-mimetic genres (including supernatural horror fiction), but will also accept that even though most sf texts appeal to most readers in much the same way as texts belong to other fantasy genres, there *are* some that warrant serious consideration in terms of the arguments advanced by Campbell, Heinlein, and Asimov.

## GENRE SF AND THE SF GENRE

The confusions surrounding the relationship of "sf" and "fantasy" would be less acute if it were not for the fact that both terms have been adopted as labels for commercial genres, while also being used by critics and historians to refer to a much larger population of texts. For this reason, a reference to "the sf genre"—meaning all texts whose themes and narrative methods comply with a particular functional description of sf—carries implications that are markedly different from a reference to "genre sf," which refers specifically to texts published under that label. In the same way, a reference to "the fantasy genre" carries different implications from a reference to "genre fantasy."

Furthermore, the fact that the word "genre" has these two different fields of implication causes acute problems in the identification of texts as "sf" or "fantasy" because the fact that commercially labeled sf and fantasy are widely considered to be despicable routinely causes writers anxious to retain respectability to deny vehemently that anything they have written could legitimately be called "sf" or "fantasy," no matter how closely its themes and motifs might resemble those routinely to be found in texts produced for publication under those labels. Strange as it may seem, writers who produce texts that have science-fictional themes but that are not to be marketed under the label are virtually obliged to disparage the genre as contemptuously as they can when publicizing their endeavor.

For this reason, critics often find it convenient to invent special terms to refer to that category of works that belongs to "the sf genre" without being "genre sf." This remainder may be described as "literary sf," "mainstream sf," or "slipstream," according to taste. "Mainstream fiction" is a term that has little use outside genre criticism, in much the same way that only blind people need a word with which to describe the "sighted," but the sf community has always been anxiously preoccupied with the relationship between sf and the wider literary spectrum. Reginald Bretnor commissioned essays on "Science Fiction and the Mainstream" for *Modern Science Fiction* and the second critical anthology with which he followed it up in 1974, although the term became much less fashionable in the 1990s, when it was largely replaced in critical and commercial discourse by "literary fiction." Some genre critics in the 1970s and 1980s attempted to reverse the pejorative implications of the mainstream/genre distinction by referring to nonspeculative fiction as "mundane fiction"—much as sf fans sometimes refer to nonfans as "mundanes"—but the practice never caught on. In much the same way, critics were eventually forced to make routine references to "literary fantasy" in order to distinguish that fraction of works that belonged to "the fantasy genre" while not being marketed as "genre fantasy."

From a publisher's point of view, of course, an item of product is sf if, and only if, it seems likely to sell more copies bearing the label than without it; content is quite irrelevant. When sf was the only kind of fantastic fiction to enjoy a seemingly secure status as a commercial genre, magical fantasy and sword-and-sorcery fiction were often published under that label; now that genre fantasy routinely outsells sf, however, there is a marked tendency for publishers to avoid using the sf label, preferring to package some books whose content would once have been marketable only beneath that label as "fantasies," "thrillers," or simply as "novels." The commercial genre is unlikely to disappear, although many writers might be glad to be free of its stigmatization, but sf might well suffer the kind of partial eclipse to which horror fiction has always been subject—perhaps not unnaturally, given that sf, like horror fiction, is defined more by the effect it is supposed to have on its readers than by its contents.

There is a sense in which it is surprising that sf ever became a commercial genre in the first place. The whole point of commercial branding is to adapt products to serve well-defined consumer tastes; the evolution of commercial genres in the 19th century was, in essence, a search for endlessly repeatable narrative patterns that could be matched up to aspects of reader demand. The French feuilletonists, whose serial fiction briefly became an important weapon in newspaper circulation wars, rapidly discovered that the key to keeping large numbers of readers interested was the dramatic tension developed by subjecting innocent protagonists to long, drawn-out threats. To provide the threats, they needed villains; to oppose the villains, they needed heroes. When popular fiction made the leap from periodical serials to series of books, writers were quick to discover that one key to endless repeatability was a cycle in which a potentially endless series of threats is initiated and intensified by villainous antagonists before being climactically thwarted by heroic protagonists. The resultant story-arcs were essentially "normalizing," in that they consisted of contriving malevolent disturbances of the status quo that were eventually cancelled out by way of narrative closure.

The majority of successful commercial genres—including genre fantasy—fit this pattern, often extending the careers of successful heroes through dozens or hundreds of encounters with various adversaries, all of whose nefarious efforts are successfully neutralized. Most of the remainder employ the one obvious alternative to the normalizing story-arc, in which different heroes (or, more usually, heroines) battle their way from positions of relative social deprivation through a long obstacle course to obtain the rewards of love, money, and status. This story-arc follows a similarly well-defined pattern in which dramatic tension is maintained by withholding ardently desired success until the moment of climactic delivery.

Many individual sf stories have attempted to use one of these two fundamental patterns, but however successful the stories in question might be when viewed in isolation, their assembly into a genre has consequences that are flagrantly absurd. To treat all the inventions of sf as threats to be cancelled out is to tacitly assume that all innovation is evil—which stands in flagrant contradiction to common sense as well as the ambitions entertained for sf by its most fervent adherents. By the same token, to treat the inventions of sf merely as a means to obtain currently conventional social rewards is such a drastic diminution of their potential to transform the underlying spectrum of social opportunity that it too is a frank betrayal of the ambitions of serious practitioners. Serious sf always aspires to deal with processes of change, and that aspiration makes it extremely difficult, if not frankly impossible, to fit sf stories into the kind of endlessly repetitive pattern that genre publication requires. The sf series is an inherently problematic literary form whose discussion requires discrimination between different kinds of series, in a way that is not relevant to such genres as detective stories, thrillers, westerns, and most—but not all—of the other kinds of fantasy that can be contrasted with sf.

In a sense, speaking of "genre science fiction" is a contradiction in terms—a contradiction that becomes more obvious if one substitutes "speculative fiction" for "science fiction," as many commentators on the genre prefer to do. Speculation is innately defiant of formularization, so commercial genre fiction cannot be speculative, nor can speculative fiction be commercially generic. The fact that sf ever became established as a commercial genre must, therefore, be regarded as a perverse anomaly—and many of the problems involved in defining and marketing "genre sf" arise quite naturally from that inherent perversity. In order to understand how the anomaly came about, it is necessary to look more closely at the economic history of the genre.

## THE ECONOMIC HISTORY OF SCIENCE FICTION

Although sf is often considered to be an aspect of "popular culture," the genre has always been economically marginal. Some texts describable in retrospect as sf—for example, Louis-Sebastien Mercier's *L'an 2440* and Edward Belamy's *Looking Backward, 2000–1887*—have been spectacular best-sellers in spite of being assertively controversial, but modern commercial publishers are routinely wary of innovative works because innovation is inherently risky. Genre sf's tendency to innovate seems, in consequence, to be awkward and it tends to be regarded as hazardous territory by commercial editors—who are, in consequence, avidly addicted to the promotion of sequels and series.

Sf is also economically problematic because those readers who are prejudiced in its favor have always been outnumbered by those who manifest a quasi-allergic reaction to it. This is, in part, a difficulty of comprehension; readers uneducated in science have difficulty understanding the language of scientific exposition and the logic of the extrapolative development of ideas. There is also a frequent failure of sympathy; many adults are so fearful of change that they react with reflexive hostility to any reminder of its inevitability, let alone any advocacy of its virtue.

British "scientific romance" flourished briefly while a new generation of middlebrow magazines was going through an experimental phase in the 1890s, but was squeezed out of the commercial sector in the 1900s when editors realized how limited its reader appeal was, and how deeply prejudiced against its ambitions some readers were. The career paths followed by many writers enthusiastic to write scientific romance testify very clearly to the relevant economic disincentives. The American pulp sf magazines were never as popular as their rivals in other genres and would almost certainly have been aborted in the early 1930s had their proprietors not been so concerned to occupy as much "rack space" as possible by multiplying brands and titles.

Had it not been for the priority this policy of aggressive competition placed on literary branding, American speculative fiction might have occupied the same marginal fringe that British scientific romance occupied in the 1930s and 1940s, and continued to occupy that fringe until the year 2000. As things were, however, the continuation of a similar competitive policy by rival paperback publishers not only allowed sf to hold its place within the spectrum of American genre fiction but to participate in the deluge that American commercial fiction unleashed upon the rest of the world in the wake of World War II. The attempts made by magazine and paperback publishers to crowd one another out of the available shelf space by publishing far more titles than could possibly be profitable gave late 20th-century publishing a reputation for inevitable loss-making that might have forced a revolution in the industry by the 1970s had the individual companies not been gathered into conglomerates prepared to use profits from elsewhere to subsidize them, in the hope that the few left standing when all the weaker competitors had been forced out would eventually be able to form a highly profitable cartel. In the meantime, however, that competition sustained a marketplace in which catering to specialized literary tastes was strongly favored—even tastes as inherently esoteric as a taste for sf.

Pulp sf survived and thrived in the 1930s, despite the fact that so many people hated and despised it, long enough to demonstrate that it had one considerable economic advantage. Although the great majority of readers found sf profoundly off-putting, severely limiting its mass-market potential, those who liked it tended to like it a lot—almost obsessively, in some cases—thus allowing it to build up what would nowadays be called a "cult following." This helped to preserve sf magazines against the dramatic decline that overtook the other fiction magazines in the 1950s when paperback books took over the popular fiction market. While readers of other genres found paperbacks far more convenient, sf readers clung hard to the idols they regarded as vital to the collective enterprise. By the end of the century, a handful of sf magazines comprised the most substantial surviving enclave of a medium of fiction that had reached the brink of extinction in the 1960s.

A few paperback publishers were able to make steady money from sf during the 1950s and 1960s, although the profits were considerably less than those returned by other genres. Such was the pressure to increase the volume of titles, however, that competition was increased regardless of the fact that the paperback sf market had reached saturation point in the early 1970s. There followed a cycle of booms and busts as publishers cut back loss-making lines several times, only to return to the fray more aggressively than before in the hope of colonizing the empty shelf space. Even a superficial study of the publication dates attached to the products of many authors annotated in these pages offers eloquent testimony to the fact that the sf paperback market fell apart three times between 1970 and 1990, each collapse being more devastating than the previous one.

Other economic factors—particularly a dramatic increase in the popularity of sf movies and TV shows—widened the market space available to sf in that period, but only for the kinds of sf readily adaptable to those media, which were limited by the technologies of visual display. TV, because of its scheduling system, became even more heavily dependent on repetitive generic patterns than paperback series, and its producers tried far harder than any pulp or paperback editor to force the genre into a straitjacket that could not possibly contain its innovative ambitions. The influence of TV spin-offs on the paperback market—directly in the case of tie-ins, indirectly in the case of attempts to appeal to media fans by imitating tie-ins—was so drastic that pressure built up to devise a new term for that kind of narrowly repetitive kind of genre fiction that could distinguish it from other paperback sf; a cable channel specializing in such material obligingly did so by co-opting the term "sci-fi," presumably blissfully unaware of the fact that it had formerly been widely used within the sf community as a term of abuse.

This situation assisted the abrupt take-off in the late 1970s of genre fantasy, which met the imaginative requirements of readers who were interested in exotic costume-drama just as well as the "softer" kinds of sf, while posing no difficulties of comprehension or sympathy. When sf lines—which had previously accommodated a few titles in other fantasy genres because there was nowhere else to file them—became sf-and-fantasy lines, the priority immediately switched to genre fantasy because the universal familiarity of its basic vocabulary of ideas did not alienate as many potential readers as the occasionally overdemanding intellectual resources of hard sf.

Although hard sf retained its market viability after 1980 by virtue of maintaining its own narrow cult following, it gradually lost the best-selling potential it had briefly enjoyed in the 1970s; the success of some individual titles in the 1990s was almost entirely a product of the rapid decline in competition within that sector of the marketplace. A sharp decline of the reading habit in teenagers—who had previously constituted an important sector of sf's core following—was supplemented by a corollary decline of literary studies in the academy, kicking away a crutch from which sf had derived some benefit in the 1980s. By the early years of the 21st century, the true status of sf as an aspect of "unpopular culture" had become obvious, and a marked division had developed between those kinds of futuristic fiction that could be formularized and "genrified" in a narrow sense, and those kinds that could not.

By 2000 it was already the case that many leading sf writers—including Arthur C. Clarke, William Gibson, Iain M. Banks, and Neal Stephenson—were being marketed as "brand name authors" rather than as participants in a genre, much as leading writers of horror fiction were. To those members of the sf community who had always wanted intellectually respectable sf to be removed from its genre "ghetto" and reunited with the "mainstream," this seemed a healthy development, but it was not without a certain cost. Although genre sf had always been an economic anomaly, perversely opposed to the common pattern of genre publication, there are factors of a very different kind that bind sf texts together in a spirit of common enterprise. It is not only the economics of the genre that are peculiar, but also its aesthetics.

## THE AESTHETICS OF SCIENCE FICTION

Apologists for science fiction resentful of assaults on the genre by literary critics—whose quasi-allergic reactions tend to be even fiercer than those manifested by ordinary readers—sometimes attempt to defend it by arguing that it has distinctive aesthetic ambitions and ought not to be evaluated solely, or even primarily, by the criteria applicable to naturalistic fiction.

Such arguments are usually allied to the proposition—advanced by such early popularizers of science as Robert Hunt in *The Poetry of Science* (1848)—that science has an aesthetic dimension of its own. Because sf shares something of the method of science, it is argued, it also shares some of the intellectual rewards of science: the appreciation of a well-wrought chain of argument and the pleasure of making new discoveries—especially the sense of welcome revelation attendant upon a "paradigm shift" or "conceptual breakthrough." Although reference is occasionally made by sf critics to the idea of "sublimity" developed in Edmund Burke's enquiry into the *Origin of Our Ideas of the Sublime and the Beautiful* (1757), most arguments of this kind rely heavily on the idea that sf appeals to a "sense of wonder." Attempts to define this phrase are as troublesome as attempts to define sf itself, but it seems to be a combination of the aesthetic appeal of well-constructed arguments that lead to a revelatory sense of discovery and a delight in exoticism for its own sake.

In this view, scientific discoveries are wonderful because they increase our knowledge, not by mere accretion of information but by the ingenious application of logic to achieve dramatic transformations of our understanding. The evolution of sf has been closely associated with a number of scientific discoveries that have demonstrated the true scale of the universe in time and space: the extrapolation of complex evidence into theories of geological and biological evolution, and the ingenious conversion of astronomical data into revelations of interstellar and intergalactic distances. By comparison with the scales on which everyday life is measured out, and the assumptions of myth and traditional religion, these discoveries place human existence on a vast stage whose imaginative effect is an unusual alloy of intimidation and intoxication. The disposition of these two effects, in various tense combinations, is the essence of the reader's experience of sf.

Although the sense of wonder seems to be a straightforward product of the discoveries, the role played by well-wrought chains of argument is crucial. Attempts to generate a sense of wonder by assertions of the marvelous unsupported by cogent argument are very common, and many such attempts routinely pretend to be scientific; this is what is meant by "pseudoscience." Without the legitimating support of the aesthetics of logical argument, however, the aesthetics of wonder are devalued. The aesthetics of logic—especially the arcana of advanced mathematics—are certainly esoteric, and often seem intimidating in consequence, but there is an intense exhilaration in being able to appreciate them as far as one can, and in learning to follow them a little further. Literary versions of logical puzzles are by no means restricted to sf—they are central to detective fiction—but the enigmas of detective fiction are "closed" in the sense that the solution has to be built in. Logical extrapolation in sf is open-ended; it surprises the writer before it surprises the reader, and there is a particular delight for both in being led inexorably by a narrative to a conclusion never previously glimpsed or seriously entertained. When the conclusion in question has a spectacular quality, the pleasure of the revelation is considerably amplified.

The kind of climactic revelation associated with what philosophers of science call a paradigm shift changes the way the world is seen, as if providing a set of intellectual lenses that bring it into a new focus. If the "new" world seems more glamorous or grandiose than the old, the shift seems all the more rewarding. Paradigm shifts refresh vision, not merely by substituting one perspective for another but by reminding us that any perspective, no matter how secure, may yet be subject to subversion or refinement—and that the refreshed vision may well be more adventurous and exciting than the old. Pseudoscience attempts to capture the sense of revelation without paying the price of coherent argument, and much sf does likewise—but the aesthetics of the genre, when rigorously applied, demand that the sensation of "breaking through" a barrier to greater conceptual freedom and wider imaginative horizons is honestly acquired.

Naturalistic fiction is, of course, equipped with its own transformative power. Its readers routinely refer to books that have changed or enriched their lives—but the changes and enrichments involved are different in kind, almost invariably relating to matters of self-perception and social relationships. The aesthetics of naturalistic fiction are intimately bound up with moral rearmament, and it is entirely natural that critics of such fiction should be far more interested in the scale of human affairs than the universal one, with the cultivation of common sense rather than rigorous argument, with the flexibility of existing paradigms rather than their collapse, and with meticulous characterization rather than ideative abstraction. Sf has other priorities.

Modern critical theories that put a high value on characterization are bound to be antipathetic to conscientious sf, in which characterization is usually (though not invariably) secondary to the extrapolation of a story's scientific and technological premises. Writers of mimetic fiction can do the work of characterization by providing exemplary vignettes that display a character's idiosyncratic responses to familiar situations, but writers dealing with exotic settings are forced to invert that process, revealing the idiosyncrasies of the setting through the observations and responses of a character whose relative familiarity has to be assumed. The result of this inversion is what led Kingsley Amis to call attention to the importance in sf of "idea-as-hero" stories. Mimetic fiction is bound to favor narrative techniques that render the author "invisible"—or at least unobtrusive—in order to maximize the reader's identification with the world within the text, but the subject matter of hard sf and the manner of its extrapolation often require elaborate expository explanation. Narrative flow and pace—highly valued within the conventional aesthetics of popular fiction—may be difficult to sustain in stories that require elaborate explanation of underlying scientific theories and the logic of their idiosyncratic extrapolation. These factors make the straightforward application of the conventional assumptions of literary criticism to sf difficult, if not flagrantly inapt.

The aesthetics of commercial genres other than sf are clearly bound up with the repetitive story formulas that define them. There is obviously a comfort and consolation to be found in such repetition, akin to the comfort and consolation to be found in the repetitive rituals of religion and play, and the small rituals of everyday life that serve to maintain our sense of social order and consistency. Although individual sf stories may borrow those same ritualistic story formulas, they are bound to stand in stark contradiction to those aesthetic aspects of science that are transferable to sf, whose rewards are dependent on breaking out of the comfort zones of everyday experience in search of novelty and discovery. This does not mean, however, that sf is not an essentially collective enterprise—quite the reverse, in fact. Just as the vision of science is cumulative, adding up to more than the sum of its individual calculations and discoveries, so the vision of sf is cumulative, and it too adds up to something more than the sum of its constituent parts.

Although some philosophical studies of futuristic fiction—notably Fred Polak's *The Image of the Future* (1973)—are critical of sf because they consider its vast variety symptomatic of an unfortunate loss of consensus regarding social and political goals, the merits of that kind of consensus are questionable. The problem with focusing attention on one particular shape that the future ought to take is that it overlooks the manifest fact that every present moment holds the seeds of countless potential futures, from which one will emerge as the result of numerous discoveries not yet made and innumerable choices not yet taken. Our ability to anticipate future possibilities, and the routes of attainment and choice that might favor or inhibit their realization, is the essence of rational thought; the worst news imaginable would be that there really is a destiny that can and will defy every attempt we might make to shape or alter it. Sf, insofar as it attempts to make a serious study of what might be (rather than what must be or could not be), is a mirror of rational thought; the essence of its aesthetics is the celebration of the potential triumphs of rational thought.

No matter how inadequate individual works of sf may prove to be as items of prediction, therefore, when seen as a whole, the genre presents a collective image of the future as a vast array of possibilities, whose actualization will depend on the sum of multitudinous discoveries and choices yet to be made. Extensions of the genre such as the alternative history story further emphasize that the present we inhabit, no matter how inevitable it may seem in the light of the pattern of cause and effect that generated it, is likewise merely one of a vast number of possible presents in which we might be living had chance and choice made slightly different intersections in the past. It is not required that any of the worlds depicted in sf should "come true" or "be true" in order for this collective effect to be achieved; the point is that this depiction is far more aesthetically edifying, as well as far more philosophically realistic, than any image of the future specified by a theory of destiny or any image of the present that takes its limited configuration entirely for granted.

Methods of characterization are not the only aspect of narrative strategy that cannot be applied in sf in the same ways that they can be applied in naturalistic fiction. Every world within a text is, in principle, unique; for that reason, the founder of aesthetic philosophy, Alexander Baumgarten, called worlds within texts "heterocosms." The heterocosms of mimetic fiction are constructed within the reader's consciousness by calling attention to their similarities with the world that the reader actually inhabits; "telling details" are used to establish the story's setting within a preexistent frame of geography and history, and critical value is attached both to the accuracy of the representation and the narrative elegance of its construction. Some fantastic heterocosms can be constructed in the same way, by reference to preexistent shared notions; the opening formula "once upon a time" refers the reader immediately to a set of commonplace assumptions about an imaginary past in which certain mythical and magical assumptions are easily enshrined. (The extent to which modern genre fantasy embraces a similar set of common assumptions is satirically analyzed in Diana Wynne Jones's *Tough Guide to Fantasyland*, 1996.) Most fantastic heterocosms, however—including all sf heterocosms—have to be constructed within the reader's consciousness by calling attention to their difference from the reader's own world, to the logic of their differentiation, and to their setting within a vastly expanded cosmography and timescale. Critical value cannot be attached to the *accuracy* of the representation, but must instead be attached to its plausibility as an invention. Narrative elegance still adds value, but the elegance of the logic must be accommodated as well as the elegance of the prose.

The difficulty of constructing a science-fictional heterocosm is twofold. On the one hand, so much narrative labor has to be done to construct a radically different heterocosm that the potential range of sf short stories is very limited. The "slices of life" conventionally featured by naturalistic short stories are founded on methods of narrative economy that sf can only duplicate in its most imaginatively constrained examples. On the other hand, the density of detail and the complexity of characterization favored by the naturalistic novel are also enormously difficult to achieve in sf. The imaginative labor of creating a finely detailed heterocosm radically different from any familiar world would be vast; most sf heterocosms are more effectively, as well as more easily, constructed as impressionistic sketches. For these reasons, sf often works far better in intermediate formats than in short stories or long novels—a fact reflected in the structuring of the field's major awards, which routinely employ multiple categories, including novelettes (usually defined as 7,500–17,500 words) and novellas (usually defined as 17,500–40,000 words) rather than simply distinguishing between long and short fiction. The fact that U.S. pulp magazines routinely made far more use of stories of intermediate length than any previous or subsequent medium was undoubtedly a major factor in assisting the birth and growth of genre sf, and the fact that early paperback formats usually defined a novel as a work between 50,000 and 65,000 words—routinely abridging longer texts—greatly assisted the migration of the genre to that new format. When post-1985 paperback contracts routinely began to specify a minimum length of 120,000 words for genre fiction, on the assumption that many readers construed expanded page count as "value for money," it caused problems for sf writers, who were routinely forced to inflate their texts by borrowing narrative methods from naturalistic genres or genre fantasy that were ill adapted to the specific aesthetic requirements of sf.

The fact that sf has particular and peculiar aesthetic merits means that critics to whom these merits are invisible are apt to condemn the entire genre as a literary disaster area, excepting only a handful of texts whose strictly limited speculative ambitions leave abundant narrative scope for conventional aesthetic merit. It also means, however, that sf has more scope to fail than any other genre; there are so many more ways in which a science fiction text can be bad that the genre's worst examples are spectacularly awful, in ways to which other texts could never aspire. Adherents of sf who claim that the genre has been unfairly stigmatized because outsiders often judge it by its most horrible examples may be missing the point, although their attempts dramatize the extent to which even the most eloquent apologist for the genre is embarrassed by its worst excesses.

No matter how bad a genre romance or crime story may be, its badness is restricted to a mere failure to produce a recognizable simulacrum of the experienced world and its everyday affairs; bad sf novels can create entirely ludicrous universes. Oddly enough, though, such errors may be so garish, and ill-constructed heterocosms so bizarre, that bad science fiction can sometimes inspire a perverse affection of its own. Although this is most easily seen in the comic book medium, where the colorfulness of some imaginative constructions easily eclipses all consideration of their rational plausibility, genre sf has always played host to some texts whose flagrant and unashamed awfulness attracts a certain paradoxical regard; the checkered history of "space opera" is to some extent a reflection of this aesthetic inversion.

The sum of all these considerations goes a long way to explaining the peculiar nature and history of sf, and no attempt to map the genre and its evolution can make much sense unless they are taken into consideration. Hopefully, this brief summary will be adequate, in association with the summary chronology, to allow users of this dictionary to see how its individual entries fit into a larger pattern.

## THE SCOPE OF THE DICTIONARY

A dictionary is, by definition, concise; it attempts to pack a great deal of information into a relatively small space. In order to facilitate the specific task of this dictionary, policies had to be devised to restrict the extent, nature, and form of the information given.

Most terms defined herein have been selected for definition because of the frequency of their use or their particular significance within the discourse of sf criticism. Although a few new terms have been improvised to facilitate the description and analysis of individual texts and subgenres, the chief priority has been to explain as succinctly as possible those that are commonly in use and those that are most useful in enhancing understanding.

Authors have been selected for annotation according to the historical significance, rather than the number, of their contributions to the genre; the lists of titles credited to individual authors are often selective, on the same basis. Little or no mention is made of titles whose contents lie entirely outside the genre, and little attention is paid to calculatedly formulaic works. Biographical information has been kept to a minimum; mention is only made of other professions and particular experiences where these have a direct bearing on the content of a writer's sf.

In order to list as many relevant titles as possible, descriptions of all but the most important have been restricted to succinct categorization, and the bibliographical information relating to them has usually been limited to the dates of original publication and variant titles. Because sf has been so heavily dependent on magazine publication for most of its history, however, dates of magazine and book publication are sometimes given separately; where texts have been significantly expanded or revised, the dates of the new versions are usually indicated. The titles of magazine publications are contained in quotation marks, the titles of books set in italics, the latter taking priority when the same title was used in different media.

# The Dictionary

## - A -

**ABBOTT, EDWIN A. (1839–1926).** British writer. His classic **dimensional fantasy** *Flatland: A Romance of Many Dimensions* (1884), originally published under the byline A Square, explains how an inhabitant of a two-dimensional world comes to terms with the notion of a third dimension.

**ACKERMAN, FORREST J. (1916– ).** U.S. pioneer of **sf fandom** and **fanzine** writing who worked in the field as a **magazine** editor and literary agent and assembled the largest collection of sf literature. His fondness for wordplay—which led him to coin the term **sci-fi**, little realizing the ignominy that would come to be heaped upon it—is often reflected in the titles of his **anthologies**, including items from the specialist Sense of Wonder Press such as *Ackermanthology*, *Rainbow Fantasia: 35 Spectrumatic Tales of Wonder*, *Sci-Fi Womanthology* (with Pam Keesey), and *Martianthology* (all 2003).

**ADAMS, DOUGLAS (1952–2001).** British writer who began converting the scripts of his 1978 radio serial *The Hitch-Hiker's Guide to the Galaxy* into a series of best-selling novels in 1979, continuing in *The Restaurant at the End of the Universe* (1980), *Life, the Universe and Everything* (1982), and *So Long, and Thanks for All the Fish* (1984). The **series** evolved from absurdist **satirization** of **sf** tropes to maudlin black comedy, which reached its darkest extreme in the belated *Mostly Harmless* (1992). The exotic genre-mingling mysteries *Dirk Gently's Holistic Detective Agency* (1987) and *The Long Dark Tea-Time of the Soul* (1988) followed a similar trajectory; chapters from an incomplete third volume were published with other trivia in *The Salmon of Doubt: Hitchhiking the Galaxy One Last Time* (2002).

**ADAMS, ROBERT (1932–1990).** U.S. writer whose long and violent **series** of **postholocaust** novels begun with *The Coming of the Horseclans* (1975) provided a significant prototype for **survivalist fiction**.

**ADVENT.** U.S. **small press** publisher specializing in **sf**-related nonfiction. It issued several important collections of sf **criticism** by genre sf writers, including **Damon Knight's** *In Search of Wonder* (1956, revised 1967); a symposium on *The Science Fiction Novel* (1959); **James Blish's** *The Issue at Hand* (1964) and *More Issues at Hand* (1970), both as "William Atheling Jr."; **Alexei Panshin's** *Heinlein in Dimension* (1968); and **Donald H. Tuck's** *The Encyclopedia of Science Fiction and Fantasy through 1968* (3 vols., 1974–1982).

**ALDISS, BRIAN W. (1925– ).** British writer; one of the central figures of the British genre, whose attempts to apply a more accomplished literary craftsmanship to the development of its motifs produced a remarkably varied and ambitious body of work. His **far-futuristic fantasies**, including stories collected in *The Canopy of Time* (1959) and *Galaxies like Grains of Sand* (1960; restored text, 1979) and the novel *Hothouse* (1962, aka *The Long Afternoon of Earth*) are crucial contributions to that subgenre. *Non-Stop* (1958, aka *Starship*) is a **conceptual breakthrough** story set on a **generation starship**. *The Primal Urge* (1961) and *The Dark Light-Years* (1964) are excursions into social **satire**. *Greybeard* (1964) is a meditative and elegiac **postholocaust fantasy**.

In keeping with the spirit of the **new wave**, Aldiss's **sf** became more conspicuously experimental in the late 1960s. *An Age* (1967, aka *Cryptozoic*) features counterclockwise time, *Report on Probability A* creates **parallel worlds** distinguished according to Heisenberg's uncertainty principle, and *Barefoot in the Head* (1969) is concerned with the fallout from psychotropic chemical warfare. The collections *The Saliva Trees and Other Strange Growths* (1966), *Intangibles Inc.* (1969), and *The Moment of Eclipse* (1970) reprint early work; *Last Orders and Other Stories* (1977) and *New Arrivals, Old Encounters* (1979) are more whimsically inclined. His informal history of sf, *Billion Year Spree* (1973; expanded in **collaboration** with **David Wingrove** as *Trillion Year Spree*, 1986), proposes that it is essentially a "post-Gothic genre" rooted in **Mary Shelley's** *Frankenstein*. This thesis underlies the novel *Frankenstein Unbound* (1973)—which was eventually followed by further homages in *Moreau's Other Island* (1980) and *Dracula Unbound* (1991)—and informed some of the many **anthologies** Aldiss edited in the 1970s (often in collaboration with **Harry Harrison**), which included a significant definitive anthology, *Space Opera* (1974). The speculative essays collected in *This World and Nearer Ones* (1979) and *The Detached Retina* (1995) further elaborated his critical perspectives. Aldiss's major genre work of the 1980s was a vast planetary romance contained in *Helliconia Spring* (1982), *Helliconia Summer* (1983), and *Helliconia Winter* (1985). *White Mars; or, The Mind Set Free* (1999) is a **Utopian** fantasy written in collaboration with Sir Roger Penrose. *Super-State* (2002) is a futuristic satire. Further short sf is featured in *A Tupolev Too Far* (1993) and *Supertoys Last All Summer Long and Other Stories of Future Time* (2001). His memoir *Bury My Heart at W. H. Smith's: A Writing Life* (1990) is typically idiosyncratic.

**ALIEN.** In the context of **sf**, the ordinary meanings of "alien"—*foreign* and *very different*—are extrapolated to refer to creatures from other worlds. The notion that such creatures would be adapted to their specific physical environments is glimpsed in **John Kepler's** *Somnium* (1634), but would not become commonplace until the Chevalier de Lamarck's theory of **evolution** as a process of gradual adaptation was popularized in the 19th century; it was first given extravagant fictional extrapolation in **Camille Flammarion's** *Lumen* (1866–1869; in book form, 1872). Two images that became fundamental to sf's deployment of aliens were introduced by **H. G. Wells**: invaders of Earth bent on genocidal conquest in *The War of the Worlds* (1898), and members of a hyperorganized hive in *The First Men in the Moon* (1901).

Alien imagery in **pulp sf** exhibited a marked biological chauvinism, meek and benevolent aliens usually being modeled on noncarnivorous mammals and birds, while nasty ones tended to be **chimerical** compounds of reptilian, insectile, and arachnid characteristics. Entities of "pure energy" tended to recapitulate religious symbolism in being imbued with quasi-angelic characteristics. **Stanley Weinbaum** introduced an elementary awareness of ecology into the design of alien biospheres, which was sophisticated by such writers as **Hal Clement**, but the imperatives of **melodrama** maintained the popularity of alien menace stories long after thoughtful writers became anxious about their tacit xenophobia. A greater sensitivity to matters of political correctness became manifest after 1960, but sf's dealings with alien beings continued to prejudice its public image; the genre is irredeemably associated in popular parlance with the imagery of **little green men** and **bug-eyed monsters**.

The problem of alien characterization is acute, and perhaps insoluble; the extent to which human writers can place themselves imaginatively in alien existential situations is severely limited. Even so, anticipation of a **first contact** between human and alien is one of the key themes of sf; the routine insistence that common intellectual ground can and must be found is an assertion of the universality of scientific reasoning and the logical necessity of fundamental social contracts rather than a failure of imagination.

**ALLEN, GRANT (1848–1899).** British writer. His pioneering contributions to **scientific romance** include the suspended animation story "Pausodyne" (1881), the Utopian ***conte philosophique*** "The Child of the Phalanstery" (1884), and a critical study of *The British Barbarians* (1895) in which a **time-traveling** anthropologist is employed as a mouthpiece.

**ALLEN, ROGER MCBRIDE (1957– ).** U.S. writer whose early **space operas** *The Torch of Honor* (1985), *Rogue Powers* (1986), and *Farside Cannon* (1988) were followed by the anthropological fantasy *Orphan of Creation* (1988), the carefully extrapolated **disaster story** *Supernova* (1991, with Eric Kotani), and the **existentialist fantasy** *The Modular Man* (1992). The Hunted Earth **series** begun with *The Ring of Charon* (1990) and *The Shattered Sphere* (1994) is sophisticated space opera. *The Depths of Time* (2000) and *The Ocean of Years* (2002) are the first volumes of the Chronicles of Solace, a **far-futuristic fantasy** involving **time travel** and **terraforming**.

**ALTERNATIVE HISTORY.** An account of a hypothetical past or present that might have been realized had some crucial historical event worked out differently. Some critics prefer the term "alternate history" and individual works occasionally style themselves Uchronias, by analogy with Utopias. The virtue of this kind of intellectual exercise was proclaimed by Isaac d'Israeli in an essay in *The Curiosities of Literature* (1791–1823) before Louis-Napoléon Geoffroy's *Napoleon apocryphe* (1836) and Charles Renouvier's *Uchronie* (1857) provided paradigmatic examples. Early examples in English include Nathaniel Hawthorne's "P's Correspondence" (1845) and Edward Everett Hale's "Hands Off" (1881). G. M. Trevelyan's essay "If Napoleon Had Won the Battle of Waterloo" and Joseph Chamberlain's collection *The Ifs of History* (both 1907) inspired the classic anthology *If It Had Happened Otherwise* (1931, expanded 1972; aka *If; or, History Rewritten*); Niall Ferguson's anthology *Virtual History: Alternatives and Counterfactuals* (1997) is a more recent exercise in the same vein.

The core of the alternative history genre consists of accounts of alternative outcomes to significant wars, the American Civil War and World War II being the favorite variables. The subgenre was introduced into **pulp sf** by **Murray Leinster's** "Sidewise in Time" (1934), and the notion of potential alternative histories competing for the privilege of actuality became a staple melodramatic formula in the wake of **Jack Williamson's** *The Legion of Time* (1938, book 1952). Many subsequent **sf** stories hypothesize a **multiverse** of **parallel worlds** as a framework in which many alternative worlds can be simultaneously held, sometimes interacting with one another; an important variant is the **time police** story, in which alternative worlds require organized protection against perversion and conquest. L. Sprague de Camp's *Lest Darkness Fall* (1939; book, 1941) provided a crucial exemplar by bringing questions of **technological determinism** to center stage. In subsequent work, they are often entangled with hypotheses regarding religious determinism by virtue of extrapolations of Max Weber's thesis regarding *The Protestant Ethic and the Spirit of Capitalism* (1901). Alternative history enjoyed a boom in the 1980s and 1990s, encouraging writers like **Harry Turtledove** to become virtual specialists therein and greatly assisting the proliferation of the **steampunk** subgenre. The renewed interest of academic historians coincided with a marked increase in the sophistication of novels, exemplified by such texts as **Kim Stanley Robinson's** *The Years of Rice and Salt* (2002).

Alternative histories of a more extravagant kind feature Earths with variant evolutionary histories and universes where the laws of physics developed differently; new speculations of cosmological theory encouraged prolific production of "alternative cosmic histories" after 1990. A comprehensive annotated bibliography of alternative history stories, compiled by Robert B. Schmunk, is available at www.uchronia.net.

***AMAZING STORIES.*** The first specialist **sf** magazine, founded by **Hugo Gernsback** as "the magazine of **scientifiction**" in 1926. Its early issues reprinted a good deal of work by **Jules Verne** and **H. G. Wells** and made much of the educational and inspirational value of the new genre, much of the original work written for the **magazines** being unashamedly didactic in its narrative construction and manner. A supplementary *Amazing Stories Annual* (1927) was converted into the companion magazine *Amazing Stories Quarterly*. When Gernsback lost control of the two magazines in 1929, his assistant T. O'Conor Sloane (1851–1940) took over their editorship. Initially larger and better produced than the general run of **pulp** magazines, they reverted to a more conventional format in 1933. The quarterly ceased publication in 1934 and *Amazing* surrendered its last pretensions to earnest didacticism in 1938 when it was sold to the Ziff-Davis chain, which installed **Ray Palmer** as editor.

Palmer revived *Amazing*'s economic fortunes by slanting the magazine toward a juvenile audience and concentrating on exotic action-adventure fiction. The companion magazine he introduced in 1939, *Fantastic Adventures*, was primarily an sf magazine, although it did use some magical fantasy and comic fantasy. The bulk of the magazines' contents was supplied by a stable of hack writers, mostly operating under "house pseudonyms," whose formulaic output was devoid of the missionary zeal animating **John Campbell's *Astounding***. Their down-market slide was hastened by Palmer's promotion of a bizarre **pseudoscience-**fictional conspiracy theory originated by Richard S. Shaver (1907–1975) and his subsequent fascination with **flying saucers**. The editors who replaced him in the early 1950s, Howard Browne and Paul Fairman, were content to let *Amazing* continue in the same rut, although Browne briefly tried to vary the formula in 1952 by introducing a new companion, *Fantastic*, which absorbed *Fantastic Adventures* in 1953 before devolving into a clone of *Amazing*. Both magazines acquired a new respectability when **Cele**

**Goldsmith** became their editor in 1958; her fondness for avant-garde **fabulation** might have made more impact within the field had the titles not been sold again in 1965, after which they became reprint magazines cannibalizing their own heritage until 1978, when **Ted White** became editor and tried to recover a viable market position for the magazine. After *Amazing*—which had merged with *Fantastic* in 1980—was bought by the marketers of the successful role-playing **game** *Dungeons & Dragons* in 1982, three more editors (George Scithers, Patrick Lucien Price, and Kim Mohan) tried to resuscitate it before it expired in 1995. It was briefly revived in 1998 but folded again in 2000.

**AMBIGUOUS TEXTS.** Texts whose generic status is difficult to determine because the scientific status of the premises they employ is unclear. The status of many of the "human sciences" remains dubious because of philosophical reservations about their claims of proof, and some of the boundaries between science and **pseudoscience** remain controversial. The most obvious category of ambiguous texts in the **sf** field is that dealing with **psi powers**, enthusiastically promoted in **John Campbell's** ***Astounding*** in spite of reservations about their rational plausibility. Ambiguous texts need to be contrasted with the **chimerical** and **hybrid texts** making up the subgenre of **science-fantasy**.

**AMIS, KINGSLEY (1922–1995).** British writer of literary fiction whose apologetic survey of genre **sf**, *New Maps of Hell* (1960), praised the satirical slant of the 1950s **magazines** and attempted to explain the distinctive appeal of sf by categorizing its typical form as the "idea-as-hero" story. He coedited the Spectrum **series** of showcase **anthologies** (5 vols., 1961–1966) with Robert Conquest before writing the **alternative history** *The Alteration* (1976) and the futuristic **satire** *Russian Hide-and-Seek* (1980).

**AMIS, MARTIN (1949– ).** British writer of literary fiction, son of **Kingsley Amis**. His black comedies—including the novels *Dead Babies* (1975) and *London Fields* (1989) and a few of the stories in *Einstein's Monsters* (1987)—sometimes employ near-future scenarios, while *Time's Arrow* (1991) employs time reversal as a narrative device.

***ANALOG.*** U.S. **sf magazine** directly descendant from ***Astounding***, whose title embodied editor **John W. Campbell Jr.'s** conviction that sf is analogous to science in its use of a rational extrapolative method. The new title gradually replaced its predecessor in 1960; it was intended to be the paradigm example of and principal vehicle for a kind of **hard sf** that is as uncompromising in its **libertarian** politics as its celebrations of future hardware. Although that policy was softened slightly when **Ben Bova** succeeded Campbell as editor in 1972, it was reinstated by **Stanley Schmidt** in 1978. *Analog* was acquired by Davis Publications in 1980, thus becoming a companion to its chief rival, ***Asimov's Science Fiction***; both were sold to Dell Magazines in 1992. *Analog*'s circulation declined from six figures in the 1970s to circa 78,000 in 1992 and circa 42,000 in 2002, in line with that of other magazines.

**ANDERSON, KEVIN J. (1962– ).** U.S. writer who began publishing **sf** in 1985. In *Resurrection, Inc.* (1988), artificial zombies put the living out of work. *Climbing Olympus* (1994) describes the tribulations of men modified to live on **Mars**. *Blindfold* (1995) is an account of subversion in a telepathy-dependent society. Anderson's **hard-sf** novels in **collaboration** with Doug Beason include *Lifeline* (1990), in which space colonies must fend for themselves when Earth suffers a nuclear holocaust; *The Trinity Paradox* (1991), a **timeslip romance** about an **alternative history** in which Nazi Germany developed an atom bomb; *Assemblers of Infinity* (1993), about a **nanotechnological** plague; the **ecocatastrophe** novel *Ill Wind* (1995); and a **technothriller series** comprising *Virtual Destruction* (1996), *Fallout* (1997), and *Lethal Exposure* (1998). He collaborated with **Brian Herbert** on a trilogy of prequels (1999–2001) to **Frank Herbert's** *Dune*. *Hidden Empire* (2002) launched "The Saga of the Seven Suns," a **space opera** series featuring several exotic **alien** species, continued in *A Forest of Stars* (2003). His short fiction is sampled in *Dogged Persistence* (2001). He became one of the most successful massproducers of movie **tie-ins** and similarly formulaic works.

**ANDERSON, POUL (1926–2001).** U.S. writer of Scandinavian descent; he was one of the central figures of the **hard-sf** tradition, combining a keen extrapolative intelligence with **libertarian** political ideals and a poetic **sense of wonder**. *Brain Wave* (1954) examines the impact of a sudden planetwide increase in intelligence but most of his sf of the 1950s and 1980s is space fiction, much of it comprising two sprawling and loosely connected **series**. One features the buccaneering traders of the Polesotechnic League—most notably the items in the omnibus *The Earth Book of Stormgate* (1978)—and the other features Dominic Flandry, a swashbuckling agent of an interstellar Terran Empire.

*The Enemy Stars* (1959, expanded 1987) is Anderson's most ambitious early space story in a more realistic vein, while *The High Crusade* (1960) is a broader comedy, and *Fire Time* (1974) and *The Winter of the World* (1975) are ecologically ingenious **planetary romances**. The space fiction series comprising *Harvest of Stars* (1993), *The Stars Are Also Fire* (1994), *Harvest the Fire* (1995), and *The Fleet of Stars* (1997), and the **SETI** romance *Starfarers* (1998) were crucial contributions to the sophistication of space opera. Another series launched in the 1950s chronicled the adventures of a **time police** organization called the Time Patrol; omnibuses are *Annals of the Time Patrol* (1984) and *Time Patrol* (1991). Other short fiction is collected in many volumes, the most notable of which include *Strangers from Earth* (1961), *Time and Stars* (1964), *Beyond the Beyond* (1969), *The Queen of Air and Darkness and Other Stories* (1973), *Space Folk* (1989), and *Kinship with the Stars* (1991). *The Boat of a Million Years* (1989) is an ambitious novel in which a small population of immortals witnesses the progress of human society from the dawn of civilization to the advent of interstellar exploration. The elegiac **far-futuristic fantasy** *Genesis* (2000) and the nostalgic mystery *For Love and Glory* (2003), in which a human archaeologist and her saurian partner investigate **alien** artifacts, provided capstones to his career.

**ANDROID.** A term originated in alchemical literature, with reference to the creation of artificial humans. In the context of **sf** it is usually employed, in contrast to **robot**, to identify artificial humanoids made from synthetic flesh rather than inorganic components—but the situation is confused by the fact that **Karel Čapek's** robots would now be thought of as androids and the exceptional usage of **Philip K. Dick**, who routinely referred to robots designed to pass for human as androids. The term was introduced into **pulp sf** by **Jack Williamson** in *The Cometeers* (1936); the conventional distinction from "robot" was popularized by **Edmond Hamilton's** tales of Captain Future, whose mechanical and fleshy sidekicks required different labels. Androids are often employed in accounts of hypothetical emancipatory movements, as in **Robert Silverberg's** *Tower of Glass* (1970).

**ANSIBLE.** An imaginary device employed for instantaneous interstellar communication in **Ursula le Guin's** Hainish **series**. The term was borrowed by other writers, including **Orson Scott Card**, and adopted by **David Langford** as the title of a long-running monthly newsletter, initially produced between 1979 and 1987 and revived by popular demand in 1991, which is a key cementing agent of modern **sf fandom**.

**ANTHOLOGIES.** "Showcase" anthologies designed to display and define the field for new audiences played an important role in **sf's** expansion into the hardcover and **paperback** book markets in the late 1940s and 1950s, highly significant examples being edited by **Donald A. Wollheim**, **Groff Conklin**, and **August Derleth**, although the most influential of all was the 997-page *Adventures in Time and Space* (1946) edited by Raymond J. Healy (1907–1969) and J. Francis McComas (1911–1978). Healy also compiled the field's first anthologies of original material, *New Tales of Space and Time* (1951) and *9 Tales of Space and Time* (1954). When **magazines** went into a long, drawn-out, but seemingly terminal decline, numerous attempts were made to substitute paperback anthology **series**, most notably **John Carnell's** *New Writings in SF* (1964–1978), **Damon Knight's** *Orbit* (1965–80), **Terry Carr's** *Universe* (1971–1987), and **Robert Silverberg's** *New Dimensions* (1971–1981). **Harlan Ellison's** *Dangerous Visions* (1968) and *Again, Dangerous Visions* (1972) became key documents of U.S. **new wave** sf, but the majority of sf anthologies from the 1970s onwards have been theme anthologies collecting stories that look at a particular motif from multiple viewpoints. The most important showcases of the latter part of the century were the **cyberpunk** anthology *Mirrorshades* (1986), edited by **Bruce Sterling**, and the annual series sampling the year's best stories, edited by **Gardner R. Dozois** (1984– ).

**ANTHONY, PATRICIA (1947– ).** U.S. writer who began publishing **sf** in 1987. *Cold Allies* (1993) introduces enigmatic **aliens** into an **ecocatastrophe**-afflicted near future (1993). *Brother Termite* (1993), *Happy Policeman* (1994), and *God's Fires* (1997) continued her exploration of the alien, while *Conscience of the Beagle* (1993) and *Cradle of Splendor* (1996) are futuristic thrillers. Her short fiction is collected in *Eating Memories* (1997).

**ANTHONY, PIERS (1934– ).** U.S. writer who began publishing **sf** in 1963 and achieved best-selling status in the 1980s with a **series** of humorous magical fantasies. *Chthon* (1967) displayed a penchant for methodically constructed **pseudoscience**-based allegory that was further extrapolated in *Macroscope* (1969), the trilogies collected in the omnibuses *Of Man and Manta* (1986) and *Tarot* (1987), and the five-volume Cluster series (1977–1982). *Battle Circle* (1978) collects a **postholocaust fantasy** trilogy. The Bio of a Space Tyrant series extended over five volumes (1983–1986) until *The Iron Maiden* (2002) was added to it. The series comprising *Virtual Mode* (1991), *Fractal Mode* (1991), *Chaos Mode* (1993), and *DoOon Mode* (2001) is lighthearted, but the Geodyssey series comprising *Isle of Woman* (1993), *Shame of Man* (1994), *Hope of Earth* (1997), and *Muse of Art* (1999) carries forward the author's philosophy in his typical fashion.

**ANTIGRAVITY.** A hypothetical force of repulsion reversing the effect of gravity. Its use as a method of spacecraft propulsion dates back to *The History of a Voyage to the Moon* (1864) by "Chrysostom Trueman," Percy Greg's *Across the Zodiac* (1880), and **Robert Cromie's** *A Plunge into Space* (1890), although none used the term; Greg called his propulsive force "apergy." **H. G. Wells's** employment of the gravity-shielding Cavorite in *The First Men in the Moon* (1901) continued the tradition. The idea was adopted into genre **sf** in such works as **James Blish's** "Bridge" (1952), which explains the theory and origins of the "spindizzy"; **Raymond F. Jones's** combative ***conte philosophique*** "Noise Level" (1952); and **Arthur C. Clarke's** "What Goes Up" (1955).

**ANTIMATTER.** Substance formed out of antiparticles whose properties invert those of the subatomic particles making up Earthly matter, so that positively charged positrons orbit a negatively charged nucleus. The theoretical possibility was broached by physicist Paul Dirac in 1930; fugitive antiparticles have been observed, although matter and antimatter suffer a mutual annihilation whenever they come into contact. The possibility of using the energy of this annihilation to drive spaceships became a staple facilitating device in **sf**, introduced by **Jack Williamson's** Seetee series (whose title is a contraction of the alternative term "contraterrene matter"), and employed by such **hard-sf** writers as **Arthur C. Clarke** and **Charles R. Pellegrino**.

**APOCALYPTIC FANTASY.** A subgenre of **religious fantasy** that took aboard **sf** motifs in the 19th century as its practitioners began to pay more attention to the means by which the world might be ended. Although stories in which accidents of nature or man-made catastrophes put an end to the world without any mention of divine motive belong unambiguously to sf, the language available for the representation of such events is heavily loaded with religious imagery; in addition to apocalypse itself, such terms as deluge, Armageddon, doom(sday), judgment (day), holocaust, and Omega provide end-of-the-world sf with its fundamental metaphorical vocabulary, with the result that even the purest examples of the sf subgenre retain a **chimerical** aspect. By the same token, modern religious fantasies of world termination routinely borrow ideas from sf in order to imagine how the divine motive might be implemented. There are numerous writers whose contribution to sf consists entirely of accounts of apocalyptic nuclear holocaust stories; notable examples include "Pat Frank" (Harry Hart, 1907–1964), author of *Mr. Adam* (1946), *Forbidden Area* (1956, aka *Seven Days to Never*), and *Alas, Babylon* (1959); Peter George (1924–1966), the author of *Two Hours to Doom* (1958, aka *Dr. Strangelove*); and Mordecai Roshwald (1921– ), the author of *Level 7* (1959).

**ARNASON, ELEANOR (1942– ).** U.S. writer whose early work included a thoughtful analysis of an **sf** writer's mind-set, "The Warlord of Saturn's Moons" (1974). Most of her sf belongs to an anthropologically informed **planetary romance series** comprising the novels *A Woman of the Iron People* (1991) and *Ring of Swords* (1993), and several short stories, including "The Gauze Banner" (1998), "Stellar Harvest" (1999), and "The Potter of Bones" (2002).

**ARTIFICIAL INTELLIGENCE (AI).** A term used in computer science since the late 1970s to describe the development of programs duplicating various aspects of intelligent thought. It was immediately taken up by **sf** writers to describe the range of hypothetical entities manifesting such abilities: sentient computers, **robots**, and networks of various kinds, especially those giving rise to diffuse, godlike entities resident in **cyberspace**. "Mechanical brains" appeared in sf in the 19th century, in such stories as **Edward Page Mitchell's** "The Ablest Man in the World" (1879) but those that did not have to be accommodated within real or artificial skulls were usually imagined as actual giant brains, as in **Miles J. Breuer's** "Paradise and Iron" (1930). Partly because it troubled **John Campbell**, the idea that artificial intelligence was bound to outstrip human intelligence became a key item of the genre sf agenda, displayed in hundreds of stories in which humans feel obliged to rebel against the dictatorship of godlike machines, no matter how benevolent their rule might be.

When the first actual computers were displayed to the public after World War II, the sight of huge arrays of transistors set in sterile surroundings greatly encouraged the image of AIs as vast entities intolerant of the least untidiness, with the result that the casually unreliable personal computer came as a complete surprise, although "A Logic Named Joe" (1946) by Will F. Jenkins (**Murray Leinster**) was retrospectively established as a **prophetic** work. The spontaneous evolution of self-consciousness by AIs became a central theme of 1970s **existentialist fantasies**; the extravagant extrapolation of the notion in such novels as Rudy Rucker's *Software* (1982) and William Gibson's *Neuromancer* (1984) was a central project of **cyberpunk** fiction, along with the notion that the "uploading" of human minds into machines might be a means of achieving immortality—a notion taken to its logical extremes in the sf of **Greg Egan**.

**ASARO, CATHERINE (1955– ).** U.S. physicist and writer. Her Skolian Empire **series**, which **hybridizes** exuberant sophisticated **space opera** with offbeat genre romance, comprises *Primary Inversion* (1995), *Catch the Lightning* (1996), *The Last Hawk* (1997), *The Radiant Seas* (1998), *The Quantum Rose* (2000), *Ascendant Sun* (2000), *Spherical Harmonic* (2001), *The Moon's Shadow* (2003), and *Skyfall* (2003). *The Veiled Web* (1999), which reflects her passion for ballet, and *The Phoenix Code* (2000), about a self-aware **android**, are futuristic thrillers.

**ASHER, NEAL (1961– ).** British writer who began publishing **sf** in 1996. *Gridlinked* (2001) is a convoluted thriller set on a planet where a **terraforming** project has gone awry. *The Skinner* (2002) is an **Odyssean fantasy** set on an ocean world. *The Line of Polity* (2003) is another sophisticated **planetary romance** featuring ingeniously designed life-forms. The background common to the novels is also featured in some of the short stories in *The Engineer* (1998) and *Runcible Tales* (1999).

**ASHLEY, MIKE (1948– ).** British **bibliographer** and historian. The first version of his most important **sf** project, issued in four volumes as *The History of the Science-Fiction Magazines* (1974–1978), was primarily an **anthology**, but its nonfiction component, much expanded and refined, was carried forward into a three-volume work begun with *The Time Machines: The Story of the Science-Fiction Pulp Magazines from the Beginning to 1950* (2000). His then-definitive guide to *Science Fiction, Fantasy, and Weird Fiction Magazines* (1985) was co-edited with Marshall B. Tymn (1937– ).

**ASHWELL, PAULINE (1928– ).** U.S. writer who published almost all her work in ***Analog***, beginning with the zestful comedy "Unwillingly to School" (1958), integrated with its sequel "The Lost Kafoozalum" (1960) into the **mosaic** *Unwillingly to Earth* (1992). Her more earnest work often appeared under the byline Paul Ash, two such stories being combined in *Project FarCry* (1995). A **time police series** launched in 1995 includes "Elsewhere" (2001).

**ASIMOV, ISAAC (1920–1992).** U.S. writer born in Russia, resident in the United States from 1923. He made a crucial contribution to the development of **Campbellian pulp sf** before becoming the leading American popularizer of science. He wrote two enormously popular and highly influential **sf series**. The original elements of the Foundation series (1942–1950) were assembled into a **mosaic** trilogy comprising *Foundation* (1951), *Foundation and Empire* (1952), and *Second Foundation* (1953) before being reprinted in a 1963 omnibus regarded by many readers as *the* central document of genre sf even though it is a **transfiguration** of Roman history examining the impact of an imaginary and impossible science upon an imaginary and impossible social structure. Early **robot** stories featuring the "Three Laws of Robotics"—first outlined in "Reason" (1942)—were collected in *I, Robot* (1950) and *The Rest of the Robots* (1964, incorporating the novels *The Caves of Steel*, 1954, and *The Naked Sun*, 1957). In addition to these series, Asimov produced numerous inventive ***contes philosophiques*** in the 1940s, most famously "Nightfall" (1941), which provide cardinal illustrations of the fact that the "hardness" of **hard sf**—or, in his own terminology, the scientific aspect of "social science fiction"—had more to do with its philosophical stance than its scientific content. The apparent centrality of the Foundation series was largely determined by the fact that the **galactic empire** became *the* key facilitating device of 1950s sf.

Asimov's sf of the 1950s includes three pre-Foundation accounts of the formulation of the series' galactic empire—*Pebble in the Sky* (1950), *The Stars Like Dust* (1952), and *The Currents of Space* (1952)—and the **time police** novel, *The End of Eternity* (1955). His short fiction of the period was collected in *The Martian Way and Other Stories* (1955), *Earth Is Room Enough* (1957), and *Nine Tomorrows* (1959). A series of **children's sf** novels featured the exploits of space ranger Lucky Starr (6 vols., 1952–1958; initially bylined Paul French). After devoting himself almost exclusively to popular science during the 1960s, Asimov returned to sf with an account of an exotic **alien** society *The Gods Themselves* (1972) and added several more existential *contes philosophiques* to the robot series, collected with other material in *The Bicentennial Man* (1976). His subsequent fictional endeavors were mainly devoted to a series of volumes that fused the **future histories** sketched out in his two series, filling them out but not extrapolating them substantially: *The Robots of Dawn* (1983), *Robots and Empire* (1985), *Prelude to Foundation* (1988), *Foundation's Edge* (1982), *Foundation and Earth* (1986), and *Forward the Foundation* (1993). He lent the selling power of his name to a large number of **sharecropping** works by other hands, including Foundation novels. His second wife, Janet Opal Jeppson (1926– ), published a series of children's stories featuring *Norby, the Mixed-up Robot* (1983) and a number of other sf novels, some of them **collaborative.**

***ASIMOV'S SCIENCE FICTION.*** U.S. **magazine** founded in 1977 as *Isaac Asimov's Science Fiction Magazine* by Davis Publications. George H. Scithers edited it for five years and Shawna MacCarthy for three before **Gardner Dozois** took over in 1986. Under Dozois' guidance, it became the leading magazine in the field in terms of reputation, although its sales always lagged behind ***Analog***, which Davis Publications had bought in 1980. Both magazines were acquired by Dell Magazines in 1992, when the title of *Asimov's* was shortened. Its circulation declined, in line with other sf magazines, from an early six-figure peak to circa 73,000 in 1992 and circa 32,000 in 2002.

***ASTOUNDING.*** U.S. **magazine**, originated as *Astounding Stories of Super-Science* by William Clayton's **pulp** chain in 1930 under the editorship of **Harry Bates**. It paid a higher word rate than ***Amazing*** or ***Wonder*** and had none of their didactic pretensions. When the Clayton chain collapsed in 1933, the title was bought by Street & Smith, who abbreviated it to *Astounding Stories* and installed **F. Orlin Tremaine** as editor. He began a process of sophistication that was considerably accelerated when **John W. Campbell Jr.** took over editorial responsibility in 1937, altering the title to *Astounding Science Fiction*. From 1938–1950 it was the paradigm example of what a serious **sf** magazine might aspire to be, even within a medium as inherently frivolous as pulp fiction, and was the primary venue of what came to be seen by many fans as sf's **golden age**. It carried popular science articles and stoutly maintained the not-altogether unjustified pretense that its stories were rational extrapolations of scientific and technological possibility—except for those featured in the column "Probability Zero," whose vignettes were calculatedly **chimerical** representations of the superficially plausible. It lost its perceived leadership of the field after 1950, when it became bogged down in the **psi** boom. It maintained its publication schedule during World War II by adopting a digest format, which it retained thereafter. It became ***Analog*** in 1960.

**ATTANASIO, A. A. (1951– ).** U.S. writer who made his debut in 1974. His **series** of **far-futuristic fantasies** comprising *Radix* (1981), *In Other Worlds* (1984), *Arc of the Dream* (1986), and *The Last Legend of Earth* (1989) exhibits an unusually flamboyant **decadence**. The stories collected in *Beastmarks* (1985) are similar in spirit. *Centuries* (1997) is an epic novel spanning the history of the next millennium.

**ATWOOD, MARGARET (1939– ). Canadian** writer of literary fiction whose **feminist** polemic *The Handmaid's Tale* (1985) is framed as a poignantly ironic futuristic **dystopia**. *Oryx and Crake* (2003) is an **apocalyptic fantasy** about **biotechnology**.

**AUSTRALIAN SCIENCE FICTION.** Australia featured in numerous **Utopian** romances and lost race stories before generating any **sf** of its own, and that imaginative heritage is reflected in G. MacIver's *Neuroomia: A New Continent* (1894) and G. Firth Scott's *The Last Lemurian* (1896; book, 1898), the latter being the obvious model for Earle Cox's *Out of the Silence* (1919). Robert Potter's *The Germ Growers* (1892) is a **religious fantasy** about demonic biological warfare, but fear of Asian invasion was a more frequent stimulus to Australian **future war** novels such as Kenneth Mackay's *The Yellow Wave* (1895).

**Scientific romance** never took firm root in Australia but when **pulp sf** was imported it gained enough adherents to generate a **fandom**, which produced such writers as **A. Bertram Chandler**, Wynne Whiteford (1915– ), and **George Turner** and gave rise to **Donald H. Tuck's** pioneering sf encyclopedia. Subsequent recruits included Jack Wodhams (1931– ), **Lee Harding**, and John Baxter (1939– ), while **Bruce Gillespie's** *SF Commentary* (1969– ) became one of the world's leading **fanzines**. Early **anthologies** of Australian sf edited by Baxter and Harding paved the way for **Paul Collins** (1954– ) to venture into **small press** publication.

Australian sf became considerably more inventive in the 1980s as writers like **David Lake**, **Damien Broderick**, **Cherry Wilder**, and **Greg Egan** rose to prominence. Domestic sf publishing became more enterprising in the 1990s, especially in its promotion of the work of **Terry Dowling** and **Sean McMullen**, and writers like **Sean Williams** continued to raise the profile of Australian sf in the United States. McMullen **collaborated** with Russell Blackford and Van Ikin on *Strange Constellations: A History of Australian Science Fiction* (1999); Graham Stone's *Notes on Australian Science Fiction* (2001) is another useful reference source.

**AWARDS.** The principal awards within the **sf** field are the **Hugo** and the **Nebula**. ***Locus*** also has a multicategory series of awards and the sf **convention** Readercon dispenses annual **small press** awards. Other annual awards for best sf novel are the **John W. Campbell** Memorial Award and the U.K.–administered **Arthur C. Clarke** Award. Campbell is also commemorated by an annual award for the best new writer. Other U.S. writers commemorated by annual awards include **Philip K. Dick** (for the best novel published as a **paperback** original), **James Tiptree Jr.** (for sf challenging gender assumptions), **Theodore Sturgeon** (for best short story), and **James White**. French writers thus commemorated are **Jules Verne** and **J. H. Rosny aîné**, while **Germany** honors **Kurt Lasswitz**. Other awards for sf in languages other than English include the **French** Prix Apollo, the **Spanish** Gigamesh Award, and the **Japanese** Seiun Award. **Canada's** Aurora and **Australia's** Ditmar also honor locally produced sf. Thematically limited awards include the Prometheus Award for **libertarian sf** and the Sidewise Award for **alternative history**. The Rhysling Award is for sf **poetry**. Academic awards for sf studies include the **Science Fiction Research Association's** Pilgrim and Pioneer Awards, the **International Association for the Fantastic in the Arts'** Distinguished Scholarship Award, and the J. Lloyd Eaton Award.

**AYERDAHL (1959– ). French** writer in various fantasy genres, very prolific in the 1990s. His **sf** extends from the colorful **space operas** *La Bohême et l'Ivraie* (1990) and *Mytale* (1991) through the complex and sophisticated *L'Histrion* (1993) and *Sexomorphoses* (1994) to such **political fantasies** as *Parleur* (1997). He edited an important showcase **anthology** of modern French sf, *Génèses* (1996). English translations include "Flickering" (2001) in ***Interzone***.

## - B -

**BACON, FRANCIS (1561–1626).** English philosopher and statesman, one of the pioneers of the scientific method. His incomplete **Utopian** *New Atlantis* (1627) is an adventurous catalogue of potential technologies, probably written as a manifesto for a Royal College of Science that he hoped to persuade King James I to endow.

**BAEN BOOKS.** A specialist **sf**/fantasy publishing company founded in 1983 by James Patrick Baen (1943- ), who had previously edited ***Galaxy*** and worked for Tor Books (1980–83). Many writers who contributed to his Tor original **anthology series** *Destinies* became regular Baen Books writers. Baen Books replaced **Donald Wollheim's DAW Books** at the **pulpish** end of the **paperback** sf spectrum when DAW began to specialize in genre fantasy, enthusiastically promoting **military sf** of a conspicuously **libertarian** stripe, and launching numerous **sharecropping** projects and **shared-world** series; it played a crucial role in the careers of **Lois McMaster Bujold**, **David Drake**, **S. M. Stirling**, and **David Weber**.

**BAILEY, J. O. (1903–1979).** U.S. scholar whose *Pilgrims through Space and Time: Trends and Patterns in Scientific and Utopian Fiction* (1947), based on a 1934 Ph.D. thesis, was the first academic study of the major themes of **sf** (although it avoids use of the term). The book's bibliography of "**scientific romances**" was an important document in the retrospective identification of the genre's roots.

**BAKER, KAGE (1952– ).** U.S. writer who began publishing **sf** with the first of the Company **series**, *In the Garden of Iden* (1997), in which immortal secret agents born in a variety of past eras—and equipped with **cyborg** augmentations following their recruitment by the 24th century-based Doctor Zeus—embark on various exotic missions of conservation. Later volumes are *Sky Coyote* (1999), *Mendoza in Hollywood* (2000), *The Graveyard Game* (2001), and *Black Projects, White Knights: The Company Dossiers* (2002). Another series featuring a different cast of superhuman heroes includes "The Likely Lad" (2002).

**BALLARD, J. G. (1930– ).** British writer born in Shanghai, where he was interned by the Japanese during World War II. He began publishing **sf** in 1956, quickly becoming an ardent propagandist for **inner space** sf and the chief exemplar for the emergent **new wave**, with such groundbreakingly mannered and stylish stories as "The Voices of Time" (1960) and "The Terminal Beach" (1964). "The Cage of Sand" (1962) was the first of several stories that took it for granted that the **space age** would be a short-lived folly whose forgotten debris would be rusting on Cape Canaveral within half a century.

Ballard's early novels were calmly meditative anticipations of disastrous **ecocatastrophes**. *The Wind from Nowhere* (1962) was followed by a highly distinctive triptych comprising *The Drowned World* (1962), *The Drought* (1965; abridged version U.S. 1964 as *The Burning World*), and *The Crystal World* (1966). Sf elements were marginalized in his subsequent work, although the corrosive effects of technology on human psychology remained a central theme in *Crash* (1973), *Concrete Island* (1974), and *High-Rise* (1975).

Some of Ballard's short stories retained the **decadent** exoticism of his tales of the futuristic artists' colony *Vermilion Sands* (1971; exp., 1973), but the broad range of such U.K.–published collections as *The Four-Dimensional Nightmare* (1963), *The Terminal Beach* (1964), and *The Disaster Area* (1967) gave way to the flagrantly avant-gardist "condensed novels" of the **mosaic** *The Atrocity Exhibition* (1970, aka *Love and Napalm: Export USA*) and then to the more narrowly focused *Low-Flying Aircraft* (1976), *Myths of the Near Future* (1982), *Memories of the Space Age* (1988), and *War Fever* (1990). Almost all his short fiction is in the omnibus *The Complete Short Stories* (2002). Although several of his later novels—including *The Day of Creation* (1987), *Rushing to Paradise* (1994), and *Super-Cannes* (2000)—feature fugitive sf elements, Ballard's last wholehearted exercise in futuristic fiction, *Hello America* (1981), was atypically frivolous. There is a certain irony in the fact that his highly controversial anticipations of the early abortion of the space age eventually proved him to be the only **prophetic** sf writer of his generation.

**BANKS, IAIN M. (1954– ).** Scottish writer who distinguished his **sf** from the literary fiction on which his reputation is principally based by including his middle initial in the byline he attached to it, although there had already been some thematic overlap in the **hallucinatory** sf motifs invoked in *Walking on Glass* (1985). *Consider Phlebas* (1987) launched a **series** of gaudy **space operas** set in and around the Culture, a loosely knit and far-ranging interstellar society, which has **Utopian** socialist elements as well as playing host to a great deal of zestful violence; it extended through *The Player of Games* (1988), *Use of Weapons* (1990), the 1989 title novella and other items in *The State of the Art and Other Stories* (1991), *Against a Dark Background*

(1993), *Feersum Endjinn* (1994), *Excession* (1996), *Inversions* (1998), and *Look to Windward* (2000). The series established Banks as the most popular sf writer in Britain and helped pave the way for a British renaissance of sophisticated space opera, whose participants included **Stephen Baxter**, **Peter Hamilton**, **Alastair Reynolds**, **Charles Stross**, and Banks's close friend **Ken MacLeod**.

**BARBET, PIERRE (1925–1995).** Pseudonym of **French** writer and biologist Claude Pierre Marie Avice. A prolific writer of action-adventure **sf**, his novels range from *Vers un avenir perdu* (1962) to *L'Ere du Spatiopithéque* (1991). Those translated into English include *The Napoleons of Eridanus* (1970, tr. 1976) and its sequel *The Emperor of Eridanus* (1982, tr. 1983), *Baphomet's Meteor* (1971, tr. 1972), and *Games Psyborgs Play* (1971, tr. 1973).

**BARJAVEL, RENÉ (1911–1985). French** novelist who wrote several angrily pessimistic **scientific romances** during and shortly after World War II, those translated being *Ashes, Ashes* (1943, tr. 1967) and *Future Times Three* (1944, tr. 1970). *L'homme fort* (1946) and *Le diable l'emporte* (1948) are in the same vein. His later work, including *The Ice People* (1968, tr. 1970) and *Une rose au paradis* (1981), is similarly pessimistic but less acerbic.

**BARNES, JOHN (1957– ).** U.S. writer who began publishing **sf** with the **space operas** *The Man Who Pulled Down the Sky* (1987) and *Sin of Origin* (1988); their interest in the politics of development and religion was carried forward into the Thousand Cultures **series** comprising *A Million Open Doors* (1992), *An Earth Made of Glass* (1998), and *The Merchant of Souls* (2001); the panoramic *Kaleidoscope Century* (1995); and the **alternative history** *Finity* (1999). *Orbital Resonance* (1991), *Candle* (2000), and *The Sky So Big and Black* (2002) are set in the same universe as *Kaleidoscope Century*. *Mother of Storms* (1994) is a **disaster story**. The Timeline Wars series comprises *Patton's Spaceship* (1997), *Washington's Dirigible* (1997), and *Caesar's Bicycle* (1997). *Encounter with Tiber* (1996) and *The Return* (2000) were written in **collaboration** with astronaut Buzz Aldrin. The trilogy comprising *The Duke of Uranium* (20002), *A Princess of the Aerie* (2003), and *In the Hall of the Martian King*

(2003) is a **Heinleinesque** series of **political fantasies**. His short fiction is sampled in . . . *And Orion* (1989) and *Apostrophes and Apocalypses* (1998), which also includes essays.

**BARNES, STEVEN (1952– ).** U.S. writer best known as a **collaborator** of **Larry Niven**, with whom he wrote *Dream Park* (1981) and its sequels, about futuristic role-playing **games**; the **disaster story** *The Descent of Anansi* (1982); the future sports story *Achilles' Choice* (1991); and the maritime **technothriller** *Saturn's Race* (2000). With Niven and **Jerry Pournelle** he wrote a **transfigurative planetary romance** comprising *The Legacy of Heorot* (1987) and *Beowulf's Children* (1995). His solo works, including *Streetlethal* (1983) and its sequel *Gorgon Child* (1989), *The Kundalini Equation* (1989), and *Firedance* (1993), display a similar fascination with real and imagined violence. In *Charisma* (2002) a behavioral engineering experiment goes wrong. *Lion's Blood* (2002) and its sequel *Zulu Heart* (2003) are **alternative histories** in which Africans colonize the New World.

**BARRETT, NEAL JR. (1929– ).** U.S. writer who began publishing **sf** in the 1960s. The short fiction collected in *A Different Vintage* (2001) is more enterprising and darker in tone than his early novels, with the exception of the surreal **planetary romance** *Stress Pattern* (1974), although the four-volume action-adventure **series** begun with *Aldair in Albion* (1976) is enlivened by the existential troubles of its hero, a **biotechnologically** humanized pig. *Through Darkest America* (1987) and its sequel *Dawn's Uncertain Light* (1989) broke new ground in their portrait of a ruined future United States; similar dark anxieties are displayed in *The Hereafter Gang* (1991) and in the collections *Slightly Off Center: Eleven Extraordinarily Exhilarating Tales* (1992) and *Perpetuity Blues and Other Stories* (2000).

**BARRON, NEIL (1934– ).** U.S. librarian and bibliographer whose library guide *Anatomy of Wonder: A Critical Guide to Science Fiction* (1976; 2nd ed. 1981; 3rd ed. 1987; 4th ed. 1995; 5th ed. projected for 2004) grew from its tentative beginning to become a very useful reference source, annotating thousands of works of fiction and hundreds of historical and critical studies. Many items covered in the third edition—

including an extensive section on foreign-language **sf**—were dropped from the fourth to make way for new material.

**BARTON, WILLIAM R. (1950– ).** U.S. writer who was inactive for some years after publishing *Hunting on Kunderer* (1973) and *A Plague of all Cowards* (1976) but resumed with **hard-sf** novels written with Michael Capobianco (1950– ): *Iris* (1990), about the colonization of an exotic world; *Fellow Traveler* (1991), featuring U.S./Soviet conflict over space travel; *Alpha Centauri* (1997), in which terrorists plague the colony ship that is humankind's last hope; and *White Light* (1998), in which families fleeing a dying Earth make contact with a godlike entity. His solo works include the **space operas** *Dark Sky Legion: An Ahrimanic Novel* (1992) and *Acts of Conscience* (1997); the **military sf** novel *When Heaven Fell* (1995); *The Transmigration of Souls* (1996), featuring an artificial **multiverse**; and *When We Were Real* (1999) in which various modified humans work for a galaxy-ruling corporation. "The Engine of Desire" (2002) launched a series of **far-futuristic** space operas.

**BASS, T. J. (1932– ).** U.S. writer and pathologist whose most significant **sf** is a **series** comprising the **mosaic** novel *Half-Past Human* (1971) and *The Godwhale* (1974), set on a future Earth whose problems of overpopulation have been ingeniously addressed by exotically nightmarish **biotechnology**.

**BATES, HARRY (1900–1981).** U.S. editor and writer who was the first editor of ***Astounding***. He **collaborated** with his assistant Desmond W. Hall (1909–1992) on an early **series** of western-influenced **space operas** in 1931–1932, collected with a belated 1942 addition as *Space Hawk* (1952). His solo work—including "A Matter of Size" (1935), "Alas, All Thinking" (1935), and "Death of a Sensitive" (1952)—was never collected, even though his most famous story, "Farewell to the Master" (1940), was the basis of the famous movie *The Day the Earth Stood Still* (1951).

**BAXTER, STEPHEN M. (1957– ).** British writer whose first **sf** story, "The Xeelee Flower" (1987), became the launchpad for an extensive **series** featuring exotic artifacts left behind by the enigmatic Xeelee, some of which are collected in *Vacuum Diagrams* (1997). His early novels *Raft* (1992), *Timelike Infinity* (1992), *Flux* (1993), and *Ring* (1994) are all set in the same universe, although the last-named is the only one focused on a Xeelee artifact; the remainder are highly sophisticated **hard-sf** novels set in extremely exotic environments—a universe subject to enormously strong gravitational forces in *Raft* and a fluid enclave inside a neutron star in *Flux*. *Anti-Ice* (1993) is a **steampunk Vernian** romance, while *The Time Ships* (1995) is a sequel to **H. G. Wells's** *The Time Machine*, ingeniously consonant with modern cosmology. *Voyage* (1996) offers an **alternative history** of the U.S. space program, while *Titan* (1997) describes a successful extrapolation of it. *Moonseed* (1998) is a large-scale **disaster story**.

The Manifold trilogy, comprising *Time* (1999), *Space* (2002), and *Origin* (2002), is an epic account of a space program in decline, compensated by displacements into alternative universes and transformative **SETI** contacts; the background is extended in *Phase Space: Stories from the Manifold and Elsewhere* (2002) and its scientific bases are further explored in the nonfictional *Deep Future* (2001). *The Light of Other Days* (2000 with **Arthur C. Clarke**) extrapolates the theme of **T. L. Sherred's** classic "E for Effort." Non-Xeelee short fiction is collected in *Traces* (1998). For younger readers, Baxter produced two **virtual reality** stories in the **shared-world** Web series, *Gulliverzone* (1997) and *Webcrash* (1998), and the Mammoth trilogy comprising *Silverhair* (1999), *Longtusk* (1999), and *Icebones* (2001), which extends from the remote past to the near future. *Evolution* (2003) is a similarly extensive panorama of human evolution.

**BAYLEY, BARRINGTON J. (1937– ).** British writer who began publishing **sf** in 1954 and often wrote as "P. F. Woods" before his friend **Michael Moorcock** became editor of ***New Worlds*** and encouraged him to produce ***contes philosophiques*** of a more ambitious stripe, many of which are collected in *The Knights of the Limits* (1978) and *The Seed of Evil* (1979), and one of which was expanded into his first novel, *The Star Virus* (1964, exp. 1970). His novels, a curious amalgam of *conte philosophique* and **pulp sf**, include the baroque **space operas** *Annihilation Factor* (1972), *Empire of Two Worlds* (1972), *The Garments of Caean* (1976), *The Grand Wheel* (1977), *Star Winds* (1978), *The Pillars of Eternity* (1982), *The Zen Gun* (1983), and *The*

*Great Hydration* (2003). *Collision Course* (1973, aka *Collision with Chronos*) and an epic tale of a "Chronotic Empire," *The Fall of Chronopolis* (1974), tamper with time, while *The Soul of the Robot* (1974), its sequel *The Rod of Light* (1985), and *The Sinners of Erspia* (2002) are **existentialist fantasies**.

**BEAR, GREG (1951– ).** U.S. writer who began publishing **sf** in 1967. After publishing the **planetary romance** *Hegira* (1979), he made rapid progress to become one of the leading practitioners of **hard sf**. *Psychlone* (1979, aka *Lost Souls*), *Beyond Heaven's River* (1980), *Strength of Stones* (1981), and the stories in *The Wind from a Burning Woman* (1983; expanded as *The Venging*, 1992) are imaginatively varied. *Blood Music* (1985) is a tour de force describing the wholesale transformation of the ecosphere—and humankind—by rapidly evolving artificial microorganisms, which foreshadowed anxieties about a **nanotechnological** "gray goo disaster."

The cosmological epic begun in *Eon* (1985) and continued in *Eternity* (1988) established a backcloth further employed in the biological fantasy *Legacy* (1995). *The Forge of God* (1987) is a large-scale **disaster story** whose sequel, *Anvil of Stars* (1992), expands into sophisticated **space opera**. *Queen of Angels* (1990) is an ambitious **Utopian** murder mystery extrapolating the social impacts of advanced information technology; it was eventually supplemented by a sequel, *Slant* (1997). *Moving Mars* (1993) moves from futuristic **political fantasy** to the promise of a metamorphosis akin to that featured in *Blood Music*. *Dinosaur Summer* (1998) is a lighthearted but reverent sequel to **Arthur Conan Doyle's** *The Lost World*, aimed at younger readers. *Darwin's Radio* (1999) and its sequel *Darwin's Children* (2003) describe a biological disaster and its aftermath; the conspiracy thriller *Vitals* (2002) is also biological **sf**. The contents of *Tangents* (1989) were combined with earlier and later material in *The Collected Stories of Greg Bear* (2002). Bear edited a notable showcase **anthology** of 1990s sf, *New Legends* (1995).

**BELL, NEIL (1887–1964).** Pseudonym of British writer Stephen Southwold, who was born Stephen Henry Critten but adopted the name of his birthplace. His first **scientific romances**, *The Seventh Bowl* (1930) and *The Gas War of 1940* (1931, aka *Valiant Clay*)—both initially published under the byline Miles—comprise a bitterly sarcastic **future history** in which the self-serving deployment of a technology of longevity precipitates an **apocalyptic** catastrophe. A similar bitterness is displayed in the apocalyptic black comedy *The Lord of Life* (1933) and the **sf** stories in *Mixed Pickles* (1935). *Precious Porcelain* (1931), *The Disturbing Affair of Noel Blake* (1932), and *Life Comes to Seathorpe* (1946) are mysteries with sf solutions.

**BELLAMY, EDWARD (1850–1898).** U.S. journalist who wrote a **hallucinatory fantasy** with an **sf** motif, *Dr Heidenhoff's Process* (1880), and the 1885 allegory that became the title story of *The Blindman's World and Other Stories* (1898) before writing the **Utopia** that became the best-selling book of America's fin de siècle: *Looking Backward, 2000–1887* (1888). The novel offers a vision of a future made comfortable by the application of advanced technologies within a socialist framework that owes more to Henry George's *Progress and Poverty* (1879) than to Karl Marx. As well as having a profound influence on the development of American socialism, *Looking Backward* inspired a great many imitations and ideological replies, the most significant of the latter being *News from Nowhere* (1890) by **William Morris**. Bellamy responded to his critics in a sequel, *Equality* (1897); his influence was extrapolated into genre sf by **Hugo Gernsback** and thoughtfully elaborated by **Mack Reynolds**.

**BELYAEV, ALEXANDER (1884–1942). Russian** writer who pioneered the writing and **criticism** of Soviet **scientific romance**, beginning with the novel translated as *Professor Dowell's Head* (1925, tr. 1980), about an isolated brain. Two other translations are *The Struggle in Space: Red Dream; Soviet-American War* (1927, tr. 1965) and *The Amphibian* (1929, tr. 1959), the latter describing an experiment in **biotechnology**. Moscow's Foreign Languages Publishing House led off its first showcase **anthology** of Soviet sf, *A Visitor from Outer Space* (1961, aka *Soviet Science Fiction*) with the "Belayev" novella "Hoity-Toity," about an elephant scientifically gifted with the power of speech.

**BENFORD, GREGORY (1941– ).** U.S. writer and physicist. The coeditors of a **fanzine** he produced in his teens included **Ted White** and

**Terry Carr** and he went on to produce occasional items of fiction with a remarkable number of **collaborators**, including his twin brother James, **Gordon Eklund** (the episodic *If the Stars Are Gods*, 1977, and *Find the Changeling*, 1980), **William Rotsler** (the **disaster story** *Shiva Descending*, 1980), **David Brin** (the sophisticated **space opera** *Heart of the Comet*, 1986), **Paul A. Carter** (the 1988 novella "Proserpina's Daughter," aka *Iceborn*), and Elisabeth Malartre (the 1997 novella "A Cold, Dry Cradle," subsequently incorporated into *The Martian Race*, 1999). He also wrote sequels to novels by **Arthur C. Clarke** (*Beyond the Fall of Night*, 1990) and **Isaac Asimov** (*Foundation's Fear*, 1997).

Benford's first professionally published story was "Stand-In" (1965). *Deeper Than the Darkness* (1970; revised as *The Stars in Shroud*, 1979) introduced one of his favorite themes, describing humankind's first, deeply disturbing, confrontation with **alien** life; the title story of his first collection, *In Alien Flesh* (1986), is another variant. *Jupiter Project* (1972; in book form 1975; rev. 1980) is a **children's sf** novel whose background was further elaborated in *Against Infinity* (1983). The ambitious "**mosaic** novel" *In the Ocean of Night* (1977) became the foundation stone of an extensive **series** in which the entire galaxy is a battlefield where self-reproducing and continually evolving machines are engaged in a war of extermination against all organic life, continued in *Across the Sea of Suns* (1984), *Great Sky River* (1987), *Tides of Light* (1989), *Furious Gulf* (1994), and *Sailing Bright Eternity* (1995).

Benford transposed his theoretical work on tachyons into the laboratory in *Timescape* (1980), a meticulously detailed account of scientists at work. *Artifact* (1985) and *Chiller* (1993, as by Sterling Blake) are **technothrillers**. *Cosm* (1998) and *Eater* (2000) are exemplary exercises in intellectually ambitious **hard sf**. His other story collections are *Matter's End* (1995), *Worlds Vast and Various* (2000), and *Immersion and Other Short Novels* (2002).

**BERESFORD, J. D. (1873–1947).** British writer whose first novel was the classic **scientific romance** *The Hampdenshire Wonder* (1911, aka *The Wonder*), an account of the career of an extraordinarily intelligent child. *Goslings* (1913, aka *A World of Women*) tracks the effects of a plague that selectively kills human males. His early short fiction, collected in *Nineteen Impressions* (1918) and *Signs and Wonders* (1921), mostly consists of speculative ***contes philosophiques***, but he found it impossible to sell such work thereafter and abandoned scientific romance (although his 1921 *Revolution* is an account of a future socialist revolution in England) until World War II renewed his philosophical ambitions. In "*What Dreams May Come . . .*" (1941), a young man temporarily drawn into a **Utopian** future returns to undertake a hopeless messianic quest in the war-ravaged present. *A Common Enemy* (1942) is a **Wellsian disaster story**. *The Riddle of the Tower* (1944), written with Esme Wynne-Tyson, is a striking **visionary fantasy** of a **future history** in which humankind evolves inexorably toward a state of "automatism." Beresford's ***H. G. Wells*** (1915) was the first major critical study of that writer's work.

**BERNAL, J. D. (1901–1971).** British scientist and philosopher whose **Today & Tomorrow** pamphlet *The World, the Flesh and the Devil* (1929) outdoes **J. B. S. Haldane's** boldest essays in providing an early blueprint for **sf** speculations about humankind's expansion throughout the universe and long-term evolutionary future.

**BESANT, SIR WALTER (1836–1901).** British writer who occasionally dabbled in **scientific romance**. *The Revolt of Man* (1882), originally issued anonymously, features a male revolt against a female-dominated future England. *The Inner House* (1888; reprinted in *The Holy Rose, etc.*, 1890) is a significant early **dystopia** in which a technology of immortality results in social and spiritual stagnation. "The Memory Cell" in *A Five Years' Tryst* (1902) is similarly suspicious of technologically facilitated social change.

**BESHER, ALEXANDER (?– ).** Chinese-born writer of Russian descent, raised in Japan and resident in the United States, who began publishing **sf** in 1993. *RIM: A Novel of Virtual Reality* (1994) is an **Orphean fantasy** involving a **virtual** world. *Mir* (1998) and *Chi* (1999) are further post-**cyberpunk** extrapolations of the same **future history**. *Hanging Butoh* (2003) launched a trilogy of futuristic paranormal detective stories.

**BESTER, ALFRED (1913–1987).** U.S. writer who began publishing **sf** in 1939. A brief burst of creativity in the 1950s produced his best work in the field, including most of the material in the collections *Starburst* (1958) and *The Dark Side of the Moon* (1964), and two classic novels, *The Demolished Man* (1953) and *The Stars My Destination* (1956 as *Tiger! Tiger!*, revised 1957). The former is a **transfiguration** of Fyodor Dostoyevsky's *Crime and Punishment* set in a society of telepaths, the latter the best of several sf versions of Alexandre Dumas's *The Count of Monte Cristo*, here recast as a story of burgeoning superhumanity. He returned to the genre with *The Computer Connection* (1974), *Golem*$^{100}$ (1980), and *The Deceivers* (1981), but never recovered the energy of his earlier work.

**BETANCOURT, JOHN GREGORY (1963– ).** U.S. writer and editor who began publishing **sf** in 1984. His own writings are mostly **tie-ins**, the most notable exception being the **cyberpunk** thriller *Johnny Zed* (1988). His work as a magazine editor, book packager, and **small press** publisher eventually led to his founding of Wildside Press, the first print-on-demand publisher to establish a steady production line. Although its selection was dominated by public domain reprints, Wildside provided a useful refuge for sf writers abandoned by the marketplace and expanded its scope considerably in the early 21st century. It issued Betancourt's own collections *Performance Art* (1992) and *Playing in Wonderland* (1995).

**BIBLIOGRAPHY.** The **sf** genre is remarkably well supplied with bibliographical information and support, thanks to heroic labors undertaken within **fandom** by such meticulous hobbyist scholars as **Everett F. Bleiler**, **Donald H. Tuck**, **Pierre Versins**, and **Philip Harbottle**. Fan-constructed checklists and indexes of **magazine** sf and **anthologies**, including a pioneering *Index to the Science-Fiction Magazines* (1952) by Donald B. Day, paved the way for the databases maintained by ***Locus*** Press CD-ROMs and the **Internet Speculative Fiction (SF) Database** and for the compilers of such reference books as the **Clute/Nicholls** *Encyclopedia*, **Neil Barron's** *Anatomy of Wonder*, and the St. James Press *Guide to Science Fiction Writers*. Useful work in constructing bibliographies of individual sf writers has been done by **Philip Stephensen-Payne** and such collector/dealers as **Lloyd W. Currey** and **George Locke**.

**BIGGLE, LLOYD JR. (1923–2002).** U.S. writer who began publishing **sf** in 1956. Many of his novels belong to a **series** featuring futuristic private eye Jan Darzek. More provocative is a series tracking the endeavors of a "cultural survey" team who always contrive to work around the regulations forbidding them to interfere with the **alien** cultures they study, including *The Still, Small Voice of Trumpets* (1961 as "Still Small Voice," exp. 1968), *The World Menders* (1971), and "The King Who Wasn't" (2001), as is the political allegory *Monument* (1962, exp. 1974). His short fiction, often involving ruminations on the future of music, is collected in *The Rule of the Door and Other Fanciful Regulations* (1967, aka *Out of the Silent Sky* and *The Silent Sky*), *The Metallic Muse* (1972), and *A Galaxy of Strangers* (1976). He completed **T. L. Sherred's** *Alien Main* (1985). *The Chronocide Mission* (2002) is a **postholocaust fantasy**. Biggle founded the Science Fiction Oral History Association (SFOHA) in 1975, which built up a considerable archive of interviews with the genre's pioneers.

**BINDER, EANDO (1911–1975).** Signature used by U.S. writer Otto Binder, initially (from 1932–1940) in collaboration with his brother Earl (1904–1965); he also wrote as John Coleridge and Gordon A. Giles and used his own forename on his final publications in 1972–1973. "I, Robot" (1939; integrated into the **mosaic** *Adam Link, Robot*, 1965) launched the craze for sympathetic **robots** that was subsequently dominated by **Isaac Asimov**, defining and dramatizing the **Frankenstein syndrome**. Other **series** assembled into the mosaics *Anton York, Immortal* (1937–1940, book 1965) and *Puzzle of the Space Pyramids* (1937–1942, book 1971), and such novels as *Enslaved Brains* (1934, book 1965) and *Five Steps to Tomorrow* (1939, book 1970) feature interesting ideas hamstrung by poor composition.

**BIOTECHNOLOGY.** The technological manipulation and creation of living organisms, often involving **genetic engineering**. **Vera Zaronovich's** *Mizora* (1880–1881) is an early example of biotechnological **sf** but the literary influence of **J. B. S. Haldane's** *Daedalus; or,*

*Science and the Future* (1923) was much greater, inspiring **Julian Huxley's** "The Tissue Culture King" (1926) and **Aldous Huxley's** *Brave New World* (1932). **Pulp sf** graphically illustrated Haldane's contention that the automatic first response to all "biological inventions" was one of **horror**, avoiding any support for biotechnological progress—Norman L. Knight's "Crisis in Utopia" (1940) is a partial exception—until **James Blish's** "Beanstalk" (1952) and **Damon Knight's** "Natural State" (1954) restored the issue to the genre's agenda. It was not until the 1970s that sf writers like **Samuel R. Delany** and **John Varley** began to assume that biotechnologies would make benign and life-enhancing contributions to future society. Although their lead was followed by such writers as **Brian Stableford** and **Joan Slonczewski**, positively inclined works remained vastly outnumbered by alarmist products of the **Frankenstein syndrome**. The advent of biotechnologies like in-vitro fertilization, cloning, and genetically modified foodstuffs in the 1990s made little difference to the tenor of near-future sf, which displayed scant confidence in the potential of biotechnology to ameliorate the impending **ecocatastrophe**, but the sophisticated **space operas** of that decade embraced the assumption that the postponed **space age** must, of necessity, be a posthuman project preceded by a dramatic biotechnological revolution.

**BISCHOFF, DAVID F. (1951– ).** U.S. writer who began publishing **sf** in 1975, writing action-adventure sf in **collaboration** with such writers as **Ted White** (*Forbidden World*, 1978), Dennis R. Bailey (*Tin Woodman*, 1979), and **Thomas F. Monteleone** (the **series** launched by *Day of the Dragonstar*, 1983). His solo works include the **horror-steampunk hybrid** *Nightworld* (1979), the lightheartedly **pulpish** *Star Fall* (1980), and the **military sf** novel *The Infinite Battle* (1985), all of which spawned sequels. Most of his 1990s work consisted of **tie-ins** and **sharecropping** projects but *Dr. Dimension* (1993, with John deChancie) and its sequel are tongue-in-cheek exercises, as is *Philip K. Dick High* (2000). *The Diplomatic Touch* (2001) is an erotic comedy about intergalactic diplomats.

**BISHOP, MICHAEL (1945– ).** U.S. writer who began publishing **sf** in 1970. His early work, including "Death and Designation among the Asadi" (1973; integrated into the **mosaic** *Transfigurations*, 1979) often applied anthropological perspectives to **alien** and futuristic societies. *A Funeral for the Eyes of Fire* (1975; revised 1980, initially as *Eyes of Fire*) is a conventional sf adventure, but *And Strange at Ecbatan the Trees* (1976, aka *Beneath the Shattered Moons*), *A Little Knowledge* (1977), the mosaic *Catacomb Years* (1979), *Stolen Faces* (1980), and *Under Heaven's Bridge* (1981, with **Ian Watson**) are intense exercises in exotic social speculation, as are many of the stories collected in *Blooded on Arachne* (1982) and *One Winter in Eden* (1984); they established Bishop as one of the leading practitioners of serious sf based in the human sciences. *No Enemy but Time* (1982) and *Ancient of Days* (1985) are extended ***contes philosophiques*** meditating upon the early evolution of humankind. Bishop's output diversified thereafter, involving excursions into **metafictional** and allegorical **horror** as well as the reverent homage to **Philip K. Dick**, *The Secret Ascension* (1987; aka *Philip K. Dick is Dead, Alas*) and the offbeat **metaphysical fantasies** in the collection *Close Encounters with the Deity* (1986). *Count Geiger's Blues* (1992) is a comedy about an sf editor who develops superpowers. In the poignant *Brittle Innings* (1994), Frankenstein's monster befriends a traumatized youth while playing minor league baseball during World War II. Later short fiction is collected in *At the City Limits of Fate* (1996), *Blue Kansas Sky* (2000), and *Brighten to Incandescence* (2003).

**BISSON, TERRY (1942– ).** U.S. writer in various genres who first edged into **sf** in *Fire on the Mountain* (1988), an **alternative history** story with **Utopian** elements. *Voyage to the Red Planet* (1990) is a futuristic comedy in which an abortive trip to **Mars** is re-created as a movie. *Pirates of the Universe* (1996) is a similarly mordant account of astronauts who dream of escaping their dangerous work by retiring to live in a theme park. *The Pickup Artist* (2001) is a **satire** about a civil servant who collects redundant art in order to make room for new work. Some sf is included in *Bears Discover Fire* (1993) and *In the Upper Room and Other Likely Stories* (2000). He completed the final phase of **Walter M. Miller's** *Saint Leibowitz and the Wild Horse Woman* (1997).

**BLAYLOCK, JAMES P. (1950– ).** U.S. writer who made several crucial contributions to the **steampunk** subgenre between his early magical fantasies and his later supernatural fictions. *The Digging Leviathan* (1984) is a politely ironic homage to the excesses of **pulp** fiction in which the eponymous machine promises much while making no actual progress. *Homunculus* (1986) is an exuberant adventure story set in an **alternative** Victorian London, whose aristocratic hero and ingenious villain continue their technologically assisted conflict in the **mosaic** *Lord Kelvin's Machine* (1992) and in some of the stories in *Thirteen Phantasms* (2000). The **time-tripping** *Land of Dreams* (1987) retains a few **sf** motifs in its **chimerical** mix. Like his friend **Tim Powers**, Blaylock developed an unusually supple narrative method that cut across genre boundaries with considerable and highly distinctive dramatic effect.

**BLAYRE, CHRISTOPHER (1861–1943).** Pseudonym of British writer and biologist Edward Heron-Allen, who displayed a tongue-in-cheek skepticism in his collections of exotic comedies, *The Purple Sapphire* (1921; expanded as *The Strange Papers of Dr. Blayre*, 1932) and *Some Women of the University* (1932). A novella advertised on the title page of *The Purple Sapphire* as having been suppressed by the printer, *The Cheetah Girl* (1923), is a bold exercise in biological **sf**; it was recombined with the rest of the **series** in *The Collected Strange Papers of Christopher Blayre* (1998, as by Edward Heron-Allen).

**BLEILER, EVERETT F. (1920– ).** U.S. scholar and editor whose *The Checklist of Fantastic Literature* (1948, revised 1979 as *The Checklist of Science-Fiction and Supernatural Literature*) was one of the foundation stones of **sf bibliography** and served generations of book collectors as an invaluable guide. His painstakingly taken notes on the books and stories included in the checklist were elaborated into the comprehensively annotated accounts of *Science Fiction: The Early Years* (1990) and *Science Fiction: The Gernsback Years* (1998, with his son Richard J. Bleiler). These works, along with numerous insightful critical articles on 19th-century sf, secured his status as the field's leading historian. In **collaboration** with the checklist's publisher, **T. E. Dikty**, Bleiler edited the first **series** of annual **anthologies** of stories selected from the sf **magazines** from 1949–1954. While working for Dover Publications from 1955–1977 he reprinted a great deal of historically important supernatural fiction and some antique sf, notably material from the **dime novel** medium. For Scribner's he edited *Science Fiction Writers: Critical Studies of the Major Writers from the Early Nineteenth Century to the Present Day* (1982; 2nd ed., with Richard J. Bleiler, 1999).

**BLISH, JAMES (1921–1975).** U.S. writer whose involvement with **sf** began with the **Futurians**; his earliest publications were in **pulps** edited by fellow members **Donald A. Wollheim** and **R. A. W. Lowndes** (with whom he wrote *The Duplicated Man*, 1953; book 1959) and from 1947–1963 he was married to Virginia Kidd (1921–2003), who set up a successful specialist literary agency. In 1950 he published the first of a **series** of stories whose **future history** owes much to Oswald Spengler's *The Decline of the West* (1918–1922), in which Earth's cities are driven by economic recession to become gargantuan spaceships powered by "spindizzies," wandering the galaxy as "Okies" in search of work. The early stories were assembled into the **mosaics** *Earthman, Come Home* (1955) and *They Shall Have Stars* (1956, aka *Year 2018!*); the series was further augmented by the **apocalyptic fantasy** *The Triumph of Time* (1958, aka *A Clash of Cymbals*) and the juvenile *A Life for the Stars* (1962); *Cities in Flight* (1970) is an omnibus.

Other books based on **magazine** stories include *Jack of Eagles* (1949 as "Let the Finder Beware"; exp. 1952; aka "ESP-er"); *Titan's Daughter* (1952 as "Beanstalk," aka "Giants in the Earth"; exp. 1961); *The Seedling Stars* (1957), a mosaic collecting the "pantropy" series based on a classic study of **miniaturized** humanity, "Surface Tension" (1952), in which **genetic engineering** becomes the key to humankind's colonization of the galaxy; and *A Case of Conscience* (1959), in which a Jesuit confronted with a seemingly sinless **alien** world must reconcile its existence with his faith. The last-named was a key element of a boom in sf stories about religion, discussed in "Cathedrals in Space," one of the critical essays Blish wrote as William Atheling Jr., collected as *The Issue at Hand* (1964) and *More Issues at Hand* (1970); Blish eventually placed the novel as the middle item of a trilogy collectively entitled "After Such Knowledge," whose first element was a historical novel about Roger Bacon, *Doctor Mirabilis* (1964, rev. 1971) and whose third was a **religious fantasy** published in two volumes in 1964 and 1971 before being reintegrated in *Black Easter and the Day after Judgment* (1980, aka *The Devil's Day*).

Blish's remaining short fiction from the 1950s was collected in *Galactic Cluster* (1959, rev. 1960) and *So Close to Home* (1961). Other novels of the period include *The Frozen Year* (1957, aka *Fallen Star*) and *VOR* (1958). His work became sporadic thereafter, the most notable additions to his canon being the mosaic *A Torrent of Faces* (1967, in **collaboration** with Norman L. Knight), the juvenile *Welcome to Mars!* (1967), and the **far-futuristic fantasy** *Midsummer Century* (1972). He achieved a belated celebrity when he was hired to turn *Star Trek* **TV** scripts into collections of short stories and wrote the early **tie-in** novel *Spock Must Die* (1970). *Tesseract: The Life and Work of James Blish* (1988) by **David Ketterer** pays tribute to his achievements as one of the most intellectually adventurous sf writers of his era.

**BLOCH, ROBERT (1917–1994).** U.S. writer famous for offbeat crime thrillers, including *Psycho* (1959), and slick horror stories. From his debut in 1935, a small but significant part of his output was **sf**; although his only specialized collection was *Atoms and Evil* (1962), he wrote three futuristic **satires**: *This Crowded Earth* (1958), *Ladies Day* (1968, combined with the former item), and the novel *Sneak Preview* (1959, exp. 1971). His **Cthulhu Mythos** stories include the novel *Strange Eons* (1978) and the stories in *Mysteries of the Worm* (1981). *The Jekyll Legacy* (1990 with **Andre Norton**) is a sequel to **Robert Louis Stevenson's** classic.

**BOND, NELSON S. (1908– ).** U.S. writer who began publishing **sf** in 1937. He attained his greatest success as a comic fantasist, importing the anarchic spirit of such works into an sf **series** featuring *The Remarkable Exploits of Lancelot Biggs, Spaceman* (1939–1943, book 1950) and the crazy inventor Pat Pending. Many of his sf stories were **transfigurations** of myths, including numerous **Shaggy God stories** and a tetralogy of novels comprising *Exiles of Time* (1940, book 1949), *Sons of the Deluge* (1940), *Gods of the Jungle* (1942), and *That Worlds May Live* (1943, book 2002). The collections *The 31st of February* (1949), *No Time Like the Future* (1954), and *Nightmares and Daydreams* (1968) include some sf; *The Far Side of Nowhere* (2002) is a sampler.

**BORDAGE, PIERRE (1955– ). French** writer, one of the leading contributors to French **sf** in the 1990s. *Les guerriers du silence* (1993), *Terra mater* (1994), and *La citadelle Hypénéros* (1995) comprise an epic **space opera**, while *Wang: Les portes d'Occident* (1996) and *Wang: Les aigles d'Orient* (1997) make up a complex political allegory.

**BORGES, JORGE LUIS (1899–1986).** Argentinian writer, one of the 20th century's leading writers of ***contes philosophiques***. *Labyrinths* (1944–1961, tr. 1962) includes two tales of ultimate extrapolation, "The Library of Babel" and "Funes the Memorious"; the **alternative history** story "The Garden of Forking Paths"; and "Tlön, Uqbar, Orbis Tertius," about a peculiar **parallel world**. The title story of *The Aleph and Other Stories* (1949, tr. 1970) is an exotic **microcosmic romance**; also included is the convoluted **fabulation** "The Immortal." The title story of *The Book of Sand* (1975, tr. 1977) is about an infinite book; also included are the bleak "Utopia of a Tired Man" and a homage to **H. P. Lovecraft**, "There Are More Things." *Collected Fictions* (1999) is an omnibus.

**BOSTON, BRUCE (1943– ).** U.S. writer whose surreal work made increasing use of **sf** motifs as his work progressed from the 1970s to the 1990s, most significantly in the story collections *Skin Trades* (1988) and *Short Circuits* (1991) and the poetry collections *Nuclear Futures* (1987), *Cybertexts* (1991), *Chronicles of the Mutant Rain Forest* (1992, with Robert Frazier), *Cold Tomorrows* (1998), and *The Lesions of Genetic Sin* (2000). *Masque of Dreams* (2001) is an eclectic sampler.

**BOUCHER, ANTHONY (1911–1968).** Pseudonym of U.S. writer and editor William Anthony Parker White, who dabbled in fantasy genres—including the **sf** novella "The Barrier" (1942)—alongside his crime fiction, which includes *Rocket to the Morgue* (1942, originally as by H. H. Holmes), a murder mystery set in the world of sf **fandom**. "Q. U. R." and "Robinc" (both 1943, originally as by Holmes) champion "usuform" **robots** against the humanoid models favored by **Isaac Asimov** and others; the Roman Catholic faith that inspired this dissent also underlies "The Quest for St. Aquin" (1951). His most substantial contribution to the field was as editor of ***The Magazine of Fantasy & Science Fiction*** from 1949–1958, initially in **collaboration** with J. Francis McComas. *Far and Away* (1955) and *The Compleat Werewolf* (1970) mingle sf stories with other kinds of fantasy.

**BOULLE, PIERRE (1912–1994). French** writer, primarily a **satirist** and **fabulist**, whose *La planète des singes* (1963, tr. as *Planet of the Apes* and *Monkey Planet*)—travestied by the movie series spun off from it—carries forward a long French tradition rooted in Léon Gozlan's *The Emotions of Polydore Marasquin* (1857). *Le jardin de Kanashima* (1964, tr. as *Garden on the Moon*) is a meditative **sf** novel about the ambitions of the space program. *Jeu d'esprit* (1971, tr. as *Desperate Games*) is a **Utopian** satire. Boulle's story collections include numerous sf ***contes philosophiques***, including those translated as "The Perfect Robot" and "The Lunians" in *Time Out of Mind and Other Stories* (1966) and as "The Heart of the Galaxy" in *Because It Is Absurd: On Earth as It Is in Heaven* (1971). A homage to **Robert Louis Stevenson's** *Jekyll and Hyde* is translated as "The Angelic Monsieur Edyh" in *The Marvelous Palace and Other Stories* (1977).

**BOVA, BEN (1932– ).** U.S. writer and editor whose early **children's sf** novels include *The Star Conquerors* (1959), *The Weathermakers* (1967), *Out of the Sun* (1968), *Escape!* (1970), and the trilogy comprising *Exiled for Earth* (1971), *Flight of Exiles* (1972), and *End of Exile* (1975). He began to write for adults in the early 1960s, eventually expanding *The Dueling Machine* (1963, with Myron R. Lewis; book 1969) into a novel and integrating three other stories into the **mosaic** *As on a Darkling Plain* (1972). When he became editor of ***Analog*** in 1971 he became a key advocate for and skilled practitioner of **hard sf**; he was fiction editor of the popular science magazine *Omni* from 1978–1982. A comic roman à clef about an ill-fated **TV** series, *The Starcrossed* (1975), was followed by the **technothriller** *The Multiple Man* (1976) and *Millennium: A Novel about People and Politics in the Year 1999* (1976), which was subsequently elaborated by the mosaic prequel *Kinsman* (1979) and the sequel *Colony* (1978). *Voyagers* (1981), *Voyagers II: The Alien Within* (1986), and *Voyagers III: Star Brothers* (1990) comprise an epic **space opera** whose political values are more wryly echoed in *Privateers* (1985) and its sequel *Empire*

*Builders* (1993). *Cyberbooks* (1989) is a futuristic **satire**. *To Save the Sun* (1992) and its sequel *To Fear the Light* (1994), both in **collaboration** with A. J. Austin, are unusually moderate **far-futuristic fantasies**. *Mars* (1992) is an account of colonization that became a prelude to a loosely knit **future history series** retrospectively labeled the Grand Tour, including the couplet *Moonrise* (1996) and *Moonwar* (1998), *Return to Mars* (1999), *Venus* (2001), *Jupiter* (2001), and *Saturn* (2003). The Asteroid War series launched in *The Precipice* (2001) was continued in *The Rock Rats* (2002). *Triumph* (1993) is an **alternative history**. *Death Dream* (1994) and *Brothers* (1995) are **technothrillers**, the first featuring **virtual reality** and the second a breakthrough in medical **biotechnology**. Bova's short story collections include *Forward in Time* (1973), *Maxwell's Demons* (1978), *Prometheans* (1986), and *Challenges* (1993).

**BOWKER, RICHARD (1950– ).** U.S. writer who began publishing **sf** in 1982. *Forbidden Sanctuary* (1982) is a humorous ***conte philosophique*** in which an **alien** attempts to claim protection from a church skeptical of his possession of a soul. *Replica* (1987) is a near-future political thriller, while *Marlborough Street* (1987) and *Summit* (1989) are conventional thrillers with a hint of **existentialist fantasy**. The **postholocaust fantasy** *Dover Beach* (1987) is more earnest.

**BOYCE, CHRIS (1943–1999).** Scottish writer who began publishing **sf** in 1964. His stirring proto-**cyberpunk space opera** *Catchworld* (1975) was joint winner of a competition sponsored by the *Sunday Times* and the publisher Victor Gollancz. *Brainfix* (1980) is a dour near-future thriller.

**BOYD, JOHN (1919– ).** Pseudonym of U.S. writer Boyd Bradfield Upchurch, who made his debut with *The Last Starship from Earth* (1968), a complex **alternative history** story whose **time-traveling** hero sets out to assassinate Jesus (whose career was more extensive in his **dystopian** world than in ours). *The Rakehells of Heaven* (1969) is a **satire** whose heroes corrupt a **Utopian** world by introducing religion and clothing. *The Pollinators of Eden* (1969) features seductive plants. The provocative satire *Sex and the High Command* (1970) was followed by biological thrillers *The Organ Bank Farm* (1970),

*The Gorgon Festival* (1972), *The I.Q. Merchant*, and *The Doomsday Gene* (1973), and the **sf** western *Andromeda Gun* (1974). *Barnard's Planet* (1975) and *The Girl with Jade Green Eyes* (1978) revisited the old ground of his earlier satires.

**BRACKETT, LEIGH (1915–1978).** U.S. writer in various genres and media. She was married to **Edmond Hamilton** from 1946 until his death. Her first **sf** story, "Martian Quest" (1940), was in ***Astounding***, but she was primarily associated with *Planet Stories*, for which she wrote numerous exceedingly lush **planetary romances**, including "Lorelei of the Red Mist" (1946, with **Ray Bradbury**), "Queen of the Martian Catacombs" (1949; exp. by Hamilton, uncredited, as *The Secret of Sinharat*, 1964), and "Black Amazon of Mars" (1951; exp. by Hamilton as *People of the Talisman*, 1964). *Shadow over Mars* (1944; book 1951; aka *The Nemesis from Terra*) and *The Sword of Rhiannon* (1949 as "Sea-Kings of Mars"; expanded 1953) are equally exotic. The **mosaic** *Alpha Centauri—or Die!* (1953–1955; 1963) was also improvised by Hamilton. Her **pulp sf** is collected in *The Coming of the Terrans* (1967) and *The Halfling and Other Stories* (1973), sampled in *The Best of Leigh Brackett* (1977) and chronologically reordered in *Martian Quest: The Early Brackett* (2003). *The Starmen* (1952, aka *The Galactic Breed* and *The Starmen of Llyrdis*) and *The Big Jump* (1955) are more restrained. *The Long Tomorrow* (1955) is a sober **postholocaust fantasy**. Brackett tried to recapture the spirit of her *Planet Stories* work in the trilogy comprising *The Ginger Star* (1974), *The Hounds of Skaith* (1974), and *The Reavers of Skaith* (1976), but its time had passed. Her work in the 1940s, like that of **C. L. Moore**, helped lay the foundations for the **hybrid** subgenre of **science-fantasy** by integrating imaginative materials pioneered by pulp fantasists **Edgar Rice Burroughs** and **A. Merritt** into the fabric of the myth of the **space age**.

**BRADBURY, RAY (1920– ).** U.S. writer in various genres who began publishing **sf** in 1939. His sf includes two works of cardinal importance: the loosely knit **mosaic** *The Martian Chronicles* (1950; revised as *The Silver Locusts*, 1951) and the heartfelt **dystopian** novel *Fahrenheit 451* (1953 with two short stories; revised 1979), in which the job of "firemen" is to burn books, thus protecting the population from potentially disturbing thoughts. The former was the first genre sf book to appeal to a wider audience and obtain some credit as literary fiction, which it achieved by pioneering a fabular format in which sf motifs are denuded of any rational plausibility or extrapolative context, employed purely for their symbolic and sentimental value. Its success caused writers loyal to the **Campbellian** manifesto to mount a spirited defense of the aesthetic merits of what they now had to differentiate as **hard sf** against the supposedly debilitating effects of whimsical **fabulation**, but their efforts eventually proved futile. A few sf stories are mingled with other kinds of fantasy in Bradbury's multitudinous collections, most notably *The Illustrated Man* (1951), *The Golden Apples of the Sun* (1953), *A Medicine for Melancholy* (1959, revised as *The Day It Rained Forever*), *R is for Rocket* (1962), and *S is for Space* (1966). There is some sf poetry in *They Have Not Seen the Stars: The Collected Poems of Ray Bradbury* (2003).

**BRADLEY, MARION ZIMMER (1930–1999).** U.S. writer who carried forward the **hybrid science-fantasy** tradition pioneered by **Leigh Brackett** and **C. L. Moore** in a long **series** of **planetary romances** set on the world of Darkover, begun with *The Planet Savers* (1958, book 1962), *The Sword of Aldones* (1962; extensively revised as *Sharra's Exile*, 1981) and *The Bloody Sun* (1964, revised 1979). Darkover was the first **sf** scenario to be opened up and advertised as a **shared world** by a living author, and it was carried forward after Bradley's final solo contribution, *The Heirs of Hammerfell* (1989) in **sharecropping** exercises by Mercedes Lackey, Adrienne Martine-Barnes, and Deborah J. Ross. Begun as a relatively orthodox action-adventure series, it was transformed after *The Shattered Chain* (1976) into a combative sexual-political fantasy, often focused on the society of the Free Amazons. Bradley's other sf includes the proto-Darkoverian adventure stories *The Door through Space* (as "Bird of Prey" 1957, exp. 1961) and *Falcons of Narabedla* (1957, book 1964); *Seven from the Stars* (1962); *The Dark Intruder and Other Stories* (1964); *Endless Voyage* (1975; expanded as *Endless Universe*, 1979); *The Ruins of Isis* (1978); and *Survey Ship* (1980). After the enormous success of the feminized Arthurian fantasy *The Mists of Avalon* (1983), the sf elements of her work—which had always been peripheral—were minimal.

**BRAZILIAN SF.** See LATIN AMERICAN SF.

**BRETNOR, REGINALD (1911–1992).** U.S. writer born in Siberia, resident in the United States from 1919. His own **sf** stories, which began to appear in 1947, are light and witty, but the critical **anthologies** he edited—the groundbreaking *Modern Science Fiction: Its Meaning and Its Future* (1953, expanded 1979), *Science Fiction, Today and Tomorrow* (1974), and *The Craft of Science Fiction* (1976)—demonstrate his serious intellectual interest in the genre's evolution and potential. The Papa Schimmelhorn **series** begun with "The Gnurrs Come from the Woodwork Out" (1950), which culminated in the collection *The Schimmelhorn File* (1979) and the novel *Schimmelhorn's Gold* (1986), deftly mingles motifs from sf and other kinds of fantasy, extracting abundant humor from the **chimerical** confusion. *Gilpin's Space* (1983, expanded 1986) is a **hard-sf** parody originated in ***Analog***. As the anagrammatic "Grendel Briarton," Bretnor wrote a long series of brief "shaggy dog stories" chronicling the misadventures of a space explorer, collected in *Through Time and Space with Ferdinand Feghoot* (1962; exp. as *The Compleat Feghoot*, 1975; further exp. as *The (Even) More Compleat Feghoot*, 1980, and *The Collected Feghoot*, 1992). His interest in the theory of warfare is reflected in a series of exemplary anthologies of **military sf** collectively entitled *The Future at War*, comprising *Thor's Hammer* (1979), *The Spear of Mars* (1980), and *Orion's Sword* (1980).

**BREUER, MILES J. (1889–1947).** U.S. writer whose M.D. was added to his byline by **Hugo Gernsback**, for whom he began writing with "The Man with the Strange Head" (1927). He was one of the most inventive of the early genre writers, but his short fiction—including the **dimensional fantasy** "The Appendix and the Spectacles" (1928), the domestic drama "A Baby on Neptune" (1929, with **Clare Winger Harris**), the political parable "The Gostak and the Doshes" (1930), and the proto-**hard-sf** story "The Fitzgerald Contraction" (1930)—was never collected, and his graphic novel of **Utopia** laid waste by technology in revolt, "Paradise and Iron" (1930), was never reprinted in book form. *Birth of a New Republic* (1930, book 1981), written in **collaboration** with **Jack Williamson**, is a **transfiguration** of the American War of Independence. He published a handful of minor tales after 1932 but never accommodated his narrative method to the action-adventure mold of orthodox **pulp** fiction.

**BRIN, DAVID (1950– ).** U.S. writer educated in physics and astronomy whose Uplift **series**, begun with his first novel *Sundiver* (1980), became a paradigm example of sophisticated **space opera** informed by the intellectual demands of **hard sf**. The series continued in *Startide Rising* (1983), *The Uplift War* (1987), and the trilogy comprising *Brightness Reef* (1995), *Infinity's Shore* (1997), and *Heaven's Reach* (1998), coping cleverly with the problems of **melodramatic inflation**. His **postholocaust fantasy** *The Postman* (1985) is a pugnacious exercise in **libertarian sf**, as is the modestly space-operatic *Heart of the Comet* (1986, with Gregory Benford). *Earth* (1990) is a wide-ranging account of a global **ecocatastrophe** complicated by the cataclysmic results of an unfortunate experiment in physics. *Glory Season* (1993) is a thoughtful **planetary romance** featuring an all-female society, the most ambitious exercise of that kind by a male author. *Kiln People* (2002, aka *Kil'n People*) depicts a near-future society in which people can delegate aspects of their lives to temporary "golem" copies with various ability levels. Brin's inventive short fiction is collected in *The River of Time* (1986), *Otherness* (1994), and *Tomorrow Happens* (2003); his strong interest in the controversies of **technological determinism** is further extrapolated in a provocative nonfiction analysis of *The Transparent Society: Will Technology Force Us to Choose between Freedom and Privacy?* (1998).

**BRITISH SCIENCE FICTION ASSOCIATION, THE (BSFA).** Although the name had been used in the mid-1930s, the organization that became the central organizing force of British **fandom** was founded in 1958, along with its principal printed vehicle, the critical journal *Vector*. Other periodicals spun off from *Vector* include the news magazine *Matrix* and a forum for would-be **sf** writers, *Focus*. The organization initiated an annual British Fantasy Award in 1966, which became the British Science Fiction Awards in 1970.

**BRODERICK, DAMIEN (1944– ). Australian** writer and critic. His first **sf** story was "The Sea's Furthest End" (1964; exp. as a **children's sf** novel, 1993). His first novel, *Sorceror's World* (1970; revised as *The Black Grail*, 1986) displayed a fascination with **far-futuristic**

**fantasy** that was more elaborately and ingeniously displayed in *The Judas Mandala* (1982) and ultimately led to the compilation of a definitive **anthology** mixing fiction and nonfiction, *Earth Is But a Star: Excursions through Science Fiction to the Far Futures* (2001). *The Dreaming Dragons* (1980; revised as *The Dreaming*, 2001) and the comedy *Striped Holes* (1988) are unusually elaborate exercises in **science-fantasy** that, together with the earlier sf novels and the non-sf novel about sf **fandom** *Transmitters* (1984), comprise the Faustus Hexagram sequence. *The Spike: Accelerating into the Unimaginable Future* (1997; revised as *The Spike: How Our Lives Are Being Transformed by Rapidly Advancing Technology*, 2001) is **speculative nonfiction**—the "spike" being similar to **Vernor Vinge's** notion of a technological **singularity**—some of whose ideas are extrapolated in *Transcension* (2002). *The Last Mortal Generation: How Science Will Alter Our Lives in the 21st Century* (1999) carries forward the argument. *The White Abacus* (1997) is a **transfiguration** of *Hamlet*. Broderick's novels written in **collaboration** with Rory Barnes—*Valencies* (1983); *Zones* (1997), about phone calls from the future; *Stuck in Fast Forward* (1999), about a bubble in space-time that becomes an unreliable **time machine**; and *The Book of Revelation* (1999)—are more economical in their use of sf motifs than his solo work. He compiled three showcase anthologies of **Australian sf** before producing the meticulous academic studies *The Architecture of Babel: Discourses of Literature and Science* (1994) and *Reading by Starlight: Postmodern Science Fiction*. His short fiction is collected in *A Man Returned* (1965) and *The Dark between the Stars* (1991).

**BROOKE, KEITH (1966– ).** British writer who began publishing **sf** in 1989. *Keepers of the Peace* (1990) offers a grim account of a failed peacekeeping exercise in a fragmented near-future United States. *Expatria* (1991) and *Expatria Incorporated* (1992) offer a bleak account of extraterrestrial colonization. *Parallax View* (2000) is a collection of stories written in **collaboration** with **Eric Brown**. Brooke's **Infinity Plus** website, launched in 1997, rapidly became a significant focal point of the British sf community.

**BROWN, ERIC (1960– ).** British writer who began publishing **sf** in 1987. His early fiction, much of it concerning artists working with advanced technologies, was collected in *The Time-Lapsed Man and*

*Other Stories* (1990) before *Meridian Days* (1992) offered a more detailed overview of an extraterrestrial artists' colony. *Engineman* (1994) is a **space opera**. Two contributions to a **children's sf series** about **virtual reality**, *The Web: Untouchable* (1997) and *The Web: Walkabout* (1999), were followed by the futuristic detective story *Penumbra* (1999) and the **cyberpunkish** Virex trilogy, set in a ruined Untied States where virtual realities offer welcome escapism, comprising *New York Nights* (2000), *New York Blues* (2001), and *New York Dreams* (2003). His other short story collections are *Blues Shifting* (1995), *Parallax View* (2000, with Keith Brooke), and *Deep Future* (2001).

**BROWN, FREDRIC (1906–1972).** U.S. writer best known for crime fiction, whose first **sf** was published in 1941. His short sf, which includes a great many vignettes and inflated jokes—notably "Answer" (1954)—as well as more extended comedies, made a crucial contribution to the development of humorous sf; it was mingled with other kinds of fantasy in *Space on My Hands* (1951), *Angels and Spaceships* (1954), *Honeymoon in Hell* (1958), *Nightmares and Geezenstacks* (1961), *Daymares* (1968), and *Paradox Lost* (1973). The novel *What Mad Universe?* (1946) constructs a farcical **alternative history** out of sf clichés. *Rogue in Space* (1949–1950, book 1957) is a **space opera**. *The Lights in the Sky Are Stars* (1953, aka *Project Jupiter*) is a sensitive analysis of the power of the myth of the **space age**. *Martians Go Home* (1955) mercilessly **satirizes** the cliché that envisages **aliens** as **little green men**. *The Mind Thing* (1961) is a **horror-sf** thriller. All Brown's sf is in the omnibuses *From These Ashes: The Complete Short SF of Fredric Brown* (2001) and *Martians and Madness: The Complete SF Novels of Fredric Brown* (2002).

**BROWN, ROSEL GEORGE (1926–1967).** U.S. writer who began publishing **sf** in 1958. Her early short fiction is collected in *A Handful of Time* (1963). *Sibyl Sue Blue* (1966, aka *Galactic Sibyl Sue Blue*) and *The Waters of Centaurus* (1970) are interstellar cases from the files of a future cop, while *Earthblood* (1966, with **Keith Laumer**) is a downbeat **space opera**.

**BRUNNER, JOHN (1934–1995).** British writer who published his first novel, *Galactic Storm* (1951, as by Gill Hunt), while still at school. He published "Thou God and Faithful" (1953) as John Loxmith and "The Wanton of Argus" (1953; reprinted as *The Space-Time Juggler*, 1963) as Kilian Houston Brunner before settling on his familiar byline. The **far-futuristic fantasy** "Earth Is But a Star," reprinted as *The Hundredth Millennium* (1959; revised as *Catch a Falling Star*, 1968) and *Threshold of Eternity* (1959) launched a flood of novels from U.S. publisher Ace, some of them as Keith Woodcott; most are routine **space operas**, some of which he rewrote and repackaged in later years. His most ambitious **sf** of this period included the notable **mosaics** *Times without Number* (1962), featuring **time police**, and *The Whole Man* (1964, aka *Telepathist*), about psychotherapeutic applications of **psi** powers. His production slowed after the success of *Stand on Zanzibar* (1968), a sprawling portrait of an overpopulated future world whose patchwork narrative technique was borrowed from John Dos Passos; it was followed by the similarly alarmist *The Jagged Orbit* (1960), *The Sheep Look Up* (1972), and the proto-**cyberpunk** novel *The Shockwave Rider* (1975), which helped to popularize the notions of computer "viruses" and "worms." *Total Eclipse* (1974) offers an account of an "archaeological autopsy" of an extinct **alien** culture whose fate humankind is likely to share.

Brunner fell silent for some years when his attempt to write a massive historical novel about Mississippi steamboats was dogged by persistent health problems and he never recovered his earlier energy or imaginative scope. His late work included an interesting mosaic tracking the troubled history of an exotic alien race, *The Crucible of Time* (1983), and the space opera *A Maze of Stars* (1991). His numerous collections of short sf include *No Future in It* (1962), *Now Then* (1965), *No Other Gods But Me* (1966), *Out of My Mind* (1967), *Not before Time* (1968), and *From This Day Forward* (1972).

**BUCK ROGERS.** A character who became an archetypal **sf** hero when **Philip Francis Nowlan** adapted the substance of two **pulp sf** stories, "Armageddon 2419 A.D." (1928) and "The Airlords of Han" (1929) into the pioneering **comic** strip *Buck Rogers in the 25th Century* (1929–1967). An air force lieutenant transported into the future, Rogers battles his chief adversary Killer Kane, and many others, on and beyond the Earth; his further adaptation to **cinema** serials and **TV** shows greatly encouraged the casual definition of sf as "that Buck Rogers stuff."

**BUDRYS, ALGIS (1931– ).** U.S. writer of Lithuanian descent, resident in the United States since 1936. He began publishing **sf** in 1952, his early work being collected in *The Unexpected Dimension* (1960), *Budrys' Inferno* (1963, aka *The Furious Future*), and *Blood and Burning* (1978). His **postholocaust fantasy** *False Night* (1954) was butchered by the publisher, the restored text being issued as *Some Will Not Die* (1961, rev. 1978). *Man of Earth* (1955, as "The Man from Earth"; rev. 1958) and *The Falling Torch* (1957–1959, book 1959; restored text, 1991) are **political fantasies**. *Who?* (1958) is an **existentialist fantasy** couched as a tense Cold War thriller, whose basic themes are further extrapolated in the more intricate *Rogue Moon* (1960, aka *The Death Machine*), in which a lethal **alien** labyrinth is explored by artificial duplicates of the increasingly disturbed protagonist. *The Amsirs and the Iron Thorn* (1967) is an eccentric **robinsonade**. *Michaelmas* (1977) is a megalomaniac fantasy. *Hard Landing* (1993) is a **UFOlogy** fantasy. Budrys was a considerable polemical force within the genre as a book reviewer for ***Galaxy*** and other periodicals from 1965 until 1980, when he took charge of an annual "Writers of the Future" sf story competition.

**BUG-EYED MONSTER (BEM).** A term coined as an item of ironic abuse in 1939, when Martin Alger announced in a **fanzine** the establishment of a Society for the Prevention of Bug-Eyed Monsters on the Covers of Science Fiction Publications; in correspondence relating to the issue, it was often represented by the acronym BEM, which achieved sufficient currency to be featured in Funk & Wagnall's dictionary in the 1950s but had fallen into disuse by the end of the century. Its reference was not restricted to insectile eyes, referring to any eyes that "bugged out" in a monstrous fashion. The fad that inspired Alger's complaint was launched by the covers of the first two issues (August and October 1936) of *Thrilling Wonder Stories*.

**BUJOLD, LOIS MCMASTER (1949– ).** U.S. writer who began publishing **sf** in 1985 and soon established herself as a highly popular writer of wittily exuberant novels whose usual classification as **military sf** overlooks the diplomatic aspects of their plots. *Shards of Honor* (1986) and *Ethan of Athos* (1986) provided much of the back story of the hero of *The Warrior's Apprentice* (1986), Miles Vorkosigan, a physically handicapped military genius who lives a double life as an officer in the tightly rule-bound Barrayaran Space Navy and the founder of a blithely deregulated mercenary space fleet. His family history is further elaborated in a **series** of comedy thrillers gently satirizing **Gordon R. Dickson's** pioneering Dorsai series, whose earlier components hop back and forth within the chronological sequence of Miles' life story. These include the collection *The Borders of Infinity* (1989) and the novels *Brothers in Arms* (1989), *The Vor Game* (1990), *Barrayar* (1991), *Mirror Dance* (1994), *Cetaganda* (1996), *Memory* (1996), *Komarr* (1998), *A Civil Campaign* (1999), and *Diplomatic Immunity* (2002). *Falling Free* (1988), situated in the same **future history** 200 years earlier, is a **libertarian sf** novel in which childlike human quadrumanes, **genetically engineered** to live in zero gravity, fight to win free of the exploitative corporation that created them.

**BULGAKOV, MIKHAIL (1891–1940). Russian** writer whose satirist tendencies were suppressed in the Stalinist era, although he was able to leave his masterpiece, *The Master and Margarita*, for posthumous publication. His most important **sf satires** are translated as "The Fatal Eggs" (1924; in *Diaboliad and Other Stories*, 1972) and *The Heart of a Dog* (written 1925; 1968). The former is a **Wellsian** extravaganza transplanting the thesis of *The Food of the Gods*, the latter a scathing political parable whose canine antihero stubbornly resists revolutionary humanization.

**BULMER, KENNETH (1921– ).** British writer who sometimes signed himself H. K. Bulmer and employed many pseudonyms during his extraordinarily prolific career, including Alan Burt Akers, Nelson Sherwood, Rupert Clinton, and Tully Zetford. He was active in **fandom** before publishing his first two novels, *Space Treason* (1952) and *Cybernetic Controller* (1952), in **collaboration** with fellow fan A. V. Clarke. His best early works are mostly novellas, including two accounts of senescent **galactic empires**, *Of Earth Foretold* (1960, aka *The Earth Gods Are Coming*) and *Earth's Long Shadow* (1960, aka *No Man's World*); an account of an aquatic human culture's reconquest of the land, *Beyond the Silver Sky* (1960, book 1961); the dimensional fantasy "The Map Country" (1961; exp.

as *Land beyond the Map*, 1965), which became the basis of an extensive **series**; and the **far-futuristic fantasies** "Scarlet Denial" and "Scarlet Dawn" (both 1962, as by Sherwood), combined as *The Million Year Hunt* (1964). He wrote a great many **space operas**, notably *Worlds for the Taking* (1966), and several **dystopias**, including *The Ulcer Culture* (1969, aka *Stained-Glass World*). His writing became more mechanical in the 1970s, mostly consisting of **Edgar Rice Burroughs**–imitations and historical novels reflecting his interest in Napoleonic war-gaming. He took over the editorship of the *New Writings in SF* **anthology** series after the death of **John Carnell**.

**BULYCHEV, KIR (1934–2003).** Pseudonym of **Russian** writer Igor Vsevlodovich Mozheiko. He is best known in his homeland for his zestful and witty contributions to **children's sf**, including the **series** translated as *Alice: The Girl from Earth* (2001). A similar spirit is manifest in the adult sf stories translated in *Half a Life* (1977) and *Gusliar Wonders* (1983). *Those Who Survive* (2000) is a **robinsonade**.

**BUNCH, DAVID R. (1925–2000).** U.S. writer of surreal **sf** fables, many of which are set within a **future history** in which humankind transforms itself by gradual **cyborgization** into a new race devoid of moral and emotional sensitivity, assembled into the highly distinctive **mosaic** *Moderan* (1971). Stories from other futuristic scenarios, developed with similar stylistic idiosyncrasy, are collected in *Bunch!* (1993).

**BURDEKIN, KATHARINE (1896–1963).** British writer whose early work was sometimes bylined Kay Burdekin and whose later work was published under the pseudonym Murray Constantine. Her **timeslip romance** *The Burning Ring* (1929) and her time-spanning **visionary fantasy** *The Rebel Passion* (1929) are marginal to the genre. The striking **scientific romances** *Proud Man* (1934, as Constantine), an **existentialist fantasy** employing a superhuman viewpoint for an inquiry into sexual politics, and *Swastika Night* (1937, as Constantine), which describes an emergent society resulting from a Nazi victory in Europe, were ahead of their time. The **Utopian** fantasy *The End of This Day's Business* (1989), which inverts the sexual-political pattern of *Swastika Night*, was one of several novels that Burdekin could not publish during her lifetime.

**BURGESS, ANTHONY (1917–1993).** British writer of literary fiction who despised **sf** but wrote a good deal of sarcastic futuristic fantasy, including the notorious **dystopian** novella *A Clockwork Orange* (1962), the futuristic **satire** *The Wanting Seed* (1962), the counter-**Orwellian** *1985* (1978), and the **apocalyptic** final segment of the eccentric **mosaic** *The End of the World News* (1983).

**BURROUGHS, EDGAR RICE (1875–1950).** U.S. writer who became one of the most popular and influential writers of **pulp** fiction after making his debut with *A Princess of Mars* (1912 as "Under the Moons of Mars"; book 1917), which became the foundation stone of an 11-volume **series**. It spawned an entire pulp subgenre, whose designation as **interplanetary romance** has been replaced in modern parlance by the more apt term **planetary romance**. Burroughs specialized in an unprecedented exuberant and uninhibited kind of action-adventure in which daydream-like fantasies of heroism ran unbridled as muscular heroes battled exotic monsters to win pulchritudinous heroines. He developed several other scenarios designed to accommodate this kind of fiction, including Pellucidar, a world *At the Earth's Core* (1914, book 1922); the prehistoric era of *The Eternal Lover* (1914–15, book 1925); the **postholocaust** era of *Beyond Thirty* (1916, aka *The Lost Continent*); *The Land That Time Forgot* (1918, book 1922); and the moon's hollow core in *The Moon Maid* (1923–25, book 1926). He also introduced **sf** motifs into the African wilderness lorded over by his most famous hero, Tarzan, and **satirized** his own formula in the role-reversal comedy *The Cave Girl* (1913–1917, book 1925). **Hugo Gernsback** and **Ray Palmer** persuaded him to write for their sf pulps, and imitations of his work were still being churned out wholesale in the 1970s by such writers as "Alan Burt Akers" (**Kenneth Bulmer**) and **Lin Carter**. The unfettered and blithely naive romanticism of his work was adopted into a good deal of **space opera** and was fundamental to early **science-fantasy**.

**BURROUGHS, WILLIAM S. (1914–1997).** U.S. writer whose drug-inspired avant-gardist fantasies sometimes made casual use of **sf** motifs; they came to the fore in the scabrously phantasmagoric **apocalyptic fantasies** *Nova Express* (1964), *The Wild Boys: A Book of the Dead* (1971, revised 1979), and *Cities of the Red Night*

(1981). He was a considerable influence on such **new wave** sf as **J. G. Ballard's** *The Atrocity Exhibition* and **Michael Moorcock's** Jerry Cornelius **series**.

**BUSBY, F. M. (1921– ).** U.S. writer long active in **fandom**, who published his first professional **sf** in 1957. The **space opera** series initiated by his first novel, *Cage a Man* (1974), was eventually collected in *The Demu Trilogy* (1980). His next novel in a similar vein was divided in two as *Rissa Kerguelen* and *The Long View* (both 1976) before being recombined in 1977 and split into three when reissued in 1984. *Zelde M'Tana* (1980) is set in the same fictional world, as is a **series** of novels placing Rissa Kerguelen's eventual husband in the foreground, comprising *Star Rebel* (1984), *Alien Debt* (1984), *Rebel's Quest* (1985), and *Rebel's Seed* (1986). *All These Earths* (1978) is a more relaxed **mosaic**. *The Breeds of Man* (1988) is an AIDS-inspired biological sf novel. *Slow Freight* (1991) features a damaged **alien** spacecraft that destroys worlds. *The Singularity Project* (1993) tracks the invention of a **matter transmitter**. *Islands of Tomorrow* (1994) is a **time-travel** fantasy about overpopulation. *Arrow from Earth* (1995) and *The Triad Worlds* (1996) are **space operas**. His short fiction is sampled in *Getting Home* (1987).

**BUTLER, OCTAVIA E. (1947– ).** U.S. writer who began publishing **sf** in 1971. Her early novels—*Patternmaster* (1976), *Mind of My Mind* (1977), *Survivor* (1978), *Wild Seed* (1980), and *Clay's Ark* (1984)—sampled a history extending from the 17th century far into the future; its key character is an African immortal whose attempts to control the selection of superhumanity lead via contemporary California to the establishment of a **psi**-powered Patternist culture, which faces a crisis when it must cope with the metamorphic effects of an extraterrestrial virus. *Kindred* (1979) is a **timeslip romance** exposing a modern black woman to the indignities of slavery. The adventurous biological sf story "Bloodchild" (1984) served as a preliminary sketch for the more elaborate Xenogenesis trilogy, comprising *Dawn* (1987), *Adulthood Rites* (1987), and *Imago* (1989), in which exotic aliens attempt to exchange genetic material with a human race on the brink of extinction. *Parable of the Sower* (1993) and *Parable of the Talents* (1998) launched a new **series** set in California in the late

2020s, in which the shards of a collapsed American society search for a new ideological impetus that will assist humankind's expansion into space.

**BUTLER, SAMUEL (1835–1902).** British writer whose flamboyant **Utopian satire** *Erewhon; or, Over the Range* (1872) includes "The Book of the Machines," a mock history representing technological progress as a mock Darwinian process of unnatural selection fated to culminate in the enslavement of men by machines. The sequel, *Erewhon Revisited* (1901), is dominated by satire directed against religion.

**BUZZATI, DINO (1906–1972).** Italian writer whose fiction mostly consists of bleak **existentialist fantasies**. Those cast as **sf** include the novel translated as *Larger Than Life* (1960, tr. 1962), in which a huge computer with a human personality sets out on an irresistible path to mechanical domination of the world; "The Slaying of the Dragon" in *Catastrophe* (1965), in which the last surviving dinosaurs are ruthlessly hunted down and their progeny slaughtered; "The Colomber" in *Restless Nights* (1983), an account of a sea monster; and three early stories in *The Siren* (1984): "The Saucer Has Landed," "Appointment with Einstein," and "The Time Machine."

**BYRNE, EUGENE (1959– ).** British writer who began publishing **sf** in 1991 in **collaboration** with **Kim Newman**, with the first of a series of **metafictions** assembled into an **alternative history mosaic** in which America undergoes a socialist revolution, *Back in the USSA* (1997). His solo novel, *ThiGMOO* (1999), is a comedy featuring **artificial intelligences** configured as characters "resurrected" from various periods of history. *Things Unborn* (2001) is a **chimerical** alternative history in which casualties of the atom war of 1962 return as "retreads."

## – C –

**CADIGAN, PAT (1953– ).** U.S. writer who relocated to the U.K. in 1996. Her early involvement with **sf** was as editor of the **fanzine** *Shayol* (1977–1985), where she published her first fiction in 1978. Her early short fiction, collected in *Patterns* (1989), *Dirty Work* (1993), and the **mosaic** novel *Mindplayers* (1987), included significant contributions to the **cyberpunk** movement, whose fascinations are ingeniously extrapolated in the novels *Synners* (1989) and *Fools* (1992). *Tea from an Empty Cup* (1998), its sequel *Dervish Is Digital* (2000), and *Reality Used to Be a Friend of Mine* (2003) are suspenseful mysteries involving crimes that must be investigated in **cyberspace**.

**CAIDIN, MARTIN (1927–1997).** U.S. writer and aerospace journalist. Many of his novels are paradigmatic **technothrillers**, including *The Long Night* (1956), *The Last Fathom* (1967), *No Man's World* (1967), and *The Mendelov Conspiracy* (1969). *Marooned* (1964) and *Four Came Back* (1968) derive their suspense from the hazards of the space program. *Cyborg* (1972) and its three sequels inspired the **TV series** *The Six Million Dollar Man. The God Machine* (1968) and *Three Corners to Nowhere* (1975) began to extrapolate his ideas into more ambitious kinds of **sf**, but he remained committed to thriller plot formulas in such paranoid fantasies as *The Messiah Stone* (1986) and *Dark Messiah* (1990). *Killer Station* (1984), in which medical **cyborgs** are recruited for dangerous work in space, and the **space opera** *Prison Ship* (1989) are his most extravagant works.

**CALDER, RICHARD (1956– ).** British writer, resident in Thailand from 1990–1996, who began publishing sf in 1989. His early short stories and the trilogy comprising *Dead Girls* (1992), *Dead Boys* (1994), and *Dead Things* (1996) are post-**cyberpunk** thrillers. *Cythera* (1998) and *Frenzetta* (1998) form a thematic bridge between those works and the **chimerical** combinations of sf and mythical fantasy wrought in *The Twist* (1999), *Malignos* (2000), and the **mosaic** *Lord Soho: A Time Opera* (2002).

**CALVINO, ITALO (1923–1985).** Italian writer famous for his highly inventive **fabulations** and ***contes philosophiques***. Those that employ **sf** devices include breezy cosmological fantasies starring the immortal Qfwfq in the collections translated as *Cosmicomics* (1965, tr. 1968) and *t zero*, (1967, tr. 1969; aka *Time and the Hunter*), and some of the items in *Invisible Cities* (1972, tr. 1974).

**CAMPBELL, JOHN W. JR. (1910–1971).** U.S. writer and editor who began publishing **sf** in 1930 while he was at college studying physics.

He soon established himself as a leading practitioner of the nascent subgenre of **space opera**, striving to outdo the narrative extravagance of his chief rival, **E. E. Smith**. The **series** comprising the **mosaic** *The Black Star Passes* (1930, book 1953), *Islands of Space* (1931, book 1956), and *Invaders from the Infinite* (1932, book 1961) demonstrated the subgenre's vulnerability to **melodramatic inflation**. *The Mightiest Machine* (1934; book 1947) launched another series, but its sequels did not see print until they were collected as *The Incredible Planet* (1949). "The Last Evolution" (1932) sketched out a **future history** in which a **decadent** human species is replaced by intelligent machines, which are themselves replaced by "Beings of Force." The evolutionary pattern was further explored in two classic **far-futuristic fantasies** published under the byline Don A. Stuart: "Twilight" (1934) and "Night" (1935). Subsequent Stuart stories elaborated the thesis in various ways, attempting to find a way out of what seemed to Campbell to be an impasse; the potential solution laid out in "Forgetfulness" (1937)—in which humankind outgrows dependence on machinery by developing **psi powers**—dominated the image of the future that he spent the next 33 years nurturing as editor of ***Astounding***.

The classic **horror-sf** story "Who Goes There?" (1939)—which became the title story of a 1948 collection, subsequently retitled *The Thing and Other Stories* and *The Thing from Outer Space* to cash in on the movie based on it—ended this phase of Campbell's career because his employers forbade him to publish more of his own work; this work is assembled in *A New Dawn: The Complete Don A. Stuart Stories* (2003). He did publish one more sf novel under his own name, *The Moon Is Hell!* (1951, with one other story)—although *Empire* (1951), bylined **Clifford D. Simak**, is also his—but he compensated by passing on his own story ideas to his inner circle of writers, while his editorial requirements exerted a general pressure on all his contributors. He shaped the central tradition of genre sf by his insistence on the conscientious choice of story premises and methods of **extrapolation**, and a bold determination to track the possible social impact of new technologies. **Robert A. Heinlein's** *Sixth Column* (1949) is a revision of his "All" (reprinted with two other antique items in *The Space Beyond*, 1976) and he fed ideas for development to **Isaac Asimov**, **L. Ron Hubbard**, **Fritz Leiber**, **Mark Clifton**, **Randall Garrett**, **Mack Reynolds**, and many others, although the extent to which he "**collaborated**" on such novels as **Jack**

**Williamson's** *The Humanoids*, **Frank Herbert's** *Dune*, and **Anne McCaffrey's** *Dragonflight* remains conjectural.

Campbell regarded the actualization of his fervent anticipation of the development of atomic power and space rockets as firm proof of his prescience, although his championship of psi powers and his determined human chauvinism were more narrow-minded and less intelligent than he was ever prepared to concede. He was a unique individual, the only person except for **H. G. Wells** about whom it can be confidently said that the evolution of sf would have been very different without his input.

**CANADIAN SCIENCE FICTION.** As in **Australia**, the British genre of **scientific romance** had no significant extension into Canada—despite the precedent provided by James de Mille's inventive **satirical Utopia** *A Strange Manuscript Found in a Copper Cylinder* (1888)—but the importation of U.S. **magazines** was a much more powerful stimulant. **Laurence Manning**, **A. E. van Vogt,** and **Gordon R. Dickson** all moved south to pursue their careers but there was a compensating counterflow that became a tide in the 1970s when **Judith Merril**, **William Gibson**, **Donald Kingsbury**, **Spider Robinson**, **Crawford Kilian**, and **Robert Charles Wilson** moved north to join such English expatriates as **Michael G. Coney**, **Monica Hughes**, and **Edward Llewellyn** in a loosely knit Canadian **sf** community whose principal native exemplar was **Phyllis Gotlieb**. *Other Canadas* (1979) edited by John Robert Colombo was an early showcase **anthology** of Canadian sf, but the Tesseracts **series** launched in 1985 by Merril and continued by other editors was more influential.

Canadian sf made rapid strides in the 1980s with the emergence of writers like **Robert J. Sawyer**, **Candas Jane Dorsey**, and **S. M. Stirling**, and critics like **Douglas Barbour**, **David Ketterer**, and the expatriate **John Clute**. Those who followed in the 1990s, with the support of the **small press** magazine *On Spec*, include **Peter Watts**, **Karl Schroeder**, and **James Alan Gardner**. Interest in sf was also generated among **French** speakers in Quebec, where showcase anthologies began to appear in 1983. By the end of the 20th century, French-Canadian sf was thriving, in spite of difficulties obtaining distribution in France; its most significant writers included **Elisabeth**

**Vonarburg**, Jean-Louis Trudel, and Agnès Guitard. Ketterer's *Canadian Science Fiction and Fantasy* (1992) is a comprehensive history and **bibliography**.

**ČAPEK, KAREL (1890–1938).** Czech writer who often worked in **collaboration** with his brother Josef, who died in Belsen. His mordant **satires** include several significant works treating **sf** motifs with **Swiftian** suspicion. The play *R.U.R.* (1921, tr. 1923) introduced the term **robot** into several languages, with the consequence that its assault on capitalist labor relations is sometimes mistakenly read as a critique of automation. *The Makropoulos Secret* (1922; tr. 1925) contrasts sharply with **George Bernard Shaw's** near-contemporary *Back to Methuselah* in suggesting that longevity would be intolerably burdensome. Čapek's novels include *The Absolute at Large* (1922; 1927), a **religious fantasy** in which a new technology that released the primal energy of Creation wreaks havoc; *Krakatit* (1924, tr. 1925; aka *An Atomic Phantasy*), about an atomic explosive whose symbolic quality is less elevated; and his masterpiece *War with the Newts* (1936, tr. 1937), a highly effective account of the ominously rapid progress made by a newly discovered race of intelligent amphibians from contented primitivism to ambitiously destructive fascism.

**CARD, ORSON SCOTT (1951– ).** U.S. writer whose first **sf** story, "Ender's Game" (1977), became the basis of a **series** comprising *Ender's Game* (1985), *Speaker for the Dead* (1986), *Xenocide* (1991), and *Children of the Mind* (1996), and spawned the related series begun with *Ender's Shadow* (1999), *Shadow of the Hegemon* (2000), and *Shadow's Puppets* (2002); related short fiction is collected in *First Meetings: In the Enderverse* (2002; exp. 2003). The **mosaics** *Capitol* (1979) and *Hot Sleep* (1979) were reworked as *The Worthing Chronicle* (1990; exp. as *The Worthing Saga*, 1990). *A Planet Called Treason* (1979) was rewritten as *Treason* (1988). The messianic theme of the mosaic *Songmaster* (1980) is recapitulated in *Wyrms* (1987). The Homecoming series comprising *The Memory of Earth* (1992), *The Call of Earth* (1993), *The Ships of Earth* (1994), *Earthfall* (1995), and *Earthborn* (1995) is a **transfiguration** of *The Book of Mormon*, and followers of that scripture take center stage in the mosaic **postholocaust fantasy** *The Folk of the Fringe* (1989). *Lovelock* (1994, with

Kathryn H. Kidd) is a **space opera** advertised as volume one of the Mayflower trilogy. *Pastwatch: The Redemption of Christopher Columbus* (1996) toys with the notion of erasing U.S. history in favor of a politically correct alternative. Card's short fiction is collected in the omnibus *Maps in a Mirror: The Short Fiction of Orson Scott Card* (1990, 4 vols. in **paperback**).

**CARNELL, E. JOHN (1912–1972).** British editor. He edited a **fanzine** version of ***New Worlds*** in the 1930s before the professional **magazine** was launched in 1946; he took over its companion *Science-Fantasy* in 1949. He acted as literary agent to many British **sf** writers, forming a close relationship with U.S. publisher **Donald A. Wollheim**. After his magazines were taken over in 1964, he edited the **anthology series** *New Writings in SF* until his death.

**CARR, JAYGE (1941– ).** Pseudonym of U.S. physicist Marj Krueger. She published her first **sf** in 1976. In *Leviathan's Deep* (1979), an **alien** female from a society whose males are inherently inferior is understandably bewildered by contact with humans. *Navigator's Sindrome* (1983), *The Treasure in the Heart of the Maze* (1985), and *Rabelaisian Reprise* (1988) comprise a similarly witty **series** about attempts to recover a female castaway from a society in which sexual slavery is institutionalized.

**CARR, TERRY (1937–1987).** U.S. writer and editor prominent in **fandom** before he began to work as an editor and occasional writer in the early 1960s. His short fiction, collected in *The Light at the End of the Universe* (1976), is more enterprising than the novels *Warlord of Kor* (1963) and *Invasion from 2500* (1964, with **Ted White** as Norman Edwards). *Cirque* (1977) is a **far-futuristic fantasy**. Carr's editorial endeavors included the highly influential Ace Special **series** of the late 1960s, which specialized in **sf** of more sophisticated varieties than the **space operas** and **planetary romances** favored by his colleague **Donald A. Wollheim**. His original **anthology** series *Universe* (1971–1987) was similarly inclined.

**CARTER, ANGELA (1940–1992).** British writer who became the leading literary fantasist of her generation. *Heroes and Villains*

(1969) and *The Passion of New Eve* (1977) are **postholocaust fantasies**, the latter offering a phantasmagoric account of the collapse of a **decadent** United States. *The Infernal Desire Machines of Dr. Hoffman* (1972, aka *War of Dreams*) includes a few **sf** motifs in a vivid **visionary fantasy**.

**CARTER, LIN (1930–1988).** U.S. writer and editor who laid the groundwork for the development of genre fantasy in the early 1970s. His own work was relentlessly imitative, including many pastiches of **Edgar Rice Burroughs**. *The Man Who Loved Mars* (1973) is one of several **science-fantasies** modeled on **Leigh Brackett**, while *Time War* (1974) takes its inspiration from **A. E. van Vogt**.

**CARTER, PAUL A. (1926– ).** U.S. scholar who published a handful of **sf** stories from 1946 onwards, most notably "Proserpina's Daughter" (1989, with Gregory Benford; aka *Iceborn*). His study of *The Creation of Tomorrow: Fifty Years of Magazine Science Fiction* (1977) is a significant academic analysis.

**CARTMILL, CLEVE (1908–1964).** U.S. writer who contributed to the **sf pulps** in the 1940s, including the stories assembled in the **mosaic** *The Space Scavengers* (1949–1950; 1975). He achieved a certain notoriety when **John Campbell** gleefully revealed that his atomic bomb story "Deadline" (1944) had drawn the attention of the security services to ***Astounding*'s** long-standing championship of atomic power and its potential spin-off.

**CARVER, JEFFREY A. (1949– ).** U.S. writer who began publishing **sf** in 1974. *Seas of Ernathe* (1976), *Star Rigger's Way* (1978), and *Panglor* (1980, revised 1996) laid the groundwork for the "Star Rigger Universe" used as a setting in such further works as *Dragons in the Stars* (1992), its sequel *Dragon Rigger* (1994), and *Eternity's End* (2000). *The Infinity Link* (1984) is an account of a **first contact** invested with transcendental significance. *The Rapture Effect* (1987) employs art as a mediating influence in a contest between warring **artificial intelligences**. Similar themes are carried forward on a grander scale in the Starstream **series**, comprising *From a Changeling Star* (1989) and *Down the Stream of Stars* (1990), and the Chaos Chronicles, comprising *Neptune Crossing* (1994), *Strange Attractors* (1995), and *The Infinite Sea* (1997).

**CASTRO, ADAM-TROY (1960– ).** U.S. writer who began publishing **sf** in 1989. "The Funeral March of the Marionettes" (1997) and "The Tangled Strings of the Marionettes" (2003) offer a striking account of a mysterious **alien** species; "Unseen Demons" (2002) is a similar exercise. *Vossoff and Nimmitz: Just a Couple of Idiots Reupholstering Time and Space* (2002) is a humorous picaresque adventure. Some of his short sf is collected in *An Alien Darkness* (2000), whose companion volume features **horror** fiction.

**CHALKER, JACK L. (1944– ).** U.S. writer active in **fandom** as a **small press** publisher before launching his professional career with the **space opera** *A Jungle of Stars* (1976) and the exotic **planetary romances** *Midnight at the Well of Souls* (1977) and *Dancers in the Afterglow* (1978). The interest in godlike **aliens** and evolving superhumanity displayed in these novels was carried forward into numerous **series**—the first of them, extrapolated from the second title cited, extending to *Ghosts of the Well of Souls* (2000)—whose **sf** elements were gradually overwhelmed by other kinds of fantasy as rational extrapolation was sacrificed to hectic narrative pace and relentless **melodramatic inflation**.

Chalker's nonseries thrillers, including *A War of Shadows* (1979), *The Identity Matrix* (1982), and *Downtiming the Night Side* (1985), exhibited a similar pattern of evolution. *The Cybernetic Walrus* (1995) is a **virtual reality** fantasy paying homage to Philip K. Dick. *Priam's Lens* (1999) is a **far-futuristic fantasy** in which the survival of the human race is at stake. The Three Kings trilogy, comprising *Balshazzar's Serpent* (2000), *Melchior's Fire* (2001), and *Kaspar's Box* (2003), is a far-futuristic fantasy in which an interstellar civilization collapses when its connecting **wormholes** are obliterated. *The Moreau Factor* (2000) is a near-future thriller involving **genetic engineering**. *Chameleon* (2003) launched a series of futuristic espionage thrillers. Chalker's collections of short fiction include *Dance Band on the Titanic* (1988) and *Dancers in the Dark* (2000).

**CHANDLER, A. BERTRAM (1912–1984).** British-born writer who served in the Merchant Navy from 1928, immigrating to **Australia** in

1956. He began publishing **sf** in 1944, drawing on his experience of life at sea in an extensive **series** of **space operas** set in the Rim Worlds on the edge of an interstellar civilization, begun with "The Outsiders" (1959; exp. as *The Ship from Outside*, 1963) and *The Rim of Space* (1961) and concluded with *The Wild Ones* (1984). His other novels include the **dystopian** fantasy *The Bitter Pill* (1974) and the Australian **alternative history** *Kelly Country* (1983). *From Sea to Shining Star* (1990) samples his short fiction.

**CHARNAS, SUZY MCKEE (1939– ).** U.S. writer in various genres whose **sf** comprises a **series** of **postholocaust fantasies** in which women serve as scapegoats for the disastrous results of male technological hubris in urban strongholds, but fare better in matriarchal societies that flourish in the wilderness: *Walk to the End of the World* (1989), *Motherlines* (1978), *The Furies* (1994), and *The Conqueror's Child* (1999).

**CHERRYH, C. J. (1942– ).** U.S. writer who began publishing **sf** in 1968. Her novels are mostly set within a **future history** spanning more than two millennia, in which a fragile galactic culture is held together by a Merchanter culture whose members stubbornly maintain their benign trading activities while being continually caught up in fierce disputes—often caused by the more oppressive activities of the empire-building Union—and making conscientious attempts to protect idiosyncratic planetary societies from cultural or actual devastation. High points in the series' main sequence include the Faded Sun trilogy (1978–1979); *Downbelow Station* (1981), the first of its many sophisticated **space operas**; *Merchanter's Luck* (1982); the extraordinarily elaborate *Cyteen* (1988); the prequel series begun with *Heavy Time* (1991); and *Tripoint* (1994). Notable peripheral texts include the extended ***conte philosophique*** *Wave without a Shore* (1981), the **metafictional** *Port Eternity* (1982), the avant-gardist space opera *Voyager in Light* (1984), and several ingeniously constructed accounts of **alien** life, culture, and psychology, including the Chanur sequence (1982–1992), *Cuckoo's Egg* (1985), and the series comprising *Foreigner* (1994), *Invader* (1995), *Inheritor* (1996), *Precursor* (2000), *Defender* (2001), and *Explorer* (2002). The Gene Wars series begun with *Hammerfall* (2001) carries forward **biotechnological** themes from *Cyteen*. *Sunfall* (1981) is a collection of **far-futuristic fantasies**

depicting **decadent** versions of Earth's major cities—a fascination also manifest in the Merovingen series, launched with *Angel with the Sword* (1985) and carried forward as a **shared-world** enterprise. Cherryh's other short sf is sampled in *Visible Light* (1986).

**CHIANG, TED (1967– ).** U.S. writer who began publishing **fabular *contes philosophiques*** with **sf** elements with the alternative universe story "Tower of Babel" (1990). His production was sparse but his stories won several awards before being collected in *Stories of Your Life and Others* (2002). The most wholeheartedly **science-fictional** are "Understand" (1991), an account of **artificially boosted intelligence**, and "Story of Your Life" (1998), a complex **first contact** story.

**CHILDREN'S SF. Jules Verne** did not consider himself an author of children's books, but his publisher serialized them in his "family magazine" and the resultant subgenre of Vernian romance consisted almost entirely of juvenile fiction—especially in Britain, where it was an important enclave of the "boys' book" market. Notable British writers of boys' book **sf** included "Fenton Ash" (Francis Henry Atkins, 1840–1927)—whose **planetary romances**, notably "A Son of the Stars" (1907–1908) and "A King of Mars" (1907; book as *A Trip to Mars* 1909), anticipated the work of **Edgar Rice Burroughs**—"Herbert Strang" (George Herbert Ely, 1866–1958, and C. J. L'Estrange, 1867–1947), and **George C. Wallis**. The tales of technological invention featured in American **dime novels** were also aimed specifically at younger readers. Although very few **pulp** magazines advertised themselves as juvenile fare, their letter columns and the memoirs of those readers who came together to constitute sf **fandom** suggest that most readers of the sf pulps were teenage boys. There is, therefore, a sense in which sf—unlike **scientific romance**—was essentially a genre of children's fiction, at least until **John W. Campbell Jr.** undertook the process of sophistication that began when he took over ***Astounding*** in 1937, and that it remained primarily a children's genre until the 1950s, when a clear distinction first began to be drawn in the U.S. marketplace between "adult" and "children's" sf—when adult sf remained largely becalmed in **magazines** and **paperbacks** and children's sf was mostly issued in a far more respectable hardcover format. For this reason, many of the more ambitious writers of Campbellian sf—including **Robert A. Heinlein**, **Isaac Asimov**, **James Blish**, and **Lester del Rey**—took advantage of a brief interval when **hard sf** for children was promoted by U.S. publishers for its supposed educational value. **Arthur C. Clarke** and **Patrick Moore** did similar work in Britain.

Although children's publishers soon realized that the **soft sf** pioneered in the United States by **Andre Norton** and **Madeleine l'Engle** and in the United Kingdom by **John Christopher** had more sales potential—because hard sf content was a deterrent to all but a small fraction of (mostly male) readers—the educational value of hard sf helped maintain its production, allowing subsequent hard sf specialists like **Ben Bova**, **Gregory Benford**, **Charles Sheffield**, and **Stephen Baxter** to work productively in the medium. As in the adult market, the use of planetary romance as an alternative format to **parallel-world** fantasy became increasingly common in the 1960s and 1970s; **postholocaust fantasies** also became increasingly common, in spite of editorial anxieties about promoting alarmism. **Timeslip romances** and **portal fantasies**, already established as important subgenres of children's fantasy, began to take on more sf elements. Writers who routinely **hybridized** sf with other kinds of fantasy include **Nicholas Fisk**, **Sylvie Louise Engdahl**, **Peter Dickinson**, **Louise Lawrence**, **H. M. Hoover**, **Cherry Wilder**, **Monica Hughes**, **William Sleator**, and **Diana Wynne Jones**. Most children's sf is necessarily aimed at older children but the imagery of sf gradually permeated fiction for younger independent readers in the 1980s, notably in the work of Eleanor Cameron and **Douglas Hill**, and the use of such imagery in picture books was considerably diversified in the 1990s as **TV** sf popularized a wider range of motifs.

**CHIMERICAL TEXTS.** Texts that combine elements of **sf** with elements drawn from other fantasy genres in spite of the fact that they are based on fundamental assumptions that are opposed and irreconcilable. Many **religious fantasies** and **horror-sf** stories adopt sf motifs without regard to the fact that they are the produce of an intrinsically secular and progressive genre. Early chimerical texts drew **humorous** or surreal narrative energy from the irreconcilability of the conflict, as in the kind of fantasy favored by ***Unknown*** or many of the works of **R. A. Lafferty**, but such combinations had become sufficiently familiar by the end of the 20th century for chimerization to be employed earnestly in such texts as China Miéville's *Perdido Street Station* (2000) and for the open defiance of genre boundaries and conventions to justify the campaign by Delia Sherman, Terri Windling, and others for a category of "interstitial fiction"—within an interstitial arts movement—that is far more assertive than the mere recognition of a literary **slipstream**. Chimerical texts may be regarded as examples of **science-fantasy**, but need to be contrasted with **ambiguous** and **hybrid** texts.

**CHINESE SF. Science-fictional** themes appeared only sporadically in Chinese fiction before the establishment of the People's Republic in 1949, the most significant examples being a 1904 account of the colonization of the **moon** by Huangjiang Doaosuo, a 1933 **satire** featuring catlike **Martians** by Lao She, and several stories attempting to popularize science via **sf** by Gu Jungzheng. It was the last example that was carried forward into communist society, where sf of a **Vernian** stripe was regarded as a useful educational subgenre of children's fiction until the cultural revolution of the late 1960s, when sf was stigmatized as a "**decadent**" Western genre and some writers—most notably Zheng Wenguang (1929–2003), an enormously influential writer and editor of **children's sf** and pioneer of Chinese sf for adults—underwent painful programs of political reeducation. After 1978 there was a brief resurgence in Chinese sf, involving such writers as Ye Yonglie and the publication of a great deal of work in translation, but the political climate cooled again after 1983. By the end of the decade, however, Yang Xiao's *Kehuan Shijia* (*SF World*), launched in 1979, had by far the largest circulation of any sf **magazine** in the world; from 1986 she hosted annual colloquia in Chengdu—including the 1991 **World SF** conference—at which the Milky Way Awards were presented; its winners include Liu Ci Xin, Wang Kin Jang, Zhao Haihong, and Wang Ya Nan. *Science Fiction from China* (1989), edited by Wu Dingbo and Patrick Murphy, is a showcase **anthology**.

**CHRISTOPHER, JOHN (1922– ).** British writer who began publishing **sf** in 1949; his early stories are collected in *The Twenty-Second Century* (1954). The near-future thriller *The Year of the Comet* (1955, aka *Planet in Peril*) was followed by a **disaster story** imitative of **John Wyndham**, *The Death of Grass* (1956, aka *No Blade of Grass*). Other exercises in a similar vein are *The World in Winter* (1962, aka *The Long Winter*), *A Wrinkle in the Skin* (1965, aka *The Ragged Edge*), and *Pendulum* (1968). His most successful project was the **children's sf series** comprising *The White Mountains* (1967), *The City of Gold and Lead* (1967), *The Pool of Fire* (1968), and the belated prequel *When the Tripods Came* (1988), in which **alien** Tripods reminiscent of the invaders in **H. G. Wells's** *The War of the Worlds* have reduced human society to a quasi-medieval state. Almost all of his subsequent fiction was for children, the most notable sf inclusions being *The Guardians* (1970), *Dom and Va* (1973), *Empty World* (1977), and *A Dusk of Demons* (1994). *Bad Dream* (2003) is an adult mystery involving **virtual reality**.

**CINEMA.** As a visual medium, cinema always found the explanatory aspects of **sf** impossible to accommodate, and the history of sf films has been governed by the evolution of special effects that have gradually facilitated the incorporation of sf imagery without the least trace of extrapolative seriousness. Fritz Lang's *Metropolis* (1926) was a major force in popularizing the idea of the **robot** and *Die Frau im Mond* (1929) attempted to advertise the imminence of the **space age**, but with the sole exception of Alexander Korda's version of **H. G. Wells's** *Things to Come* (1936), there was no serious attempt to accommodate the themes of **scientific romance** to the film medium. In 1930s Hollywood, sf motifs were used in a few exotic crime thrillers, numerous **horror** movies, and various serials based on **comic** strips; very little changed in the succeeding decades, although ultracheap movies designed to aid the attempted teenage seductions for which drive-in movies provided an important arena in the 1950s and 1960s reduced the scabrous public image of sf to abysmal levels.

Unlike sf comic strips, sf novels are essentially impossible to film, although a number of artistically successful movies have been based on the bare bones of stories extracted from sf texts, including *Invasion of the Body Snatchers* (1956, based on Jack Finney's *The Body Snatchers*), *Charly* (1966, based on **Daniel Keyes**' "Flowers for Algernon"), *A Clockwork Orange* (1971, based on **Anthony Burgess's** novella), *Solaris* (1972, based on **Stanislaw Lem's** novel), *Who?*

(1974, based on **Algis Budrys's** novel), *A Boy and His Dog* (1975, based on **Harlan Ellison's** short story), *Blade Runner* (1982, based on **Philip K. Dick's** *Do Androids Dream of Electric Sheep?*), and *Harrison Bergeron* (1995, based on **Kurt Vonnegut's** story). The influence of cinema on sf has mostly consisted of inspiring scathing **satires**, but Stanley Kubrick's *2001: A Space Odyssey* (1968), scripted with **Arthur C. Clarke**, inspired a **series** of novels that transcended the inherent absurdities of their original. Thanks to the success of *Star Wars* (1977) as a marketing instrument, movie **tie-ins** are now an important sector of the sf book marketplace, and are sometimes skillfully done (**Alan Dean Foster** handles such work with unparalleled deftness), but they are essentially an extension of "**sci-fi**" into the print medium rather than a subspecies of literary sf.

**CLARESON, THOMAS D. (1926–1993).** U.S. scholar. A significant pioneer of the academic study of **sf**, he edited the journal *Extrapolation* from 1959–1989. He compiled several significant **anthologies** of sf **criticism**, including *SF: The Other Side of Realism* (1971) and the *Voices for the Future* series (3 vols., 1976–1983), a useful annotated bibliography of *Science Fiction in America, 1870s–1930s* (1984), and a significant study of that era, *Some Kind of Paradise: The Emergence of American Science Fiction* (1985). He was the first president of the **Science Fiction Research Association** (1970–1976).

**CLARION SF WRITERS' WORKSHOP.** An annual summer school at which many leading **sf** writers have served as guest tutors. Its teaching methods were modeled on the **Milford** workshop. It was launched at Clarion State College, Pennsylvania, in 1968, under the directorship of Robin Scott Wilson. It divided into two in 1971; the "original" Clarion settled at Michigan State University from 1972, while the less regular "Clarion West" was based at the University of Seattle until 2003, when it moved to the University of Washington. Many contemporary sf writers attended the workshop before building substantial careers, including **Octavia Butler**, **Vonda McIntyre**, **Kim Stanley Robinson**, and **Lucius Shepard**.

**CLARKE, SIR ARTHUR C. (1917– ).** British writer, long resident in Sri Lanka. Like **Isaac Asimov**, he was both a definitive writer of

**hard sf** and a highly effective popularizer of science. He was the most vocal **prophet** of the **space age**, which he advertised in *Interplanetary Flight* (1950) before obtaining his first big commercial success with *The Exploration of Space* (1951). He is sometimes credited with the "invention" of the communications satellite, having laid out the case for some such technology in "Extraterrestrial Relays" (1945). His early novels *Prelude to Space* (1951, rev. 1954), *Earthlight* (1951, exp. 1955), *The Sands of Mars* (1951), and the juvenile *Islands in the Sky* (1952) were calculatedly propagandistic dramatizations of these speculations; his contribution to **Reginald Bretnor's** definitive account of *Modern Science Fiction* (1953) declared sf to be "Preparation for the Age of Space."

Clarke began publishing sf in 1946. His first novel, *Against the Fall of Night* (1948, book 1953; revised as *The City and the Stars*, 1956) is a **far-futuristic fantasy** combining the visionary range and philosophical depth of **Olaf Stapledon** with the narrative drive and gaudy lyricism of **pulp sf** to contrive an ingenious fusion. When he expanded "Guardian Angel" (1950) into *Childhood's End* (1953), he added a similar visionary element, coincidentally producing an image of humankind's evolutionary future reminiscent of Teilhard de Chardin's **Omega Point**. The similarly pretentious "Sentinel of Eternity" (1951, aka "The Sentinel") became the basis of Stanley Kubrick's film *2001: A Space Odyssey* (1968, novelization 1968). The short fiction collected in *Expedition to Earth* (1953), *Reach for Tomorrow* (1956), *The Other Side of the Sky* (1958), *Tales of Ten Worlds* (1962), and *The Nine Billion Names of God* (1967) is mostly hard sf of a restrained kind but "The Star" describes the discovery by space travelers of worlds devastated by the explosion of the Star of Bethlehem. *The Deep Range* (1954) also adds a visionary element to its prospectus for the future exploitation of the oceans. *A Fall of Moondust* (1961), a thriller set on the **moon**, was followed by *Dolphin Island* (1963), a juvenile cast in a similar mold.

When *2001: A Space Odyssey* made him famous, Clarke returned to writing sf with a sequence of flamboyant hard sf novels that became best sellers: *Rendezvous with Rama* (1973), *Imperial Earth* (1975, restored text 1976), and *The Fountains of Paradise* (1979). He intended the last of these—which describes the building of a space elevator—to be his fictional swan song, but his mind remained sharp in spite of his health problems and further elaborations continued to occur to him. *2010: Odyssey Two* (1982) was eventually followed by *2061: Odyssey Three* (1988) and *3001: The Final Odyssey* (1997). *The Songs of Distant Earth* (1986) greatly elaborated a 1958 short story. After extrapolating one of Clarke's ideas into *Cradle* (1988), Gentry Lee was entrusted with writing *Rama II* (1989), *The Garden of Rama* (1991), and *Rama Revealed* (1993). Although Clarke managed to produce a memoir, *Astounding Days* (1989), and *The Hammer of God* (1993) without assistance, the more substantial *The Trigger* (1999, with **Michael Kube-McDowell**) and *The Light of Other Days* (2000, with **Stephen Baxter**) were also done in **collaboration**. *The Collected Stories* (2000) is a massive omnibus.

**CLARKE, I. F. (1918– ).** British scholar who published an annotated **bibliography** of *The Tale of the Future* (1961; 2nd ed. 1972; 3rd ed. 1978). *Voices Prophesying War 1763–1984* (1966; revised 1992 as *Voices Prophesying War: Future Wars 1763–3749*) is a definitive study of the **future war** subgenre. *The Pattern of Expectation 1644–2001* (1979) is a wide-ranging history of images of the future. Clarke compiled an eight-volume showcase **anthology** of *British Future Fiction 1700–1914* (2001).

**CLEMENT, HAL (1922–2003 ).** Pseudonym of U.S. science teacher and writer Harry Clement Stubbs, who began publishing **sf** with "Proof" 1942. His work for ***Astounding*** rapidly became the epitome of **hard sf**, subsuming all other narrative considerations to the bold extrapolation and clear exposition of scientific ideas. His pioneering short fiction was sampled in *Natives of Space* (1965) and *Small Changes* (1969, aka *Space Lash*); *The Essential Hal Clement, Volume 2: Music of Many Spheres* (2000) is a comprehensive collection. His first novel, *Needle* (1950), attempted to provide a more reader-friendly account of a parasitic **alien** policeman in pursuit of a fugitive; it seems to have been intended as a juvenile—as, presumably, were its sequel *Through the Eye of a Needle* (1978) and the castaway drama *Close to Critical* (1958, book 1964).

*Iceworld* (1951, book 1953), which offers an account of Earth through exotic alien eyes, was followed by the classic *Mission of Gravity* (1953, abridged book 1954; restored text 1978) and the similarly designed *Cycle of Fire* (1957), which construct unprecedentedly elaborate descriptions of radically alien ecospheres. *Ocean on Top* (1967, book 1973), *The Nitrogen Fix* (1980), *Still River* (1987), *Half Life* (1999), and *Noise* (2003) are cast in a similar mold. *Star Light* (1971) revisits the rapidly rotating setting of *Mission to Gravity* and was reprinted with it and other connected materials in *The Essential Hal Clement, Volume 3: Variations on a Theme by Isaac Newton*, 2000). Volume 1 of the series, *Trio for Side Rule & Typewriter* (1999) includes *Needle*, *Iceworld*, and *Close to Critical*. As well as complex scientific exposition, Clement's work is notable for its steadfast refusal to employ villains, on the grounds that the universe is sufficiently hostile and challenging without requiring further assistance from human or alien evil.

**CLIFTON, MARK (1906–1963).** U.S. writer who channeled the results of his work as a personnel profiler into the **sf** he began publishing in 1952. His early work, done for ***Astounding*** at the height of the **psi** boom, includes a **series** of stories about the search for wild talents and the fervently propagandistic *They'd Rather Be Right* (1954, with Frank Riley; book 1957, aka *The Forever Machine*), whose concluding lecture is pure **John Campbell**. *Eight Keys to Eden* (1960), a striking work of **ecological mysticism**, was a marked change of direction. *When They Come from Space* (1962) is a comedy. *The Science Fiction of Mark Clifton* (1980), edited by **Barry N. Malzberg**, is a sampler of his short fiction.

**CLUTE, JOHN (1940– ). Canadian** writer whose primary contributions to the genre are the trenchant reviews and critical articles collected in *Strokes: Essays and Reviews 1966–1986* (1988), *Look at the Evidence* (1996), and *Scores: Reviews 1993–2003* (2003) and his coeditorship with **Peter Nicholls** of *The Encyclopedia of Science Fiction* (1979; 2nd ed. 1993), a then-definitive guide to the field that remains immensely useful. *Appleseed* (2001) is a baroque **far-futuristic space opera**.

**COBLENTZ, STANTON A. (1896–1982).** U.S. writer who published poetry and nonfiction before **Hugo Gernsback's sf pulps** provided a market for his eccentric **Utopian satire** *The Sunken World* (1928;

book 1948). More novels followed in rapid succession, including the inventive *After 12,000 Years* (1929; book 1950), "Reclaimers of the Ice" (1930, book 1964 as *The Lost Comet*), and the unsubtle political satires *The Blue Barbarians* (1931) and *In Caverns Below* (1935, book 1957 as *Hidden World*). He struggled to adjust such works as "Planet of the Knob Heads" (1939) to the requirements of down-market pulps and his later books—including *Next Door to the Sun* (1960), *The Crimson Capsule* (1967, aka *The Animal People*), and *The Island People* (1971)—seemed anachronistic.

**COGNITIVE ESTRANGEMENT.** A term used by **Darko Suvin** to define the fundamental method and effect of **sf**; it concentrates critical attention on the process by which the reader "gets to know" the world within the text. In this view, becoming acquainted with the fictitious worlds of mimetic fiction only requires the reader to refine and reconstruct the stocks of knowledge used in the understanding of actual situations, while reading "fantasy" only requires the partial and temporary suspension of such stocks (thus lacking "cognitive believability"); **science fiction**, by contrast, requires those stocks to be elaborated and metamorphically transformed, with some intellectually or socially constructive end in view.

**COLLABORATION.** An unusually high proportion of **sf** stories are written in collaboration, partly because sf writers are more likely than writers in other genres to be personally acquainted with one another (thanks to sf **conventions**). Writers recruited from **fandom** often collaborate on their early works, as the **Futurians** did, and sometimes retain the habit. The most celebrated collaborative team of the 1940s consisted of **Henry Kuttner** and his wife, **C. L. Moore**, while **Robert Silverberg**, **Harlan Ellison**, and **Randall Garrett** formed a "fiction factory" in the 1950s, some of whose produce ended up in Ellison's collection of collaborations *Partners in Wonder* (1971). Other significant writing teams include **Frederik Pohl** and **C. M. Kornbluth**, **Larry Niven** and **Jerry Pournelle** (sometimes with **Steven Barnes**), **Arthur C. Clarke** and Gentry Lee, and **William Barton** and Michael Capobianco. **Gregory Benford** and **David Bischoff** have worked with astonishingly long lists of collaborators. The frequency with which collaborative bylines appeared on sf books was dramatically increased in the 1970s and 1980s by the advent of **shared-world** and **sharecropping** exercises. Seen as a whole, sf is an innately collaborative genre in which writers routinely react to one another's inventions by extending or challenging the logic of their extrapolations.

**COLLINS, PAUL (1954– ).** English-born writer and **small press** publisher resident in **Australia** from 1972. His **fanzine** *Void* (1975–1981) was eventually transformed into an **anthology series**. He and Rowena Cory formed Cory and Collins, whose publications in 1980–1985 included books by **A. Bertram Chandler** and **David Lake**. His **children's sf** includes *The Earthborn* (2003). *Cyberskin* (2000) is a post-**cyberpunk** thriller. *The Government in Exile* (2000) samples his short fiction.

**COMICS. Pulp sf** spilled over into the comic strip medium in the 1930s, when the pioneering example of **Buck Rogers** was followed by Brick Bradford and **Flash Gordon**. The **superhero** pulps were a key model for early comic books, including Action Comics (launched 1938), from which *Superman*—edited by sf pulp editor Mort Weisinger—was rapidly spun off. Weisinger recruited such sf writers as **Edmond Hamilton**, **Henry Kuttner**, and **Alfred Bester** to write for him, while **Otto Binder** worked for rival publication *Captain Marvel*. In the early 1950s **Jack Williamson** wrote scripts for *Beyond Mars* based on his Seetee series, while **Harry Harrison** was instrumental in the founding of *Weird Science*, which often adapted stories by such writers as **Ray Bradbury**. The development of British sf comic strips was held up by World War II paper shortages, but they made rapid progress in the 1950s, when Frank Hampson's *Dan Dare—Pilot of the Future* was a fixture in the *Eagle* from 1950–1969; Dare's adversary, the Mekon, probably helped establish the cliché that **aliens** were **little green men**. British sf writers who worked in the comic medium in the 1950s included **Michael Moorcock** and **Barrington J. Bayley**.

The most pivotal historical development in the American comic book medium was the resuscitation of Marvel Comics in the early 1960s by Stan Lee, whose new generation of angst-ridden superheroes forced main rival DC Comics to respond in kind. The subsequent boom in more complex—but relentlessly exotic—heroes, often working in teams rather than individually, opened up opportunities for more sophisticated **graphic novels**, whose breakthroughs included a good deal of work by British recruits to the American scene, including Alan Moore (*Watchmen*, 1987), Brian Talbot (the Luther Arkwright series, 1989), and Neil Gaiman.

Comic strips won greater respect in France as *bandes dessinées*, where artist René Pellos outshone writer Martial Cendres in the *Futuropolis* strip (1937–1938). **French** and Belgian writers and artists flourished during the war when American imports were banned from occupied territory, and the ground they gained was held after 1945 when the Catholic Church (which considered U.S. comics immoral) and socialist politicians (who considered them imperialistic) formed an unlikely alliance to hold them at bay. *Bande dessinée* sf for adults, pioneered by Jean-Claude Forest's *Barbarella* (1964) and Philip Druillet's *Lone Sloane* (1966), laid the groundwork for *Métal Hurlant* (launched 1974) and numerous graphic novels. The other nation that developed a distinctive comic book tradition in the postwar era was **Japan**, where *manga* became an important 1950s medium for the Japanese fascination with destructive giant **robots**, gradually paving the way for such huge hits as *Akira* (launched 1982).

Comic strip sf was unable to take aboard the least hint of expository sophistication or extrapolative rigor, which made it the ideal feeder medium for **cinema** and **TV**—although producers in both media were slow to realize the fact—and it was, therefore, the comic strip medium that first defined the concerns, methods, and attitudes of "**sci-fi.**"

**COMPTON, D. G. (1930– ).** British writer in various genres, whose **sf** mostly consists of alarmist fantasies. In *The Quality of Mercy* (1965) governments take direction to reduce overpopulation. In *Farewell Earth's Bliss* (1966) dissidents are shipped to **Mars**. *Synthajoy* (1968) and *The Steel Crocodile* (1970) feature misuses of new technologies. *Chronocules* (1970) and *The Missionaries* (1972) are jaundiced treatments of the classic sf themes of **time travel** and **alien** invasion. *The Continuous Kathrine Mortenhoe* (1974, aka *The Unsleeping Eye & Death Watch*) is an intense **existentialist fantasy** in which a man's eyes are adapted for use in reportage; *Windows* (1979) is a sequel. In *A Usual Lunacy* (1978), love turns out to be a curable virus. In *As-*

*cendancies* (1980) free energy proves less than a boon, while in *Ragnarok* (1991, with **John Gribbin**) a well-intentioned scientist precipitates worldwide disaster. In *Nomansland* (1993) women can no longer bear male children. *Justice City* (1994), set in a high-tech prison, and *Back of Town Blues* (1996) are exotic mysteries.

**CONCEPTUAL BREAKTHROUGH.** A term employed by **Peter Nicholls** in *The Encyclopedia of Science Fiction* to define a fundamental theme of **science fiction**, derived from the model of scientific progress as a series of "paradigm shifts," set out in Thomas Kuhn's *The Structure of Scientific Revolutions* (1962). The notion is attractive to **sf** writers because it offers a possibility of contriving climaxes that are both dramatic and progressive—a radical alternative to the normalizing story-arcs typical of **pulp** fiction. One of the reasons that **psi powers** became so attractive to sf writers in the 1950s was that the acceptance of their possibility—a paradigm shift in itself—opened the way for climactic attainments of superhuman enlightenment like those featured in **Charles L. Harness's** "The Rose" (1953) and **Theodore Sturgeon's** *More Than Human* (1953). Such tales are more flamboyant than parables that place their characters in a state of artificial ignorance in order to celebrate their breakthrough to an awareness we already possess, classic examples of which include **Isaac Asimov's** "Nightfall" (1941) and **James Blish's** "Surface Tension" (1952). Conceptual breakthroughs are difficult to contrive in quantity, but such writers as **Greg Egan** and **Charles Stross** have demonstrated that heroic efforts are feasible.

**CONEY, MICHAEL G. (1932– ).** British-born writer, resident in **Canada** since 1973, who began publishing **sf** in 1969; his early short stories are collected in *Monitor Found in Orbit* (1974). *Mirror Image* (1972) and *Brontomek!* (1976) feature **alien** "amorphs" who mimic humans so well that they believe themselves human. The ecological mystery *Syzygy* (1973) shares the same background. *Charisma* (1975) is a **parallel-worlds** story. The **mosaic** *Friends Come in Boxes* (1973) offers an unorthodox solution to the problem of overpopulation. *Winter's Children* (1974) is a **postholocaust fantasy**. *Hello Summer, Goodbye* (1975, aka *Rax & Pallahaxi Tide*) is a wistful love story in an exotic setting. Several stories set in a futuristic artists' colony are collected in *The Girl with a Symphony in Her Fingers* (1975, aka *The Jaws That Bite, the Claws That Catch*). The **dystopian** *The Ultimate Jungle* (1979) and the thriller *Neptune's Cauldron* (1981) were followed by a **series** of **far-futuristic fantasies** whose core item, The Song of Earth—comprising *The Celestial Steam Locomotive* (1983) and *Gods of the Greataway* (1984)—was preceded by *Cat Karina* (1982); later works in the series dispensed with its fugitive sf elements.

**CONKLIN, GROFF (1904–1968).** U.S. editor whose **anthology** of *The Best of Science Fiction* (1946) was one of the genre's first important hardcover showcases. He followed it up with *A Treasury of Science Fiction* (1948), *The Big Book of Science Fiction* (1950), and *The Omnibus of Science Fiction* (1952), then became a prolific producer of theme anthologies, most significantly *Invaders of Earth* (1952), *Science Fiction Adventures in Dimension* (1953), *Science Fiction Thinking Machines* (1954), and *Science Fiction Adventures in Mutation* (1955).

**CONRAD, JOSEPH (Josef Korzeniowski 1857–1924).** Polish-born writer whose only **scientific romance**, *The Inheritors* (1901, with Ford Madox Ford), is a **dimensional fantasy**, although other works—especially *Heart of Darkness* (1902)—have become favorite items for **transfiguration** into **sf** by such writers as **Robert Silverberg**, **J. G. Ballard**, **Michael Moorcock**, **Michael Bishop**, and **Lucius Shepard**.

**CONSTANTINE, STORM (1956– ).** British writer whose trilogy of **postholocaust fantasies** featuring the androgynous Wraeththu—*The Enchantments of Flesh and Spirit* (1987), *The Bewitchments of Love and Hate* (1988), and *The Fulfillments of Fate and Desire* (1989)—flamboyantly extrapolated the poses and interests of the Goth subculture of which she was an ardent adherent. *The Wraiths of Will and Pleasure* (2003) returned to the scenario. *The Monstrous Regiment* (1989) and *Aleph* (1991) are **planetary romances** featuring a **dystopian** matriarchal society. Her short fiction is sampled in *Oracle Lips* (1999).

***CONTE CRUEL.*** A term used (in the plural) as the title of a collection of stories by **Villiers de l'Isle Adam** before being more widely applied to a subgenre of short fiction whose cynical and skeptical worldview is neatly encapsulated in ironic climactic twists. British **scientific romance** was very hospitable to parables of this kind; much of the futuristic short fiction produced by **H. G. Wells**, **J. D. Beresford**, and other important contributors to that genre consists of *contes cruels*. Early American **sf** was less hospitable to sarcasm, or to a jaundiced view of future possibility, but the attractions of the narrative form proved irresistible to many sf writers of the 1950s, most notably **C. M. Kornbluth**, **Damon Knight**, **Frederik Pohl**, **Robert Sheckley**, and **Robert Silverberg**; it was their fondness for *conte cruel* story-arcs that led **Kingsley Amis**, in *New Maps of Hell*, to identify them as **satirists**. The skeptical outlook of the **new wave** often gave rise to scathing exercises in black comedy, and writers like **John Sladek** and **Thomas M. Disch** helped bring the sf *conte cruel* to new extremes of inventive acidity. By the 1980s the *conte cruel* was the standard narrative form of **soft sf**. The format offers a useful means of tackling the paradox identified by **Anatole France** in *The White Stone* (1905), which observes that writers who accept that the moral order of future society will be different from that of their own are bound to get a poor reception, especially if their anticipations are well calculated; the progressive writer's most powerful narrative weapon is, in consequence, an assertive insistence that the existing moral order is woefully inadequate to answer the challenges of the future.

***CONTE PHILOSOPHIQUE*.** A term employed by **Voltaire** to describe his works of fiction, one of which—"Micromegas" (1752)—provided a key model for writers of **speculative fiction**. While ***conte cruel*** provides an apt description of the narrative format most useful to serious writers of speculative fiction, *conte philosophique* usefully embraces some of their key objectives: the exploration of the ways in which conceivable innovations might transform future society; the use of hypothetical viewpoints (**aliens**, **artificial intelligences**, etc.) to illustrate and illuminate issues in philosophy; the use of fictional instruments to address such questions as how human life might best be lived, what "being human" ought to mean, and so on. Many classic short sf stories, including **Isaac Asimov's** "Nightfall," **Daniel Keyes's** "Flowers for Algernon," and **Bob Shaw's** "Light of Other Days," are *contes philosophiques* cast in the form of *contes cruels*; this became the standard strategy of such prolifically inventive writers as **Michael Bishop** and **Greg Egan**. Although the use of the word *conte* ("tale") implies shortness, several of Voltaire's paradigmatic *contes philosophiques* are novellas and *Candide* is a novel; unlike *conte cruel*, therefore, the term has routinely been applied to fictions of all lengths.

**CONVENTION.** One of the central institutions of **sf fandom** (the other being the **fanzine**). The term is often shortened to "con." Conventions are social gatherings, usually involving a program of discussions featuring guests and other attending professionals, which many participants routinely ignore. There is usually a book room, and sometimes a masquerade. The first sf convention took place in Leeds in 1937, the first U.S. convention being held in 1938 in New York; the annual World SF Convention (or Worldcon), at which the **Hugo** awards are presented, was inaugurated in 1939; annual conventions were subsequently instituted in various U.S. cities and many European nations. Since 1980, sf literature has been gradually sidelined at most conventions (Readercon and WisCon are notable exceptions) although writers continue to be featured as guests because they are extremely cheap and flexible by comparison with media celebrities.

**COOK, WILLIAM WALLACE (1867–1933).** U.S. writer prolific in **dime novel** and **pulp** formats. His **sf** mostly consists of lively **satirical** parodies of **Vernian** romance, including the novels *A Round Trip to the Year 2000* (1903, book 1908) and its sequel "Castaways of the Year 2000" (1912–1913), *Cast Away at the Pole* (1904, book 1927), *Adrift in the Unknown* (1904–1905, book 1908), *Marooned in 1492* (1905, book 1908), and *The Eighth Wonder* (1906–1907, book 1926). The reprints were early **paperbacks**, somewhat ahead of their time; *Around the World in Eighty Hours* (1925) was his only sf hardcover book. The six-part **series** "Tales of Twenty Hundred" (1911–1912) is more earnest, although its subject matter—straightening the world's axis in order to stabilize its climate—now seems ill suited to serious treatment.

**COOPER, EDMUND (1926–1982).** British writer who began publishing **sf** in 1954, much of his early sf being mingled with other fantasies in the overlapping collections *Tomorrow's Gift* (1958), *Voices in the Dark* (1960), and *Tomorrow Came* (1963). *The Uncertain Midnight* (1958, aka *Deadly Image*) and *Seed of Light* (1959) are thrillers in which humankind narrowly avoids extinction. *Transit* (1964) and *All Fools' Day* (1966) are equally pessimistic. *A Far Sunset* (1967) is a **robinsonade** whose protagonist fails to reform a brutal **alien** culture. *Five to Twelve* (1968), *Sea-Horse in the Sky* (1969), *The Last Continent* (1969), *The Overman Culture* (1971), and *The Cloud Walker* (1973) are similarly grim, but *Son of Kronk* (1970, aka *Kronk*) is a lively **satire** whose tone is carried forward into the crude antifeminist parable *Who Needs Men?* (1972). Cooper's later novels—including four **space operas** bylined Richard Avery—became increasingly less coherent.

**CORELLI, MARIE (1855–1924).** British writer of best-selling **religious fantasies**, significant in the history of **sf** by virtue of her use of ideas borrowed from science, **pseudoscience**, and **scientific romance** to add imaginative fiber to the unorthodox beliefs fervently expressed in *A Romance of Two Worlds* (1886) and *Ardath* (1889). *The Young Diana* (1915), which features a technology of rejuvenation, and *The Secret Power* (1921) are more closely akin to scientific romance.

**CORNELL, PAUL (1967– ).** British writer who began publishing **sf** in 1990. He moved on from **tie-ins** to *Something More* (2001), a hectic **metaphysical fantasy** whose vision of 23rd-century Britain blends futuristic and primitive imagery and features reclusive **aliens**. *British Summertime* (2002) ranges from the far future to the Acts of the Apostles.

**CORREY, LEE (1928– ).** Pseudonym of U.S. writer G. Harry Stine, used on almost all his **sf** before the late 1980s, although he used his own byline on his first story, published in 1951, and many articles popularizing the space program, before reverting to it in the extensive warbots **series** (1988–1992). His work as Correy, ranging from the **children's sf** novel *Starship through Space* (1954) to such thrillers as *Shuttle Down* (1981) and *Manna* (1984) is **hard sf** designed as **space-age** propaganda.

**COSMIC BREAKOUT.** One of two conventional climaxes that became commonplace in 1950s **sf**, the other being **conceptual breakthrough**. The moment of cosmic breakout—almost invariably symbolized by the liftoff of a spaceship from a doomed or **decadent** Earth—became the central ritual of the sf myth of the **space age**. Although its significance was drastically reduced by its actualization in the Apollo program, the notion that the future of humankind must involve some such gigantic leap if the species is not to decay into sterility or self-destruction remains powerful within genre sf, clearly expressed and extravagantly developed in such sophisticated **space operas** as **Poul Anderson's** *Starfarers* (1998) and **Vernor Vinge's** *A Deepness in the Sky* (1999). It is, in effect, an extrapolation of the United States' own "creation myth," similarly celebrated in the western genre: the notion of adventurers and outcasts from a decadent Old World heroically pioneering a new frontier in spite of all obstacles. Understandably, it is not nearly so prominent in European sf.

**COULSON, JUANITA (1933– ).** U.S. writer who coedited the **fanzine** *Yandro* with her husband, Robert (1928–1999), from 1953–1986. She began publishing professionally in 1963, following the early **planetary romance** *Crisis on Cheiron* (1967) with the **dystopian** *Unto the Last Generation* (1975), the **first contact** story *Space Trap* (1976), and an extensive **space operatic** family saga comprising *Tomorrow's Heritage* (1981), *Outward Bound* (1982), *Legacy of Earth* (1989), and *The Past of Forever* (1989). *Star Sister* (1990) is similar. Robert's work, much of it done in **collaboration** with Gene deWeese, is mostly lightweight comedy.

**COVER ART.** While the primary media of genre **sf** were **magazines** and **paperbacks**, the problem of finding appropriate visual images to represent it to the reader was vexatious. **Hugo Gernsback**, desirous of avoiding the kind of garish imagery favored by other fiction **pulps**, employed Frank Paul to provide futuristic cityscapes overflown by massive vehicles, often reducing human figures to miniature status—although larger figures wearing jet packs or clad in space suits were also considered appropriate. Extraterrestrial landscapes were usually desolate, often viewed from a very distant viewpoint. When the Gernsback-founded magazines reverted to a conventional pulp format, however, their covers slowly evolved toward the gaudier plumage adopted by the Clayton ***Astounding***, without quite getting there until new publishers wrought abrupt transformations in the late 1930s. **Aliens** were then much more frequently featured and spaceships were usually shown engaged in violent conflict. **Ray guns** of various dimensions were a great boon to sf cover artists, whose rivals were only able to show the muzzle-flashes of conventional weapons. The down-market pulps of the 1940s often employed a formula favored by Earle K. Bergey, in which a lightly dressed female—often clad in a stereotyped combination of metallic bra, miniskirt, and boots—is threatened or seized by a monster (often of the **bug-eyed** variety) while a muscular hero makes ready to intervene. Extraterrestrial landscapes tended to be lushly furnished with exotic vegetation.

Ironically, while the Gernsback-originated titles were undergoing this metamorphosis, their primary model, *Astounding*, was moving in the opposite direction under the control of **John Campbell**, who was eager to find imagery representative of his earnest ambitions. When he increased *Astounding* to "bedsheet" size, he briefly forsook cover art entirely, but when the U.S. entry into World War II put an end to that experiment, he tried to give the covers of the digest *Astounding* more dignity. Cityscapes, big machines, space suits, and desolate extraterrestrial terrain were all extensively featured, though placed under the pressure of a more stringent realism. He also began to use covers redolent with the symbolism of **Promethean fantasy**. When covers of this era showed faces in close-up, the expressions were usually meditative, if not quizzical, reflecting the problematic quality of the fiction.

The 1950s digests were considerably more relaxed in their use of cover images of aliens, **robots**, and other by-now-stereotypical sf images, frequently indulging in whimsical humor and gentle parody of such notions as **little green men**. On the other hand, their use of spaceships—save for **flying saucers**—and space stations became more earnestly realistic, supporting the imagery of **cosmic breakout** employed in the stories. Depictions of extraterrestrial landscapes became much more sophisticated; the leading digests made considerable use of the pioneering "space artist" Chesley Bonestell and imitators of his work. Ace paperback editor **Donald A. Wollheim** formulated a long-standing policy by which every sf cover had to include either a spaceship or an alien, those being the crucial identifiers of the genre in the public mind, but Ace's chief rival Ballantine made abundant use of Richard Powers, who replaced representational cover art with amorphous surrealist imagery—an initiative that proved highly influential when Ace eventually needed to distinguish **Terry Carr's** upmarket "specials" from Wollheim's standard fare.

British sf cover art followed a similar divided trajectory, the magazines of the 1950s and 1960s mingling surreal and symbolic covers with representations of spaceships, aliens, and extraterrestrial landscapes, while paperback publishers used the contrasting styles to distinguish sophisticated fare—especially **new wave** material—from **space-operatic** entertainment. It was, however, British artists who pioneered a new vogue in the 1970s for complex cityscapes and huge "spiky spaceships" that eliminated human (and humanoid) figures from consideration while looking to new astronomical imagery for backgrounds incandescently spangled with stars, galaxies, and colored dust clouds.

Space art and surrealism remained highly significant in sf cover art during the last decades of the 20th century, primarily associated in the former instance with **hard sf** and in the latter with literary ambition. The major trend, however, was associated with the growing influence of feminized **soft sf**, which brought human and near-human figures into the foreground and relegated other signifiers—including all manner of hardware—to the backcloth. By 1990 such figures were frequently in uniform, thanks to the prevalence of **military sf**, but their faces were routinely used to express character and emotion in a far more wide-ranging fashion than the terrified heroines and quizzical heroes of old.

**COWPER, RICHARD (1926–2002).** Pseudonym of British writer John Middleton Murry Jr., who switched from literary fiction to **sf** after publishing the **ESP** novel *Breakthrough* (1967). His elegant and heartfelt short fiction, collected in *The Custodians* (1976), *The Web of the Magi* (1980), and *The Tithonian Fator* (1984), is more effective than his novels. *Phoenix* (1968), *Domino* (1971), *Kuldesak* (1972), and *Time Out of Mind* (1973) are futuristic thrillers. *The Twilight of Briareus* (1974) is a **postholocaust fantasy**. *Clone* (1972), *Worlds Apart* (1974), and *Profundis* (1979) are comedies. A **series** of sequels to the novella "Piper at the Gates of Dawn" (1976), comprising *The Road to Corlay* (1978), *A Dream of Kinship* (1981), and *A Tapestry of Time* (1982), tracks the emergence of a new religion in the wake of a second Deluge.

**CRAWFORD, WILLIAM L. (1911–1984).** U.S. **small press** publisher who published occasional **magazines** and **anthologies** in the 1930s and 1940s before becoming the proprietor of the Fantasy Publishing Company Inc. (FPCI) in 1947; it was the first of several such operations publishing hardcover editions of notable **pulp** fiction in various fantasy genres.

**CRICHTON, MICHAEL (1942– ).** U.S. writer, initially of thrillers, who began to make use of **sf** motifs in *The Andromeda Strain* (1969). *The Terminal Man* (1972), *Westworld* (1974, a novelization of his own film script), *Sphere* (1987), *Jurassic Park* (1990), and its sequel *The Lost World* (1995) are similarly alarmist. The exotic historical fantasy *Eaters of the Dead* (1976) is a **transfiguration** of *Beowulf*, and *Congo* (1980) transfigures one of **Edgar Rice Burroughs's** later Tarzan novels. *Timeline* (1999) features **time travel**, while *Prey* (2002) is deeply suspicious of **nanotechnology**.

**CRITICISM.** Early works of **sf** criticism by **J. O. Bailey** and **Patrick Moore** tended to summarize themes rather than risk aesthetic evaluation—a tradition carried forward by **Sam Moskowitz**, W. H. G. Armytage's *Yesterday's Tomorrows* (1968), and **I. F. Clarke**. Aesthetic criticism, introduced into the **fanzines** and **magazine** book-review columns by **Damon Knight** and **James Blish**, was carried forward by **Reginald Bretnor's** *Modern Science Fiction* (1953) and **Kingsley Amis's** *New Maps of Hell* (1963). In the 1960s **Thomas Clareson's** *Extrapolation* and Leland Sapiro's fanzine *Riverside Quarterly* prepared the way for the launch of *Foundation* in 1972 and ***Science-Fiction Studies*** in 1973. This academic formalization—assisted by the emergence of literary theories specifically geared to the study of "**fabulation**"—tipped the balance of authority in favor of those who wished to subject sf to orthodox critical analysis rather than examining the evolution of its themes in the context of the history of ideas. Academic studies of sf appeared in some profusion in the last quarter of the 20th century, often prefaced by apologetic arguments explaining why such peculiar labor was worthwhile. Much intelligent work on the aesthetics of sf (and other kinds of fantasy) was done by writers active within the genre, including **Brian Aldiss**, **Samuel Delany**, and **Ursula le Guin**, who understood the complexity of the task better than academics trained to analyze the mimetic strategies of naturalistic fiction. The "History of Science Fiction Criticism" in *Science Fiction Studies* 78 (1999) includes a comprehensive chronological **bibliography**.

**CROMIE, ROBERT (1856–1907).** Irish writer whose contributions to the emergent genre of **scientific romance** are the interplanetary fantasy *A Plunge into Space* (1890)—whose second edition had a preface by **Jules Verne**—and the protoatomic bomb story *The Crack of Doom* (1895).

**CROWLEY, JOHN (1942– ).** U.S. writer in various fantasy genres. **Sf** motifs are subtly deployed in *The Deep* (1975), *Beasts* (1976), and the elegiac fantasy *Engine Summer* (1979). The collection *Novelty* (1989) includes an account of the futile exploits of **time police**, *Great Work of Time* (separate edition 1991). *Antiquities: Seven Stories* (1993) also includes some sf.

**CTHULHU MYTHOS.** A fantastic history used as a backcloth in many of the later work of **H. P. Lovecraft**, which obtained its name and definition from the posthumous critical writings and pastiches of **August Derleth**. Lovecraft invited other writers to use his fictional apparatus while he was still alive, thus setting a significant example to later writers who opened up more limited scenarios as **shared worlds**, and he often introduced elements of it into works by other writers that he revised. Derleth elaborated it considerably, as did many other writers, to the extent that it ultimately became a subgenre in its own right, sustaining a rich subculture of **small press magazines** and showcase **anthologies**. It is, in essence, a distillation of the sensation of "cosmic **horror**" allegedly generated by too keen an awareness of human and scientific ambition as impotent and futile follies; it imagines a universe dominated by malevolent godlike **aliens**, whose apocalyptic reemergence is inevitable even though their present dormancy restricts them to relatively tentative abominations.

**CUMMINGS, RAY (1887–1957).** U.S. writer who launched a prolific career as a **pulp** fantasist with the pioneering **microcosmic romance** *The Girl in the Golden Atom* (1919, combined with a sequel in the 1922 book). In addition to other microcosmic romances, he wrote **time-travel** adventures, including *The Men Who Mastered Time* (1924, book 1929), *The Shadow Girl* (1929, book 1946), and *Exile of Time* (1931, book 1964); pioneering **space operas**, including *Tarrano the Conqueror* (1925, book 1930), *A Brand New World* (1928, book 1964), and *Brigands of the Moon* (1930, book 1931); **dimensional fantasies**, including *Into the Fourth Dimension* (1926, book 1943); and **planetary romances**, including *Tama of the Light Country* (1930, book 1965). The innovative nature of his work was undermined by the limitations of his prose and plot construction, but he charted a course for later writers.

**CURREY, L. W. (1942– ).** U.S. collector, book dealer, bibliographer and (in **collaboration** with **David Hartwell**) **small press** publisher. His **bibliographical** work—most notably *Science Fiction and Fantasy Authors: A Bibliography of Their Fiction and Selected Nonfiction* (1979)—displays a fanatical fascination with the minutiae of book production.

**CURVAL, PHILIPPE (1929– ).** Pseudonym of **French** writer Philippe Tronche, a key member of the French **sf** community from the 1950s to the 1970s. His novels range from early **space operas** like *Les fleurs de Vénus* (1960) to dark social **satires** like *Le dormeur s'éveillera-t-il?* (1979) and *L'arc tendu de désir* (1995); *Cette chère humanité* (1976) was translated as *Brave Old World* (1981).

**CYBERPUNK.** A term employed by **Gardner Dozois** to characterize a movement of writers spearheaded by **Bruce Sterling**, **William Gibson**, and **John Shirley**; it had previously been used as the title of a story by Bruce Bethke (which Dozois might have seen in the ***Asimov's*** slush pile). The "cyber" element, borrowed from "cybernetics," refers to hypothetical sophistications of information technology that permit more intimate interactions with the human body and brain, while the "punk" element relates to the adventurous exploitation of these opportunities by an outlaw fringe modeled on streetwise drug culture.

The central documents of the movement, Gibson's *Neuromancer* (1984) and Sterling's showcase **anthology** *Mirrorshades* (1986), were read far beyond the usual limits of the **sf** audience, permeating the burgeoning community of enterprising personal computer users, many of whose members so ardently desired to become (or at least to imagine themselves as) cyberpunks that they appointed Gibson and Sterling as their gurus. The cyberpunk subgenre thus became the literary arm of a nascent cyberculture; its fascination with **virtual reality** and the subjectively constructed realm of **cyberspace** endeared it to champions of **postmodernism** because its inevitable tendency to question the nature and limits of "reality" seemed to be in tune with the methods and concerns of their own literary and social **criticism**—a case argued by Larry McCaffery's *Storming the Reality Studio: A Casebook of Cyberpunk and Postmodern Science Fiction* (1992).

As a manifest movement, cyberpunk did not last long (Sterling proudly declared that the term was "obsolete before it was coined") and in 1987 the **fanzine** *Science Fiction Eye* began its first issue with a "Requiem for the Cyberpunks." This reproduced a **Science Fiction Research Association** panel discussion on "Cyberpunk or Cyberjunk"—in which **Norman Spinrad** belatedly argued that "Neuromantics" would have been a much better label—and promulgated a rival "Humanist Manifesto," issued in contradiction to Sterling's *Mirrorshades* introduction by **John Kessel**, following **Michael Swanwick's** lead. The cyberpunk label was insuppressible, but the subgenre's favorite "cyber" motifs held so narrow a lead over actual developments that they soon ceased to inspire amazement and became taken-for-granted aspects of all images of the near future, carefully sophisticated by such writers as **Pat Cadigan** and **Neal Stephenson**. The "punk" elements of the thriller format were carried forward into a "post-cyberpunk" phase that relied even more heavily on the cynical tone of "noirish" crime fiction. Max More proposed in 1991 that "cyberfiction" would be a more useful term for fiction employing the technological ideas of cyberpunk without the "amoralism" and "nihilism" of the punk element, but it never caught on.

**CYBERSPACE.** A term popularized by **William Gibson's** *Neuromancer* (1984); it easily outstripped such competitors as "virtual space" and "software space" to become the definitive term for a "consensual hallucination" that allows the data stored in the multitudinous switches of networked microchips, and entities mapped out thereby to become visible and tangible. The obsolescence of the **cosmic breakout** climax in the wake of the Apollo program had left a gap within genre **sf** that was partly filled, for a while, by "cyberspatial breakthroughs" in which human characters forsake the flesh in favor of a new and better life in cyberspace—a transcendence most eloquently celebrated in the work of **Greg Egan**.

**CYBORG.** A contraction of "cybernetic organism" referring to products of organic/inorganic—particularly human/machine—chimerization. David Rorvik's *As Man Becomes Machine* (1971) popularized the notion, anticipating a new era of "participant evolution." Martin Caidin's *Cyborg* (1972) was quick to pick it up; the **TV series** based on the book, *The Six Million Dollar Man* (1973–1978), popularized the alternative term "bionic man." Primitive medical cyborgs—people with prosthetic limbs or pacemakers—were already familiar by the end of the 20th century; **sf** also features functional cyborgs (people modified to perform specific tasks) and adaptive cyborgs (people redesigned to operate in **alien** environments). Cyborgization and **genetic engineering** can be seen as opposed strategies for adaptation to extreme environments, as in **Bruce Sterling's** Shaper/Mechanist series. The functional cyborgs most commonly featured in sf are those modified for the purpose of space travel, as in **Cordwainer Smith's** "Scanners Live in Vain" (1950) and **Anne McCaffrey's** *The Ship Who Sang* (1961), and those modified for espionage and warfare, as in **Poul Anderson's** "Kings Who Die" (1962) and **Keith Laumer's** *A Plague of Demons* (1965). Donna J. Haraway's influential essay "A Cyborg Manifesto: Science, Technology, and Socialist-Feminism in the Late Twentieth Century" (1985) invested the motif with a new ironic significance.

**CYRANO DE BERGERAC (Savinien Cyrano, 1619–1655). French** soldier and writer, famous as the eponymous hero of a play by Edmond Rostand (1897). The latter phases of his pioneering interplanetary

**satire** *L'Autre monde* were lost, but the surviving texts, first published in censored form in 1656 and 1662, were restored in 1920 and translated as *Voyages to the Moon and Sun* (1923; new translation as *Other Worlds*, 1965).

## – D –

**DANIEL, TONY (1963– ).** U.S. writer who began publishing **sf** in 1990. *Warpath* (1993) is an **alternative history** in which Native Americans invent space flight. The 1996 title story of *The Robot's Twilight Companion* (1999), about an abandoned mining **robot** that develops self-consciousness, was integrated into the time-spanning **mosaic** *Earthling* (1996). *Metaplanetary* (2001) is an epic account of a future rebellion involving **virtual** personalities, **nanotechnological artificial intelligences**, and conglomerate LAPs (large arrays of persons) while godlike Cloudships look on with Olympian disdain.

**DANN, JACK (1945– ).** U.S. writer but long resident in **Australia**, whose first **sf** publications in 1970 were **collaborations** with **George Zebrowski**. *Junction* (1973, exp. 1981) is an avant-gardish account of its hero's progress from sterile stability to promising chaos—a pattern recapitulated in the **mosaic space opera** *Starhiker* (1977), the items collected in *Timetipping* (1980), and the **Orphean fantasy** *The Man Who Melted* (1984). *High Steel* (1993, with **Jack C. Haldeman III**) is a space program fantasy. "Da Vinci Rising" (1995) is an **alternative history** ingeniously redeploying material from a historical novel about Leonardo da Vinci's technological speculations, *The Memory Cathedral* (1995). *Jubilee* (2001) and *Visitations* (2003) collect more short fiction. Dann's many **anthologies** include *Wandering Stars* (1974) and *More Wandering Stars* (1981), dedicated to Jewish sf and fantasy; *In the Field of Fire* (1987, with Jeanne van Buren Dann), a showcase of sf stories about the Vietnam War; and numerous theme anthologies edited in collaboration with **Gardner Dozois**.

**DANVERS, DENNIS (1947– ).** U.S. writer in various genres, who first ventured into **sf** in *Circuit of Heaven* (1998) and *End of Days* (1999), in which a vast **virtual reality** Bin offers immortality for all;

the former **transfigures** *Romeo and Juliet. The Fourth World* (2000) is an **Orphean fantasy** and political thriller. In *The Watch: Memoirs of a Revolutionist* (2002), a visitor from the far future arrives at Pyotr Kropotkin's deathbed to offer him a new life in the United States in 1999.

**DATLOW, ELLEN (1949– ).** U.S. editor who was fiction editor of *Omni* from 1981–1998 before moving to the *Event Horizon* website (1998–1999). In 2000 she became fiction editor for the **Sci-Fi** Channel website SciFiction. Her **anthologies** range across the fantasy spectrum, those with most sf inclusions being *Alien Sex* (1990) and *Vanishing Acts* (2000).

**DAVIDSON, AVRAM (1923–1993).** U.S. writer who began publishing **sf** in 1954. His quirky short fiction paid little attention to genre boundaries and was well suited to ***The Magazine of Fantasy & Science Fiction***, which he edited from 1962–1964. *Joyleg* (1962, with **Ward Moore**) is a **satire** about an immortal eccentric. His sf novels—including *Rogue Dragon* (1965), *The Masters of the Maze* (1965), and *The Enemy of My Enemy* (1966)—are mostly potboilers, but *Clash of the Star Kings* (1965) makes use of a linguistic skill and visionary imagination that were more profitably deployed in other fantasy genres. Short story collections of sf interest include *Or All the Seas with Oysters* (1962), *What Strange Stars and Skies* (1965), *Strange Seas and Shores* (1971), *The Enquiries of Doctor Esterhazy* (1975, expanded 1990 as *The Adventures of Doctor Esterhazy*), and *The Other Nineteenth Century* (2001, edited by Grania Davis and Henry Wessells).

**DAVY, SIR HUMPHRY (1778–1829).** British scientist who published romantic poetry in his youth and included a cosmic vision in the posthumous *Consolations in Travel; or, The Last Days of a Philosopher* (1830), which imagines life as a series of incarnations—some of them in radically **alien** biospheres—in which the soul has the opportunity to ascend (or slip back down) a creationist scale of moral perfection. **Camille Flammarion** translated it into French while writing *Lumen*, whose most adventurous sections are inspired by it.

**DAW BOOKS.** A specialist publishing company founded by **Donald A. Wollheim** in 1972. DAW (an acronym of Wollheim's initials) issued its books in a numbered **series**, appealing to collectors, and its products were slightly cheaper than their competitors; the consequent deterrent effect of paying lower-than-average advances to authors was partly offset by importing titles by British writers and translations. Although Wollheim was primarily interested in **sf**, DAW published a good deal of genre fantasy before other publishers became interested; when he fell ill in 1985 his daughter dropped most of the label's sf writers and it had little impact on the genre thereafter, although it continued to publish **C. J. Cherryh**.

**DECADENCE.** The notion that civilizations have a natural life cycle, and that their senescence involves jaded, morally anaesthetized aristocrats following sybaritic lifestyles, originated in 19th-century literature, but was taken sufficiently seriously by such 20th-century social philosophers as Oswald Spengler and Arnold Toynbee to license conscientious attempts by **sf** writers like **James Blish** and **Charles L. Harness** to use it as a basis for projecting **future histories**. Fantasies of future decadence tend to be recounted in an artificially ornate style, whose key features were detailed by Théophile Gautier's analysis of the work of Charles Baudelaire. Decadent style was imported into **pulp** fiction and carried to its furthest extreme by **Clark Ashton Smith's** tales of Zothique, but it is reproduced to some degree in almost all **far-futuristic fantasies**, which often dramatize the notion of entropy in a similar elegiac spirit. Images of decadence abound in the far-futuristic **space operas** of **A. A. Attanasio**, **Tony Daniel**, and **John C. Wright**.

**DE CAMP, L. SPRAGUE (1907–2000).** U.S. writer who became a key contributor to **John Campbell's** ***Astounding*** after making his debut there in 1937, although he also became an important practitioner and popularizer of the sword-and-sorcery genre. He had already written a **satirical timeslip romance** in **collaboration** with **P. Schuyler Miller** in which humankind's place in nature is eventually usurped by other great apes, *Genus Homo* (1941; book 1950). De Camp produced a great deal of **chimerical** comic fantasy for ***Unknown***, much of it in collaboration with **Fletcher Pratt**. His standards of plausibility were so high that he did not think his classic timeslip romance *Lest Darkness Fall* (1939, book 1941; revised

1949) belonged in *Astounding*, despite its earnest consideration of problems of **technological determinism**; the **alternative history** "The Wheels of If" (1940; reprinted in *The Wheels of If and Other Science-Fiction*, 1948) also appeared there.

Early stories developing the Viagens Interplanetarias **future history**, in which interstellar exploration is dominated by Brazil, were collected in *The Continent Makers and Other Tales of the Viagens* (1953) and *Sprague de Camp's New Anthology of Science Fiction* (1953). With the exception of *Rogue Queen* (1951), *The Stones of Nomuru* (1988), and *The Venom Trees of Sunga* (1992), the **planetary romances** in the **series** detailed the history and geography of the planet Krishna: *The Queen of Zamba* (1949, 1954 book as *Cosmic Manhunt*; aka *A Planet Called Krishna*); *The Hand of Zei* (1950; 1962–1963 book version divided in two, the first aka *The Floating Continent*); *The Virgin of Zesh* (1953; first collected in *The Virgin and the Wheels*, 1990); *The Tower of Zanid* (1958, combined with the former item in 1983); *The Hostage of Zir* (1977); *The Prisoner of Zhamanak* (1982); *The Bones of Zora* (1983); and *The Swords of Zinjaban* (1991). The last two were cocredited to de Camp's wife, Catherine, whose collaborations with him were more numerous than the bylines of his books acknowledge.

De Camp's other **sf** includes the romanesque *The Glory That Was* (1952, book 1960); *The Great Fetish* (1978), which parodies creationist resistance to evolutionary theory; and *Rivers of Time* (1933), which collects a series of stories extrapolated from "A Gun for Dinosaur" (1956). He compiled a guide to the writing and marketing of sf, *The Science Fiction Handbook* (1953, revised 1975) and wrote *Lovecraft: A Biography* (1975) as well as numerous books on the technology of the ancient world and several historical novels paying detailed attention to technological matters.

**DELANY, SAMUEL R. (1942– ).** U.S. writer whose first novel, *The Jewels of Aptor* (1962), was a remarkably vivid **hybrid science-fantasy**. *The Fall of the Towers* (1963–1965 in three volumes as *Captives of the Flame*, aka *Out of the Dead City, The Towers of Toron*, and *City of a Thousand Suns* 1965; revised omnibus 1970), *The Ballad of Beta-2* (1965), and *Empire Star* (1966) are of a similar ilk, displaying an increasing complexity of language and imaginative reach.

The continuing trend bore spectacular fruit in an ultrasophisticated **space opera** about the deciphering of an **alien** language, *Babel-17* (1966); the complex **metafictional postholocaust fantasy**, *The Einstein Intersection* (1967); and the supercharged **Promethean fantasy**, *Nova* (1968). Together with the short stories collected in *Driftglass* (1971; aka *Starshards*, rev. as *Aye, and Gomorrah*, 2003) and *Distant Stars* (1981), these were key documents of American **new wave sf**; Delany and Marilyn Hacker edited four volumes of a new wave **anthology series**, *Quark* (1970–1971).

Delany broke further new ground in the countercultural epic *Dhalgren* (1975), which brought his **decadent** imagery and earnest reflections on the social role of the artist much closer to home. This was followed by the "ambiguous heterotopia" *Triton* (1976; aka *Trouble on Triton*), an analysis of future social possibilities whose complexity transcends the tacit assumptions built into the notion of **Utopia**. Delany's intense interest in the language of **science fiction** was developed in a series of important critical writings, including the essays in *The Jewel-Hinged Jaw* (1977) and *Starboard Wine* (1984), and his minute dissection of **Thomas M. Disch's** "Angouleme," *The American Shore* (1978). Delany's academic exploration of semiotics and poststructuralist literary theory strongly influenced his subsequent works, which moved into other genres. A long two-volume sf novel begun with *Stars in My Pocket Like Grains of Sand* (1984) remained incomplete, but he did complete a novel abandoned in the 1960s, *They Fly at Çiron* (1993).

**DEL REY, LESTER (1915?–1993).** The name adopted by a U.S. writer and editor who fabricated his life history up to the point when he began to write **sf** in 1938. He became a member of **John Campbell's *Astounding*** stable in spite of the sentimental tendencies of such works as the **robot** love story "Helen O'Loy" (1938). *Nerves* (1942, exp. 1956; rev. 1976), about the aftermath of an accident in a nuclear power plant, is atypically gritty. He published numerous works of **children's sf**, some under the pseudonym Philip St. John, but several bearing his own byline were actually written by Paul W. Fairman (1916–1977). Del Rey **collaborated** with **Frederik Pohl** on *Preferred Risk* (1955; initially bylined Edson McCann) and "No More Stars" (1954 as by Charles Satterfield; rev. as the first item in *The Sky is Falling & Badge* *of Infamy*, 1963). *Police Your Planet* (1953; book 1956; rev. 1975), bylined Erik van Lhin, is a hard-boiled account of the **Martian** frontier. *The Eleventh Commandment* (1962; rev. 1970) is an early melodrama of overpopulation. *Pstalemate* (1971) is a **psi** novel. His short fiction is collected in *And Some Were Human* (1948), *Robots and Changelings* (1957), and *Gods and Golems* (1973).

Del Rey's fourth wife, Judy-Lynn Benjamin (1943–1986), became Ballantine's sf editor in the mid-1970s; when Del Rey joined the company as editor of its pioneering genre fantasy line in 1977, their purchases were issued under the imprint Del Rey Books. *The World of Science Fiction: 1926–1976; The History of a Subculture* (1979) is a fan's-eye view.

**DERLETH, AUGUST W. (1909–1971).** U.S. writer and editor who founded the **small press** Arkham House in association with **Donald Wandrei** to issue the works of **H. P. Lovecraft**; it went on to reprint a great deal of classic supernatural fiction. Derleth completed numerous Lovecraft fragments; the novel *The Lurker at the Threshold* (1945) and the collection *The Survivor and Others* (1957) were combined and augmented in *The Watcher Out of Time and Others* (1974). His own contributions to the **Cthulhu Mythos**—a term he defined and popularized—were collected in *The Mask of Cthulhu* (1958) and the **mosaic** novel *The Trail of Cthulhu* (1962). All of Derleth's orthodox **sf** is collected in *Harrigan's File* (1975), but he made a more substantial contribution to the genre in a **series** of showcase **anthologies** comprising *Strange Ports of Call* (1948), *The Other Side of the Moon* (1949), *Beyond Time and Space* (1950), *Far Boundaries* (1951), and *The Outer Reaches* (1951).

**DESMOND, SHAW (1877–1960).** Irish writer whose **scientific romances** include the **apocalyptic future war** stories *Ragnarok* (1926) and *Chaos* (1938), the **Stapledonian** *World-Birth* (1938), and the slightly less pessimistic *Black Dawn* (1944).

**DICK, PHILIP K. (1928–1982).** U.S. writer who achieved a wide readership and extravagant critical attention posthumously, thanks to **cinema** adaptations of his work and the innate appeal of his reality-questioning themes to **postmodernist** critics—circumstances that facilitated belated publication of the abundant mainstream fiction he had written in the 1950s. His reputation only gained from the revelation in such biographies as Lawrence Sutin's *Divine Invasions* (1989) that he was a lifelong neurotic, addicted for most of his career to amphetamines whose induced paranoid delusions lingered long after he was forced to kick the habit.

Dick's first **sf** stories, "Beyond Lies the Wub" (1952) and "Roog" (1953), already encapsulated the whimsical paranoia that characterizes almost all his work in the genre. Many of his early stories focus on the difficulty of distinguishing real individuals from ersatz imitations, as in tales of mechanical **androids** like "Second Variety" (1953), accounts of **aliens** like "The Father-Thing" (1954), and **political fantasies** like "The Variable Man" (1953) and *Vulcan's Hammer* (short version 1956; expanded 1960). *Solar Lottery* (1955, aka *World of Chance*) attempts conventionality, as does *Dr. Futurity* (1954 as "Time Pawn," exp. 1960), but *The World Jones Made* (1956) and *The Man Who Japed* (1956) are more distinctive. The **hallucinatory fantasies** *Eye in the Sky* (1957)—in which a group of tourists caught in a freak accident experience a series of distorted worlds, each based in the beliefs of one of their number—and *Time Out of Joint* (1959) further refined his idiosyncratic method.

The **alternative history** *The Man in the High Castle* (1961) displays wild mood swings, but the relentlessly downbeat *We Can Build You* (1972)—which interprets schizophrenia as an "androidal" condition—written in 1962, was slow to sell, and the bleakness of the similarly themed *Martian Time-Slip* (1964) and *The Simulacra* (1964), the **postholocaust fantasy** *Dr. Bloodmoney* (1965), and the hallucinatory fantasies *The Three Stigmata of Palmer Eldritch* (1965) and *Now Wait for Last Year* (1966) is carefully ameliorated. Given that Dick produced the potboilers *The Game-Players of Titan* (1963), *Clans of the Alphane Moon* (1964), *The Penultimate Truth* (1964), *The Crack in Space* (1966), *The Unteleported Man* (1966 in abridged form; 1983 as *Lies Inc*), *Counter-Clock World* (1967), *The Zap Gun* (1967), and *The Ganymede Takeover* (1967, with Ray Nelson) alongside them, the achievements of these novels are even the more remarkable. He followed them up with two books—*Do Androids Dream of Electric Sheep?* (1968) and *Ubik* (1969)—which brought his preoccupation with the relationship between real and ersatz entities to its highest level of complexity and intensity.

With the exception of *Our Friends from Frolix 8* (1970), the remainder of Dick's sf-related works are all **metaphysical fantasies**. A loosely knit sequence comprising *Galactic Pot-Healer* (1969), *A Maze of Death* (1970), and *Deus Irae* (1976)—a planned **collaboration** that **Roger Zelazny** had to complete unaided—was far outshone by the hallucinatory fantasy *Flow My Tears, the Policeman Said* (1974) and the expiatory drug-abuse fantasy *A Scanner Darkly* (1977), whose writing was interrupted (in February–March 1974) by a series of "visions" that obsessed Dick for the remainder of his life, shaping the concerns of *Radio Free Albemuth* (1985, but written 1976), its wholesale revision as *VALIS* (1981), and *The Divine Invasion* (1981). A five-volume set of his complete short fiction, annotated by **Paul Williams**, was issued in 1987.

Like **Ray Bradbury**, Dick used sf imagery without supplying any underlying explanations to its conformation or applying any rational logic to its extrapolation, and many of his readers were grateful for it. The plights of his protagonists, adrift in treacherous worlds of deceptive appearance, struck a chord with many people confused by modernity as well as those impatient to transcend it.

**DICKINSON, PETER (1927– ).** British writer prolific in the fields of juvenile fiction and detective fiction; some of his works in the latter genre are modest **alternative histories**. His only adult **sf** novel is the **satire** *The Green Gene* (1973) but his **children's sf** includes *Healer* (1983), about the attempted exploitation of a talented child; *Eva* (1988), about a girl resurrected after an accident into the body of a chimpanzee; and the scrupulous evolutionary fantasies *A Bone from a Dry Sea* (1992) and *The Kin* (1998; U.S. publication in four vols.).

**DICKSON, GORDON R. (1923–2001). Canadian**-born writer resident in the United States from 1936, who began publishing **sf** in 1950. *Alien from Arcturus* (1956) was the first of many novels to feature sympathetic **aliens**, whose cute cuddliness is only occasionally compromised by carnivorous habits. Other examples include the imitative Hokas featured in comedies written in **collaboration** with **Poul Anderson**, collected in *Earthman's Burden* (1957) and *Hoka!* (1982), and the races described in *Space Winners* (1965), *The Alien Way* (1965), *Alien Art* (1973), and *Masters of Everon* (1980). Less appealing aliens are featured in *Wolfling* (1969), *Hour of the Horde* (1970), and *Way of the Pilgrim* (1980).

Dickson's major literary project was the Childe Cycle—which was planned to include historical novels as well as sf—tracking the evolution of an ethically responsible humankind. The "warrior phase" of this evolution (the other phases being "philosopher" and "faith-holder") is represented in a definitive series of **military sf** stories, including *Dorsai!* (1959; book 1960 as *The Genetic General*, rev. 1976), *Soldier, Ask Not!* (1964, exp. 1967), *The Tactics of Mistake* (1971), *The Spirit of Dorsai* (1979), and *Lost Dorsai* (1980). *Necromancer* (1962) is a prequel to the Dorsai series, while *The Final Encyclopedia* (1984), *The Chantry Guild* (1988), *Young Bleys* (1991), and *Other* (1994) carried the **future history** forward without fully fleshing out the later phases of the scheme.

Dickson's other sf of note includes the **robinsonade** *The Lifeship* (1976, with **Harry Harrison**); the offbeat **disaster story** *Time Storm* (1977); the space program thriller *The Far Call* (1978); and a meticulous depiction of an interspecific relationship forged under stress, *Wolf and Iron* (1990). His many short story collections include *Danger—Human* (1970), *The Star Road* (1973), *Love Not Human* (1981), *Beginnings* (1988), and *Ends* (1988).

**DI FILIPPO, PAUL (1954– ).** U.S. writer who published one **sf** story in 1977 although his career did not get under way until 1985. Most of his work consists of inventive **satirical fabulations**, like the **metafictional** novellas comprising *The Steampunk Trilogy* (1995). *Ribofunk* (1996) is a collection dealing with possibilities of **biotechnology**. *Ciphers* (1997) is a subversively surreal account of the revelation of America's secret past. Other collections include *Strange Trades* (2001), *Little Doors* (2002), and *Babylon Sisters and Other Posthumans* (2002), the last featuring stories of future evolution. *A Mouthful of Tongues: Her Totipotent Tropicanalia* (2002) is a biotechnologically assisted erotic fantasy. *A Year in the Linear City* (2002) is an **Odyssean fantasy** set on an infinite street whose hero is a writer of "cosmogonic fiction." *Fuzzy Dice* (2003) is an elaborate **existentialist fantasy** featuring a transmultiversal odyssey to the **Omega Point**.

**DIKTY, T. E. (1920–1991).** U.S. editor and **small press** publisher, married to **Julian May** from 1953 until his death. He and Earle Korshak founded Shasta to issue **Everett F. Bleiler's** *Checklist of Fan-*

*tastic Literature* (1948) and went on to publish **John W. Campbell Jr.'s** *Who Goes There?* (1948), early volumes of **Robert A. Heinlein's future history series,** and **Alfred Bester's** *The Demolished Man* (1953) before running into financial difficulties that consigned the winner of a competition they had sponsored (**Philip José Farmer's** *I Owe for the Flesh*) to a frustrating limbo. Dikty was involved in several other small press projects, including Fax Collector's Editions (1972–1977) and Starmont House (1977–1991); the latter, like **Robert Reginald's** Borgo Press, specialized in critical monographs. He coedited an early **series** of year's best selections (1949–1954) and several other **anthologies** with Bleiler.

**DIME NOVELS.** The major U.S. medium of cheap popular fiction prior to the emergence of the **pulp magazines**, dime novels were prolifically produced between the 1860s and 1890s; the term encompasses **serial** publications akin to the British boys' papers as well as paperbound individual works selling at five or ten cents; the most stereotypical format of the latter was 215mm × 280mm (the "bedsheet" size later employed by ***Amazing Stories***). The division of fiction into commercial genres began in the dime novel, whose crime melodramas were roughly divided into detective dramas set in the eastern United States and tales of outlaw gunslingers set in the still-wild west. Dime novel proto-**sf** consisted almost entirely of "inventor stories" aimed at young readers, whose juvenile heroes were budding Thomas Edisons. Many such works, including Edward S. Ellis's pioneering *The Steam Man of the Prairies* (1868) and an imitation of it that launched a long-running series, *Frank Reade and His Steam Man of the Plains* (1876, book 1892), were westerns celebrating the technological advantages that would allow invading colonialists to exterminate the Native Americans. Frank Reade spawned such imitators as Jack Wright and Tom Edison Jr., their collective exploits running into the hundreds. By the late 1880s **melodramatic inflation** had forced the dime novel writers to much more adventurous extremes of invention, involving exotic monsters, scientific supercriminals, and occasional interplanetary excursions and **alien** visitations. Although dime novels per se had virtually died out by 1900, the production methods they encouraged—especially the establishment of syndicates to organize and commission series by teams of authors—persisted well into the 20th century, and the spirit of dime novel sf lived on in the Great Marvel series of **Vernian** and interplanetary adventures bylined Roy Rockwood (1906–1913) and various Tom Swift series (1910–1938, 1954–1971, 1981–1984, and 1991–1993).

**DIMENSIONAL FANTASY.** Human senses perceive three spatial dimensions, but mathematics can deal with many more; graphical analysis often plots time along an axis, encouraging the idea that it can be imagined as "the fourth dimension," which is extrapolated in various fanciful ways in **C. H. Hinton's speculative nonfiction** and was adopted into **sf** by **H. G. Wells** in *The Time Machine* (1895). The idea of a fourth spatial dimension licensed the notion of an infinite array of **parallel worlds** lying "alongside" ours, and many occultists and **pseudoscientists** borrowed dimensional jargon to support the idea of an astral plane. The limitations of human perception were allegorized in such dimensional fantasies as **Edwin Abbott's** *Flatland* (1884) and **E. V. Odle's** *The Clockwork Man* (1923) before **Miles J. Breuer** and **Donald Wandrei** imported the subgenre into **pulp sf**. The notion that interstellar spaceships might use a fourth-dimensional **hyperspace** to avoid crippling Einsteinian limitations became commonplace in sf, while a **multiverse** of parallel worlds became a convenient framework for **alternative histories** and **time police** stories. The elaboration of dimensional fantasies for their own sake is much rarer in sf than their use as facilitating devices, although **Rudy Rucker** has done notable work in this vein.

**DISASTER STORIES.** Disaster stories became a commercial genre in their own right in the 1970s, although the best-selling examples were mostly limited to naturalistic accounts of huge fires, violent storms, endangered aircraft, floods, earthquakes, and so forth. The principal **sf** variants have always been the cosmic disaster story—usually involving a comet or asteroid strike, as popularized by **Camille Flammarion**—and the man-made catastrophe story, in which disaster is precipitated by reckless technological mismanagement. Stories of naturally generated plagues also extend into sf, after the fashion of **George R. Stewart's** *Earth Abides*. Any large-scale disaster is bound to edge into the imaginative territory of **postholocaust fantasy**, if not that of **apocalyptic fantasy**.

**DISCH, THOMAS M. (1940– ).** U.S. writer who began publishing **sf** in 1962. He became associated with the British **new wave** while living in the United Kingdom, many of his early black comedies being collected in *One Hundred and Two H-Bombs* (1966; revised 1971, exp. as *White Fang Goes Dingo and Other Funny SF Stories*; further exp. as *The Early Science Fiction Stories of Thomas M. Disch*, 1977) and *Under Compulsion* (1968, aka *Fun With Your New Head*). The **apocalyptic fantasy** *The Genocides* (1965) and the expanded version of "White Fang Goes Dingo" (1965), *Mankind under the Leash* (1966, aka *The Puppies of Terra*), are similarly scathing. *Echo Round His Bones* (1967) moves in the direction of **existentialist fantasy**, a trend continued in the highly ambitious *Camp Concentration* (1968), which tackles the problem of representing the evolution of superhumanity with unprecedented forthrightness. The **mosaic** *334* (1972) is a bleak account of a near-future United States sliding toward **dystopia**. His subsequent work was mostly in other genres, but *On Wings of Song* (1979) is an elegant futuristic **satire** built on allegorical foundations. The sf stories in *Getting into Death* (1973), *Fundamental Disch* (1980), and *The Man Who Had No Idea* (1982) are slickly satirical. *The Dreams Our Stuff Is Made Of: How Science Fiction Conquered the Worlds* (1998) considers sf as a revealing reflection of the ideas and ideals of American culture.

**DNA PUBLICATIONS.** U.S. **small press** owned by Warren Lapine. Initially the publisher of *Absolute Magnitude*, it gradually accumulated a stable of small press **magazines** by assuming responsibility for such established titles as *Weird Tales* and *Aboriginal Science Fiction* (from 1986 to 2001). Andrew Porter's newszine *Science Fiction Chronicle*, which had long competed with *Locus* for advertising support without ever attaining the same readership or regularity of production, joined the group in 2001. DNA revived **Amazing Stories'** one-time companion *Fantastic* in 2003.

**DOCTOROW, CORY (1971– ). Canadian** writer who began publishing **fabulations** employing **sf** motifs in 1990, increasing his production considerably after the success of "Craphound" (1998). He has collaborated with **Karl Schroeder** and **Charles Stross**, whose cutting-edge irreverence he shares. *Down and Out in the Magic Kingdom*

(2003) is a surreal **satire** about future life in the Bitchun Society's Disneyland-writ-large; "Truncat" (2002) is set in the same fictional milieu. His short fiction is sampled in *A Place So Foreign and Eight More* (2003).

**DONALDSON, STEPHEN R. (1947– ).** U.S. writer whose early work helped define and popularize genre fantasy. His **space opera** series comprising *The Gap into Conflict: The Real Story* (1990), *The Gap into Vision: Forbidden Knowledge* (1991), *The Gap into Power: A Dark and Hungry God Arises* (1992), and *The Gap into Madness: Chaos and Order* (1994) is a **transfiguration** of Richard Wagner's Ring Cycle.

**DONNELLY, IGNATIUS (1831–1901).** U.S. writer and politician, famous for his **pseudoscientific** account of *Atlantis: The Antediluvian World* (1882). *Caesar's Column* (1890, early editions bylined Edmund Boisgilbert) reacted to Edward Bellamy's *Looking Backward, 2000–1887* (1888) by providing the first significant American **dystopia**. Other political **satires** with **sf** elements are *Doctor Huguet* (1891), whose racist protagonist exchanges bodies with a black man, and *The Golden Bottle* (1892), in which a technology for manufacturing gold puts an end to capitalism.

**DORSEY, CANDAS JANE (1952– ). Canadian** writer best known as a poet. The title story of her collection of **fabulations** *Machine Sex—and Other Stories* (1988) deftly deploys **cyberpunk** imagery in a **feminist** parable whose protagonist was borrowed from *Hardwired Angel* (1985, with Nora Abercrombie). *Black Wine* (1997) is an intricate avant-gardist coming-of-age story. In *A Paradigm of Earth* (2001) a child-care specialist is hired to educate an **alien** visitor. Some items in *Vanilla and Other Stories* (2000) feature **sf** motifs.

**DOWLING, TERRY (1947– ). Australian** writer who began publishing **sf** in 1982. The collections *Rynosseros* (1990), *Blue Tyson* (1992), and *Twilight Beach* (1993) feature a series of lyrical futuristic fantasies in which the outback is a "dry ocean" transformed by the detritus of high-tech Ab'o society and navigated by the questing masters of baroque sandships. The stories in *Wormwood* (1991) are set in the aftermath of an enigmatic **alien** invasion. *Antique Futures: The Best of Terry Dowling* (1999) is an eclectic sampler.

**DOYLE, SIR ARTHUR CONAN (1859–1930).** British writer best known for detective fiction. His early **scientific romance** *The Doings of Raffles Haw* (1891) is an account of a disenchanted gold maker. His **horror-sf** stories include "The Los Amigos Fiasco" (1892), about an experimental electric chair, and "The Horror of the Heights" (1913), about strange life-forms in the upper atmosphere. *The Lost World* (1912), a classic novel about a geographical enclave where dinosaurs still survive, launched the Professor Challenger **series** continued in the **disaster story** *The Poison Belt* (1913) and—following Doyle's conversion to spiritualism—the dispirited **religious fantasy** *The Land of Mist* (1926). *The Professor Challenger Stories* (1952, aka *The Complete Professor Challenger*) also includes two horror-sf stories earlier reprinted in *The Maracot Deep and Other Stories* (1929). The **future war** story "Danger!" (1914; reprinted in *Danger! and Other Stories*, 1918) was rapidly overtaken by events. *The Best Science Fiction of Arthur Conan Doyle* (1981) includes all of his relevant short fiction except for the oblique **alternative history** "The Death Voyage" (1929).

**DOZOIS, GARDNER (1947– ).** U.S. writer and editor, whose control of ***Asimov's Science Fiction*** (1986– ) and the largest annual *Year's Best Science Fiction* collection (1984– ) made him the most influential short fiction editor in the field. He began publishing **sf** in 1966, much of his early short fiction being collected in *The Visible Man* (1977; exp. as *Geodesic Dreams: The Best Short Fiction of Gardner Dozois*, 1992); later work is in *Strange Days: Fabulous Journeys with Gardner Dozois* (2001). His fondness for **collaboration** is more productively demonstrated by the stories assembled in *Slow Dancing through Time* (1990) and many **anthologies** coedited with **Jack Dann** than the futuristic thriller *Nightmare Blue* (1975, with **George Alec Effinger**). *Strangers* (1974, exp. 1978) is a careful revisitation of the theme of **Philip José Farmer's** *The Lovers* (1961).

**DRAKE, DAVID A. (1945– ).** U.S. writer who began publishing in various fantasy genres in the 1960s, becoming prolific when the **military**

**sf** stories collected in *Hammer's Slammers* (1979) gave rise to a **series** continued in the novels *Cross the Stars* (1984), *At Any Price* (1985), *Counting the Cost* (1987), *Rolling Hot* (1989), *The Warrior* (1991), and *Paying the Piper* (2001). He participated in numerous **shared-world** and **sharecropping** exercises, adding a sequel, "To Bring the Light," to a new edition of **L. Sprague de Camp's** *Lest Darkness Fall* (1996). His other **time-travel** stories include the **mosaic** *Time Safari* (1982), *Birds of Prey* (1984), and *Bridgehead* (1986). Other military sf includes *Skyripper* (1983) and its sequel *Fortress* (1987), the stories in *The Military Dimension* (1991), *The Sharp End* (1993), *Redliners* (1996) and the series begun with *With the Lightnings* (1998), and *Lt. Leary, Commanding* (2000). In *Ranks of Bronze* (1986) **aliens** unwisely recruit a Roman legion. In *Starliner* (1992) a passenger ship gets caught up in an interstellar war. *The Voyage* (1994) **transfigures** the *Argonautica* much as *Cross the Stars* had transfigured the *Odyssey*. *Patriots* (1996) is a transfiguration of prerevolutionary American history.

**DUNN, J. R. (1953– ).** U.S. writer who began publishing **sf** in 1987. *This Side of Judgment* (1995) is a post-**cyberpunk** thriller featuring "chiphead" **cyborgs**. *Days of Cain* (1996) employs the viewpoint of an **Omega Point** intelligence in order to understand what happened in Auschwitz. *Full Tide of Night* (1998) is a **hybrid** fusion of mythological fantasy and extraterrestrial colonization, whose plot **transfigures** John Webster's *Duchess of Malfi*.

**DUNYACH, JEAN-CLAUDE (1957– ). French** writer and aerospace engineer, whose early stories were collected in *Autoportrait* (1986). In the four-volume *Étoiles mortes* series (1991–92) businesslike **aliens** facilitate human expansion into the galaxy, charging high fees. Translations of his short fiction began appearing in ***Interzone*** in the late 1990s.

**DVORKIN, DAVID (1943– ).** British-born U.S. writer whose debut novel *The Children of Shiny Mountain* (1977, aka *Shiny Mountain*) was followed by a **satire** on religion, *The Green God* (1979), and the convoluted **Wellsian** homage, *Time for Sherlock Holmes* (1983). *Budspy* (1987) is an **alternative history**. *The Seekers* (1988) is an antireligious satire. *Central Heat* (1988) is a **disaster story** in which the sun vanishes. *Ursus* (1989) is tongue-in-cheek **horror-sf** featuring **miniature** bears. In *Pit Planet* (2003) a hero searches the planet Colliery for the secret of a mysterious mineral.

**DYSON SPHERE.** A shell built around a star to make the maximum possible use of its radiant energy. Freeman Dyson borrowed the idea from **Olaf Stapledon's** *Star Maker* to characterize the central project of a civilization whose technology would exploit the entire energy resources of a star. In a classification devised by Nikolai Kardaschev, such civilizations are type II, type I civilizations being those that exploit the entire energy resources of a planet, and type III civilizations the entire energy resources of a galaxy. As usually imagined, Dyson spheres suffer from the technical difficulty that gravity would not anchor anything to the inner surface of the sphere; for this reason they require further modification in **hard sf** stories such as **James White's** *Federation World*, **Bob Shaw's** *Orbitsville*, and **Stephen Baxter's** *The Time Ships*. More modest megastructures constructed by type I civilizations evolving toward type II status include **Larry Niven's** *Ringworld*.

**DYSTOPIA.** A term used (and perhaps coined) by John Stuart Mill in 1868 as an antonym of **Utopia**, tacitly construing the latter term as "eutopia" (good place) rather than "outopia" (no place), as Thomas More originally intended. It describes hypothetical societies that are considerably worse than our own, tending toward the worst imaginable, although that extreme is hardly ever attained. Although many societies described in **satire** are implicitly dystopian, the term is usually reserved for earnest images of a future where the forces of **technological determinism** have made civilization hellish. *Le monde tel qu'il sera* (1846) by Émile Souvestre established the pattern in **France**, while **Walter Besant's** *The Inner House* (1888) and **Ignatius Donnelly's** *Caesar's Column* (1890) provided important English-language precedents. Anticapitalist and antisocialist sentiments were prolific sources of 20th-century dystopian fiction, extreme examples on both sides employing the image of the anthive as an ultimately undesirable but terrifyingly plausible end point. Writers of **scientific romance** and genre **sf** have made more use of images of

**decadence**, usually associated with excessive dependence on technology. The literary paradigm established by **E. M. Forster's** skeptical response to **Wellsian** optimism, "The Machine Stops" (1909), was imported into **pulp sf** by "City of the Living Dead" (1930) by **Laurence Manning** and **Fletcher Pratt** before becoming a particular preoccupation of **John W. Campbell Jr.** Revolution against some sort of dystopian regime rapidly became a standard plot formula in sf, and the domination of 20th-century futuristic fiction by dystopian imagery owes a great deal to its melodramatic potential, which Utopian fiction cannot match.

## – E –

**EASTON, THOMAS A. (1944– ).** U.S. writer who began publishing **sf** in 1974. He took over ***Analog's*** book review column in 1979. His Organic Future novels *Sparrowhawk* (1990), *Greenhouse* (1991), *Woodsman* (1992), *Tower of the Gods* (1993), and *Seeds of Destiny* (1994) depict a future in which **genetic engineering** has facilitated the replacement of almost all inorganic machinery by living equivalents. *The Electric Gene Machine* (2000) is a collection of stories about future **biotechnology**. In *Unto the Last Generation* (2000) and *Stones of Memory* (2000) human minds are uploaded into gravestones. *Alien Resonance* (2003) is a **first contact** story featuring tiny **aliens** whose spacecraft resemble Easter eggs. *Firefight* (2003) is a **technothriller** about environmental terrorism.

**ECOCATASTROPHE.** A term popularized by the **futurologist** Paul Ehrlich, who used it in 1969 as the title of a documentary summary of his anxieties about the compound threat of overpopulation and environmental pollution. The greenhouse effect and the erosion of the ozone layer were subsequently added to the ominous combination. Alvin Toffler's *Ecospasm* (1975) offered a less popular alternative term. Almost all post-1980 **sf** stories dealing with the near future take it for granted that a 21st-century global ecocatastrophe is inevitable, although artificial nostalgia for an imaginary golden age of ecological harmony encourages some writers to argue that a retreat from modern technology would be a good thing; Richard Jefferies's *After*

*London; or, Wild England* (1885) set an early precedent for this kind of exercise in future pastoralism. Notable ecocatastrophic fantasies include John Brunner's *The Sheep Look Up* (1972), Philip Wylie's *The End of the Dream* (1972), and David Brin's *Earth* (1990).

**ECOLOGICAL MYSTICISM.** Ecology is the study of organisms in relation to their environment; ecological mysticism adds a quasi-supernatural dimension to such associated notions as the "balance" or "harmony" of nature. A reverent awareness of humankind's integration into a complex network of interspecific relationships was displayed in W. H. Hudson's *A Crystal Age* (1887) long before "ecology" became a branch of biological science in the 1920s. Similar supernaturalizations resurfaced in genre **sf** in such works as Robert F. Young's "To Fell a Tree" (1959), Mark Clifton's *Eight Keys to Eden* (1960), and Richard M. McKenna's "Hunter, Come Home" (1963), alongside popularizations of the political and economic significance of humankind's ecological relationships by such alarmist **futurologists** as Paul Ehrlich, the **prophet** of **ecocatastrophe**; Garrett Hardin, whose essay on "The Tragedy of the Commons" (1968) provided a succinct account of an irreconcilable conflict between the assumptions of economic theory and the imperatives of ecology; and Barry Commoner, author of *The Closing Circle: Man, Nature, and Technology* (1971).

Much modern ecological mysticism is associated with exaggerations of the hypothesis outlined in James Lovelock's *Gaia: A New Look at Life on Earth* (1979), some of which has transferred its focus from Earth to **Mars** in the wake of Lovelock's essay on *The Greening of Mars* (1984, with Michael Allaby). **Isaac Asimov** relocated the hypothesis to a much larger stage in *Foundation's Edge* (1982), where "Galaxia" is a curious hybrid of Gaia and the **Omega Point**. Ernest Callenbach's *Ecotopia* (1975), which recommends ecological mysticism as a substitute for traditional religion, describes the creed in terms that licensed the commonplace description of ecological mystics as "tree huggers"—a tendency reflected in such forest-worshipping sf stories as **Ursula le Guin's** *The Word for World Is Forest* (1972) and Cynthia Joyce Clay's *Zollocco: A Novel of Another Universe* (2000). Callenbach's neologism was taken up and its reference broadened by **Kim Stanley Robinson's** sf **anthology** *Future Primitive: The New Ecotopias* (1994).

**EDISONADE.** A term used by **John Clute** in the *Encyclopedia of Science Fiction* to categorize tales in which heroic inventors devise technological fixes to save their communities from disaster. The word echoes **robinsonade**, similarly celebrating individual heroic improvisation under the spur of necessity.

**EDMONDSON, G. C. (1922–1995).** U.S. writer long resident in Mexico who began publishing **sf**-based tall tales in 1955, some of which are collected in *Stranger Than You Think* (1965). *The Ship That Sailed the Time Stream* (1965, rev. 1978) and *To Sail the Century Sea* (1978) are **Odyssean fantasies**. *Chapayeca* (1971, aka *Blue Face*) and *The Aluminum Man* (1975) introduce **aliens** to a Native American context. *The Man Who Corrupted Earth* (1980) and *The Takeover* (1984, with C. M. Kotlan) are strident exercises in **libertarian sf**. Kotlan also collaborated on the trilogy comprising *The Cunningham Equations* (1986), *The Black Magician* (1986), and *Maximum Effort* (1987), in which **genetically engineered** humans battle **AIs** to determine the course of future evolution.

**EFFINGER, GEORGE ALEC (1947–2002).** U.S. writer who began publishing **sf** in 1971. His enterprising short fiction, collected in *Mixed Feelings* (1974), *Irrational Numbers* (1976), *Dirty Tricks* (1978), *Idle Pleasures* (1983), and *The Old Funny Stuff* (1989), outshone his surreal novels *What Entropy Means to Me* (1973), *Relatives* (1973), *Those Gentle Voices* (1976), *Death in Florence* (1978, aka *Utopia 3*), and *Heroics* (1979). The grimness displayed in *The Wolves of Memory* (1981) was, however, productively combined with the playfulness of *The Nick of Time* (1985) and *The Bird of Time* (1986) in the **cyberpunk** trilogy *When Gravity Fails* (1987), *A Fire in the Sun* (1989), and *The Exile Kiss* (1991). Short stories and unfinished works belonging to the latter series were posthumously assembled in *Budayeen Nights* (2003).

**EGAN, GREG (1961– ). Australian** writer and computer programmer who began publishing **sf** in 1983. He became the outstanding **hard sf** writer of the 1990s with a series of unprecedented adventurous and philosophically sophisticated novels that combine ideas drawn (with uncompromising theoretical exactitude) from physics, cosmology, and biology. *Quarantine* (1992) extrapolates the uncertainty principle to a new extreme. *Permutation City* (1994) finds new potential in the idea of **cyberspace**, which is carried to extremes in the far-reaching cosmological extravaganza *Diaspora* (1997). *Schild's Ladder* (2002) tracks the creation of a "novo-vacuum" that begins to expand as new cosmos. The **political fantasy** *Distress* (1995) and the ecological fantasy *Teranesia* (1999) are modest by Egan's standards, but not by comparison with anyone else's work. The collections *Axiomatic* (1995) and *Luminous* (1998) contain some of the finest modern ***contes philosophiques***, including "Learning to Be Me" (1990), "Transition Dreams" (1993), "Reasons to be Cheerful" (1997), and "The Planck Dive" (1998); a third collection appeared in Japanese in 2000.

**EKLUND, GORDON (1945– ).** U.S. writer who began publishing **sf** in 1970. *The Eclipse of Dawn* and the **alternative history** of American socialism *All Times Possible* (1974) are enterprising **political fantasies**. The **mosaic** *If the Stars Are Gods* (1977, with **Gregory Benford**) features **aliens** whose religion is founded on that belief. After *The Garden of Winter* (1980) he devoted himself to the production of **tie-ins** and **sharecropping** exercises.

**ELGIN, SUZETTE HADEN (1936– ).** U.S. writer who began publishing **sf** in 1969. Most of her work extrapolates her expertise in linguistics into accounts of human/**alien** communication. *The Communipaths* (1970) and *Furthest* (1971), combined in *Communipath Worlds* (1980), began a **space opera series** continued in *Star-Anchored, Star Angered* (1979) and *Yonder Comes the Other End of Time* (1986) and linked to the **planetary romance** trilogy *Twelve Fair Kingdoms* (1981), *The Grand Jubilee* (1981), and *There'll Be Fireworks* (1981). *Native Tongue* (1984), *The Judas Rose* (1987), and *Earthsong* (1993) are **feminist** fantasies about the creation of a language for the exclusive use of oppressed women. Elgin founded the Science Fiction Poetry Association (SFPA) in 1978 and a newsletter on *Linguistics and Science Fiction* in 2000.

**ELLISON, HARLAN (1934– ).** U.S. writer, celebrated in **fandom** for his extraordinary showmanship, who defined American **new wave sf**

with his "taboo-breaking" **anthologies** *Dangerous Visions* (1969) and *Again, Dangerous Visions* (1972). He began publishing sf in 1955, although he was ambitious to work in several genres and media, always resisting attempts to "pigeonhole" him as an sf writer. The early fiction assembled in the **mosaic** *The Man with Nine Lives* (1960) and the collections *A Touch of Infinity* (1960) and *Ellison Wonderland* (1962; revised as *Earthman, Go Home*) is relatively orthodox, but the **fabulations** collected in *Paingod and Other Delusions* (1965, expanded 1975), *I Have No Mouth and I Must Scream* (1967, revised 1967), and *The Beast That Shouted Love at the Heart of the World* (1969) are more distinctive and idiosyncratic, the most effective displaying a remarkable stylistic and moral intensity. Ellison found it difficult to sustain his creative energy beyond the short story format, his ambition to expand his famous ***conte cruel*** "A Boy and his Dog" (1969) to novel length remaining long unfulfilled. The **bibliography** of his short fiction, which made progressively less use of sf motifs as it evolved, is complex; *The Essential Ellison* (1987) is an eclectic sampler.

**ELWOOD, ROGER (1933– ).** U.S. anthologist who was extraordinarily prolific from 1969–1978, producing thematically defined original **anthologies** in such profusion that he was estimated to constitute a quarter of the marketplace for short **sf**. He quit the genre abruptly after the failure of the determinedly formulaic Laser Books sf line he originated for **Canadian** publisher Harlequin. His own novels are mostly **religious fantasies**; those with sf elements include *Frankenstein Projects* (1991) and *Shawn Hawk: A Novel of the 21st Century* (1995).

**EMORTALITY.** A term coined by Alvin Silverstein and popularized in his *Conquest of Death* (1979), referring to a condition in which an organism does not age, and is therefore potentially capable of living indefinitely, while remaining vulnerable to violent death. Its preference to "immortality" in an **sf** context—because the older term implies an absolute immunity to destruction—is argued in such works as **Brian Stableford's** *Architects of Emortality* (1999).

**EMSHWILLER, CAROL (1921– ).** U.S. writer who began publishing **fabulations** with **sf** elements in 1957. *Carmen Dog* (1988) is a comedy of transformations. *The Mount* (2002) is a **satire** in which

**aliens** use humans as a means of transport. Her short fiction is collected in *Joy in Our Cause* (1974), *Verging on the Pertinent* (1989), *The Start of the End of It All* (1990), and *Report to the Men's Club and Other Stories* (2002). Her husband, Ed Emshwiller (1925–1990), was a notable sf illustrator who signed himself Emsh.

**EMTSEV, MIKHAIL (1930– ). Russian** writer who began writing sf in collaboration with fellow-scientist Eremei Parnov (1935– ) in 1961. **Hard-sf** stories featured in showcase **anthologies** include the title story of *The Last Door to Aiya* (1968), "He Who Leaves No Trace" in *The Ultimate Threshold* (1970), "The Snowball" in *Journey across Three Worlds* (1973), "Bring Back Love" in *Everything but Love* (1973), and "The Pale Neptune Equation" in *New Soviet Science Fiction* (1979). Their novel *World Soul* (1964; tr. 1978) is a more philosophically inclined account of telepathic communism.

**ENGDAHL, SYLVIA LOUISE (1933– ).** U.S. writer of **children's sf**. *Enchantress from the Stars* (1970), its sequel *The Far Side of Evil* (1970), and the trilogy comprising *This Star Shall Abide* (1972, aka *Heritage of the Star*), *Beyond the Tomorrow Mountains* (1973), and *The Doors of the Universe* (1981) are thoughtful exercises in **soft sf**.

**ENGH, M. J. (1933– ).** U.S. writer. *Arslan* (1976, aka *A Wind from Bukhara*) is a meticulously drawn portrait of a future world dictator. "The Oracle" (1980) is a ***conte philosophique***. *Wheel of the Winds* (1988) attempts to get to grips with an **alien** viewpoint. *Rainbow Man* (1993) is a study of the inflexibility of faith.

**ENGLAND, GEORGE ALLAN (1877–1936).** U.S. writer active in the early **pulp magazines**. His **sf** includes the exotic **existentialist fantasy** "The Elixir of Hate" (1911); the anticapitalist parables *The Air Trust* (1915) and *The Golden Blight* (1912, book 1916); the languorous **postholocaust mosaic** *Darkness and Dawn* (1912–1913, book 1914; in five volumes 1964–1967) and the **apocalypse**-anticipation story "The Nebula of Death" (1918). His short sf remains uncollected.

**ESHBACH, LLOYD ARTHUR (1910–2003 ).** U.S. writer and **small press** publisher. He began publishing **sf** in 1931 but his genre creations, collected in *Tyrant of Time* (1955), were sparse. In 1946 he founded Fantasy Press, which reprinted notable **pulp sf** by **E. E. Smith**, **Stanley Weinbaum**, **John W. Campbell Jr.**, **Jack Williamson**, and others. He edited a pioneering collection of essays on sf writing, *Of Worlds Beyond: The Science of Science Fiction Writing* (1947), which included manifestos by Campbell and **Robert A. Heinlein**.

**EVANS, CHRISTOPHER (1951– ).** Welsh writer, not to be confused with the psychologist Christopher (Riche) Evans (1931–1979), who edited two **anthologies** of psychology-related **sf**. *Capella's Golden Eyes* (1980), which features problematic contact with **aliens**, laid the groundwork for the intense **existentialist fantasies** *The Insider* (1981) and *In Limbo* (1985). The **mosaic** *Chimeras* (1992) describes the emergence of a new art form. *Aztec Century* (1993) is an **alternative history**. *Mortal Remains; or, Heirs of the Noosphere* (1995) is a convoluted **space opera**. With Robert P. Holdstock, Evans co-edited the original anthology **series** *Other Edens* (3 vols., 1987–1989).

**EVOLUTIONARY FANTASY.** The development of evolutionary philosophy in the Chevalier de Lamarck's *Philosophie zoologique* (1809) and Charles Darwin's *Origin of Species* (1859) was crucial to the early development of **sf**, shaping the imagery deployed in representing the past and future of humankind and estimations of the nature of **alien** life. **French** evolutionary fantasy, pioneered by Camille Flammarion's *Lumen* (1872), retained a framework of **religious fantasy** into the 20th century, but British **scientific romance** followed **H. G. Wells's** example in accepting that the theory of natural selection had rendered God's creativity redundant. American sf accepted from the beginning that one of its central tasks was to figure out where future human evolutionary progress might lead—a prospect dominated by **psi powers** until a mature appreciation of the transformative potential of **biotechnology** emerged in the 1970s. Some **far-futuristic fantasy** looks forward to a time when humankind's descendants will have given way to other life-forms, but designing the posthuman superman—or whole series of descendant species, as in **Olaf Stapledon's** *Last and First Men* (1930) and **Robert Silverberg's** *Son of Man* (1971)—has always been the subgenre's core enterprise.

**EXISTENTIALIST FANTASY.** The philosophical tradition of existentialism, founded by Søren Kierkegaard and carried forward by Martin Heidegger and Jean-Paul Sartre, attempts to define and evaluate the fundamental conditions of human identity and agency; it lends itself very readily to literary extrapolation and might itself be regarded as an essentially literary project. The sector of existentialist fantasy colonized by **sf** consists of texts that explore the nature and possibilities of consciousness in an innovative manner, routinely comparing and contrasting the mind-sets of such hypothetical constructs as **artificial intelligences** and **aliens** with those of human beings. This can only be done in written texts, and thus belongs exclusively to sf literature; **cinema** and **TV sci-fi** can only offer oblique hints.

**EXTRAPOLATION.** The process by which conclusions are drawn out of a set of premises. Although it is essentially a matter of logical calculation, extrapolation requires considerable artistry and intellectual ambition if it is to bear abundant fruit. The aesthetics of extrapolation are central to the enjoyment of **sf**, at least in its harder manifestations—a circumstance reflected in **Thomas Clareson's** decision to use that title on the first academic journal devoted to sf, launched in 1959; *Extrapolation* was initially published by the College of Wooster, Ohio, but moved to Kent State University Press in 1979 and the University of Texas at Brownsville in 2002.

**EXTRASENSORY PERCEPTION (ESP).** A term popularized by J. B. Rhine's *Extra-Sensory Perception* (1935), which repackaged folkloristic notions of "second sight" and a "sixth sense" in **pseudoscientific** jargon, whose central terms included "telepathy" and "precognition." A supernaturally assisted "empathy," in which feelings rather than thoughts are directly perceived, was added to **sf** versions of ESP in the 1950s by such writers as **Theodore Sturgeon**. Rhine's experimental investigations of ESP broadened to embrace the wider spectrum of wild talents routinely described in sf as **psi powers**. Some sf stories of the 1950s—notably **Alfred Bester's** *The Demolished Man* (1953)—briefly popularized the term "esper," but it soon fell into disuse.

## – F –

**FABULATION.** A term introduced into critical theory by **Robert Scholes** in *The Fabulators* (1967; rev. as *Fabulation and Metafiction*, 1979) to describe "ethically constrained fantasy"—or "didactic romance"—characterized by an acute consciousness of artifice (other kinds of fantasy being "pure romance"). The fabulator's calculated departure from naturalistic representation, in Scholes's view, is undertaken in the hope of obtaining a more accurate account of mental experience, which is itself conceived as a kind of fantasy in which dreams are inescapable and daydreams always available. Scholes subsequently placed **sf** within this fantasy spectrum by characterizing it as "structural fabulation," a subcategory of "speculative fabulation" (as opposed to "dogmatic fabulation"), in *Structural Fabulation* (1975). Other critics, including **John Clute** in *The Encyclopedia of Science Fiction*, define fabulation in a slightly different way, but retain the essential notion of the fabulator's delight in and strategic use of the manifest artificiality of the narrative. A good deal of sf is "pure romance" in Scholes's sense, but seriously intended sf is indeed didactic and ethically constrained, speculative rather than dogmatic, and carefully structured in terms of its **extrapolative** coherency. Although Scholes places no limit on the length of fabulations, the term is most commonly applied to short fiction, in which the art of fabulation may be displayed in its purest form without the distractions of novelistic narrative conventions.

**FANDOM.** The community of **sf** fans, whose larger meetings are **conventions** and whose routine communications are channeled through **fanzines**. Although the formal organization of fandom was encouraged by **Hugo Gernsback** when he used ***Wonder Stories*** to promote a Science Fiction League with chapters in many U.S. states, **Britain**, and **Australia**, some such spontaneous process had already become manifest in the letter columns of his magazines. The natural tendency of sf readers to flock together and exchange ideas—the basis of the "cult following" that allowed the genre to thrive in spite of its esotericism—is sometimes misunderstood as a mere matter of nerdish outsiders huddling together for comfort, but it actually reflects the essentially collective nature of the genre's aesthetics. Sf stories are far less significant when consumed individually and independently than they are when read in the context of a much larger body of work by a reader conscious that each one is a fragment of a vast spectrum of possibilities. Sf readers therefore have a strong incentive to associate with one another to compare notes on the range and merits of available texts. Writers enthusiastic to work seriously within the genre also benefit from this kind of consciousness, so many sf writers emerge from within fandom, and many of those who come to the genre by other routes subsequently find participation in fandom rewarding. Many sf fans were among the first prolific users of the Internet, so sf fandom is a very obvious aspect of the World Wide Web; by 2000, its many bases on the Internet were at least as important as fanzines and conventions in maintaining and shaping the sf community.

**FANTHORPE, R. LIONEL (1935– ).** British writer who began publishing **sf** in 1952, working almost exclusively for Badger Books, one of many **paperback** publishers that sprang up in the United Kingdom as World War II paper rationing was relaxed; his mostly pseudonymous contributions to their sf and supernatural fiction lines (between 80 and 90 volumes in each case) helped to keep the firm in business until 1966. His sf, improvised into a Dictaphone by night (he always had a day job) is ludicrously bad, but its ludicrousness has a perverse entertainment value and his oeuvre is an eccentric summation of the motifs and devices assembled by **pulp sf**.

**FANZINE.** An amateur **magazine** produced by **sf** fans. The term soon became commonplace after being coined by Russ Chauvenet (in opposition to "prozine") in 1940. It was subsequently adopted by fans of many other kinds, especially those of popular music and sports teams, but the range and diversity of sf fanzines is unparalleled. Early examples of sf fanzines were **Ray Palmer's** *The Comet* and Allen Glasser's *The Planet*, both of which made their debut in 1930, although members of **H. P. Lovecraft's** circle had been involved in similar exercises in the 1920s, a notable example being W. Paul Cook's *The Recluse*. By 2000 there were more than 500 sf fanzines, ranging from small "personalzines" through "reviewzines" and "newszines" to serious critical journals like A. Langley Searles's *Fantasy Commentator* (1943– ) and **Bruce Gillespie's** *SF Commentary*. ***Locus*** became sufficiently professional in its production standards and practices in the 1980s to require the invention of a new category of "semi-prozines," although the publishers of many **small press** fiction magazines had always considered them slightly grander than mere fanzines. All such publications, however, are essentially labors of love.

The vital role played by fanzines in constituting and sustaining **fandom** was recognized by the formation in 1937 of **Donald A. Wollheim's** Fantasy Amateur Press Association (FAPA)—modeled on the National Amateur Press Association founded in 1869—to facilitate the production and distribution of individual fanzines within a larger network. As well as providing much of the glue that holds the sf community together, fanzines have always made a vital contribution to the scholarship that is vital to the genre's collective effect. A great deal of **bibliographical** and critical endeavor is channeled through fanzines; very few (if any) academic scholars would ever be prepared to take on the heroic labors undertaken by fan bibliographers, because it would serve no purpose in the context of an academic career. Fan critics often seem intellectually gauche but are able to view sf texts within their natural context (which academic critics routinely refuse even to attempt), and the best fanzines have therefore retained some advantages over the academic journals. Were it not for the effort put into such long-running fanzines as *Fantasy Commentator* and Camille Cazedessus II's *PulpDom*, much of the heritage of **pulp** fantasy would have been lost for lack of collation, comparison, and analysis.

**FAR-FUTURISTIC FANTASY.** In the terminology of Fred Polak's *The Image of the Future*, fantasies of the near future represent "the future of history," while fantasies of the far future represent "the future of destiny" and are therefore different in kind rather than degree. Far-futuristic fantasies are usually replete with images of **decadence** and are often narrated in a conspicuously decadent style. Early scientifically inspired images of the far future—like those produced by **Camille Flammarion**, **H. G. Wells**, and **William Hope Hodgson**—employed a calculation of the sun's likely lifetime made by Lord Kelvin, who assumed that its heat was produced by gravitational collapse, but later **sf** writers adjusted their timescales to take account of the revelation that the sun's heat is actually produced by nuclear fusion, implying a lifespan in billions, rather than millions of years. **Clark Ashton Smith's** representation of the far future as a new age of magic was carried forward by **Jack Vance**, whose tokenistic suggestion that the "magic" in question is the result of the decay of awesomely powerful but long-forgotten technologies provided a license for those who came after, notable late-20th century examples including **Gene Wolfe's** New Sun **series** and **Paul J. McAuley's** Confluence trilogy. The notion of **nanotechnology** reinforced its plausibility in the 1990s—by which time far-futuristic imagery was often **chimerically** alloyed with notions drawn from cosmology and **evolutionary** theory, especially those that imagine the ultimate destiny of life in terms of some kind of **Omega Point**. One of the most significant developments in sf of the 1990s was the fusion of far-futuristic fantasy with **space opera**, extending its images of decadence across a vast stage and refreshing both subgenres.

**FARMER, PHILIP JOSÉ (1918– ).** U.S. writer who began publishing **sf** in 1946. His career began in earnest with a groundbreaking account of human/**alien** sex, *The Lovers* (1952; exp. 1961, rev. 1979), whose scandalous impact Farmer tried hard to replicate, most notably in the stories collected in *Strange Relations* (1960). His second novel, set against the same background, *A Woman a Day* (1953, rev. 1960; aka *The Day of Timestop* and *Timestop!*) displayed more interest in religion than sex, and he became particularly fascinated by hypothetical experiences of godhood and life after death—fascinations amply displayed in the **series** collected in *Father to the Stars* (1955–1961, book 1981), one of whose elements was expanded into the novel *Night of Light* (1966); the third novella in *The Alley God* (1962); and the novels *Flesh* (1960), *Inside Outside* (1964), and *Traitor to the Living* (1973).

Two novels from the early 1950s that languished unpublished for many years were the mildly erotic *Dare* (1965) and the afterlife fantasy *I Owe for the Flesh*, which was extensively rewritten as *To Your Scattered Bodies Go* (1965–1966, book 1971) before something nearer to the original was reprinted as *River of Eternity* (1983). In the meantime, Farmer relaxed into the prolific production of calculatedly bizarre **Odyssean fantasies**, most notably *The Green Odyssey* (1957) and *The Maker of Universes* (1965), although he found it far easier to start such stories than to bring them to a conclusion. In the 1970s he published several incomplete texts of this kind; the two series that he took furthest were the World of Tiers sequence begun with *Maker of Universes* and the Riverworld sequence begun with *To Your Scattered Bodies Go*, which meandered on and on, but contrived nevertheless to establish key exemplars for a new kind of chimerical **science-fantasy**.

Most of Farmer's subsequent work belongs to other similarly blended genres, including erotic thrillers and extravagantly **metafictional** homages to such **pulp** heroes as Tarzan and Doc Savage; the most interesting include the **Vernian** fantasy *The Other Log of Phileas Fogg* (1973) and the **Kurt Vonnegut** pastiche *Venus on the Half-Shell* (1975, bylined Kilgore Trout). *Dark of the Sun* (1979) and *Jesus on Mars* (1979) are similarly chimerical, but Farmer returned to sf of a more orthodox kind in *The Unreasoning Mask* (1981) and the trilogy comprising *Dayworld* (1985), *Dayworld Rebel* (1987), and *Dayworld Breakup* (1990). His short fiction showed his inventiveness to greater advantage; *The Classic Philip José Farmer* (2 vols., 1984) is an eclectic sampler.

**FARREN, MICK (1943– ).** British musician and writer who edited the underground newspaper *IT* (1970–1973) after the demise of his band, The Deviants, and founded the **comic** *Nasty Tales*. *The Texts of Festival* (1973) and the **series** comprising *The Quest of the DNA Cowboys* (1976), *Synaptic Manhunt* (1976), *The Neural Atrocity* (1977), and *The Last Stand of the DNA Cowboys* (1990) are **postholocaust fantasies**. *The Feelies* (1978) is a **satire**. *Protectorate* (1984) describes the **decadent** society of an **alien**-dominated future Earth. *Corpse* (1986, aka *Vickers*), *The Long Orbit* (1988, aka *Exit Funtopia*), and *The Armageddon Crazy* (1989) are hard-boiled near-future thrillers. *Their Master's War* (1987) is a **space-operatic political fantasy**. *Mars—the Red Planet* (1990) is an atypical experiment in **hard sf**.

**FARRÈRE, CLAUDE (1876–1957).** Pseudonym of **French** writer Charles Bargone. His **sf** includes *The House of the Secret* (1911, tr. 1923), a fantasy of longevity; and *Useless Hands* (1920, tr. 1926), in which a protest by industrial workers rendered redundant by automation is ruthlessly put down. *Contes d'outre et d'autres mondes* (1923) includes the adventurous **dimensional fantasy** "Où?" and a parable describing the explosive formation of the asteroids, "Fin de planète."

**FAUST, JOE CLIFFORD (1957– ).** U.S. writer who began publishing **sf** in 1983. *A Death of Honor* (1987) is a near-future mystery. *The Company Man* (1988) is a **cyberpunk** thriller. The trilogy comprising *Desperate Measures* (1989), *Precious Cargo* (1990), and *The Essence of Evil* (1990) tracks the **space-operatic** misadventures of the starship *Angel's Luck*. *Ferman's Devils* (1996) and *Bodekker's Demons* (1997) make up a **satirical** couplet combined in *Handling IT; How I Got Rich and Famous, Made Media Stars Out of Common Street Scum, and Almost Got the Girl* (1998).

**FAWCETT, EDGAR (1847–1904).** U.S. writer whose ventures into **hallucinatory fantasy** include the identity-exchange story *Douglas Duane* (1887); *Solarion* (1889), about a dog with artificially augmented intelligence; *The Romance of Two Brothers* (1889), about a problematic elixir of life; and the serial killer story *The New Nero* (1893). The preface to his most adventurous work, *The Ghost of Guy Thyrle* (1895), which includes a far-reaching comic voyage, is a manifesto for a new species of "realistic romance"—**sf** by another name. "In the Year Ten Thousand" in *Songs of Doubt and Dream* (1891) is an early example of sf **poetry**.

**FEARN, JOHN RUSSELL (1908–1960).** British writer who began writing for the **sf pulps** in 1933 with the garish **superman** story, *The Intelligence Gigantic* (book 1943). A **mosaic** about a superwoman, *The Golden Amazon* (1939–1943, book 1944) became the basis for a long **series** of novels (1945–1949) in the *Toronto Star Weekly*. His other pulp sf, which included an uninhibited account of *Liners of Time* (1933, book 1947), the **space opera** "The Blue Infinity" (1935; rev. as *The Renegade Star*, 1951), and the **microcosmic romance** "Worlds Within" (1937; rev. as *The Inner Cosmos*, 1952) is sampled in *The Best of John Russell Fearn, Volume One: The Man Who Stopped the Dust and Other Stories* and *Volume Two: Outcasts of Eternity and Other Stories* (both 2001) edited by **Philip Harbottle**. Most of this work was cannibalized after World War II when he produced **paperbacks** on a weekly basis, most of his sf appearing under the pseudonyms Vargo Statten—a name carried forward by the short-lived *Vargo Statten's Science Fiction Magazine* (1954–1956)—and Volsted Gridban.

**FEINTUCH, DAVID (1944– ).** U.S. writer of **military sf**. *Midshipman's Hope* (1994) launched a long **series** of novels **transfiguring** C. S. Forester's Horatio Hornblower as "Nicholas Seafort."

**FELICE, CYNTHIA (1942– ).** U.S. writer who began publishing **sf** in 1976. In *Godsfire* (1976) feline **aliens** inhabit a world of ceaseless rain. *The Sunbound* (1981), *Eclipses* (1983), *Downtime* (1985), *The Khan's Persuasion* (1991), and *Iceman* (1991) combine elements of sf and genre romance. *Double Nocturne* (1986) is an **Odyssean fantasy**. Her **collaborations** with **Connie Willis**, *Water Witch* (1982), *Light Raid* (1989), and *Promised Land* (1997), are breezy action-adventure stories.

**FEMINIST SF.** Because feminists have an active interest in precipitating and shaping social change, they have an intrinsic interest in **Utopian** fantasy, but images of hypothetical societies in which men and women are truly equal are rare. Even the most adventurous attempts—in **Theodore Sturgeon's** *Venus Plus X* (1960) and **Marge Piercy's** *Woman on the Edge of Time* (1976)—are conspicuously hesitant and ambivalent. There is, however, no shortage of horrific fantasies that employ **sf** devices to produce images of worlds where the plight of women is utterly desperate; the feminist movement increased their production dramatically in the last quarter of the 20th century. Nor is there any shortage of Utopian societies whose perfection is assured by the exclusion or elimination of the male of the species; the account of Whileaway in Joanna Russ's *The Female Man* (1975) began a boom, further increased by the production of **small presses** specializing in lesbian fiction. What this pattern of preferences might signify, in terms of the likelihood of the feminist cause making further progress, or the precise direction that progress might take, remains open to conjecture.

Sarah Lefanu's study of feminist sf *In the Chinks of the World Machine* (1988, aka *Feminism and Science Fiction*) draws a careful distinction between feminist sf and "feminized sf"; while the former examines sexual-political power structures and their underlying logic with conscientious skepticism, the latter extols the virtues of femininity, valuing empathy more highly than technical competence, passivity more highly than assertiveness, and—in its more extreme forms—intuition more highly than rationality. Although **soft sf** is primarily defined by the hardness it lacks, there is a good deal of it whose softness arises from calculated feminization; such material provides a counterweight to the absurdly uncompromising masculinity of the more extreme forms of action-adventure sf. The sf subgenre most hospitable to both feminist and feminized sf is **military sf**, whose celebration of the fact that advanced weaponry renders minor physical differences irrelevant has paved the way for shrewd and witty examinations of hypothetical gender roles in the works of such writers as **Lois McMaster Bujold** and **Catherine Asaro**.

**FERMI PARADOX.** An enigma posed by the physicist Enrico Fermi, which asks why, if the evolution of intelligent life on the planets of other suns is a matter of routine, there is no discernible evidence of its existence. The argument arises from the philosophical "principle of mediocrity," which suggests that it is highly unlikely that our sun is the only one among billions equipped with a planet capable of supporting life, or that our planet might be the first one on which life happened to appear. Further arguments suggest that a sophisticated technological species ought to be able to build **von Neumann machines** capable of exploring the galaxy within ten million years, or change their own environment in easily detectable ways (e.g., by the construction of megastructures like **Dyson spheres**) but there is no evidence of any such activity. Hypothetical solutions to this conundrum became increasingly melodramatic in the last quarter of the 20th century in the work of **hard sf** writers like **Gregory Benford**, **David Brin**, **Charles Pellegrino**, and **Stephen Baxter**. Notable examples include *The Coming* (2000) by **Joe Haldeman** and "Lying to Dogs" (2002) by Robert Reed; *Where Is Everybody? Fifty Solutions to the Fermi Paradox and the Problem of Extraterrestrial Life* (2002) by Stephen Webb summarizes contemporary thinking on the issue.

**FINCH, SHEILA (1935– ).** British-born writer resident in the United States since the early 1960s, who began publishing **sf** in 1977. *Infinity's*

*Web* (1985) is a convoluted **alternative history** story. *Triad* (1986) is a complex account of human/**alien** communication. The **planetary romance** comprising *The Garden of the Shaped* (1987), *Shaper's Legacy* (1989), and *Shaping the Dawn* (1989) tracks the result of an experiment in human population dynamics involving three artificially created races. *Tiger in the Sky* (1999) is a juvenile in which children battle aliens on a space station. *Birds* (2003) is a mystery with a NASA setting. In *Reading the Bones* (1998, exp. 2003) an unlucky xenolinguist seizes an opportunity to redeem himself and transform an alien language.

**FINNEY, JACK (1911–1995).** U.S. writer in various genres, whose collections *The Third Level* (1957; aka *The Clock of Time*, 1958) and *I Love Galesburg in the Springtime* (1963) mingle lightheartedly sentimental **sf** with other kinds of fantasy. *The Body Snatchers* (1955, aka *Invasion of the Body Snatchers*) is derivative of **Robert A. Heinlein's** *The Puppet Masters* (1951), similarly catching the mood of Cold War paranoia. *The Woodrow Wilson Dime* (1968) is a comedy of escape to a **parallel world**. *Time and Again* (1970) is an earnest escapist fantasy cast as a **timeslip romance**.

**FIRST CONTACT.** Humankind's first contact with an **alien** species is one of the fundamental themes of **sf**, capable of infinite variation; it is frequently envisaged as a pivotal moment in **future history**, even when it is made at a vast distance, as in **SETI** fantasies. The social-Darwinian assumptions of **H. G. Wells**, which led inexorably to the conclusion that any alien species we might encounter would be competitors in a cosmic struggle for existence, have always played a prominent part in the thinking of genre sf writers, although **Camille Flammarion's** contrary assumption that all sentient species have identical interests within the cosmic scheme has served to counterbalance it. The political significance of such differences of opinion is reflected in the fact that the Soviet sf writer **Ivan Yefremov** felt compelled to frame "Cor Serpentis" (1959) as an explicit ideological reply to **Murray Leinster's** tacitly paranoid "First Contact" (1945), proposing that any society sufficiently advanced to go spacefaring must have evolved a communist society, no matter how alien it might be in biological terms. Exotic and problematic first contacts are an equally prominent feature of the work of such ultra-**hard** sf writers as **Hal Clement** and **Robert L. Forward** and such earnestly **soft** sf writers as **Patricia Anthony** and **Nancy Kress**.

**FISK, NICHOLAS (1923– ).** Pseudonym of British children's writer David Higginbottom, whose **sf** stories have a harder edge, and are frequently darker in implication, than those of his contemporaries. *Space Hostages* (1967) and the Starstormer series (5 vols., 1981–1983) are derivative space fiction, but *Trillions* (1971), about an odd **alien** invasion, and *Time Trap* (1976) are more enterprising. *A Rag, a Bone, and a Hank of Hair* (1980) and *A Hole in the Head* (1991) are bleak futuristic fantasies. His short fiction is collected in *Sweets from a Stranger and Other Strange Tales* (1982) and *Living Fire and Other S-F Stories* (1987).

**FIX-UP.** A term used by **A. E. van Vogt** (sometimes unhyphenated) to describe the novels he improvised from previously published **magazine** stories, some of which had no intrinsic connection with one another until they were rewritten. The **Nicholls/Clute** *Encyclopedia* uses the term to apply to all books marketed as novels whose parts had seen previous independent publication but not to collections of linked short stories. Critics who dislike the term include Eric Rabkin, who suggested the alternative "composite novel," and **Gregory Benford**, who suggested "**mosaic** novel"; this book employs mosaic in a slightly wider sense.

**FLAMMARION, CAMILLE (1842–1925). French** astronomer and writer, and a leading exponent of the popularization of science. *La pluralité des mondes habités* (1862) was a pioneering work of **speculative nonfiction** about life on other worlds, and the survey of relevant fictional images contained in *Les mondes imaginaires et les mondes réels* (1864, expanded 1892) is an early history of proto-**sf**. Three fictionalized essays are collected in *Récits de l'infini* (1872, tr. as *Stories of Infinity*), the most substantial being *Lumen* (1866–1869, separate ed. 1887; expanded 1906), in which a disembodied spirit who is free to roam the universe at will relates observations of otherworldly life adapted to **alien** physical conditions, extrapolating an example provided by **Humphry Davy**. The ideas were further developed in the bildungsroman *Stella* (1877) and the patchwork *Uranie* (1889, tr. as

*Urania*). Flammarion also popularized the vulnerability of the Earth to a comet strike—a notion that he employed in the first part of *La fin du monde* (1893–1894, tr. as *Omega; The Last Days of the World*), whose second part extends into a languid futuristic fantasy. Some further sf is collected, with other items, in *Contes philosophiques* (1911) and *Rêves étoilés* (1914, abridged tr. as *Dreams of an Astronomer*).

**FLASH GORDON.** U.S. **comic** strip conceived in 1934 by Alex Raymond as a rival to **Buck Rogers**, which soon became more adventurous in its use of **planetary romance**, especially in the eponymous hero's battles with arch villain Ming the Merciless on the planet Mongo. Like its rival, it spun off **cinema** and **TV** serials as well as a **pulp magazine** (which never published a second issue) and a handful of **tie-in** novels.

**FLINT, HOMER EON (1892–1924).** U.S. writer whose first **pulp sf** stories, "The Planeteer" and "The King of Conserve Island" (both 1918), were near-future **political fantasies**. A **series** of **planetary romances** comprising "The Lord of Death," "The Queen of Life" (both 1919, omnibus 1965), "The Devolutionist," and "The Emancipatrix" (both 1921, omnibus 1965) is more ambitious, although their political speculations are undermined by the implausibility of their plots. Flint collaborated with **Austin Hall** on a feverish **dimensional fantasy**, *The Blind Spot* (1921, book 1951).

**FLYING SAUCER.** A term popularized in the early 1950s in the wake of an alleged sighting in 1947 of a group of strange flying objects. Although sightings of a similar kind had been collated by **Charles Fort**, with precedents extending back to biblical times, the post–World War II sightings began a craze, greatly encouraged by Cold War paranoia. The notion of furtive **alien** observers echoed the paranoid fantasies of Richard S. Shaver, to which **Ray Palmer** had given abundant publicity in ***Amazing Stories***, and Palmer latched on to it enthusiastically, although other **sf magazines** maintained a scrupulous skepticism that soon turned to mocking disdain. Such texts as *The Flying Saucers Are Real* (1950) by Donald Keyhoe and *Flying Saucers Have Landed* (1953) by George Adamski were only taken seriously by a tiny minority, but the craze was sufficiently widespread and bizarre to attract the interest of sociologists and psychologists, including Carl Jung in *Flying Saucers* (1958, tr. 1959). The term soon acquired sufficient pejorative overtones to be substituted by the seemingly more neutral Unidentified Flying Object (UFO). The popular delusion that sf fans are likely to believe in the reality of flying saucers deeply offended scrupulous skeptics within the sf community, many of whom became scathing critics of **UFOlogy**.

**FLYNN, MICHAEL F. (1947– ).** U.S. writer who began publishing **sf** in 1984. *In the Country of the Blind* (1987; book 1990) is an **alternative history** novel featuring a 19th-century computer. "The Washer at the Ford" (1989), an early thriller about **nanotechnology**, was integrated into the **mosaic** *The Nanotech Chronicles* (1991). *Fallen Angels* (1991, with **Larry Niven** and **Jerry Pournelle**) is a **political fantasy**. The **series** comprising *Firestar* (1996), *Rogue Star* (1998), *Lodestar* (2000), and *Falling Stars* (2001) offers a minutely detailed account of a space program designed to protect Earth from asteroid strikes. In *The Wreck of The River of Stars* (2003), disaster strikes an obsolete spaceship. His short fiction is sampled in *The Forest of Time and Other Stories* (1997).

**FORCE FIELD.** In the vocabulary of **sf**, a force field is a transparent shield, impenetrable by matter or radiation (at least until it is overloaded). In **cover art**, force fields often enclose cities like domes, and they were routine defenses for spaceships in early **space opera**. **Charles Harness** modified the notion in *Flight into Yesterday* (1949) to permit the penetration of slow-moving objects, thus forcing future warriors to employ swords rather than guns—a useful **melodramatic** asset. **Poul Anderson's** *Shield* (1963) is the most sustained attempt to analyze the logical implications of such a device.

**FORD, JOHN M. (1957– ).** U.S. writer who began publishing **sf** in 1975. *Web of Angels* (1980) anticipates **cyberpunk** motifs. *The Princes of the Air* (1982) is a flamboyant **space opera**. *The Dragon Waiting* (1983) is an **alternative history** set in medieval Europe. *Growing Up Weightless* (1993) is a rite of passage novel set on the moon. His **poetry** collection *Timesteps* (1993) includes a sonnet cycle on "SF Clichés."

**FORSTCHEN, WILLIAM R. (1950– ).** U.S. writer who began publishing **sf** with a trilogy comprising *Ice Prophet* (1983), *The Flame upon the Ice* (1984), and *A Darkness upon the Ice* (1984), about the messianic revival of science in a pusillanimous **postholocaust** society. His later works—including the **series** comprising *Star Voyager Academy* (1994), *Article 23* (1998), and *Prometheus* (1999); *In the Sea of Stars* (1986); and *We Look Like Men of War* (2001)—similarly contrive futuristic situations in which violent conflicts are routine. The **alternative histories** *1945* (1995) and *Gettysburg* (2003) are **collaborations** with Republican politician Newt Gingrich.

**FORSTER, E. M. (1879–1970).** British writer of literary fiction whose early fantasy stories included the ***conte philosophique*** "The Machine Stops" (1909), a response to the **Utopias** of **H. G. Wells**, which argues that human overdependence on machines would lead inexorably to disaster—a key theme of 20th-century **sf**.

**FORT, CHARLES (1874–1932).** U.S. journalist who compiled four collections of "damned data" (reportage of events discounted by the "scientific priesthood" as impossible) beginning with *The Book of the Damned* (1919) and *New Lands* (1923). A thoroughgoing skeptic, Fort delighted in the **extrapolation** of wryly bizarre hypotheses from these strange assemblies, lending enormous encouragement to occultists, **pseudoscientists**, and fantasists, including such **sf** writers as **Eric Frank Russell** and **Damon Knight**. *Lo!* (1931; reprinted in ***Astounding***, 1934) and *Wild Talents* (1932), which laid the groundwork for the modern mythology of **extrasensory perception** and **psi powers**, had a particularly profound impact on genre sf. A Fortean Society was formed in 1931 to celebrate and carry forward Fort's work; the International Fortean Organization published *INFO Journal* while the U.K. branch published the slightly more lighthearted *Fortean Times*. A *Fortean TV* show was launched in Britain in 1997, presented by **Lionel Fanthorpe**.

**FORWARD, ROBERT L. (1932–2002).** U.S. physicist and writer who began publishing **sf** in 1979. *Dragon's Egg* (1980) and its sequel *Starquake!* (1985) are ultra-**hard sf** stories in the tradition of **Hal Clement**, describing the evolution of an ecosphere on the surface of a neutron star and the interaction of its sentient species with humankind. *The Flight of the Dragonfly* (1985; exp. as *Rocheworld*, 1990) speculates about the ecosphere of a double planet linked by a bridge; two sequels, *Return to Rocheworld* (1993) and *Rescued from Paradise* (1995), were written with his daughter, Julie Forward Fuller, and a further two, *Marooned on Eden* (1993) and *Ocean under the Ice* (1994), with his wife, Martha Dodson Forward. *Martian Rainbow* (1991) is a restrained **political fantasy** whose **libertarian** rhetoric is further **extrapolated** in *Timemaster* (1992). *Camelot 30K* (1993) is a puzzle story set on an ice world in the Oort cloud. *Saturn Rukh* (1997) is about an expedition to mine the Saturnian atmosphere and its interaction with native life-forms. *Indistinguishable from Magic* (1995) mingles short fiction with **speculative nonfiction**.

**FOSTER, ALAN DEAN (1946– ).** U.S. writer who began publishing **sf** in 1971. *The Tar-Aiym Krang* (1972) launched a long **series** set within the galactic civilization of the Humanx Commonwealth, whose name reflects the rhetoric of the stories, which strongly favors the establishment of harmoniously liberal and mutually rewarding social relationships. The most notable works in the series include the **planetary romances** *Icerigger* (1974) and its sequels; *Midworld* (1975); *Voyage to the City of the Dead* (1984); and the subseries about the Commonwealth's founding comprising *Phylogenesis* (1999), *Dirge* (2000), *Diuturnity's Dawn* (2002), and *Drowning World* (2003). The planetary romances *Cachalot* (1980) and *Life Form* (1995); the Earth-set thrillers *Cyber Way* (1990) and *Cat-a-Lyst* (1991); and the **parallel worlds** story *Parallelities* (1998) are similar in spirit. Although similarly prolific in other fantasy genres, Foster continued to extend his range in such sf novels as *The Mocking Factor* (2002), a near-future detective story. From 1974 onward he was the most sought-after writer of sf movie novelizations, largely because he took that kind of work more seriously than most of his rivals. His short fiction is sampled in *Impossible Places* (2002).

**FOSTER, M. A. (1939– ).** U.S. writer whose first **sf** project was a **series** of novels about a future race of **genetically engineered** superhumans comprising *The Warriors of Dawn* (1975), its prequel *The Gameplayers of Zan* (1979), and its sequel *The Day of the Klesh*

(1979). *Waves* (1980) is a **planetary romance** featuring a sentient ocean. The possibilities of genetically engineered shape-shifting are explored in *The Morphodite* (1981), *Transformer* (1983), and *Preserver* (1985). *Owl Time* (1985) collects four exercises in pastiche.

**FOWLER, KAREN JOY (1950– ).** U.S. writer who began publishing **sf** in 1985. Her delicate work lies on the margins of the genre but addresses some of its basic motifs with unusual subtlety and seriousness. *Sarah Canary* (1991) tells the story of an **alien** visitor to the late 19th-century United States, whose unintelligible speech reflects the communicative difficulties of the many underdogs and outsiders she encounters. Her short sf is collected in *Artificial Things* (1986) and *Black Glass* (1999).

**FOY, GEORGE (1952– ).** U.S. writer who first ventured into **sf** in a near-future **series** that follows a standard trajectory in evolving from post-**cyberpunk** thriller to exotic **political fantasy**, comprising *The Shift* (1996), *Contraband* (1997), *The Memory of Fire* (2000), and *The Last Harbor* (2000).

**FRANCE, ANATOLE (Anatole-François Thibault, 1844–1924). French** writer whose **mosaic** *Sur la pierre blanche* (1905, tr. as *The White Stone*) scrupulously carried forward Félix Bodin's analysis of the potential of futuristic fiction, pointing out that any writer who successfully anticipated the moral order of the future would be deemed dangerously subversive of contemporary morality. This did not prevent him from attempting, in the book's final ***conte philosophique***, to analyze the prospects of a Marxist **Utopia**, nor scathingly **satirizing** French history and politics in *L'île des pingouins* (1908, tr. as *Penguin Island*), nor championing corrosive skepticism against dogmatic religion in *Le révolte des anges* (1914, tr. as *The Revolt of the Angels*).

**FRANKE, HERBERT W. (1927– ).** Austrian-born writer resident in **Germany** from 1950, who began publishing sf in the 1950s. The novels translated as *The Mind Net* (1961, tr. 1974), *The Orchid Cage* (1961, tr. 1973), and *Zone Null* (1970, tr. 1974) are typical of his output in featuring humans placed under extreme stress by exotic circumstances.

**FRANKENSTEIN SYNDROME.** A term coined by **Isaac Asimov**—although the case had been made in **Eando Binder's** "I, Robot"—in the course of explaining that his stories about the socially beneficial use of **robots** were intended to counteract the common assumption that any such invention would be a hubristic usurpation of divine prerogatives that could only lead to disaster. The melodramatic convenience of normalizing story-arcs had ensured that the fundamental pattern of **Mary Shelley's** novel was repeated incessantly, and unthinkingly accepted into **pulp sf**, in spite of the fact that its standardization tacitly implies that all invention is evil. In spite of the heroic efforts of Asimovian apologists for technological progress, the attitudinal effects of the Frankenstein syndrome remained very evident in sf and the real world as the 21st century began. The proposition that the myth of progress is both false and pernicious is the basis of continued cultural **criticism** of sf in such works as Ernest Yanarella's *The Cross, the Plow, and the Skyline* (2001).

**FRANKLIN, H. BRUCE (1934– ).** U.S. critic who taught one of the first university courses in **sf**, in 1961 at Stanford. His critical **anthology** *Future Perfect: American Science Fiction of the Nineteenth Century* (1966, revised 1968 and 1978) is a model of its kind. After his dismissal from Stanford for protesting against the college's involvement in the Vietnam War, he directed his future researches to sf's reflections of and participation in American attitudes to the politics of war; his findings are summarized in *Robert A. Heinlein: America as Science Fiction* (1980) and the wide-ranging *War Stars: The Superweapon and the American Imagination* (1988). He edited an exemplary anthology of stories about nuclear weapons, *Countdown to Midnight* (1984).

**FRENCH SCIENCE FICTION.** Almost all the significant 19th-century innovations in **speculative fiction** were first made in French literature, although a lack of translations meant that many had to be independently rediscovered by English writers. France's unusually rich tradition of fantastic voyages and **Utopian** romances gave rise to a 36-volume series of reprints edited by Charles Garnier, *Voyages imaginaires, songes, visions, et romans cabalistiques* (1787–1789), which would presumably have extended further had it not been interrupted by the revolution. It includes such **interplanetary romances** as **Voltaire's** "Micromégas" (1750), the Chevalier de Béthune's *Relation du monde de Mercure* (1750), Marie-Anne de Roumier's *Voyages de Mylord Céton dans les sept planètes* (1765–1766), and **Louis-Sebastien Mercier's** "Nouvelles de la lune" (1788), all of which—in addition to the pioneering **planetary romance** *Star; ou Psi de Cassiopée* (1854, tr. as *Star*) by Charles de Fontenay—were key influences on the work of **Camille Flammarion**, who summarized them in *Les mondes imaginaires et les mondes réels* (1864) before importing the revelations of modern astronomy into their metaphysical framework. Achille Eyraud's tale of a spaceship powered by a "reaction engine," *Voyage à Vénus* (1865), laid the foundations for more realistic accounts of interplanetary travel.

The huge success of Mercier's pioneering futuristic Utopia, *L'an 2440* (1771, tr. as *Memoirs of the Year 2500*), laid the groundwork for the first theoretical discussion of the potential scope of futuristic fiction, Félix Bodin's *Le roman d'avenir* (1834) and the first **dystopia**, Émile Souvestre's *Le monde tel qu'il sera* (1846). **Alternative history** was introduced into French literature by Louis-Napoléon Geoffroy's *Napoleon apocryphe* (1836). **Jules Verne** might have continued the futuristic tradition had he not accepted the guidance of his publisher P.-J. Hetzel and concentrated on his *Voyages extraordinaires*, which became the exemplars of a subgenre of romances of exploration aimed primarily at younger readers, whose main contributors included **André Laurie** and Paul d'Ivoi and whose main vehicle was the weekly *Journal des Voyages* (1885–1915).

Although **sf** had made no inroads into the popular *roman* feuilleton in the mid-19th century, the popularization of Vernian fiction meant that it obtained a much more obvious presence there by 1900; sf very similar to that which appeared in the early U.S. **pulps** was developed by such writers as Jules Lermina, **Maurice Renard**, Jean de la Hire, and Paul Féval *fils*. The illustrator **Albert Robida** launched his career as a writer with Vernian parodies in a feuilleton format, in much the same spirit as Eugène Mouton's parodies of Flammarion. Up-market variants of the Vernian format included George Sand's *Laura: voyage dans le cristal* (1865). **Wellsian** fiction was imported into France, and its influence combined with that of Flammarion, by **J. H. Rosny aîné**. Such "middlebrow" fiction was further popularized by H.-J.

Proumen, André Couvreur, and Gustave le Rouge, while the native tradition of ***contes philosophiques*** was carried forward to considerable effect by such writers as **Anatole France** and George Pawlowski.

France's burgeoning tradition of **speculative fiction** was interrupted by World War I in much the same fashion as British **scientific romance**, but not as drastically; Rosny, Renard, le Rouge, and Proumen continued their careers, while notable new work was done by **Claude Farrère**, Noëlle Roger (Helen Pittard), **André Maurois**, José Moselli, and Théo Varlet. World War II proved, however, to be more decisive; when American sf began to flood the French market after the war's conclusion, French writers had not the same opportunities as their English counterparts to climb on the bandwagon.

Although the pulpish sf that flooded the postwar **paperback** market provided opportunities for such native writers as Maurice Limat and Jimmy Guieu, more serious material struggled to avoid eclipse by imported sf. Such writers as **Pierre Boulle**, **René Barjavel**, **Pierre Barbet**, **Gérard Klein**, **Jacques Sternberg**, **Philippe Curval**, and **Michel Jeury** found themselves faced with stiff domestic competition from imported materials, while their own penetration of the English-language market was very limited. As the end of the century approached and the English language market became steadily more conservative, even the finest French sf writers—including **Pierre Bordage**, **Jean-Marc Ligny**, **Ayerdahl**, **Laurent Genefort**, and **Jean-Claude Dunyach**—found it very difficult to publish their work in English translation. In spite of this virtual imprisonment, however, domestic sf continued to thrive in France to a greater extent than in any other nation outside the English-language marketplace.

**FUTURE HISTORY.** In the context of **sf**, a future history is a framework external to a **series** of stories, which serves as a backcloth for its further extension and elaboration. Individual works containing extensive histories of the future are sometimes included under the label, although **Olaf Stapledon's** *Last and First Men* would qualify anyway because of its backcloth's further use in *Last Men in London*. Knowledge of an imaginary history carried forward by readers from earlier works can save the author a good deal of narrative labor, although the assumption of familiarity may make it difficult for new readers to get to grips with the material in later works. **Laurence Manning** and **Neil R. Jones** produced early genre examples, but the first future history to be given considerable publicity was the one tying together **Robert A. Heinlein's** early work for ***Astounding***, for which he briefly reserved his own name while publishing nonseries stories under pseudonyms. The history of the **galactic empire** sketched out in **Isaac Asimov's** Foundation series was far more influential, foreshadowing such future histories as those developed by **Poul Anderson**, **Gordon R. Dickson**, and **Lois McMaster Bujold**.

**FUTURE WAR.** Future war stories became the core subgenre of British **scientific romance** in the 1890s, as the opinion became widespread that there would have to be a crucial settlement of affairs between the British Empire and other colonial powers resentful of its powers and extent—especially Germany, whose military might had been demonstrated in the Franco-Prussian War. The realization that new technologies would make wars much more destructive had been growing for some time, anticipated by such fictions as *The Air Battle* (1859) by Herrmann Lang. George T. Chesney's account of *The Battle of Dorking* (1871) caused a sensation, although his other futuristic novella, *The New Ordeal* (1879)—which suggested that it might be possible to find alternatives to technologically sophisticated warfare—attracted far less attention. Future war fiction was firmly reestablished in the public consciousness by **George Griffith's** *The Angel of the Revolution* (1893), which launched a deluge of newspaper serials, one of which—**Louis Tracy's** *The Final War*—helped plant the treacherous idea that the next war would be a final settlement of world politics: a war to end war that would secure Anglo-Saxon hegemony indefinitely. The prewar acceptance of that myth generated a violent postwar backlash when it was realized that all the destruction and slaughter had been for nothing—a disenchantment vividly reflected in such **apocalyptic fantasies** as Edward Shanks's *People of the Ruins* (1920). When British future war fiction was revived in the 1930s, its bitterly pessimistic tone helped to create very different expectations of World War II.

The United States came late into both world wars and its territory was virtually untouched by their effects; this assisted American futuristic fiction to maintain a much more positive attitude to war, whose history is tracked in **H. Bruce Franklin's** *War Stars: The Superweapon and the American Imagination* (1988). The advent of the atom bomb caused considerable anxiety, even before the USSR obtained the weapon, but alarmist **apocalyptic fantasies** never went unchallenged in U.S. futuristic fiction; **libertarian sf** routinely celebrated armed might as the only effective guarantee of freedom—a philosophy treated with far greater skepticism in Europe. The innate belligerence of the subgenre was one reason why European writers were slow to get involved in **space opera**; **military sf** remained an exclusively American subgenre until the end of the 20th century.

**FUTURIANS.** A group of **sf** fans, almost all of them would-be professionals, resident in New York from 1938. The group disintegrated after the end of World War II, split asunder when **James Blish** sued **Donald A. Wollheim** for slander, although its residue continued to form a focal point of a loosely knit New York-based community of sf writers for some years thereafter. **Frederik Pohl**, **C. M. Kornbluth**, **Damon Knight**, **Judith Merril**, Virginia Kidd, **Robert A. W. Lowndes**, and **Richard Wilson** were all key members; peripheral associates included **Isaac Asimov**. Pohl and Knight both published memoirs of their association with the group.

**FUTUROLOGY.** A term coined in 1943 by Ossip Flectheim as propaganda for a concerted effort by social scientists to develop methods of trend analysis as a means of **prediction**. It was popularized by **Aldous Huxley**, who tried to practice what he preached in *Brave New World Revisited* (1958). The origins of futurological ambition can, however, be found in T. R. Malthus's *Essay on the Principle of Population* (1798), whose second edition of 1803 was obliged to admit that the disasters held to be inevitable in the first version might, in fact, be avoided by the exercise of "moral restraint." Modern futurologists are usually careful to admit that their work is necessarily speculative, given that the future is inherently unpredictable, but the temptation to believe that the future can be "discovered" is so strong that even **H. G. Wells** fell prey to it after writing the essays collected in *Anticipations* (1901), which set a pattern for many subsequent futurological enterprises. The principal disadvantage of exercises in futurology is that their excessive reliance on trend analysis anchors them even more securely to the present than near-future sf but the exceptions are spectacular; sf took a long time to catch up with the imaginative scope casually deployed by **J. B. S. Haldane** and **J. D. Bernal's** contributions to the **Today & Tomorrow series** of futurological pamphlets (1923–1930), although the other 106 essays now seem ludicrously unadventurous. In spite of continual lapses of individual writers into predictive folly, when futurological enterprises are viewed as a collective they have the same mutually contradictory virtue as sf.

## – G –

**GAIL, OTTO WILLI (1896–1956). German** writer whose novels about space travel aimed for verisimilitude—although *The Shot into Infinity* (1925, tr. 1929) is more convincing than its sequel "The Stone from the Moon" (1926, tr. 1930)—and provided inspiration to the German Rocket Society, of which **Willy Ley** was a member.

**GALACTIC EMPIRE.** A term used in **sf** to describe any far-flung interstellar society, whether or not it is an empire in political terms; **Iain M. Banks's** Culture would qualify in spite of its socialist leanings. The term was popularized by **Isaac Asimov's** Foundation **series**, whose early volumes were a **transfiguration** of the history of the Roman Empire. Such entities were a standard feature of early **space opera**, where evil empires tyrannizing hundreds of subject worlds were rapidly generated to fill antagonistic roles by the process of **melodramatic inflation**. Despite its essential improbability, the idea of a vast interstellar culture harboring many exotic backwater worlds was a useful facilitating device for framing serious **planetary romances**, whose proliferation was a core enterprise of 1950s and 1960s sf. The refinement of the idea of the galactic empire became a key element in the sophistication of space opera required by more adventurous celebrations of the **space-age** and **military sf**, although the idea that any kind of political power could be exercised or any kind of effective trade conducted over interstellar distances is hard to swallow.

***GALAXY.*** U.S. **magazine** whose founding in 1950, paying the same word rate as ***Astounding***, offered serious **sf** writers an alternative market to the increasingly dogmatic and **psi**-obsessed **John Campbell**. *Galaxy*'s first editor (1950–1961), H. L. Gold, had no alternative manifesto to offer, but the writers who gravitated toward *Galaxy* no longer needed charismatic leadership and discipline, only opportunities to carry through their own purposes. Gold was more liberal than Campbell, politically and aesthetically, and *Galaxy* was particularly hospitable to **soft sf** with a **satirical** flavor, as practiced by **William Tenn** and **Damon Knight**; and he was equally sympathetic to **Theodore Sturgeon's** sentimentality and **Robert Sheckley's** humor, although a fantasy companion he founded, *Beyond* (1953–1955), proved short-lived. His hesitations over material that seemed too outré—like **Fritz Leiber's** *The Big Time*—and his blind spot regarding downbeat endings were compensated by the advocacy of his long-time assistant and eventual successor, **Frederik Pohl**, who remained in charge until 1969.

Pohl broadened the magazine's range, making *Galaxy* and its recently recruited stablemates *If* and *Worlds of Tomorrow* useful vehicles for **Cordwainer Smith's** Instrumentality series and **Jack Vance's** exotic planetary romances as well as liberal **political fantasy**; the stable went into a decline following his departure, but that had more to do with changing market conditions—because of the **paperback** sf boom—than any incapacity of his successors, who included James **Baen** (1974–1977). *Galaxy* folded in 1979, although it published one more issue in 1980 when an abortive attempt was made to revive it as a companion to the short-lived *Galileo* (1976–1980). Although the sf published in *Galaxy* was less given to heavy exposition than that in *Astounding*, the magazine ran an inventive science column by **Willy Ley** from 1952–1969, which provided a model for **Isaac Asimov's** column in ***The Magazine of Fantasy & Science Fiction***. The title of *Galaxy's* companion series of *Galaxy Science Fiction Novels* (1950–1959) enjoyed a bizarre paperback afterlife (1959–1961) when it was promoted by Beacon Books as if its graphically retitled inclusions were pornographic.

**GALLUN, RAYMOND Z. (1911–1994).** U.S. writer who began publishing **pulp sf** in 1929. "Old Faithful" (1934) was an ideological protest against the frequent depiction of **aliens** as monstrous antagonists. The best of his unusually inventive pulp output was collected as *The Best of Raymond Z. Gallun* (1978). He reprocessed early material into *People Minus X* (1957) and *The Planet Strappers* (1961) before publishing an **existentialist fantasy** about extreme longevity, *The Eden Cycle* (1974), and the biological sf novels *Skyclimber* (1981) and *Bioblast* (1985).

**GALOUYE, DANIEL F. (1920–1976).** U.S. writer who began publishing **sf** in 1952. *Dark Universe* (1961) is an ingenious account of a sightless society. *Lords of the Psychon* (1963), *Counterfeit World* (1964; aka *Simulacron-3*), and *The Lost Perception* (1966, aka *A Scourge of Screamers*) share a concern with deceptive appearances with the contemporary works of **Philip K. Dick**. Galouye's interest in evolving superhumanity is displayed in *The Last Leap and Other Stories of the Super-Mind* (1964) and *The Infinite Man* (1973); his other story collection was *Project Barrier* (1968).

**GAMES.** The advent of **sf**-based role-playing games (RPGs) in the 1970s and sf-based computer games in the 1980s offered fans new opportunities to participate in **science-fictional** action-adventure scenarios, although the extent to which this contributed to a subsequent decline in reading sf among teenage boys remains conjectural. As computer games played in arcades and on PCs became more complicated, tending toward excursions in **virtual reality**, the sf scenarios entertained therein benefited from successive generations of new special effects. Fantasy war-gaming occasionally makes use of **space-operatic** elements, as in Games Workshop's *Warhammer 40,000*, but cannot offer the same participative intensity. Many classic works of sf have been adapted into RPG and computer-game formats, although any fashionability they may enjoy tends to wane rapidly as obsolescence sets in. **Tie-in** novels based on games are difficult to write, because universes designed to facilitate incessant combat have little room for characterization, explanation, or rumination, but may well have a role to play in informing the imaginative aspect of the game-playing experience.

**GAMOW, GEORGE (1904–1968). Russian**-born physicist resident in the United States from 1935, having earlier participated in the development of quantum theory. An ardent popularizer of science, he employed **fabular visionary fantasies** to make the physics of relativity and the atomic microcosm imaginatively accessible to lay readers in *Mr. Tompkins in Wonderland* (1939) and *Mr. Tompkins Explores the Atom* (1944), combined in *Mr. Tompkins in Paperback* (1965) and carefully updated by Russell Stannard in *The New World of Mr. Tompkins* (1999). *Mr. Tompkins Learns the Facts of Life* (1953, expanded 1967 with Martynas Ycas as *Mr. Tompkins Inside Himself*) deals with human biology.

**GANSOVSKY, SEVER (1918–1990). Russian** poet and writer of stridently pacifist **hard sf**. His best work, including the novellas "Vincent van Gogh" and "Part of This World," is sampled in the translated collection *The Day of Wrath* (1989), whose title story can also be found in *World's Spring* (1981, ed. Vladimir Gakov), along with "Testing Grounds." "The New Signal Station" is in *Last Door to Aiya* (1968, ed. Mirra Ginsburg) and "The Two" is in *Journey across Three Worlds* (1973).

**GARCIA Y ROBERTSON, R. (1949– ).** U.S. writer who began publishing **sf** in 1987, his imaginatively exuberant work being sampled in *The Moon Maid and Other Fantastic Adventures* (1998). *The Virgin and the Dinosaur* (1996) and *Atlantis Found* (1997) are **time-travel** fantasies. His ambiguous "paranormal romances" have some slight sf interest. "Starfall" (1998) launched a typically extravagant **series** of comic **space operas**.

**GARDNER, JAMES ALAN (1955– ). Canadian** writer who began publishing **sf** in 1990. A **series** set against the **future history** of the League of Peoples, usually featuring diplomat Admiral Festina Ramos, comprises *Expendable* (1997), *Vigilant* (1999), *Aftermath* (1999), *Hunted* (2000), *Ascending* (2001), and *Trapped* (2002). *Commitment Hour* (1998) is set in a world in which adult gender is a matter of choice.

**GARDNER, MARTIN (1914– ).** U.S. popularizer of mathematics, famous as a debunker of **pseudoscience**. Many of his mathematical puzzles are framed as stories, including those collected as *Science*

*Fiction Puzzle Tales* (1981) and *Puzzles from Other Worlds* (1984). More orthodox stories are collected in *The No-Sided Professor* (1987). Several essays on **sf** are included in *From the Wandering Jew to William F. Buckley, Jr.* (2001).

**GARNETT, DAVID S. (1947– ).** British writer and editor who initially signed himself Dav Garnett and then David S. Garnett to distinguish himself from David Garnett (1892–1981) of the Bloomsbury Group. *Mirror in the Sky* (1969), *The Starseekers* (1971; revised as *Stargonauts*, 1994), and *Time in Eclipse* (1974) are routine **sf** adventures, although the revision of the second item recast it as a comedy in the same vein as *Bikini Planet* (2000) and *Space Wasters* (2001). He made a more considerable contribution to sf by editing two *Zenith* **anthologies** (1989–1990) and four volumes of ***New Worlds*** (1991–1994).

**GARRETT, RANDALL (1927–1987).** U.S. writer who began publishing **sf** in 1944 and became a fixture in the ***Analog*** stable during the 1950s, sometimes publishing as David Gordon and Darrel T. Langart. As Robert Randall he **collaborated** with **Robert Silverberg** on a **mosaic planetary romance** comprising *The Shrouded Planet* (1957) and *The Dawning Light* (1958), and as Mark Phillips he collaborated with **Laurence M. Janifer** on a series of **psi** stories. His most interesting solo work was the **series** collected in the omnibus *Lord Darcy* (1983), set in an **alternative** 17th century in which sympathetic magic works, and is therefore a science subject to methodical research and technological development.

**GEIS, RICHARD E. (1927– ).** U.S. writer who published a series of **fanzines** from 1953 onward, including *Psychotic*, *Science Fiction Review,* and *The Alien Critic*. Geis championed the entertainment value of **sf** against all pretension; most of his own fiction was pornographic, including sf novels with such titles as *The Sex Machine* (1967), *Canned Meat* (1978), and *Star Whores* (1981). He published two issues of the **small press magazine** *Taboo Science Fiction* (1995–1996).

**GENEFORT, LAURENT (1968– ). French sf** writer who made his debut with *Le Bagne des Ténèbres* (1988), the first of a loosely knit and intricately subdivided **series** of **far-futuristic fantasies** and **planetary romances** featuring mysterious **alien** artifacts and peculiar ecospheres.

**GENERATION STARSHIP.** The idea that human colonization of the galaxy, unaided by faster-than-light travel, would necessitate the building of self-enclosed and self-sufficient "worldlets" was first broached in **speculative nonfiction** of the 1920s by **Konstantin Tsiolkovsky** and **J. D. Bernal**. It was imported into **pulp sf** in the 1930s, its most dramatic treatment there being **Robert A. Heinlein's** "Universe" (1941), one of many stories in which the ship's inhabitants rediscover the nature and purpose of their worldlet by means of a **conceptual breakthrough**. Later variants include **Gene Wolfe's** Long Sun **series**.

**GENETIC ENGINEERING.** A term coined in the late 1940s, imported into **sf** by **Jack Williamson** in *Dragon's Island* (1951) and subsequently adopted into common parlance—although the idea of a **biotechnology** enabling the purposive manipulation of genetic material had been introduced into **pulp sf** by Clement Fézandie in the first of his "Doctor Hackensaw" stories (1921) in **Hugo Gernsback's** *Science and Invention*. Norman L. Knight's "Crisis in Utopia" (1940) called such manipulation "tectogenesis." The notion became fashionable in sf of the 1970s and was a standard element of sf's images of the near future by the end of the 20th century, its potential explored in many stories by **Brian Stableford**.

**GERMAN SCIENCE FICTION. German** writers produced some important early **speculative nonfiction**—most notably **John Kepler's** *Somnium* (1634) and Immanuel Kant's *Universal Natural History and Theory of the Heavens* (1755)—and a few 18th-century **Utopian** fantasies set in an interplanetary framework, including a 1744 story by the astronomer Eberhard Christian Kindermann that features a journey to **Mars**. The third volume of Heinrich Zschokke's *Die schwarzen Brüder* (1795) is a notable futuristic fantasy. E. T. A. Hoffmann's widely translated stories "Der Sandmann" (1816) and "Automata" (1818), which invest humanoid machinery and its makers with quasi-demonic qualities, became key exemplars of antiscience fiction, but it was not until English **future war** stories sparked retaliation in kind—rapidly followed by the importation of **Vernian** romance by such writers as Robert Kraft and Friedrich Mader, and **Wellsian** fiction by **Kurt Lasswitz**, that a coherent tradition of German sf was launched. Early participants included the artist Paul Scheerbart, whose *Astrale Noveletten* (1912) offered **Flammarionesque** visions of a cosmos filled with exotic life. German writers like Carl Grunert and Oskar Hoffmann soon adopted **sf** motifs to **pulpish** popular fiction; the 165 issues of *Der Luftpirat und sein Lenkbares Luftschiff* [The Air Pirate and His Dirigible Airship] (1908–1911), whose adventures range throughout the solar system, might be regarded as the first specialist sf **magazine**.

Ironically, Germany's defeat in World War I had a less dispiriting effect on native futuristic fiction than the war's legacy had on British and **French scientific romance**. Germany soon forged its own distinctive tradition of the *zukunftsroman* [technological novel], which celebrated the efficiency and ambition of German engineers. The genre's key exemplars were established by Hans Dominik (1872–1945), whose first novel was *Die Macht der Drei* (1922); one of his works was translated in **Gernsback's** *Air Wonder Stories* in 1930, but U.S. pulp readers got a far better appreciation of the German genre's concerns and tone from five novels by Otfrid von Hanstein that the German-speaking Gernsback published thereafter, most notably "Electropolis" (1930), "Utopia Island" (1931), and "In the Year 8000" (1932). Other German novels featured in the Gernsback pulps included "The Cosmic Cloud" (1931) by Bruno H. Burgel, "Druso" (1932) by Friedrich Freksa, and two by **Otto Willi Gail**.

The sentiments expressed by these novels and the genre from whence they came overlapped considerably with those that inspired the burgeoning Nazi movement, for which reason the tradition was eclipsed after World War II. It was not unopposed between the wars, but socialist Utopianism as featured in Werner Illing's *Utopolis* (1930) and enthusiastically promoted by Weimar minister of culture Walter Rathenau was quickly suppressed by the Nazis. Alfred Döblin—whose *Berge, Meere und Giganten* (1924, revised as *Giganten*) was an early celebration of the transformative potential of **biotechnology**—went into exile in 1933, quickly followed by Thea von Harbou, whose novelizations of two films made by her husband,

Fritz Lang, *Metropolis* (1926) and *The Girl in the Moon* (1928), must have been far more widely read in the United States than the German sf in Gernsback's pulps.

German sf produced for **paperback** publication alongside imported U.S. material was—as in France and Britain—mostly downmarket pulp sf, but such fiction took a much firmer hold in West Germany. Walter Ernsting, who wrote as Clark Darlton and K. H. Scheer, founded the long-running *Perry Rhodan* **series** in 1961, which continued into the 21st century (having published more than 2,000 issues). Although *Perry Rhodan* and its many imitators were aimed at a juvenile audience, their profusion limited the market opportunities available to writers of adult sf. Writer/editors like **Herbert W. Franke** and **Wolfgang Jeschke** had more difficulty establishing a domestic tradition of sf than their counterparts in Britain and France, although their heroic efforts—begun in the early 1960s—became increasingly fruitful in the 1980s.

In East Germany, from which American sf was excluded, domestic sf made little progress in the 1950s and 1960s despite the availability of **Russian** models, but began to appear in greater profusion in the 1970s, notable material being produced by two husband-and-wife teams, Johanna and Günter Braun and Karlheinz and Angela Steinmüller. By the time of reunification, sf **fandom** in East Germany had become an important focus of a youth culture whose rebelliousness had to be, by necessity, carefully muted. Reunification made manifest some deep cultural and ideological differences between the sf communities of the West and East but the gradual fusion of the two had begun to result in a new **hybrid** vigor by the end of the 20th century; significant writers active at that time included Birgit Rabisch, author of *Jonas 7: Clone* (1992); Andreas Eschbach, author of *Das Jesus Video* (1998); Oliver Henkel, author of *Die zeitmaschine Karls des Grossen* (2001), and Marcus Hammerschmitt, author of *Polyplay* (2002).

**GERNSBACK, HUGO (1884–1967).** Luxembourg-born entrepreneur who immigrated to the United States in 1904. He set up in business as an importer of technical equipment from Germany, and quickly developed his mail-order catalogues into the magazine *Modern Electrics*, whose features celebrated the social transformations that were soon to be precipitated by his wares. He wrote the novel *Ralph 124C41+*

(1911–1912, book 1925) for serialization there, becoming very interested in the possibilities of fiction as a medium of advertising. When the magazine became *Electrical Experimenter*, he wrote a **series** of stories transforming the notorious teller of tall tales Baron Munchausen [*sic*] into an inventor, and when it became *Science and Invention,* **scientifiction** by other hands became a regular feature. After testing the waters with an all-fiction issue in 1923 he launched ***Amazing Stories*** as a companion in 1926. Practicing what he preached, Gernsback invested heavily in radio, and it was the loses of his radio station that bankrupted his company. When *Amazing* was sold off, he started a rival group whose core product was ***Wonder Stories***, but eventually sold it and concentrated his efforts thereafter on the more profitable magazine *Sexology*—until **Sam Moskowitz** persuade him to finance a new sf **magazine**, *Science Fiction Plus* in 1953, which proved short-lived. Gernsback was termed "the father of Science Fiction" by Moskowitz and the **Hugo** award took its nickname from him, but some of his successors felt that the didactic emphasis and stylistic insensitivity of scientifiction were as deleterious to the emergent genre's image as the excesses of **pulp** action-adventure fiction.

**GERROLD, DAVID (1944– ).** U.S. writer who sold **TV** scripts in the late 1960s before **collaborating** with **Larry Niven** on the **planetary romance** *The Flying Sorcerers* (1971). *Space Skimmer* (1972) and *Yesterday's Children* (1972, rev. 1980; aka *Starhunt*) are **space operas**, as are the War against the Chtorr **series** begun with *A Matter for Men* (1983) and the trilogy comprising *Star Wolf* (1990), *The Voyage of the Starwolf* (1990), and *The Middle of Nowhere* (1995). *When Harlie Was One* (1972; rev. as *When H.A.R.L.I.E. Was One (Release 2.0)*, 1988) is an **existentialist fantasy**, as are the narcissistic *The Man Who Folded Himself* (1973) and some of the stories collected in *With a Finger in My I* (1972). *Moonstar Odyssey* (1977) examines a hermaphroditic **alien** society. *Jumping Off the Planet* (2000), *Bouncing Off the Moon* (2001), and *Leaping to the Stars* (2002) comprise a trilogy of **children's sf** stories. The quasi-autobiographical *The Martian Child* (1994; exp. 2002) was misleadingly marketed as sf.

**GESTON, MARK S. (1946– ).** U.S. writer whose **far-futuristic fantasies** *Lords of the Starship* (1967) and *Out of the Mouth of the*

*Dragon* (1969) are earnestly stylish studies of terminal cultural **decadence** that employ symbolic **cyborgs** in a manner echoing **David R. Bunch's** *Moderan*. *The Day Star* (1972) and *The Siege of Wonder* (1976) attempted to carry similar themes forward into **chimerical science-fantasy**. *Mirror to the Sky* (1992) is more restrained.

**GIBSON, WILLIAM (1948– ).** U.S. writer who moved to **Canada** in 1968 and began publishing **sf** in 1977. Some of the early stories collected in *Burning Chrome* (1986), especially "Johnny Mnemonic" (1981), together with his novel *Neuromancer* (1984), became the definitive examples of **cyberpunk** fiction. *Neuromancer* became a modern classic by virtue of its status as a handbook of cybercultural aspirations, but its sequels *Count Zero* (1985) and *Mona Lisa Overdrive* (1988) struggled to find anything substantial to add to it in that respect, although their fast-paced plots perfected Gibson's futuristic **transfiguration** of noirish hard-boiled crime fiction. A further loosely knit trilogy in a similar vein, comprising *Virtual Light* (1993), *Idoru* (1996), and *All Tomorrow's Parties* (1999), kept abreast of new developments in cyberculture and its associated technologies, but had no chance of repeating the impact of *Neuromancer*. With cyberpunk's chief propagandist, Bruce Sterling, Gibson wrote the **steampunk** novel *The Difference Engine* (1990), set in an **alternative history** in which Victorian England has undergone a sweeping technological revolution thanks to the development of Charles Babbage's mechanical computer. This novel testifies even more clearly than the noirish edge of the futuristic thrillers to the deep skepticism with which Gibson regards the progressive potential of technology—a skepticism forgiven by the worshipful pioneers of cyberculture but admired by the celebrants of **postmodern sf**, who are more appreciative of his ambivalence.

**GILLESPIE, BRUCE (1947– ). Australian small press** publisher and critic whose **fanzine** *SF Commentary*, launched in 1969, became one of the primary vehicles of serious **sf criticism**. He cofounded Norstrilia Press, whose products included his **anthology** *Philip K. Dick: Electric Shepherd* (1975).

**GILLINGS, WALTER (1912–1979).** British journalist active in **fandom** from the early 1930s. His *Scientifiction: The British Fantasy*

*Review* (1937–1938) was produced to a much higher standard than any of its rival **fanzines**. He was editor of the first British **sf pulps**, *Tales of Wonder* (1937–1942) and *Fantasy* (1946–1947), and copro-prietor with pulp sf writer Benson Herbert of the specialist **small press** Utopian Publications. He revived his fanzine as *Fantasy Review* in 1947; it became *Science-Fantasy Review* in 1949 and *Science-Fantasy* in 1950; its editorship was transferred to **John Carnell** in 1951. Gillings's history of British fandom, "The Impatient Dreamers," began serialization in *Vision of Tomorrow* in 1969. He published his first sf story in 1938 under the pseudonym Thomas Sheridan, but wrote few others.

**GILMAN, CHARLOTTE PERKINS (1860–1935).** U.S. pioneer of **feminism** whose most famous work of fiction was the **hallucinatory fantasy** "The Yellow Wallpaper" (1892, as by Charlotte Perkins Stetson) until her contributions to her political periodical *The Forerunner* (1909–1916) were rediscovered in the 1970s; its serial fiction included the futuristic feminist **Utopia** *Moving the Mountain* (1911), whose reprinting as a **small press** publication had similarly passed unnoticed. A reprint of her account of an all-female society, *Herland* (1914, book 1979) was followed by *The Yellow Wallpaper and Other Writings* (1989) and a sequel to *Herland*, *With Her in Ourland* (1916, book 1997). The three novels are combined in the omnibus *Charlotte Perkins Gilman's Utopian Novels* (1999).

**GLOAG, JOHN (1896–1981).** British writer in several genres, whose contributions to **scientific romance** between the wars were second in distinction only to those of his friend **Olaf Stapledon**. *Tomorrow's Yesterday* (1932) fits a **satirical** frame around an unproduced **Wellsian** film script in which humankind's replacements (descended from cats) review the story of its decline to extinction, using notions carried forward from the **Today & Tomorrow** essay *Artifex; or, The Future of Craftsmanship* (1926). *The New Pleasure* (1933) is a drug whose side effects heighten the sense of smell, persuading its users that modern civilization stinks. *Winter's Youth* (1934) is a political satire about rejuvenation. *Manna* (1940) features a new foodstuff whose **Utopian** potential has to be shelved because of the necessity of fighting World War II. *99%* (1944), about a drug that revives ancestral memories, echoes a conviction expressed in the short stories "Pendulum" and "The Slit" and the novel *Sacred Edifice* (1937) that civilization is but a temporary folly of a Stapledonian "World Spirit" whose components include human thought. *Slow* (1954) is a crime thriller featuring a time-retardant device.

**GODWIN, TOM (1915–1980).** U.S. writer who began publishing **sf** in 1953. The 1954 title story of *The Cold Equations and Other Stories* (2003) became one of the most celebrated and bitterly controversial of sf's modern ***contes cruels***. *The Survivors* (1958, aka *Space Prison*) and its sequel *The Space Barbarians* (1964) are a defiant exercise in human chauvinism. *Beyond Another Sun* (1971) is a thoughtful anthropological sf novel.

**GOLDEN AGE OF SF.** A term initially invented by fans who became nostalgic for the **pulp** era of **sf** when it was over—particularly for the uniquely exciting years of 1938–1941, when **John Campbell** transformed ***Astounding*** and demonstrated the potential that sf might have for embedding serious **speculative fiction** within marvelous tales of adventure. Readers of later generations sometimes applied it to other supposedly revolutionary eras, particularly to the first few years of the 1950s, suggesting that the idea of a golden age was subjective rather than objective, recalling an individual's first dramatic exposure to the **sense of wonder**. This notion gave birth to the oft-quoted saw that "the golden age of science fiction is 13" (or 12, in **David Hartwell's** preferred version).

**GOLDIN, STEPHEN (1947– ).** U.S. writer who began publishing **sf** in 1965. His early novels, including *Herds* (1975), *Caravan* (1975), and numerous **sharecropping** enterprises, were routine adventure sf, as is the Jad Darcy **series** launched in 1990 in **collaboration** with Mary Mason. *The Eternity Brigade* (1980) is a ghoulish vision of **future wars** fought by artificially reincarnated soldiers. *Mindflight* (1978), *And Not Make Dreams Your Master* (1981), and *A World Called Solitude* (1981) have elements of **existentialist fantasy**.

**GOLDING, WILLIAM (1911–1993).** British writer of literary fiction who was persuaded to minimize the **postholocaust sf** elements of his first novel, *The Lord of the Flies* (1954), before publication. *The Inheritors* (1955) is one of the earliest prehistoric fantasies to side with Neanderthal humankind against its Cro-Magnon conquerors; the novella "Clonk Clonk" in *The Scorpion God* (1971) is similar in spirit. "Envoy Extraordinary" (1956), an ingenious historical fantasy in which a Roman emperor turns down the opportunity to institute an industrial revolution, was adapted into the play *The Brass Butterfly* (1957).

**GOLDSMITH, CELE (1933–2002).** U.S. editor who took over ***Amazing Stories*** and its companion *Fantastic* in 1958, after two years as assistant to Paul Fairman. She rapidly transformed the **magazines** into cutting-edge instruments of a pre-**new wave** avant-gardism, helping to revitalize the career of **Fritz Leiber** and publishing numerous pioneering **fabulations** by **David R. Bunch**, **Roger Zelazny**, **Thomas M. Disch**, and **Ursula le Guin**. The magazines were sold not long after her marriage in 1964, when she became Cele G. Lalli; she then became editor of *Modern Bride*.

**GOONAN, KATHLEEN ANN (1952– ).** U.S. writer who began publishing **sf** in 1991. The **series** comprising *Queen City Jazz* (1994), *Mississippi Blues* (1999), *Crescent City Rhapsody* (2000), and *Light Music* (2002) is set in the surreal wake of a disaster precipitated by rogue **nanotechnology**, whose dire effects are eventually complicated by **alien** intrusion. *The Bones of Time* (1996) is a thriller involving illicit cloning.

**GORDON, REX (1917– ).** Pseudonym of British writer Stanley Bennett Hough, who published the alarmist thrillers *Extinction Bomber* (1956) and *Beyond the Eleventh Hour* (1961) under his own name. *Utopia 239* (1955) is similarly obsessed with the possibility of nuclear war, but reacts to it far more imaginatively. *No Man Friday* (1956, aka *First on Mars*) and *First to the Stars* (1959, aka *The Worlds of Eclos*) are **robinsonades**, while *First through Time* (1962, aka *The Time Factor*) and *Utopia Minus X* (1966; revised as *The Paw of God*, 1967) are **existential fantasies**. *The Yellow Fraction* (1966) is a **political fantasy**.

**GORDON, STUART (1947– ).** Scottish writer who distinguished himself from a famous namesake by writing as Richard A. Gordon in the late 1960s. His new byline (which duplicated that of a U.S. actor/director who wrote and produced a notable item of **sf theater**, *Warp!*, in 1971) first appeared on *Time Story* (1972). After the **postholocaust** trilogy *One-Eye* (1973), *Two-Eyes* (1974), and *Three-Eyes* (1975) and a slyly **satirical** account of a new messiah, *Smile on the Void* (1981), he returned to the **time-travel** theme in an effective account of an Elizabethan naval hero's experiences in an **apocalyptic** near future, *Fire on the Abyss* (1983), and the complex trilogy comprising *Archon* (1987), *The Hidden World* (1988), and *The Mask* (1989), which juxtaposes a similar future scenario with medieval France.

**GOTLIEB, PHYLLIS (1926– ). Canadian** writer, best known as a poet, who began publishing **sf** in 1959. *Sunburst* (1964) is a tale of superhuman coming-of-age deftly echoing **Theodore Sturgeon's** *More than Human*, some of whose concerns are carried over into the **planetary romance** comprising *O Master Caliban!* (1976) and *Heart of Red Iron* (1989). The trilogy comprising *A Judgment of Dragons* (1980), *Emperor, Swords, Pentacles* (1982), and *The Kingdom of Cats* (1985) is **chimerical science-fantasy**. *Flesh and Gold* (1998) and *Violent Stars* (1999) are complex futuristic thrillers, ***Mind*Worlds*** (2002) offers an elaborate account of various **alien** species, involving telepathic contacts of considerable—but not quite transcendental—existential significance. Her short fiction is sampled in *Son of the Morning and Other Stories* (1983) and *Blue Apes* (1995).

**GOULART, RON (1933– ).** U.S. writer in various genres who began publishing **sf** in 1952. The bulk of his sf is uninhibited and relentlessly superficial comedy, which works better in the short stories sampled in *What's Become of Screwloose? and Other Stories* (1971) and two volumes of "Troubles with Machines," *Broke Down Engine* (1971) and *Nutzenbolts* (1975), than in the novels he published in great profusion after *The Sword Swallower* (1968). The **apocalyptic** black comedy *After Things Fell Apart* (1970) was followed by four sequels set in "fragmented America." Alongside novels under his own byline, he produced scores of pseudonymous works and ghosted an sf **series** for a media personality.

**GOULD, STEVEN (1955– ).** U.S. writer who began publishing **sf** in 1980. *Jumper* (1992) features a **psi-powered** young runaway. *Wildside*

(1996) describes a pristine **alternative world** devoid of humankind. *Greenwar* (1997) is a **technothriller** written in **collaboration** with his wife, **Laura J. Mixon**. In *Helm* (1998) refugees from **ecocatastrophe** flee to a **terraformed** world. *Blind Waves* (2000) is a thriller set after the melting of the ice caps.

**GRANT, DONALD M. (1927– ).** U.S. **small press** publisher who was involved in the Hadley Publishing Company before setting up his own imprint to issue high-quality illustrated books. His **sf** publications include numerous books by **Jack Vance**, including editions of *The Dying Earth* (1976) and *Big Planet* (1978), several collections of stories by **William Hope Hodgson**, and **C. L. Moore's** *Scarlet Dream* (1981).

**GRAPHIC NOVEL.** An extended **comic** book with modest—and by no means unjustified—delusions of grandeur; the term was coined to describe Will Eisner's **mosaic** *A Contract with God* (1978). Fugitive examples can be identified from the 1920s but the format became commonplace in the 1980s, when a copiously advertised **series** of releases included Alan Moore's *Watchmen* (1987). Although most graphic novels were mosaics formed out of comic book serials, serials were soon being written with eventual graphic novel publication in mind, offering new narrative opportunities that were grasped enthusiastically by such writers as Neil Gaiman. ***Locus*** 510 (July 2003) was a special issue devoted to graphic novels.

**GREEN, JOSEPH L. (1931– ).** U.S. writer who began publishing **sf** in U.K. **magazines** in 1962. *The Loafers of Refuge* (1965) and *Conscience Interplanetary* are **mosaics** about human/**alien** relationships; *The Horde* (1976) is similar. *Gold the Man* (1971, aka *The Mind behind the Eye*) is an account of a human endoparasite within the head of a giant alien. *Star Probe* (1976) is a less ambitious account of bodily displacement. *An Affair with Genius* (1969) collects early short stories.

**GREENBERG, MARTIN (1918– ).** U.S. **small press** publisher, not to be confused with **Martin H. Greenberg**. He was cofounder in 1948 of Gnome Press, whose publications included the first book edition of **Isaac Asimov's** Foundation **series**, and operated solo in the late 1950s under his own name. The showcase **anthologies** he edited for

Gnome included *Men against the Stars* (1950), *Travelers of Space* (1951), and *Journey to Infinity* (1951).

**GREENBERG, MARTIN H. (1941– ).** U.S. editor who began producing **sf anthologies** as teaching aids for various social science subjects in **collaboration** with Joseph D. Olander and others in the mid-1970s. He also edited several anthologies of critical writings about sf writers. The expertise thus gained was channeled into a vast **series** of reprint and original theme anthologies bylined as collaborations, often with various prominent authors. From the mid-1980s Greenberg was by far the most prolific anthologist in the field, providing permission-clearing services to many other anthologists from whom he received unobtrusive acknowledgments rather than collaborative bylines, and also organizing single-author collections and omnibuses. The company he set up to manage these endeavors, Tekno Books, went from strength to strength in the 1990s, and expanded its operations in 2001 to begin packaging a line of books for Five Star. As with **Roger Elwood**, Greenberg's salesmanship was a boon to the writers who benefited from the additional market space he created, although would-be rivals regarded his near-monopolistic position with envy.

**GREENLAND, COLIN (1954– ).** British writer who published a study of British **new wave sf**, based on his Ph.D. thesis, as *The Entropy Exhibition* (1983) shortly after publishing his first sf story in 1982. His early novels were pensive pastoral fantasies, but he struck out in a new direction with the colorful **space opera** *Take Back Plenty* (1990) and its sequel, *Harm's Way* (1993).

**GREENWOOD PRESS.** U.S. academic publishing house, one of whose lines specializes in **sf**-related books. As well as numerous commentaries and **anthologies**, it has published several notable reference books, including **Mike Ashley** and Marshall Tymn's definitive guide to *Science Fiction, Fantasy, and Weird Fiction Magazines* (1985), and microfiche editions of complete sets of several sf **magazines**, including ***Amazing Stories*** and ***Starling Stories***.

**GRIBBIN, JOHN (1946– ).** British journalist who became a leading popularizer of science in the 1980s. His ventures into **sf** often entrust collaborators with the task of fictionalizing his meticulously extrapolated scientific projections, although Douglas Orgill, who cowrote *Sixth Winter* (19790 and *Brother Esau* (1982), and Marcus Chown, who cowrote *Double Planet* (1980) and its sequel *Reunion* (1991), were not ideal partners in this regard. **D. G. Compton**, who cowrote *The Ragnarok Alternative* (1991), had better literary credentials, but the resultant **apocalyptic** thriller makes less productive use of Gribbin's abilities than his solo novels *Father to the Man* (1989), which dramatizes an ideological contest between a geneticist and a creationist, and *Innervisions* (1993), a painstaking account of a logically derived **conceptual breakthrough**.

**GRIFFIN, RUSSELL M. (1943–1986).** U.S. writer whose first excursion into **sf** was the interplanetary fantasy *The Makeshift God* (1979). The millennial **satire** *Century's End* (1981) and the **existentialist fantasy** *The Blind Men and the Elephant* (1982) are black comedies, while *The Timeservers* (1985) reverted to the earlier template.

**GRIFFITH, GEORGE (1857–1906).** British journalist whose 1893 commission to write a gripping **future war** serial for *Pearson's Weekly* produced "The Empress of the Earth," in which an organization of self-proclaimed terrorists uses airships, submarines, and high explosives to obliterate the world's tyrants. The book version, *The Angel of the Revolution* (1893), launched a flood of similar exercises, many of them cast as ideological replies. After adding an **apocalyptic** sequel, "The Syren of the Skies" (1893–1894; book 1894 as *Olga Romanoff*), Griffith toned down his own socialism in *The Outlaws of the Air* (1895) and then began repeating himself in such retreads as *The Great Pirate Syndicate* (1899), *The World Masters* (1903), and *The Great Weather Syndicate* (1906). He imitated popular novels in various genres, his most interesting **sf** projects being the **disaster story** "The Great Crellin Comet" (1897; exp. as *The World Peril of 1910*, 1907) and the interplanetary fantasy *A Honeymoon in Space* (1900). The posthumously published future war novel *The Lord of Labour*, whose principal weapons are atomic missiles fired from bazookas and disintegrator **rays**, suggests that his political position had moved some way to the right. His short fiction is collected in *Gambles with Destiny* (1898) and *The Raid of "Le Vengeur"* (1974).

**GRIFFITH, NICOLA (1960– ).** British-born writer resident in the United States since 1989, who began publishing sf in 1986. *Ammonite* (1993) is a **feminist planetary romance** featuring an all-female society. *Slow River* (1995) is a tense near-future thriller.

**GRIMWOOD, JON COURTENAY (1953– ).** Maltese-born British writer whose *neoAddix* (1997) launched a series of post-**cyberpunk** novels continued in *Lucifer's Dragon* (1998), *reMix* (1999), and *red-Robe* (2000). *Pashazade* (2001), *Effendi* (2002), and *Felaheen* (2003) are similarly grim thrillers set in an **alternative history**.

**GUIN, WYMAN (1915–1989).** U.S. writer who began publishing **sf** in 1950. He was primarily associated with ***Galaxy***, where he published the **existentialist fantasy** "Beyond Bedlam" (1951), reprinted in *Living Way Out* (1967, aka *Beyond Bedlam*). *The Standing Joy* (1969) is a story of evolving superhumanity.

**GUNN, JAMES E. (1923– ).** U.S. writer and academic who began publishing **sf** in 1949. *This Fortress World* (1955) and *Star Bridge* (1955, with **Jack Williamson**) are polished **space operas**. The **mosaic** *Station in Space* (1958) is an account of the troubled advent of the **space age**. Like **James Blish**, Gunn—who was ambitious to use sf for more philosophically ambitious purposes but acutely aware of the difficulties he would have in selling such work to the **magazines**—carefully grafted his bolder speculations onto **pulp** fiction rootstocks in mosaics built out of sets of novellas. The most ambitious is a neatly argued and boldly extrapolated account of a spoiled **Utopia** founded by technologically assisted hedonists, *The Joy Makers* (1961); it was followed by the *The Immortals* (1962), whose **TV** adaptation Gunn renovelized as *The Immortal* (1970); the poignant **SETI** fantasy *The Listeners* (1972); the **postholocaust fantasy** *The Burning* (1972); *The Dreamers* (1980, aka *The Mind Master*), which offers an account of the development of technologies based in the biochemistry of memory; *Crisis!* (1986), which attempts to define solutions to problems that other writers were content to dramatize despairingly; and *The Millennium Blues* (2000). His nonmosaic novel *Kampus* (1977) is dourly **satirical**; the best of his short stories are assembled in *Breaking Point* (1972) and *Human Voices* (2002).

Gunn's critical work, first displayed when excerpts from his M.A. thesis were published in *Dynamic Science Fiction* in 1953–1954, was extrapolated in the coffee-table book *Alternate Worlds: The Illustrated History of Science Fiction* (1975). *The New Encyclopedia of Science Fiction* (1988), which he edited for a packager, was rendered redundant by the second edition of the **Clute/Nicholls** *Encyclopedia*, but his **series** of illustrative **anthologies** *The Road to Science Fiction* (4 vols., 1977–1982; expanded to 6 vols., 1998) and the essays collected in *The Science of Science Fiction Writing* (2000), including lecture notes from his pioneering course in writing sf, display his well-informed critical intelligence to better advantage.

## – H –

**HABER, KAREN (1955– ).** U.S. writer who began publishing **sf** in 1988. She edited numerous **anthologies** in **collaboration** with her husband, **Robert Silverberg**, one of whose stories she expanded as *Mutant Season* (1989), the first of a **series** about an endangered subculture of **psi-powered** people, followed by *The Mutant Prime* (1990), *Mutant Star* (1992), and *Mutant Legacy* (1993). *The War Minstrels* (1995), *Woman without a Shadow* (1995), and *Sister Blood* (1996) are **space operas.**

**HAIBLUM, ISIDORE (1935– ).** U.S. writer whose first work employing **sf** motifs was the **chimerical** comedy *The Tsaddik of the Seven Wonders* (1971). *The Return* (1973) and *Transfer to Yesterday* (1973) feature flawed **Utopias** in a state of incipient disintegration; the latter is framed as a detective story, as are most of the author's other works, including the **series** comprising *Interworld* (1977), *Outerworld* (1979), *Spectreworld* (1991), and *Crystalworld* (1992), and the couplet comprising *The Identity Plunderers* (1984) and *The Hand of Ganz* (1985). *The Wilk Are among Us* (1975) and *The Mutants Are Coming* (1984) are frenetic comedies; the more earnest *Out of Sync* (1990) is set in the same world as the latter. *Nightmare Express* (1984) is an intricate **alternative history** story.

**HALDANE, J. B. S. (1892–1964).** British biologist whose excursions into fiction, including the children's fantasies collected in *My Friend*

*Mr. Leakey* (1937) and the incomplete **sf** novel *The Man with Two Brains* (1976), are less adventurous than his endeavors in **speculative nonfiction.** The anticipations of future **biotechnology** in *Daedalus; or, Science and the Future* (1923) provided a blueprint for **Aldous Huxley's** *Brave New World*. The **future history** sketched out in "The Last Judgment" in *Possible Worlds and Other Essays* (1927) was the main inspiration of **Olaf Stapledon's** *Last and First Men*. "Possibilities of Human Evolution," "Man's Destiny," and "Some Consequences of Materialism" in *The Inequality of Man and Other Essays* (1932) offer further **extrapolations.**

**HALDEMAN, JACK C. II (1941–2002).** U.S. writer who began publishing **sf** in 1971. Many of his works are comedies about future sports. He often worked in **collaboration**, most frequently with **Jack Dann**, as on *Echoes of Thunder* (1991) and the space-colonization novel *High Steel* (1993). *There Is No Darkness* (1983), written with his younger brother **Joe Haldeman**, is an action-adventure **mosaic**. *Vector Analysis* (1978) is a space-set mystery.

**HALDEMAN, JOE W. (1943– ).** U.S. writer whose experiences in Vietnam colored much of his subsequent fiction, including the **sf** he began publishing in 1969. *The Forever War* (1972–1974, book 1974) is an effective skeptical antidote to the more enthusiastic kinds of **military sf.** Another **mosaic** featuring a surgically and hypnotically modified interplanetary spy, *All My Sins Remembered* (1971–1977, book 1977), similarly counts the cost of effective competition. Personality modification also features in *Mindbridge* (1976), employed in **alien** contact. The trilogy comprising *Worlds* (1981), *Worlds Apart* (1983), and *Worlds Enough and Time* (1992) is a meticulous **apocalyptic fantasy.** *Tool of the Trade* (1987) and *The Long Habit of Living* (1989, aka *Buying Time*) are chase thrillers involving **science-fictional** objects of desire. *The Hemingway Hoax* (1990) is cast in a similar mold, complicated by the involvement of **time police.** *Forever Peace* (1997) reexamines the concern raised in *The Forever War* as to whether humankind can possibly outlive its addiction to war. *Forever Free* (1999) is a sequel to *The Forever War* in which the lead characters exploit relativistic distortions to travel 40 millennia into the future. *The Coming* (2000) is a **SETI** fantasy with apocalyptic overtones. *Guardian* (2002) is a **hallucinatory** pastiche of 19th-century fiction. His short fiction is sampled in *Dealing in Futures* (1985) and *None So Blind* (1996).

**HALE, EDWARD EVERETT (1822–1909).** U.S. writer who dabbled in **Utopian** fiction as well as producing the supernaturally framed **alternative history** story "Hands Off" (1881) and a groundbreaking **satirical** account of an unlikely artificial satellite, "The Brick Moon" (1869), which was combined with its sequel, "Life in the Brick Moon" (1871), in book versions.

**HALL, AUSTIN (c1885–1933).** U.S. writer of **pulp** fiction. He developed **sf** motifs within the conventional frameworks of pulp fantasy in "Almost Immortal" (1916), "The Rebel Soul" (1917), and its novel-length sequel, "Into the Infinite" (1919). "The Man Who Saved the Earth" (1919) established a significant narrative template when it was reprinted in an early issue of ***Amazing Stories***. The confusions of the **dimensional fantasy** he wrote with **Homer Eon Flint**, *The Blind Spot* (1921, book 1951), were intensified rather than illuminated in his solo sequel, *The Spot of Life* (1932, book 1964). "Hop o'my Thumb" (1923, book 1948 as *People of the Comet*) is a **microcosmic romance.**

**HALLUCINATORY FANTASY.** A subdivision of **visionary fantasy.** The implication of quasi-divine revelation carried by pretentious visionary fantasy is unsuited to accounts of the future constructed as aspects of an infinite array of possibilities. Paradoxical as it may seem, the futures and other speculative constructions of 19th-century **sf** were more appropriately accommodated within admitted hallucinations. Hallucinations are usually of shorter duration than delusions, and are generally recognized as hallucinations by the experiencing party as soon as they are terminated, so delusional fantasy is much more closely associated with other fantasy genres. The didactic utility of hallucinatory fantasy is illustrated by **George Gamow's** accounts of alternative universes. Hallucinations also fit more comfortably into the calculated paradoxicality of **chimerical** texts, as in the work of **Josephine Saxton.**

**HAMILTON, CICELY (1872–1952).** Pseudonym of British writer Cicely Mary Hamill. *Theodore Savage* (1922; rev. as *Lest Ye Die*, 1928) is one of the most striking **future war** stories reflecting the deep disenchantment inflicted on **scientific romance** by World War I. A less **apocalyptic** Second World War is featured in *Little Arthur's History of the Twentieth Century* (1933), cast as a parody of a popular Victorian educational text.

**HAMILTON, EDMOND (1904–1977).** U.S. writer, who began publishing unashamedly melodramatic **pulp sf** in 1926. He was one of the pioneers of interstellar **space opera**, in the **series** collected in *Crashing Suns* (1928–1930, book 1965) and *Outside the Universe* (1929, book 1964), but he retained a certain anxiety about the tacit xenophobia of his many **alien** menace stories, counteracting it in such cautionary tales as "A Conquest of Two Worlds" (1932) and the deeply skeptical 1952 title story of *What's It Like Out There? and Other Stories* (1974). The **planetary romance** trilogy making up *Kaldar, World of Antares* (1933, book 1998) anticipates the **science-fantasies** of **Leigh Brackett**, to whom he was married in 1946. Unwilling to make the effort to meet **John Campbell's** exacting standards, Hamilton remained a fixture in the more down-market pulps. He wrote a long series of juvenile space adventures featuring *Captain Future* for a magazine of that name. His later novels for its companion ***Startling Stories***, including *The Star of Fire* (1947; rev. 1959) and *The Valley of Creation* (1948; rev. 1964), borrow more colorful apparatus from his wife. *The Star Kings* (1947, book 1949; aka *Beyond the Moon*) is a space-operatic **transfiguration** of Anthony Hope's *The Prisoner of Zenda*, which he was to copy again in "Starman Come Home" (1954; book 1959, as *The Sun Smasher*). With the partial exceptions of *City at World's End* (1951) and *The Haunted Stars* (1960) his novels never forsook the formulas of pulp fiction—the *Starwolf* trilogy (1967–1969, omnibus 1982) and the **mosaic** *Return of the Star Kings* (1970) are calculatedly old-fashioned—but **fabular** short stories such as "Requiem" (1962), "After a Judgment Day" (1963), and "The Pro" (1964) displayed the more thoughtful aspects of his profound neoromanticism.

**HAMILTON, PETER F. (1960– ).** British writer who began publishing **sf** in 1991. *Mindstar Rising* (1993), *A Quantum Murder* (1994), and *The Nano Flower* (1995) are tightly organized futuristic mysteries that contrive an unusually effective fusion of the sf and detective genres. The epic Night's Dawn trilogy, comprising *The Reality Dysfunction* (1996), the *Neutronium Alchemist* (1997), and *The Naked God* (1999) is an ambitious fusion of **hard sf**, sophisticated **space opera**, **military sf**, and **horror-sf**, whose success helped to launch a new vogue for sprawling melodramatic space opera in the United Kingdom. The novel-length title story of *A Second Chance at Eden* (1998) is a mystery set in the same **future history**, to which *The Confederation Handbook* (2000) is a reader's guide. *Fallen Dragon* (2001) is another weighty space opera set against a more **decadent** background. *Misspent Youth* (2002) is a near-future family drama featuring the first rejuvenated human.

**HAND, ELIZABETH (1957– ).** U.S. writer in various fantasy genres. The trilogy comprising *Winterlong* (1990), *Aestival Tide* (1992), and *Icarus Descending* (1993) employs ideas drawn from biological **sf** to underpin an unusually detailed account of a **decadent** future Earth. Some of the stories in *Last Summer at Mars Hill* (1998) and *Bibliomancy* (2003) have sf elements.

**HARBOTTLE, PHILIP (1941– ).** British editor and **bibliographer**. He edited the **magazine** *Vision of Tomorrow* (1969–1970) and various **small press anthologies** as well as writing *The Multi-Man* (1968), a biography and bibliography of **John Russell Fearn.** With Steven Holland, an expert on early British **paperbacks**, he wrote *Vultures of the Void: A History of British Science Fiction, 1946–1956* (1992) and compiled a bibliography of *British Science Fiction Paperbacks, 1949–1956* (1992).

**HARDING, LEE (1937– ). Australian** writer who began publishing **sf** in 1961 with the first version of a story he reshaped into the **children's sf** novel *Displaced Person* (1979, aka *Misplaced Persons*); others include *Fallen Spaceman* (1973, rev. 1980) and the bleak *Waiting for the End of the World* (1983). His sf novels for adults are the identity-exchange story *A World of Shadow* (1975) and the **hallucinatory fantasy** *Future Sanctuary* (1976).

**HARD SF.** A term coined in 1957 by **P. Schuyler Miller**, who recognized that it had become necessary to draw a distinction between

Campbellian **sf** and the sf produced by such recent trends as ***Galaxy*'s** promotion of social **satire** and **Ray Bradbury's fabulations.** Key examples cited by Miller were **John Campbell's** *Islands of Space*, **Murray Leinster's** *Colonial Survey*, and **Hal Clement's** *Cycle of Fire*, the last-named being the most paradigmatic. Some subsequent users took the term to mean sf based in the "hard sciences" (physics and chemistry; biology is included by some users and excluded by others) rather than the "soft sciences" (psychology, sociology, and economics), thus licensing the antonym **soft sf**—while others took it to be a contraction of "hard-core," meaning the sf that lay at the heart, rather than the periphery, of the genre. Such innovations as **new wave** sf and the increasing use of sf motifs by **mainstream** fabulators caused later users—including **David Hartwell**, in his showcase **anthologies** *The Ascent of Wonder* (1994) and *The Hard SF Renaissance* (2002)—to attribute "hardness" to any sf story containing quasi-scientific exposition or explicitly championing science against superstition.

Attempts to draw a boundary around hard (or hard-core) sf are inevitably confused by the ambiguous situation of the marginal sciences of biology and psychology, the hospitability of the Campbellian tradition to **psi** stories—which many skeptics consider essentially **pseudoscientific**, or so soft as to be vaporous—and the tendency of stories that once seemed rationally plausible to be exposed by the passage of time as flagrant impossibilities. The concept of hard sf is so closely linked to the myth of the **space age** and its associated hardware that it is intricately interwoven with the political imperatives of the "conquest" of space; for this reason, hardness in sf is closely associated with **libertarian** and militaristic hard-headedness, and softness with "woolly" liberalism and sentimentality.

**HARNESS, CHARLES L. (1915– ).** U.S. writer who began publishing **sf** with "Time Trap" (1948), a convoluted **time paradox** story involving tremendous off-stage forces, which grants its hero a quasi-transcendental experience in the climax. All these elements were appropriated from **A. E. van Vogt** but Harness proved more adept at their manipulation and sophistication than his model. *Flight into Yesterday* (1949, exp. 1953; aka *The Paradox Men*) and *The Ring of Ritornel* (1968) develop the same template with unprecedented panache. "The Rose" (1953) is a remarkable allegory of burgeoning superhumanity. "An Ornament to His Profession" (1966), "The Alchemist" (1966), and "Probable Cause" (1968) drew on the experience as a patent attorney that he had had earlier exploited in whimsical items of **speculative nonfiction** bylined Leonard Lockhard, often written in **collaboration** with **Theodore L. Thomas.** *Wolfhead* (1978) is an **Orphean fantasy.** *The Catalyst* (1980) features a quasi-miraculous scientific discovery. *Firebird* (1981), *Krono* (1988), and *Lurid Dreams* reiterate the transcendental time-bending of the earlier novels. *Redworld* (1986) and *Cybele, with Bluebonnets* (2002) are eccentric pseudo-autobiographical bildungsromans. *The Venetian Court* (1982) and *Lunar Justice* (1991) are melodramatic courtroom dramas. *An Ornament to His Profession* (1998) is an eclectic sampler of short fiction; the omnibus of four time-looping novels, *Rings* (1999) includes the previously unpublished "Drunkard's Endgame."

**HARRIS, CLARE WINGER (1891–1968).** U.S. writer who began publishing **pulp sf** in 1926, producing early examples of both **feminist** and feminized **sf**, the most conspicuous examples of the latter in **collaboration** with **Miles J. Breuer.** All of her sf is reprinted in *Away from the Here and Now* (1947).

**HARRISON, HARRY (1925– ).** U.S. writer born Henry Maxwell Dempsey; his father changed the surname soon after his birth. He became involved with **sf comic** book **illustration** before publishing his first short story in 1951. ***Astounding*** became his primary market after the first of his picaresque stories featuring *The Stainless Steel Rat* (1961) appeared there in 1957; the **mosaic's** several sequels were further supplemented by **sharecropping** exercises. The melodramatic *Deathworld* (1960) was also extrapolated into a series of bleak **planetary romances**, later volumes of which were written specifically for the Russian market. John Campbell was not, however, sympathetic to Harrison's scathing parody of the tradition he had shaped, *Bill the Galactic Hero* (1965), which also became the basis of a sharecropping **series**; the same corrosive spirit is displayed in the stories collected in *War with the Robots* (1962), *The Technicolor Time Machine* (1967), the proto-**steampunk** novel *Tunnel through the Deeps* (1972; aka *A Transatlantic Tunnel, Hurrah!*), and *Star Smashers of the Galaxy Rangers* (1973).

Notable among Harrison's more earnest works are the population explosion story *Make Room! Make Room!* (1966); the mosaics *One Step from Earth* (1970) and *The Daleth Effect* (1970, aka *In Our Hands, the Stars*), one tracking the development of **matter transmitters**, the other of an **antigravity** device; and the **technothriller** *Skyfall* (1976). The trilogy comprising *West of Eden* (1984), *Winter in Eden* (1986), and *Return to Eden* (1988) is set in an unusually ambitious **alternative history** in which the dinosaurs never died out, evolving instead into sentient species skilled in **biotechnology**. A more conventional alternative history is the backcloth to a trilogy co-written with "John Holm" (Tom Shippey), *The Hammer and the Cross* (1993), *One King's Way* (1995), and *King and Emperor* (1996). *The Turing Option* (1992), written with Marvin Minsky, dramatizes Minsky's ideas about the evolution of **artificial intelligence.** *Stars & Stripes Forever* (1998), *Stars & Stripes in Peril* (2000), and *Stars & Stripes Triumphant* (2002) comprise a trilogy of sarcastic alternative history stories. Harrison edited numerous **anthologies**, mostly in **collaboration** with his friend **Brian W. Aldiss**, and compiled *Great Balls of Fire: A History of Sex in Science Fiction Illustration* (1977).

**HARRISON, M. JOHN (1945– ).** British writer who began publishing **sf** in 1968, quickly becoming a leading figure in **Michael Moorcock's new wave**; his early work in that vein is collected in *The Machine in Shaft Ten and Other Stories* (1975). *The Committed Men* (1971) is a **postholocaust fantasy** and *The Centauri Device* (1974) a parodic **space opera**; between the two, he wrote the **far-futuristic fantasy** *The Pastel City* (1971), which launched a patchwork **series** set in the **decadent** city of Viriconium—some sf motifs are employed in its second volume, *A Storm of Wings* (1980). *Signs of Life* (1997) links dreams of flying to experimental **biotechnology.** *Light* (2002) is a mystery set on the edge of an "ocean of radiant energy" deep in the galaxy. *Things That Never Happen* (2002) is an omnibus of his short fiction. His choice of byline avoided confusion with British writer Michael Harrison (1907–1981), whose early works had included the **Wellsian** fantasies *Higher Things* (1945) and *The Brain* (1953).

**HARTWELL, DAVID G. (1941– ).** U.S. editor and **small press** publisher. He began working in the **sf** field in 1971, editing sf lines for various **paperback** publishers before settling at Tor in 1984. When

**Donald A. Wollheim** became inactive, Hartwell became the only editor in the field with a purposive agenda, although his first attempt to implement it—via Pocket Books' Timescape imprint in the early 1980s—had gone awry, forcing him to be more cautious thereafter. Unlike Wollheim, who remained committed to the **pulp**-engendered notion that sf is primarily light entertainment, Hartwell was ambitious to import the sophistications of literary fiction into **hard sf**, hoping to produce fertile **hybrids** rather than bizarre **chimeras.** The background to this program is set out in *Age of Wonders: Exploring the World of Science Fiction* (1984), and carried forward in the showcase **anthologies** *The Ascent of Wonder: The Evolution of Hard SF* (1994) and *The Hard SF Renaissance* (2002), both edited in **collaboration** with his wife, Kathryn Cramer. ***The New York Review of Science Fiction*** was launched in 1988 by Hartwell's Dragon Press, which had earlier published important sf **criticism** by **Samuel R. Delany**; it became the genre's most enterprising critical periodical, its regular contributors including **John Clute**, **Damien Broderick**, **Michael Swanwick**, and Michael M. Levy.

**HAWTHORNE, NATHANIEL (1804–1864).** U.S. writer whose classic short fiction includes a few antiscientific parables employing **sf** motifs, including "The Birthmark" (1843), "The Artist of the Beautiful" (1844), and most notably, "Rappaccini's Daughter" (1844), whose unlucky heroine's immunity to the world's toxicity is bought at too high a cost.

**HEARD, H. F. (1889–1971).** British writer resident in the United States from 1937. His U.K. publications continued to carry the byline Gerald Heard, which he had used on his early **speculative nonfiction**, including a **Today & Tomorrow** pamphlet *Narcissus: An Anatomy of Clothes* (1924). Much of his work in that vein indulged in scientific and **pseudoscientific** speculation while offering panoramic accounts of human and social evolution. His fiction includes two volumes of ***contes philosophiques***: *The Great Fog and Other Weird Tales* (1944, rev. 1946 as *The Great Fog: Weird Tales of Terror and Detection*), whose title story is a classic parable in which humankind is saved by a seeming disaster, and *The Lost Cavern* (1948). *Doppelgängers: An Episode of the Fourth, the Psychological Revolution* (1947) and

*Gabriel and the Creatures* (1952, aka *Wishing Well*) develop his unorthodox evolutionary ideas in fictional form, the latter intended for children. Three of his crime novels—*A Taste for Honey* (1941, aka *A Taste for Murder*), *Reply Paid* (1942), and *Murder by Reflection* (1942)—involve **science-fictional** methods of murder.

**HEINLEIN, ROBERT A. (1907–1988).** U.S. writer who began writing **pulp sf** when a political campaign undertaken after he was invalided out of the navy, in connection with Upton Sinclair's EPIC (End Poverty in California) movement, left him with a mortgage to pay off. After selling "Life-Line" (1939) to ***Astounding*** he became a determined member of **John Campbell's** nascent stable, adapting himself more closely to Campbell's ambitions than anyone else. He published five definitive stories in 1940: "If This Goes On—" transfigured his memories of growing up in the Bible Belt into a cautionary tale of a future America ruled with totalitarian rigor by a Prophet Incarnate; "Requiem" is a Hemingwayesque tale in which the man whose entrepreneurial efforts gave birth to the **space age** evades well-meant efforts to stop him making a fatal voyage to the **moon**; "The Roads Must Roll" is about a near-future labor dispute; "Blowups Happen" is about the social and psychological tensions generated by a nuclear power plant; "Coventry" describes life in a reservation to which dissidents from a formal social contract are banished, stubbornly reproducing all the social problems that it has negotiated away.

By taking technological innovations for granted and focusing on the social and psychological corollaries of their integration into the pattern of everyday life, Heinlein imported a new realism into pulp sf and pioneered a new method of carrying forward the Campbellian prospectus. The ideological legacy of his aborted career in politics was a way of thinking about the future framed by practical political concerns, whose hypothetical solutions are generated by innovative radical pragmatism. In order to facilitate the equipment of his stories with telling details, Heinlein linked them together with a common historical background, whose chart Campbell published, proposing in consequence that Heinlein should reserve his own name for stories set within that **future history.** Heinlein agreed, putting the byline Anson MacDonald on *Sixth Column* (1941, book 1949; aka *The Day* *after Tomorrow*). The future history extended beyond Earth in "Logic of Empire" (1941), the **generation starship** stories "Universe" and "Common Sense" (1941; combined in *Orphans of the Sky*, 1963), and the **Odyssean fantasy** *Methuselah's Children* (1941; book 1958). When the United States became embroiled in World War II, Heinlein was recalled to military service. Although Campbell had a few stories in hand, including the quasi-**Utopian** novel *Beyond This Horizon* (1942, book 1948), Heinlein's career as a pulp writer was over; when he returned to sf writing, he approached the prospect very differently, producing work aimed at a variety of more prestigious markets. He sold stories set in the nearer reaches of his **future history** to *The Saturday Evening Post*, beginning with "The Green Hills of Earth" (1947), and he began to write **children's sf** because that was the only way in which sf could then be sold to mass-market publishers.

*Rocket Ship Galileo* (1947), the first of the juveniles Heinlein produced annually for Scribner's until 1958, provided a basis for the script he wrote for the George Pal film *Destination Moon* (1950); the second, *Space Cadet* (1948), inspired the **TV** show *Tom Corbett—Space Cadet*. He wrote "Gulf" (1949) as a favor to Campbell but treated the pulps as a market of last resort, although he allowed specialist **small presses** to reprint his early pulp work and wrote a new novella to round out *The Man Who Sold the Moon* (1950). He aimed his new novels—the paranoid thriller *The Puppet Masters* (1951) and the **transfigurations** of classic popular fictions *Double Star* (1956) and *The Door into Summer* (1957)—at commercial publishers; the sf **magazines** were only permitted to buy subsidiary serial rights. His radical pragmatism crept into *Space Cadet* and *Between Planets* (1951), and his subsequent juveniles became increasingly ambitious. *Red Planet* (1949), *The Rolling Stones* (1952), and *Starman Jones* set new standards for technical sophistication and narrative skill, while *The Star Beast* (1954), *Tunnel in the Sky* (1955), *Time for the Stars* (1956), and *Citizen of the Galaxy* (1957)—a transfiguration of **Rudyard Kipling's** *Kim*—were more sophisticated than his work aimed at adults. *Have Space Suit—Will Travel* (1958) was combatively contentious and *Starship Troopers*—a transfiguration of Leon Uris's *Battle Cry* (1953)—tested his editor's tolerance too far causing it to be rerouted to an adult market that had now become wide open to sf. When Heinlein eventually decided to write one more juvenile, *Pod-*

*kayne of Mars* (1963), he was initially determined to violate the last and most sacred taboo of children's fiction, but he bowed to editorial pressure and let his heroine live.

*Stranger in a Strange Land* (1961), an account of a fledgling messiah and his opinionated mentor, began a new and uncompromising phase of Heinlein's career. *Farnham's Freehold* (1964), a transfiguration of *The Swiss Family Robinson*, became the prototype of **survivalist fiction.** *The Moon Is a Harsh Mistress* (1966), a stirring replay of the American Revolution, popularized the acronymic motto TANSTAAFL (There Ain't No Such Thing as a Free Lunch). In *I Will Fear No Evil* (1970) the mind of a crotchety old man is displaced into the brain of a young woman. The **mosaic** *Time Enough for Love* (1973), an episodic bildungsroman that takes up the threads of *Methuselah's Children*, and *The Number of the Beast* (1980) are exercises in wish fulfillment; *The Cat Who Walked through Walls* (1985) and *To Sail Beyond the Sunset* (1987) are only slightly less narcissistic. Even *Friday* (1982), an energetic action-adventure story with little incidental axe-grinding, was a far cry from the revolutionary work he had done in 1940–1941, which facilitated a rapid maturation that John Campbell might not have been able to achieve without his timely input.

**HENDERSON, ZENNA (1917–1983).** U.S. writer who began writing **sf** in 1951, soon importing her experience as an elementary school teacher into the **series** of stories collected in *Pilgrimage: The Book of the People* (1961) and *The People: No Different Flesh* (1966), in which **psi-powered** castaways exemplify ways of coping with the predicaments of outsiders in human society. Her other stories, collected in *The Anything Box* (1965) and *Holding Wonder* (1971), are similarly sentimental.

**HENDRIX, HOWARD V. (1959– ).** U.S. writer who began publishing **sf** in 1986. *Testing, Testing, 1, 2, 3* (1990) is a small sampler of short fiction. *The Vertical Fruit of the Horizontal Tree* (1994) is a novella about a symbiotic alliance of psychotropic fungi, crystals, and computers. *Lightpaths* (1997) is a mystery set in a **Utopian** orbital habitat; its sequel, *Standing Wave* (1998), is a complex account of evolutionary transcendence embedded within a murder mystery, while its prequel, *Better*

*Angels* (1999), tracks the discovery of the remains of an **alien** "angel" in a tar pit. *Empty Cities of the Full Moon* (2001) is a **postholocaust fantasy** in which a **biotechnological** plague has created shape-shifters.

**HERBERT, BRIAN (1947– ).** U.S. writer, the son of **Frank Herbert**, with whom he **collaborated** on *Man of Two Worlds* (1986). His solo **sf**, all of which is **satirical**, includes *Sidney's Comet* (1983) and its sequel, *The Garbage Chronicles* (1985), as well as the surreally bizarre *Sudanna, Sudanna* (1985) and *Prisoners of Arionn* (1987), in which San Francisco's Bay Area is abducted by **aliens.** *The Race for God* (1990), in which humans are invited to meet God in a distant galaxy, and *Memorymakers* (1991), in which the future belongs to cannibals, were both written in collaboration with Marie Landis. He wrote several prequels to his father's Dune **series** in collaboration with **Kevin J. Anderson.**

**HERBERT, FRANK (1920–1986).** U.S. writer who began publishing **sf** in 1952. His **technothriller** *The Dragon in the Sea* (1956, aka *21st Century Sub & Under Pressure*) is an exceptionally adept example of the subgenre. His epic novel *Dune* (1965), about the advent of a messiah on the desert world that produces the life-preserving spice on which a **galactic empire** is built, caught the mood of the day with its intense **ecological mysticism** and was elaborated by five sequels. Ecological mysticism also formed the basis of *The Green Brain* (1966) and *Hellstrom's Hive* (1973). Herbert's fascination with religion was further developed in *The God Makers* (1960 as "The Priests of Psi," exp. 1972) and in a **series** of sequels to his solo novel *Destination: Void* (1966), written in **collaboration** with Bill Ransom: *The Jesus Incident* (1979), *The Lazarus Effect* (1983), and *The Ascension Factor* (1988). His fascination with immortality was also displayed in *The Eyes of Heisenberg* (1966) and *The Heaven Makers* (1968, rev. 1977). *The Santaroga Barrier* (1968) tackles the problem of depicting superhuman intelligences with some ingenuity, but several similar projects are not as clearly focused. *Whipping Star* (1970, rev. 1977) and its sequel, *The Dosadi Experiment* (1977), struggle to model **alien** intelligences. *The White Plague* (1982) is a sexual-political **disaster story.** His short fiction is assembled in several overlapping collections, most notably *The Worlds of Frank Herbert* (1970) and *Eye* (1985).

**HERZOG, ARTHUR (1927– ).** U.S. writer whose early **sf** novels were alarmist **disaster stories**; *The Swarm* (1974) features killer bees, *Earthsound* (1975) earthquakes, *Heat* (1977) the greenhouse effect, and *IQ 83* (1978) **biotechnology** gone awry. *Make Us Happy* (1978) and *Glad to Be Here* (1979) are accounts of **dystopian** futures and their psychological foundations. The collection *Body Parts* (2002) includes some **horror-sf.**

**HIGH, PHILIP E. (1914– ).** British writer who began publishing **sf** in 1955. *The Prodigal Sun* (1964), in which a human "**alien**" redeems Earth from disaster, set a pattern for many later novels; *No Truce with Terra* (1964), *The Mad Metropolis* (1966, aka *Double Illusion*), *These Savage Futurians* (1967), *Twin Planets* (1967), *Reality Forbidden* (1967), and *Invader on My Back* (1968) vary the formula by adding extra exoticism to the redeemer, the threat, and/or the act of redemption. In *The Time Mercenaries* (1968) the saviors are resurrected submariners unconstrained by the moral qualms of future **Utopians**, and thus qualified to repel alien invaders. *Butterfly Planet* (1971) and *Speaking of Dinosaurs* (1974) ventured into exotic mystery fiction. *The Best of Philip E. High* (2002) samples his short fiction.

**HILL, DOUGLAS (1935– ). Canadian** writer resident in the United Kingdom since 1959. He worked in the field as an editor in the late 1960s before turning his hand to **children's sf.** He was one of the first writers to adapt traditional **space opera** for younger readers (aged 9 to 12) in three **series** begun with *Galactic Warlord* (1979), *The Huntsman* (1992), and *Exiles of ColSec* (1984), and the trilogy comprising *Galaxy's Edge* (1996), *The Moons of Lannamur* (1996), and *The Phantom Planet* (1997). *Space Girls Don't Cry* (1998) and *Alien Deeps* (2000) are among his works for even younger readers. His adult space operas, *The Fraxilly Fracas* (1989) and *The Colloghi Conspiracy* (1990), are confections in a similar vein.

**HINTON, C. H. (1853–1907).** British writer whose ***Scientific Romances*** (1886) featured essays in **speculative nonfiction** that laid the groundwork for the subgenre of **dimensional fantasy** (including the "explanation" of **H. G. Wells's time machine**) and a **religious fantasy** about the mathematics of redemption. The novellas *Stella* and

*An Unfinished Communication* (1895)—the first of which features a technology of invisibility, the second a **time-traveling** afterlife—were combined with more essays in *Scientific Romances: Second Series* (1902). *An Episode of Flatland* (1907) describes life on the rim of a circle.

**HOBAN, RUSSELL (1925– ).** U.S. writer resident in the United Kingdom since 1969. The literary fiction he wrote alongside his many children's books sometimes used **sf** motifs. *Riddley Walker* (1980) is a **postholocaust fantasy** told in the deftly transformed language of the neoprimitives whose way of life is threatened by the reinvention of gunpowder. *The Medusa Frequency* (1987) is a phantasmagoric **Orphean fantasy.** The **existentialist fantasy** *Fremder* (1996) follows the sobering experiences of the sole survivor of a space disaster. *Amaryllis Night and Day* (2001) is a **hallucinatory fantasy** about the topography of memory and time.

**HODGSON, WILLIAM HOPE (1877–1918).** British writer who ran away to sea in his youth and was deeply affected by his experiences aboard ship. Many of the fantastic sea stories he published in the wake of "From the Tideless Sea" (1906) are classic examples of **horror-sf**—notably "The Voice in the Night" (1907), in which castaways are transformed by a fungus they have been obliged to eat, and "The Stone Ship" (1914), in which an ancient wreck thrust up from the depths by a volcanic eruption bears a weird living cargo. In *The Boats of the Glen Carrig* (1907), shipwreck survivors take refuge on an island near a mass of floating seaweed inhabited by bizarre life-forms. The remarkable **visionary fantasy** *The House on the Borderland* (1908) includes an allegorical cosmic journey. *The Ghost Pirates* (1909) is a vivid **dimensional fantasy.** The phantasmagoric **Orphean fantasy** *The Night Land* (1912; abridged as *The Dream of X*, 1912) helped set the pattern for subsequent **far-futuristic fantasies.** His fantastic stories are collected in *Deep Waters* (1967) and *Out of the Storm* (1975).

**HOGAN, JAMES P. (1941– ).** British-born writer resident in the United States since 1979. He began publishing **sf** with *Inherit the Stars* (1977), a **hard-sf** mystery story whose puzzles were further unraveled in *The Gentle Giants of Ganymede* (1978), *Giants' Star* (1981), and *Entoverse* (1991). Scientists with strong **libertarian** inclinations play similarly heroic roles—usually meeting stubborn opposition from socialist bureaucrats, and occasionally from crooked businessmen—in the **technothriller** *The Genesis Machine* (1978); the **time-paradox** story *Thrice upon a Time* (1980); the giant computer story *The Two Faces of Tomorrow* (1979); the **space operas** *Voyage from Yesteryear* (1982), *Code of the Lifemaker* (1983), and *Cradle of Saturn* (1999); the **alternative history** stories *The Proteus Operation* (1985) and *Paths to Otherwhere* (1996); the **political fantasy** *Endgame Enigma* (1987); the **virtual reality** story *Realtime Interrupt* (1995); and the **miniaturization** story *Bug Park* (1997). Later works, including the **existential fantasy** *The Multiplex Man*, the meditative study of **alien** life *The Immortality Option* (1993), and the witty scientific mystery *Out of Time* (1993) moderated his ideologically stridency. In *Star Child* (1998) sapient machines tell their story to human children; *Outward Bound* (2000) is also a juvenile. *Cradle of Saturn* (1999) and its sequel, *The Anguished Dawn* (2003), are tales of cosmic catastrophe. *The Legend That Was Earth* (2000) is a political fantasy.

**HOOVER, H. M. (1935– ).** U.S. writer of **children's sf.** *Children of Morrow* (1973) and its sequel *Treasures of Morrow* (1976) are **postholocaust fantasies.** *The Delikon* (1977) is a **political fantasy.** *The Rains of Eridan* (1978), *The Lost Star* (1979), *Return to Earth* (1980), and *This Time of Darkness* (1980) employ mystery and thriller frameworks to nurture the earnest exploration of **sf** motifs. *Another Heaven, Another Earth* (1981), *The Shepherd Moon* (1984), *Orvis* (1987, aka *Journey through the Empty*), *Away Is a Strange Place to Be* (1990), *Only Child* (1992), and *The Winds of Mars* (1995) are accounts of ingenious survival in exotically hostile conditions.

**HOPKINSON, NALO (1961– ).** Jamaican-born writer resident in **Canada** since 1977, who began publishing **sf** in 1997. *Brown Girl in the Ring* (1998) is a **chimerical** near-future thriller fusing sf motifs with voodoo-rooted mythical fantasy. *Midnight Robber* (2000) is an even-more-phantasmagoric mélange set on the colony world of Toussaint at carnival time. Her short fiction is collected in *Skin Folk* (2001).

**HORNIG, CHARLES D. (1916–1999).** U.S. editor. His early **fanzine**, *The Fantasy Fan* (1933–1935), brought him to the attention of **Hugo Gernsback**, who hired him to edit ***Wonder Stories*** before he had finished high school. As the administrator of the Science Fiction League, he played a leading role in the early organization of **fandom.** He subsequently edited the **magazines** *Science Fiction*, *Future Fiction,* and *Science Fiction Quarterly* from 1939–1941, until he was replaced by **Robert A. W. Lowndes.**

**HORROR-SF.** Much early **sf** was cast as horror fiction, partly because technophobia was a more powerful stimulus to imaginative effort than technophilia and partly because the horror-fiction story formula—a nasty threat intensified by degrees until it can be melodramatically exorcized by a deus ex machina—is so very convenient. The school of futuristic thought implicit within horror-sf was stigmatized by **Isaac Asimov** as the **Frankenstein syndrome** but **Brian Aldiss**, identifying *Frankenstein* as the first sf novel, suggested that the whole genre has descended from gothic fiction and is typically cast in a "post-gothic mode." The case is certainly arguable, given the manner in which **aliens**, biological **mutants**, **supermen**, and **artificial intelligences** have so often been used as straightforward substitutes for the traditional antagonists of horror fiction, and the many **hybrid** stories in which those very antagonists—vampires, werewolves, ghosts, zombies, and so forth—are carefully **transfigured** by "scientific" explanations. On the other hand, the intellectual descendants of the 18th-century philosophers of progress—including **Utopian technological determinists** like **Edward Bellamy**, **Hugo Gernsback**, and **J. B. S. Haldane**, and genre sf writers loyal to **John Campbell's** manifesto—see the demolition of the anxieties generating the Frankenstein syndrome as an essential component of their mission. For this reason, **hard-sf** writers are apt to react to horror-sf in much the same way that the heroes of horror-sf react to their antagonists, seeing it as a hideously **chimerical** subgenre whose betrayal of their ideals is even more pernicious than that of **science-fantasy.**

This situation is further complicated by philosophical analysis of the idea of "horror." Distinctions between "terror" and "horror" can be drawn in several ways, but while terror is usually a response to an immediate and perceptible stimulus, the origins of unease in horror fiction are often less certain, the consequent distress being further intensified by the lack of any obvious source. That fraction of horror fiction that belongs to such subgenres as **metaphysical fantasy** and **existentialist fantasy** draws its impact from doubt as to the coherence and reliability of perceived reality—and modern science, in revealing that the world of sensory experience and mundane time calculation overlies the complex anticommonsensical realities of cosmology, atomic physics, and geological time, does have innately horrific aspects. Such subgenres as the "cosmic horror" fiction identified by **H. P. Lovecraft** are hybrid rather than chimerical and it was inevitable that 20th-century horror fiction would make ever-more-prolific use of sf motifs, as exemplified by some of the work of **Stephen King** and **Dean R. Koontz.** Even if the traditional antagonists of horror fiction had retained a fuller measure of plausibility, the resources of the scientific imagination and the exploitability of the "yuck factor" of **biotechnology** would have opened up irresistible opportunities, providing ample scope for **melodramatic inflation** (only sf can provide whole worlds populated by vampires, shapeshifters, and monsters, and the prospect of their eternal dominion). That very inevitability increased the burden of responsibility that writers of hard sf undertook, forcing them to insist more loudly and more ingeniously than before that progress *is* possible, and that the **sense of wonder** really ought to prove more powerful, if only in the long run, than panic born of paranoia.

**HOYLE, SIR FRED (1915–2001).** British astronomer and writer notorious for his opposition to the cosmological theory he dismissed contemptuously as "the Big Bang" and for his vociferous advocacy of the notion that life, having originated in **outer space**, was first brought to Earth by comets that still visit diseases upon us. The latter thesis, popularized in such works of **speculative nonfiction** as *Lifecloud* (1979), *Evolution from Space* (1981), and *The Intelligent Universe* (1983), developed from ideas broached in his first **sf** novel, *The Black Cloud* (1957). *Ossian's Ride* (1959) is a more conventional mystery thriller, while *A for Andromeda* (1962) and *The Andromeda Breakthrough* (1964), both with John Elliot, are novelizations of **TV** serials. After the enterprising **timeslip romance** *October the First Is Too Late* (1966), Hoyle mostly worked in **collaboration** with his son Geoffrey

(1942– ), much of their work being **children's sf** derived from the popularizing efforts of the Molecule Club, which mounted educational plays and displays in schools and theaters. The most interesting are the tentatively **Stapledonian** *The Incandescent Ones* (1977) and the **disaster story** *The Inferno* (1973). Hoyle used a late solo effort, *Comet Halley* (1985), as a vehicle for his unorthodox ideas.

**HUBBARD, L. RON (1911–1986).** U.S. **pulp** writer, initially of westerns, who was recommended to **John Campbell** as a craftsmanlike hack but was transformed under that editor's influence into a highly idiosyncratic writer. He was more comfortable working for ***Unknown***, but ***Astounding*** published his early **psi** story "The Tramp" (1938); a grim account of the utter devastation of Europe by World War II, *Final Blackout* (1940, book 1948); the **space opera** "The End Is Not Yet" (1947); the medical **sf series** collected in *Old Doc Methuselah* (1947–1950 as Rene Lafayette, book 1970); and the time-dilatation story "To the Stars" (1950, book 1954 as *Return to Tomorrow*), which ends with the most extreme of *Astounding*'s many diatribes on humankind's universe-conquering destiny. Hubbard returned to the field after a long absence with the space opera *Battlefield Earth* (1982) and the Mission Earth dekalogy (1985–1987), which attempt a drastic minimalization of literary style. His name is associated with an annual Writers of the Future contest founded in 1985 by followers of a religion he invented.

**HUDSON, W. H. (1841–1922).** British naturalist and writer born and long resident in Argentina. His **far-futuristic fantasy** *A Crystal Age* (1887) imagined that what would later be called ecological relationships might one day evolve into a state of supernatural harmony. *Green Mansions* (1904) attempts to go beyond the *Heart of Darkness* identified by **Joseph Conrad** in search of a similar ideal state of being, here represented by the sole survivor of an extinct tribal society.

**HUGHES, MONICA (1925–2003).** British-born writer for children who immigrated to **Canada** in 1952. Her earliest **sf** novels, *Crisis on Conshelf Ten* (1975) and its sequel, *Earthdark* (1977), describe variously restricted colonial societies, while *Beyond the Dark River* (1979) and *Ring-Rise, Ring-Set* (1982) examine Native American cultures in futuristic settings. Crises of adolescence are modeled in *The Tomorrow City* (1978); the trilogy comprising *Guardian of Isis* (1980), *Keeper of the Isis Light* (1981), and *The Isis Pedlar* (1982), which offer a painstaking account of their heroine's attempts to come to terms with her chimerical identity; and two couplets set in grim futures: *Devil on My Back* (1984) and *The Dream Catcher* (1986), and *Sandwriter* (1985) and *The Promise* (1989). *Invitation to the Game* (1990), in which a future society attempts to secure its **Utopian** ambitions by exporting its troublesome adolescents, is similar in spirit. *The Crystal Drop* (1992), *A Handful of Seeds* (1993), and *The Golden Aquarians* (1994) are environmentalist fantasies.

**HUGHES, ZACH (1928– ).** Pseudonym used on most of his **sf** by U.S. writer Hugh Zachary. He followed an early exercise in sf pornography with *The Book of Rack the Healer* (1973), a **postholocaust fantasy** whose sequel *Thunderworld* (1982) follows the example of *The Legend of Miaree* (1974) in entwining humankind's fate problematically with **alien** species. The interplanetary confederation in *Thunderworld* also serves as a background to *Gold Star* (1983), *Closed System* (1986), *Sundrinker* (1987), *The Dark Side* (1987), *Life Force* (1988), and *Mother Lode* (1991). *Seed of the Gods* (1974) parodies then-fashionable **pseudoscience**, although *Pressure Man* (1980) treats similar subject matter sympathetically. *Tide* (1974) and *The St. Francis Effect* (1976) are **ecocatastrophe** novels. *The Stork Factor* (1975) is an account of emergent superhumanity. *Killbird* (1980) is a postholocaust fantasy. As Evan Innes, he wrote the *America 2040* **series** (5 vols., 1986–1988). *The Omnificence Factor* (1993) is a mystery involving a vanished civilization.

**HUGO.** The nickname (honoring **Hugo Gernsback**) of the Science Fiction Achievement Award, given annually in numerous categories by the World Science Fiction Convention, as voted by its members. Introduced in 1953, the Hugos have been awarded continuously from 1955. The award is shaped like a spaceship standing on its fins.

**HUMOROUS SF.** Humor was an essential component of **Hugo Gernsback's scientifiction**, which routinely used levity as a means of sugaring its didactic pills. The tall tales so frequently featured in

*Science and Invention* were, however, less prevalent in ***Amazing Stories***, which favored earnest action-adventure. Although most of the **chimerical** fiction published in ***Unknown*** was humorous, **John Campbell** took ***Astounding's*** manifesto much more seriously, and comedy remained fugitive there until the effects of World War II limited his options, creating an opening for the consistently irreverent solo work of **Henry Kuttner**, whose tales of drunken inventor Galloway Gallagher (1943–1948, collected as *Robots Have No Tails*) were far more sophisticated than Gernsback's accounts of "Baron Munchausen's Scientific Adventures," establishing a useful template for writers like **Fredric Brown.** Many of the Gallagher stories featured **robots**, whose alloy of human and mechanical features was a fertile source of mistaken identity jokes that had already been exploited by such writers as J. Storer Clouston in *Button Brains* (1933). Naive **aliens** could also be comic figures, and Campbell's human chauvinism encouraged writers averse to genocidal violence—most notably **Eric Frank Russell**—to dramatize human/alien conflicts in humorous terms, with human sharp operators continually making fools of unimaginatively arrogant aliens.

The increasing importance of sf ***contes cruels*** helped black comedy to flourish, especially when the advent of ***Galaxy*** and ***The Magazine of Fantasy & Science Fiction*** made the field much more hospitable to such work—an opportunity taken up with alacrity by **C. M. Kornbluth**, **Damon Knight**, **William Tenn**, **Robert Sheckley**, and many others, and exploited outside the magazines by **Kurt Vonnegut.** The spectrum of 1950s humorous sf extended from maliciously dark **satire** to the calculated silliness exemplified by **Reginald Bretnor's** shaggy dog stories; the latter kind of humor was ancestral to a whole tradition of slapstick sf eventually brought to a curious perfection by such writers as **Douglas Adams**. There was a good deal in **pulp sf** that was innately preposterous, or was rendered preposterous by overfamiliarity, and which therefore lent itself to outrageous parody. The black comedies of the 1960s and 1970s became slicker and more sophisticated in the works of such writers as **Thomas M. Disch** and **John Sladek**, whose **new wave** surrealism, allied with the increasing importance of **fabulation**, facilitated the development of quirkier kinds of comedy sf in the work of such writers as **R. A. Lafferty** and **Howard Waldrop.**

Fan writing was always a significant medium of humor; writers like **Bob Shaw** and **David Langford** were much funnier in their fan writing than their professional sf.

**HUNT, ROBERT (1807–1887).** British scientist who became the most important British pioneer of the popularization of science, to which end he wrote an account of *The Poetry of Science* (1848), whose ardent enthusiasm prompted **William Wilson** to invent the term "**science-fiction**" in 1851. *Panthea, the Spirit of Nature* (1849) is a **chimerical** bildungsroman whose hero experiences two remarkable symbolic cosmic visions by courtesy of a Rosicrucian guru but eventually forsakes occultism for the more rewarding vocation of empirical scientific inquiry and technological development.

**HUXLEY, ALDOUS (1894–1963).** British writer of literary fiction. His biologist brother Julian (1887–1975) extrapolated the substance of J. B. S. Haldane's *Daedalus* (1923) into the cautionary **satire** "The Tissue Culture King" (1926); Aldous combined this inspiration with the sketch of a future "Rational State" he had set out in *Crome Yellow* (1920) to produce the classic **Utopian** satire *Brave New World* (1932), whose scathing black comedy was taken very seriously by many of its readers. *After Many a Summer Dies the Swan* (1939, aka *After Many a Summer*) takes a jaundiced view of the prospect of immortality. *Ape and Essence* (1948) is a vitriolic **postholocaust fantasy** based on an unproduced film script. The earnestly Utopian *Island* (1962) proposes that only **pseudoscience** based in Eastern mysticism can save the world from the scientifically engendered horrors sketched out in *Brave New World Revisited* (1958).

**HYAMS, EDWARD S. (1910–1975).** British writer in various genres. *Not in Our Stars* (1949) earnestly expresses anxieties about the advent of biological warfare. *The Astrologer* (1950) couches its fear of possible **ecocatastrophe** in a **satirical transfiguration** of *Lysistrata*. *Sylvester* (1951: aka *998*) gently satirizes the militarization of science. *The Final Agenda* (1973) and *Prince Habib's Iceberg* (1974) are marginal **political fantasies.** *Morrow's Ants* (1975) is an enterprising account of an allegorical social experiment.

**HYBRID TEXTS.** Texts in which elements drawn from **sf** are combined with elements drawn from other genres of fantasy in such a way as to harmonize them, by providing a speculative "rational explanation" for motifs that would be seen as magical or supernatural in another context. Such examples as **Jack Williamson's** *Darker Than You Think* (1940) and **James Blish's** "There Shall Be No Darkness" (1950) transform their materials in such a way as to remove the resultant stories from the **horror-sf** category to which they would otherwise have belonged, but **science-fantasies** like **C. L. Moore's** *The Dark World* (1946) and **Anne McCaffrey's** *Dragonflight* (1968) retain their heroic fantasy flavor. Many **transfigurations** of myths, including **shaggy God stories**, are similar in kind. Hybrid texts may be regarded as examples of **science-fantasy**, but need to be contrasted with **ambiguous** and **chimerical** texts.

**HYNE, C. J. CUTCLIFFE (1866–1944).** British writer in various genres. There are **sf** elements in *Beneath Your Very Boots* (1889), about a subterranean world under England, the **robinsonade** *The New Eden* (1892), and the thriller *The Recipe for Diamonds* (1893), but Hyne's most explicit early sf is to be found in stories in *The Adventures of an Engineer* and *The Adventures of a Solicitor* (both 1898, bylined Weatherby Chesney) that feature fanciful mechanical inventions. His later works, including the world-blackmail story *Empire of the World* (1910, aka *Emperor of the World*) and the similar items in *Man's Understanding* (1933), are much darker in tone, although *Abbs, His Story through Many Ages* (1929) retains an amiable levity.

**HYPERSPACE.** A term introduced into **sf** in **John Campbell's** *Islands of Space* (1931), referring to a medium through which spaceships can take "shortcuts" in order to avoid the Einsteinian limitation on traveling faster than light. It is usually conceived as a **parallel dimension** with a distinct topography—hence, the alternative name of "warp space," although some writers prefer to consider hyperspace as a more limited, artificially generated phenomenon, in which case they are more likely to describe it as a "space warp" (a term also used in *Islands in Space*). Other writers prefer the term "subspace," but hyperspace is far more common than any of its rivals. The notion lacks rational plausibility, having no answer to Einsteinian objections, but serves as the fundamental facilitating device of interstellar **space operas** and **galactic empires.**

## – I –

**ILLUSTRATION.** Although **magazine** and **paperback cover art** is the most obvious arena of **sf** illustration, visual imagery supporting text (or vice versa) has a much longer history. *Un autre monde* (1844), by a **French** illustrator who signed his drawings Taxile Delord and the accompanying text as Isidore Grandville, provided a crucial exemplar for the work of later French illustrators, most notably **Albert Robida. Jules Verne's** novels and **Camille Flammarion's** *Uranie* were published in lavishly illustrated editions. Robida's nearest equivalent in Britain was **Fred T. Jane**, who illustrated many of the **future war** novels issued by Tower Publications, including **George Griffith's** *Angel of the Revolution*. The **scientific romance** published in the British **magazines** of the 1890s was usually illustrated, but rarely to much effect; Warwick Goble could not do justice to **H. G. Wells's** *War of the Worlds*, nor could Stanley Wood render much assistance to the magazine version of Griffith's *Honeymoon in Space*.

The internal illustration of early sf **pulps** was often crude, but artists whose work assisted and enhanced the fiction include Frank R. Paul and Virgil Finlay. The digest magazines that replaced them made less use of internal illustration but substantial contributions to ***Astounding/Analog*'s** ambience were made by Kelly Freas and John Schoenherr. With the exception of **children's** books, few sf books were illustrated in the first half of the 20th century, but the Earl of Birkenhead's **futurology** book *The World in 2030 A.D.* (1930) features some interesting examples of artistic futurism and futuristic nonfiction spawned a distinctive imagery of its own, lavishly displayed in such popular science periodicals as *Modern Wonder* (1937–1940). In the latter part of the century, sf illustration achieved a degree of independence, eventually giving rise to such retrospective assemblies as *Barlowe's Guide to Extraterrestrials* (1979) by Wayne Douglas Barlowe and Ian Summers and such **collaborative** efforts as

*Planet Story* (1979) by Harry Harrison and Jim Burns. The book-packager Byron Preiss became a prolific producer of illustrated sf books, notable examples including *The Illustrated Roger Zelazny* (1978) and **Ray Bradbury's** *Dinosaur Tales* (1983). Speculative projects originated as art books include Dougal Dixon's *After Man: A Zoology of the Future* (1981) and James Gurney's *Dinotopia* (1992).

**IMAGINARY VOYAGES.** The literary tradition most obviously ancestral to **sf** is that of the imaginary voyage. *Voyages imaginaires* was the leading term in the 36-volume series of proto-sf works compiled by Charles Garnier in 1787–1789, having existed as a category since the late 17th century; it served so well as a generic description that the **French** language did not require any such supplement as **scientific romance** or **science fiction** until the latter was imported from America. Vernian romance was initially distinguished from more fanciful *voyages imaginaires* by the invention of a modest subcategory of *voyages extraordinaires*. Long before sf began its earnest evangelism on behalf of the **space age**, the **moon** was seen as the ultimate destination of the fanciful traveler's tale—the final, most preposterous fiction in the great liar's armory. It held that status from the second century, when Lucian wrote his *True History*, until 1840, when **Edgar Allan Poe** added an introductory call for "verisimilitude" to the second version of "The Unparalleled Adventure of One Hans Pfaall" in the same ironic spirit—although it can be read in a different light today. **Jules Verne** was, in consequence, a truly revolutionary writer, who had an enormous burden of expectation to overcome in presenting *his* travelers' tales as plausible accounts rather than exercises in transparent mendacity. **H. G. Wells** drew enough narrative energy from the tradition of imaginary voyages in *The Time Machine* and *The First Men in the Moon* for his work in that vein to be regarded as deftly **chimerical**, using the semblance of the big lie to sugarcoat the bitter truth lurking within it. Most of those who followed his example were less conscious of the chimerical quality of their work, but it is a narrative condition from which **time travel** stories, **microcosmic romances**, and **space operas** never escaped—and which very few literary accounts of space travel have contrived to transcend, in spite of the powerful advocacy of the **prophets** of **hard sf.**

**INFINITY PLUS.** A website at www.infinityplus.co.uk operated by **Keith Brooke**, launched in 1997. It is the leading **sf** site in the United Kingdom, including a huge archive of interviews, feature articles, fiction, and links to all the major **magazines** and sf publishers. ***Interzone*** 177 (April 2002) was a special *Infinity Plus* issue. **Anthologies** linked to the site, edited by Brooke and Nick Gevers, are *Infinity Plus One* (2001) and *Infinity Plus Two* (2003).

**ING, DEAN (1931– ).** U.S. writer who began publishing **sf** in 1955. *Soft Targets* (1979) is a tale of future terrorism. *Pulling Through* (1983) and the trilogy comprising *Systemic Shock* (1981), *Single Combat* (1983), and *Wild Country* (1985) provided prototypes for **survivalist fiction.** The novel-length lead story in *Anasazi* (1979, book 1980) is a graphic account of **alien** parasitism. *The Big Lifters* (1988) is a **libertarian satire**. Ing completed six novels drafted by **Mack Reynolds**: the **Utopian** fantasies *The Lagrangists* (1983), *Home Sweet Home 2010 A.D.* (1984), and *Trojan Orbit* (1985); the **alternative history** *The Other Time* (1984); the exotic mystery *Eternity* (1984); and the futuristic thriller *Deathwish World* (1986).

**INGS, SIMON (1965– ).** British writer who began publishing **sf** in 1990. *Hot Head* (1992) is a taut post-**cyberpunk** thriller whose antagonist, only slightly inconvenienced by death and **transfiguration**, reappears in *Hotwire* (1995). *Headlong* (1999) carries forward similar themes with considerable ingenuity.

**INNER SPACE.** A term derived by inverting **outer space**, popularized by J. B. Priestley in "They Came from Inner Space" (*New Statesman*, 1954), who argued that it was a mistake for **sf** to try to explore realms beyond the Earth's atmosphere rather than attempting to plumb the hidden depths of the human psyche. **J. G. Ballard** made a similar plea in ***New Worlds*** in 1962, laying important groundwork for **new wave** sf. The label was not applied to **microcosmic romance** or such **pulp sf** stories as "Into the Subconscious" (1929) by Ray Avery Myers because "outer space" did not enter everyday parlance until the 1953 release of the movie *It Came from Outer Space*. By the end of the 20th century, inner space was used promiscuously to refer to the spaces of the mind, the subatomic microcosm, and the ocean depths.

In 2003 the University of Michigan launched an "inner space program" using nanoprobes to observe chemical activity in living cells.

**INTERNATIONAL ASSOCIATION FOR THE FANTASTIC IN THE ARTS (IAFA).** An organization formed in 1982 to maintain an annual International Conference on the Fantastic in the Arts (ICFA), whose scope extends far beyond **sf** but usually includes more papers on sf than the smaller annual conference of the **Science Fiction Research Association.** The ICFA had been inaugurated in 1980, under the sponsorship of Margaret Gaines Swann, the mother of fantasy writer Thomas Burnett Swann (1928–1976), as a memorial to her son. IAFA continued the tradition of inviting professional guests—including "permanent special guest" **Brian Aldiss**—in order to maintain a more eclectic input than the general run of academic conferences. The organization introduced an annual Distinguished Scholarship Award in 1986 and created its own *Journal of the Fantastic in the Arts* in 1988.

**INTERNET SPECULATIVE FICTION DATABASE (ISFDB).** A website established by Al von Ruff in 1995, hosted by Texas A&M University, which maintains **bibliographies** of all novels and most short fiction produced by writers in the **sf** field and other genres of fantasy, along with various supplementary features. The data held on the site overlaps considerably with that available at ***Locus*** Online, but has usually been updated more rapidly. After a brief shutdown in 2003 it resumed operations at www.isfdb.org.

**INTERPLANETARY ROMANCE.** A subgeneric term whose paradigm examples were **Edgar Rice Burroughs's Martian** stories; it was still in use when Gary K. Wolfe reported it in *Critical Terms for Science Fiction and Fantasy* (1986) but **John Clute** replaced it in the second edition of the *Encyclopedia of Science Fiction* with **planetary romance**, on the reasonable grounds that the works in question pay no significant attention to the process of interplanetary travel. The term retains a certain currency, however, because there is a significant category of works—key examples include **H. G. Wells's** *The First Men in the Moon* and **James Blish's** *Welcome to Mars!*—in which the interplanetary voyage *is* a key element, but which nevertheless qualify as "romances" rather than realistic accounts of plausible space programs.

***INTERZONE*.** British **magazine** founded in 1982. Initially a slim quarterly edited by a cumbersome collective, it came under the editorial control of **David Pringle** in 1988, when it moved to a bimonthly schedule, becoming a monthly in 1990. It provided a vital anchorage for the British **sf** community and a ready market for new British writers like **Stephen Baxter** and **Eric Brown**, whose careers it helped to launch.

**INVENTION.** One of the basic story forms of **sf** is that in which a new invention is made and employed for the first time. Many sf **series extrapolate** the gradually unfolding transformative consequences of a technology's adoption; classic examples include the **mosaics** assembled in **Isaac Asimov's** *I, Robot* and **Bob Shaw's** *Other Days, Other Eyes*. Normalizing story-arcs, in which inventions are obliterated in climactic restorations of the status quo—as featured in **Mary Shelley's** *Frankenstein*—make little sense, given that any invention made by the application of the scientific method is, ipso facto, infinitely replicable, so the progressive story **series** is fundamental to the imaginative endeavor of sf. This is one reason why sf is essentially a collective enterprise, in that the extrapolative process may—and perhaps ought—to be carried forward by many different hands, forming a branching pattern of alternatives rather than a single line. Invention stories were first formularized as **Edisonades** in U.S. **dime novels. Hugo Gernsback's magazines** made extravagant use of that formula, but one of the key points of **John Campbell's** new prospectus was the recognition that technological progress is less a matter of sporadic triumphs by magically talented geniuses than the aggregate of extensive experiments carried out by large numbers of individuals applying the scientific method. This notion of invention as a **collaborative** process of trial and error is intrinsic to such Campbellian classics as **George O. Smith's** *Venus Equilateral* mosaic; the same insistence had been imported into **scientific romance** by **M. P. Shiel**, who often waxed eloquent on the subject.

## – J –

**JABLOKOV, ALEXANDER (1956– ).** U.S. writer who began publishing **sf** in 1985. *Carve the Sky* (1991) is a baroque futuristic thriller whose fervent exoticism and melodramatic flair are recapitulated in the **cyberpunk** murder mystery *Nimbus* (1993), the **Martian political fantasy** *River of Dust* (1996), and the sophisticated **space opera** *Deepdrive* (1998). *A Deeper Sea* (1989; exp. 1992) tracks the consequences of human communication with dolphins. Jablokov's early short fiction, including several expansive **time-travel** stories, is collected in *The Breath of Suspension* (1994).

**JAEGER, MURIEL (c1893–?).** British writer whose **sf** consists of meditative ***contes philosophiques***. *The Question Mark* (1926) wonders whether human beings are ready for **Utopian** society. *The Man with Six Senses* (1927) is an **existentialist fantasy** about **ESP.** *Hermes Speaks* (1933) examines the perils of widely believed **prophecy.** *Retreat from Armageddon* (1936) is a conversation piece in which intellectuals hiding out from a second world war discuss humankind's long-term prospects, treating the prospectus of **J. B. S. Haldane's** *Daedalus* with far more reverence than Jaeger's fellow Bloomsbury Group hanger-on **Aldous Huxley.** Her own **Today & Tomorrow** pamphlet was *Sisyphus: The Limits of Psychology* (1928).

**JAKES, JOHN (1932– ).** U.S. writer who worked extensively in **sf** from 1950 until the mid-1970s, when he achieved best-seller status as a writer of historical fiction. His short sf, collected in *The Best of John Jakes* (1977), is darker in tone than most of the **paperback** novels he published profusely between 1967—when he launched a **space opera** sequence with *When the Star Kings Die*—and 1973. *The Asylum World* (1969) is a media **satire**. *Six-Gun Planet* (1970) is an amusing account of a theme-park planet. *Black in Time* (1970) is a didactic trawl through African American history. *Monte Cristo #99* (1970) **transfigures** the Alexandre Dumas classic. *Time Gate* (1972) is an **alternative history** romp. *On Wheels* (1973) is a love story set in a trailer-trash community forbidden by law ever to stop moving.

**JAMESON, MALCOLM (1891–1945).** U.S. writer who began publishing **sf** in 1938, when he was already terminally ill. His novels

*Time Column* (1941), *Tarnished Utopia* (1943, book 1956), and *The Giant Atom* (1944, book 1945 as *Atomic Bomb*) showed more imaginative enterprise than was then common in the more colorful **pulps.** The items making up the **mosaic** *Bullard of the Space Patrol* (1940–1945, book 1951) are representative of the short fiction he produced with astonishing rapidity as his time ran out.

**JANE, FRED T. (1865–1916).** British illustrator famed for his official record of *Jane's Fighting Ships* (1898– ). He turned his expertise to good use in the **illustration** of **George Griffith's** early **future war** stories, and soon wrote one of his own, *Blake of the "Rattlesnake"* (1895). His "Guesses at Futurity" (1894–1895) in the *Pall Mall Magazine* are pale shadows of the work of **Albert Robida.** His other **scientific romances** were the moralistic fantasy *The Incubated Girl* (1896), the improbable interplanetary comedy *To Venus in Five Seconds* (1897), and the melodramatic **apocalyptic fantasy** *The Violet Flame* (1899).

**JANIFER, LAURENCE M. (1933–2002).** U.S. writer born Larry Mark Harris, who used that name on his fiction until 1963, when he recovered the family name abandoned by his Polish-born parents. He began publishing **sf** in 1953. He often wrote in **collaboration**, producing a trilogy of **psi** stories with **Randall Garrett**, bylined Mark Phillips, and three **space operas** with S. J. Treibich. His solo novels *Slave Planet* (1963) and *You Sane Men* (1965, aka *Bloodworld*) are calculatedly provocative. *Power* (1974) is an earnest **political fantasy**; a cynical comedy **series** in the same vein, featuring the aptly named Gerald Knave, comprises *Survivor* (1977), *Knave in Hand* (1979), the **mosaic** *Knave and the Game* (1987), *Alienist* (2001), *The Counterfeit Heinlein* (2001), and *Two* (2003).

**JAPANESE SCIENCE FICTION.** During a late 19th-century phase of rapid modernization, **Vernian** romance was imported into Japan as an inspirational medium; it was soon adapted by such writers as Shunro Oshikawa (1877–1914) to the production of **future war** fiction. U.S. **pulp sf** had some influence in the 1930s, in the work of such writers as Juza Unno (1897–1949), but was regarded as a kind of **children's** fiction—a reputation that the genre retained. Japan proved less vulnerable to the influx of translated American sf after the end of World War II than France or Germany because cultural differences were more extreme, but Hayakawa—which began publishing its first sf line in 1957—established a position as a central supplier of both Western and domestic sf. Takumi Shabano's **fanzine** *Uchujin* ("Comic Dust"), also launched in 1957, became the principal vehicle of Japanese sf **fandom.** As sf imagery became ever more prolific in the media of *manga* **comics** and monster movies, much fiction produced under the sf label retained a similar superficiality, despite the attempts of writers like Taku Mayumura to found a tradition of Japanese **hard sf** and Mototo Arai's introduction of a more conversational style to accounts of encounters with **aliens.** The works that gained the highest reputation were produced by writers of literary fiction like Kobo Abe, author of *Inter Ice Age 4* (1959, tr. 1970) and Sakyo Komatsu, author of *Japan Sinks* (1973, abridged tr. 1976). It was not until **cyberpunk** fiction—much of which makes extravagant use of Japanese decor—was imported in the 1980s that such writers as Chohei Kanbayasi and Mariko Ohara began to produce sf with a confident hard edge. ***Science Fiction Studies*** 88 (November 2002) is a special issue on Japanese sf; other critical studies include Robert Matthew's *Japanese Science Fiction* (1989).

**JARRY, ALFRED (1873–1907). French** avant-garde writer who invented the antiscience of pataphysics, which supposedly deals with the exceptions excluded by scientific laws. His speculative essay "How to Construct a Time Machine" (1899) is typically perverse, but *The Supermale* (1901; tr. 1964) is an unrepentantly frank account of the manner in which a hero endowed with superhumanity might seek to demonstrate his prowess. "Exploits and Opinion of Dr. Faustroll, Pataphysician" (1911; tr. in *Selected Works of Alfred Jarry*, 1965), which advertises itself as a "neoscientific romance," reverted to a more challenging mode of discourse.

**JESCHKE, WOLFGANG (1936– ).** German writer and editor who played a central role in the development of **German sf** as the editor of Heyne Verlag's sf line from 1973–2002, for which he produced more than a hundred showcase **anthologies** mingling domestic and translated work, including material drawn from further afield than the United States and Britain. His first novel, translated as *The Last Day* *of Creation* (1981, tr. 1984) is a **time-paradox** story involving attempts to hijack Middle Eastern oil supplies. *Midas* (1987, tr. 1990) is a near-future thriller involving the production of short-lived human replicates. The novellas "The King and the Dollmaker" (1970, tr. 1976) and "The Land of Osiris" (tr. 1982) further indicate the range and imaginative depth of his work.

**JETER, K. W. (1950– ).** U.S. writer who wrote the avant-gardist **Philip K. Dick**–influenced *Dr. Adder* (1984) in 1972 but only began publishing **sf** with the offbeat thriller *Seeklight* (1975) and the eccentric **visionary fantasy** *The Dreamfields* (1976). *Morlock Night* (1979), a "gonzo-historical" sequel to **H. G. Wells's** *The Time Machine*, helped pioneer the **steampunk** subgenre, to which *Infernal Devices* (1987) is a more self-conscious contribution. When *Dr. Adder* made it into print on the back of the **cyberpunk** movement, Jeter followed it with the sequels *The Glass Hammer* (1985) and *Death Arms* (1987). In *Farewell Horizontal* (1989) biker gangs parasitize the outer surface of an incalculably tall skyscraper. *Madlands* (1991) is a more conventional futuristic thriller. Two sequels to the Philip K. Dick–based movie *Blade Runner* (1995–1996) laid the groundwork for *Noir* (1998), a calculated fusion of sf and film noir aesthetics appreciative of the dominant tone of post-**cyberpunk** fiction.

**JEURY, MICHEL (1934– ). French** writer who published two **sf** novels in 1960 as Albert Higon before reemerging as a central figure of a French sf **new wave** in 1973 with the publication of *Le temps incertain* (tr. 1980 as *Chronolysis*), in which possible futures compete to establish historical roots in the present. His subsequent novels echo the work of **Philip K. Dick** in offering painstaking portraits of ordinary people struggling to get by in worlds whose reality is under threat of disintegration. Some of his later work, including *Le chat venu du futur* (1998), was written in **collaboration** with his daughter Dany.

**JONES, D. F. (1917–1981).** British writer whose first venture into **sf** was *Colossus* (1966), whose eponymous giant computer also featured in *The Fall of Colossus* (1974) and *Colossus and the Crab* (1977). His subsequent **disaster stories** were relentlessly downbeat. *Implosion* (1967) features a plague of sterility; *Denver Is Missing*

(1971, aka *Don't Pick the Flowers*), a geological cataclysm; *The Floating Zombie* (1975), superweapons hijacked by terrorists; *Earth Has Been Found* (1979, aka *Xeno*), an **alien** invasion; and *Bound in Time* (1981), an ill-fated experiment in **time travel**.

**JONES, DIANA WYNNE (1934– ).** British writer, mostly of **children's** fiction, whose unusually inventive fantasies often involve **sf** motifs. *The Homeward Bounders* (1981) is a vivid **Promethean fantasy** involving a **multiverse** of alternative worlds employed as gaming arenas by godlike **aliens.** *Archer's Goon* (1984) is a convoluted sf mystery. *A Tale of Time City* (1987) features a precarious **Utopia** whose control of the time-stream goes gradually awry. *A Sudden Wild Magic* (1992) and *Hexwood* (1993) are **chimerical texts** cleverly juxtaposing sf motifs with magical devices.

**JONES, GWYNETH (1952– ).** British writer who uses her own name for adult work and writes most of her **children's** fiction as Ann Halam. Her first **sf** novel, *Divine Endurance* (1984), follows the adventures of a female **android** in Southeast Asia; *Flowerdust* (1993) is a sequel. *Escape Plans* (1986) describes a computerized **dystopia.** *Kairos* (1988) features a reality-dissolving drug. The trilogy comprising *White Queen* (1991), *North Wind* (1994), and *Phoenix Café* (1997) tracks the progress of an **alien** invasion. The Halam trilogy comprising *The Daymaker* (1978), *Transformations* (1988), and *The Skybreaker* (1989) is a **chimerical** fantasy featuring magic in a postindustrial futuristic setting. *The Hidden Ones* (1988), a children's novel bylined Gwyneth A. Jones, and the adult couplet *Bold as Love* (2001) and *The Burning of the Midnight Lamp* (2003) are similarly chimerical. The Halam novel *Dr. Franklin's Island* (2001) pays homage to **H. G. Wells**, using **biotechnology** to invert the pattern of Dr. Moreau's exploits. *Taylor Five* (2002 as Halam) features a cloned girl on the run with an intelligent orangutan.

**JONES, NEIL R. (1909–1988).** U.S. writer who claimed that his first **pulp sf** story, "The Death's Head Meteor" (1930), included the first appearance in English of the word "astronaut" (it had previously been used in French by **J. H. Rosny aîné**). Almost all his work shares a common **future history** background, much of it comprising a long

**series** begun in "The Jameson Satellite" (1931) whose human hero, resurrected in a **robot** body in the distant future, undertakes a tour of the universe. Sixteen stories were collected in *The Planet of the Double Sun* (1967), *The Sunless World* (1967), *Space War* (1967), *Twin Worlds* (1967), and *Doomsday on Ajiat* (1968) but seven stories from 1940–1951 remained unreprinted when the series was suspended and a previously unpublished item appeared in the **small press** magazine *Astro-Adventures* in 1987.

**JONES, RAYMOND F. (1915–1994).** U.S. writer who began publishing **sf** in 1941. The **pulp** stories collected in *The Toymaker* (1951), the **parallel worlds** novel *Renaissance* (1944, book 1951; aka *Man of Two Worlds*) and *The Cybernetic Brains* (1950, book 1962) show the influence of **A. E. van Vogt.** *The Alien* (1951) is an account of a nasty **alien** discovered in suspended animation. *Syn* (1950 as "Divided we Fall," exp. 1969) describes an **android** revolt. The **mosaic** *This Island Earth* (1952) is about alien interference in human affairs. The **series** comprising "Noise Level" (1952), "Trade Secret" (1953), and "The School" (1954) tracks the development of **antigravity** following a deceptively forced paradigm shift. *The Secret People* (1956, aka *The Deviates*) tracks the replacement of humankind by new species after a nuclear war. Jones also wrote three **children's sf** novels in the 1950s. *Weeping May Tarry* (1978)—cocredited to **Lester del Rey** because it extrapolates his "For I Am a Jealous People" (1954)—is a futuristic **religious fantasy.**

**JÜNGER, ERNST (1895–1998). German** writer who often used **sf** motifs, most significantly in *The Glass Bees* (1957, tr. 1960), a powerful antitechnological allegory, and *Eumeswil* (1980, tr. 1983), in which a historian in an overorganized future society employs a "luminar" to search through time for guidance as to how it might be constructively subverted.

## – K –

**KADREY, RICHARD (1957– ).** U.S. writer who began publishing **sf** in 1985. *Metrophage* (1988) is a near-future thriller whose **cyberpunk**

hardware is earnestly moderated, as might be expected of a writer who went on to produce two *Covert Culture Sourcebooks* and other nonfiction tracking the forms of emergent cyberculture. *Kamikaze l'Amour* (1995) is a surreal futuristic fantasy echoing the work of **J. G. Ballard**.

**KAGAN, JANET (1945– ).** U.S. writer who followed up a **TV tie-in** with the similarly inclined *Hellspark* (1988) before developing a **mosaic** account of a colony on *Mirabile* (1991), where the consequences of the inefficient compaction of gene banks brought from Earth unfold with bizarrely humorous consequences.

**KANDEL, MICHAEL (1941– ).** U.S. writer active as a translator of **Stanislaw Lem** from 1974. His own novels are **satirical** comedies. In *Strange Invasion* (1989) Earth becomes a tourist resort. *In between Dragons* (1990) features an allegorical library whose volumes are **portals** to **chimerical** game worlds. In *Captain Jack Zodiac* (1991) insanity proves to be the last defense and ultimate deterrent in **postholocaust** America. *Panda Ray* (1996) ingeniously mixes mathematics and **mutants**.

**KAPP, COLIN (1928– ).** British writer who began publishing **sf** in 1958, making an early impact with "The Railways Up on Cannis" (1959), one of several accounts of silly solutions to exotic problems provided by *The Unorthodox Engineers* (1979). *Transfinite Man* (1964, aka *The Dark Mind*) is a carbon copy of **Alfred Bester's transfiguration** of *The Count of Monte Cristo*. *The Patterns of Chaos* (1972) echoes **A. E. van Vogt** in similar fashion; *The Chaos Weapon* (1977) revisits its theme. *Cageworld* (1982, aka *Search for the Sun!*), *The Lost Worlds of Cronus* (1982), *The Tyrant of Hades* (1982), and *Star-Search* (1983) are set in a solar system enclosed by a series of **Dyson spheres**.

**KARINTHY, FRIGYES (1887–1938).** Hungarian **satirist** whose works include two sequels to **Jonathan Swift's** *Gulliver's Travels*, combined in translation as *Voyage to Faremido and Capillaria* (1916 and 1921, tr. 1965). Faremido is a machine society whose members communicate musically; Capillaria is a nation on the ocean bed whose inhabitants exhibit an extreme sexual dimorphism, much to the disadvantage of the male of the species.

**KELLER, DAVID H. (1880–1966).** U.S. physician and psychiatrist who was a hobbyist writer for many years before **Hugo Gernsback** recruited him to work for ***Amazing***; his first appearance there was "The Revolt of the Pedestrians" (1928), one of many parables complaining about the dehumanizing effects of technology. Although the ideological thrust of his work was diametrically opposed to Gernsback's, Keller wrote **sf** in some profusion until Gernsback left the field, after which he continued to work for the same patron in the pages of *Sexology*. His novels are mostly **disaster stories**; *The Human Termites* (1929, book 1979) features a dramatic enslavement of humankind; "The Metal Doom" (1932) celebrates the destruction of mechanical civilization; the 1934 title story of *Life Everlasting and Other Tales of Science, Fantasy, and Horror* (1947) depicts the advent of immortality as a tragedy. The second novella in *The Solitary Hunters and The Abyss* (1948) features a drug that obliterates repression of the unconscious, with hideous results. Keller's sf—the best of which is collected, with other material, in *Tales from Underwood* (1952)—provides numerous examples of the **Frankenstein syndrome** at work.

**KELLOGG, M. BRADLEY (1946– ).** U.S. writer who began publishing **sf** with *A Rumor of Angels* (1983). The Lear's Daughters couplet, comprising *The Wave and the Flame* (1986) and *Reign of Fire* (1986), written in **collaboration** with William B. Rossow, is a detailed account of the tribulations of establishing a colony on an **alien** world. *Harmony* (1991) is an ecological fantasy about life on a polluted future Earth.

**KELLY, JAMES PATRICK (1951– ).** U.S. writer who began publishing **sf** in 1975. His friend **John Kessel** named him as a key example of the **cyberpunk**-opposing "Humanist Movement," even though he had a story in *Mirrorshades*; although he denied any such allegiance, his work is consistently interested in social science and suspicious of mechanization. *Planet of Whispers* (1984) and its sequel *Look into the Sun* (1989) comprise an intriguing exercise in "**alien** anthropology."

The **mosaic** *Freedom Beach* (1985) assembles some of his **collaborations** with Kessel. *Wildlife* (1994) is an intense **existentialist fantasy**. *Ninety Per Cent of Everything* (2001 with Kessel and **Jonathan Lethem**) is a **satire** featuring alien "shit dogs." Kelly's short fiction is collected in *Think Like a Dinosaur and Other Stories* (1990) and *Strange but Not a Stranger* (2002).

**KENYON, KAY (?– ).** U.S. writer who began publishing **sf** with *The Seeds of Time* (1997), in which travelers in space and time seek sources to restock the dying Earth. *Leap Point* (1998) describes the invasion of a small town by **aliens** and exotic technology. In *Rift* (1999) a **terraforming** project goes awry. *Tropic of Creation* (2000) is a **planetary romance** featuring an empty world riddled with tunnels. In *Maximum Ice* (2002) and its sequel, *The Braided World* (2003), survivors of a catastrophe in which most humans have been mysteriously transformed into raw information are lured to a distant planet by a message promising to restore missing data.

**KEPLER, JOHN (1571–1630). German** astronomer whose *Somnium* (1634 in Latin, tr. 1967) set a **visionary** frame around a speculative essay attempting to popularize Copernican theory by describing observations of the Earth made from a viewpoint on the **moon**. The conclusion digresses into an account of the way in which lunar life might be adapted to the long day/night cycle—a proto-**evolutionary fantasy** far ahead of its time.

**KESSEL, JOHN (1950– ).** U.S. writer who began publishing parables, **fabulations**, and **metafictions** involving **sf** motifs in 1978; the **mosaic** *Freedom Beach* (1985 with **James Patrick Kelly**) and the stories collected in *Meeting in Infinity* (1992) and *The Pure Product* (1997) are typical of his method. *Good News from Outer Space* (1989) is a **mosaic** account of millenarian anxieties. *Corrupting Dr. Nice* (1997) is a **chimerical** comedy involving time-tourists gathered in Jerusalem to observe the crucifixion.

**KETTERER, DAVID (1942– ).** British-born **Canadian** critic whose *New Worlds for Old: The Apocalyptic Imagination, Science Fiction, and American Literature* (1974) attempts to place **sf** themes in a wider cultural context. He followed up his biography of **James Blish**, *Imprisoned in a Tesseract* (1987), with a similarly intensive study of **John Wyndham**. He wrote a definitive study of *Canadian Science Fiction and Fantasy* (1992).

**KEYES, DANIEL (1927– ).** U.S. writer who became associate editor of the short-lived *Marvel Science Fiction* in 1951, publishing his first **sf** story there in 1952. His work is sparse but includes the classic "Flowers for Algernon" (1959), a fine ***conte cruel*** whose history is chronicled in the memoir *Algernon, Charlie and I: A Writer's Journey* (2000). The novel version issued in 1966 sacrificed the advantages of the form. *The Touch* (1968, aka *The Contaminated Man*) is an account of the psychological trauma of nuclear contamination. His collected short fiction was published in Japanese in 1993.

**KEYES, J. GREGORY (?– ).** U.S. writer in various fantasy genres. The Age of Unreason sequence comprising *Newton's Cannon* (1998), *A Calculus of Angels* (1999), *Empire of Unreason* (2000), and *The Shadows of God* (2001) is set in an **alternative** world where alchemy works; Benjamin Franklin is its protagonist.

**KILIAN, CRAWFORD (1941– ).** U.S.-born writer resident in **Canada since** 1967 who began writing **sf** with *The Empire of Time* (1978), which sets up a **series** of **alternative histories** as dubious escape routes from a near-future **apocalypse**; *The Fall of the Republic* (1987) and *Rogue Emperor: A Novel of the Chronoplane Wars* (1988) are sequels. *Icequake* (1979) and *Tsunami* (1983) track a **disaster** caused by melting icecaps. *Eyas* (1982) is a **far-futuristic fantasy**. In *Brother Jonathan* (1985) **artificial intelligences** intrude upon human/animal communication. *Lifter* (1986) is a juvenile involving mentally powered flight. *Gryphon* (1989) is a humorous account of an **alien** invasion.

**KILLOUGH, LEE (1942– ).** U.S. writer who began publishing **sf** in 1970. *A Voice Out of Ramah* (1979) describes a society in which matriarchy is assured by mass murder. *The Monitors, the Miners, and the Shree* (1980) is a **political fantasy**. *Aventine* (1982) is a **mosaic** set in an extraterrestrial artists' colony. Most of her other novels are futuristic police procedurals.

**KILWORTH, GARRY (1941– ).** British writer whose first **sf** story, "Let's Go to Golgotha" (1975), won a contest sponsored by Gollancz and the *Sunday Times*. The sf novels he wrote before moving on to other genres, including *In Solitary* (1977), *The Night of Kadar* (1978), *Split Second* (1979), *Gemini God* (1981), *A Theatre of Timesmiths* (1984), and *Abandonati* (1988), are tense **existentialist fantasies** whose protagonists struggle to come to terms with exotically stressful situations. His early short fiction is collected in *The Songbirds of Pain* (1984).

**KING, STEPHEN (1947– ).** U.S. writer of best-selling **horror** fiction. His early horror-sf often featured **Fortean** wild talents running out of control, as in *Carrie* (1974), *The Dead Zone* (1979), and *Firestarter* (1980). Some later works, including *The Tommyknockers* (1987) and *Dreamcatcher* (2001), employ **alien** antagonists, following a calculatedly vague precedent set in "The Mist" (1980). *The Stand* (1978, restored text 1990) is a **hybrid apocalyptic fantasy**. The novels King published as Richard Bachmann include the **dystopian** *The Running Man* (1982).

**KINGSBURY, DONALD (1929– ).** U.S. writer resident in **Canada** since 1948, who began publishing **sf**, sparsely, in 1952. *Courtship Rite* (1982, aka *Geta*) is an unusually rich and complex **planetary romance**. *The Moon Goddess and the Son* (1979, book 1986) is a remote prequel about the beginnings of the **space age**; "Shipwright" (1978) belongs to the same **series**. "The Cauldron" (1994) is an excerpt from the unpublished novel *The Finger Pointing Solward*. *Psychohistorical Crisis* (1995 as "Historical Crisis," exp. 2001) is an **Asimovian** fantasy in which **psychohistorians** realize their ambition in a second **galactic empire**. He contributed two novellas (1991–1994) to the Man-Kzin War **sharecropping** enterprise based on **Larry Niven's** Known Space series.

**KIPLING, RUDYARD (1865–1936).** British writer. His **scientific romances** include the **timeslip** fantasy "Wireless" (1902) and, more importantly, the couplet "With the Night Mail" (1905) and "As Easy as A.B.C." (1912), which describes a future society dominated by the Aerial Board of Control. Michael Arlen's *Man's Mortality* (1933) is set in the same **future history**.

**KLEIN, GÉRARD (1937– ). French** writer and critic who began publishing **sf** in 1955. He was sf editor for Robert Laffont in the 1970s and became a prolific writer of analytical nonfiction about the nature and evolution of the genre. His translated novels are *Starmaster's Gambit* (1958, tr. 1973), *The Day before Tomorrow* (1963, tr. 1972), *Mote in Time's Eye* (1965, tr. 1975), and *The Overlords of War* (1971, tr. 1973).

**KNIGHT, DAMON (1922–2002).** U.S. writer and editor who recalled his membership in the famous fan group in *The Futurians* (1977). Like many other members of the group, he published his first **sf** story in one of the **pulps** edited by **Donald A. Wollheim**, but followed Wollheim's example after 1943 by working primarily as an editor. His pioneering digest *Worlds Beyond* (1950–1951) failed after three issues, and his tenure as editor of *If* (1958–1959) was equally brief, but he had greater success with the influential original **anthology series** *Orbit* (21 vols., 1966–1980), which helped to establish the career of **Gene Wolfe** and bring the work of **Kate Wilhelm** (Knight's third wife) to an effective maturity. He began publishing trenchant **criticism** in the late 1940s, complaining bitterly about the logical and aesthetic failings of pulp sf; his reviews were collected in *In Search of Wonder* (1956, revised 1967). He cofounded the **Milford** workshop in 1956 in order to press such demands more urgently, and was also instrumental in founding the **Science Fiction Writers of America** in 1965. His own sf is mostly humorous, his short fiction being collected in *Far Out* (1961), *In Deep* (1963), *Off Center* (1965), and *Turning On* (1966). Notable novellas included "Natural State" (1954; exp. as *Masters of Evolution*, 1959) and the 1954 title story of *Rule Golden* (1979). The **mosaic** *Hell's Pavement* (1955; aka *Analogue Men*) and *The People Maker* (1959; rev. as *A for Anything*) are sober **satires**. His production dwindled while he was busy with *Orbit* but resumed in a more earnest vein in the reformist trilogy comprising *CV* (1985), *The Observers* (1988), and *A Reasonable World* (1991). The elegiac **apocalyptic fantasy** *Why Do Birds?* (1992) is deftly ironic. *Humpty Dumpty: An Oval* (1996) is a surreal fantasy in which the fabric of reality cracks.

**KOONTZ, DEAN R. (1945– ).** U.S. writer who wrote a good deal of **sf** between 1967 and the mid-1970s, after which he concentrated on the thrillers and **horror** novels that boosted him to best-seller status. Many of his early novels, including *Beastchild* (1970), *Dark Symphony* (1970), *A Darkness in My Soul* (1973), and *Nightmare Journey* (1975), make abundant use of the element of horror that was to become his chief stock in trade, albeit in contexts remote from the everyday. He continued to use sf motifs as facilitating devices to pressurize his characters, as in *Twilight Eyes* (1985), *Strangers* (1986), *Watchers* (1987), *Lightning* (1988), *Mr. Murder* (1993), and *Sole Survivor* (1997). *Fear Nothing* (1998) is a story of **genetic engineering** gone awry. *From the Corner of His Eye* (2000) involves quantum mechanics. *By the Light of the Moon* (2002) is a chase thriller whose protagonists are infested with transformative nanobots. *Strange Highways* (1995) includes some sf stories.

**KORNBLUTH, C. M. (1923–1958).** U.S. writer associated with the **Futurians**, who was the most prolific contributor to the **pulp** magazines edited by **Donald A. Wollheim** and **Robert A. W. Lowndes** in 1940–1942, using several pseudonyms and often working in **collaboration**. After active service in World War II he resumed sf writing in 1947, producing a number of classic black comedies and **satirical contes cruels**, including "The Little Black Bag" (1950) and "The Marching Morons" (1951); his work in this vein is collected in *The Explorers* (1954), *A Mile beyond the Moon* (1958), and *The Marching Morons* (1959). His solo novels—*Takeoff* (1952), *The Syndic* (1953), and *Not This August* (1955; aka *Christmas Eve*)—are routine, but he did more interesting work in **collaboration** with **Judith Merril** as "Cyril Judd" in *Outpost Mars* (1952, aka *Sin in Space*) and *Gunner Cade* (1952) before establishing a far more productive partnership with **Frederik Pohl**. Their novels include the classic satirical account of a world ruled by advertising, *The Space Merchants* (1953), the satirical **Odyssean fantasy** *Search the Sky* (1954), the vividly **dystopian** *Gladiator-at-Law* (1955), and the surreal thriller *Wolfbane* (1957). Their collaborative short fiction—some of it posthumous, completed by Pohl after Kornbluth's career was cut short—is collected in *The Wonder Effect* (1962) and *Critical Mass* (1977).

**KRESS, NANCY (1948– ).** U.S. writer who began publishing **sf** in 1976. After several novels in other fantasy genres she published *An*

*Alien Light* (1988), in which **aliens** find human aggression puzzling, and the **dystopian** *Brain Rose* (1990), before extrapolating her ***conte philosophique*** *Beggars in Spain* (1991, exp. 1993) into a **series** of novels in which a technology that frees a new *priviligentsia* from the necessity of sleep greatly enhances the intelligence of its recipients; in *Beggars and Choosers* (1994) and *Beggars Ride* (1996), the new elite institutes a **Utopian** society, which is brought down by the resentment of unenhanced humans and the failure of the sleepless to respond understandingly to further improvements in the superhumanity of their own descendants. *Oaths and Miracles* (1995) and *Stinger* (1998) are **technothrillers**. *Maximum Light* (1998) is a dystopia featuring a plague of sterility. The trilogy comprising *Probability Moon* (2000), *Probability Sun* (2001), and *Probability Space* (2002) is sophisticated **space opera** in which anthropologists investigate alien artifacts, perhaps influenced by her marriage to **Charles Sheffield**. *Crossfire* (2003) has human colonists caught between conflicting alien societies. *Nothing Human* (2003) is a variation on the evolutionary theme of *Beggars Ride*. Kress's inventive short fiction is collected in *Trinity and Other Stories* (1985), *The Aliens of Earth* (1993), and *Beaker's Dozen* (1998).

**KUBE-MCDOWELL, MICHAEL P. (1954– ).** U.S. writer who attached his wife's surname to his own in order to avoid confusion with another writer named McDowell. He began publishing **sf** in 1979. The trilogy comprising *Emprise* (1985), *Enigma* (1986), and *Empery* (1987) is **libertarian space opera** whose darker undercurrents are extrapolated in the **space-age** fantasy *The Quiet Pools* (1990). *Alternities* (1988) juggles **alternative histories**. *Exile* (1992) examines an extraterrestrial **dystopia**. *The Trigger* (1999) is a thriller written in **collaboration** with **Arthur C. Clarke**. In *Vectors* (2002) evidence of a lover's reincarnation challenges a neuroscientist's assumptions.

**KURLAND, MICHAEL J. (1938– ).** U.S. writer whose first **sf** story, published in 1964, was a **collaboration** with **Laurence M. Janifer**. His first novel, *Ten Years to Doomsday* (1964) was a collaboration with Chester Anderson; his second, the **chimerical** *The Unicorn Girl* (1969), was the middle element in a whimsical trilogy whose other volumes were by Anderson and T. A. Waters. His most notable solo work is the political **alternative history** *The Whenabouts of Burr* (1975); *The Last President* (1980, with "S. W. Barton" [Barton S. Whaley]) is in a similar vein.

**KUTTNER, HENRY (1914–1958).** U.S. writer who published a **Lovecraftian** fantasy in ***Weird Tales*** before branching out into the **sf pulps** in 1937. His early work was mostly slapdash **space opera**, including the blithely extravagant novellas "Time Trap" (1938)—one of two "spicy" stories he wrote for *Marvel Science Stories*, whose attempt to eroticize pulp sf was swiftly aborted—and "When New York Vanished" (1940) and "A Million Years to Conquer" (1940, book 1968 as *The Creature from Beyond Infinity*). When he married **C. L. Moore** in 1940, however, the two entered into a close partnership, most of their subsequent work being to some extent **collaborative**. Her stylistically lavish but essentially earnest romanticism counterbalanced his tendency to frivolity and subjected his fertile imagination to a valuable narrative discipline; the alchemical combination of their talents allowed them to become highly prolific and remarkably versatile. They worked for Campbell's ***Astounding***, mostly as Lewis Padgett and Laurence O'Donnell, while simultaneously supplying ***Startling Stories*** with some of the cardinal examples of pulp **science-fantasy**, mostly as "Henry Kuttner" (although Moore was the more active writer of the works in question) and Keith Hammond. Kuttner's chief near-solo contributions appear to have been two **series** of **humorous** stories, one collected as *Robots Have No Tails* (1943–1948, book 1952; aka *The Proud Robot*) and the other (1947–1949) featuring the mutant hillbilly Hogbens; the classic "Mimsy Were the Borogoves" (1943), whose Lewis Carroll influences are further displayed in the remarkable couplet *Tomorrow and Tomorrow* and *The Fairy Chessmen* (1946–1947; book 1951, aka *The Far Reality* and *Chessboard Planet*); and *Fury* (1947, book 1950; aka *Destination Infinity*), a sequel to Moore's novella "Clash by Night."

## – L –

**LAFFERTY, R. A. (1914–2002).** U.S. writer who began publishing **sf** in 1960, soon establishing a reputation for quirky **humorous sf**, although the full extent of his originality only became evident when **small presses** began issuing work that commercial markets had refused. His witty, surreal, and flagrantly **chimerical fabulations** contrive oblique collisions between sf motifs, mythology, and theology, as in *Past Master* (1968), which tracks the investigation of a failed **Utopia** by an artificially reincarnated St. Thomas More. *Space Chantey* (1968) is a **transfiguration** of the *Odyssey*. *The Reefs of Earth* (1968) describes a failed attempt by **alien** children to rid the Earth of humankind. *Fourth Mansions* (1969) is a vivid account of incomprehensible conspiracies contesting the determination of future spiritual evolution. His subsequent sf novels, most notably *Arrive at Easterwine: The Autobiography of a Ktitsec Machine* (1971), the two items in *Apocalypses* (1977), and *The Annals of Klepsis* (1983), became increasingly idiosyncratic. A similar evolution was evident in his short work, the exuberantly inventive collections *Nine Hundred Grandmothers* (1970), *Strange Doings* (1972), and *Does Anyone Else Have Something Further to Add?* (1974) being followed by many others whose inclusions were unrepentantly whimsical. Although he was a writer sui generis, Lafferty's contributions to the **soft** end of the sf spectrum serve to illustrate the remarkable elasticity of that sector of the genre.

**LAGRANGE COLONY.** A term used in **sf** to describe clusters of space habitats aggregated at the "Lagrange points" in the **moon's** orbit around the Earth; they often figure in **space-age** stories published after the notion was popularized by Gerard K. O'Neill's **speculative nonfiction** book *The High Frontier* (1977). The 18th-centurty mathematician Joseph Lagrange had calculated that there would be several points in Jupiter's orbit around the sun where objects could be stably accumulated; two groups of asteroids were eventually found at relevant points. Of the five Lagrange points in the moon's orbit (which form a hexagon with the moon at the sixth point), the one O'Neill reckoned most convenient for colonization is L-5, so that abbreviation is often applied to the relevant Lagrange colonies in sf. Notable examples include *Lagrange Five* (1979) and its sequels by **Mack Reynolds** and **Joe Haldeman's** *Worlds* **series** (1981–1992).

**LAIDLAW, MARC (1960– ).** U.S. writer whose first **sf** publication in 1968 was a **collaboration** with **Gregory Benford**, and who did some subsequent short fiction in collaboration with **Rudy Rucker.** He was included in the **cyberpunk** showcase *Mirrorshades* but *Dad's Nuke* (1985), *Neon Lotus* (1988), and *Kalifornia* (1993) are **satirical** comedies and *The 37th Mandala* (1996) is **horror-sf.**

**LAKE, DAVID J. (1929– ).** Indian-born writer and critic who was a U.K. citizen before immigrating to **Australia** in 1967. His **sf** novels are mostly **planetary romances** that infuse the flamboyant imagery typical of the subgenre with ironic doses of rationalism. *Walkers on the Sky* (1976) features an exotically **terraformed** world. *The Right Hand of Dextra* (1977) and *The Wildings of Westron* (1977) are set on a colony world whose native ecosystems employ dextro-rotatory organic molecules. *The Gods of Xuma* (1978) and *Warlords of Xuma* (1983) offer a skeptical analysis of a world uncannily like **Edgar Rice Burroughs's** Barsoom. *The Fourth Hemisphere* (1980) is a political **satire.** Lake's strong interest in **H. G. Wells**—reflected in his critical work and his compilation of a definitive critical edition of *The First Men in the Moon*—gave rise to the ingenious *Time Machine* sequel *The Man Who Loved Morlocks* (1981). *The Ring of Truth* (1982) is an account of a scientifically guided **conceptual breakthrough** in a world radically different from ours.

**LANDIS, GEOFFREY A. (1955– ).** U.S. space scientist and writer who began publishing **sf** in 1984 with "Elemental," a hybrid **science-fantasy** about a future in which law-governed magic works in parallel with science. Other works ingeniously varying traditional themes include the **time-paradox** story "Ripples in the Dirac Sea" (1988); the Sherlock Holmes story "The Singular Habits of Wasps"; "A Walk in the Sun" (1991), in which a castaway on the **moon** must make heroic efforts to survive; and "Across the Sea of Darkness" (1995), about the lingering effects of a heroic sacrifice on the crew of a starship. His early short fiction is collected in *Impact Parameter and Other Quantum Realities* (2001). *Mars Crossing* (2000) is a paradigm example of modern **hard sf**.

**LANGFORD, DAVID (1953– ).** British writer and critic best known for his fan writing—for which he has won a record number of Hugo awards—and for his newsletter *Ansible*. He began publishing **sf** professionally in 1975. *An Account of a Meeting with Denizens of Another World, 1871, by William Robert Loosely* (1979) is a hoax in which he poses as an editor using modern scientific theory to cast new light on a record of an **alien** encounter allegedly made by a 19th-century cabinetmaker. *The Space Eater* (1992) is a **space opera** spun off from the **speculative nonfiction** book *War in 2080* (1979). *The Leaky Establishment* (1984) is a comedy drawing upon his experiences working as a physicist at the Atomic Weapons Research Establishment at Aldermaston. *The Third Millennium: A History of the World 2000–3000 A.D.* (1985, with **Brian Stableford**) is another exercise in speculative nonfiction. *Earthdoom!* (1987, with "John Grant" [Paul Barnett]) is a **satire** on **disaster stories**. *The Dragonhiker's Guide to Battlefield Covenant at World's Edge: Odyssey Two* (1988) is a collection of parodies. Langford is an exceptionally perceptive **critic** as well as an accomplished humorist; his essays are collected in *Critical Assembly* (1987; rev. 1992), *Critical Assembly II* (1992; combined with the former item as *The Complete Critical Assembly*, 2002) and *Up through an Empty House of Stars: Reviews and Essays* 1980–2002 (2003).

**LANIER, STERLING E. (1927– ).** U.S. writer who began publishing **sf** in 1961. His Münchhausen-esque tall stories, many of which deploy sf motifs, are collected in *The Peculiar Exploits of Brigadier Ffellowes* (1972) and *The Curious Quest of Brigadier Ffellowes* (1986). *Hiero's Journey* (1973) and its sequel, *The Unforsaken Hiero* (1983), comprise a phantasmagoric **Orphean fantasy** set in a **postholocaust** world. *Menace under Marswood* (1983) is a similar exercise with an extraterrestrial setting.

**LARGE, E. C. (?–1976).** British plant pathologist who wrote three notable **scientific romances**. *Sugar in the Air* (1937) is a fierce critique of capitalism's stewardship of technological progress featuring a process of artificial photosynthesis. *Asleep in the Afternoon* (1939) and *Dawn in Andromeda* (1956) are wide-ranging **satirical fabulations**.

**LASSWITZ, KURT (1848–1910).** German historian and writer whose sprawling novel *Auf Zwei Planeten* (1897; abridged tr. as *Two Planets*, 1971) is a crucial landmark of **German sf**. His analysis of the philosophical method employed in his many speculative short stories, contained in the introduction to *Bilder aus der Zukunft* (1878, one item translated 1890 as "Pictures of the Future") anticipates **John Campbell's** manifesto for sf in many important respects. Other ***contes philosophiques*** are collected in *Seifenblasen* (1890) including the **hybrid** texts translated as "When the Devil Took the Professor" (1953), "Aladdin's Lamp" (1953), "Psychotomy" (1955), "The Universal Library" (1958), and *Nie und Nimmer* (1902). He wrote two other sf novels, *Aspira* (1906) and *Sternentau* (1909).

**LATHAM, PHILIP (1902–1981).** Pseudonym used by U.S. astronomer Robert Shirley Richardson on the **sf** that he began publishing in 1946. He wrote two **children's sf** novels in the early 1950s but his **speculative nonfiction**—including *Second Satellite* (1956, as Robert S. Richardson)—and his short fiction, including the cosmological fantasies "The Xi Effect" (1950) and "The Dimple in Draco" (1967), are more significant contributions to the genre.

**LATIN AMERICAN SCIENCE FICTION.** The great success enjoyed in the English-speaking world by such writers of ***contes philosophiques*** as **Jorge Luis Borges** and such "magic realist" writers as Gabriel Garcia Marquez and Paolo Coelho helped to establish the notion that Latin American literature had its own unique claims to greatness, and something of that confidence spilled over into the organization, activity, and assertiveness of **sf** communities. The broad history of Latin American sf is conscientiously mapped out in the showcase **anthology** *Cosmos Latinos* (2003), edited by Andrea L. Bell and Yolanda Molina-Gavilán

The South American nation that developed the most prolific domestic publication in the 1950s and 1960s was Argentina, where several sf **magazines** were produced; Eduardo Goligorsky and Alberto Vanasco put together two notable showcase anthologies in 1966–1967. *Kalpa Imperial* (tr. by **Ursula K. le Guin**, 2003), a **mosaic** history of an imaginary empire by Angélica Gorodischer, is the most significant work of Argentinian sf to have been translated into English. Cuban sf production, following Soviet models, became abundant in the mid-1960s. Mexican sf took off in the same period, its achievements after 1984 being summarized in Ramón López Castro's *Expedición a la Ciencia*

*Ficción Mexicana* (2001). The advent of the Internet helped to forge links between **Spanish**-language sf communities throughout the world; Latin American writers play a prominent role in the *Rede Global Paraliterária* (RPG) or Global Paraliterary Network set up by **Bruce Sterling** and Roberto de Sousa Causo to communicate news and promote discussion of sf throughout the world.

Brazilian sf—represented in the Encounters **series** by contributions from Gerson Lodi-Ribeiro—followed much the same pattern of evolution as Latin American Spanish-language sf, with the support of the publisher Gumercindo Rocha Dorea and Marcelo Branco's **fanzine** *Magelon* (1988– ). Braulio Tavares's *Fantastic, Fantasy and Science Fiction Literature Catalog* (1993) is a comprehensive annotated guide (in English) to Brazilian sf, subsequently supplemented by Roberto S. Causo's *Ficção Cientifica, Fantasia e Horror no Brasil: 1875–1950* (2003). See also SPANISH SCIENCE FICTION and PORTUGUESE SCIENCE FICTION.

**LAUMER, KEITH (1925–1993).** U.S. writer who began publishing **sf** in 1959, soon building a reputation for colorful adventure stories, including works collected in *Nine by Laumer* (1967), *Greylorn* (1968, aka *The Other Sky*), and *Once There Was a Giant* (1971, the 1984 book of the same title has different contents) and a **series** of ironic **political fantasies** starring the unorthodox diplomat Jaime Retief, based on Laumer's own experience in the U.S. diplomatic corps; early examples were collected in *Envoy to New Worlds* (1963; expanded as *Retief: Envoy to New Worlds*, 1987), *Galactic Diplomat* (1965), *Retief: Ambassador to Space* (1960), and *Retief of the CDT* (1971) and recombined in the omnibus *Retief!* (2001). His early novels include an extravagant **time police** series comprising *Worlds of the Imperium* (1962), *The Other Side of Time* (1965), and *Assignment in Nowhere* 1968); a series of enterprising comedies involving **parallel worlds**, beginning with *The Time Bender* (1966); and a series highlighting the nightmarish experiences of **cyborg** soldiers, including *A Plague of Demons* (1965) and the **mosaics** *Bolo: The Annals of the Dinochrome Brigade* (1976) and *Rogue Bolo* (1986). Laumer's favorite theme for independent novels was that of burgeoning superhumanity, presented with **van Vogtian** bravura in such works as *A Trace of Memory* (1963), *The Long Twilight* (1969), and *The Infinite*

*Cage* (1972). The health problems he began to suffer in 1973 never relented; his work after that date became repetitive and dispirited.

**LAURIE, ANDRÉ (1845–1909).** Pseudonym of **French** writer and political activist Paschal Grousset, who began writing **sf** while in exile after the demise of the Paris commune of 1871; a draft of *Les cinq cents millions de la bégum* was given to **Jules Verne**, who rewrote it for publication in 1879 (tr. as *The Begum's Fortune*); three other novels followed the same route, Laurie finally getting a joint byline on the fourth. He then began to write Vernian romances of his own, starting with the wildly improbable *Le exiles de la Terre* (1887, tr. as *The Conquest of the Moon*), in which a giant magnet draws the **moon** out of its orbit and into the Earth's atmosphere. The novels translated as *New York to Brest in Seven Hours* (1888, tr. 1890), *The Secret of the Magian* (1890, tr. 1891), and *The Crystal City under the Sea* (1895, tr. 1896) are moderate by comparison. His lineal descendant Alain Grousset became a popular writer of **children's sf** and fantasy at the end of the 20th century.

**LAWRENCE, LOUISE (1943– ).** Pseudonym of British children's writer Elizabeth Rhoda Wintle Holden, whose first **sf** novel was *Andra* (1971), about teenage rebellion in a claustrophobic future society. *The Power of Stars* (1972) is an unusual account of extraterrestrial oppression. *The Star Lord* (1978) features an **alien** castaway protected by a human teenager. *Children of the Dust* (1985) is an ambitious **postholocaust fantasy**. *The Warriors of Taan* (1986) is a **planetary romance**. In *Dream-Weaver* (1995) a psychic girl anticipates the arrival on her world of human colonists. *The Crowlings* (1999) describes social tensions arising from a human/alien marriage. Her short sf is collected in *Extinction Is Forever and Other Stories* (1990).

**LEE, TANITH (1947– ).** British writer in several fantasy genres. Her **sf** includes the **far-futuristic fantasy** couplet *Don't Bite the Sun* (1976) and *Drinking Sapphire Wine* (1977), the **fabular** *Electric Forest* (1979) and *Day by Night* (1981), and the unconventional love story *The Silver Metal Lover* (1981).

**LE GUIN, URSULA K. (1929– ).** U.S. writer in various genres. As befits the daughter of anthropologist Alfred Kroeber, most of her **sf** novels are painstaking and elegant thought experiments in human science. The majority are set against the common background of the Ekumen, in which many Earth-clone worlds (including Earth) seeded from the planet Hain have developed a wide spectrum of human societies before being regathered into a loose confederation. *Rocannon's World* (1966), *Planet of Exile* (1966), and *City of Illusions* (1967) focus on the social and psychological problems associated with the evolution of telepathic "mindspeech." *The Left Hand of Darkness* (1969) offers a detailed and sympathetic critique of a society of human hermaphrodites. *The Word for World Is Forest* (1972; book 1976) is a heartfelt condemnation of colonialism and imperialism. *The Dispossessed: An Ambiguous Dystopia* (1974) is a tour-de-force contrasting the quasi-**Utopian** anarchist society of an arid **moon** with the capitalist system of its technologically developed parent world. The novellas collected in *Four Ways to Forgiveness* (1995) are set in the deeply problematic aftermath of a slave revolt in a double-planet culture. In *The Telling* (2001) an Ekumen observer visits a remote planet in order to compare and contrast the society of the Maoist Aka with that of fundamentalist UNists. Six of the eight stories in *The Birthday of the World and Other Stories* (2002)—which also includes the **generation starship** novella "Paradises Lost"—are set in the Hainish universe.

Outside the Hainish sequence are *The Lathe of Heaven* (1971), a **metaphysical fantasy** with echoes of **Philip K. Dick**, about dreams that alter reality; the **political fantasy** *The Eye of the Heron* (1978, book 1982); *Always Coming Home* (1986), which describes in great detail the folkways, myths, and artwork of the "posttechnological" society of the Kesh, future inhabitants of northern California; and the **mosaic** *Changing Planes* (2003), which offers an account of a **multiverse** of worlds linked by the investigations of the Interplanary Agency. Le Guin's short sf is mingled with other fantasies in *The Wind's Twelve Quarters* (1975) and *The Compass Rose* (1982). Her highly perceptive critical essays are collected in *The Language of the Night* (1979, rev. 1989) and *Dancing at the Edge of the World* (1989).

**LEIBER, FRITZ (1910–1992).** U.S. writer in several fantasy genres. The early novella *The Dealings of Daniel Kesserich*—written in 1936 but unpublished until 1997—is a **Wellsian** romance but he concentrated on other kinds of fantasy until **John Campbell** persuaded him to write **sf** again after he became a regular in ***Unknown***. In *Gather, Darkness!* (1943; book 1950) future revolutionaries against a technologically sophisticated religious dictatorship disguise their own superscientific armory as witchcraft. *Destiny Times Three* (1945; book 1957), a tale of **alternative histories** at war, laid the groundwork for his liveliest sf enterprise, the Change War **series**, comprising *The Big Time* (1958; book 1961) and the short stories combined with it in the omnibus *The Change War* (1978). Having never succeeded in adapting himself comfortably to Campbell's requirements, Leiber found the new **magazines** of the 1950s more hospitable to such stylish **fabulations** as the heartfelt **postholocaust fantasies** "Coming Attraction" (1951) and the title story of *A Pail of Air* (1964). His most ambitious sf novel, *The Wanderer* (1964), is a striking **disaster story** that was ahead of its time. *The Silver Eggheads* (1958, exp. 1962) and *A Specter Is Haunting Texas* (1969) are amiable **satires**. Later work employing sf motifs included the blithely **chimerical** "Ship of Shadows" (1969) and the surreal alternative-world story "Catch that Zeppelin" (1975). His son Justin (1938– ), an academic philosopher, cast two ***contes philosophiques*** as futuristic novels: *Beyond Humanity* (1987) and *Beyond Gravity* (1988).

**LEINSTER, MURRAY (1896–1975).** Pseudonym of U.S. writer William Fitzgerald Jenkins, who began publishing **sf** in 1919 with the extravagant **timeslip romance** "The Runaway Skyscraper." Much of his early work in the genre—including his first novel, *Murder Madness* (1931)—was fantastic crime fiction, although "The Mad Planet" (1920) and its sequel "The Red Dust" (1921) were adventures in **miniaturization** belatedly aggregated in the **mosaic** *The Forgotten Planet* (1954). His contributions to the sf **pulps** included the pioneering **alternative history** story "Sidewise in Time" (1934), a controversial account of "First Contact" (1945), whose assumptions were questioned in "The Ethical Equations" (1945), and the first desktop computer story "A Logic Named Joe" (1946 as Will F. Jenkins).

Leinster became much more prolific in the 1950s, following up a notable **series** about an eccentric team of troubleshooters, collected in *Colonial Survey* (1955–1956, book 1956), with the more extensive Med Ship series about an interstellar flying doctor (1957–1966), its book versions comprising *The Mutant Weapon* (1959), *This World Is*

*Taboo* (1961), and the collections *Doctor to the Stars* (1964) and *S.O.S. from Three Worlds*, 1967), all assembled in the omnibus *Med Ship* (2002). Leinster's novels were formulaic by comparison with his short fiction; his many **paperback** potboilers included *The Pirates of Zan* (1959), *Time Tunnel* (1964; not to be confused with his 1967 novelization of an episode from the **TV** series *The Time Tunnel*), and *The Duplicators* (1964). *First Contacts: The Essential Murray Leinster* (1998) is the most wide-ranging sampler of his short sf.

**LEM, STANISLAW (1921– ).** Polish writer who began publishing **sf** in 1951, hitting his stride in the latter part of the decade with three **series** of stories, one about space pioneer Ijon Tichy, translated into English in the collections *The Star Diaries* (1976) and *Memoirs of a Space Traveler* (1982); one featuring the more modest adventures translated in *Tales of Pirx the Pilot* (1979) and *More Tales of Pirx the Pilot* (1982); and a set of **fabular contes philosophiques** featuring two inquisitive **robots**, some of which are translated in *The Cyberiad* (1974) and *Mortal Engines* (1977). His translated novels include the grotesque **planetary romance** *Eden* (1959; tr. 1989), an account of an equally grotesque Earth discovered by an astronaut suffering the effects of time-dilatation in *Return from the Stars* (1961, tr. 1980), and two classic accounts of painful confrontation with incomprehensible **aliens**, *Solaris* (1961, tr. 1970) and *The Invincible* (1964, tr. 1973).

Lem's subsequent work built on foundations laid in the earlier period to construct a more blackly comic and scathingly **satirical** commentary on the utter folly of all human attempts to understand the world or other people. This thesis is developed in the **metafictional** works translated as *His Master's Voice* (1968, tr. 1983); *A Perfect Vacuum* (1971, tr. 1978), a collection of introductions to nonexistent texts; and *Imaginary Magnitude* (1973, tr. 1984); and the more orthodox novels translated as *The Futurological Congress* (1971, tr. 1974), *Memoirs Found in a Bathtub* (1971, tr. 1973), *Fiasco* (1986, tr. 1987), and *Peace on Earth* (1987, tr. 1994). This philosophical position caused him to be derisively critical of American sf, with the exception of the more paranoid works of **Philip K. Dick**.

**L'ENGLE, MADELEINE (1918– ).** U.S. writer who published an **sf** story in 1956 and produced a good deal of other work for adults and children before breaking new ground in the graphic **Orphean fantasy** *A Wrinkle in Time* (1962), whose enterprising heroine must win her father back from an oppressive **alien** computer. The heroine's other adventures in the same spirit are *A Wind in the Door* (1973), *A Swiftly Tilting Planet* (1978), *Many Waters* (1986), and *An Acceptable Time* (1989). The couplet comprising *The Arm of the Starfish* (1965) and *The Young Unicorns* (1968) makes more tentative use of sf motifs.

**LE QUEUX, WILLIAM (1864–1927).** French-born British journalist who incorporated **sf** elements into such thrillers as *A Madonna of the Music Halls* (1897) and leapt onto the **future war** bandwagon in *The Great War in England in 1897* (1894) and *The Invasion of 1910* (1906); he also directed his paranoid fantasies about Germany's "invisible hand" into the pioneering of the spy story genre. When World War I began he accepted that he had been wrong to neglect the destructive power of aircraft and tried to make amends in *The Zeppelin Destroyer* (1916). *The Terror of the Air* (1920) is a belated attempt to renew anti-German alarmism.

**LESSING, DORIS (1919– ).** Writer of literary fiction born in what is now Iran and self-exiled to the United Kingdom, from what is now Zimbabwe, since 1959. *The Four-Gated City* (1969) carried her "Children of Violence" sequence into the near future. *Memoirs of a Survivor* (1974) is a measured **apocalyptic fantasy.** The Canopus in Argos **series**—comprising *Shikasta* (1979), *The Marriage between Zones Three, Four, and Five* (1980), *The Sirian Experiments* (1981), *The Making of the Representative for Planet 8* (1982), and *Documents Relating to the Sentimental Agents in the Volyen Empire* (1983)—uses a **galactic empire** as background for a **hybrid religious** and **political fantasy.** *The Fifth Child* (1988) features an **alien** baby. *Mara and Dan: An Adventure* (1998) is a **far-futuristic fantasy** set in the aftermath of an **ecocatastrophic** Ice Age.

**LETHEM, JONATHAN (1964– ).** U.S. writer who began publishing **fabulations** including **sf** motifs in 1989. *Gun, with Occasional Music* (1994) is surrealized noir fiction. *Amnesia Moon* (1995) is a hectic **Orphean fantasy** in a **postholocaust** setting. In *As She Climbed across the Table* (1997) a particle physicist creates an artificial void that comes between her and her lover. *Girl in Landscape* (1998) describes its heroine's sexual awakening in a new frontier world. *This Shape We're In* (2000) is a surreal fabulation. His short fiction is collected in *The Wall of the Sky, the Wall of the Eye* (1996).

**LEVI, PRIMO (1919–1987).** Italian chemist and writer famed for his accounts of Auschwitz. His short story collections include numerous **fabulations** and ***contes philosophiques*** based in scientific ideas, especially those translated as *The Periodic Table* (1974, tr. 1984) and *The Sixth Day and Other Stories* (1966 and 1977, tr. 1990). The fabulations in *The Mirror Maker* (1989) are **chimerical.**

**LEVIN, IRA (1929– ).** U.S. writer in various genres. His **sf** consists of the **dystopian** *This Perfect Day* (1970) and two **satires** cast as thrillers; *The Stepford Wives* (1972) disguises an account of female paranoia as a **feminist** parable, while *The Boys from Brazil* (1976) employs multiple clones of Hitler to illustrate the folly of extreme genetic determinism.

**LEVINSON, PAUL (1947– ).** U.S. writer who began publishing **sf** in 1993. His sophisticated **hard sf** is closely related to his work in the popularization of science and Internet education, and as editor of the *Journal of Social and Evolutionary Systems*. *The Silk Code* (1999), *The Consciousness Plague* (2002), and *The Pixel Eye* (2003) are elements of a **series** of forensic science detective stories. In *Borrowed Tides* (2001) the first mission to Alpha Centauri is led by a philosopher of science and specialist in Native American mythology. Anxieties about the future of the space program illustrated in the novella "Loose Ends" (1997) are amplified in his **speculative nonfiction** book *Realspace: The Fate of Physical Presence in the Digital Age, on and off Planet* (2003).

**LEVY, ROGER (1955– ).** British writer who began publishing **sf** with *Reckless Sleep* (2000), a thriller set in a disaster-prone world whose inhabitants use **virtual reality** to distract themselves from their plight; the sequel, *Dark Heavens* (2003), features an epidemic of suicide. *Reckless Days* (2001) and *Bad Memory* (2002) are similarly dour extrapolations of contemporary crises.

**LEWIS, C. S. (1898–1963).** British writer famed for the ingenuity of his exercises in Christian apologetics. Those co-opting **sf** motifs include the Cosmic Trilogy comprising *Out of the Silent Planet* (1938), *Perelandra* (1943), and *That Hideous Strength* (1945), which persecute the alleged heresies of **H. G. Wells** and **J. B. S. Haldane** with inquisitorial zeal.

**LEWITT, SHARIANN (1954– ).** U.S. writer who began publishing **sf** in 1982. *White Wing* (1985), written with **Susan M. Shwartz** and bylined Gordon Kendall, was followed by several solo ventures in **military sf** signed S. N. Lewitt, including *Angel at Apogee* (1987), *Cyberstealth* (1989), *Dancing Vac* (1991), and *Blind Justice* (1991). Her **cyberpunk** thriller, *Cybernetic Jungle* (1992) and **biotechnological** fantasy *Songs of Chaos* (1993) carried the same byline, but she used her full name on *Memento Mori* (1995), in which an **AI** takeover on a bleak world is opposed by artists and philosophers; *Interface Masque* (1997), featuring intrigues in future Venice; and *Rebel Sutra* (2000), a love story set in a society stratified by genetic enhancement.

**LEY, WILLY (1906–1969).** German-born rocket pioneer who immigrated to the United States in 1935. He was one of the first and most enduring **prophets** of the **space age**, and one of the first popularizers of science to work in the pages of the **sf magazines.** He announced "The Dawn of the Conquest of Space" in ***Astounding*** in 1937, and published in several other **pulps** before becoming science editor of ***Galaxy*** from 1952–1969. He published four sf stories bylined Robert Willey in 1937–1940.

**LIBERTARIAN SF.** The political philosophy of libertarianism aims at the maximization of individual freedom by the careful minimization of government into a "night-watchman state" whose obligations are confined to robust defense and a streamlined criminal justice system. Its orthodox **elaboration** by Robert Nozick's *Anarchy, State and Utopia* (1974) is paralleled by the "objectivist" writings of **Ayn Rand**, who routinely used fiction, including **sf**, as a means of popularization. Much U.S. sf, especially that developing the core mythology of the **space age**, showed libertarian leanings in the 1940s, encouraged by the radical pragmatism of **John Campbell** and **Robert A. Heinlein.** Such political philosophizing became increasingly commonplace and strident during the 1960s, sporadically evident in the work of writers such as **Poul Anderson** and **Vernor Vinge** and consistently assertive in the work of writers like **James P. Hogan**, **Jerry Pournelle**, and libertarian activist **L. Neil Smith.** The Libertarian Futurist Society sponsors the annual Prometheus Award for the best libertarian sf novel of the year.

**LICHTENBERG, JACQUELINE (1942– ).** U.S. writer who began publishing **sf** in 1969. Almost all of her relevant work is **ambiguous science-fantasy** examining intimate interspecies relationships in a **galactic empire** setting; the most significant of three subsidiary series is the Sime/Gen sequence launched in *House of Zeor* (1974), to which other writers also contributed.

**LIGHTMAN, ALAN P. (1948– ).** U.S. physicist and writer whose account of *Einstein's Dreams* (1993) deftly combines scientific and literary notions of the relativity of time and space. *Good Benito* (1995) is a bildungsroman about a scientist. *Reunion* (2003) is an ingenious **timeslip romance.** His **poetry** includes items in the journal *Science* (1982). His essays on the "human side of science" collected in *Time Travel and Papa Joe's Pipe* (1984) and *A Modern-Day Yankee in a Connecticut Court* (1986) include several **fabular** parables.

**LIGNY, JEAN-MARC (1956– ). French** writer in various fantasy genres whose first **sf** novels, *Temps blancs* (1979) and *Biofeedback* (1979), featured worlds exotically perverted by the power of dictatorial computers. The five-volume *Chroniques des nouveaux mondes* (1991) explores aspects of a **galactic empire**, while *Cyberkiller* (1993) and *Inner City* (1996) are **cyberpunk** thrillers.

**LINAWEAVER, BRAD (1952– ).** U.S. writer who began publishing **sf** with the **alternative history** *Moon of Ice* (1982, exp. 1988), in which Joseph Goebbels becomes a pragmatic defender of rationalism following a Nazi victory in World War II. "Destination: Indies" (1992) features an alternative Christopher Columbus, "Unmerited Favor" (1993) a more militant Jesus, and *Anarquía* (2003, with J.

Ken Hastings) an alternative Spanish Civil War. His short fiction is sampled in *Clownface* (1999).

**LITTLE GREEN MEN.** The representation of **aliens** as diminutive green humanoids, often with antennas sprouting from their heads, became conventional among cartoonists in the 1940s; after 1950 such beings were routinely equipped with **flying saucers.** Although the derisive image was resented by **sf** readers and writers, it was too tempting for ever-desperate providers of **cover art** to resist, and was mischievously adopted into such **satirical** fantasies as **Fredric Brown's** *Martians Go Home* (1955). The symbolic utility of the image went into an inevitable decline when "alien abductees" began insisting in the 1980s that the navigators of flying saucers were actually gray.

**LLEWELLYN, EDWARD (1917–1984).** Welsh-born **Canadian** writer who began publishing **sf** with *The Douglas Convolution* (1979), in which a **time-traveling** mathematician helps to solve the social problems consequent upon a plague of sterility. *The Bright Companion* (1980) is a sequel, *Prelude to Chaos* (1983) a prequel. *Salvage and Destroy* (1984) and *Fugitive in Transit* (1985) extrapolate the same **future history** into **space opera**, while *Word-Bringer* (1986) describes an **alien**-inspired technological revolution on Earth.

**LOCKE, GEORGE W. (1936– ).** British **small press** publisher and **bibliographer**, who published six **sf** stories between 1957 and 1966, all but the first bylined Gordon Walters, but made a more substantial contribution to the genre in the annotated bibliographies issued by his Ferret Fantasy imprint, especially *Voyages in Space: A Bibliography of Interplanetary Fiction, 1801–1914* (1975) and the bibliography of his own collection *A Spectrum of Fantasy* (three vols., 1980–2002). Other books issued by the press include the **anthology** *Worlds Apart* (1972) and **George Griffith's** *The Raid of "Le Vengeur"* (1974).

***LOCUS.*** U.S. periodical founded in 1968 as a **fanzine** newsletter, which soon came under the sole editorship of Charles N. Brown (1937– ), who retired from his job in 1976 to devote himself to it full-time. By that time it was the field's trade journal, showcasing interviews with writers, reviewing the leading books and **magazines**, conducting an annual reader survey (in association with which it made its own annual awards in numerous categories), issuing regular lists of forthcoming books, and heroically attempting to maintain a record of every work of fantastic fiction published in the United States. By 1980 it was indispensable to anyone professionally involved in the field. *The Locus Index to Science Fiction*, comprehensive since 1984, was integrated with William G. Contento's *Index to Science Fiction Anthologies and Collections* for regular publication in CD-ROM form in 1998 and was made available at the *Locus* On-Line website at www.locusmag.com, which also carries news, comprehensive lists of forthcoming books, links to news items and articles on **sf** in other online publications, and so forth. Locus Press also produced a companion CD-ROM version of Stephen T. Miller and Contento's *Science Fiction, Fantasy, and Weird Fiction Magazine Index (1890–1998)*.

**LONDON, JACK (1876–1916).** U.S. writer in various genres whose first **sf** story was "A Thousand Deaths" (1899), one of several accounts of extraordinary **inventions.** He also wrote a number of prehistoric fantasies, including the novel *Before Adam* (1906). His sf became stridently serious as it took aboard his political passions; *The Iron Heel* (1907) is a **dystopian** account of capitalism rampant, viewed from the perspective of the socialist historians of a more remote future; "Goliah" (1908) and "The Dream of Debs" (1909) are optimistic companion pieces. Similar anxieties about the likelihood of things getting far worse before they get better are displayed in the classic **disaster story** *The Scarlet Plague* (1912, book 1914) and the epic **visionary fantasy** *The Star Rover* (1915, aka *The Jacket*). "The Red One" (1918) is a parable in which Stone Age tribesmen worship an extraterrestrial object. Most of London's short sf is collected in *The Science Fiction of Jack London* (1975), edited by Richard Gid Powers.

**LONG, FRANK BELKNAP (1903–1994).** U.S. writer associated with ***Weird Tales*** in the 1920s, who knew **H. P. Lovecraft** and became a notable contributor to the **Cthulhu Mythos**, some of the relevant stories being collected in *The Hounds of Tindalos* (1946). His early stories for the **sf pulps** included the **far-futuristic fantasies** "The Last

Men" (1934) and "Green Glory" (1935); *The Rim of the Unknown* (1972) collects all of his work in that vein except a **series** about a "botanical detective" collected as *John Carstairs: Space Detective* (1949). *Space Station No. 1* (1957) and the mildly erotic *Woman from Another Planet* (1960) were followed by many other **paperback** potboilers, of which the most notable is the paranoid fantasy *Lest Earth Be Conquered* (1966, aka *The Androids*).

**LONGYEAR, BARRY B. (1942– ).** U.S. writer who began publishing **sf** in 1978. His early short stories were collected in *Manifest Destiny* (1980) and *It Came from Schenectady* (1984), most notably the melodramatic novella "Enemy Mine" (1979), in which stranded human and **alien** enemies must forge an alliance in order to survive; it became the basis of a convoluted **series** collected in the **mosaic** omnibus *The Enemy Papers* (1998). The mosaic trilogy comprising *City of Baraboo* (1980), *Circus World* (1981), and *Elephant Song* (1982) follows the adventures of a castaway circus troupe. The **dystopian** *Sea of Glass* (1987) and the **satirical** *Naked Came the Robot* (1988) are conspicuously downbeat by comparison.

**LORRAINE, LILITH (1894–1967).** Pseudonym of U.S. writer Mary Maude Wright, née Dunn. Her first **sf** story, *The Brain of the Planet* (1929), was issued as a booklet by **Hugo Gernsback**, perhaps because he feared that its Marxist **Utopianism** might be too controversial for ***Wonder Stories***. He did publish the similarly socialist "Into the 28th Century" (1930) and three minor items in his magazines, but Lorraine became frustrated with the difficulty of expressing her ideas in **magazine** fiction and switched to **poetry**; she was probably the first person to conceive of some of her work as sf poetry; in 1940 she founded the **small press** Avalon, which issued her long poem *They* (1943) and the first sf poetry magazine *Challenge*, although her collection *Wine of Wonder* (1952) appeared under another imprint. *Ape into Pleiades* (1998) adds a biography and **bibliography** to several similar items.

**LOST WORLD STORIES.** The "lost race" genre of popular fiction—a subcategory of **imaginary voyages**—was a useful medium for some kinds of **speculative fiction** in the early days of **scientific ro-**

**mance** and **pulp** fiction, although the world ran short of useful terra incognita early in the 20th century. In order for such a fictional milieu to qualify as "lost," it needs to feature a civilization built by people displaced from known history in the distant past, like the technologically sophisticated societies featured in Joseph Shield Nicholson's *Thoth* (1888) or Jules Lermina's *Mystère-ville* (1904, book 2002), or survivals from prehistory, as in Charles Derennes' *Le peuple du pôle* (1907) or **Conan Doyle's** *The Lost World* (1912). Examples of the latter kind need not feature a human society—hence the preference for "lost world" over "lost race"—although they usually do, no matter how anachronistic such an inclusion may be.

The development of the **galactic empire** scenario in the 1950s facilitated the evolution of a directly descendant subgenre whose lost worlds are Earth-clone colonies. The new subgenre provided a convenient framework device for a good deal of human science-based sf, including **Ursula K. Le Guin's** Hainish series and various works by **Jack Vance**, **Lloyd Biggle Jr.**, and **H. Beam Piper.** The **steampunk** subgenre has also renewed the format by featuring Earthly lost worlds redolent with **metafictional** nostalgia; notable examples include "Black as the Pit, from Pole to Pole" (1977) by **Steven Utley** and **Howard Waldrop** and *The Hollow Earth* (1990) by **Rudy Rucker.**

**LOUDON, JANE, née Webb (1807–1858).** British writer who was inspired by the example of **Mary Shelley's** *Frankenstein* to produce the anonymous *The Mummy! A Tale of the Twenty-Second Century* (1827, rev. 1828; abridged 1995), an elaborate **political fantasy** whose background includes numerous technological innovations.

**LOVE, ROSALEEN (1940– ). Australian** writer who began publishing **fabulations** involving **sf** motifs in 1985; her collections are *The Total Devotion Machine and Other Stories* (1989) and *Evolution Annie and Other Stories* (1993).

**LOVECRAFT, H. P. (1890–1937).** U.S. writer who joined the United Amateur Press Association in 1914 and produced much of his early fiction in connection with that enterprise. It put him in contact with **Clark Ashton Smith**, **Frank Belknap Long**, and others, with whom he formed a neoromantic *cénacle* dedicated to the production of weird fiction adapted for survival in a rationalistic era. The **mosaic** *Herbert West—Reanimator* (1922, booklet 1977) is tongue-in-cheek **horror-sf** but most of his work for ***Weird Tales*** is in deadly earnest. Although he turned down the editorship of the magazine in 1924, he exerted a considerable influence on many of its key contributors by means of voluminous correspondence; his disciples included **Donald Wandrei**, **August Derleth**, **Robert Bloch**, **Henry Kuttner**, and **Fritz Leiber.** Derleth and Wandrei founded Arkham House to reprint his work, providing a vital haven for many other writers of offbeat fiction.

Lovecraft's later works, especially those belonging to the **Cthulhu Mythos**, used motifs drawn from sf—including **aliens**, **parallel worlds**, and **biotechnological** experimentation—to develop a distinctive kind of "cosmic horror" based on the notion that human delusions of intellectual grandeur are absurd in a vast and implicitly hostile universe. The distinctive prose style of such fictions extended by degrees from a quasi-clinical mode into passages of adjective-dense exposition; those making the most conspicuous use of sf motifs are the novellas *The Shadow over Innsmouth* (1936), *The Shadow Out of Time* (1936, restored text 2002), and "At the Mountains of Madness" (1936, abridged), all of which were included in the first Arkham House collection *The Outsider and Others* (1939). Lovecraft's complete works were subsequently re-edited in three volumes: *The Dunwich Horror and Others* (1963, corrected 1985); *At the Mountains of Madness and Other Novels* (1964, corrected 1985); and *Dagon and Other Macabre Tales* (1965, corrected 1986).

**LOVEGROVE, JAMES (1966– ).** British writer in various genres, whose first (marginal) **sf** story, *The Hope* (1990), features a ship adrift for decades and the society that evolves thereon. *Days* (1997) is a **satire** set in a future department store. *The Foreigners* (2000) is a detective story in which benevolent **aliens** are tempted to leave Earth when one of their company is murdered. *Untied Kingdom* (2003) is a postdisaster **Odyssean fantasy.** His short fiction is sampled in *Imagined Slights* (2001).

**LOWNDES, ROBERT A. W. (1916–1998).** U.S. editor and writer who, like fellow members of the **Futurians**, wrote much of his early

**sf** pseudonymously and in **collaboration**. Like **Donald A. Wollheim** he became a **pulp** editor, taking over *Future Fiction* and *Science Fiction Quarterly* in 1941–1943 and resuming his position when they were revived after the war in 1950. He also edited *Dynamic Science Fiction* and *Science Fiction Stories* in the 1950s; when the chain to which they belonged folded in 1960 he began working for Health Knowledge Inc., gradually accumulating a number of fantasy **magazines** under that imprint—including *Famous Science Fiction*—until its demise in 1970. He also edited Avalon Books' sf line in the late 1950s and early 1960s. He wrote a novel in collaboration with **James Blish**, *The Duplicated Man* (1953; book 1959), but his most notable sf work is *Believers' World* (1952 as "A Matter of Faith," exp. 1961) featuring an odd religion invented by the inhabitants of a **lost world.**

**LUNDWALL, SAM J. (1941– ).** Swedish writer, editor, and translator who became the central figure of the Swedish **sf** community in the mid-1950s and began publishing sf in 1963. He translated his own survey of the genre as *Science Fiction: What It's All About* (1969, tr. 1971) and four of his novels as *Alice's World* (1970), *No Time for Heroes* (1970), *Bernhard the Conqueror* (1973), and *A.D. 2018, or the King Kong Blues* (1974, tr. 1975). The last-named—a vitriolic futuristic **satire**—is more typical of his subsequent work than the earlier items. Lundwall edited an sf line for an established publisher from 1970–1973 before founding his own specialist press, Delta, which issued more than 300 books before its demise in 1991; he also revived the Swedish sf magazine *Jules Verne-Magasinet*, whose original incarnation had run from 1940–1948. He served as the European representative of the **Science Fiction Writers of America** until 2003.

**LUPOFF, RICHARD A. (1935– ).** U.S. writer active in **fandom** before writing professionally. He published a study of *Edgar Rice Burroughs: Master of Adventure* (1965, rev. 1968 and 1975) before his first novel, the **far-futuristic fantasy** *One Million Centuries* (1967, rev. 1981). He carried forward a strong interest in parody and pastiche from his fan-writing days, lending his professional work an offbeat **metafictional** quality, which became increasingly surrealized in the material gathered into the **mosaics** *Sacred Locomotive Flies* (1971) and *Space War Blues* (1978). *Into the Aether* (1974) pays eccentric homage to **Vernian** romance, *The Triune Man* (1976) to **comic** book **sf**, and the brief *Nebogipfel at the End of Time* (1979) to **H. G. Wells**, while *Circumpolar!* (1984) and *Countersolar!* (1986) set **steampunk** adventures on the flat disk of an alternative Earth. He returned to far-futuristic fantasy more earnestly in *Sun's End* (1984) and *Galaxy's End* (1986) but never completed the projected trilogy. *Lovecraft's Book* (1985) and stories in *The Digital Wristwatch of Philip K. Dick* (1985) were further homages. *Claremont Tales* (2001) and *Claremont Tales II* (2002) collect stories in various genres.

**LYMINGTON, JOHN (1911–1983).** Pseudonym used for adult **sf** by British writer John Newton Chance, who published detective stories under his own name. He employed sf motifs in a number of **children's** stories before inventing "John Lymington" in a blatant attempt to cash in on the success of **John Wyndham.** His **disaster stories**, usually embellished with **alien** intrusions, include *Night of the Big Heat* (1959), *The Giant Stumbles* (1960), *The Grey Ones* (1960), *The Coming of the Strangers* (1961), *A Sword above the Night* (1962), *The Sleep Eaters* (1963), *The Screaming Face* (1963), and the atypically **satirical** *Froomb!* (1964). His work became more various thereafter, often employing occult fiction motifs within **horror-sf** formulas, as in *Ten Million Years to Friday* (1967), *A Caller from Overspace* (1979), and *Voyage of the Eighth Mind* (1980).

**LYNN, ELIZABETH A. (1946– ).** U.S. writer who began publishing **sf** in 1976. Most of her work is in other fantasy genres, but her early sf stories are mingled with other material in *The Woman Who Loved the Moon and Other Stories*. Her first novel, *A Different Light* (1978), is an **existential fantasy** making unusual use of **hyperspace.** Her other sf novel, *The Sardonyx Net* (1981), is a complex **political fantasy** about the evils of slavery.

## – M –

**MACAPP, C. C. (1913–1971).** Byline used on all but one of his books by U.S. writer Carroll M. Capps, who began publishing **sf** in 1960 after illness forced him to retire from salaried employment. The **mosaic**

*Omha Abides* (1964–1966, book 1968), in which humans rebel against their **alien** masters, established a pattern, reiterated in *Prisoners of the Sky* (short version 1966, book 1969) and *Recall Not Earth* (1970), in which heroic individuals recover from despair to carry forward bold projects. *Secret of the Sunless World* (1969) carried his own name. *Worlds of the Wall* (1964, exp. 1969) develops a conventional quest fantasy in an exotic setting. In *Subb* (1968, exp. 1971) aliens donate a technology of artificial resurrection to humankind. *Bumsider* (1972) contrasts the worlds of Inside and Outside.

**MACISAAC, FRED (1886–1939).** U.S. writer of **pulp** fiction, prolific between 1925–1936. He first ventured into **sf** in *The Vanishing Professor* (1926, book 1927), a routine thriller. "The Seal of Satan" (1926) and "The Great Commander" (1926), both published anonymously, and "World Brigands" (1928) are vivid **political fantasies**, the second recounting the rise and fall of an American dictator and the third featuring an Anglo-American war fought over unpaid war debts, settled by the threat of an atomic bomb. After *The Last Atlantide* (1927–1928, book 2000) and *The Hothouse World* (1931, book 1965)—a messianic fantasy in which the survivors of a global catastrophe huddle in a single building for fear that the air outside is not breathable—MacIsaac attempted another explicit **political fantasy** in "The Tyrant of Technocracy" (1933), but then returned to conventional ground in "The Lost Land of Atzlan" (1933).

**MACKAY, SCOTT (1957– ). Canadian** writer who began publishing **sf** in 1990. In *Outpost* (1998) **aliens** interfere with human history. *Orbis* (2002) extends the theme considerably in an **alternative history** story in which the Roman Empire is exported to the stars.

**MACLEAN, KATHERINE (1925– ).** U.S. writer whose first **sf** publication was "Defense Mechanism" (1949), an early contribution to the ***Astounding*** **psi**-boom. Other groundbreaking stories included "Incommunicado" (1950), which describes the acceleration of spacecraft by "slingshot effect"; "Syndrome Johnny" (1951, published under the name of her then-husband Charles Dye), which features virus vectors used to achieve genetic transformations; and "The Snowball Effect" (1952), which sets out the theory that subsequently became known as a pyramid scheme. The problematically assisted evolution of mankind also provided the theme of the 1953 novella that became the title story of *The Diploids* (1962). MacLean's later work failed to sustain this innovative flair. "Second Game" (1958, exp. as *Cosmic Checkmate* 1962; further exp. 1981), written with Charles V. deVet, is a **political fantasy**, as is the **mosaic** *The Missing Man* (1975). *Dark Wing* (1979 with Carl West) is a juvenile about a future in which medicine is outlawed. More short fiction is collected in *The Trouble with You Earth People* (1980).

**MACLEOD, IAN R. (1956– ).** British writer who began publishing **sf** in 1989. He was a prolific short story writer, his early work being collected in *Voyages by Starlight* (1997). *The Great Wheel* (1997) is a futuristic thriller in which a priest in Africa investigates a mysterious disease. The **SETI** fantasy "New Light on the Drake Equation" (2001) is a poignant commentary on the demise of 20th-century sf's mythical future. The **far-futuristic fantasy** "Breathmoss" (2002) is part of a **series** set in the Ten Thousand and One Worlds. *The Light Ages* (2003) is a **hybrid alternative history** in which technology is based on a substantial "aether" discovered in the Renaissance, which permits the promiscuous manipulation of matter.

**MACLEOD, KEN (1954– ).** Scottish writer who began publishing **sf** with *The Star Fraction* (1995), a futuristic thriller set in a fragmented Britain. Almost all his works are loosely organized into a **future history** with **alternative historical** branches. His explicit **political fantasies**—*The Star Fraction*, *The Stone Canal* (1996), in which **artificial intelligences** play a crucial role in the colonization of New **Mars**, and *The Sky Road* (1999), in which the space program is problematically reborn after a catastrophic collapse of civilization—adopt a left-wing stance rare in **hard sf**, although its anarchistic elements are attractive to some American **libertarians.** Later volumes in the **series**—*The Cassini Division* (1997) and the Engines of Light sequence, comprising *Cosmonaut Keep* (2000), *Dark Light* (2001), and *Engine City* (2002)—employ a much larger stage. In the unconnected novella *The Human Front* (2002), **aliens** tamper with human history.

**MACLEOD, SHEILA (1939– ).** Scottish writer whose second novel, *The Snow-White Soliloquies* (1970), is a **feminist transfiguration** of the fairy tale with a **hard sf** edge. *Xanthe and the Robots* (1977) is a conscientious ***conte philosophique*** describing the development of **artificial intelligence.** The **ambiguous existentialist fantasy** *Circuit-Breaker* (1978) strikes a careful balance between **inner** and **outer space.**

**MAD SCIENTISTS.** A class of villains employed in popular fiction, whose prototypes include **Mary Shelley's** Victor Frankenstein and **Robert Louis Stevenson's** Henry Jekyll. Insofar as **sf** is subject to the demands of melodrama, its plot formulas require antagonists to oppose its protagonists, but scientists are more likely to be featured as heroes than villains; the tacit assumption that scientists would have to be mad to be plausibly cast as villains is actually a compliment rather than an insult. In **pulp sf** scientists were more often featured as reluctant accomplices of villainous paymasters, or as unwitting dupes (in accordance with the "absent-minded professor" stereotype, which suggests that scientists' minds are too preoccupied with abstract matters to pay much attention to mundane circumstances) than as active agents of evil; examples abound in the work of **Jack Williamson** and **Edmond Hamilton.**

**Hard sf** writers are bound to regard efficient scientific thought as a model of mental health and a good in itself, thus crediting scientists with an innate sanity and virtuousness, but literary forms that are inherently antiscientific (like **Swiftian satires** and **technothrillers** bound to the **melodramatic** formula that generates the **Frankenstein syndrome**), do tend to embody a more negative view. In the latter kinds of fiction, "mad scientists" are more likely to be morally reckless practitioners of "mad science" rather than dangerous lunatics equipped with scientific expertise; nuclear physics and **biotechnology** are favorite examples of supposedly insane science. To the extent that sf is a significant factor in determining the public image of science and scientists, this ideological conflict is one of the most important aspects of the contemporary genre.

***MAGAZINE OF FANTASY & SCIENCE FICTION, THE*** **(F&SF).** U.S. digest **magazine** launched in 1949 as *The Magazine of Fantasy*; the full title was used from the second issue. Its first editors, **Anthony Boucher** and J. Francis McComas, were both mystery writers who had dabbled in **sf**; their brief was to replace the obsolete tone and manner of **pulp sf** with the informal stylistic gloss of streetwise crime fiction. They reprinted a good deal of literary fantasy in the magazine's early years to help set the new standard, and attracted such writers as **C. S. Lewis** and **H.F. Heard** to its pages. The mingling of sf with slick contemporary fantasy made *F&SF* seem slightly more sophisticated, but slightly less serious, than ***Galaxy.*** While *Galaxy* attracted writers of a **satirical** bent, *F&SF* became the principal market for the **softest** forms of sf, including the sentimental stories of **Zenna Henderson** and Mildred Clingerman, and the whimsical **fabulations** of writers like **Reginald Bretnor** and **Avram Davidson** (who edited the magazine briefly in 1962–1964), although its ventures into avant-gardism were rarely as bold as those of **Cele Goldsmith's *Amazing*** and *Fantastic*. A short-lived companion dealing in more traditional action-adventure sf, *Venture* (1957–1958), seemed somewhat out of keeping with *F&SF*'s philosophy; its second incarnation in 1970 was even briefer. Boucher remained editor of *F&SF* until 1958, the last four years in sole charge; the longest subsequent editorial term was served by Edward L. Ferman, the son of publisher Joseph L. Ferman, from 1966–1991. Two years after Gordon van Gelder replaced **Kristine Kathryn Rusch** as editor in 1998, he became the magazine's proprietor as well. Its sales declined, in line with those of its rivals, from circa 68,000 in 1991 to circa 24,000 in 2002.

**MAGAZINES.** For its first 30 years as a commercial genre (circa 1930–circa 1960) **sf** was primarily a magazine medium, in that magazines were the immediate target market of all self-defined sf writers; book publication was regarded as a remote possibility of little significance. When the **pulp** magazines died in the aftermath of World War II they were replaced by "digests" (modeled on the *Reader's Digest*) whose activities changed the image and stylistic gloss of sf but not its essence. From the very beginning, digest magazines faced opposition from a booming **paperback** book market, which embraced sf along with other pulp genres, but the sf magazines proved uniquely robust in resisting that competition. When other fiction magazines faced an extinction crisis in the 1960s, the core of the sf magazine market proved surprisingly resilient, to the extent that by the end of the 20th century the sf magazines were almost the last commercial fiction magazines in existence. Their economic hegemony had been lost in the 1960s when advances on paperback royalties became the commercial engine of the field and serial rights became as peripheral to writers' economic calculations as book publication had been in the 1940s, but the magazines nevertheless retained a crucial role.

The persistence of the magazine medium had something to do with the cultish quality of sf **fandom**—all the sf magazines had unusually large subscription lists and were not as vulnerable as other genre fiction magazines to a rapid decline in "newsstand sales"—but was mainly a consequence of the genre's peculiar aesthetics. From the very beginning, the establishment of sf magazines solved one of the fundamental problems of exotic fiction—that of addressing a story to a reader whose "default assumption," on starting to read, was that it would be set in the known world and in the present day. Writers of naturalistic fiction had only to invoke a date and a place name to signal modifications of that expectation, but writers whose stories were set in distant futures or on **alien** planets had a great deal more narrative labor to do. Publication in a magazine exclusively devoted to sf reversed the preliminary expectations that readers brought to each individual story, considerably reducing the burden of explanation borne by the writer.

Read in a genre magazine, every story set in a hypothetical future or on an alien world was immediately placed within a vast spectrum of alternatives (which eventually expanded to encompass **alternative histories**). This had the double effect of making each individual story more easily comprehensible to habitual readers and emphasizing the holistic aspect of the genre's aesthetic appeal. It is for this reason that the distinct editorial philosophies that differentiated ***Astounding*** from the ***Amazing*** and ***Wonder*** groups in the 1930s, changed the character of *Astounding* in such a way as to distinguish it from the likes of ***Startling*** in the 1940s, and permitted ***Galaxy*** and the ***Magazine of Fantasy and Science Fiction*** to bring a new diversity to the field in the 1950s, were so vitally important to the evolution of the genre. Such supplementary materials as a magazine's editorial, book review column, and popular science articles were powerful instruments in enhancing reader awareness of the field as a whole entity with a purpose and a philosophy extending far beyond the rhetoric of any one story or writer.

**MAINE, CHARLES ERIC (1921–1981).** Pseudonym used by British writer David McIlwain on all his **sf**, which he began publishing in 1938 in his own **fanzine**, making his professional debut in 1952 with a **radio** play about an artificial satellite, novelized as *Spaceways* (1953). *Timeliner* (1955) also novelized a radio script and the first of his several **technothrillers**, *The Isotope Man* (1957), adapted his script for the movie *Timeslip* (1955). As his media work dried up, Maine transferred his efforts to imitations of **John Wyndham** in such **disaster stories** as *Crisis 2000* (1955), *The Tide Went Out* (1958), *The Darkest of Nights* (1962), and *The Random Factor* (1971). He varied his output with the space-set thriller *High Vacuum* (1957), ventures into **soft sf** in *World without Men* (1958; revised as *Alph*, 1972) and *He Owned the World* (1960, aka *The Man Who Owned the World*), and the extended ***contes philosophiques*** *The Mind of Mr. Soames* (1961) and *B.E.A.S.T.* (1966). Illness cut his career short before he had time to exploit the new publishing opportunities of the 1970s.

**MAISON D'AILLEURS, LA ["The House of Elsewhere"].** An establishment founded by **Pierre Versins** in 1975, in Yverdon, Switzerland, to serve as a "museum of **Utopia.**" He donated his personal collection to form the basis of its holdings, and it began to receive municipal support in 1989. It is the most important research center in France and formed a model for such institutions as the **SF Foundation.** Its holdings are less numerous than those of library collections in California, Texas, Toronto, and Sydney but remain uniquely valuable in their assembly of **French**-language materials.

**MALZBERG, BARRY N. (1939– ).** U.S. writer who began publishing **sf** in 1967, quickly becoming extremely prolific within the genre, although he continued to operate in other genres with a similar breathtaking facility. He claimed the world record for writing at speed when he completed a 60,000-word novel in 15 hours, but his compositional fervor arose out of profound involvement rather than casual haste; his best works are unparalleled in their furious narrative pace, acute psychological intimacy, and blackly comic imaginative intensity. His early sf, collected in *Final War and Other Fantasies* (1969) and *In the Pocket and Other Science Fiction Stories* (1971) was bylined K. M. O'Donnell, as were *The Empty People* (1969), the **satirical** farces *Dwellers of* *the Deep* (1970) and *Gather in the Hall of the Planets* (1971), and the **mosaic** *Universe Day* (1971). The first sf novels to appear under his own name were skeptical commentaries on the space program featuring astronauts as paradigmatic case studies in alienation. *The Falling Astronauts* (1971) is a tense psychological drama. *Revelations* (1972) broached the possibility that the **moon**-landings had been faked in a **TV** studio. *Beyond Apollo* (1972) is a phantasmagoric satire.

Malzberg's subsequent sf novels often invoke **aliens** as incomprehensible, taunting persecutors of protagonists caught in existential traps, as in *Overlay* (1972), *The Day of the Burning* (1974), and *The Tactics of Conquest* (1974). *Galaxies* (1975) extrapolates alienation to its extreme in an account of a corpse-laden spaceship's fall into a black hole. *Scop* (1976) is a **time-traveler** whose desperate attempts to change the history that created his intolerable world are futile. The antihero of *Herovit's World* (1973) is an sf writer whose fantasies are impotent to alleviate his own distress, giving eloquent voice to a deep disenchantment with the genre's market situation—further explained in the essay collection *The Engines of the Night: Science Fiction in the Eighties* (1982)—that caused Malzberg to abandon his vocational involvement in despair, save for occasional heartfelt revisitations such as *Chorale* (1978), *The Cross of Fire* (1982), and *The Remaking of Sigmund Freud* (1985) and vivid **fabulations**, some of which are collected in *The Man Who Loved the Midnight Lady* (1980), *The Passage of the Night: The Recursive Science Fiction of Barry N. Malzberg* (1994), and *In the Stone House* (2000).

**MANN, PHILIP (1942– ).** British-born writer resident in New Zealand since 1969, whose first **sf** publication was *The Eye of the Queen* (1982), which features an unusually detailed account of a radically **alien** society. *Master of Paxwax* (1986) and its sequel *The Fall of the Families* (1987) describe the disintegration of a fledgling interstellar empire. *Pioneers* (1988) and *Wulfsyarn: A Mosaic* (1990) are **existentialist fantasies**, the former focusing on humans adapted for life in alien environments, the latter on an unfulfilled starship captain. The **series** collectively titled *A Land Fit for Heroes*, comprising *Escape to the Wild Wood* (1993), *Stand Alone Stan* (1994), *The Dragon Wakes* (1995), and *The Burning Forest* (1996), features an **alternative history** where 20th-century Britain is still part of the Roman Empire.

**MANNING, LAURENCE (1899–1972).** Canadian-born writer, resident in the United States from 1920, whose first story for **Hugo Gernsback's pulps**, "The City of the Living Dead" (1930, with **Fletcher Pratt**), was a striking **dystopian** fantasy about a society's retreat into **virtual reality.** He was a founding member of the American Interplanetary Society and wrote an early **space-age** fantasy comprising "The Voyage of the *Asteroid*" and "The Wreck of the *Asteroid*" (both 1932). His **future history mosaic** *The Man Who Awoke* (1933, book 1975) was his only work to reach book form, although the Stranger Club sequence launched with "The Call of the Mech-Men" (1933) was similarly adventurous. He quit the field along with Gernsback after publishing the novella "The World of Mist" (1935).

**MARLEY, LOUISE (1952– ).** U.S. writer who began publishing **sf** with the trilogy comprising *Sing the Light* (1995), *Sing the Warmth* (1996), and *Receive the Gift* (1997) about **psionic** singers on an ice-bound planet. In *The Terrorists of Irustan* (1999) women are oppressed in a quasi-Islamic culture on a mining planet. In *The Glass Harmonica* (2000) musicians in 1761 and 2018 are linked by their love of an instrument invented by Benjamin Franklin. *The Maquisarde* (2002) is a **hybrid** futuristic **political fantasy.**

**MARS.** Mars has always held a special place in the mythology of the **space age**, and hence of **sf**. The speculatively adventurous popularization of astronomical observations made in the late 19th century by Giovanni Schiaparelli, Percival Lowell, and others established the planet in the public imagination as a likely abode of life, far more interesting than the obviously lifeless **moon.** It became a key source of **alien** invaders, a key target of exploratory expeditions, and a key venue of lushly romantic adventure stories. Its mythic history moved through several distinct phases, mapped out by **Stephen Baxter** in "Martian Chronicles: Narratives of Mars in Science and SF" (1996) as (**Edgar Rice Burroughs's**) "Barsoom," "Arid Mars," and "Viking Mars." Each phase cast a long shadow over the next, reflected in such determinedly anachronistic fantasies as **Ray Bradbury's** *Martian Chronicles* and such skeptical tragedies as **Ludek Pesek's** *The Earth Is Near*. The notion that there might be life on Mars was such an important aspect of the space program's utilization of space-age mythology that James Lovelock's conclusion in the 1960s that its chemically neutral atmosphere as sufficient proof of its lifelessness was extremely unwelcome—although Lovelock's subsequent interest in **terraforming** Mars, detailed in *The Greening of Mars* (1984, with Michael Allaby), was a significant influence on a flood of novels that restored the colonization of Mars as a major topic of fin-de-siècle sf, most notably on **Kim Stanley Robinson's** Martian trilogy. An ingenious anti-Lovelock argument was set out in **Gregory Benford's** *The Martian Race* (1999) but the cause of indigenous Martian life was effectively lost by the end of the 20th century, as evidenced by the elegiac tone of most of the stories in Peter Crowther's anthology *Mars Probes* (2002).

**MARTIN, GEORGE R. R. (1948– ).** U.S. writer who began publishing **sf** in 1971. His most successful early works were novellas, including the 1974 title story of *A Song for Lya and Other Stories* (1976), featuring **aliens** whose religion is founded in a biologically guaranteed afterlife; "The Storms of Windhaven" (1975, with Lisa Tuttle), a **planetary romance** extended into the **mosaic** *Windhaven* (1981); the 1979 title story of *Sandkings* (1981), about an artificial **miniature** world; and the 1980 title story of *Nightflyers* (1985), a taut thriller set aboard a starship. His other collections are *Songs of Stars and Shadows* (1976) and *Portraits of His Children* (1987). *Dying of the Light* (1977) is a planetary romance set on a temporarily defrosted ice world. The mosaic *Tuf Voyaging* (1986) assembles comedies about a peripatetic ecological engineer. Martin edited five volumes of novellas by nominees for the **John W. Campbell** Award for the best new sf writer, *New Voices* (1977–1984), but moved into other fantasy genres thereafter.

**MARTIN, GRAHAM DUNSTAN (1932– ).** Scottish writer, mostly of **children's** fantasy. His adult **sf** novels are pessimistic extended ***contes philosophiques.*** *Time-Slip* (1986) imagines the notion of **alternative** worlds being used as an excuse for moral apathy. *The Dream Wall* (1987) is an **Orwellian dystopia.** *Half a Glass of Moonshine* (1988) is about sensory censorship by natural selection.

**MARVELL, ANDREW (1896–1985).** Pseudonym used on three **satirical scientific romances** by British journalist Howell Davies. *Minimum*

*Man; or, Time to be Gone* (1938) is a fervent **political fantasy** in which a race of **miniaturized** humans is recruited to a war against fascism. *Three Men Make a World* (1939) is an ambivalent **disaster story** about a petrol-devouring bacterium. *Congratulate the Devil* (1939) sarcastically describes the dire fate of the inventors of a drug that makes people happy.

**MASON, DOUGLAS R. (1918– ).** British writer who began publishing **sf** as John Rankine in 1964, retaining that name for numerous routine **space operas** while attaching his own to works embodying his favorite theme: a retreat to pastoral self-sufficiency from comfortable but excessively regimented civilizations controlled by **artificial intelligences.** Examples include *From Carthage Then I Came* (1966, aka *Eight against Utopia*), *Ring of Violence* (1968), *Matrix* (1970), and *The End Bringers* (1973).

**MASON, LISA (1953– ).** U.S. writer who began publishing **sf** in 1987 with a story subsequently expanded into her first novel, the **feminized cyberpunk** thriller *Arachne* (1990); *Cyberweb* (1995) is a sequel. *Summer of Love* (1994) brings a dour **time-traveler** to Haight-Ashbury in 1968 to track down the flower child on whom the shape of the future will depend. *The Golden Nineties* (1995) takes a time-traveler back to San Francisco in 1895. The Pangaea **series** of **far-futuristic fantasies** launched with *Imperium without End* (1999) and *Imperium Afire* (2000) tracks a rebellion against institutional dream-control.

**MASSON, DAVID I. (1915– ).** Scottish writer whose linguistically inventive time-twisting contributions to **new wave sf**, begun in 1965, were assembled in *The Caltraps of Time* (1968, exp. 2003).

**MATHESON, RICHARD (1926– ).** U.S. writer best known for his work in other media and other fantasy genres, who began publishing **sf** in 1950 with the **horror-sf** title story of his most relevant collection, *Born of Man and Woman* (1954, abridged as *Third from the Sun*). *I Am Legend* (1954) is a classic attempt to **hybridize** supernatural horror and sf by extrapolating the notion of a literal plague of vampirism. *The Shrinking Man* (1956) is a similarly hybridized account of progressive **miniaturization.** *The Shores of Space* (1957) mingles a substantial number of sf stories with other kinds of fantasy, but all his subsequent work—including the **timeslip romance** *Bid Time Return* (1975)—dispensed with rationalizing artifice.

**MATTER TRANSMITTER.** A hypothetical technology for transporting objects or people from one place to another without their passing tangibly through the intervening space—effectively, an artificial form of the **psi power** of teleportation (for which reason matter transmitters are sometimes called teleporters). Early examples can be found in late 19th-century stories of invention. The matter transmitter's utility as a facilitating device in literary work is limited, although it eventually proved a boon to **TV space opera.** Some genre **sf** developments of the idea are akin to **time-paradox** stories, in that they revel in the absurdity of consequences that can be extrapolated from the premise—some ghoulish examples are featured in *Earthdoom!* (1987) by **David Langford** and John Grant and some tricky ones in **Harry Harrison's mosaic** *One Step from Earth* (1970)—but the novellas comprising *Three Trips in Time and Space* (1973) edited by **Robert Silverberg** are earnest **extrapolations** of the transformative effects such a technology might have on global society, which were subsequently taken further by two of the authors, **John Brunner** and **Larry Niven.** If what is actually being transmitted is encoded information rather than a package of "disassociated matter," then matter transmitters might better be regarded as matter duplicators—a conclusion exploited in such works as *Rogue Moon* (1960) by **Algis Budrys.**

**MATTHEWS, SUSAN R. (1954– ).** U.S. writer who began publishing **sf** with *An Exchange of Hostages* (1997), the first of the Jurisdiction Universe **series** featuring military inquisitor Andrej Kosciusko, a surgeon with a conscience-troubling talent for torture; it was followed by *Prisoner of Conscience* (1998), *Hour of Judgment* (1999), *Angel of Destruction* (2001), and *The Devil and Deep Space* (2002). *Avalanche Soldier* (1999) is a thriller in which terrorism on the planet Creation precipitates the heroine's crisis of faith. *Colony Fleet* (2000) features colonists about to make landfall whose **Utopian** ideals have been severely corroded.

**MAUROIS, ANDRÉ (1885–1967).** Pseudonym of French writer Émile Salomon Wilhelm Herzog, who dabbled in **fabulation** from 1903 onward, producing several fragments of a **future history**, including a cautionary account of *The Next Chapter: The War against the Moon* (1928). Other translated works include three extended ***contes philosophiques***: the **Utopian satire** *A Voyage to the Island of the Articoles* (1927, tr. 1928); the **metaphysical fantasy** *The Weigher of Souls* (1931); and a sober account of the **invention** and deployment of *The Thought-Reading Machine* (1937, tr. 1938).

**MAY, JULIAN (1931– ).** U.S. writer who published her first **sf** story in ***Astounding*** in 1951 but dedicated her subsequent efforts to educational nonfiction and assisting her husband, **T. E. Dikty**, in his publishing ventures until she returned with the epic Saga of the Pliocene Exile, comprising *The Many-Colored Land* (1981), *The Golden Torc* (1982), *The Nonborn King* (1984), and *The Adversary* (1984), which **hybridized** motifs from **hard sf** with genre fantasy materials to pioneer a new kind of mature **science-fantasy.** *Intervention* (1987), *Jack the Bodiless* (1992), *Diamond Mask* (1994), and *Magnificat* (1996) comprise a sequel quartet moving the action from a prehistoric stage to a contemporary one, enthusiastically embracing all the **extrapolative** intricacies necessary to that adjustment and adding further complications adapted from Teilhard de Chardin's **Omega Point** theory. The Rampart Worlds sequence comprising *The Perseus Spur* (1998), *Orion Arm* (1999), and *Sagittarius Whorl* (2000) is a sophisticated **space opera.**

**MCALLISTER, BRUCE (1946– ).** U.S. writer who began publishing **sf** in 1963. *Humanity Prime* (1971) describes a society of humans adapted for undersea life. *Dream Baby* (1989) is a harrowing account of the experiences of a **psi-powered** nurse in the Vietnam War. The title story in his **anthology** of novellas *Their Immortal Hearts* (1980) is an earnest ***conte philosophique*.**

**MCAULEY, PAUL J. (1955– ).** British writer who began publishing **sf** in 1984. *Four Hundred Billion Stars* (1988) is a mystery set on an **alien** world whose solution necessitates a **conceptual breakthrough.** *Of the Fall* (1989, aka *Secret Harmonies*) and *Red Dust* (1993) are similarly structured accounts of problematic colonization whose climactic revelations are relatively modest. *Eternal Light*

(1991) is a sophisticated **space opera** embodying bold cosmological speculations. *Pasquale's Angel* (1994) is an **alternative history** set in Renaissance Italy. *Fairyland* (1995) is a **cyberpunk** thriller about **nanotechnology.** The Confluence trilogy comprising *Child of the River* (1997), *Ancients of Days* (1998), and *Shrine of Stars* (1999) is a **far-futuristic fantasy.** *The Secret of Life* (2001) tracks the contest to explain and exploit a mysterious alien life-form. *Whole Wide World* (2001) is a futuristic murder mystery. McAuley's short fiction is collected in *The King of the Hill* (1991) and *The Invisible Country* (1996). "Dr. Pretorius and the Lost Temple" (2002) is a **steampunk** fantasy featuring Isambard Kingdom Brunel.

**MCCAFFREY, ANNE (1926– ).** U.S. writer, resident in Ireland since 1978, who began publishing **sf** in 1953. Her production was sparse until she published her first novel, *Restoree* (1967), but included the unconventional love story "The Ship Who Sang" (1961), which became the basis of a 1969 **mosaic** and a **sharecropping** franchise. Two carefully **hybridized** ***Analog*** novellas that employed **Campbellian** rationalization to accommodate quasi-mythical dragons to the **lost world** of Pern were combined as *Dragonflight* (1968), launching an extensive **series** whose quasi-scientific basis was soon eroded; its enormous success in the marketplace was an early demonstration of the hitherto-untapped commercial potential of genre fantasy. Other exercises in hybridization include the series begun with the mosaics *To Ride Pegasus* (1973) and *The Crystal Singer* (1974–1975, book 1982) and the novels *Dinosaur Planet* (1978) and *The Rowan* (1990). Some similar short fiction is to be found in *Get Off the Unicorn* (1977), which owes its title to a copy editor who misunderstood the significance of "Get" and added a second "f" to McCaffrey's "of." The series begun with *Freedom's Landing* (1995), *Freedom's Choice* (1996), *Freedom's Challenge* (1998), and *Freedom's Ransom* (2003), in which Earth has been conquered by **aliens** and humans exported as slaves to various alien worlds, is more wholeheartedly **science-fictional**.

**MCCARTHY, WIL (1966– ).** U.S. writer who began publishing **sf** in 1990. The **first contact** novel *Aggressor Six* (1994) and its sequel, *The Fall of Sirius* (1996), are **space operas.** *Murder in the Solid State* (1996) is a thriller featuring early developmental stages of **nanotechnology.**

*Flies from Amber* (1995) features the discovery of **alien** life adapted for existence inside a black hole; *Bloom* (1998) is a further exercise of the same kind, featuring organic nanotechnology. *The Collapsium* (2000) is a **hybrid** comedy set in the 26th-century Queendom of Sol, transformed by **matter-transmitting** "fax" machines; its sequel, *The Wellstone* (2003), follows the adventures of unruly adolescents on a makeshift spaceship. Some of the ideas underlying McCarthy's fiction are explored in *Hacking Matter: Levitating Chairs, Quantum Mirages, and the Infinite Weirdness of Programmable Atoms* (2003).

**MCCOLLUM, MICHAEL A. (1946– ).** U.S. writer who began publishing **sf** in 1979. His early novels, including the **mosaic** *A Greater Infinity* (1982) and the two **series** commenced with *Life PROBE* (1983) and *Antares Dawn* (1986), are hectic **space operas.** *Thunderstrike!* (1989) is a **disaster story.** *The Clouds of Saturn* (1991) explores the possibility of colonizing a gas giant world. In *The Sails of Tau Ceti* (1992) **alien** refugees settle on Earth. *A Greater Infinity* (1999) is adventure sf facilitated by a Paratime shuttle. *Gibraltar Earth* (1999) is a **first contact** story.

**MCDEVITT, JACK (1935– ).** U.S. writer who began publishing **sf** in 1981. *The Hercules Text* (1986) is a **SETI** fantasy whose interest in the potential impact of exotic revelations on dogmatic religious faiths is echoed in *A Talent for War* (1988), *Engines of God* (1994), and *Ancient Shores* (1996). *Eternity Road* (1997) is a **postholocaust** novel. *Moonfall* (1998) is a melodramatic catastrophe story. The techniques of **hard sf** are cleverly employed to tighten the threads of suspenseful plots in *Infinity Beach* (2000), a **first contact** story cast as a well-crafted mystery, and *Deepsix* (2001), a race-against-time thriller in which castaways must be rescued from a disintegrating planet. *Chindi* (2002) is an **Odyssean fantasy** in which a starship tracks **alien** signals. McDevitt's short fiction is sampled in *Standard Candles* (1996).

**MCDONALD, IAN (1960– ).** British writer, a native of Ulster, who began publishing **sf** in 1982. His remarkably inventive early short fiction was collected in *Empire Dreams* (1988) and *Speaking in Tongues* (1992). The multifaceted **fabulation** *Desolation Road* (1988) tells the story of a community of misfits and exiles struggling to get by while **Mars** is **terraformed** and politically transformed; *Ares Express* (2001) is a sequel. *Out on Blue Six* (1989) is a **dystopian** fantasy. *King of Morning, Queen of Day* (1985, exp. 1991) is an unusually clear-cut **chimerization** of fairy tale and sf whose self-contradictions reflect the changing condition of Ireland. *Hearts, Hands and Voices* (1992, aka *The Broken Land*), *Necroville* (1994, aka *Terminal Café*), and *Chaga* (1995, aka *Evolution's Shore*) carry forward a fascination with settings descended to varying degrees from today's developing world but dramatically transmuted by biological innovations. The novella *Scissors Cut Paper Wrap Stone* (1994) features powerful computer-generated images. *Sacrifice of Fools* (1996) is a thriller set in the wake of an incursion of **alien** refugees. *Kirinya* (1998) is a sequel to *Chaga* that further extrapolates its phantasmagoric transmutations; the novella *Tendeléo's Story* (2000) shares the same background.

**MCHUGH, MAUREEN F. (1959– ).** U.S. writer who began publishing **sf** in 1979, her first two short stories subsequently being integrated into the **mosaic** *China Mountain Zhang* (1992), a **dystopian** account of an overcrowded future dominated by oriental culture. *Half the Day Is Night* (1994) is a thriller set in cities built on the seabed to accommodate the ever-expanding population. *Mission Child* (1998) is a coming-of-age story set on a colony world disrupted by **alien** invasion. The heroine of *Nekropolis* (2001), whose unconventional love for an **artificial intelligence** proves less hopeless than might be assumed, carries forward an emerging pattern in which the rewards available to oppressed individuals in difficult circumstances have to be won by difficult means.

**MCINTOSH, J. T. (1925– ).** Pseudonym of Scottish writer James Murdoch MacGregor, sometimes rendered M'Intosh on early work. He began publishing **sf** in the U.S. **magazines** in 1950 and his fiction retained an American flavor through a tentative account of "The E.S.P. Worlds" (1952, exp. 1964 as *The Noman Way*), the **van Vogtian** *World Out of Mind* (1953), the **political fantasy** of extraterrestrial colonization *Born Leader* (1954), and the **mosaic** account of a hasty world-evacuation and its aftermath *One in Three Hundred*

(1954). *The Fittest* (1955, aka *Rule of the Pagbeasts*) moved into the **disaster** subgenre opened up in the United Kingdom by **John Wyndham.** Once he had used up the last resources of his one productive decade in the **dystopian** fantasy *The Million Cities* (1958, exp. 1963), the **generation starship** story *200 Years to Christmas* (1959, book 1961), and "Immortality for Some" (1960, exp. as *Flight from Rebirth* 1971), his work became repetitive and formulaic.

**MCINTYRE, VONDA N. (1948– ).** U.S. writer who began publishing **sf** in 1971. Her archetypal example of **feminized** sf "Of Mist and Grass and Sand" (1973) was expanded into the **mosaic** *Dreamsnake* (1978), its background having been further elaborated in *The Exile Waiting* (1975), whose heroine escapes local troubles by setting off for the stars. The heroine of *Superluminal* (1983), expanded from the novella "Aztecs" (1977), takes the same option in a more decisive manner. After her early short fiction was collected in *Fireflood and Other Stories* (1979), McIntyre produced numerous *Star Trek* **tie-ins**, and her subsequent **series** comprising *Starfarers* (1989), *Transition* (1991), *Metaphase* (1992), and *Nautilus* (1994) employed a similar backcloth and narrative method. *The Moon and the Sun* (1997) introduces an enigmatic sea monster to the court of Louis XIV.

**MCKILLIP, PATRICIA A. (1948– ).** U.S. writer in various fantasy genres. Her ventures into **sf** are the juvenile couplet *Moon-Flash* (1984) and *The Moon and the Face* (1985), which follows a symbolic quest from an Edenic enclave to the shore of an interstellar empire, and the **Orphean fantasy** *Fool's Run* (1987).

**MCLAUGHLIN, DEAN (1931– ).** U.S. writer who began publishing **sf** in 1951. He wrote numerous novellas for ***Analog***, including one expanded into *Dome World* (1958; book 1962), three collected in *Hawk among the Sparrows* (1976)—including the combative ***conte philosophique*** "The Brotherhood of Keepers" (1960)—and the moral tales "Ode to Joy" (1991) and "Mark on the World" (1992). *The Fury from Earth* (1963) and the **mosaic** *The Man Who Wanted Stars* (1965) attempt to embed similar assertions of **libertarian** ideals within action-adventure formulas.

**MCMULLEN, SEAN (1948– ). Australian** writer who began publishing **sf** in 1986. Several of his early stories, collected in *Call to the Edge* (1992), use **time travel** and other devices to draw connections between the distant past and the near future—a stratagem repeated in *The Centurion's Empire* (1998). Similar imagistic **hybridization** is employed in the design of the futuristic world of Greatwinter, phases of whose history are **extrapolated** in *Voices in the Light* (1994) and *Mirrorsun Rising* (1995)—which were combined and revised as *Souls in the Great Machine* (1999)—*The Miocene Arrow* (2000), and *Eyes of the Calculor* (2001). The hybrid **science-fantasy** *Voyage of the Shadowmoon* (2002) similarly features a low-tech postcatastrophe scenario, although the eponymous vessel seeks the magical Silverdeath on a moon of a gas giant.

**MCQUAY, MIKE (1949–1995).** U.S. writer who began publishing **sf** with the futuristic thriller *Life-Keeper* (1980), followed by four novels explicitly modeled on Raymond Chandler's private eye novels. *Jitterbug* (1984) is a **dystopian** fantasy. In *Memories* (1987) a psychiatrist seeks a more profound version of Freudian abreaction via **time travel**; *The Nexus* (1989) similarly imports a ***conte philosophique*** element into a near-future thriller. *Richter Ten* (1996, with **Arthur C. Clarke**) is about earthquake prediction.

**MEANEY, JOHN (1957– ).** British writer who began publishing **sf** in 1992. *To Hold Infinity* (1998) is a post-**cyberpunk** thriller. The Nulapeiron trilogy launched by *Paradox* (2000) and *Context* (2002) tracks the unfolding consequences of a rebellion against Oracles whose ability to foresee the future has facilitated the establishment of an oppressive aristocracy.

**MELODRAMATIC INFLATION.** All **series** fiction tends to be afflicted by the necessity of increasing the magnitude of the threats that the hero is required to overcome. Fiction featuring heroes equipped with new technologies or superhuman powers has no intrinsic limits, so the necessity of making each new threat bigger and nastier than the one before routinely produces rapid escalations of scale. **Space opera** series that begin by employing everyday criminals or relatively ordinary **aliens** as antagonists tend to make rapid progress to the sun-smashing stage; by the time the elements of **E. E. Smith's** Lensman series were gathered into a multivolume **mosaic**, it was insufficient to progress from the thwarting of mundane space pirates to the summary dispatch of entire interstellar empires; even the **galactic empires** had to be unwitting tools of godlike entities whose conflict ranged across the entirety of space and time.

Melodramatic inflation is not entirely inconvenient, given that the expansion of perspective by means of a series of **conceptual breakthroughs** is one of the fundamental aesthetic rewards of reading sf. The process provides useful opportunities to writers who continually discover new ways to stretch their devices a little further—as, for instance, **Frederik Pohl** did in the Heechee series. The constant temptation to move all the way from here and now to the edge of the universe and the **Omega Point** in a hop, a skip, and a jump can, however, be deleterious to the meticulous logical **extrapolation** supposedly required of **hard sf**, and the consequent excesses—very obvious in bad sf—have intensified the genre's image problems. The demands of melodramatic inflation are responsible for producing the exotic superheroes of **comic** book sf, whose grandiosity is always in peril of dissolving into silliness, and similar demands continually nudge all sf extrapolations toward the edge of a slippery slope.

**MERCIER, LOUIS-SEBASTIEN (1740–1814). French** political philosopher who pioneered futuristic **Utopian** fiction in *L'an 2440* (1771, tr. as *Memoirs of the Year 2500*), which became a huge best seller in the prerevolutionary era despite its publication being unauthorized. It laid the groundwork for the first theoretical discussion of the potential scope of futuristic fiction, Félix Bodin's *Le roman d'avenir* (1834), and the first **dystopia**, Émile Souvestre's *Le monde tel qu'il sera* (1846). Mercier's earlier ***contes philosophiques***, collected in *Songes et Visions Philosophiques* (1768), include "Nouvelles de la lune," in which the news in question is conveyed by means of a concentrated beam of light that burns an inscription on planks of wood laid out to receive it; it describes a universe in which the disincarnate souls of the dead are free to roam while making progress (or not) toward further phases of **evolution**—an obvious precursor of **Camille Flammarion's** *Lumen*.

**MEREDITH, RICHARD C. (1937–1979).** U.S. writer who began publishing **sf** in 1962. *The Sky Is Filled with Ships* (1969) and *We All Died at Breakaway Station* (1969) are stirring **space operas**, whose imaginative boldness is carried forward into the **apocalyptic time-tripping** trilogy comprising *At the Narrow Passage* (1973), *No Brother, No Friend* (1976), and *Vestiges of Time* (1978) and the deftly paradoxical *Run, Come See Jerusalem!* (1976).

**MERLE, ROBERT (1908– ).** Algerian-born **French** writer of literary fiction. Three novels embodying **sf** motifs have been translated: *The Day of the Dolphin* (1967, tr. 1969) explores the consequences of human communication with dolphins; *Malevil* (1972, tr. 1974) is a **postholocaust fantasy**; and *The Virility Factor* (1974, tr. 1977) is a **satire** about a plague that spares women and sexually incapable males.

**MERRIL, JUDITH (1923–1997).** U.S. writer and anthologist, resident in Canada from 1968. Born Josephine Juliet Grossman, she changed her first name before becoming Judith Zissman by marriage, then changed her surname. She was a late recruit to the **Futurians** fan group, marrying **Frederik Pohl** in 1949 (they divorced in 1953). She began publishing **sf** with the classic ***conte cruel*** "That Only a Mother" (1948). *Shadow on the Hearth* (1950) is an account of a nuclear war as experienced by a housewife. She wrote *Outpost Mars* (1952) and *Gunner Cade* (1952) in collaboration with **C. M. Kornbluth** as "Cyril Judd." Several notable stories in which established sf motifs are reexamined from female viewpoints, deftly fusing studied compassion with cool skepticism, are collected with other material in *Out of Bounds* (1960), *Daughters of Earth* (1968), and *Survival Ship and Other Stories* (1974). *The Tomorrow People* (1960) is an intricate futuristic mystery story. Merril edited several theme **anthologies** before embarking on a **series** of "year's best" samplers launched in 1956, which ran until 1966 with an addendum in 1968. She set out to broaden the scope of the genre considerably, campaigning in favor of the replacement label **speculative fiction**, seeking out material published outside the genre **magazines** and juxtaposing **hard sf** stories with contemporary fantasies and—as soon as they became available—avant-gardist **new wave fabulations.** Her donation of sf books and magazines to the Toronto Public

Library formed the nucleus of that city's valuable research collection, which was known for a while as the Spaced Out Library.

**MERRITT, A. (1884–1943).** U.S. journalist whose "The Moon Pool" (1918, combined with a sequel in the 1919 book) launched a sequence of lush escapist fantasies that were among the greatest successes of **pulp** fiction. Although he made little use of **sf** motifs, Merritt was one of **Hugo Gernsback's** favorite writers, and Gernsback prompted him to give more emphasis to the sf element in *The Metal Monster* (1920)—an **alien** life-form—to adapt it for reserialization in *Science and Invention*. "The Snake Mother" (1930) similarly extrapolated *The Face in the Abyss* (1923; **mosaic** 1931) by filling its **lost world** setting with sf devices, but Merritt was never comfortable with such materials. He was a powerful influence on several writers recruited by the sf pulps, most obviously **Jack Williamson** and **C. L. Moore**—whose definitive **science-fantasy** *The Dark World* (1946, as by **Henry Kuttner**) is a **transfiguration** of Merritt's *The Dwellers in the Mirage* (1932), and was itself further transfigured by **Marion Zimmer Bradley** in *Falcons of Narabedla* (1957). Merritt helped to establish **portal fantasies** as a significant subgenre of modern fantasy, employing a dimensional jargon that facilitated their adaptation into pulp sf.

**MERWIN, SAM JR. (1910–1996).** U.S. writer and editor who began publishing **sf** in 1939. He was editor of ***Startling Stories*** and *Thrilling Wonder Stories* from 1944–1951 and worked briefly on several sf digests before quitting the field. He wrote a good deal of sf for his own **magazines**, the most notable items being the **time police** stories *The House of Many Worlds* (1951) and "Journey to Miseneum" (1953, book 1955 as *The Three Faces of Time*). *The Time Shifters* (1971) was a belated revisitation of the theme.

**METAFICTION.** A term defined by **Robert Scholes** (who credits its coinage to William Gass) in *Fabulation and Metafiction* (1979) as "experimental **fabulation.**" It usually refers to fiction whose acute consciousness of its own fictionality involves the explicit redeployment of material from other texts in order to lay bare or explore their hidden subtexts. Much **science-fictional** fabulation is metafictional, not so much because **sf** is innately experimental in Scholes's sense as because the collective nature of the enterprise means that sf writers routinely respond to other writers' stories, challenging or further extrapolating their logical development for the purposes of reemphasis or subversion. The use of **transfiguration** as a compositional strategy also generates a good deal of metafiction. The **Clute/Nicholls** *Encyclopedia* uses the term "recursive sf" to refer to sf stories whose subject matter is other sf stories, but metafiction is broader and more flexible.

**METAPHYSICAL FANTASY.** Given that metaphysics is, by definition, that which lies outside the scope of science, it may seem that metaphysical fantasy is one genre of fantasy from which sf is rigorously excluded. In fact, metaphysical systems are constructed in order to contain what is known about the world, in the hope of discovering more coherence therein than the logical extrapolation of actual observations can provide. As knowledge of the world changes, therefore, the spectrum of metaphysical possibility changes with it and the advancement of science inevitably gives rise to metaphysical extensions. Such scientific disciplines as cosmology and evolutionary theory are host to as much metaphysics as physics and biology, and their conscientious **extrapolation** demands some consideration of metaphysical as well as physical implications. For this reason, there is a metaphysical aspect even to the **hardest sf**—most obvious when it deals with cosmology—as well as to philosophically inclined products of **dimensional fantasy**, especially those dealing with **alternative histories** and **time paradoxes**, and to **evolutionary fantasies** and **existential fantasies.** All **hybrid texts** may be regarded as metaphysical fantasies, because the process of hybridization inevitably involves some kind of metaphysical reconstruction; this is one of the factors differentiating hybrid texts from **chimerical** ones. Those subgenres of metaphysical fantasy that may seem incompatible with science-fictional speculation—most notably **religious fantasy**—are actually very hospitable to it.

**METZGER, ROBERT A. (1956– )** U.S. physicist and writer who began publishing **sf** in 1987, appearing regularly in the **small press magazine** *Aboriginal SF*. In *Quad World* (1991) an engineer is transplanted to a **parallel world** where prominent figures from history are engaged in an eternal war. *Picoverse* (2002) is an enterprising **alternative history** in which our world is a by-product of a particle accelerator experiment that is in danger of being closed down by omnipotent **aliens.**

**MICROCOSMIC ROMANCE.** The word "microcosm" is one element of a contrasting pair whose partner is "macrocosm"; traditionally, microcosm was used to refer to the Earth or the human body, while macrocosm was applied to the whole universe. Some occult traditions allege that there is an important analogy to be drawn between the two, summarized in the slogan "as above, so below"—the philosophical basis of the **pseudoscience** of astrology.

Following the invention of the microscope, microcosm began to be applied to the world of microbes, and the revival of atomic theory in the 19th century initiated talk of a subatomic microcosm. Several 19th-century **sf** stories offered glimpses into the microscopic world, most notably **Fitz-James O'Brien's** "The Diamond Lens." Microcosmic romance, pioneered by **Ray Cummings's** "The Girl in the Golden Atom" (1919) as a variant of **Burroughsian planetary romance**, exploited a literal interpretation of early 20th-century atomic models that likened electrons orbiting nuclei to planets orbiting stars. Examples from the sf pulps include "Awlo of Ulm" (1931) by Sterner P. Meek and "The Green Man of Graypec" (1935, book 1936 as *The Green Man of Kilsona*) by Festus Pragnell.

As atomic models became more sophisticated, microcosmic romance lost its imaginative warrant, although ventures into the exotic microcosms hypothesized by modern physics continued to feature in such stories as **James Blish's** "Nor Iron Bars" (1957) and **Robert L. Forward's** *Dragon's Egg*. Journeys into a macrocosm in which our solar system is merely an atom are rarer, one notable example being **Donald Wandrei's** "Colossus" (1934).

**MIÉVILLE, CHINA (1972– ).** British writer. *Perdido Street Station* (2000) is an elaborate **hybrid science-fantasy** presenting a vividly exotic spectrum of disparate elements, including **aliens**, **artificial intelligences**, and theoretical aeronautics. *The Scar* (2002) is an **Odyssean fantasy** set in the same world, mostly in the floating city of Armada.

**MILFORD SCIENCE FICTION WRITERS' CONFERENCE.** An annual writers' workshop founded in 1956 in Milford, Pennsylvania, attendance being limited to active professionals; it was hosted for many years by **Damon Knight**, latterly with **Kate Wilhelm**—whom he met through the workshop and subsequently married—and retained its name after Knight left Milford. When **James Blish** moved to Britain he set up an English version in 1972, selecting an initial site in Milford-in-Sea, Hampshire, for the sake of propriety. The system of workshop practice established at Milford was based on a method developed by the University of Iowa's M.A. program in creative writing, but it became an influential model in its own right, copied by the **Clarion** workshop and scores of other **sf** workshops; those for professional writers include the Sycamore Hill workshop cohosted by **John Kessel**, the Turkey City workshop hosted by **Bruce Sterling**, and the Rio Hondo workshop cohosted by **Walter Jon Williams.** Workshopping is particularly useful in the sf genre because of the **collaborative** nature of the genre and the dependence of individual exercises on ingenious but logical **extrapolation**.

**MILITARY SF.** Stories dealing with future military organization and warfare were extensively featured in **sf** from the earliest days of its incorporation as a **pulp** genre, and **future war** fiction had earlier been one of the foundation stones of **scientific romance.** A distinct subgenre of military sf began to emerge in the 1950s when a number of writers—notably **Gordon R. Dickson** in the Dorsai **series**, and **Robert A. Heinlein** in *Starship Troopers*—deepened their use of such motifs to address more serious consideration to the role of military forces, and of warfare, in social evolution. **Reginald Bretnor's** Future at War **anthology** series, *Thor's Hammer* (1979), *The Spear of Mars* (1980), and *Orion's Sword* (1980), brought such questions into clearer focus, and the topic became an important aspect of **libertarian sf**, stridently carried forward by **Jerry Pournelle's** *There Will Be War* anthology series (9 vols.; 1984–1990). It has become an important area of specialization, ardently promoted by James Baen as an editor for Tor and publisher of **Baen Books.** Although some Baen writers, like **David Weber** and **David Feintuch**, have contented themselves with relatively straightforward **transfigurations** of historical war stories, others—including **David Drake** and **Lois McMaster Bujold**—have been much more sensitive to the political and philosophical subtexts of their work, often employing a deftly ironic tone.

**MILLER, P. SCHUYLER (1912–1974).** U.S. writer and critic, who began publishing **sf** in 1930. His **pulp sf**, including *Genus Homo* (1941 with **L. Sprague de Camp**, book 1950) and the stories collected in *The Titan* (1952), was often groundbreaking, but he abandoned it to concentrate on his work as ***Astounding*'s** book reviewer from 1945 until his death. This was an important supportive role in the **Campbellian** cause, helping to identify, celebrate, and promote the collective project to which he eventually attached the label **hard sf.**

**MILLER, WALTER M. JR. (1922–1996).** U.S. writer who began publishing **sf** in 1951, rapidly moving on to the earnestly meditative ***contes philosophiques*** collected in *Conditionally Human* (1962)—most notably the theatrical allegory "The Darfsteller" (1955)—and *The View from the Stars* (1965). His finest work was a classic **mosaic** built from three novellas tracking the role played by an ironically reconstituted Catholic Church in ameliorating a new **postholocaust** Dark Age, *A Canticle for Leibowitz* (1955–1957, rev. 1960). The text hovers uneasily between **hybrid** and **chimerical** status, and also between **satire** and tragedy, eventually cultivating a melancholy indecision so painfully profound that Miller was unable to complete the interstitial companion piece on which he labored until he died, *Saint Leibowitz and the Wild Horse Woman* (1997); the text was completed by **Terry Bisson.**

**MILNE, ROBERT DUNCAN (1844–1899).** Scottish-born journalist, resident in the United States from the mid-1860s, who produced numerous **sf** stories for various West Coast periodicals, which were forgotten until **Sam Moskowitz** exhumed them. Moskowitz argued persuasively for their exemplary importance in *Science Fiction in Old San Francisco* (1980), whose first volume is a *History of the Movement from 1854–1890* and whose second is a sampler of Milne's work, *Into the Sun and Other Stories*. The 1882 title story and its sequel describe a cataclysmic comet strike and its aftermath, while "Ten Thousand Years in Ice" and its sequel "The World's Last Cataclysm" (both 1889) feature relics of a similar prehistoric incident. "A New Palingenesis" (1883) **hybridizes** spiritualism and electrical theory.

**MINIATURIZATION.** Miniature humans have been a standard motif in fantasy fiction for centuries, although the notion that fairies are tiny is of relatively recent provenance. The Lilliputians described in **Jonathan Swift's** *Gulliver's Travels* (1726) have been abundantly copied. Stories in which ordinary humans are miniaturized in order to see the world—including aspects of it invisible to the naked eye—from a different viewpoint were a natural development, and the invention of hypothetical machines to facilitate the process was equally natural, in spite of obvious rational objections regarding the mass and density of the miniaturized individual. Edwin Pallander's *Adventures of a Micro-Man* (1902) is an early example and **Harry Bates's** "A Matter of Size" (1934) an early adaptation of the theme to **pulp sf. James Blish's** "Surface Tension" (1952) remains the most impressive, although movie variants provided the theme with a much higher profile thereafter. The artificial creation of miniature worlds, as in **Jack Williamson's** "Pygmy Planet" (1932), **Theodore Sturgeon's** "Microcosmic God" (1941), and **Frederik Pohl's** "The Tunnel under the World" (1954) is an enterprising variant.

**MITCHELL, EDWARD PAGE (1852–1927).** U.S. journalist who wrote a number of **sf** stories, mostly accounts of bizarre **inventions**, for newspapers and periodicals, beginning with the mathematical fantasy "The Tachypomp" (1871). "The Man without a Body" (1877) features a **matter transmitter** and "The Ablest Man in the World" (1879) a **cyborg** with a computer for a brain (although none of the relevant descriptive terms had yet been invented). **Sam Moskowitz** tracked down numerous forgotten items in order to compile the definitive collection *The Crystal Man* (1973).

**MITCHELL, J. LESLIE (1901–1935).** Scottish writer. He followed his flippant contribution to the **Today & Tomorrow series**, *Hanno; or, The Future of Exploration* (1928) with the earnest **timeslip romances** *Three Go Back* (1932) and *Gay Hunter* (1934), which take representative parties of contemporary humans into the remote past and near future—where they find similar situations that cast a melancholy shadow over the delusions of civilization. A third extended ***conte philosophique*** with a similar structure was left incomplete on the author's sudden death; John Gawsworth published an edited version of it, along with two other brief **scientific romances**—one of them bearing Mitchell's better-known pseudonym, Lewis Grassic Gibbon—in the **anthology** *Masterpiece of Thrills* (1936).

**MITCHELL, JOHN A. (1845–1918).** U.S. writer in several genres. *The Last American* (1889) is a **satirical** novella in which future archaeologists from Persia investigate an **ecocatastrophically** devastated America. The **hybrid science-fantasy** *Drowsy* (1917) involves a trip to the moon whose **illustration** (by Angus Peter Macdonald) is exceptionally interesting.

**MITCHELL, SYNE (1970– ).** U.S. writer in various fantasy genres. Her **sf** includes *Murphy's Gambit* (2000), in which a "floater" raised in zero gravity is the only person able to fly a mysterious spaceship, and the post-**cyberpunk** thriller *Technogenesis* (2002). *The Changeling Plague* (2003) is an intense account of illicit **biotechnology** running out of control.

**MITCHISON, NAOMI (1897–1999).** British writer in several genres, best known for anthropologically informed historical fantasies that sometimes strayed into the margins of **sf**. As **J. B. S. Haldane's** sister, she took an interest in his speculative ideas; *Memoirs of a Spacewoman* (1962) is a thoughtful account of communication with various **alien** species extrapolating ideas broached in "Possible Worlds," but she politely waited until he was dead before expressing her skepticism and dissent regarding the theses of *Daedalus* in *Solution Three* (1975) and *Not by Bread Alone* (1983).

**MIXON, LAURA J. (1957– ).** U.S. writer married to **Steven Gould.** Her first ventures into **sf** were the near-future thrillers *Glass Houses* (1992) and *Proxies* (1998), the latter involving a technology facilitating the transmission of consciousness whose applications include the ability to "inhabit" distant **android** bodies. *Burning the Ice* (2002) is set in the same universe on a cold colony world.

**MODESITT, L. E. (1943– ).** U.S. writer who began publishing **sf** in 1973. A complex **metaphysical fantasy series** involving **time travel** comprises *The Fires of Paratime* (1982), *The Timegod* (1993), *Timediver's Dawn* (1992), and the collection *Timegods' World* (2000).

Much of his sf addresses ecological themes; a keen awareness of Earth's likely near-future spoliation is unblunted by the action-adventure frameworks employed in the **space opera** series comprising *Dawn for a Distant Earth* (1987), *Silent Warrior* (1987), *In Endless Twilight* **(1988)**, and *The Forever Hero* (1999) and the **political fantasy** series comprising *The Ecologic Envoy* (1986), *The Ecolitan Operation* (1989), *The Ecologic Secession* (1990), *The Ecolitan Enigma* (1997), and *Empire and Ecolitan* (2001). *Of Tangible Ghosts* (1994) and its sequel *Ghost of the Revelator* (1998) are **alternative history** espionage thrillers. *The Parafaith War* (1996) is **military sf.** *Gravity Dreams* (1999) is a far-ranging space opera.

**MOFFETT, JUDITH (1942– ).** U.S. writer whose first venture into **sf** was a 1986 story subsequently reprinted in *Two That Came True* (1991). In the earnest moral fantasy *Pennterra* (1987), an extraterrestrial colony established by Quakers fares better than one founded with more exploitative intentions. **Aliens** assist a devastated Earth in the **mosaic** *The Ragged World* (1991) and its sequel *Time, Like an Ever-Rolling Stream* (1992).

**MOFFITT, DONALD (1936– ).** U.S. writer who began publishing **sf** with *The Jupiter Theft* (1977), whose epic ambitions were extended to a wider stage in the couplet comprising *The Genesis Quest* and *Second Genesis* (both 1986). The couplet comprising *Crescent in the Sky* (1990) and *A Gathering of Stars* (1990) develops more easily manageable **hard sf** themes within the framework of a **political fantasy** in which the troubled relations between Islam and the West are extrapolated into space. *Jovian* (2002) describes the Jupiter-born hero's adventures on Earth and Venus.

**MONSTERS.** The evolution of **sf** has dramatically increased the catalogue of monsters available to writers of **horror** fiction. **Mary Shelley's** *Frankenstein* stands at the head of a vast series of exercises in teratology, whose produce includes exotic evolutionary products of Earth's ecosphere—including survivals from remote prehistory—**aliens**, **mutants**, amoral **supermen**, and sinister machines. Many **hybrid texts** have been produced with the specific objective of "rationalizing" the traditional monsters of other kinds of fantasy, including vampires, shape-shifters, and zombies. Monstrous antagonists became less fashionable when the **pulp** era ended as writers became more anxious about stigmatizing scientific discovery and promoting xenophobia, but the advent of **genetic engineering** added considerably to the available resources for monster creation. The visual dimension of **sf cinema** has offered unique opportunities for the development of monsters, from *King Kong* to *Alien*, but such imagery often draws inspiration from classic literary texts, including **H. G. Wells's** *The War of the Worlds* (1898), **A. E. van Vogt's** "Discord in Scarlet" (1939), and **Robert A. Heinlein's** *The Puppet Masters* (1951).

**MONTELEONE, THOMAS F. (1946– ).** U.S. writer who began publishing **sf** in 1973, his early work being collected in *Dark Stars, and Other Illuminations* (1981). *Seeds of Change* (1975), the first of **Roger Elwood's** ill-fated Laser Books, was given away as a promotional item. Powerful computers are featured in the **mosaic** *The Time-Swept City* (1977) and the couplet comprising *Guardian* (1980) and *Ozymandias* (1981). *The Secret Sea* (1979) is a proto-**steampunk Vernian metafiction**. He wrote the Dragonstar trilogy (1983–1989) in **collaboration** with **David Bischoff** before redirecting his attention to other fantasy genres.

**MOON, THE.** The moon has a unique significance in the evolution of **sf**, having been important in the genre's history as a key venue of **Utopian satire** and becoming even more important in the mythology of the **space age** by virtue of being the most immediate destination of space travel. This importance became problematic after 1969, when the first moon landing actually took place, advertised as "a giant leap for mankind." Doubts as to whether that landing actually took place rather than being faked in a **TV** studio need not be taken seriously to be seen as significant; the point is not that the moon landing might never have happened but that it might just as well not have happened, for all the lasting difference it made. The famous passage in Ludovico Ariosto's *Orlando Furioso* (1516) in which the moon is represented as a storehouse of everything wasted on Earth—including unfulfilled desires and intentions—had come to seem strangely **prophetic** by the end of the 20th century, when the futuristic dreams and ambitions reflected and embodied in so much sf seemed to have been abandoned along with the manned space program.

**MOON, ELIZABETH (1945– ).** U.S. writer who began publishing **sf** in 1986. Her experience in the U.S. Marine Corps provided some of the inspiration for a tongue-in-cheek **military sf series** comprising *Hunting Party* (1993), *Sporting Chance* (1994), *Winning Colors* (1995), *Once a Hero* (1997), *Rules of Engagement* (1998), *Change of Command* (1999), and *Against the Odds* (2000); *Trading in Danger* (2003) began a new series of a similar stripe. *Remnant Population* (1996) is a **first contact** story. *The Speed of Dark* (2003) confronts its autistic protagonist with a choice as to whether to employ new technology to change his personality. Moon's short fiction is collected in *Lunar Activity* (1990) and *Phases* (1997).

**MOONEY, TED (1951– ).** U.S. writer whose first novel, *Easy Travel to Other Planets* (1981), is an unusual futuristic fantasy featuring the advent of a new emotion and the effect of various technological innovations on human relationships. *Traffic and Laughter* (1990) is an **alternative history** of a world without nuclear power.

**MOORCOCK, MICHAEL (1939– ).** British writer and editor. His early publications were mostly in other fantasy genres, although *The Sundered Worlds* (1962–1963, book 1965) is a **metaphysical space opera** that introduced the idea of the **multiverse**, a concept which he subsequently used to bind together all his works into an unrepentantly **chimerical** whole. He took over the editorship of ***New Worlds*** in 1964 with a missionary zeal, intending to bring about an avant-gardist revolution within **sf**. His Jerry Cornelius stories, including the tetralogy comprising *The Final Programme* (1968), *A Cure for Cancer* (1971), *The English Assassin* (1972), and *The Condition of Muzak* (1977), are paradigm examples of the **new wave** sf he promoted. The character was made available to other writers in stories such as those featured in *The Nature of the Catastrophe* (1971) edited by Moorcock and Langdon Jones, and **transfigured** in numerous other works in various genres into more exotic characters (often with the same initials). These include Jherek Carnelian, in the series of **far-futuristic fantasies** featuring the Dancers at the End of Time, including the novels *An Alien*

*Heat* (1972), *The Hollow Lands* (1974), and *The End of All Songs* (1976). A different Jerry Cornelius is the hero of *The Distant Suns* (1969, with James Cawthorn; book 1975), while *Behold the Man* (1969) features a **time-traveling** search for Jesus Christ that proves more challenging than anticipated.

Moorcock's other early sf includes the gaudy futuristic fantasies *The Fireclown* (1965, aka *the Winds of Limbo*) and *The Twilight Man* (1966, aka *The Shores of Death*); *The Wrecks of Time* (1965–1966, 1967; aka *The Rituals of Infinity*), a thriller borrowing imagery from **J. G. Ballard**; *The Black Corridor* (1969), a bleak account of space travel; *The Ice Schooner* (1969), a far-futuristic transfiguration of **Joseph Conrad**; and some of the short stories collected in *The Deep Fix* (1966) and *The Time Dweller* (1969). The trilogy comprising *The Warlord of the Air* (1971), *The Land Leviathan* (1974), and *The Steel Tsar* (1981) is a significant precursor of the **steampunk** subgenre. Almost all of these texts were revised for republication, along with material from other fantasy genres, in a 14-volume **series** of omnibuses (1992–1993) collectively entitled *The Tale of the Eternal Champion*.

**MOORE, C. L. (1911–1987)** U.S. writer whose first publication in ***Weird Tales***, "Shambleau" (1933), pioneered a new kind of **science-fantasy** hybridizing post-**Burroughsian planetary romance** with mythical fantasy. Several sequels followed, the **series** initially being mingled with a heroic fantasy series in *Shambleau and Others* (1953) and *Northwest of Earth* (1954) before being brought together in *Scarlet Dream* (1981, aka *Northwest Smith*). She began publishing similar material in ***Astounding*** in 1934 and continued to do so after **John Campbell** took charge. After marrying **Henry Kuttner** in 1940, she worked in close association with him under several different names. Moore's subsequent solo contributions to *Astounding* included the colorful **space opera** used as the title story of *Judgment Night* (1943, book 1952); the classic proto-**feminist cyborg** story "No Woman Born" (1944); several stories as Laurence O'Donnell, including the **Venus-set** romance "Clash by Night" (1943); and the classic tale of time tourism "Vintage Season" (1946).

After publishing the **far-futuristic fantasy** *Earth's Last Citadel* (1943, book 1964) in *Argosy* under a collaborative byline, Moore continued to develop her distinctive brand of science-fantasy in the pages of ***Startling Stories***; because Kuttner had already published two novels there, she used his name, as well as the byline Keith Hammond, for a series of works to which his contributions were probably peripheral. These included *The Dark World* (1946, book 1965), *Valley of the Flame* (1946, book 1964), "Lands of the Earthquake" (1947), *The Mask of Circe* (1948, book 1971), *The Time Axis* (1949, book 1965), "The Portal in the Picture" (1949, book 1954 as *Beyond Earth's Gates*), and *The Well of the Worlds* (1952, book 1965). She wrote one more solo sf novel, the **disaster story** *Doomsday Morning* (1957), but mostly worked in other genres and other media from 1956 until 1963, when she abandoned writing.

**MOORE, PATRICK (1923– ).** British amateur astronomer and **TV** presenter who wrote an early book on **sf**, *Science and Fiction* (1957), and a number of **children's sf** novels, beginning with *Master of the Moon* (1952); 18 of these were issued in 1952–1969 and 6 more in the late 1970s. Some of his later books are comedies with **sf** elements, including a proto-**steampunk** account of *How Britain Won the Space Race* (1982, with Desmond Leslie) in the 19th century.

**MOORE, WARD (1903–1978).** U.S. writer in several genres, who first ventured into **sf** in the **satirical disaster story** *Greener Than You Think* (1947). A more cynical study of reaction to disaster, comprising "Lot" (1953) and "Lot's Daughter" (1954), casts Los Angeles as Sodom afflicted by a nuclear rain of fire. *Bring the Jubilee* (1953) is a classic **alternative history** story in which the United States is a 20th-century technological backwater following the Confederacy's victory in the Civil War. *Caduceus Wild* (1959, with Robert Bradford; book 1978) satirizes a future run by the U.S. medical profession. The novella "Transient" (1960) is a surreal **hybrid** text. *Joyleg* (1962, with **Avram Davidson**), featuring a long-lived hillbilly, is much lighter in tone.

**MORGAN, DAN (1925– ).** British writer who began publishing **sf** in 1952. *CeeTee Man* (1955) and *The Uninhibited* (1957, book 1961) are action-adventure novels. *The Richest Corpse in Show Business* (1966) is a farce **satirizing** sf clichés. The **psi** series comprising *The New Minds* (1967), *The Several Minds* (1969), *Mind Trap* (1970), and

*The Country of the Mind* (1975) is a sympathetic reappraisal of familiar themes. *Inside* (1971) describes a sociological experiment. *The High Destiny* (1973) is a folkloristic fantasy set in a **miniature galactic empire.** *The Concrete Horizon* (1976) is an alloy of **existentialist fantasy** and **disaster story.** In **collaboration** with John Charles Hynam (1915–1974), who wrote as John Kippax, Morgan produced a **space opera series** comprising *A Thunder of Stars* (1968), *Seed of Stars* (1972), *The Neutral Stars* (1973), and *Where No Stars Guide* (1975); the fourth volume was written by Hynam alone.

**MORGAN, RICHARD (1956– ).** British writer. *Altered Carbon* (2002) is a convoluted post-**cyberpunk** thriller set against the background of a ramshackle **galactic empire.** In the sequel, *Broken Angels* (2003), the protagonist acquires a new "sleeve" (body) in order to investigate a **Martian** artifact.

**MORRIS, JANET E. (1946– ).** U.S. writer in various fantasy genres. Some of her work is hybrid **science-fantasy**, including her early Silistra sequence (1977–1979) and the trilogy comprising *Dream Dancer* (1980), *Cruiser Dreams* (1981), and *Earth Dreams* (1982). Her other sf was mostly written in collaboration, either with her husband, Chris Morris—with whom she produced the **disaster story** *The 40-Minute War* (1984); the **military sf** novel *Outpassage* (1988); and the **space opera** trilogy *Threshold* (1990), *Trust Territory* (1992), and *The Stalk* (1994)—or with **David A. Drake**, with whom she wrote several futuristic spy thrillers.

**MORRIS, WILLIAM (1834–1896).** British artist and writer. His heartfelt opposition to the technologies of mass production led him to compose *News from Nowhere, or An Epoch of Rest* (1890), in which **Utopia** is achieved by employing craftsmanship to supply carefully moderated material needs, as a reply to **Edward Bellamy's** *Looking Backward, 2000–1887* (1888).

**MORROW, JAMES (1947– ).** U.S. writer who produced some **children's sf** in connection with experiments in multimedia education before his first novel, the **satirical** allegory *The Wine of Violence* (1981), in which a castaway on a **lost world** inadvertently precipitates disaster in a society whose members exorcise their violent impulses by means of technologically assisted catharsis. *The Continent of Lies* (1984) similarly delves into the murkier depths of human psychology in a colorful **Orphean fantasy** featuring trees genetically engineered to produce dream-inducing fruit. The heart-rending **postholocaust fantasy** *This Is the Way the World Ends* (1986) is a **hybrid** text, and Morrow's subsequent novels, *Only Begotten Daughter* (1989) and the trilogy comprising *Towing Jehovah* (1994), *Blameless in Abaddon* (1996), and *The Eternal Footman* (1999), are all futuristic **religious fantasies** whose most conspicuous **sf** elements are passionate skepticism and relentless extrapolative fervor. The novella *City of Truth* (1991) is a satirical **Utopia**; other spirited **contes philosophiques** are collected in *Bible Stories for Adults* (1996).

**MOSAIC.** A term used by **Gregory Benford** (in the phrase "mosaic novel") to refer to his exercises in fictional accretion, by which short stories are extrapolated into **series** collectible in book form. It embraces what the **Clute/Nicholls** *Encyclopedia* calls **fix-ups** and collections of sequentially linked stories, but not series of novels.

**MOSKOWITZ, SAM (1920–1997).** U.S. historian and editor. He became a central figure of **sf fandom** in the mid-1930s, his passionate interest in the genre eventually leading him to embark on numerous biographical and **bibliographical** studies. His essays on sf's precursors, collected in *Explorers of the Infinite* (1963), were followed by studies of the major genre writers, collected in *Seekers of Tomorrow* (1966); a third collection, *Strange Horizons* (1976), included some addenda alongside essays on various themes and motifs.

Although he worked as an editor outside the field, Moskowitz's editorial ventures within it were confined to the short-lived **Gernsback**-funded magazine *Science Fiction Plus* and numerous **anthologies**, those from commercial publishers often being "ghost-edited" for Leo Margulies, **Roger Elwood**, or Alden H. Norton. Far more significant were the historical anthologies and collections he released through **small presses**, many of which recovered long-forgotten and long-unavailable works of considerable historical significance. These included *Science Fiction by Gaslight: A History and Anthology of Science Fiction in the Popular Magazines, 1891–1911* (1968), *Under* *the Moons of Mars: A History and Anthology of the Scientific Romance in the Munsey Magazines, 1912–1920* (1970), and *When Women Rule* (1972), and collections by **David H. Keller**, **Stanley G. Weinbaum**, **Edward Page Mitchell**, **Olaf Stapledon**, **William Hope Hodgson**, **George Griffith**, and **Robert Duncan Milne.**

All of these volumes were liberally equipped with editorial commentary, embodying original biographical research and tracking the histories of the ideas deployed by individual stories with such avid exactitude that Moskowitz was often accused of assuming influences where none really existed. Thanks to the assiduousness with which he located, collated, and put into print a great deal of material that would otherwise have remained obscure, he made an unparalleled contribution to the retrospective construction of the genre's history.

**MULTIVERSE.** An infinite array of **parallel worlds** displaced from ours in a fourth spatial dimension, often playing host to a similarly infinite array of **alternative histories.** The term was popularized within the genre by **Michael Moorcock**, who used it as a framing concept to link the very various worlds described within his texts into an inherently **chimerical** superstructure; it had previously been used in the **metaphysical fantasies** of John Cowper Powys. The "many worlds interpretation" of quantum-mechanical uncertainties gave a gloss of theoretical respectability to the notion that all possible universes might actually exist, organized into such a manifold—as in **Stephen Baxter's** Manifold trilogy. *Scientific American* devoted a special issue to the question in May 2003—thus emphasizing the extent to which science, and **sf**, remain intricately interlinked with metaphysical fantasy.

**MUNRO, JOHN (1849–1930).** British popularizer of science who wrote a handful of didactic stories for **magazines**, the first of which—"A Message from Mars" (1894)—was expanded into the awkwardly constructed *A Trip to Venus* (1897), whose second chapter is an earnest discussion of the possibility of space travel, which includes (but does not favor) rockets fired in stages.

**MURPHY, PAT (1955– ).** U.S. writer who began publishing **sf** in 1979. *The Shadow Hunter* (1982) displaces a Stone-Age man into the future; *The Falling Woman* (1986) equips an archaeologist with the psychic gift of seeing into the past; "Rachel in Love" (1987) examines the existential plight of a chimpanzee with artificially enhanced intelligence. *The City, Not Long After* (1988) is a **hybrid post-holocaust fantasy** meditating upon the social functions of art. *There and Back Again* (1999) is a lighthearted **space-operatic transfiguration** of J. R. R. Tolkien's *The Hobbit*, credited to the imaginary Max Merriwell—star of *Adventures in Time and Space with Max Merriwell* (2001)—whose alter ego Mary Maxwell (aka Mary Merriwell) also writes sf, including the ironically feminized Tarzan transfiguration *Wild Angel* (2000). Murphy's early short fiction is collected in *Points of Departure* (1990).

**MUTANT.** A term whose importance in evolutionary theory was secured by Hugo de Vries' *Die Mutationstheorie* (1901–1903), although de Vries had gross physical deformities in mind rather than the minute variations of DNA base sequences that inherited the term when the chemical mechanisms of heredity were clarified. The word has always retained de Vriesian implications in the popular imagination, and in much **sf**. Wilhelm Müller's discovery in 1927 that mutations could be induced in fruit flies by irradiation was rapidly taken up by **pulp sf**, where the notion served so well as an apologetic jargon for the creation of **monsters** that melodramatic "mutational romance" became a significant subgenre, vividly pioneered by **John Taine** in *The Iron Star* (1930) and *Seeds of Life* (1931). Mutants became a standard feature of stories set in the aftermath of a nuclear holocaust, where mutational variations in evolution became convenient as a means of generating climactic light at the end of the narrative tunnel. The mutational romances of the 1950s **magazines** were more inclined to follow the pattern of **Wilmar H. Shiras's** *Children of the Atom* (1948–1950) and **John Wyndham's** *The Chrysalids* (1955) than Taine's exercises in teratology, although sf **cinema** remained a generation in arrears. Mutational miracles continued to supply sf with deus-ex-machina climaxes until the end of the century, although such sophisticated examples as **Greg Bear's** *Blood Music* (1985) are careful to incorporate rapid natural selection into the scenario in order to simulate progressive purpose.

## – N –

**NAGATA, LINDA (1960– ).** U.S. writer who began publishing **sf** in 1987. Her work, from *The Bohr Maker* (1995) on, makes extravagant use of **nanotechnology**; *Tech-Heaven* (1995) also involves cryonics and longevity technology. *Deception Well* (1997) is a **van Vogtian Orphean fantasy**; *Vast* (1998) is set in the same seemingly crumbling galactic civilization. *Limit of Vision* (2001) is a near-future thriller about **biotechnology** run amok. *Memory* (2003) is an Orphean fantasy featuring a ring-shaped planet afflicted by mysterious nanotechnological fog controlled by insectile mechanical "kobolds."

**NANOTECHNOLOGY.** A term coined and popularized by K. Eric Drexler in his highly influential work of **speculative nonfiction** *Engines of Creation* (1987). It refers to the use of very tiny machines capable of manipulating individual atoms and molecules, thus simulating—and vastly extending—the "natural technologies" used by living cells to manufacture proteins, organs, and whole bodies. Drexler proposed that the difficulties faced by human inventors working with imperceptible materials could be overcome by a stepwise process of making generations of machines to manufacture even smaller machines, with the aid of self-improving **artificial intelligence** programs that would make ever-more-rapid progress as they descended the space-time scale. **Sf** writers, who joined very enthusiastically in the business of further elaborating the terminology, rapidly took up these notions. Drexler called the tiny machines "assemblers" but many sf writers preferred "nanobots" (a contraction of "nano-**robots**").

The idea that nanobots could be used to process extremely raw material into any object of desire prompted speculation about amorphous "utility mists" awaiting metamorphosis, whose inverse was described in melodramatic accounts of "gray goo" catastrophes precipitated by out-of-control nanotechnologies; variants of the latter scenario often employed goo of other colors—green, gold, and red being favorites, blue being conventionally reserved for defensive goo preventing such catastrophes.

By the end of the 20th century, the evolution of nanotechnology was taken for granted in most of the futuristic scenarios of **hard sf**, although writers offered widely different estimates of the pace of that progress; some who embraced the second part of Drexler's thesis, most notably **Vernor Vinge**, extrapolated the idea of ever-accelerating self-directed technological progress to embrace the notion of a technological **singularity.** The medical usefulness of nanotechnology is so obvious that it hardly features as a specific subject matter, although **Greg Bear's** *Queen of Angels* (1990) speculates about its potential impact on mental health. *Nanotech* (1998) edited by **Jack Dann** and **Gardner Dozois** is a notable theme **anthology**.

**NASIR, JAMIL (1955– ).** U.S.-born writer of Palestinian descent who began publishing **sf** in 1988, putting his experiences of life in the Middle East to good use in establishing settings dramatically dissimilar to those usually deployed in Anglo-American sf. *Quasar* (1995) is a thriller featuring a psychiatric technician's descents into **inner space** and an actual underworld. The hero of *The Higher Space* (1996) is involved with the **chimerical** discipline of Thaumatomathematics. *Tower of Dreams* (1999) is a **hybrid** text in which expert media exploitation of mythic imagery becomes surreally confused. The protagonist of *Distance Haze* (2000) is an sf writer who joins a search for God and struggles to reconcile seemingly incompatible worldviews.

**NEBULA.** The annual award given by the **Science Fiction Writers of America** since 1966, in the usual categories: novel, novella, novelette, and short story. An award for best dramatic presentation or writing was introduced in 1973 but abandoned in 1975. A Grand Master Award was added in 1975. The qualification period for the award was initially restricted to the previous calendar year, but the rules were changed in the 1990s, allowing works to retain their eligibility for a longer period in order to diminish the relative advantage enjoyed by works published in the earlier months of the year. The award-winners in the shorter categories and a selection of other short-listed items were reprinted in an annual **anthology**, although changes in its publisher occasionally resulted in production falling behind schedule; its editorship was rotated annually until the mid-1980s, when editors began to serve terms of three years.

**NEEPER, CARY (1937– ).** U.S. writer whose first venture into **sf** was *A Place beyond Man* (1975), a hard-edged philosophical romance in which **aliens** become involved in planning humankind's response to an inevitable **ecocatastrophe.** A revised version, *The View beyond Earth* and excerpts from sequels *The Unheard Song*, *The Webs of Varok*, *Conn: The Alien Effect*, and *Shawne: An Alien's Quest* were posted on the author's website at www.caryneeper.com along with other items.

**NELSON, RAY FARADAY (1931– ).** U.S. writer and cartoonist who began publishing **sf** with the vivid **dystopian** fantasy "Turn Off the Sky" (1963), whose effect he never contrived to recapitulate, although *The Ganymede Takeover* (1967, with **Philip K. Dick**) is a lively comedy and *Blake's Progress* (1975; revised as *Timequest*, 1985) is an effective account of inspirational excursions in time undertaken by the romantic poet and his talented wife. The **Utopian** arguments extrapolated in the couplet comprising *Then Beggars Could Ride* (1976) and *The Revolt of the Unemployables* (1978) are masked by their **pulpish** narrative framework; their recontextualizations in the melodrama *The Prometheus Man* (1982) and the **planetary romance** *The Ecolog* (1977) were similarly awkward. *Virtual Zen* (1996) is a thriller set in near-future Tokyo.

**NESFA PRESS.** The New England Science Fiction Association (NESFA) first got involved in **small press** publication when it was still known as the MIT Science Fiction Society, under which imprint it issued Erwin S. Strauss's *Index to the S-F Magazines, 1951–65* (1966). The organization began producing small books of stories by the guests of its annual convention, Boskone, in the 1980s—early examples included *The Men from Ariel* (1982) by **Donald A. Wollheim** and *Compounded Interests* (1983) by **Mack Reynolds**—and branched out into the production of similar booklets for other conventions. The expertise thus gained became a springboard for much more adventurous publishing ventures in the 1990s, when NESFA Press became the most important small press in the field; it began issuing a **series** of omnibuses featuring the complete short **sf** of important writers, including **Cordwainer Smith** (1993), **C. M. Kornbluth** (1997), **William Tenn** (2 vols., 2001–2002), and "Don A. Stuart" (**John W. Campbell Jr.**) (2003), and published extensive multivolume samplers of the work of such writers as **Hal Clement** (3 vols.,

1999–2000), **Charles L. Harness** (2 vols., 1998–1999), and **Fredric Brown** (2 vols., 2001–2002).

**NESVADBA, JOSEF (1926– ).** Czech psychiatrist and writer in several genres, whose ***contes philosophiques*** cleverly carried forward the **satirical** tradition of **Karel Čapek**. Selections from his early **sf** (1958–1962) were translated in the overlapping collections *Vampires Ltd.* (1964) and *In the Footsteps of the Abominable Snowman* (1970, aka *The Lost Face*).

**NEVILLE, KRIS (1925–1980).** U.S. writer who began publishing **sf** in 1949. His short fiction, sampled in the **mosaic** *Bettyann* (1970), about an adopted child of extraterrestrial origin, and the collections *Mission: Manstop* (1971) and *The Science Fiction of Kris Neville* (1984, edited by **Barry N. Malzberg**), is more varied and enterprising than his formulaic novels, which include *The Mutants* (1953, exp. 1966) and *The Unearth People* (1964).

**NEWMAN, KIM (1959– ).** British film critic and writer, primarily of **postmodern horror** fiction, who began publishing **sf** in 1984. His lavish use of **metafictional alternative histories** sweeps sf motifs into a uniquely capacious generic melting pot. His first novel, the **virtual-reality** thriller *The Night Mayor* (1989), and the **mosaic** *Back in the USSA* (1997, with **Eugene Byrne**) make the most conspicuous use of sf devices, although the revisionist vampire **series** begun with *Anno Dracula* (1992) applies a scrupulous extrapolative method to its exotic premise. *Orgy of the Blood Parasites* (1994, as Jack Yeovil) is tongue-in-cheek horror-sf. His short fiction is collected in *The Original Dr. Shade and Other Stories* (1994), *Famous Monsters* (1995), *Seven Stars* (2000), and *Unforgivable Stories* (2000).

**NEW WAVE SF.** "New wave" became a fashionable term in **cinema criticism** in the early 1960s, translated from the French *nouvelle vague*. It was co-opted into the jargon of **sf fandom** in 1964, being applied to a group of British **fanzines** before being employed—initially by **Christopher Priest**—as a label for the avant-gardist sf of **J. G. Ballard** and **Brian W. Aldiss**, especially in the context of **Michael Moorcock's** use of those writers as key models for the kinds of fiction he was anxious to showcase in ***New Worlds*** from 1964 onward. Other exemplars included Langdon Jones, **M. John Harrison**, and such U.S. imports as **Thomas M. Disch** and **John Sladek**, the whole enterprise being contextualized by the criticism of **John Clute.** The term was soon taken up by the U.S. sf community, where it was applied to the works of such writers as **Samuel R. Delany**, **Roger Zelazny**, **Harlan Ellison**, and **Barry N. Malzberg**, and to the kinds of work showcased in Ellison's "taboo-breaking" **anthology** *Dangerous Visions* (1967). More writers strove to deny that the label had any relevance to them than rushed to embrace it, and its promiscuous use made easy definition or characterization of its content impossible. The illusion of a movement was connected with the importation into labeled sf of calculated surrealism and **fabulation**, a **satirical** concern with the media landscape and its subcultural undergrowth, tentative experimentation with nonlinear narrative techniques, and a newfound freedom to write about sex.

***NEW WORLDS.*** British **magazine** that carried forward the name of a late 1930s **fanzine.** It was launched professionally in 1946 by Steven Frances's Pendulum Publications and was saved from folding after three issues by a group of fans, including **John Carnell**, who had earlier edited the fanzine version. They founded Nova Publications, which published 138 further issues between 1949–1964 under Carnell's editorship, soon gathering *Science-Fantasy* into the stable and continuing *Science Fiction Adventures* (1958–1963) for 27 further issues after the demise of the U.S. magazine whose produce its first five had reprinted. The title was then sold to Roberts and Vinter, who installed **Michael Moorcock** as the new editor. It folded in 1967 (along with *Science-Fantasy*, whose last 12 issues, edited by **Keith Roberts** and **Harry Harrison**, were retitled *Impulse*), but Moorcock resurrected it with the aid of an arts council grant and occasional editorial assistance from his then-wife, Hilary Bailey, and **Charles Platt**; it folded again in 1969 but was revived as a supposedly quarterly **paperback series**, publishing 10 issues from 1971–1976. Such was its talismanic significance that it was revived twice more as a fanzine before a new paperback series edited by **David S. Garnett** published four more issues in 1991–1994. Under Carnell, *New Worlds* was a relatively conservative **sf** digest that played a vital role in developing the careers of such writers as **Kenneth**

**Bulmer**, **E. C. Tubb**, **James White**, and **John Brunner** before more adventurous input from **Brian W. Aldiss** and **J. G. Ballard** helped to inspire the drastic change of direction instituted by Moorcock, who made it the flagship of **new wave** sf.

***NEW YORK REVIEW OF SCIENCE FICTION, THE*** **(NYRSF).** U.S. **small press** periodical founded in 1988 by **David Hartwell** and produced with the aid of a small group of fellow editors, whose population never stabilized—in spite of which, the magazine has contrived to maintain a regular monthly schedule for 15 years, giving it a far greater immediacy than any of the academic quarterlies. Although it often published papers presented at the **International Conference on the Fantastic in the Arts** and other academic essays, it mingled such materials with high-quality fan writing; its reviews and regular "Read This" columns are as argumentative as they are eclectic. Far more combative than the advertising-supported ***Locus***, NYRSF has complemented that journal very well in maintaining a lively running commentary on the fortunes and progress of the field.

**NICHOLLS, PETER (1939– ). Australian** academic who became the first administrator of the **Science Fiction Foundation** and editor of its journal from 1971–1977, when he left to concentrate his efforts on the first edition of *The Encyclopedia of Science Fiction* (1979, in collaboration with **John Clute** and others). The *Encyclopedia's* packager, Roxby Press, also commissioned *The Science in Science Fiction* (1983), which Nicholls wrote in **collaboration** with **David Langford** and **Brian Stableford.**

**NIVEN, LARRY (1938– ).** U.S. writer who began publishing **sf** in 1964, quickly establishing a reputation as a definitive writer of **hard sf** and an important pioneer of sophisticated **space opera.** His exercises of the latter kind were mostly set within a common **future history** of "Known Space," which he began developing in his earliest short stories—assembled, along with an explanatory chronology, in *Tales of Known Space* (1975)—and extrapolated considerably in the novels *World of Ptavvs* (1966), *Protector* (1967, exp. 1973), *A Gift from Earth* (1968), and the classic *Ringworld* (1970). His determination to maintain the consistency of the backcloth while refining its individual inventions to overcome logical objections is amply displayed in the *Ringworld* sequels *Ringworld Engineers* (1979), *The Ringworld Throne* (1996), and *Ringworld's Children* (2003). Other notable Known Space stories include the futuristic mysteries assembled in *The Long ARM of Gil Hamilton* (1976) and *The Patchwork Girl* (1980) and a bold exercise in world building describing a peculiar planetless ecosphere, comprising *The Integral Trees* (1984) and *The Smoke Ring* (1987). The scenario was opened up to other writers in a **series** of **shared-world anthologies** about *The Man-Kzin Wars* (4 vols., 1988–1991).

Niven's other solo work includes a series of **time-paradox** comedies featuring Hanville Svetz, some of which were collected in *A Hole in Space* (1974) and the novel *Rainbow Mars* (1999); the epic time-spanning **mosaic** *A World Out of Time* (1976); and the grim **planetary romance** *Destiny's Road* (1997). His most frequent **collaborator** has been **Jerry Pournelle**, with whom he wrote the fervently **libertarian** space opera *The Mote in God's Eye* (1974) and its sequel *The Gripping Hand* (1993, aka *The Moat around Murcheson's Eye*); the **disaster story** *Lucifer's Hammer* (1977); the **political fantasy** *Oath of Fealty* (1981); and the **alien** invasion story *Footfall* (1985). The **transfigurative** planetary romance comprising *The Legacy of Heorot* (1987) and *Beowulf's Children* (1995) brought in **Steven Barnes** as a third partner, while **Michael Flynn** was the third participant in the political fantasy *Fallen Angels* (1991). With Barnes, Niven also wrote a series about **virtual reality** gaming, the disaster story *The Descent of Anansi* (1981), and the thrillers *Achilles' Choice* (1991) and *Saturn's Race* (2000).

**NOLAN, WILLIAM F. (1928– ).** U.S. writer in several genres, who began publishing **sf** in 1954. His short fiction is sampled in *Dark Universe* (2001). *Logan's Run* (1967, with George Clayton Johnson), about a **Utopian** society that resists overpopulation by executing its citizens at the age of 21, became a best-seller when film rights were sold, but the belated movie (1976) did not excite demand for Nolan's solo sequels *Logan's World* (1977) and *Logan's Search* (1980). His other sf series features hard-boiled future detective Sam Space in *Space for Hire* (1971), *Look Out for Space* (1985), and the collection *3 for Space* (1992).

**NOON, JEFF (1957– ).** British writer whose first novel, *Vurt* (1993), is a spectacular near-future fantasy in which society is transformed by the use of portable devices giving their users access to all manner of **virtual** experience, further enhanced by psychotropic drugs. A similar hectic surrealism is displayed in the exotic **disaster story** *Pollen* (1995) and *Nymphomation* (1997), and is carried to even further extremes in the Carrollian *Automated Alice* (1996). *Pixel Juice* (1998) assembles 50 short stories into a kaleidoscopic multigeneric **mosaic.** *Cobralingus* (2000) includes a guide to Noon's exotic literary methodology.

**NORTON, ANDRE (1912– ).** U.S. writer born Alice Mary Norton, who wrote **children's** fiction in other genres before venturing into **sf** in the groundbreaking **postholocaust fantasy** *Star Man's Son* (1952, aka *Daybreak 2250 A.D.*). She followed it with several **space operas**, including three bylined Andrew North and two couplets, one comprising *Star Rangers* (1953, aka *The Last Planet*) and *Star Guard* (1955), the other *The Stars Are Ours!* (1954) and *Star Born* (1957). *The Crossroads of Time* (1956) and *The Time Traders* (1958) launched two brief **time police series**. Because sf was considered at the time to be a boys' genre, most of these works are determinedly masculine, even though their harder elements are rather tokenistic, but her work became **softer** in texture as it moved away from space opera into **planetary romances** like *The Beast Master* (1959), *Secret of the Lost Race* (1959, aka *Wolfshead*), and *Catseye* (1961).

Norton's books were successfully reprinted in Ace Books' adult **paperback** line, prompting her to move to an opposite extreme in the thoroughly feminized **hybrid science-fantasy series** launched with *Witch World* (1963). The series soon minimized its fugitive sf elements, and much of her subsequent work was in other fantasy genres, although she continued to use sf motifs in many novels for younger readers, most impressively in *Dark Piper* (1968), *Breed to Come* (1972), and *Outside* (1974). Norton played a pivotal role in the softening of children's sf, arguably more significant as a recruiter of female readers to the genre—in that she was extending its limits rather than preaching to the converted—than **Robert Heinlein** had been as a recruiter of young males to the causes of **hard sf**.

**NORWOOD, WARREN C. (1945– ).** U.S. writer who first ventured into **sf** in a four-volume **series** chronicling the adventures of a star-faring soldier of fortune from the viewpoint of his sentient spaceship, launched in *The Windhover Tapes* (1982). They were followed by another **space opera** series begun with *Midway Between* (1984). *Shudderchild* (1987) is a **postholocaust** fantasy. The **time police** series initiated by *Vanished!* (1988) was continued with the assistance of Mel Odom when Norwood fell ill.

**NOURSE, ALAN E. (1928–1992).** U.S. physician and writer who began publishing **sf** in 1951, with stories subsequently integrated into the **mosaic** *The Universe Between* (1966). Best known within the genre for his **children's sf**—including *Trouble on Titan* (1954), *Raiders from the Rings* (1957), and *Star Surgeon* (1960)—he achieved far greater success outside it with material more directly related to his medical expertise. His adult sf includes *The Invaders Are Coming!* (1959, with J. A. Meyer) and the collections *Tiger by the Tail* (1961, aka *Beyond Infinity*) and *The Counterfeit Man and Others* (1963); its most interesting inclusions are the future medical **series** launched with "Nightmare Brother" (1953)—which includes *A Man Obsessed* (1959, revised as *The Mercy Men*) and stories collected in *Rx for Tomorrow* (1971)—the thriller *The Bladerunner* (1974), and the plague story *The Fourth Horseman* (1983).

**NOVUM.** A term employed by **Darko Suvin** to define an essential feature of an **sf** story: its central "idea" or "motif." The significance of characterizing it as a "new thing" is to emphasize the effect that Suvin calls **cognitive estrangement**—the displacement of the reader's consciousness into a framework of awareness that is not merely different from the one employed in understanding the real world but different in a new way. Merely returning to a familiar imaginary world, in the latest item of a segmental **series**, does not count as an authentic **science-fictional** experience in Suvin's view, although returning to an imaginary world that is to be further transformed by an additional novum, as in an expansive series, is a different matter. Because the idea in an sf story functions as a novum, it can acquire the special status observed in **Kingsley Amis's** characterization of sf stories as "idea-as-hero" stories.

**NOWLAN, PHILIP FRANCIS (1888–1940).** U.S. writer whose first **pulp sf** story, "Armageddon—2419 A.D." (1928) and its sequel "The Airlords of Han" (1929) launched the multimedia career of **Buck Rogers.** He published four more stories, including the novella "The Prince of Mars Returns" (1940), before dedicating himself entirely to **comic** books.

## – O –

**OBERNDORF, CHARLES (1959– ).** U.S. writer who began publishing **sf** with the **existentialist fantasy** "Mannequins" (1988). *Sheltered Lives* (1992) is a futuristic thriller in which the United States is devastated by a new plague. *Testing* (1993) is a **political fantasy** in which **virtual reality** games are used to test the moral fiber of college students. *Foragers* (1996) is an anthropological study of an **alien** race, set against the backcloth of an interstellar war.

**O'BRIEN, FITZ-JAMES (1828–1862).** Irish-born writer resident in the United States from 1852, active in several fantasy genres. **Hybrid** stories involving **sf** motifs include "The Diamond Lens" (1858), about a microscopic femme fatale; "What Was It?" (1859), about an invisible creature; "The Wondersmith" (1859), about an army of **miniature** automata; and the **hallucinatory fantasy** "How I Overcame My Gravity" (1864).

**ODLE, E. V. (1890–1942).** British writer whose only published **scientific romance** (a second was lost) was the inventive ***conte philosophique*** *The Clockwork Man* (1923), in which inhabitants of an English village respond in various way to a **timeslipped cyborg** from a distant and radically different future.

**O'DONNELL, KEVIN JR. (1950– ).** U.S. writer who began publishing **sf** in 1973. *Bander Snatch* (1979) is a futuristic thriller involving **extrasensory perception.** *Mayflies* (1979) is a **generation starship** story whose viewpoint character is immortally enshrined within the ship's governing **artificial intelligence.** Similarly quasi-godlike **hybrids** are featured in the four-volume *Journeys of McGil Feighan*

(1981–1986) and *ORA:CLE* (1984). *War of Omission* (1982) features a weapon that obliterates segments of space-time. *Fire on the Border* (1990) is a hectic **space opera.**

**ODYSSEAN FANTASY.** Homer's *Odyssey* is the literary work most frequently **transfigured** into **sf**, notable versions including **Fletcher Pratt's** "The Wanderer's Return" (1951), Stephen Barr's "The Homing Instinct of Joe Vargo" (1959), **R. A. Lafferty's** *Space Chantey* (1968), and **David Drake's** *Cross the Stars* (1984). Its attraction is mainly due to its basic narrative structure—a long series of extraordinary encounters invested with dramatic tension by the hero's urgent desire to return home—which makes an ideal framework for sf stories whose primary agenda is to parade a series of exotic entities and societies before the reader. Although the subgenre is also important in other fantasy genres, the relative dearth of alternative frameworks in sf, the greater variety of metaphorical meanings that sf stories can attach to the idea of "home," and the special significance of **series** in sf combine to give Odyssean fantasy a particular importance. Employed in early **pulp sf** by **Stanley G. Weinbaum**, it became a favorite device of **Jack Vance. E. C. Tubb's** Dumarest series is an extraordinarily extended example. It has obvious affinities with **Orphean fantasy** and **Promethean fantasy.**

**O'LEARY, PATRICK (1952– ).** U.S. writer who first employed **sf** motifs in *Door Number Three* (1995), a psychoanalytic fantasy about a patient claiming to be an **alien.** In *The Impossible Bird* (2002) humans gifted with an artificial afterlife by **aliens** defiantly assert their right to die. *Other Voices, Other Doors* (2000) mingles short fiction, essays, and poems.

**OLIVER, CHAD (1928–1993).** U.S. anthropologist and writer, who began publishing **sf** in 1950. His most effective stories—including many of those collected in *Another Kind* (1955) and *The Edge of Forever* (1971)—draw on his anthropological expertise to construct intriguing **alien** societies, as he does in *Unearthly Neighbors* (1960; rev. 1984). The juvenile *Mists of Dawn* (1952) draws on physical rather than cultural anthropology, as do *The Shores of Another Sea* (1971) and *Giants in the Dust* (1976). *Shadows in the Sun* (1954) is a mystery formulated in calculated opposition to the then-prevalent paranoia about the possibility of aliens living unobtrusively among us.

**OLSEN, LANCE (1956– ).** U.S. writer in various genres who began publishing **sf** in 1989. He followed up a 1992 critical study of **William Gibson** with *Tonguing the Zeitgeist* (1994), a macabre fantasy about the future of the music industry. *Time Famine* (1996) juxtaposes vivid images of a **decadent** and disintegrating near-future United States with the cannibalistic exploits of the doomed Donner party. *Burnt* (1996) is a **dystopian** "eco-novel" and "academentic **satire.**" *Freak Nest* (2000) is set in a quasi-Dickensian near-future England, featuring feral children and nanodrugs. His short story collections include *Scherzi, I Believe* (1994) and *Sewing Shut My Eyes* (2000), "an avant-pop concept album in prose."

**OMEGA POINT.** A term invented by the Jesuit evolutionary philosopher Pierre Teilhard de Chardin, who began to formulate the thesis in the 1920s but was forbidden to publish; it was posthumously popularized in *The Phenomenon of Man* (1955, tr. 1959), which hypothesizes that the sum of Earth's sentient beings constitutes a "noosphere" analogous to the ecosphere, whose future evolution will bring about a climactic "concurrence of human monads." Initially conceived as a local phenomenon, the Omega Point was transplanted to a universal stage in a 1945 lecture reprinted in *The Future of Man* (1959, tr. 1964), which suggested that the Earthly noosphere might detach itself from the planet in order to join a universal collective—an image prefigured in the work of **Olaf Stapledon** and echoed in **Arthur C. Clarke's** *Childhood's End*. Teilhard's version of the Omega Point was appropriated and further modified by such **sf** writers as **George Zebrowski**, **A. A. Attanasio**, and **Damien Broderick.**

The Omega Point was dramatically reconfigured by the physicist Frank Tipler in *The Physics of Immortality* (1994), where Teilhard's model is combined with inspiration drawn from Freeman Dyson's "Time without End: Physics and Biology in an Open Universe" (1979) and *Infinite in All Directions* (1988) in the proposition that the mechanical descendants of all the sentient beings in the universe—whose ultimate survival will depend on their minds being uploaded into more durable bodies—must eventually combine into a single godlike entity whose researches into its own origins will cause it to resurrect all the minds that ever existed into a **virtual** universe. Sketchily prefigured in such sf stories as **John Campbell's** "The Last Evolution" (1932) and **Isaac Asimov's** "The Last Question" (1956), this schema was appropriated into such works as **Frederik Pohl's** Eschaton **series** (Eschaton being the principal alternative term, also favored in **Charles Sheffield's** *Tomorrow and Tomorrow* and **Charles Stross's** *Singularity Sky*), **William Barton** and Michael Capobianco's *White Light*, **J. R. Dunn's** *Days of Cain*, and **Robert Charles Wilson's** *Darwinia*, rapidly becoming a standard element of sf's **far-futuristic fantasies.**

**O'NEILL, JOSEPH (1886–1953).** Irish politician and writer. He followed his **timeslip romance** *The Wind from the North* (1933) with two **scientific romances**: the striking subterranean **dystopia** *Land under England* (1935) and the **apocalyptic future war** novel *Day of Wrath* (1936).

**ORE, REBECCA (1948– ).** Pseudonym of U.S. writer Rebecca B. Brown, who began publishing **sf** in 1986. The trilogy comprising *Becoming Alien* (1988), *Being Alien* (1989), and *Human to Human* (1990) relocates a human misfit to a multicultural environment in which a series of exotic encounters prepare him for life on a universal stage. *The Illegal Rebirth of Billy the Kid* (1991) is a similar account of the gradual cultivation of an intelligence capable of adjusting to vastly expanded cultural horizons. *Gaia's Toys* (1995) combines character studies of three individuals alienated from a complex near-future society in various literal and metaphorical ways. *Outlaw School* (2000) is a cautionary tale about the perils of nonconformity. Ore's short fiction is collected in *Alien Bootlegger and Other Stories* (1993).

**ORPHEAN FANTASY.** A subgenre of fantasies echoing the myth of Orpheus' descent into the underworld on an ultimately frustrated quest to recover his lost wife, Eurydice, which is transfigured into **sf** almost as frequently as the *Odyssey*; there are notable versions by **Charles L. Harness**, **Tim Powers**, and **Jeff VanderMeer.** The pattern is particularly useful in sf as a model for descents from a rarefied and civilized interstellar culture to the dismal surfaces of primitive and dangerous planets. The object of the quest need not be a wife, but has to be someone (or something) of very intimate value; if it is not, the text moves into the neighboring subgenre of Dantean fantasy, in which underworld tours are educational in a broader sense. Orphean fantasy is primarily a matter of self-discovery, being more inclined to the exploration of the depths of the unconscious mind than discoveries about the nature of the universe.

**ORWELL, GEORGE (1903–1950).** Pseudonym of British writer Eric Arthur Blair, whose trenchant social commentary, undertaken from a socialist viewpoint, gave way to the deep disillusionment with the development of Soviet communism that saturates the spectacular **dystopian** fantasy *Nineteen Eighty-Four* (1949). The novel's imagery—the metaphorical Big Brother who keeps everyone under constant oppressive observation; the permanent fictitious war maintained as an instrument of propaganda and social control; the reduction of Britain to an American satellite "Airstrip One"; and Room 101, in which customized torture has been refined to the point of irresistible perfection—was soon absorbed into the routine parlance of political discourse.

**OUTER SPACE.** A popular phrase whose fine ring makes up for its pleonastic quality, the only function of "outer" being to emphasize the reference to space outside the Earth's atmosphere. Having featured in such titles as "From Outer Space" (1952) by Robert Zacks, it caught on rapidly—especially in citing the probable source of **flying saucers**—after its popularization by the movie *It Came from Outer Space* (1953) and Donald Keyhoe's *Flying Saucers from Outer Space* (1953), almost immediately generating the complementary term **inner space.**

## – P –

**PALMER, RAY A. (1910–1977).** U.S. editor who published an early **sf fanzine**, *The Comet*, in 1930. He became editor of ***Amazing Stories*** when it was bought by Ziff-Davis in 1938. The chain's system of operating a stable of house writers was presumably foisted on him, but he must have decided to recruit the conspiracy theory fantasist Richard S. Shaver to the **magazine** (and probably wrote a good deal of "Shaver Mystery" fiction himself) before he became entranced with the idea of **flying saucers**, none of which helped the genre's reputation. In 1948 he founded the occult magazine *Fate* and prepared the way for his exit from Ziff-Davis by founding sf magazine *Other Worlds* in 1949. He created *Imagination* in 1950 to supply employment for another unhappy employee, William L. Hamling, but the magazines carried forward too many Ziff-Davis practices to provide significant opposition to ***Galaxy*** and ***The Magazine of Fantasy & Science Fiction***. After being forced to give up *Imagination* and *Other Worlds* by the latest in a series of accidents that blighted his health throughout his life, Palmer founded *Universe* and *Science Stories* in 1953, but they never thrived; in 1955 he changed the title of *Universe* to *Other Worlds*, the earlier magazine having become defunct, expanding it to *Flying Saucers from Other Worlds* in 1957, after which his only publications were in the realm of **Fortean** fantasy.

**PALMER, STEPHEN (1962– ).** British writer who began publishing **sf** with *Memory Seed* (1996), set in the wake of an **ecocatastrophe** when the remnants of civilization are being extinguished by aggressive vegetation. *Glass* (1997) is similar in tone and structure, but features a more exotic antagonist. *Flowercrash* (2002) was planned as the third in the **series** but reconfigured when the publisher dropped it. *Muezzinland* (2002) is a post-**cyberpunk** novel set in "Aphrica," in which information technology is adapted to the local culture.

**PANGBORN, EDGAR (1909–1976).** U.S. writer in various genres whose first venture into **sf** was "Angel's Egg" (1951). *West of the Sun* (1953) is a Edenic **robinsonade** set on a planet named Lucifer. **Transfigured religious imagery** also abounds in *A Mirror for Observers* (1954), in which **Martians** play the part of guardian angels and their demonic counterparts, struggling to possess the soul of a human child with messianic potential. *The Judgment of Eve* (1966) is similar in essence, but the **postholocaust** sequence comprising the picaresque *Davy* (1964), the **mosaic** *The Company of Glory* (1975), and some of the stories collected in *Still I Persist in Wondering* (1978) and *Good Neighbors and Other Strangers* (1972) break the restraints of traditional imagery to undertake further-ranging ventures in moralistic fantasy.

**PANSHIN, ALEXEI (1940– ).** U.S. writer active in **fandom** before his first professional **sf** publication in 1963, with a story subsequently expanded into *Rite of Passage* (1968), a coming-of-age novel modeled on the work of **Robert A. Heinlein**, about whom Panshin wrote the first major critical study, *Heinlein in Dimension: A Critical Analysis* (1968). His subsequent critical works, including the essays collected in *SF in Dimension* (1976, exp. 1980), and the scrupulously researched *The World beyond the Hill: Science Fiction and the Quest for Transcendence* (1989), were written in **collaboration** with his wife, Cory. His other sf novels, *Star Well* (1968), *The Thurb Revolution* (1969), and *Masque World* (1969), are comic **space operas.**

**PAPERBACK BOOKS.** For nearly a hundred years, paperback books were unable to make substantial inroads into an English-language fiction marketplace dominated by hardcover books and **magazines**, but paper shortages caused by World War II changed the balance of power dramatically and the economically aggressive paperback companies formed in the United States and the United Kingdom immediately before the war seized an advantage they never surrendered. Cheaper digest magazines replaced the U.S. **pulps**, but the paperback publishers were always winning the subsequent battle for the low- and middlebrow ground. Although hardcover publication was still considered a necessity in the uppermost strata of the marketplace, hardcover publishers had to enter into a parasitic economic association with paperback publishers, multiple takeovers and mergers accomplishing an effective fusion by the end of the century.

The U.S. paperback boom that followed the end of World War II transplanted all the successful pulp genres, although sf remained on the margins until the force of its cult following became fully manifest, when the sf lines published by Ace (under the editorial auspices of **Donald Wollheim**) and Ballantine were widely imitated. By 1960 a new phase of the economic history of sf had begun: U.S. paperback publishers had replaced magazine editors as the genre's principal paymasters. In Britain, the maintenance of paper rationing after the war created a peculiar situation in which publishers anxious to exploit the new economic opportunities bought black-market paper to produce a glut of material crudely imitative of U.S. pulp fiction—including sf, thanks to the propagandizing efforts of "Hank Janson" (Steven Frances). The opportunities they offered were absurdly underpaid, but nevertheless welcome to writers like **John Russell Fearn**, **Kenneth Bulmer**, **E. C. Tubb**, and **R. Lionel Fanthorpe.** Similar phenomena were observed in **France** and **Germany**, and it was not until the late 1950s that paperback sf in these nations began to produce more sophisticated sf in considerable quantities—by which time, the tide of American imports was irresistible and native sf writers were permanently relegated to the periphery of their own domestic marketplaces.

The effects of paperback market hegemony on sf production were initially muted by the fact that paperback editors had a huge legacy of magazine material to mine, but an increasingly high proportion of 1960s and 1970s sf was written specifically for the paperback medium, so the novel replaced shorter formats as the genre's primary vehicle and novels began to get longer as publishers realized the selling power of thick spines. The crucial advantage of schooling regular readers in the skills of sf reading, which had helped sustain the magazines, was weakened as the work in question was effectively completed; control of the expectations that readers brought to texts was by then invested in the label itself—particularly to the iconic abbreviation "sf."

The rapid inflation of the standard length of an sf paperback—from an effective maximum of 60,000 words in 1970 to an oft-specified minimum of 120,000 by 1990—opened up some new narrative opportunities, but greatly encouraged the production of works whose **world-building** could be done in ways economical of narrative labor, usually involving a drastic proportional reduction of supportive explanation. Several scenarios were standardized for easy representation, including the **galactic empire** framing **planetary romances**, interplanetary fiction, and **space operas**, the near-future scenarios of post-**cyberpunk** thrillers, and the pastoral scenarios of much **postholocaust fantasy.** The conscientious expansion of **hard sf** into a long novel format requires narrative labor of such complexity as to pose a considerable challenge to readers and writers alike, so the evolution of paperback sf greatly encouraged the softening of the genre and its gradual replacement by genre fantasy.

**PARALLEL WORLD.** A world situated alongside our own, displaced from it in a fourth spatial dimension (for which reason parallel worlds are often referred to in **sf** jargon as "other dimensions"). The idea that such worlds exist is tacitly present in myth and folklore, where the world of the dead and the land of Faerie are often imagined to adjoin the perceived world and to be connected to it by a variety of permanent and temporary openings. This notion gave rise to a subgenre of **portal fantasies** long before sf writers began to adapt it to their own purposes. The concept received a substantial boost in the 19th century by virtue of the emergence of occult theories of an "astral plane." The idea of parallel worlds was foregrounded in a number of **scientific romances**, including **J. H. Rosny aîné's** "Another World" and **H. G. Wells's** "The Strange Case of Davidson's Eyes" (both 1895), and **pulp fiction** adopted them as convenient venues for exotic adventure stories some time before the advent of pulp sf, although it was sf writers who extrapolated the notion into the **multiverse.**

**PARK, PAUL (1954– ).** U.S. writer who began publishing **sf** with the **far-futuristic fantasy** *Soldiers of Paradise* (1987), the first volume of a loosely knit trilogy completed by *Sugar Rain* (1989) and *The Cult of Loving Kindness* (1991), which echo many of the themes of **Brian Aldiss's** Helliconia trilogy. *Coelestis* (1993, aka *Celestis*) is a phantasmagoric **planetary romance.** His short fiction is sampled in *If Lions Could Speak and Other Stories* (2002).

**PEIRCE, HAYFORD (1942– ).** U.S. writer who began publishing lighthearted **sf** in 1974. *Napoleon Disentimed* (1987) is a lively **alternative history** story. *The Thirteenth Majestral* (1989, aka *Dinosaur Park*) is a **far-futuristic fantasy** involving **time travel** and dinosaurs. *Phylum Monsters* (1989) employs **genetic engineering** in a wryly irreverent fashion. His short fiction is aggregated into several **mosaics**, including *Chap Foey Rider: Capitalist to the Stars* (2000); *Jonathan White, Stockbroker in Orbit* (2001); and *Sam Ferron, Time Scanner* (2001). *Flickerman* (2001), *The Spark of Life* (2001), and *Black Hole Planet* (2003) are similar in spirit. *Aliens* (2003) samples his short fiction.

**PELLEGRINO, CHARLES R. (1953– ).** U.S. scientist and writer who began publishing **sf** in 1991 with a story written in **collaboration** with **George Zebrowski.** He wrote the article on the possibility of cloning dinosaurs that prompted **Michael Crichton** to write *Jurassic Park*. *Flying to Valhalla* (1993) describes humankind's first interstellar flight, made with the aid of an **antimatter** drive, and its uncomfortable aftermath; *The Killing Star* (1995, with Zebrowski) **extrapolates** the most **melodramatic** idea broached therein into a **disaster story.** *Dust* (1998) is a more formulaic **disaster story**, in which the abrupt extinction of the world's insect life precipitates an **apocalyptic ecocatastrophe.**

**PESEK, LUDEK (1919–1999).** Czech writer and artist—a pioneer of "space art"—long resident in Germany. He first ventured into **sf** in providing text to accompany his pictorial *Log of a Moon Expedition* (1966, tr. 1969), following it up with two fine novels similarly marketed as children's books, although *The Earth Is Near* (1970, tr. 1973) is a dispassionate account of the disillusionment of expeditionaries to **Mars** whose hopes of finding life are dashed and *A Trap for Perseus* (1976, tr. 1980) is a sophisticated **dystopian** ***conte philosophique.***

**PETAJA, EMIL (1915–2000).** U.S. writer of Finnish descent who published **poetry** and fiction in **fanzines** before making his professional **sf** debut in 1942; his early work in various fantasy genres is sampled in *Stardrift and Other Fantastic Flotsam* (1971). The **series** comprising *Saga of Lost Earths* (1966), *The Star Mill* (1966), *The Stolen Sun* (1967), and *Tramontane* (1967) **transfigures** the Finnish epic *Kalevala*.

**PHILLIFENT, JOHN T. (1916–1976).** British writer in various genres who bylined much of his work John Rackham, under which pseudonym he began publishing **sf** in 1954. His most adventurous work in the genre appeared in the years immediately previous to his death, notably the **planetary romances** *Genius Unlimited* (1972), *Hierarchies* (1973), *King of Argent* (1973), and *Beanstalk* (1973, as Rackham).

**PHILLPOTTS, EDEN (1862–1960).** British writer in many genres. His first **sf** novel was a lurid thriller bylined Harrington Hext, *Num-*

*ber 87* (1922), but his most substantial **scientific romance** was *Saurus* (1938), in which a reptilian **alien** serves as an objective observer of human affairs. Phillpotts subsequently modified his opinion regarding the entitlement of aliens to pass such judgment in *Address Unknown* (1949). His other sf novel, *The Fall of the House of Heron* (1948), is a cautionary tale about overcommitment to scientific objectivity leading to moral anesthesia.

**PIERCY, MARGE (1936– ).** U.S. writer of literary fiction whose strong commitment to **feminism** led her to venture into **sf** with the exceptionally thoughtful **visionary fantasy** *Woman on the Edge of Time* (1976), which includes a rare attempt to describe a future society in which inequalities between males and females have been significantly eroded. *He, She and It* (1991, aka *Body of Glass*) is a complex **transfiguration** of the legend of the golem of Prague, set in a **cyberpunk**-influenced near future.

**PIPER, H. BEAM (1904–1964).** U.S. writer who began publishing **sf** in 1947. A contemptuous view of the common human herd, perhaps forged while he worked as a railroad policeman, found powerful expression in such archetypal **Campbellian** fantasies as "Day of the Moron" (1951) and "A Slave Is a Slave" (1962) and robust tales of uncompromising heroism like *Space Viking* (1963). The **alternative history series** launched with *Lord Kalvan of Otherwhen* (1965, aka *Gunpowder God*) is similar, but the early sf novels he wrote with John J. McGuire, "Null-ABC" (1953, book 1957 as *Crisis in 2140*) and *A Planet for Texans* (1958, aka *Lone Star Planet*) were both **satires**, and the uncollected **series** including the novella "Time Crime" (1955) was a thoughtful early example of **time police** fiction. The trilogy comprising *Little Fuzzy* (1962), *The Other Human Race* (1964, aka *Fuzzy Sapiens*), and the belatedly discovered *Fuzzies and Other People* (1984) is a wry moralistic fantasy in which cute **aliens** are protected from ruthless capitalistic exploitation. The **future history** backcloth of these books—especially its galaxy-spanning Federation—was used as the setting of much of Piper's work, including two tales of adaptation to extreme environments, "Ullr Uprising" (1953; rev. by Theodore Pratt as *Uller Uprising*, 1983) and *Four Day Planet* (1961), the stories assembled in

*Federation* (1981) and *Empire* (1981), and the tongue-in-cheek *Junkyard Planet* (1963, aka *The Cosmic Computer*).

**PISERCHIA, DORIS (1928– ).** U.S. writer who began publishing **sf** in 1966. *Mister Justice* (1973) is a **van Vogtian** vigilante drama. *Star Rider* (1974) adapts girl-and-pony fiction to a strange combination of **dimensional fantasy** and **space opera.** *Spaceling* (1978), *The Dimensioneers* (1982), and *The Deadly Sky* (1983) were apparently intended as juveniles of a similar ilk, although they were likewise released in the adult market. A remarkable imaginative fecundity, unconstrained by any robust narrative structure, is displayed in the vivid **far-futuristic fantasies** *A Billion Days of Earth* (1976), *Earthchild* (1977), *Doomtime* (1981), and *Earth in Twilight* (1981). *The Spinner* (1980) and *The Fluger* (1980) feature troublesome **alien monsters.** One of the **horror** novels Piserchia bylined Curt Selby, *I, Zombie* (1982), is also sf.

**PLANETARY ROMANCE.** A term coined by Russell Letson in a 1978 reprint of **Philip José Farmer's** *The Green Odyssey*, and subsequently popularized by **John Clute** in the second edition of his *Encyclopedia*, as a more apt description than **interplanetary romance** for exotic adventure stories in the tradition pioneered by **Edgar Rice Burroughs** and carried forward by such successors as **Leigh Brackett** and **Marion Zimmer Bradley.** Clute is adamant that the "romance" element of the phrase should exclude all seriously speculative stories set on **alien** planets, although it might profitably include **far-futuristic fantasies** set on a much-changed Earth. In fact, the term—which was taken up with alacrity—has usually been applied more promiscuously to tales of other worlds set within a **galactic empire** framework, but very rarely to far-futuristic fantasies. Given that Earth-clone worlds are no less fantastic when scattered about a galactic civilization than they are when named after planets within the solar system, it is probably appropriate to describe all stories set on such worlds as planetary romances, even when they are used as settings for serious investigations of hypothetical societies. The conspicuously alien worlds of **hard sf**, on the other hand, exempt themselves from the category by refusing to endorse the conceit that so many other worlds would be exactly like ours, save for relatively trivial matters of ecospheric decor.

**PLATT, CHARLES (1945– ).** British writer resident in the United States since 1970. He began publishing **sf** in 1965 in **Michael Moorcock's** ***New Worlds***, with which he was closely associated, occasionally serving as its coeditor as well as contributing maliciously trenchant **criticism**, but his own work does not warrant description as **new wave** sf. *Garbage World* (1967) and *Planet of the Voles* (1971) are farcical **satires**, while the **mosaic** *The City Dwellers* (1970; rev. as *Twilight of the City*, 1977) offers a grim description of progressive urban decay and *The Gas* (1970) is satirical pornography. He published two volumes of interviews with sf writers before returning to comedy sf with *Less Than Human* (1986, initially bylined Robert Clarke) and *The Free Zone* (1988). *The Silicon Man* (1991) is a **cyberpunk**-influenced **existentialist fantasy.**

**POE, EDGAR ALLAN (1809–1849).** U.S. writer who pioneered several modern genres, including the detective story and psychological **horror** fiction as well as **sf**. His unparalleled inventiveness received such a cold greeting in his homeland that one of his biographers, J. A. T. Lloyd, felt free to title his life story *The Murder of Edgar Allan Poe* (1931), but he was much more influential in France, where he was translated by Charles Baudelaire. Poe was the first writer to tackle the problem of finding appropriate narrative forms for literary extrapolations of the scientific imagination in a thoroughly experimental spirit, toying with visionary **poetry** in "Al Aaraaf" (1829); extraordinary voyages in "MS found in a Bottle" (1833), *The Narrative of Arthur Gordon Pym of Nantucket* (1838), and "The Unparalleled Adventure of One Hans Pfaall" (1835, revised 1840); mock philosophical dialogue in "The Conversation of Eiros and Charmion" (1839) and "The Colloquy of Monos and Una" (1841); **visionary fantasy** in "Mesmeric Revelation" (1844) and "A Tale of the Ragged Mountains" (1844); journalistic fakery in the material reprinted in "The Balloon Hoax" (1844); pastiche scientific reportage in "The Facts in the Case of M. Valdemar" (1845); and—most spectacularly of all—a curious alloy of **satire**, reportage, and extended prose-poetry in *Eureka* (1848). He also set important stylistic precedents for **decadent far-futuristic fantasy** in "The Masque of the Red Death" (1842). The gropingly experimental nature of this material makes much of Poe's sf seem odd to modern readers, but no one has ever matched his innovative flair and daring. It took more than a hundred years for the genius of *Eureka*—particularly its concluding vision of the death and rebirth of whole cosmic systems—to become evident, but all grandiose visions of **Omega Points** and other varieties of universal crisis owe their ultimate origin to Poe, and sf would have evolved much more rapidly and effectively had his precedents been ardently followed up instead of being allowed to fall into such long neglect.

**POETRY.** The scientific imagination was considered a perfectly apt subject by several notable poets of the 18th century, including Alexander Pope and Mark Akenside. Erasmus Darwin put many of his scientific publications into poetic form, as in *The Loves of the Plants* (1789; subsequently integrated into *The Botanic Garden*, 1791), there being no standardized form of scientific reportage at the time. Although the romantic movement encouraged hostility to the utilitarian aspects of science—especially the technologies providing the primary means of industrialization—many romantic poets, including Percy Shelley, were sympathetic to the visionary aspects of scientific discovery. William Wordsworth's preface to the *Lyrical Ballads* (3rd ed., 1802) earnestly discussed the relationship between science and poetry, establishing a topic subsequently to be addressed by Thomas Love Peacock, Herbert Spencer, and A. N. Whitehead, among many others.

Nineteenth-century scientists who dabbled in romantic verse (and prose) included **Sir Humphry Davy**, **Robert Hunt**, and Sir Ronald Ross. Edgar Allan Poe's "Al Aaraaf" (1829) offered a cosmic vision inspired by astronomical discovery, although Oliver Wendell Holmes's "medicated" poetry proved more influential in the United States in the short term. **Evolutionary** theory, as refined by Erasmus Darwin's grandson Charles, proved a powerful, if somewhat sobering, influence on poets as diverse as Alfred, Lord Tennyson, Charles Mackay, and Thomas Hardy. Modern epic poetry occasionally finds **science-fictional** themes useful in generating the scope and imaginative grandeur required by the form; notable examples include Harry Martinson's *Aniara* (1963), which features a **generation starship**, and Frederick Turner's *Genesis* (1988), about the **terraforming** of Mars.

The U.S. **pulps** had little time or place for poetry, and it was rare for the sf pulps to deviate from that policy, although a few did use poetry as fillers—many **fanzines**, however, were much more hospitable. The pioneer of labeled sf poetry, **Lilith Lorraine**, regarded poetry as an alternative medium for speculation, free of the cramping constraints of pulp fiction. The digest **magazines** did nothing to bridge this divide until the 1960s, when **new wave** sf began to encourage formal experimentation, encouraging established writers like **John Brunner** as well as newcomers like **Thomas M. Disch** and **Ursula le Guin** to publish volumes of poetry. Since the Science Fiction Poetry Association and its annual Rhysling Award were founded by **Suzette Haden Elgin** in 1978, sf poetry has gone from strength to strength, exemplified in the work of such writers as **Bruce Boston**, **John M. Ford**, and **Geoffrey A. Landis**, who were regularly featured in the pages of ***Asimov's Science Fiction*** once **Gardner Dozois** took over the editorship. Several **small press** magazines specializing in sf poetry emerged in the 1980s and Steve Sneyd undertook the difficult task of compiling a history of poetry in sf fanzines, reprinting exemplary selections, via Hilltop Press.

**POHL, FREDERIK.** U.S. writer and editor. He was a member of the **Futurians**, and was able to publish much of his own early work—most of it bylined James MacCreigh—along with that of his friends, while he was assistant editor to Alden Norton on the **pulp magazines** *Astonishing Stories* and *Super Science Stories* from 1941–1943. *The Early Pohl* (1976) mingles reminiscences with reprints of his early stories, while *The Way the Future Was: A Memoir* (1978) is a more detailed account of Futurian life. After the war he became a specialist literary agent for a while before becoming assistant editor of ***Galaxy***. He also edited the first **paperback** original **anthology series** *Star Science Fiction* (6 vols., 1953–1959).

Pohl abandoned the MacCreigh pseudonym when he produced the first of several novels in **collaboration** with **C. M. Kornbluth**, *The Space Merchants* (1953), and soon began turning out similar satires for *Galaxy*, most of which are collected in *Alternating Currents* (1956), *The Case against Tomorrow* (1957), *Tomorrow Times Seven* (1959), *The Man Who Ate the World* (1960), *Turn Left at Thursday* (1961), and *The Abominable Earthman* (1963). His early solo novels—*Slave Ship* (1957), *Drunkard's Walk* (1960), *A Plague of Pythons* (1965), and *The Age of the Pussyfoot* (1969)—were less successful than his collaborations with Kornbluth. He also seemed more comfortable working with **Jack Williamson**, on a juvenile trilogy (1955–1958) and a trilogy comprising *The Reefs of Space* (1964), *Starchild* (1965), and *Rogue Star* (1969). He also worked with **Lester del Rey** on *Preferred Risk* (1955 as by Edson McCann).

Once he had given up editing *Galaxy* and its companions, Pohl's novel-length work improved dramatically. His later short fiction, collected in *Day Million* (1970), *In the Problem Pit* (1976), and *Pohlstars* (1984), is more cleverly as well as more bleakly **satirical**, although his **extrapolation** of the classic novella "The Midas Plague" (1954) into *Midas World* (1983) and his solo sequel to *The Space Merchants*, *The Merchants War* (1984) struggled to bridge the long publication gaps. "The Merchants of Venus" (1971) was the prelude to the far-reaching Heechee series, comprising *Gateway* (1977), *Beyond the Blue Event Horizon* (1980), *Heechee Rendezvous* (1984), *The Annals of the Heechee* (1987), and the **mosaic** *The Gateway Trip* (1990).

*Man Plus* (1976) and *JEM: The Making of a Utopia* (1979) are hardheaded tales of extraterrestrial colonization. *The Cool War* (1981), *The Coming of the Quantum Cats* (1986), *Black Star Rising* (1985), *Narabedla Ltd.* (1988), and *The Day the Martians Came* (1988) are political satires. *Starburst* (short version 1971 as "The Gold at the Starbow's End"; book 1982) and *Homegoing* (1989) feature confrontations with the **alien.** *The Years of the City* (1984) is a mosaic **future history** of New York. His further collaborations with Williamson were the expansive action-adventure couplet *Farthest Star* (1975) and *Wall around a Star* (1983), the **disaster story** *Land's End* (1988), and the extravagant cosmological fantasy *The Singers of Time* (1991), which carried forward ideas Pohl had broached in *The World at the End of Time* (1999) and was to further elaborate in a **series** of **Omega Point** fantasies comprising *The Other End of Time* (1996), *The Siege of Eternity* (1997), and *The Far Shore of Time* (1999). *Stopping at Slowyear* (1991), *Mining the Oort* (1992), and *The Voices of Heaven* (1994) are further accounts of the difficulties of extraterrestrial colonization, examined in a far more lighthearted vein in *O Pioneer!* (1998). *Outnumbering the Dead* (1990) is a thoughtful ***conte philosophique*** cast as a **Utopian** satire.

Although Pohl's work was in the **soft** half of the 1950s sf spectrum, his fierce commitment to the ideals of the genre sharpened a simmering resentment of its gradual displacement in the marketplace by genre fantasy, which eventually forged him into one of the most conscientious and versatile writers of **hard sf.**

**POLITICAL FANTASY.** Political fantasy, in its **Utopian** and **satirical** aspects, has a much longer history than **sf**. Sf elements assumed an important place within the subgenre when writers realized the extent to which politics—"the art of the attainable" in one aphoristic definition—is dependent on technological resources and technological progress. The dependency is mutual and complex; technological progress embodies political hazards as well as opportunities, and consideration of the ways in which new technologies might force political change has to be complemented with consideration of the ways in which political institutions may foster or inhibit technological innovation.

In sf, political fantasies comparing and contrasting capitalism and socialism—whose contest dominates the historical backcloth to the genre's history—often investigate their relative merits as generators and exploiters of new technology, and the ways in which the instrumentality of their power might be enhanced, weakened, or transformed by the technological developments in question. Sf tends to take a much longer view than people involved in actual decision making, whose primary concern is for the immediate future; it is much more concerned with the logical end points of political and technological trends, and with questions of the ultimate purpose of political activity. The centrality within genre sf of the myth of the **space age** produced a good deal of sf that evaluated political attitudes and programs purely in terms of whether or not they are helpful to that particular dream; much **libertarian sf** seems more concerned with the freedom of the species to expand into the cosmos than with individual freedom of choice. The demise of the myth of the space age, and its replacement by a sharp awareness of the need to ameliorate the impending **ecocatastrophe**, had a marked effect on the spectrum of sf political fantasies in the 1990s.

**PORTAL FANTASY.** The **parallel worlds** of mythical and folkloristic fantasy were equipped with various kinds of permanent or temporary portals allowing a certain amount of traffic between worlds, vital to such literary subgenres as **Orphean fantasy.** Farah Mendlesohn's

"Towards a Taxonomy of Fantasy" (2003) identifies portal fantasy as one element of a fundamental trisection whose other components are "immersive fantasy" (stories which take place entirely in fantastic worlds) and "intrusive fantasy" (in which fantastic elements crop up within the real world). **Sf** portal fantasy fits into this taxonomy readily enough, but has a further dimension by virtue of the fact that sf **multiverses** and **galactic empires** often require portals for convenient transportation across their vast stages.

Magical fantasy poses few difficulties in the establishment and maintenance of arbitrary access points, but such portals pose problems of plausibility in sf stories dealing with parallel worlds and **time travel**. The problem is usually solved by the standard method of re-jargonization; sf portal fantasy routinely makes use of "dimensional doorways"—"stargates" and "timegates" located in mysterious **alien** artifacts became commonplace in the 1950s along with galactic empires and manifolds of parallel worlds. The most obvious alternative strategy is to transform the object of transportation—whether it be a person or a vehicle—so that it hauls itself across the dimensional boundary, so stories involving such facilitating technologies as **time machines** and **matter transmitters** are closely akin to portal fantasies. **Wormholes** are frequently pressed into use in portal fantasies that aspire to consideration as **hard sf.**

**PORTUGUESE SCIENCE FICTION.** Portuguese fantastic literature made little use of **sf** motifs until U.S. imports provided models in the wake of World War II, although Melo De Matos had published a vision of *Lisboa no Ano 2000* (*Lisbon in the Year 2000*) in 1906. Such remnants were gathered together into a patchwork history in the magazine *Omnia* (1988–1991) by Alvaro de Sousa Holstein and José Manuel Morais, who published a definitive *Bibliografia da Ficção Cientifica e Fantasia Portuguesa* (1993). New writers promoted in the magazine included João Barreiros and Daniel Tércio, both of whom were represented, along with Luis Filipe Silva—Barreiros's **collaborator** on the epic novel *Terrarium* (1996)—António de Macedo and Maria de Menezes, in *Non-Events on the Edge of the Empire* (1996), the first of three bilingual **anthologies** published in association with "Encounters" held in Cascais from 1996–2001. Simetria, the Portuguese Science Fiction and Fantasy Association, organized the later ones. The other anthologies in the **series** are *Side-Effects* (1997) and *Frontiers* (1998); the latter features a succinct history of "SF in Portugal" by Teresa Sousa de Almeida. *See also* LATIN AMERICAN SCIENCE FICTION.

**POSTHOLOCAUST FANTASY.** A subgenre of stories set in the aftermath of catastrophes so extreme that civilization is effectively obliterated. The term came into use in connection with the civilization-destroying potential of a nuclear holocaust, but is routinely applied to similar fantasies involving devastating plagues, deluges, and **ecocatastrophes.** The genre overlaps with **apocalyptic fantasies**, which track the progress of the relevant world-ending catastrophes. Some texts adopt an ambivalent tone combining elegiac regret for all that has been lost with a conviction that the survivors might be better off without it—examples range from Richard Jefferies' *After London* (1885) to **Russell Hoban's** *Riddley Walker* (1980), but an angry bitterness is prominent in such grim accounts of postholocaust primitivism as **Cicely Hamilton's** *Theodore Savage* (1922), **Wilson Tucker's** *The Long Loud Silence* (1952), and Robert C. O'Brien's *Z for Zachariah* (1975). The subgenre was firmly established in British **scientific romance** after World War I but it was not until the advent of the atomic bomb—whose explosion was enthusiastically greeted by **John Campbell** and others as solid proof of sf's prophetic acumen—that it made much impact in the United States.

**POSTMODERN SF.** A term that overspilled literary critical theory in the 1980s, ambitious to embrace every aspect of contemporary culture—including science. "Modernism," in this view, is conceived as a movement concerned with questions about the extent to which the world is "knowable" within the limits of our instruments of discovery. Postmodernism transforms such questions by challenging the basic assumption that the world is sufficiently definite and stable to be known, no matter what instruments might be brought to the task—in effect, by assuming that all culture, including science, is best understood as an ideologically guided system of convenient delusions. Support for this position was sought not only in philosophical skepticism about scientific knowledge but within science itself, in the anti-commonsensical confusions of quantum mechanics.

The fact that so much academic **criticism** of **sf** adopted a postmodern attitude in the late 1980s, and found similar attitudes within the fiction on which it focused, was partly a coincidence of timing—whatever critical method was in fashion at the time when sf became an object of widespread attention would inevitably have been unleashed upon it—but it is certainly arguable that the sf of that period was particularly conducive to postmodernist interpretation. Although a few sf writers, notably **Samuel R. Delany**, had been influenced by the development of postmodernist ideas, a more important factor was the emergence of **cyberpunk** fiction, which embraced and carried forward the notion of **virtual reality.** The belated recognition of the significance of **Philip K. Dick** also had much to do with the manner in which his habitual transformation of doubts about the reliability of sensory perception into doubts about the reliability of the perceptible world harmonized with postmodern skepticism.

**POURNELLE, JERRY (1933– ).** U.S. writer professionally involved in the space program, who published thrillers bylined Wade Curtis before venturing into **sf** in 1971. His early genre works, including *West of Honor* 1976) and the **mosaics** *The Mercenary* (1977) and *High Justice* (1977), were mostly **military sf** of an aggressively **libertarian** stripe. The fiction he wrote in **collaboration** with **Larry Niven**, beginning with *The Mote in God's Eye* (1974), was more varied and adventurous, although it retained the same political edge. With John F. Carr he edited a **series** of military sf **anthologies** titled *There Will Be War* (9 vols., 1984–1990) and involved himself in various other anthologies and **shared-world** projects celebrating the contribution that politically motivated violence might make to the advancement of the **space age.**

**POWERS, TIM (1952– ).** U.S. writer whose first **sf** novel, *The Skies Discrowned* (1976; rev. as *Forsake the Sky*, 1986) was a **transfiguration** of a swashbuckling formula employed by Rafael Sabatini. *Epitaph in Rust* (1976, rev. 1989) and *Dinner at Deviant's Palace* (1985) are **postholocaust fantasies**, the latter an unusually explicit transfiguration of the fundamental myth of **Orphean fantasy.** There are sf elements in many of Powers's other fantasies, but their prominence was drastically reduced after the **timeslip romance** *The Anu-*

*bis Gates* (1983). His short fiction is sampled in *Night Moves and Other Stories* (2001).

**PRATCHETT, TERRY (1948– ).** British writer famous for his **humorous** fantasies, whose two comedies **satirizing sf** motifs, *The Dark Side of the Sun* (1976) and *Strata* (1981), served as preludes to his more wide-ranging Discworld **series**. The **children's sf** novel *Only You Can Save Mankind* (1992) likewise served as a prelude to **hybrid** sequels in which the artful and skeptical application of logical extrapolation to fantastic premises generated an abundance of hilarity underlaid by cogent moralization.

**PRATT, FLETCHER (1897–1956).** U.S. writer who began publishing **sf** in 1928, much of his early work for **Hugo Gernsback's** pulps carrying fictitious **collaborative** bylines. His most impressive story, "The City of the Living Dead" (1930), was an authentic collaboration with **Laurence Manning** and he went on to do most of his best work with **L. Sprague de Camp.** He also translated **French** and **German sf** novels for Gernsback. His sf is inferior to his work in other fantasy genres, the most notable items being the **transfigurations** of Greek hero-myths "The Wanderer's Return" (1951) and "The Conditioned Captain" (1953, aka *The Undying Fire*), and the **mosaic** thriller *Double Jeopardy* (1952). As an editor for Twayne, Pratt initiated the first **shared-world** sf **anthology** *The Petrified Planet* (1952), whose three novellas juxtaposed his "The Long View" with contributions by **H. Beam Piper** and **Judith Merril.**

**PREDICTION. Sf** has often been advertised as a medium of prediction and **prophecy**, although the essential treacherousness of both terms makes such boasts ill advised. The genre's anticipations of technologies that later came to fruition were hailed as firm evidence of its virtue and utility by both **Hugo Gernsback** and **John Campbell**, although the latter was always careful to point out that all predictions obtained by **extrapolation** are conditional—a qualification often ignored or misunderstood. As the philosopher of science Karl Popper pointed out, to the extent that the future is dependent on choices and discoveries not yet made, it is implicitly unpredictable; indeed, the whole point of attempting to calculate what *might* happen is to enable constructive interventions to alter the relevant spectrum of probabilities. What sf writers seek to do—as **John Brunner** was fond of saying—is not so much to predict the future as to *prevent* it; their direst warnings are offered in the hope that they will become self-negating prophecies.

**PREUSS, PAUL (1942– ).** U.S. writer whose first venture into **sf** was *The Gates of Heaven* (1980), in which black holes are employed as space-time **portals.** *Re-Entry* (1981) extrapolated the hypothesis into **space opera.** His later novels mostly involve earnest depictions of scientists at work in near-future settings; they include *Broken Symmetries* (1983), *Human Error* (1985), and *Secret Passages* (1997). *Starfire* (1988) is a disciplined **space-age** fantasy, while *Core* (1993) moves into the world's interior in an adventurous spirit.

**PRIEST, CHRISTOPHER (1943– ).** British writer who began publishing **sf** in 1966. He seems to have been the first person to describe **Michael Moorcock's** ***New Worlds*** venture as **new wave** sf, although his own work was peripheral to the movement, the **Ballardian** aspects of his first novel, *Indoctrinaire* (1970), and the multistranded complexity of the relentlessly downbeat *Fugue for a Darkening Island* (1972, aka *Darkening Island*) notwithstanding. *Inverted World* (1974) launched an extensive sequence of novels whose protagonists retreat from the everyday world into another, usually **virtual**, whose palliative quality blurs the boundary between the subjective and the objective; other sf variants include *A Dream of Wessex* (1977) and *The Extremes* (1998), while *The Affirmation* (1981) and the related stories collected in *The Dream Archipelago* (1999) are **hybrid** texts, but the underlying theme is always more important than the ideative superstructure. Some of the stories in *An Infinite Summer* (1979) are similar. *The Space Machine* (1976) is an homage to **H. G. Wells.** *The Separation* (2002) plays teasingly with shadowy **alternative histories** of World War II.

**PRINGLE, DAVID (1950– ).** Scottish scholar and editor whose earliest publications were studies of the work of **J. G. Ballard.** He was a research fellow at the **Science Fiction Foundation** in 1978–1979 and edited its journal from 1979–1986, soon after which he took over sole editorial responsibility for ***Interzone***. He produced a number of readers' guides, including *Science Fiction: The Hundred Best Novels* (1985) and *The Ultimate Guide to Science Fiction* (1990).

**PROMETHEAN FANTASY.** A subgenre recapitulating and celebrating the myth of Prometheus's theft, on humankind's behalf, of the fire of the gods—for which he was direly punished. Prehistoric fantasies often focus on the domestication of fire as a key moment in social evolution, but the importance of the subgenre in **sf** is correlated with a wider interpretation of the relevant symbolism, in which fire—by virtue of its association with the ironmaster's forge—represents technological progress in general. The subtitle of **Mary Shelley's** *Frankenstein, or The Modern Prometheus* refers to another myth, in which Prometheus becomes the creator of humankind, but that too can be regarded as a symbolic **transfiguration** of the adage that "tools made man." Promethean fantasy was particularly pertinent to sf in the **pulp** era, when the future was more often conceived as the atomic age than the **space age**, although the fire metaphor was easily transferable from the heat of nuclear fission and fusion to the backblast of an ascendant rocket. Human scientists playing a Promethean role on behalf of their immediate kin are, however, outnumbered in postwar sf by humans bringing Promethean gifts to **aliens**, and vice versa; liver-devouring eagles are not essential to the subgenre, but equivalents thereof have an obvious melodramatic attraction. The Prometheus Award is given annually by the Libertarian Futurist Society for the best **libertarian sf** novel of the year.

**PROPHECY.** In religious scripture, a prophecy is primarily a kind of promise: a declaration that the obvious moral inequities of the present will one day be set right, by a rain of destruction from which only the righteous will be delivered. The attractions of the idea are obvious, and the hope that a power exists that is ready to make such promises and is capable of making them good has always been the chief mainstay of religious faith. Like most promises, however, a prophecy is also a kind of threat; the prospect of the rain of destruction is supposed to make the wicked mend their ways, and the hope of eventual deliverance is supposed to make the good persevere in spite of their tribulations. Although prophecy has to pretend to be based on a theory of inevitable destiny in order to maintain its authority, its utility as an instrument of thought and social control is confined to those aspects of the future that are amenable to variation.

Prophecy is, in consequence, a powerful agent in shaping the future that it pretends to predict; the fact that a prophecy is uttered may be crucial to the likelihood of its fulfillment—a confusion explored in many myths and stories, sometimes called the Oedipus Effect in recognition of one of the most ingenious. Prophecies can be self-fulfilling, as in Oedipus's case, but they are far more likely to be self-negating—anyone told that he will suffer disaster at a particular time and place is highly likely to avoid it; that is the whole point of consulting oracles before taking risks.

These observations serve to establish that **sf** is not and cannot be a medium of **prediction** and to emphasize the fact that most **science-fictional** visions of the future are consciously calculated to affect the probability of their fulfillment, usually (but not invariably) negatively. They also underpin the logic and help explain the rewards of such subgenres as **time-paradox** stories—which are, in essence, extrapolations of the Oedipus Effect—and are fundamental to the holistic aesthetics of the genre.

**PSEUDOSCIENCE.** A set of assertions devoid of any rational support, which is couched in quasi-scientific terminology in the expectation of gaining credence therefrom. Many pseudosciences handed down from remote or recent antiquity, such as astrology, numerology, phrenology, and psychoanalysis, probably originated from hopeful error rather than deceptive charlatanry, but the majority of 20th century pseudosciences are calculatedly deceptive. Where the mimicry extends beyond mere terminology to experimental methods of inquiry, as in much research into "paranormal" phenomena, it is more difficult to distinguish science and pseudoscience—a matter of particular relevance to **sf** because of the ambiguous status of research into **extrasensory perception** and **psi powers.** The alleged findings of such researches were accepted into the pages of ***Astounding*** by **John Campbell**, thus confusing—and perhaps spoiling—his ambition to set sf on firm rational foundations.

With the exception of psi powers, sf writers usually treat pseudo-scientific material satirically, often cruelly, partly because they resent being lumped together with **UFOlogists** and followers of Immanuel Velikovsky, Erich von Däniken, or Graham Hancock in the public mind. **John Sladek**, **Martin Gardner**, and Carl Sagan are conspicuous among the ranks of those who have considered it a moral duty to expose and ridicule the impostures of pseudoscience. Mild sympathy for the works of **Charles Fort** is, however, often seen as open-minded skepticism without any implied commitment to false beliefs. The sf writer who has taken the strongest and broadest interest in literary extrapolations of pseudoscience is **Piers Anthony.**

**PSI POWERS.** A term invented in the 1940s to describe the objects of research into unusual mental powers—telepathy, psychokinesis, precognition, clairvoyance, teleportation, and so on—by researchers who considered **extrasensory perception** insufficiently broad and theoretically loaded. It was rapidly adopted into **sf**, notably by **John Campbell**, whose enthusiasm prompted a "psi boom" in the early 1950s, which overspilled the pages of ***Astounding*** to make itself equally conspicuous in ***Galaxy***, although it was less prominent in ***The Magazine of Fantasy & Science Fiction***. Campbell regarded the cultivation of new mental powers as the only way in which humankind could avoid **decadence** and supercession by its own machinery. Many sf writers employed the imagery of this kind of evolutionary transcendence extravagantly, either because they genuinely believed it possible—as **A. E. van Vogt** seemed to do—or because they recognized its power as a metaphor for moral progress, as **Theodore Sturgeon** did.

**PSYCHOHISTORY.** A term coined by **Isaac Asimov** to describe the powerfully **predictive** social science underlying the activities of the Foundation in his most famous **series**. It is, in essence, a refinement of the grandiose theories of history popularized in the 19th century by G. W. F. Hegel and Karl Marx, and in the 20th by Oswald Spengler and Arnold Toynbee. Such **pseudoscientific** notions have an obvious appeal to **sf** writers whose hypothetical futures are constructed by **transfiguring** the past.

**PULP SF.** Pulp **magazines** were so called because they were printed on cheap paper made from wood pulp—although "bedsheet" magazines like the original version of ***Amazing Stories*** were a cut above the rest because they used sturdier sheets. The more expensive "slick" magazines with which the pulps coexisted used paper that was chemically reconditioned so as to be able to carry the high-quality illustrations favored by advertisers; "pulp fiction," by metaphorical extension, became that kind of fiction that only warranted reproduction in the cheapest formats, unlike the kinds of fiction that lent some kind of prestige to the ads they accompanied.

Although the pulp magazines lost their economic advantages in World War II, pulp fiction in the metaphorical sense migrated to other media, retaining its label. The movement of **sf** from pulp to digest magazines—following a trail blazed by **John Campbell's** *Astounding*—was associated with a conscious attempt to rid the genre of the "pulp fiction" stigma, but it had little chance of success while so many magazines and **paperbacks** were designed and packaged in the same manner as their predecessors. It was not until the 1980s that the pulpish aspects of sf were largely transferred to **TV**, **cinema**, and **comic** book **sci-fi**; the continued prevalence on sf shelves of **tie-ins**, **sharecropping** exercises, and **military sf** ensured that the genre carried its manifest pulp associations into the 21st century.

**PURDOM, TOM (1936– ).** U.S. writer who began publishing **sf** in 1957. His early **paperback** novels were routine action-adventure novels, but *Reduction in Arms* (1971) and *The Barons of Behavior* (1972) are more ambitious projections of the possible social impact of psychotropic technologies. His more recent short fiction, mostly published in ***Asimov's***, remains uncollected.

**PYNCHON, THOMAS (1937– ).** U.S. writer whose surreal literary fiction occasionally employs **sf** motifs to stigmatize infatuation with technology, most obviously in *Gravity's Rainbow* (1973).

## – Q –

**QUICK, W. T. (1946– ).** U.S. writer who began publishing **sf** in 1979. The trilogy comprising *Dreams of Flesh and Sand* (1988), *Dreams of Gods and Men* (1989), and *Singularities* (1990) features a **cyber-**

**punk**-influenced account of near-future information technology. *Yesterday's Pawn* (1989) and *Systems* (1989) are mysteries. *Chains of Light* (1992) is bylined Quentin Thomas, and a **series** of prehistoric novels begun with *Mammoth Stone* (1993) is bylined Margaret Allan. *Silent Plague* (1999) is a **disaster story** about a plague of deafness.

## – R –

**RADIO.** Genre **sf** and radio broadcasting originated at the same time, not entirely coincidentally; **Hugo Gernsback's** ventures into **magazine** publishing were extensions of his mail-order catalogs selling radio hardware, and it was the failure of his radio station that forced the sale of ***Amazing Stories*** in 1929. Radio dramatizations of sf, from **Buck Rogers** in 1932 to the **anthology series** *Dimension X/X Minus 1* (1950–1958), helped popularize the genre, and Orson Welles's notorious Mercury Theater adaptation of *The War of the Worlds* (1938) provided a spectacular demonstration of the power of sf imagery. Like other realized technologies, radio faded into the background of sf stories, less than half a century separating **Rudyard Kipling's** "Wireless" (1902) from **George O. Smith's** Venus Equilateral series (1942–1947), but it continued to play a vital role thereafter in **SETI** fantasies.

**RAND, AYN (1905–1982).** Pseudonym of Russian-born U.S. writer Alissa Rosenbaum, who used **sf** devices to popularize her libertarian "objectivist" philosophy in the **Promethean fantasies** *Anthem* (1938) and *Atlas Shrugged* (1957). The latter's representation and exhaustive justification of a capitalists' strike against the oppressions of labor was an inspiration to right-wing thinkers who feared that the high moral ground belonged to the opposition.

**RANDALL, MARTA (1948– ).** U.S. writer who began publishing **sf** in 1973. *Islands* (1976) is an **existentialist fantasy** about a mortal misfit in a world of **emortals.** *A City in the North* (1976) and the couplet comprising *Journey* (1978) and *Dangerous Games* (1980) are didactic accounts of costly colonization. *Those Who Favor Fire* (1984) embeds similar lessons in a **dystopian** depiction of near-future California.

**RANKIN, ROBERT (1949– ).** British writer of slapstick comedy who began using **sf** motifs as facilitating devices and objects of cheerful derision in 1981. They are most prominent in the Armageddon sequence, comprising *Armageddon: The Musical* (1990), *They Came and Ate Us* (1991), and *The Suburban Book of the Dead* (1992), in which a **time-traveling** Elvis Presley discovers that all human life is but a soap opera stage. *The Greatest Show off Earth* (1994) is a parodic **space opera.** *Apocalypso* (1998) features a Thing from **Outer Space**. *The Dance of the Voodoo Handbag* (1998) describes a contest for control of the virtual Necronet.

**RAY GUN.** The rapidly popularized discovery of X rays by Wilhelm Röntgen in 1895, followed in 1896 by Antoine Becquerel's discovery of atomic radiation, administered a powerful stimulus to the **sf** imagination. Death rays, disintegrator rays, and heat rays like those deployed by **H. G. Wells's Martians** soon became regular features of **future war** fiction. Ray guns of various kinds were staples of **pulp space opera**; **John Campbell's** "Space Rays" (1932) provided multiple examples so extravagant that **Hugo Gernsback** advertised it as a "burlesque." The **illustrative** potential of ray guns endeared them to **cover** artists, who made lavish use of "blasters" deluging their targets with spectacular radiance. The development of lasers in the 1960s was hailed by many sf fans as a successful sf **prediction.**

**REDGROVE, PETER (1932–2003).** British writer best known as a poet. His novels are **ambiguous existentialist fantasies**, those making the most use of **sf** motifs being *The God of Glass* (1979), *The Sleep of the Great Hypnotist* (1979), *The Beekeepers* (1980), and *The Facilitators, or Mister Hole-in-the-Day* (1982).

**REED, KIT (1932– ).** U.S. writer in various genres who began contributing **satirical fabulations** to ***The Magazine of Fantasy & Science Fiction*** in 1958, many of them collected in *Mister da V. and Other Stories* (1967), *The Killer Mice* (1976), *Other Stories and . . . The Attack of the Giant Baby* (1981), and *Revenge of the Senior Citizens* (1986). *Armed Camps* (1969) is an earnest study of near-future social collapse and *Fort Privilege* (1985) a tongue-in-cheek account of urban **decadence** under threat—themes deftly combined in the novella *Little Sisters of the Apocalypse* (1994; reprinted in *Seven for the Apocalypse*, 1999).

**REED, ROBERT (1956– ).** U.S. writer who began publishing **sf** in 1986. His meditative **existentialist fantasies** are located in a wide range of settings and situations, including the watery colony world of *The Leeshore* (1987), the hectically crowded solar system of *The Hormone Jungle* (1989), the **biotechnologically** sophisticated near future of *Black Milk* (1989), the **first contact** arena of *The Remarkables* (1992), the suddenly sequestered Earth of the **portal fantasy** couplet *Beyond the Veil of Stars* (1994) and *Beneath the Gated Sky* (1997), and the exotic ship-enclosed planet *Marrow* (2000). Godlike entities crop up frequently in his work, as objects of quests like that featured in *Down the Bright Way* (1991) or as active agents like those rewriting history backwards in *An Exaltation of Larks* (1995). His short fiction is sampled in *The Dragons of Springplace* (1999) and the **mosaic** *Sister Alice* (1993–2000; book 2003). "Veritas" (2002) reassesses the argument of **L. Sprague de Camp's** *Lest Darkness Fall*.

**REEVE, ARTHUR B. (1880–1936).** U.S. writer who pioneered the "scientific detective" subgenre in tales featuring Craig Kennedy, the Sherlock Holmes of *Cosmopolitan* (1910–1915); his early adventures were collected in *The Silent Bullet* (1912), *The Poisoned Pen* (1913), and *The Dream Doctor* (1914). **Hugo Gernsback** was inspired to found *Scientific Detective Monthly* in 1930 with Reeve as consultant, but it only lasted 10 issues, the last four retitled *Amazing Detective Tales*.

**REGINALD, ROBERT (1948– ).** Pseudonym of U.S. **bibliographer** and publisher Michael Roy Burgess. His most significant contribution to the field was the Borgo Press, which published numerous monographs on sf writers and several substantial critical works and collections of critical essays between 1975 and 2000. *Contemporary Science Fiction Authors* (1974), an expansion of the anonymous *Stella Nova* (1970), was further revised as a companion volume to *Science Fiction and Fantasy Literature: A Checklist, 1700–1974* (1979) before becoming the foundation of the St. James Press *Twentieth Century SF Writers* (1981; rev. as *The St. James Guide to Science Fiction Writers*,

4th ed., 1996). He was an editorial advisor on several Arno Press reprint **series**, including an sf series issued in 1975.

**RELIGIOUS FANTASY.** A subgenre dramatizing and extrapolating the substance of any one of the major religious belief systems; its Jewish and Christian variants have borrowed extensively from **sf** in the 20th century. Christian fantasy played an important ancestral role to sf in earlier centuries by virtue of its production of numerous notable works of interplanetary fiction. The *Arcana Coelestia* (1749–1756) of Emmanuel Swedenborg were represented as revelatory visions rather than fantasies, but their extraterrestrial expeditions made extensive use of Swedenborg's early education in science—a significant inspiration to many later writers, including **Restif de la Bretonne**, **Sir Humphry Davy**, **Camille Flammarion**, W. D. Lach-Szyrma, and **Marie Corelli**, all of whom used "cosmic tours" to combine ideas drawn from religion and science.

A great many 20th-century cosmic voyages retain a religious gloss in spite of its **chimerical** impositions. Materials borrowed from sf are lavishly employed in the apparatus of many religiously inspired **apocalyptic fantasies**, including Tim LaHaye and Jerry B. Jenkins' Left Behind **series** (1995–2003), and in attempts to revisualize heaven and hell in faith-based moralistic fantasies. Modern angelic fantasies often draw on sf-derived imagery in order to elaborate the missions on which such messengers are sent and the methods they employ in fulfilling them, as in Bill Myers's trilogy *Blood of Heaven* (1996), *Threshold* (1997), and *Fire of Heaven* (1999). By the same token, sf often borrows religious imagery to assist in the characterization of **aliens** and their worlds. The sociology of religion is an important aspect of the subject matter of **soft sf** in futuristic and alien settings. The clash of religion and science, especially in the context of evolutionary theory—as reflected in the promotion of creationist **pseudoscience**—has been a significant stimulus to sf **satire.** Although "religious sf" is an inherently chimerical notion, the relationships between religious fantasy and sf remain intimate and intricate.

**RENARD, MAURICE (1875–1939). French** writer in various genres, whose work had a good deal in common with U.S. **pulp** fiction. His translated **sf**—including the novella *The Flight of the Aerofix* (1909, tr. 1932), about a craft that remains stationary in midair while the Earth rotates beneath it; *New Bodies for Old* (1908, tr. 1923), a **horror-sf** story about soul transference; and *Blind Circle* (1925 with Albert Jean, tr. 1928), a mystery involving matter duplication—is less adventurous than such works as *Le péril bleu* (1912), about a bizarre atmospheric ecosystem; *L'homme truqué* (1921), about artificial sensory perception; *Un homme chez les microbes* (1928), a **miniaturization** fantasy; and *Le maître de la lumière* (1933), about a kind of glass that modifies the light passing through it in peculiar ways.

**RESNICK, MICHAEL D. (1942– ).** U.S. writer in various genres whose earliest **sf**, written in the 1960s, was mostly imitative of **Edgar Rice Burroughs**, one exception being the **postholocaust fantasy** *Redbeard* (1969). He returned to the genre in the early 1980s with such works as the lurid *Walpurgis III* (1982); *Sideshow* (1982) and other comic Tales of the Galactic Midway; and *Eros Ascending* (1984) and other erotic Tales of the Velvet Comet.

The history-spanning *Birthright: The Book of Man* (1982) established a narrative method for much of Resnick's subsequent work. *Santiago: A Myth of the Far Future* (1986) is an alloy of **fabulation** and **pulp** romance—*The Return of Santiago* (2003) is a sequel—whose **metafictional** gloss was carried forward into *The Dark Lady: A Romance of the Far Future* (1987) and *Ivory: A Legend of Past and Future* (1988), which employed Resnick's fascination with Africa and big-game hunting in the construction of an unusual mystery. Versions of Africa are featured in much of Resnick's subsequent sf; its history is ingeniously **transfigured** in *Paradise* (1989), *Purgatory* (1993), and *Inferno* (1993), cleverly altered in the two novellas collected in *Bwana and Bully!* (1991), and set within an expansive temporal panorama in the novella *Seven Views of Olduvai Gorge* (1994), which is reprinted in *An Alien Land* (1992) and in *Hunting the Snark and Other Short Novels* (2002). *A Hunger in the Soul* (1998) is similarly inspired, as are the ***contes philosophiques*** comprising the **mosaic** *Kirinyaga* (1998), set in a space habitat where the Masai have reconstituted their traditional society, whose **alien** values pose a discomfiting challenge to interested observers.

Works produced in parallel with these include several **existentialist fantasies**, including the trilogy *Soothsayer* (1991), *Oracle* (1992), and *Prophet* (1993), the singleton *A Miracle of Rare Design* (1994), and the more whimsical *contes philosophiques* collected in *Will the Last Person to Leave the Planet Please Shut Off the Sun* (1992). *The Outpost* (2001) is a bar where exceedingly tall stories are told and an alien invasion is thwarted.

**RESTIF DE LA BRETONNE (Nicolas-Anne-Edmé, 1734–1806). French** writer in various genres, whose imaginative extravagance made him an important pioneer of **sf**, most notably in *La découverte australe par un homme volant* (1781), whose airborne hero surveys a series of hypothetical societies, and *Les posthumes* (written 1787–1789, published 1802), in which correspondence from beyond the grave includes a remarkable avant-garde account of a cosmic voyage undertaken by the allegorical Multipliandre ("Everyman").

**REYNOLDS, ALASTAIR (1966– ).** British writer resident in the Netherlands, an employee of the European Space Agency from 1991. He began publishing **sf** in 1990. *Revelation Space* (2000) is a complex sophisticated **space opera**; *Redemption Ark* (2002) and *Absolution Gap* are direct sequels, completing the Inhibitors trilogy, but his other works are also set in the same fictional universe. *Chasm City* (2001) is an equally elaborate account of a one-time **Utopia** made hellish by a **nanotechnological** plague. The novellas *Diamond Dogs* (2001), about an **alien** artifact, and *Turquoise Days* (2002), set on an aquatic world, were reissued in an omnibus (2003).

**REYNOLDS, MACK (1917–1983).** U.S. writer who began writing **sf** in 1950. *The Case of the Little Green Men* (1951) is a murder mystery set in an sf **convention.** He became a regular member of **John Campbell's** stable of writers, although his politics—he was an active member of the American Socialist Party—contrasted sharply with those of his fellows. The determinedly unorthodox Campbell was happy to publish such provocative **political fantasies** as "Adaptation" (1960; exp. as *The Rival Rigelians*, 1967), which describes an experiment in economic development pitting the methods of Western capitalism and Soviet communism against one another; "Ultima Thule" (1961; integrated into the **mosaic** *Planetary Agent X*, 1965), the first item in a **series** in which a secret agent code-named "Tommy

Paine" takes a pragmatic approach to the encouragement of progress in various extraterrestrial venues; and the couplet comprising *Black Man's Burden* (1961–1962, book 1972) and *Border, Breed nor Birth* (1962, book 1972), in which similarly underhanded methods are employed with good intentions in near-future Africa.

The core of Reynolds's oeuvre is a series of **Utopian** novels carrying forward and reinterrogating the work of **Edward Bellamy**; *Looking Backward from the Year 2000* (1973) and *Equality in the Year 2000* (1977) recast Bellamy's own books, after which Reynolds examined corollary possibilities in *After Utopia* (1977) and developed parallel lines of thought in *Rolltown* (1969, exp. 1976), *Commune 2000 A.D.* (1974), *The Towers of Utopia* (1975), and the series begun with *Lagrange Five* (1979), whose later volumes were completed by **Dean Ing.** He also wrote political **satires**, including "Russkies Go Home!" (1960; exp. as *Tomorrow Might Be Different*, 1975); the couplet comprising "Mercenary" (1962; exp. as *Mercenary from Tomorrow*, 1968) and "Frigid Fracas" (1963, book as *The Earth War*); "Speakeasy" (1963; exp. as *The Cosmic Eye*, 1969); and *Of Godlike Power* (1966, aka *Earth Unaware*). Two novels in which information technology provides key instruments and targets of **future warfare**, *Computer War* (1967) and *The Computer Conspiracy* (1968), also seem farsighted in retrospect. *The Best of Mack Reynolds* (1976) samples his short sf.

**ROBERTS, ADAM (1965– ).** British writer who began publishing **sf** with *Salt* (2000), about the troubled colonization of an inhospitable world. *On* (2001) is an earnest quasi-**dimensional fantasy** about life on a vertical plane. In *Stone* (2002) a prison escapee is hired to murder a world's population. *Polystom* (2003) is a **chimerical** amalgam of quasi-Wodehousian comedy and cynical war fiction, set in a world where space travel is facilitated by an interplanetary atmosphere. *Park Polar* (2001) and *Jupiter Magnified* (2003) are enterprising novellas.

**ROBERTS, JANE (1929–1984).** U.S. writer who began publishing **fabulations** with **sf** elements in 1956. *The Rebellers* (1963) is an **apocalyptic fantasy.** *The Education of Oversoul Seven* (1973) launched an ambitious **series** of **hybrid metaphysical fantasies** whose protagonist's studies take her far and wide in time and space.

**ROBERTS, KEITH (1935–2000).** British artist and writer who began working in several fantasy genres in 1964, primarily as a short story writer. The collections *Machines and Men* (1973), *The Grain Kings* (1976), *Ladies from Hell* (1979), and *The Lordly Ones* (1986) are mostly **sf**. Items gathered into **mosaics** include *Pavane* (1968), a classic **hybrid alternative history**; *The Inner Wheel* (1970), an account of emergent superhumanity; and *The Chalk Giants* (1974), a harrowing but painstakingly elegiac image of a **postholocaust** Britain. *The Furies* (1966) is a **Wyndhamesque disaster story.** Roberts's later work became increasingly downbeat as it continually revisited his preoccupations with drastic reversals of social progress and (usually in frankly **chimerical** texts or works in other genres) adolescent female sexuality; they include the **dystopian** mosaics *Molly Zero* (1980) and *Kiteworld* (1985). Roberts's expressionist **cover art** for ***New Worlds*** and its companion, *Science-Fantasy/Impulse* (which he coedited from 1965–1967), helped to give **new wave** sf a distinctive face.

**ROBIDA, ALBERT (1848–1926). French** illustrator and writer. He first combined **illustrations** with his own text in a five-part **series** of farcical adventures parodying **Jules Verne's** *voyages extraordinaires*, *Voyages très extraordinaires de Saturnin Farandoul* (1879). He followed it up with several caricaturish works of futuristic **speculative nonfiction**, most notably *Le vingtième siècle* (1882), *La vie électrique* (1883), and two extravagant accounts of *La guerre au vingtième siècle* (1883 and, more significantly, 1887). He returned to fiction in *Jadis chez aujourd'hui* (1890), in which famous figures from the past are artificially resurrected, and *L'horloge des siècles* (1902), an early account of time marching backward.

**ROBINSON, FRANK M. (1926– ).** U.S. writer who began publishing **sf** in 1950, much of his early work being collected in *A Life in the Day of . . . and Other Short Stores* (1981). *The Power* (1956) is a **psi**-boom thriller about a problematic search for a sociopathic **superman.** Robinson returned to the margins of the genre in some of the **disaster stories** he wrote with **Thomas N. Scortia**—notably *The Nightmare Factor* (1978), about biological weaponry—but the **generation starship** story *The Dark Beyond the Stars* (1991) is more enterprising. *Waiting* (1999) is **horror-sf**. *Science Fiction of the 20th*

*Century* (1999) offers an insider's view of the genre's development. Later short fiction is collected in *Through My Glasses Darkly* (2002).

**ROBINSON, KIM STANLEY (1952– ).** U.S. writer who began publishing **sf** in 1975. His production was sparse while he wrote a doctoral thesis on *The Novels of Philip K. Dick* (1984)—whose influence is evident, though carefully modified, in the **mosaic** *Icehenge* (1984) and *The Memory of Whiteness* (1985)—but he rapidly established himself thereafter as a leading writer in the genre, with a more profound interest in **Utopian** speculation than any of his contemporaries. The **postholocaust** pastoral *The Wild Shore* (1984) was the first of several alternative versions of future California, emphasizing by contrast the **dystopian** elements of the technologically overdeveloped vision of *The Gold Coast* (1988), which contrasted in its turn with the controlled and far more life-enhancing image constructed in *Pacific Edge* (1990). His early short fiction was collected in *The Planet on the Table* (1986) and *Remaking History* (1991; exp. as *Down and Out in the Year 2000*; further exp. as *Vinland the Dream and Other Stories*, 2002).

Robinson's interest in mountaineering fuelled the stories making up the lighthearted **mosaic** *Escape from Kathmandu* (1989) and, more significantly, the novella "Green Mars" (1985). The latter became the foundation stone of an elaborate trilogy describing various phases in the colonization and **terraforming** of the planet, comprising *Red Mars* (1992), *Green Mars* (1994)—which does not include the novella of the same title—and *Blue Mars* (1996); associated items are collected in *The Martians* (1999). *Antarctica* (1997) is a similar account of awkward economic and ecological development plagued by political problems. *The Years of Rice and Salt* (2002) is an **alternative history** spanning seven centuries after the Black Death wiped out 99 percent of the population of Europe.

**ROBINSON, SPIDER (1948– ).** U.S. writer resident in **Canada** from 1973, in which year he began publishing **sf**, with the first item in an extensive **series** of tall stories set in *Callahan's Crosstime Saloon* (1977). Nonseries material was collected in *Antinomy* (1980) and *Melancholy Elephants* (1984), recombined in *User Friendly* (1998) and *By Any Other Name* (2001), and sampled in *God Is an Iron and*

*Other Stories* (2002). His mildly bawdy **humor** is routinely combined with a sentimentality that came to the fore in *Telempath* (1974) and the couplet comprising *Stardance* (1979) and *Starmind* (1995), the latter written in **collaboration** with his wife, Jeanne. The series comprising *Mindkiller* (1982), *Time Pressure* (1987), *Deathkiller* (1996), and *Lifehouse* (1997) consists of hard-boiled thrillers involving convoluted time-bending; *Night of Power* (1985) is a similarly dark tale of near-future rebellion. Robinson's enthusiastic, slangy, and occasionally combative book reviews endeared him to many fans.

**ROBINSONADE.** A subgenre of stories named after Daniel Defoe's Robinson Crusoe, in which castaways use their intelligence and technical skills to survive and thrive in exotic environments. Some 18th- and 19th-century robinsonades stray into the margins of **sf** but the most important extension of the subgenre is its adaptation to tales of castaways on **alien** worlds. These include numerous stories set on **Mars**, including **Rex Gordon's** *No Man Friday* (1956) and **James Blish's** *Welcome to Mars!* (1967) although those set on distant Earth-clones, including **Randall Garrett's** "The Queen Bee" (1958), **Edmund Cooper's** *A Far Sunset* (1967), and Charles Logan's *Shipwreck* (1975) tend to be more interestingly adventurous.

**ROBOT.** A term used by Karel Čapek in his allegory *R.U.R.* (1921) to describe the artificial laborers who represent the working class; the word was derived from *robota*, meaning forced labor. It was quickly borrowed for application to other artificial humanoids, an association with metallic simulacra being forged in the public mind by Fritz Lang's film *Metropolis* (1926), before being imported into the **sf pulps** in such alarmist fantasies as David H. Keller's "The Threat of the Robot" (1929). The use of robots as figures of menace was, however, decisively challenged in the late 1930s, first by **Eando Binder** and more effectively by **Isaac Asimov**, who established the robot as a key figure for use in **existentialist fantasies** exploring the possibilities of **artificial intelligence** and moral apprehension. The progress of robotic technology has been keenly observed within the sf field and has given risen to a good deal of extravagant **speculative nonfiction**; notable popularizers include Hans Moravec of the Robotics Institute at Carnegie Mellon University, author of *Mind Children:*

*The Future of Robot and Human Intelligence* (1988) and *Robot: Mere Machine to Transcendent Mind* (1998), and Kevin Warwick, professor of cybernetics at the University of Reading, author of *The March of the Machines* (1997) and *I, Cyborg* (2002).

**ROBSON, JUSTINA (1968– ).** British writer who began publishing **sf** in 1994. *Silver Screen* (1999) is a post-**cyberpunk** thriller with overtones of **existentialist fantasy.** *Mappa Mundi* (2001) is a similarly styled account of the possible uses of **nanotechnology** in neuropsychological research and mind control. *Natural History* (2003) is a **far-futuristic fantasy.**

**ROCKETS.** Rockets were used as fireworks and weapons long before **Konstantin Tsiolkovsky**—author of "The Probing of Space by Means of Jet Devices" (1903)—and Robert Goddard began experiments intended to lead to space flight. A **German** "Society for Space Travel" was founded in the 1920s by Hermann Oberth, which numbered **Willy Ley** and Wernher von Braun among its members. "Interplanetary Societies" were similarly established in Britain and the United States, in which rocket technologists and **sf** writers joined forces to create propaganda for an imminent **space age.** The near-unanimous testimony of rocket scientists that their first inspiration came from sf seemed to constitute evidence of the genre's potential to influence the shape of the future while it remained plausible that rockets really did have the potential to launch a space age.

**ROCKLYNNE, ROSS (1913–1988).** U.S. writer who began publishing **sf** in 1935. His early short sf was unusually enterprising. The **series** collected in *The Men and the Mirror* (1936–1946, book 1973) places spacefarers in problematic situations that require them to exercise unusual ingenuity; "The Forbidden Dream" (1940) launched a series in which an agent for the Bureau of Transmitted Egos is physically and psychologically adapted for strange missions on an assortment of **alien** worlds; the series collected in *The Sun Destroyers* (1940–1951; book 1973) is an account of living nebulas whose experiences span vast reaches of time and space. His longer stories, including "The Day of the Cloud" (1942), "Pirates of the Time Trail" (1943), and "Intruders from the Stars" (1944), are conventional action-adventure stories. He remained sporadically active until the 1970s, adapting to the changing demands of the marketplace well enough to be featured in **Harlan Ellison's** *Again, Dangerous Visions* (1972).

**ROSENBLUM, MARY (1952– ).** U.S. writer who began publishing **sf** in 1990. *The Drylands* (1994) is a **postholocaust** melodrama. *Chimera* (1993) is a post-**cyberpunk** thriller about **virtual reality.** In *The Stone Garden* (1995) asteroid miners create a new art form. The collection *Synthesis and Other Virtual Realities* (1996) includes prequels to the first two titles.

**ROSNY AÎNÉ, J. H. (1856–1940).** Pseudonym of Belgian writer Joseph-Henri Boëx, whose younger brother Justin shared the pseudonym J. H. Rosny with him from 1893–1907, although few of their works were **collaborations**. Like **Camille Flammarion**, and in stark contrast to **H. G. Wells**, Rosny saw **aliens** as companions to humankind in a progressive cosmic scheme, so the encounters featured in "Les xipéhuz" (1887, tr. as "The Shapes") and *Les navigateurs de l'infini* (1925) are much more positively inclined than *The War of the Worlds* and its successors. *La guerre du feu* (1909, heavily abridged and tr. as *The Quest for Fire*) and other novels of early human evolution, including *Vamireh* (1892), *Eyrimah* (1893), *Le félin géant* (1918; tr. as *The Giant Cat*, 1924), and *Helgvor du fleuve bleu* (1930; tr. as "Helgvor of Blue River," 1932), similarly put more stress on collaboration than competition. *La légende sceptique* (1889) is a lyrical **speculative essay** on evolution, akin to **Edgar Allan Poe's** *Eureka* as well as Victor Hugo's *Légende des siècles*, whose **poetic** inclinations were carried forward in "La mort de la terre" (1910, tr. as "The Death of the Earth"). "Un autre monde" (1895, tr. as "Another World") is a **dimensional fantasy.** *L'étonnant voyage de Hareton Ironcastle* (1922), whose translation was substantially rewritten by **Philip José Farmer** as *Ironcastle* (1976), is a **Vernian** romance.

**ROTSLER, WILLIAM (1926–1997).** U.S. writer and artist famed for his **fanzine** cartoons, who began publishing **sf** in 1970. *Patron of the Arts* (1972, exp. 1974) is an enterprising attempt to visualize future art forms. *To the Land of the Electric Angel* (1976) and the couplet comprising *Zandra* (1978) and *The Hidden Worlds of Zandra* (1983) use similar stages for conventional melodramas. *The Far Frontier* (1980) is a **space age** fantasy. *Shiva Descending* (1980, with **Gregory Benford**) is a **disaster story** about an asteroid strike.

**ROTTENSTEINER, FRANZ (1942– ).** Austrian editor and critic who edited **sf** lines for several **German** publishers and served for a while as **Stanislaw Lem's** literary agent. His academic nonfiction includes some useful accounts of the history of German imaginative fiction, although *The Science Fiction Book* (1975) is an unpretentious coffee-table book. *View from Another Shore* (1973, expanded 1999) is a showcase **anthology** of European sf.

**ROUSSEAU, VICTOR (1879–1960).** British writer resident in the United States from 1915, who used the byline H. M. Egbert on some British reprints of his **pulp** fiction. His most notable **sf** novel is *The Messiah of the Cylinder* (1917, aka *The Apostle of the Cylinder*), an ideological reply to **H. G. Wells's** *When the Sleeper Wakes*. *The Sea-Demons* (1916, book 1924) is a tale of exotic invasion. *Draught of Eternity* (1918, book 1924) is a **visionary postholocaust fantasy.** "World's End" (1933; reprinted in an omnibus with Harl Vincent's "Red Twilight," 1991) is an **apocalyptic fantasy.**

**RUCKER, RUDY (1946– ).** U.S. mathematician and writer who began publishing **sf** in 1978. *White Light* (1980) is a vivid **chimerical** fantasy in which the afterlife offers opportunities to model and explore arcane mathematical concepts and problems; *The Sex Sphere* (1983) and *The Secret of Life* (1985) are sequels. Similarly exuberant short fiction—including numerous **dimensional fantasies** paying homage to the pioneering endeavors of **Edwin Abbott** and **C. H. Hinton**, whose foundations had been laid in a nonfiction account of *Geometry, Relativity and the Fourth Dimension* (1977)—was collected in *The 57th Franz Kafka* (1983), whose contents were reprinted in the more various omnibus *Transreal!* (1991) and again in *Gnarl!* (2000). *Spacetime Donuts* (1981), which belatedly completed an aborted serial, examined the future of information technology in a more skeptical fashion than the trilogy comprising *Software* (1982), *Wetware* (1988), and *Realware* (2000), whose early volumes became key examples of **cyberpunk** fiction. *The Hacker and the Ants* (1994;

rev. as *The Hacker and the Ants, Release 2.0*, 2003) develops similar subject matter in a more broadly comic manner carried forward from the absurdist wish fulfillment fantasy *Master of Space and Time* (1984). *The Hollow Earth* (1990) is a flamboyant **steampunk** novel starring **Edgar Allan Poe.** *Saucer Wisdom* (1999) is a **metafiction** whose hypothetical narrator is abducted and enlightened about the future by **aliens**, featuring metamorphic "femtotechnology." *Spaceland: A Novel of the Fourth Dimension* (2002) further elaborates Rucker's fascination with **dimensional fantasy**.

**RUSCH, KRISTINE KATHYRN (1960– ).** U.S. editor and writer in several genres who began publishing **sf** in 1987, the year in which she and her husband, **Dean Wesley Smith**, founded the innovative **small press** Pulphouse. Pulphouse was remarkably prolific until 1992, issuing a "hardcover magazine" as well as a more orthodox one that never attained its ambition of weekly production, a **series** of "short story **paperbacks**" and the *Author's Choice Monthly* series. Rusch edited ***The Magazine of Fantasy & Science Fiction*** from 1991–1998. The **mosaic** *Alien Influences* (1994) is a **planetary romance** featuring enigmatic **alien** Dancers. The title story of *The Retrieval Artist and Other Stories* (2002) is part of an exotic thriller series including *The Disappeared* (2002) and *Extremes* (2003). Short sf is mingled with other material in *Stories for an Enchanted Afternoon* (2001). Rusch used the byline Kristine Grayson on a number of ambiguous "paranormal romances," including *Utterly Charming* (2000).

**RUSS, JOANNA (1937– ).** U.S. writer and scholar who began publishing **sf** in 1959, although her production was sparse until she published *Picnic on Paradise* (1968), in which a **time-tripping** troubleshooter has a hard time minding a party of interplanetary tourists; it became the first item in a **series** assembled in *Alyx* (1976, aka *The Adventures of Alyx*). *And Chaos Died* (1970) is an ambitious study of psychological metamorphosis. *The Female Man* (1975) is a classic of **feminist sf** in which versions of the same character drawn from widely various societies in four **alternative** worlds learn a great deal when their experiences begin to overlap and merge; "When It Changed" (1972) is a prequel to one of its narrative strands. *We Who Are About To . . .* (1977) is an account of castaways on an **alien** world that mocks the assumptions of **pulpish robinsonades.** *The Two of Them* (1978) revisits the method of *The Female Man* in a more economical fashion. Her short fiction is collected in *The Zanzibar Cat* (1983), *Extra(ordinary) People* (1984), and *The Hidden Side of the Moon* (1987).

**RUSSELL, BERTRAND (1872–1970).** British philosopher. The ***contes philosophiques*** collected in *Satan in the Suburbs and Other Stories* (1953), *Nightmares of Eminent Persons and Other Stories* (1954), and *Fact and Fiction* (1961)—subsequently reassembled as *The Collected Stories of Bertrand Russell* (1972)—include several **sf** stories, most notably "Zahatopolk" and "Planetary Effulgence." Russell's ideological reply to **J. B. S. Haldane's** *Daedalus; or, The Future of Science* (1924), sarcastically entitled *Icarus; or, Science and the Future*, prompted the extension of the multifaceted **Today & Tomorrow series** of pamphlets; its thesis—that because technological progress makes it easier for people to kill one another it will inevitably bring about the extinction of the human race—is a common theme of alarmist sf.

**RUSSELL, ERIC FRANK (1905–1978).** British writer who began publishing **sf** in 1937 and became a regular contributor to **John Campbell's *Astounding***, making an early impact with the stories assembled in the **mosaic** *Men, Martians and Machines* (1941–1943, book 1955), which includes accounts of the exotic ecospheres of "Mechanistra" and "Symbiotica." His **Fortean** fantasy *Sinister Barrier* (1939, book 1943; rev. 1948) appeared in the first issue of ***Unknown***; *Dreadful Sanctuary* (1948; rev. 1951, 1963, and 1967) is of the same ilk. After World War II he wrote a number of passionate antiwar stories, including "Late Night Final" (1948), "I Am Nothing" (1952), and the Gandhi-inspired **satire** "And Then There Were None . . ." (1951), which was integrated into the **mosaic** *The Great Explosion* (1962). He also poked fun at the limitations of the military mind in "The Waitabits" (1955), "Plus X" (1956; expanded as *The Space Willies*, 1958; rev. as *Next of Kin*, 1959), "Nuisance Value" (1957), and *Wasp* (1957). At its furthest extreme, this distaste became an earnest hope that evolution might ultimately free sentient creatures from all the follies of the flesh, as in "Metamorphosite" (1946) and "The Star Watchers" (1951; rev. as *Sentinels from Space*, 1953). His later novels, *Three to Conquer* (1956) and *With a Strange Device* (1964), are thrillers involving **psi** powers. His short story collections include *Deep Space* (1954), *Far Stars* (1961), and *Somewhere a Voice* (1965); *Major Ingredients* (2000) is an extensive sampler whose companion volume is *Entities: The Selected Novels of Eric Frank Russell* (2001).

**RUSSELL, MARY DORIA (1950– ).** U.S. writer whose **first contact** novel *The Sparrow* (1996) echoed **James Blish's** *A Case of Conscience* in testing a Jesuit's faith by confrontation with an exotic **alien** species. The sequel, *Children of God* (1998), resolves the issues raised and is less interesting in consequence.

**RUSSIAN SF.** Russian **Utopian** fiction began to take up issues of technological progress in the mid-19th century, as illustrated by a fragmentary text translated in Leland Fetzer's showcase **anthology** of *Pre-Revolutionary Russian Science Fiction* (1982) as "The Year 4338" (1840). Such issues were often sidelined as political conflicts intensified, although Alexander Bogdanov's "Red Star" (1908) is a notable exception. **Sf** motifs figure more prominently in such surreal **dystopian** fantasies as Fyodor Dostoyevsky's "Dream of a Ridiculous Man" (1877) and Valery Bryussov's "The Republic of the Southern Cross" (1907). Early Russian **hard sf**, exemplified by the work of **Konstantin Tsiolkovsky**, was more narrowly didactic, often cast as **Vernian** romance in the vein of Vladimir Obruchev's *Plutonia* (1915, tr. 1924) and *Sannikov Land* (1926, tr. 1955). Its **pulpish** popular extensions were parodied by Alexander Kuprin in "Liquid Sunshine" (1913). Following the revolutions of 1917, sf became an instrument of propaganda in Alexei Tostoy's *Aelita* (1922, tr. 1957), although its **satirical** use by **Mikhail Bulgakov** was quickly suppressed. **Yegevny Zamyatin's** *We* (written 1920, tr. 1924), written in exile, was clandestinely circulated in Soviet Russia as a *samizdat* publication.

Much early Soviet sf was didactic, as exemplified by the work of **Alexander Belyaev**, but after early promotion it was treated with suspicion in the late Stalinist era, being virtually eclipsed between the mid-1930s and the mid-1950s. Its revivification was largely due to **Ivan Yefremov**, who sparked something of a boom in both domestic and translated sf. The Foreign Languages Publishing House, later renamed Mir, began publishing showcase anthologies in English in 1961, with *The Heart of the Serpent* and *A Visitor from Outer Space*, both featuring material by the **Strugatsky** brothers alongside older material; their *Destination: Amaltheia* was the title piece of a third anthology (1962); more anthologies, novels, and collections followed. Other writers featured in the anthology **series** included Anatoly Dnieprov, **Vladimir Savchenko**, Valentina Zhuravleva, Ilya Varshavsky, **Kir Bulychev**, and **collaborators Mikhail Emtsev** and Eremy Parnov. Sf of a **softer** kind became more widespread in the 1970s, assisted by abundant adaptation in the **cinema**, although the continuing political sensitivity of sf caused the Strugatskys some difficulty. Following the collapse of communism in the late 1980s, entrepreneurial publishers rushed to bring more controversial produce from the West and open up new opportunities for more ambitious domestic sf, but their efforts were dogged by inevitable problems of economic readjustment. Studies of Soviet sf include John Glad's *Extrapolations from Dystopia* (1982) and Patrick McGuire's *Red Stars* (1985).

**RUSSO, RICHARD PAUL (1954– ).** U.S. writer who began publishing **sf** in 1986. *Inner Eclipse* (1988) features a search for **alien** intelligence by a disillusioned empath; its plaintive tone is recapitulated in such stories as "More Than Night" (1989). *Subterranean Gallery* (1990) is a near-future **dystopia** set in San Francisco, which also served as a setting for a trilogy of detective novels comprising *Destroying Angel* (1992), *Carlucci's Edge* (1995), and *Carlucci's Heart* (1997). *Ship of Fools* (2001) is a mystery story set aboard a **generation starship.** Russo's short fiction is sampled in *Terminal Visions* (2000).

**RYMAN, GEOFF (1951– ).** Canadian-born writer, resident in Britain since 1973, who began publishing surreal **fabulations** with **sf** elements in 1976. *The Unconquered Country* (1984, book 1986), set in an **alternative** Cambodia, features nightmarishly allegorical machines. *The Child Garden* (1988) is an extravagant **existential fantasy** set in an alternative near-futuristic England governed by an exotic **biotechnological** artifact whose instruments of social control are viruses to which the heroine is immune. The collection *Unconquered Countries* (1994) includes the previously unpublished novella "The

Fall of Angels, or On the Possibility of Life under Extreme Conditions," set on a colony world. The novella *VAO* (2002) is a near-future fantasy about the social effects of "Victim Activated Ordinance." *Air* (2002) is about the arrival of the Internet in a remote village.

## – S –

**SABERHAGEN, FRED (1930– ).** U.S. writer in various fantasy genres who began publishing **sf** in 1961. His chief contribution to sf is a series of **space operas** in which humankind is plagued by killing machines left over from an interstellar war, launched with the items collected in *Berserker* (1967). *The Golden People* (1964, rev. 1984), *The Water of Thought* (1965, rev. 1981), and *Specimens* (1976) all feature problematic encounters with **aliens.** *The Veils of Azlaroc* (1978) is set in a radically alien environment. *Love Conquers All* (1979, rev. 1985) is an ironic **dystopia**. *Coils* (1982 with **Roger Zelazny**) is a thriller whose subject matter was rapidly overtaken by the emergence of **cyberpunk.** *A Century of Progress* (1983) juggles **alternative histories.** *The Black Throne* (1990, with Zelazny) is a homage to **Edgar Allan Poe.** Saberhagen's **transfigurations** of classic texts *The Dracula Tape* (1975) and *The Frankenstein Papers* (1986) are **hybrid** rationalizations.

**ST. CLAIR, MARGARET (1911–1995).** U.S. writer who began publishing **sf** in 1946. Her **pulp** sf is undercut by a dark skepticism, which complicates the plot of "Vulcan's Dolls" (1952, book 1956 as *Agent of the Unknown*) and adds a nightmarish edge to "Mistress of Viridis" (1955; exp. as *The Green Queen*, 1956), *The Games of Neith* (1960), and the claustrophobic **postholocaust** fantasy *Sign of the Labrys* (1963). *The Dolphins of Altair* (1967), *The Shadow People* (1969), and *The Dancers of Noyo* (1973) extrapolate environmentalist concerns. Her short sf—including comedies bylined Idris Seabright—is sampled in *Three Worlds of Futurity* (1964), *Change the Sky* (1974), and *The Best of Margaret St. Clair* (1985).

**SARGENT, LYMAN TOWER (1940– ).** U.S. scholar whose annotated **bibliography** of *British and American Utopian Literature*

*1516–1975* (1979) was much expanded when it was updated (to 1986) in 1988. Remarkably comprehensive, it offers an invaluable overview of the **Utopian** strand in **sf** and its connections with Utopian **political fantasies** that pay less attention to matters of **technological determinism.**

**SARGENT, PAMELA (1948– ).** U.S. writer who began publishing **sf** in 1970, much of her early work collected in *Starshadows* (1977). The **mosaic existentialist fantasy** *Cloned Lives* (1976) remains the most clearheaded account of its subject. The **postholocaust fantasy** *The Sudden Star* (1979, aka *The White Death*), the **existentialist** study of longevity *The Golden Space* (1982), and the enlightenment fantasy *The Alien Upstairs* (1983) subject standard themes to thoughtful reanalysis. The trilogy of **children's sf** novels comprising *Watchstar* (1980), *Eye of the Comet* (1984), and *Homesmind* (1985) and the related *Earthseed* (1983), which elaborate motifs borrowed from the work of her husband, **George Zebrowski**, are earnestly didactic. *Alien Child* (1988) is similar in kind. *The Shore of Women* (1986) is a darkly ambivalent **feminist** fantasy. The trilogy comprising *Venus of Dreams* (1986), *Venus of Shadows* (1988), and the long-delayed *Child of Venus* (2001) is an epic account of **terraforming.** *Climb the Wind: A Novel of Another America* (1998) is an **alternative history.** Later short fiction is collected in *Behind the Eyes of Dreamers and Other Short Novels* (2002) and *The Mountain Cage and Other Stories* (2002). Sargent edited the **anthologies** *Bio-Futures* (1976) and the three-volume *Women of Wonder* series (1975–1978).

**SATIRE.** Satire was one of the primal genres, born into Greek drama alongside tragedy as its "satyr-play" counterweight. Although its theatrical manifestations were subsequently subsumed within a broader comedy genre, it retained a greater independence in prose fiction, where it made abundant use of **fantastic voyages** and **Utopian** societies, avidly taking aboard many settings and devices that were later to become important in **sf**. The satirical impulse generated both the ***conte philosophique*** and the ***conte cruel***, which became important narrative forms of sf. Although American **pulp sf** detached itself from its satirical roots in favor of action-adventure formulas carried forward from **Vernian** romance, British **scientific romance** rooted in

**Wellsian** fiction always retained a satirical core; the distinction between the two traditions became far less obvious when American sf reembraced satirical methods and purposes in the 1950s.

Although **Campbellian hard sf** routinely employs satire as a means of assaulting its skeptics, the primary aim of such fiction is to uphold the ideal of technological and social progress as a necessary and virtuous unity; critics within the genre mostly subscribe to that ideal. Critics trained in the academy, on the other hand, are far more likely to be deeply skeptical about the necessity of the connection between technological and social progress and flagrantly antipathetic to the notion that the existing connection is virtuous. In consequence, critics looking at genre sf from without are prone to conserve their applause for fiction satirizing the assumption that technology assists social progress. **Swiftian** satire—whose application to the subject matter of sf is founded in the third book of *Gulliver's Travels*—is extremely scathing about that which Campbellian sf holds most dear and there is a certain inconvenience in having to subsume the ideological backlash against it under the same category label. Given the passions aroused on either side of ongoing debates about the virtuousness of various aspects of technological progress, however, all literary camps are bound to maintain considerable stocks of satirical derision within their armories.

**SAWYER, ROBERT J. (1960– ). Canadian** writer who began publishing **sf** in 1981. *Golden Fleece* (1990; rev. 1999) carefully hybridizes a **transfiguration** of the Greek myth with a murder mystery; he continued to use mysteries as narrative frames for **hard sf** speculations in the loosely knit Quintaglio trilogy, comprising *Far-Seer* (1992), *Fossil Hunter* (1993), and *Foreigner* (1994)—in which saurian **aliens** figure out how to avoid extinction when their world comes under threat—and the **time-travel** fantasy *The End of an Era* (1994). His work became conspicuously more ambitious thereafter; although the **existentialist fantasy** *The Terminal Experiment* (1995) has a murder mystery subplot, it employs the notion of artificially split personalities to delve deep into the roots of morality. *Starplex* (1996) is a complex **portal fantasy** featuring **wormholes.** *Illegal Alien* (1997) is a courtroom drama arguing fundamental principles of moral philosophy. *Frameshift* (1997) is a conventional **techno-**

**thriller** that takes a similarly indignant argumentative line on matters of legal entitlement. The **SETI** fantasy *Factoring Humanity* (1998) and the ambiguous **disaster story** *Flashforward* (1999) attempt to rehabilitate and sophisticate the **van Vogtian** notion of a sudden access of superhumanity. *Calculating God* (2000) sets up cosmic coincidences in order to reexamine the classical argument from design. The Neanderthal Parallax **series** comprising *Hominids* (2002), *Humans* (2003), and *Hybrids* (2003) carefully compares alternative evolutionary patterns in **parallel worlds.** Sawyer's short fiction is sampled in *Iterations* (2002).

**SAXTON, JOSEPHINE (1935– ).** British writer who began publishing surreal **fabulations** with **sf** elements in 1965, her fiction in that vein being collected in *The Power of Time* (1985). "The Consciousness Machine" (1968; exp. as *The Hieros Gamos of Sam and An Smith*, 1969) and *Vector for Seven; or, the Weltanschaung* [sic] *of Mrs. Amelia Mortimer and Friends* (1970) are earnest allegories, but the **satirical** tone of *Group Feast* (1971) developed into the comedy of the **feminist hallucinatory fantasies** *The Travails of Jane Saint* (1980, reprinted as the title story of a 1986 collection) and *Queen of the States* (1986). The sequel to the former item included in *Jane Saint and the Backlash: The Further Travails of Jane Saint, and the Consciousness Machine* (1989) updates the political element by including the "new man" as a satirical target.

**SCHACHNER, NAT (1895–1955).** U.S. writer in various genres who began publishing **sf**, initially in **collaboration** with **Arthur Leo Zagat**, in 1930. Although he wrote a good deal of hackwork, some of his futuristic fiction—notably "The Robot Technocrat," "The Revolt of the Scientists," and the ironic **time-paradox** story "Ancestral Voices" (all 1933)—was energized by fervent antifascist attitudes. He carried this train of thought further in an intriguing study of a charismatic **alien**, "He from Procyon" (1934), and a five-part **series** of **political fantasies** begun with "Past, Present and Future" (1937–1939), in which he readily adapted his style to **John Campbell's** editorial requirements. He did not return to the field after World War II; his only sf to reach book form was a lighthearted **mosaic** making use of his professional experience, *Space Lawyer* (1941, book 1953).

**SCHENCK, HILBERT (1926– ).** U.S. writer who published his first **sf** story in 1953, returning to the genre in 1977 with the first of the sea stories collected in *Wave Rider* (1980), whose loose-knit **series** culminated in *At the Eye of the Ocean* (1980), a lyrical exercise in **ecological mysticism.** He redeployed New England coastal settings with similarly loving care in the poignant **apocalyptic fantasy** *A Rose for Armageddon* (1982) and the mystery *Chrono-Sequence* (1988), both of which use loops in **time** to redeem intractable situations. The short novel *Steam Bird* (1988, the book also contains the novella "Hurricane Claude") is an ironic comedy about a bizarre secret weapon.

**SCHMIDT, STANLEY (1944– ).** U.S. editor and writer who began publishing **sf** in ***Analog*** in 1968, 10 years before he took over the editorship of the **magazine**, staunchly maintaining the **Campbellian** tradition—which he fully restored after the slight relaxation indulged by his predecessor, **Ben Bova**—through the next quarter-century. *Newton and the Quasi-Apple* (1970, exp. 1975) is a paradigmatic example of Campbellian **hard sf**, describing a scientific revolution on a primitive world. The couplet comprising *The Sins of the Fathers* (1976) and the **mosaic** *Lifeboat Earth* (1978) offers a more elaborate account of an exotic **alien** society set against a more complex background. *Tweedlioop* (1986) is a lighthearted account of an alien castaway's reception on Earth. In *Argonaut* (2002) aliens use insects to reconnoiter near-future Earth. Schmidt's short fiction is sampled in *Generation Gap and Other Stories* (2002).

**SCHMITZ, JAMES H. (1911–1981). German**-born U.S. writer who began publishing **sf** in 1949, when he produced the first part of the **mosaic space opera** *Agent of Vega* (1960) and a short version of the lively **psi** story *The Witches of Karres* (exp. 1966). Almost everything he wrote rests firmly on those two foundation stones; he combined their backgrounds into an image of a sprawling **galactic** society whose Hub is ruled by an Overgovernment ambitious to extend order outward, holding chaos at bay in the meantime by a series of serendipitous discoveries and pragmatic adjustments. **Baen Books** collected his entire output in a **series** of volumes edited by Eric Flint and Gary Gordon: *Telzey Amberdon* (2000), *T'n'T: Telzey & Trigger* (2000), *Trigger*

*& Friends* (2001), *The Hub: Dangerous Territory* (2001), *Agent of Vega and Other Stories* (2001), and *Eternal Frontier* (2002).

**SCHOLES, ROBERT (1929– ).** U.S. scholar whose definitive book on narrative theory, *The Nature of Narrative* (1966, with Robert Kellogg), was followed by *The Fabulators* (1967; revised as *Fabulation and Metafiction*, 1979), *Structural Fabulation: An Essay on Fiction of the Future* (1975), and *Science Fiction: History/Science/Vision* (1977 with Eric Rabkin), all of which use the terms **fabulation** and **metafiction** to analyze and categorize 20th-century imaginative fiction, including **sf**.

**SCHOLZ, CARTER (1953– ).** U.S. writer who began publishing **sf** in 1976. "The Ninth Symphony of Ludwig van Beethoven and Other Lost Songs" (1977) was the first of several notable fantasies about music. His darkly elliptical futuristic fantasies are sampled in *Cuts* (1985) and *The Amount to Carry* (2003). *Palimpsests* (1984, with Glen Harcourt) is a **time-paradox** story cast as an archaeological mystery, which revels in its own perversity. *Radiance* (2002) is a **satire** featuring a contest between rival physicists to obtain funding for a death **ray.**

**SCHROEDER, KARL (1962– ). Canadian** writer who began publishing **sf** in 1983. He followed a **collaborative** comic fantasy with the epic **far-futuristic planetary romance** *Ventus* (2000). *Permanence* (2002) is a philosophical **space opera** examining the potential of **nanotechnology** and the philosophy of "transhumanism" (partly based on **Vernor Vinge's** anticipation of a technological **singularity**). In collaboration with **Cory Doctorow** he produced *The Complete Idiot's Guide to Publishing Science Fiction* (2001).

**SCHUYLER, GEORGE S. (1895–1977).** U.S. writer who wrote periodical fiction as Samuel I. Brooks but put his own byline on *Black No More, Being an Account of the Strange and Wonderful Workings of Science in the Land of the Free, A.D. 1933–1940* (1931), a trenchant **satire** on race relations involving a skin-bleaching technology. *Black Empire* (1936–1938 as Brooks; 1991) imagines a revolution resulting from the lack of any such literal or metaphorical adjustment and the eventual establishment of a separatist **Utopia.**

**SCIENCE-FANTASY.** A term used in several different ways, sometimes as a synonym for **science fiction** but more often in attempts to distinguish (from "real" science fiction) texts that deploy items from the imaginative lexicon of **sf** within narrative frameworks derived from other fantasy genres, with only the most superficial pretence of rational plausibility. Its most frequent use refers to a conspicuously romantic tradition of **pulp** fiction extending from the works of **Edgar Rice Burroughs**, **A. Merritt**, and **Clark Ashton Smith** through such obvious genre sf descendants as **Leigh Brackett**, **C. L. Moore**, and **Jack Vance** to a great many late 20th-century **planetary romances**, **parallel world** fantasies, and **far-futuristic fantasies.** The British **magazine** *Science-Fantasy* never focused its contents in accordance with any of the possible meanings of its title, beginning as a straightforward sf magazine and ending up playing host to **Michael Moorcock's** sword-and-sorcery fiction and Thomas Burnett Swann's mythological fantasies, but it did feature such paradigmatic neoromantic novellas as **John Brunner's** "Earth Is But a Star" (1958) and **Ken Bulmer's** "The Map Country" (1961).

Because there are so many fantastic subgenres straddling the boundaries between sf and other genres of fantasy, no matter how meticulously those boundaries are drawn, "science-fantasy" is a useful umbrella term, within whose span it is convenient to draw distinctions between texts that are **ambiguous**, **hybrid**, and **chimerical.** There was a gradual but relentless displacement of hybrid science-fantasy by chimerical science-fantasy as pulp sf gave way to digest magazines and **paperback** books; this greatly encouraged the development within the genre of **satire** and **fabulation**, both of which derive more benefit from chimerical contradiction than hybrid compromise. This evolution paved the way for **new wave** avant-gardism and the perception and promotion of a much closer relationship between certain aspects of genre sf and literary fiction; it also facilitated the market growth of genre fantasy, which overshadowed sf to such an extent by the end of the 20th century that chimerical science-fantasy was then a more abundant subgenre than **hard sf** or **soft sf.**

**SCIENCE FICTION.** The hyphenated term "**science-fiction**" was coined by the Scottish poet **William Wilson** in 1851, in response to his reading of **Robert Hunt's** *The Poetry of Science* (1848), but was not taken up by anyone else. When the existence of some such popular genre became sufficiently obvious to require a label in the 1890s,

British reviewers and journalists preferred **scientific romance**, although some of the writers to whom the label was applied—including **H. G. Wells**—were initially reluctant to accept it. Once **Hugo Gernsback** began using "science fiction" in preference to **scientifiction**, it was quickly taken up by other U.S. **magazine** publishers (although ***Astounding*** originally offered "stories of superscience") and established an unassailable dominance in the specialist **pulps** by the mid-1930s; post–World War II global marketing spread it throughout the world in the late 1940s. The **Wilsonian** hyphen made occasional fugitive reappearances, as in the original title of **Science-Fiction Studies.** If "science" is construed as "truth" and fiction as "falsehood," the compound term is an oxymoron, but there is an irreducible **speculative** (and therefore fictional) component within the hardest of sciences and the fictional goal of plausibility inevitably involves some consideration of rationality (as defined by scientific method). "Science fiction" is, therefore, more reasonably construed as a hybrid term—unlike "science-fantasy," which is blatantly **chimerical** (that being the significance of the retention of its hyphen). Attempts to define science fiction are acutely problematic, as observed and explained in the introduction to this volume.

**SCIENCE FICTION BOOK CLUB (SFBC).** Book clubs specializing in **sf** were launched in the United States and the United Kingdom in the early 1950s. The U.K. version changed proprietors several times before dying in the 1980s, but the U.S. book club, published by an associate of Doubleday, continued to thrive into the 21st century under the direction of Ellen Asher. Book clubs are powerful institutions in the United States because the geographic dispersal of the population confers unique economic privileges on mail-order distribution, and the SFBC was a significant shaping force in the evolution of sf from its inception. An early decision to offer **Isaac Asimov's** Foundation trilogy as a loss leader inducement to attract new members played a considerable role in establishing that work as a central text of genre sf, and prompted the SFBC to begin producing many more omnibuses for exclusive distribution to its members—a prominent feature of its activities from the 1970s on. This helped to encourage publishers to invest ever more heavily in trilogies and had a considerable effect on the consumption habits of an important sector of the genre's core readership.

**SCIENCE FICTION FOUNDATION (SFF).** An institution established in 1971, initially based at the North East London Polytechnic. Its principal advocate, George Hay, had imagined it as an organization of intellectuals akin to **Isaac Asimov's** Foundation (hence its name), who would endeavor to further the cause of progress by agitating for the realization of **sf's** better ideas, but its only assets were a collection of books donated by the **British Science Fiction Association** and an administrator hired by the polytechnic. The administrator chaired a council of interested persons selected from a population of "ordinary members" gathered by invitation, facilitated the use of the library as an instrument of academic research, and edited the journal *Foundation*—which, following its launch in 1972, rapidly fell into the familiar mold of academic journals, although it retained such features as a regular column of personal insider views of "The Profession of Science Fiction." **Peter Nicholls** occupied the post from 1971–1977, Malcolm Edwards from 1978–1980, after which it was frozen. The journal was run thereafter by its editors—David Pringle from 1980–1986, Edward James from 1986–2003, when he handed over primary responsibility to his long-time **collaborator**, Farah Mendlesohn; the book collection was eventually taken over by the University of Liverpool. Librarian Andrew Sawyer was hired to look after the collection, which remained connected to the journal via a loosely knit organization of volunteers styling itself the Friends of the Foundation.

**SCIENCE FICTION RESEARCH ASSOCIATION (SFRA).** A group of academics formed in 1970 to aid and encourage **sf** scholarship (which was assumed to include, or at least to overlap, **Utopian** studies and the study of other fantasy genres in all media). Its first chairman was **Thomas Clareson.** It established an annually updated membership directory and a newsletter—initially published 10 times a year—that was retitled *The SFRA Review* in 1992 and reduced by stages to a quarterly schedule. It also inaugurated an annual award, the Pilgrim (named for **J. O. Bailey's** pioneering academic study of sf), for a lifetime contribution to sf scholarship, to be awarded at the organization's annual conference. Subscriptions to the critical journals **Extrapolation** and **Science-Fiction Studies** were included in the membership fee. In 1990 SFRA created a second annual award, the Pioneer, for the best critical essay of the year; it subsequently added others, most notably the Clareson Award for lifetime contributions to the field exclusive of scholarship.

***SCIENCE-FICTION STUDIES.*** An academic journal founded in 1973, published three times a year, initially by Indiana State University, where coeditor R. D. Mullen (who worked in association with **Darko Suvin**) was based. It moved to Suvin's base—McGill University in Montreal, Canada—in 1979, after which the editorship involved a small committee with an irregular turnover of members. From 1993 onward—at which time the hyphen disappeared from the title and the page-count of its issues increased—it was based at DePauw University. It has published a number of special issues devoted to particular authors or topics, one of which—no. 78 (vol. 26, part 2, 1999)—featured a useful "History of Science Fiction **Criticism**."

**SCIENCE FICTION WRITERS OF AMERICA (SFWA).** An organization of professional writers, originally envisaged as a specialist writers' guild, founded in 1965 by writers associated with the **Milford Conference**, headed by **Damon Knight.** It established two regular publications, the *SFWA Bulletin*, accessible to interested parties outside the organization as well as its members, and the confidential *SFWA Forum*, which soon became a venue for fierce controversies. It also established the annual **Nebula** Awards and an associated banquet. In its early years, SFWA designed a model contract, whose example exerted some pressure on publishers and had a marked effect on the way that **magazine** editors and **anthologists** did business, and it produced a *SFWA Handbook* for the use of new members, which passed through various incarnations during the next 20 years.

The original qualification for full SFWA membership was that writers had to be active, and their credentials had to updated every year by new publications (a novel or three short stories in professional magazines), but this was eventually reduced so that anyone meeting the requirement once remained permanently qualified. This change boosted the membership numbers, but had a considerable diluting effect. No attempt was ever made to discriminate between **sf** and other fantasy genres in assessing membership criteria, so the advent of genre fantasy in the 1970s began a cumulative change in the composition of the membership that eventually resulted in the redefinition of the organization in 1992 as the Science Fiction and Fantasy Writers of America (a separate organization of Horror Writers of America had been founded in the 1980s).

**SCIENTIFICTION.** A contraction of "scientific fiction" used by **Hugo Gernsback** (in addition to the expanded phrase) to describe the didactically inclined fiction he featured in *Modern Electrics* (1908–1913), *The Electrical Experimenter* (1913–1920), and *Science and Invention* (1920–1931) before founding ***Amazing Stories***. Gernsback might have stuck to that label had he not lost control of *Amazing* and elected to go into competition with it by founding the ***Wonder*** group; his subsequent preference for "science fiction" presumably reflected a desire to imply that his new magazines were no mere duplicates of their forebears. Once *Amazing* had changed its subtitle from "The Magazine of Scientifiction" to "The Magazine of Science Fiction" (in the November 1932 issue), the establishment of the latter term was assured, although "scientifiction" and its abbreviation *stf* retained some lingering currency within the genre until the late 1930s; **Walter Gillings** used it as the title of a significant fanzine in 1937–1938.

**SCIENTIFIC ROMANCE.** A term applied by **C. H. Hinton** to two collections mixing speculative fiction and **speculative nonfiction.** It was taken up by journalists and reviewers in the 1890s as a convenient label for Wellsian fiction; **Wells** resisted it for some time, preferring the designation "Fantastic and Imaginative Romances" in lists of his previous works printed in his books, but capitulated by sanctioning the release of an omnibus edition of *The Scientific Romances of H. G. Wells* (1933). The designation remains useful as a means of highlighting the clear distinction that existed between the British and American traditions of **speculative fiction** until the massive importation of American **sf** into Britain in the wake of World War II brought them together in irredeemable confusion; it is employed in that fashion in **Brian Stableford's** analytical history *Scientific Romance in Britain, 1890–1950*. The term still retains some currency, occasionally used as a subtitle—or even, as in Ronald Wright's *A Scientific Romance* (1997), as a title—by writers intent on making the point that the works in question have more in common with the classics of the British tradition than those of American sf.

**SCI-FI.** An abbreviation of "**science fiction**" coined in the early 1960s by **Forrest J. Ackerman** by analogy with "hi-fi." He intended it as a complimentary term but when it began to displace **sf** in the jargon of newspaper and **TV** reporters—who thought of the genre primarily as an aspect of movie and **TV** production—the typically patronizing and casually insulting tone of such reportage, blended with blithe ignorance of the fact that sf had a long and august literary history, resulted in its falling into extreme disrepute in the 1970s within the sf community, whose members routinely insisted on pronouncing it as "skiffy" in order to make their contempt and resentment audible. Once it had been taken up as a label by the satellite-TV Sci-Fi Channel in the 1980s, however, it became a convenient way to distinguish between media sf and literary sf. Given that different media manifestations of sf are separated by a wider gulf than the respective manifestations of other genres—because of hard sf's heavy emphasis on expository explanation, which cannot be adapted to the screen—it might have been useful to retain two distinct labels. The dominance of TV and **cinema** sf ensured, however, that by the beginning of the 21st century "sci-fi" had begun to lose its pejorative connotations in the eyes of younger fans and critics and seemed increasingly likely to become established as the standard abbreviation descriptive of the entire genre.

**SCORTIA, THOMAS N. (1926–1986).** U.S. writer who began publishing **sf** in 1954. His short fiction, sampled in *Caution! Inflammable!* (1975), is uneasily meditative about the possibilities of progress; after *Artery of Fire* (short version 1960, exp. 1972) his work displayed an increasingly scathing skepticism about the capacity of human beings to use technology productively. His later works are accounts of man-made **disasters**, all but the **apocalyptic** *Earthwreck!* (1974) being written in **collaboration** with **Frank M. Robinson.**

**SCOTT, MELISSA (1960– ).** U.S. writer whose early **space operas**, *The Game Beyond* (1984) and the trilogy comprising *Five-Twelfths of Heaven* (1986), *Silence in Solitude* (1986), and *The Empress of Earth* (1987), are casually **feminized**. *A Choice of Destinies* (1986) is an **alternative history** in which Alexander the Great takes on Rome instead of invading India. *The Kindly Ones* (1987) is a

**dystopian fantasy** of social control by ostracism. *Mighty Good Road* (1990) similarly examines dilemmas of conscience set against an exotic background. *Dreamships* (1992) and *Burning Bright* (1993) are sophisticated space operas. *Trouble and Her Friends* (1994) is a **cyberpunk** thriller. *Shadow Man* (1995) features a hypothetical society whose sexual relationships are inordinately complex, thanks to the physiological and psychological side effects of a medicinal drug. In *Night Sky Mine* (1996) a survivor of a pirate raid searches for lost self-knowledge. In *Dreaming Metal* (1997), set in same world as *Dreamships*, an illusionist accidentally creates an **artificial intelligence.** In *The Shapes of Their Hearts* (1998) an **AI** merges with a brain-tape of a religious prophet. *The Jazz* (2000) is a thriller about future media. *Conceiving the Heavens: Creating the Science Fiction Novel* (1986) is a writing guide.

**SELLINGS, ARTHUR (1921–1968).** Pseudonym of British writer Robert Arthur Ley, who began publishing **sf** in 1953. His novels describe ordinary individuals struggling to come to terms with extraordinary circumstances—the acquisition of **psi** powers in *Telepath* (1962, aka *The Silent Speakers*) and *The Uncensored Man* (1964); the invention of **antigravity** in *The Quy Effect* (1966); transferred memories in *Intermind* (1967); and matter duplication in *The Power of X* (1968). The posthumous **postholocaust fantasy** *Junk Day* (1970) is the most ambitious. His short fiction is sampled in *Time Transfer* (1956) and *The Long Eureka* (1968).

**SENSE OF WONDER.** A term improvised to describe an aesthetic response to a sudden expansion of imaginative perspective induced by science or **sf**. The discoveries of 19th-century astronomy, microscopy, and geology, which revealed the limitations of human sensation and experience, were the primary generators of the response, although they often required careful dramatization—by essays in the popularization of science or by sf—to enable them to be imaginatively grasped. **Camille Flammarion's** *Lumen* is a cardinal example of a strategic attempt to invoke the sense of wonder. The response is a wasting asset, historically as well as psychologically; once the relevant **conceptual breakthrough** has occurred, on a collective or individual basis, the intensity of its first revelation is never recoverable—this is why cynics are apt to observe that "the **golden age** of sf is thirteen" and why jaded fans are inclined to employ the dismissive misspelling "sensawunda." **Space opera** was an effective generator of the sense of wonder in the 1930s for those who could entertain its ludicrous artifice but when **galactic empires** became commonplace in the 1950s, the possibilities of metamorphic mental evolution and **multiverses** of **parallel worlds** were more significant. By the end of the 20th century, cosmological fantasies had been forced to such extremes as the **Omega Point**, and evocative resources seemed to have attained their limit.

**SERIES.** The commodification of popular fiction that gave birth to commercial genres was, in essence, an attempt to regularize the process of supply and demand. The mass production of commercial fiction requires its careful formularization to fit the pattern of reader expectation, and series fiction is the ultimate evidence of that project's success. In effect, all genre fiction aspires to the condition of crime fiction, in which crime fighters arrayed along a spectrum of legitimacy extending from policemen through secret agents to vigilantes and virtuous outlaws can be confronted with a potentially infinite sequence of antagonists, generating conflicts that move through a series of fixed phases to satisfactory climactic solutions. Such series are "segmental," in the sense that each one is like a segment of an ever-growing tapeworm or a section cut from an infinite roll of wallpaper. Even segmental series, however, run into problems of **melodramatic inflation**, and genres that routinely employ improving rather than normalizing story-arcs—the group comprising love stories, rags-to-riches stories, and so forth—can only repeat their formula endlessly by using a different protagonist in each individual segment.

**Sf** stories do not fit comfortably into either of these molds; the repeated use of normalizing story-arcs inevitably led to the **Frankenstein syndrome**, and although sf has a more extensive stock of improving story-arcs than any naturalistic genre, their effectiveness in generating a **sense of wonder** is soon blunted by repetition and familiarization. Even so, insofar as sf is a commercial genre, its producers have a strong economic incentive to deal as extensively as possible in series; powerful market forces pressure publishers and writers to follow up successful works with sequels, and to continue the process until audience receptiveness is exhausted.

Sf does have a built-in tendency to generate series, albeit of a different kind from those typical of other genres. The role played in sf by **extrapolation** means that even when a particular story-arc has reached an aesthetically satisfactory conclusion, potential usually remains for the premise to generate further corollaries. This is particularly relevant to futuristic fantasies, which can be carried further forward in time for as long as further climaxes can be fitted to individual story-arcs. This kind of "expansive" series is much more prone to the problem of melodramatic inflation than segmental series—which is why sf series that begin expansively, like **Isaac Asimov's** Foundation series and **Frank Herbert's** Dune series, often lapse into segmentality by filling in gaps in the **future history** or providing prequels when no further melodramatic inflation is possible.

**SERVISS, GARRETT P. (1851–1929).** U.S. journalist and popularizer of astronomy. He first became involved with **sf** when he was commissioned to write a **serial** sequel to **H. G. Wells's** *The War of the Worlds*; *Edison's Conquest of Mars* (1898, book 1947) describes how Earth strikes back at the invaders. A new element replaces gold as a currency standard in *The Moon Metal* (1900). An atomic-powered spaceship facilitates an exploratory voyage to Venus in *A Columbus of Space* (1909, book 1911). *The Second Deluge* (1912) is a **disaster story** about a new Noah.

**SETI.** An acronym signifying the Search for Extraterrestrial Intelligence. The endeavor originated with Project Ozma, established in 1960 by Frank Drake at the National Radio Astronomy Observatory in Greenbank, Virginia, to scan G-type stars for radio signals that might be communications. Drake and others, especially Carl Sagan (1934–1996)—whose **speculative nonfiction** laid the groundwork for SETI fiction, to which he made his own lyrical contribution in *Contact* (1985)—invested much intellectual effort in trying to figure out which frequency an **alien** species might employ for such broadcasts, and how information might best be encoded within a sequence of binary digits. **Sf** writers were enthusiastic to imagine what the consequences might be of the project's fulfillment, a notable early account being *The Listeners* (1972) by **James E. Gunn.** Its lack of success called into question the so-called Drake equation, which calculated (on the basis of a series of probabilistic assumptions) that there might be hundreds of millions of potentially communicative civilizations in the galaxy, and forced interested sf writers into sharp confrontation with the **Fermi paradox.** The continuation of the search after NASA withdrew funding in 1993 generated a remarkable **collaborative** enterprise in the early 21st century, when its data-processing was dispersed to hundreds of thousands of Internet-connected PCs whose owners volunteered their use—a project explained and publicized in *Are We Alone in the Cosmos? The Search for Alien Contact* (2000), edited by **Ben Bova** and Byron Preiss.

**SF.** An abbreviation of "**science fiction**" which became the standard label applied to the genre in the letter columns of **pulp magazines**, **fanzines**, and on the spines and covers of **paperback** books. Its iconic significance encouraged the coinage of other proposed generic labels with the same initials, including **speculative fiction** and structural **fabulation.** The emergence of the rival contraction **sci-fi** initiated a contest whose initial outcome was the assignation of the two terms to separate aspects of the genre, sf being preferred with reference to printed texts, sci-fi with reference to products of the visual media. By the early 21st century, however, sci-fi seemed likely to displace its rival in all contexts.

**SF SITE.** A website at www.sfsite.com founded by John O'Neill, active since 1997 and updated twice monthly. Like ***Locus*** On-Line, it provides reviews of **sf** books, interviews with authors, lists of forthcoming titles, and links to other sites, as well as a number of columns offering informed opinions on every aspect of the genre.

**SHAGGY GOD STORIES.** A term coined by **Brian Aldiss** to describe stories whose story-arcs conclude with a revelatory dissolution into a familiar myth; in the most frequent variation, two survivors of an exotic catastrophe turn out to be Adam and Eve. Stories of this kind made up an astonishingly high proportion (up to a third in the 1970s) of the unsolicited material submitted to 20th-century **sf magazines**, partly because so few of them reach print that naive authors have no awareness of their lack of originality, although the fact that the idea occurs spontaneously to so many people is remarkable.

**SHARECROPPING.** A term borrowed by **Gardner Dozois** in the late 1980s—from a system of tenure in which farmers receive a proportion of the crop in return for cultivating land they do not own—to describe an increasingly common publishing practice. A best-selling author licenses an existing setting, or invents a new one, for use as the basis of a segmental **series** written by other writers, whose names receive second billing on the cover and who only receive a proportion of the advance and any subsequent royalties. **Baen Books** is by far the most prolific dealer in generic sharecropping exercises.

Although it only became viable once **sf** writers like **Isaac Asimov**, **Arthur C. Clarke**, and **Anne McCaffrey** had established their names as best-selling "brands," sharecropping echoed the long-standing practices of series syndicates, whose history extended back to **dime novels**; it had also been foreshadowed by a number of **shared-world** exercises whose inspiration was less crudely commercial. All genres making copious use of segmental series tend to produce heroes who outlast the creative capabilities of their originators, but the practice seems pernicious in sf because segmental series cannot—by definition—make any real progress, and are thus contrary to the spirit of a genre whose "natural" series are necessarily expansive. Sharecropping sf has been vociferously attacked on these grounds by **Norman Spinrad** and others.

**SHARED WORLDS.** Settings used by a number of different writers, usually presented in an **anthology** or **series** of anthologies. The first such **sf** project was *The Petrified Planet* (1952) edited by **Fletcher Pratt**, who supplied details of an **alien** world to **H. Beam Piper** and **Judith Merril** so that he and they could describe different phases in its colonization. The unusual level of **collaboration** in genre sf and the problematics of **world-building** encouraged other aesthetically and intellectually motivated ventures like **Roger Elwood's** *A World Named Cleopatra* (1977) and **Harlan Ellison's** *Medea* (1985), while **Marion Zimmer Bradley** set a significant precedent by inviting other writers to use Darkover as a setting.

Such game-playing was not commercially significant until the advent of genre fantasy, which is far more hospitable to segmental series, but once it had been successful there it was rapidly adapted to **military sf** by **Baen Books**, whose shared-world projects often took the form of **sharecropping** exercises. Only a few—the Man-Kzin Wars series adapted from **Larry Niven's** Known Space **future history** is the most conspicuous example—attracted the involvement of writers who had no need to indulge in hackwork. All **tie-in** fiction is, in effect, shared-world fiction, and is almost invariably produced in accordance with sharecropping principles.

**SHAW, BOB (1931–1996).** British writer born in Ulster. He became enthusiastically involved in **fandom** in his teens, and published a few **sf** stories professionally in 1954–1956, but did not begin to produce mature work until 1965. "Light of Other Days" (1966), which introduced the notion of "slow glass," was quickly recognized as a classic and a key model of the way in which "human-interest stories" could be designed to accommodate and display sf motifs. The careful extrapolation of the potential social impact of the seemingly trivial innovation eventually produced the **mosaic** *Other Days, Other Eyes* (1972). *Night Walk* (1967) features a technical device that allows a blind man on the run to borrow the sight of others. *The Two-Timers* (1968) follows the consequences of its protagonist's attempt to escape his troubles by moving into an **alternative** world. *The Shadow of Heaven* (1969) features applications of **antigravity**, which Shaw came to consider ill judged, replacing them with the more plausible applications examined in *Vertigo* (1978). *The Palace of Eternity* (1969) investigates an afterlife secured by courtesy of **aliens** under threat of extinction. *One Million Tomorrows* (1970) features a technology of longevity whose price is sexual impotence. *Ground Zero Man* (1971; rev. as *The Peace Machine*, 1985) is a world-blackmail story carefully reassessing the tactical problems exposed by previous exercises in the subgenre.

*Orbitsville* (1975) offers an account of a vast alien artifact enclosing a sun, which generated further possibilities sufficient to supply two sequels, *Orbitsville Departure* (1983) and *Orbitsville Judgment* (1990). *A Wreath of Stars* (1976) features an exceedingly odd **parallel world** whose nature is extrapolated from subatomic physics. *Medusa's Children* (1977) describes the ecosphere of an artificial worldlet composed of seawater. *Who Goes Here?* (1977), a slapstick comedy whose sequel is *Warren Peace* (1993), was Shaw's first attempt to import into his novels the comedy he had long employed in his fan writing, especially the deadpan *Serious Scientific Talks* (1984) that had become a popular feature of British **conventions.** *Ship of Strangers* (1978) pays homage to **A. E. van Vogt's** *Voyage of the Space Beagle*. Shaw's ingenuity seemed to be tiring by this time; *Dagger of the Mind* (1979) and *The Ceres Solution* (1981) suffer some confusion of effect, although the exotic **space opera** trilogy comprising *The Ragged Astronauts* (1986), *The Wooden Spaceships* (1988), and *The Fugitive Worlds* (1989) is admirably bold. His short fiction, collected in *Tomorrow Lies in Ambush* (1973), *Cosmic Kaleidoscope* (1976), *A Better Mantrap* (1982), and *Dark Night in Toyland* (1989), exhibited a similar gradual fatigue.

**SHAW, GEORGE BERNARD (1856–1950).** British playwright whose *Back to Methuselah: A Metabiological Pentateuch* (1921) is a far-reaching account of human evolution that begins and ends in allegory but develops an earnest intermediate account of social adaptation to an increase in human longevity attained by effort, as per the "Lamarckian" thesis defended in a long introduction to the printed version. His other futuristic fantasies include the "political extravaganzas" *The Apple Cart* (1930) and *Too True to Be Good* (1932) and the "political comedy" *On the Rocks* (1933).

**SHECKLEY, ROBERT (1928– ).** U.S. writer who began publishing **sf** in 1952. His mordant comedies, whose **satirical** edge is deceptively keen, became a regular feature in ***Galaxy***, many being collected in *Untouched by Human Hands* (1954), *Citizen in Space* (1955), *Pilgrimage to Earth* (1957), *Notions: Unlimited* (1960), *Store of Infinity* (1960), and *The Shards of Space* (1962). Although *Immortality Delivered* (1958, rev. as *Immortality Inc.*) and the satirical **dystopia** *The Status Civilization* (1960) contrive token thriller plots, his novels soon dispensed with such inconveniences; *Journey beyond Tomorrow* (1962) and *Mindswap* (1966) are sufficiently inventive to work in the absence of any such structure, but *Dimension of Miracles* (1968), *Options* (1975), *The Alchemical Marriage of Alistair Crompton* (1978; aka *Crompton Divided*), and *Dramocles: An Intergalactic Soap Opera* (1983) are patchy. Two sequels (1987–1988) to *The Tenth Victim*

(1966), a novelization of a film based on his short story "Seventh Victim" (1953), lack bite. His later short fiction is sampled in *Can You Feel Anything When I Do This?* (1971, aka *The Same to You Doubled*), *The Robot Who Looked Like Me* (1978), and *Uncanny Tales* (2003). Omnibuses of his work include a five-volume set of *The Collected Short Fiction of Robert Sheckley* (Pulphouse, 1991) and *Dimensions of Robert Sheckley: The Selected Novels of Robert Sheckley* (2002).

**SHEFFIELD, CHARLES (1935–2002).** British-born physicist and writer, resident in the United States from the mid-1960s, who began publishing **sf** in 1977. His early short fiction, collected in *Vectors* (1979) and *Hidden Variables* (1981), built him a reputation as a leading writer of **hard sf**, although some of his early inventions—the metamorphic **biotechnology** featured in *Sight of Proteus* (1978) and its sequels *Proteus Unbound* (1989) and *Proteus in the Underworld* (1995), and the transplanted half-brain in *My Brother's Keeper* (1982)—seem rather implausible. The stories in *The McAndrew Chronicles* (1983; exp. as *One Man's Universe*, 1993; further exp. as *The Compleat McAndrew*, 2000) constitute a wry acknowledgment and defiant rebuttal of such complaints. *The Web between the Stars* (1979) coincidentally features a device similar to the space elevator in **Arthur C. Clarke's** *The Fountains of Paradise*. *Erasmus Magister* (1982; exp. as *The Amazing Dr. Darwin*, 2002) is a **mosaic** in which Charles Darwin's grandfather brings a cannily skeptical attitude to a series of odd encounters.

*Between the Strokes of Night* (1985, rev. 2002) is a far-reaching epic including an early trip to the end of time, which laid groundwork for the **far-futuristic fantasy** *Godspeed* (1993) and the more ambitious **Omega Point** fantasy *Tomorrow and Tomorrow* (1997). Intriguing **aliens** enliven the **space operatic** *The Nimrod Hunt* (1986; exp. as *The Mind Pool*, 1993) and its sequel *Spheres of Heaven* (2001), the mosaic **postholocaust fantasy** *Trader's World* (1988), and the Heritage Universe **series** of exotic **planetary romances**, comprising *Summertide* (1990), *Divergence* (1991), *Transcendence* (1992), *Convergence* (1997), and *Resurgence* (2002). *Cold as Ice* (1992) and its sequels *The Ganymede Club* (1995) and *Dark as Day* (2002) are tense thrillers in which the development of the solar system becomes a necessity following the devastation of Earth. *Brother* *to Dragons* (1992) describes a future in which economic classes are polarized. *Aftermath* (1998) and *Starfire* (1999) comprise a **disaster story** in which Alpha Centauri goes supernova and Earth is devastated by an electromagnetic pulse. *Higher Education* (1996, with **Jerry Pournelle**), *The Billion Dollar Boy* (1997), *Putting Up Roots* (1997), and *The Cyborg from Earth* (1998) are juveniles. Sheffield's later short fiction is collected in *Dancing with Myself* (1993), *Georgia on My Mind and Other Places* (1995), *Space Suits* (2001), and *The Lady Vanishes and Other Oddities of Nature* (2002).

**SHELLEY, MARY WOLLSTONECROFT (1797–1851).** British writer whose Gothic ***conte philosophique*** *Frankenstein, or The Modern Prometheus* (1818, rev. 1831) established an important cultural archetype and a plot formula whose overuse led to the problem identified as the **Frankenstein syndrome.** *The Last Man* (1826), one of the earliest **apocalyptic fantasies** couched in **science-fictional** terms, describes the progress and aftermath of a devastating plague.

**SHEPARD, LUCIUS (1947– ).** U.S. writer who began publishing **ambiguous science-fantasies** in 1983. *Green Eyes* (1984) is **horror-sf** featuring artificial zombies. The **mosaic** *Life during Wartime* (1987) features a psychotropically embellished Vietnam-style war in Latin America; the novella *Aztechs* (2003) is a sequel. A few of the stories in *The Jaguar Hunter* (1987), *The Ends of the Earth* (1991), and *Barnacle Bill the Spacer* (1997, aka *Beast of the Heartland*) have **sf** inclusions, most notably the title story of the third collection.

**SHERRED, T. L. (1915–1985).** U.S. writer whose first **sf** publication was "E for Effort" (1947), a ***conte cruel*** in which the invention of a device for seeing through time precipitates an **apocalypse.** A similar cynicism is displayed in the other stories assembled with it in *First Person, Peculiar* (1972) and the novel *Alien Island* (1970), although the blackly comic tenor of the latter was ameliorated in the sequel *Alien Main* (1985) completed by **Lloyd Biggle** after Sherred fell terminally ill.

**SHIEL, M. P. (1865–1947).** British writer born in Montserrat, who came to the United Kingdom in his teens. He was the most conspicuous British exponent of the Baudelairean "**decadent** style," which he displayed in numerous **Poe-esque** tales in several genres. His first **sf** novel was a **future war** serial reprinted in book form as *The Yellow Danger* (1898), which set out to upstage **George Griffith.** He wrote others of a more moderate stripe, including *The Yellow Wave* (1905) and *The Dragon* (1913), but was more at home in a loosely knit trilogy of **scientific romances** offering alternative visions of the near future: *The Purple Cloud* (1901), an **apocalyptic fantasy** transfiguring the allegory of Job; *The Lord of the Sea*, an eccentric messianic fantasy espousing socialist theories similar to those of Henry George; and *The Last Miracle* (1906), which celebrates the replacement of Christianity by a humanist religion. *The Isle of Lies* (1909) is a ***conte philosophique*** tracking an experiment in education that contrives to produce a **superman** of sorts. Shiel maintained the combative attitude of these stories throughout his career, integrating his theories into most of his naturalistic novels, until he allowed it to flourish wholeheartedly again in the trenchant **visionary fantasy** *The Young Men Are Coming* (1937), which summarizes his ideas regarding humankind's place in the cosmos and the ambitions the species ought to embrace.

**SHINER, LEWIS (1950– ).** U.S. writer who began publishing **sf** in 1977. *Frontera* (1984) is a bleak account of the colonization of **Mars.** *Deserted Cities of the Heart* (1988) is a **hybrid time-travel** fantasy. His short fiction, including some deft ***contes philosophiques***, is collected in *Nine Hard Questions about the Nature of the Universe* (1990) and *The Edges of Things* (1991). "Lizard Men of Los Angeles" (1999) is blithely **chimerical.**

**SHIRAS, WILMAR H. (1908–1990).** U.S. writer who began publishing **sf** with "In Hiding" (1948), the first of a **series** of sentimental tales of mutant children, which seemed quite contrary to the ethos of **John Campbell's *Astounding*** but were welcomed as important precursors of the 1950s **psi** boom. They were collected in the **mosaic** *Children of the Atom* (1953).

**SHIRLEY, JOHN (1953– ).** U.S. writer who began publishing **sf** in 1973. His experiences as a punk rock musician heavily influenced such **dystopian fantasies** as *Transmaniacon* (1979), the **chimerical** *Three-Ring Psychus* (1980), and *City Come A-Walkin'* (1980). He was one of the original propagandists of the **cyberpunk** movement but used its typical apparatus as a relatively sober backcloth in the trilogy of **political fantasies** comprising *Eclipse* (1985), *Eclipse Penumbra* (1988), and *Eclipse Corona* (1990). *A Splendid Chaos* (1988) is a surreal **planetary romance.** Most of his subsequent work was **horror** fiction, but *Silicon Embrace* (1996) is a thriller featuring **alien** grays and . . . *And the Angel with the Television Eyes* (2002) has sf elements. Some sf stories are included in the collections *Heatseeker* (1988), *The Exploded Heart* (1996), and *Darkness Divided* (2001); a few of the surreal **fabulations** in *New Noir* (1993) have sf elements.

**SHUTE, NEVIL (1899–1960).** British writer resident in **Australia** from 1950. Several of his early novels drew on his experiences in the aeronautical industry, including the **future war** story *What Happened to the Corbetts* (1939, aka *Ordeal*), which was soon overtaken by events. *In the Wet* (1953) is a **Utopian visionary fantasy.** *On the Beach* (1957) is a striking account of the brief aftermath of a nuclear war.

**SHWARTZ, SUSAN M. (1949– ).** U.S. writer mainly active in other genres of fantasy, whose ventures into **sf** began with the **military sf** novel *White Wing* (1985), written in collaboration with **Shariann Lewitt** under the byline Gordon Kendall, and the effective **mosaic** study of genocide *Heritage of Flight* (1989). *Second Chances* (2001) is a **transfiguration** of **Joseph Conrad's** *Lord Jim*. Her short fiction is sampled in *Suppose They Gave a Peace and Other Stories* (2002). Her **anthologies** include *Habitats* (1984).

**SILVERBERG, ROBERT (1935– ).** U.S. writer who began publishing **sf** in 1954. After he published the **children's sf** novel *Revolt on Alpha C* (1955), he, **Randall Garrett**, and **Harlan Ellison** set up a "fiction factory" mass-producing work for various **magazines** under numerous pseudonyms; as the magazine market shrank he redirected his efforts into other enterprises. The most adventurous items from this phase of his career include *Master of Life and Death* (1957), in which a bureaucrat struggles to implement policies to counter overpopulation; *Invaders from Earth* (1958), in which the colonization of a Jovian moon is orchestrated by venial organizations; *Recalled to Life* (1958, book 1962), in which society is transformed by a technology of resurrection; and *Collision Course* (1959, book 1961), a sober **first contact** story rejected by **John Campbell** for its antichauvinistic inclinations. His short fiction from the period, including some neat ***contes cruels***, is most effectively sampled in *To Worlds Beyond* (1965).

Following the publication of "To See the Invisible Man" (1963), Silverberg returned to sf in a very different frame of mind, exploring the uses of its vocabulary of ideas in modeling situations of human alienation and mapping routes to psychological fulfillment. His most effective images of spiritual isolation include those in *Thorns* (1967), *Hawksbill Station* (1968, aka *The Anvil of Time*), *The Man in the Maze* (1969), *A Time of Changes* (1971), the **mosaic** *The World Inside* (1971), *Dying Inside* (1972), *The Second Trip* (1972), *The Stochastic Man* (1975), and *Shadrach in the Furnace* (1976). Works in which such situations are preludes to metamorphic transcendence include the mosaics *To Open the Sky* (1967) and *Nightwings* (1969); *Downward to the Earth* (1970), a **transfiguration** of **Joseph Conrad's** *Heart of Darkness*; the **SETI** fantasy *Tower of Glass* (1970); and *Son of Man* (1971), an allegorical **far-futuristic romance.** His children's sf of the same period, including the **alternative history** *The Gate of Worlds* (1967) and the **space opera** *Across a Billion Years* (1969), is similarly sophisticated, and he edited a large number of **anthologies**. Short fiction samplers from this phase include *The Cube Root of Uncertainty* (1970), *The Reality Trip and Other Implausibilities* (1972), *Earth's Other Shadow* (1973), *Sundance and Other Science Fiction Stories* (1974), *Born with the Dead* (1974), and *The Feast of St. Dionysus* (1975).

After five years of "retirement," Silverberg returned to genre work in the 1980s to exploit the opportunities it now presented for writing best-sellers. The **hybrid planetary romance** *Lord Valentine's Castle* (1980), which launched the Majipoor **series**, was the first item off the new production line. The most impressive items of this third phase were shorter works, including those collected in *The Conglomeroid Cocktail Party* (1984) and *In Another Country and Other Short Novels* (2002), and such novellas as *Sailing to Byzantium* (1985) and *The Secret Sharer* (1988), but Silverberg was initially resolute in excluding the depth and intensity of these works from his commercial sf novels. He encouraged more serious work by other writers in the series of original anthologies he edited or coedited, including *New Dimensions* (1971–1981) and *Universe* (1990– ), and it began to creep back in the quasi-allegorical components of the **Odyssean fantasies** *The Face of the Waters* (1991) and *Kingdoms of the Wall* (1992); the **satirical apocalyptic fantasy** *Hot Sky at Midnight* (1994); and the parable of desperation *Starborne* (1996). *The Alien Years* (1998) is an ironically sophisticated revisitation of the theme of **H. G. Wells's** *The War of the Worlds*. *The Longest Way Home* (2002) is an Odyssean fantasy. The mosaic *Roma Mater* (2003) is an alternative history in which the Roman Empire is untroubled by monotheistic religions.

**SIMAK, CLIFFORD D. (1904–1988).** U.S. journalist who began publishing **sf** in 1931 but did not begin to work seriously in the genre until **John Campbell** took over ***Astounding***, enabling its use as a vehicle for ***contes philosophiques*.** The **space opera** *Cosmic Engineers* (1939, book 1950) formed a prelude to a sequence of stories set on the various planets, including "Hermit of Mars" (1939), "Clerical Error" (1940), and "Tools" (1942). In the **future history series** assembled in the classic **mosaic** *City* (1944–1951, book 1952), humankind abandons civilization for a radically new way of life on Jupiter, Earth becoming the heritage of humanoid **robots** and dogs with **artificially enhanced intelligence**, who establish a pastoral **Utopia.**

*City*'s key themes recur throughout Simak's later work, the notion of evolutionary transcendence recurring in the time-twisting *Time and Again* (1951, aka *First He Died*) and *A Choice of Gods* (1972) and a passionate delight in pastoral life in the **parallel worlds** story *Ring around the Sun* (1953) and the meditative *Way Station* (1963)—both of which acknowledge that lifestyles of that kind are only fully sustainable within a much more elaborate technological context. The more exotic formulations of that context—including the galactic network of teleportation stations in *Way Station*, glimpsed in embryo in *Time Is the Simplest Thing* (1961)—similarly accept and assert that the sustainability of any such technological system depends on the willingness of everyone in the world, universe, or **multiverse** to get along peacefully, assisting one another in a neighborly spirit. That spirit is the essence of his cosmic vision, made manifest in the wryly ironic tales collected in *Strangers in the Universe* (1956), *The Worlds of Clifford Simak* (1960; aka *Aliens for Neighbors*), and *All the Traps of Earth* (1962).

Simak's later work became increasingly patchy, often borrowing elements from other fantasy genres to form unconvincing **hybrid** texts, but never lost its narrative energy or the fundamental coherence of its philosophy. *Cemetery World* (1973), *Shakespeare's Planet* (1976), *A Heritage of Stars* (1977), and *The Visitors* (1980) are the most notable of his later novels; the short fiction collected in *The Marathon Photograph and Other Stories* (1986) includes a few items that carried his concerns forward into new literary territory.

**SIMMONS, DAN (1948– ).** U.S. writer in several genres. His principal contribution to **sf** is a series of **metaphysical fantasies** launched with *Hyperion* (1989) and *The Fall of Hyperion* (1999)—reprinted in the omnibus *Hyperion Cantos* (1990—in which various pilgrims arrive at the eponymous planet in search of a revelation consequent upon the opening of the mysterious Time Tombs. The Keatsian implications of the title were amplified in the sequel couplet comprising *Endymion* (1996) and *The Rise of Endymion* (1997), in which an **AI** "TechnoCore" opposed to the Church Militant that has imposed peace on a sclerotized galactic civilization completes its plan to launch a new era of productive free thought heralded by a female messiah. *The Hollow Man* (1992), a **hybrid** fantasy about a bereaved telepath, echoes Dante as well as T. S. Eliot. *Ilium* (2003) launched a Homeric **transfiguration** to be completed in *Olympos*. The collection *Worlds Enough and Time* (2002) includes four sf stories, including "Orphans of the Helix" (1999), a coda to the Hyperion saga.

**SINCLAIR, ALISON (1959– ).** British-born writer mostly resident in **Canada** since 1967. Her first **sf** novel, *Legacies* (1995), describes an expedition from a colony world to its devastated parent. *Blueheart* (1996) is set on a watery colony where humans **genetically engineered** for ocean life are becoming independent of their creators. In *Cavalcade* (1998) humans offered a free ride to the stars by visiting **aliens** find the trip turning nightmarish. In *Throne Price* (2000, with Linda Williams) humans engineered for space travel find themselves in conflict with their parental species after a thousand-year separation.

**SINCLAIR, UPTON (1878–1968).** U.S. social campaigner and writer in many genres. His EPIC (End Poverty In California) crusade involved **sf** writers-to-be **Cleve Cartmill** and **Robert A. Heinlein**, the latter turning to sf to pay the expenses of a failed election campaign. A futuristic **satire** Sinclair wrote to popularize his socialist ideas, initially as a play, was novelized as *The Millennium: A Comedy of the Year 2000* (1914, book 1924). Sf elements are peripheral to the **timeslip romances** *Roman Holiday* (1931) and *Our Lady* (1938) but central to another play, *The Giant's Strength: A Three-Act Drama of the Atomic Bomb* (1947).

**SINGULARITY.** A term used in mathematics to describe critical points at which functions become indefinable, usually by tending to infinity—for instance, a number divided by zero, or what happens to collapsing matter when it is transformed into a black hole. The term was commonly encountered in **hard sf** of the 1970s and 1980s in the latter context, in association with Roger Penrose's "singularity theorem"; in the 1990s, however, that meaning was largely displaced by another, derived from the notion of a "technological singularity" first broached by **Vernor Vinge** in 1982 and popularized in a 1983 article in *Omni*. John von Neumann had earlier written about an "essential singularity" beyond which the future cannot be anticipated but Vinge's bolder proposition is that the evolution of self-transforming **nanotechnologies** and associated **biotechnologies** might accelerate to a point at which it brings about a sudden drastic transformation of human capability and nature: a breakthrough toward which various "transhumanist" and "extropian" movements soon began to work, with the further encouragement of such futurist philosophers as Hans Moravec. **Damien Broderick's** *The Spike: Accelerating into the Unimaginable Future* (1997) offers an alternative term for the same phenomenon. The notion, as dramatized in such sf stories as **Marc Stiegler's** "The Gentle Seduction" (1989) and **Charles Stross's** Accelerando **series**, is the central underlying assumption of the **far-futuristic space operas** of such writers as **Wil McCarthy** and **Karl Schroeder.**

**SITWELL, SIR OSBERT (1892–1969).** British writer, one of three famous sibling poets. The title novella of *Triple Fugue and Other Stories* (1924) paints a **satirical** picture of the post–Third World War Britain of 1948, in which "human grafting" has greatly extended the durability of the body. *The Man Who Lost Himself* (1929) is a character study of a poet whose life and work are drastically altered by a visionary encounter with his future self. *Miracle on Sinai* (1929) describes the effect of a new Mosaic revelation on a cross-sectional band of tourists, whose different reading of the new commandments precipitates a second world war.

**SLADEK, JOHN T. (1937–2000).** U.S. writer in several genres, resident in Britain from the mid-1960s to the mid-1980s, who became involved with **Michael Moorcock's *New Worlds***. His contributions to **new wave** sf are **satirical** comedies in which the mechanization of society and humanity are carefully considered in spite of the hilarity of his plots. *The Reproductive System* (1968, aka *Mechasm*) features a self-replicating technology that runs out of control. *The Müller-Fokker Effect* (1970) tracks the consequences of making multiple copies of a taped personality. Sladek's major work in this vein was to have been an epic post-**Asimovian existential fantasy** cast as the autobiography of a **robot**; its first two parts were issued as *Roderick* (1980) and *Roderick at Random* (1983) before being recombined in *The Complete Roderick* (2001) but the third was never completed; it was substituted by a conscientiously melodramatic slapstick account of a more stereotyped robot run murderously amok, *Tik-Tok* (1983). *Bugs* (1898) tracks the adventures of an innocent abroad in an irredeemably corrupt high-tech United States. Sladek's shorter satires, many with **sf** elements, are collected in *Alien Accounts* (1982), *The Steam-Driven Boy and Other Strangers* (1973), *Keep the Giraffe Burning* (1977), *The Lunatics of Terra* (1984), and *Maps: The Uncollected John Sladek* (2002).

**SLEATOR, WILLIAM (1945– ).** U.S. writer of children's fiction who first employed **sf** motifs in a didactic assault on behavioral science, *House of Stairs* (1974), but used them more enterprisingly after 1980. *Green Future of Tycho* (1981) is a **space opera. Aliens** play games with humans in *Interstellar Pig* (1984) and its sequel *Parasite Pig* (2002). *Singularity* (1985), *The Boy Who Reversed Himself* (1986), *Strange Attractors* (1990, aka *Strange Attractions*), *The Boxes* (1998), and its sequel *Marco's Millions* (2001) are **portal fantasies** exploring space, time, and other dimensions. The similar *Boltzmon!* (1999) features a remnant of a black hole. In *The Duplicate* (1988) a time-pressed teenager who thinks that multiplying himself might solve his problems inevitably learns better; *Rewind* (1999) is a similar cautionary tale.

**SLIPSTREAM.** A term coined by **Bruce Sterling** to designate "mainstream **sf**": stories that make use of sf motifs while remaining—sometimes ostentatiously—outside the labeled genre. The implication is that such works gain the benefit of the narrative vitality of the motifs without paying the customary price of public ignominy, like a cyclist who positions himself behind another vehicle to escape the full burden of wind resistance. Some **small press magazines**—notably *The Third Alternative*—began to use the term to emphasize their immunity to the commercial considerations that supposedly ruined sf's reputation. Peter Brigg's *The Span of Mainstream and Science Fiction* (2002) uses "span fiction" in a similar fashion, but the definition and manifesto for "interstitial" fiction offered on the Interstitial Arts website at www.endicott-studio.com/IA are more calculatedly and assertively **chimerical.**

**SLOANE, WILLIAM M. (1906–1974).** U.S. publisher and writer who produced two **hybrid** texts mingling **sf** and occult fiction. *To Walk the Night* (1937) is an account of an enigmatic **alien** visitation. *The Edge of Running Water* (1939) describes the hopeful construction of a machine to enable communication with the dead (a pet project of Thomas Edison's). Sloane edited two showcase sf **anthologies**, *Space, Space, Space* (1953) and *Stories for Tomorrow* (1954).

**SLONCZEWSKI, JOAN (1956– ).** U.S. writer who began publishing **sf** with *Still Forms on Foxfield* (1980), in which a Quaker **Utopia** on an Earth-clone world reluctantly restores contact with its parent culture. *A Door into Ocean* (1986) and its sequel *Daughter of Elysium* (1993) feature a similar cultural collision between an all-female **Utopia** and a militaristic male-dominated society whose invasion plans are subverted. *The Children Star* (1998), set in the same galactic culture, varies the formula by pitting a society of genetically modified orphans against ruthless **terraformers**. *The Wall around Eden* (1989) is a **postholocaust fantasy** in which human survivors must come to terms with a far more exotic communicative challenge—a theme repeated in *Brain Plague* (2000), where the challenge is provided by intelligent **nanotechnological** commensals.

**SMALL PRESS.** A publishing company established for vocational rather than commercial motives. Small presses played a vital role in the evolution of genre **sf** from its inception, and continue to do so, although their role has changed as the market space left to them by commercial publishers has altered its configuration. The **Lovecraft** school of **horror-sf** has always been associated with enthusiastic small press activity, **August Derleth** and **Donald Wandrei** following earlier precedents—most importantly that of William L. Crawford—in setting up Arkham House. From 1947 until the late 1950s, Crawford and other small press publishers, including **Lloyd Arthur Eshbach**, **Martin Greenberg**, **T. E. Dikty**, **Donald M. Grant**, and **Oswald Train**, took the leading role in giving **pulp sf** a more permanent form in hard covers. After 1960 that role became redundant, although Underwood-Miller and Donald Grant thrived by specializing in illustrated editions. Other small presses colonized such remaining niches as the publication of sf **criticism**, pioneered by **Advent** and carried forward by **Robert Reginald's** Borgo Press and Dikty's Starmont House long after academic publishers began to get tentatively involved.

While small press book publishers were in the doldrums between 1960 and 1990, small press **magazine** publishers multiplied rapidly, taking up the slack as the commercial magazines died out. Some commercial magazines retreated to small press status, most notably ***The Magazine of Fantasy & Science Fiction***, while other defunct titles were revived in that medium, including ***Weird Tales.*** As the 20th century ended, **DNA Publications** was in the process of building up a stable of small press magazines, while ***Interzone***, the Australian magazine *Aurealis*, the Canadian magazine *On Spec*, and ***Locus*** all occupied significant positions within the field.

By 2000 so many mass-market publishers had replaced sf with genre fantasy in their lists and given up on short story collections that such small presses as **Mark V. Ziesing**, **NESFA Press**, Golden Gryphon Press, and Britain's PS Publishing had begun to reclaim an increasingly important role within the genre. Many such ventures proved meteoric, after the fashion of **Kristine Kathryn Rusch** and **Dean Wesley Smith's** Pulphouse and the British Kerosina Publications, but others continually emerged to take the place of the fallen. Small press sf publication was even more significant in languages other than English; in **France** such imprints as Éditions de l'Oxymore extended the range of new material far beyond commercially defined limits and provided supportive nonfiction, while Jean-Pierre Moumon's Apex imprint resurrected classic material and such magazines as *Galaxies* provided a domestic short fiction market. *The Science-Fantasy Publishers: A Critical and Bibliographic History* (3rd ed., 1991) by **Jack L. Chalker** and Mark Owings provided a then-comprehensive guide to the Anglo-American sectors of the field.

**SMITH, CLARK ASHTON (1893–1961).** U.S. writer, most notable as a poet, who wrote prolifically for the **pulps** during the mid-1930s. Most of his work was done for ***Weird Tales***, including a groundbreaking **series** of tacitly **hybrid far-futuristic fantasies** collected in *Tales of Zothique* (1995), whose **sf** elements were teased out and further emphasized by many later writers, most notably **Jack Vance.** Smith's work for the **sf** pulps is more obviously hybridized but retains a distinctive and conspicuously **decadent** style; its most notable inclusions are the **portal fantasy** "City of the Singing Flame" (1931) and the **dimensional fantasies** "The Dimension of Chance" and "The Eternal World" (both 1932).

**SMITH, CORDWAINER (1913–1966).** The pseudonym used for **sf** by U.S. political scientist and sinologist Paul Myron Anthony Linebarger. He published at least one sf story in the late 1920s but it was the belated publication of "Scanners Live in Vain" (1950) that prompted him to write a highly distinctive **series** of **far-futuristic fantasies** set against the background of the Instrumentality of Mankind, a **galactic empire** whose human overlords are facing demands for the emancipation of their "underpeople": animals **genetically engineered** into human form and capability. The stories are lyrical **hybridizations** of sf and mythical fantasy, which featured in several collections before being drawn together, the shorter pieces initially forming a two-volume collection comprising *The Best of Cordwainer Smith* (1975, aka *The Rediscovery of Man*) and *The Instrumentality of Mankind* (1979) before they were combined in an omnibus as *The Rediscovery of Man: The Complete Short Science Fiction of Cordwainer Smith* (1993). The one novel in the series was badly butchered for publication in **magazine** and book form in the 1960s, but the text was restored to its proper form as *Norstrilia*

(1975); it tells the story of a boy from the eponymous colony planet who buys Earth and becomes the underpeople's redeemer.

**SMITH, DEAN WESLEY (1950– ).** U.S. editor and writer, cofounder with his wife **Kristine Kathryn Rusch** of the briefly prolific **small press** Pulphouse. He began publishing **sf** in 1984, most of his genre work being **tie-ins.** *Laying the Music to Rest* (1989) is a **hybrid time-travel** fantasy whose protagonist is trapped in the *Titanic*.

**SMITH, E. E. (1890–1965).** U.S. writer whose Ph.D. was appended to his byline by **pulp** editors enthusiastic to exploit its implications, with the result that he became affectionately known as "Doc" Smith to the fans entranced by his pioneering **space operas.** He had begun work on *The Skylark of Space* in 1915 but it languished unpublished after its completion in 1920 until he submitted it to ***Amazing Stories***, where it appeared in 1928, carrying a joint byline with a neighbor, Lee Hawkins Garby, who had helped him out with "the love interest." It tells the story of a young scientist's discovery of a magical metal capable of propelling ships to the stars; the galaxy became a vast playground for further adventures in *Skylark Three* (1930, book 1948), *Skylark of Valeron* (1934–1935, book 1949), and—belatedly—*Skylark Duquesne* (1966). The unashamed exuberance of the adventures in question, strongly reminiscent of **Edgar Rice Burroughs's** daydream fantasies, remained sufficiently potent to win fervent adherents of a much later generation via 1970s **paperback** editions.

After disappointing his readers with the modest *Spacehounds of IPC* (1931, book 1947), Smith put the bulk of his subsequent effort into a **series** of carefully escalated adventures that moved though several stages of **melodramatic inflation** to massive intergalactic conflicts. The human heroes become the stars of a heterogeneous team endowed with superhumanity with magical "lenses" by a godlike **alien** Mentor, who has long groomed humanity to take the lead in a celestial war against the massed forces of galactic evil. The Lensman series was eventually rewritten for book publication as *Triplanetary* (1934, rev. 1948), *First Lensman* (1950), *Galactic Patrol* (1937–1938, 1951), *Gray Lensman* (1939–1940, 1951), *Second-Stage Lensmen* (1941–1942, 1953), and *Children of the Lens* (1947–1948, 1954). A **mosaic** set in the same universe was appended to the series as *The Vortex Blaster* (1960, aka *Masters of the Vortex*). **John Campbell**, who had been a writer of Smithic space opera himself, gladly accepted the later novels for ***Astounding***, although any claim that they were rationally extrapolating sound scientific principles would have been ludicrous. The **series** was distinguished from other kinds of hybrid **science-fantasy** only by the fact that it involved fleets of spaceships at war rather than the more intimate conflicts of **planetary romance**, and yet **P. Schuyler Miller** was willing to name it as a key example of **hard sf**. Smith's later works, including *The Galaxy Primes* (1959, book 1965) and *Subspace Explorers* (1960, exp. 1965), were shadows as pale as the **sharecropping** exercises spun off in the late 1970s and 1980s.

**SMITH, EVELYN E. (1927–2000).** U.S. writer in several genres who began publishing **sf** in 1952. Most of her **magazine** sf was irreverently **humorous**; its **satirical** elements became more prominent in her novels. *The Perfect Planet* (1962) is about a colony seeded by a health farm. *Unpopular Planet* (1975) is modeled on 18th-century picaresque fiction. *The Copy Shop* (1985) features **aliens** living inconspicuously in New York.

**SMITH, GARRET (1876?–1954).** U.S. journalist and **pulp** writer, whose ventures into **sf** were sometimes enterprising. "On the Brink of 2000" (1910), "The Treasures of Tantalus" (1920–1921), and "You've Killed Privacy" (1928) feature devices for seeing through time. His sf novels were "After a Million Years" (1919), which struggles to live up to its bold title, and *Between Worlds* (1919; book 1929), in which women from Venus set out to conquer Earth. "Thirty Years Late" (1928) is a **transfiguration** of the tale of Rip van Winkle. "The Girl in the Moon" (1928) features a runaway rocket ship.

**SMITH, GEORGE O. (1911–1981).** U.S. writer who began publishing **sf** in 1942 with the first story in the **series** assembled as *Venus Equilateral* (1947, exp. 1976), which became a key example of **Campbellian hard sf** although its use of interplanetary radio relay stations now seems quaint. Some of his work was bylined Wesley Long, including the first version of the **space opera** *Nomad* (1944, book 1950). The most notable of his later novels are "The Kingdom of the Blind"

(1947, book 1958 as *Path of Unreason*), a scientific mystery story; *Troubled Star* (1953, book 1957), in which aliens make plans whose collateral damage will include the destruction of Earth; *The Fourth "R"* (1959, aka *the Brain Machine*), about the education of a child whose mentality is artificially boosted; and *Highways in Hiding* (1956), a more elaborate but equally paranoid **psi** story. *The Worlds of George O.* (1982) is a sampler of his short fiction.

**SMITH, L. NEIL (1946– ).** U.S. writer and **libertarian** activist who began publishing **sf** in 1980. An **alternative history** tracking the development of a libertarian United States forms the background to the comedy detective thrillers *The Probability Broach* (1980), *The Venus Belt* (1981), *The Nagasaki Vector* (1983), and *The American Zone* (2001). *Their Majesties Bucketeers* (1981) is another thriller set in the same milieu. The trilogy comprising *Tom Paine Maru* (1984), *The Gallatin Divergence* (1985), and *Brightsuit McBear* (1988) catapults the sequence on to a galactic stage. *The Crystal Empire* (1986) features an alternative world in which European development was halted by the Black Death—a premise differently extrapolated in **Kim Stanley Robinson's** *The Years of Rice and Salt*. *The Wardove* (1986) is a sober **political fantasy** set on the **moon** after Earth's nuclear devastation. *Contact and Commune* and *Converse and Conflict* (both 1990), recombined with their canceled sequel *Concert and Cosmos* and revised as *Forge of the Elders* (2000), feature ingenious resistance against a communist takeover of the United States. *Taflak Lysandra* (1988) is a **planetary romance.** *Henry Martyn* (1989) features an interstellar space pirate whose daughter stars in the revenge fantasy *Bretta Martyn* (1998). *Pallas* (1993) is a drama set on a prison asteroid.

**SMITH, MICHAEL MARSHALL (1965– ).** British writer of exotic thrillers and horror stories, active since 1990. There are **sf** elements in his **hybrid** novels *Only Forward* (1993) and *One of Us* (1998) but his most sustained sf exercise is the futuristic melodrama *Spares* (1996), in which imperfect clones of rich people are created and maintained as reservoirs of "spare parts." The collection *What You Make It* (1999; exp. as *More Tomorrow and Other Stories*, 2003) includes some **horror-sf.**

**SOFT SF.** The logical counterpart to **hard sf.** Few authors claim it as a label for their own work—people who like to think of themselves as "hard" far outnumber those willing to be described as "soft" (although they are themselves far outnumbered by people who loathe the kind of people who like to think of themselves as "hard"), but critics find it convenient, primarily to describe **speculative fiction** based in the "soft" (i.e., human) sciences, but also to characterize other kinds of sf that are at odds with the assertive overtones implicit in the word "hard." For this reason, **libertarian sf** and **survivalist fiction** seem "hard" to many readers and critics no matter how little science or logic is manifest therein, while liberal and sentimentally inclined sf seem "soft" no matter how detailed their scientific exposition may be.

It was the popularization of delicately softened sf by **Ray Bradbury** in the early 1950s that prompted **P. Schuyler Miller** to begin talking about "hard sf," although **Isaac Asimov's** essay on "Social Science Fiction" (1953) had already recognized that there was a problematic lack of real science in much of the fiction produced in accordance with **John Campbell's** manifesto, even by such fervent advocates thereof as himself and **Robert A. Heinlein.** Once the reader-friendliness of fiction that used sf's now-familiar vocabulary of ideas without any supportive explanations had been demonstrated, though, the advance of soft sf became relentless.

**SOMTOW, S. P. [Somtow Papinan Sucharitkul, 1952– ].** Thai writer educated in the United Kingdom and partly resident in the United States, many of whose early works were initially bylined Somtow Sucharitkul. He began publishing **sf** in 1977, his early short fiction being collected in *Fire from the Wine Dark Sea* (1983). *Mallworld* (1981; incorporated into the **mosaic** *The Ultimate Mallworld*, 2000) is a **satirical** farce in which **aliens** observe humans to be a race of shoppers. The Inquestor sequence carries forward themes from *Starship and Haiku* (1981) into a lyrical **far-futuristic** fusion of **ecological** fantasy and **space opera**, comprising *Light on the Sound* (1982, rev. 1986), *The Throne of Madness* (1983, rev. 1986), the mosaic *Utopia Hunters* (1984), and *The Darkling Wind* (1985). *The Aquiliad* (3 vols., 1983–1988) is a lighthearted **alternative history series** in which a **time-traveler** unbalances a rampant Roman Empire, while

*The Shattered Horse* (1986) imagines a different outcome to the Trojan War. Somtow's later work moved into other genres and media.

**SPACE AGE.** A characterization of the imminent future based in the notion that rocket flights into space, and particularly a landing on the **moon**, would be the first and most vital step in an inexorable historical process that would unfold as a gradual expansion of the human population throughout the solar system, and then throughout the galaxy, founding colonies wherever possible (and tolerating few limits to that possibility). David Lasser, sometime editor of ***Wonder Stories*** and the president of the American Interplanetary Society, titled his pioneering popularization of the possibility of space travel *The Conquest of Space* (1931) and that phrase soon acquired an iconic significance in **sf**. The first article in ***Astounding*** by rocket pioneer **Willy Ley** in 1935 advertised "The Dawn of the Conquest of Space," and the notion of conquest remained fundamental to sf's representations of space flight. The introduction to the showcase **anthology** *Adventures in Time and Space* (1946) blithely announced that the true significance of the explosion of the atom bomb was that "the universe is ours."

The idea of an imminent space age was most enthusiastically popularized, along with the phrase itself, by **Arthur C. Clarke**, who claimed that reading Lasser's book had changed his life; his contribution to **Reginald Bretnor's** *Modern Science Fiction: Its Meaning and Its Future* (1953) was uncompromisingly titled "Science Fiction: Preparation for the Age of Space." Clarke's early fiction and nonfiction were equally conceived as propaganda for this cause, and he considered the **prophetic** case securely made by the time he wrote *Voices from the Sky: Previews of the Coming Space Age* (1965) and edited *The Coming of the Space Age* (1967). **Donald A. Wollheim's** memoir *The Universe Makers* (1971) maps out a future history of the space age, whose consensus of support among sf writers he takes as evidence that it is what our "mental computers" calculate as "the shape of the future."

Subscribers to this myth within the genre tended to take it for granted that the social function of sf was to provide propaganda for the space age; **J. G. Ballard** was widely regarded as a traitor to this cause when he wrote stories in the 1960s that suggested that the first step into space might also prove to be the last, and that the space age might be rapidly aborted—before the end of the 20th century—when the realization sunk in that there is no point in sending human beings into unremittingly hostile environments when tiny machines can do the work of exploration far more economically, without requiring elaborate life support. Space-age enthusiasts never conceded the argument, and still regarded sf as a key vehicle of their propaganda in the early 21st century, but the mythical currency of the space age had suffered a severe devaluation by then. Images of space colonization were shunted several centuries forward in most speculative maps of future history, often to the far side of a technological **singularity**, thus shifting **space opera** into the **far-futuristic** mode of the 1990s.

**SPACE OPERA.** A term coined by **Wilson Tucker** in 1941, by analogy with "horse opera" and "soap opera," to denigrate hackneyed tales about spaceships. It caught on quickly, but was applied instead to exuberant adventure stories set on a galactic scale, as pioneered by **E. E. Smith's** *The Skylark of Space* (1928), **Edmond Hamilton's** "Crashing Suns" (1928), and **John W. Campbell's** *Islands of Space* (1931) and carried forward by such writers as **Jack Williamson** and **A. E. van Vogt.** The term retained its pejorative qualities in the 1940s and early 1950s because writers and readers anxious to see the genre become more respectable felt that it was high time such naive and essentially childish things were put away. **Isaac Asimov** specifically excluded space opera from consideration as "significant" **science fiction**, but it was not long before his own Foundation **series** and such works as **James Blish's** *Cities in Flight* came to be seen as space operas by virtue of their use of a galactic stage. Furthermore, the naive exuberance of early space opera acquired a kind of quaint charm as it came to be viewed with sentimental nostalgia; **Brian Aldiss's** showcase **anthology** *Space Opera* (1974) is warmly affectionate about exactly those aspects of space opera that early users of the term desired to stigmatize. More exotic examples of the subgenre acquired a quasi-ironic gloss, their gaudiness being construed as showmanship rather than foolishness. Writers soon began to produce new space operas intended to embody the decadent charm with which the older models now seemed to be endowed; notable examples include **Poul Anderson's** Dominic Flandry series and **van Vogtian** fantasies by such writers as **Charles L. Harness**, **Ian Wallace**, and **Barrington**

**J. Bayley**. Hamilton and Williamson easily adapted their produce to take account of the shift in perspective.

As the **galactic empire** became a conventional facilitating device supporting speculative endeavors of many other kinds, space opera became a convenient medium for **political fantasy** and **military sf**, and comfortably supported such exotic **transfigurative** projects as **Samuel R. Delany's** grail-epic *Nova* and **R. A. Lafferty's Odyssean fantasy** *Space Chantey* (both 1968). By the end of the 1980s, "space opera" was, in effect, a category description signifying stories set within a galactic civilization whose emphasis was on interstellar travel rather than events on planetary surfaces; the residue of its former pejorative intent could easily be set aside by the use of such qualifying adjectives as "sophisticated" in describing items fit for approval. The **decadent** elements of space opera were greatly enhanced in the 1990s when an inversion of elements in sf's consensual **future history**—consequent on the suspension of the **space age** and anticipation of a technological **singularity**—facilitated a fusion of space opera and **far-futuristic fantasy**, producing a plethora of **hybrid** and **chimerical** texts in the works of such writers as **Wil McCarthy**, **Peter F. Hamilton**, **Karl Schroeder**, **Alastair Reynolds**, and **John C. Wright.** ***Locus*** devoted a special issue to "the new space opera" in August 2003; the August 2003 edition of the webzine *SFRevu* featured an article by **David Hartwell** on "Space Opera Redefined," trailing a forthcoming showcase anthology.

**SPANISH SCIENCE FICTION.** No Spanish tradition of **speculative fiction** was established in the 19th century while the **French** and English traditions were developing apace, although the influence of **Jules Verne** and **Camille Flammarion** is evident in Enrique Gaspar's **time-travel** fantasy *El anacronópete* (1887) and other works identified by Nil Santiáñez-Tio's 1994 study of **sf** motifs in 19th-century Spanish literature. Thus, when U.S. sf arrived in quantity after World War II, soon generating a **fandom** according to the familiar pattern, there was no substantial domestic genre to be displaced. The emergence of sf writers in Spain thereafter was assisted by the existence of a large potential audience in South and Central America, where domestic traditions of a slightly different kind sprang up in response to the same stimulus.

The focal point of the sf community in Spain, after its establishment in 1991, was Barcelona's specialist bookshop Gigamesh, which also actively promotes Catalan sf. Notable authors include Juan Miguel Aguilera, coauthor with Javier Redal of the sophisticated **space opera** *Mundos en el Abismo* (1988), and Rafael Marin and Gabriel Bermúdez Castillo. The Polytechnical University of Catalonia sponsors an annual award for novellas that may be submitted in English, Spanish, or Catalan. The Asociación Española de Fantasia y Ciencia Ficción maintains a website at www.aefcf.es that carries news of conventions, publications, and so forth. *See also* LATIN AMERICAN FICTION.

**SPECULATIVE FICTION.** The most common alternative employed by critics, writers, and readers desirous of avoiding the pejorative implications of "**science fiction**." **Robert A. Heinlein** campaigned for it in his contribution to **Lloyd Arthur Eshbach's** *Of Worlds Beyond* (1947) and **Judith Merril** took it up in the 1960s to justify the extension of the scope of her Year's Best **anthologies** beyond conventional genre boundaries. It was often used in association with **new wave sf**, and remained popular into the 21st century, not merely in attempting to avoid stigmatization by such labels as sf and **sci-fi** but by way of providing a capsule description of the distinctive method employed by sf writers to construct the worlds within their texts.

**SPECULATIVE NONFICTION. Extrapolative** speculation plays a vital role in scientific thought, in the construction of new hypotheses for testing and the kind of imaginary trial that constitutes a "thought-experiment"—a translation of Werner Heisenberg's *Gedankenexperiment*. Philosophical analysis, especially in the philosophy of mind and moral philosophy, also involves the imaginative construction of hypothetical cases, which sometimes employ such **science-fictional** devices as **aliens** and **artificial intelligences.** Many exercises in scientific reportage produced before the standardization of the scientific paper (**John Kepler's** *Somnium* is a cardinal example) employ strategies that would now be held to belong exclusively to fiction, and might be regarded as **hybrid** texts. For these reasons, speculative nonfiction is not merely an important source of ideas developed in **sf** but a field of activity that borders it. It sometimes overflows that border, in texts that range from classical dialogues and the poetics of Lucretius' *De rerum natura* through the 19th-century popularizing endeavors of **Camille Flammarion**, **Robert Hunt**, and Percival Lowell, and the **Today & Tomorrow series** and parallel exercises by **J. B. S. Haldane**, to the modern era of Carl Sagan, Hans Moravec, R. C. W. Ettinger (the popularizer of cryonics), and Eric Drexler (the popularizer of **nanotechnology**). Sf writers who have parallel careers as popularizers of science—**Isaac Asimov** and **Arthur Clarke** are the most famous examples—routinely produce a good deal of speculative nonfiction, often blurring the boundaries between the two strands of their work. Many sf writers have flirted with mock nonfiction formats—examples can be found in the work of **Stanislaw Lem**, **Thomas M. Disch**, **R. A. Lafferty**, and **Bruce Sterling**, while ***Analog*** often features "non-fact articles"—just as popularizers of science like Jack Cohen and **Ian Stewart** have employed exemplary items of fiction to get their points across.

**SPINRAD, NORMAN (1940– ).** U.S. writer, resident in France since the late 1980s, who began publishing **sf** in 1963. *The Solarians* (1966) is a gaudy **space opera.** *Agent of Chaos* (1967) is a futuristic thriller with elements of **political fantasy**, whose themes were carried forward into *The Men in the Jungle* (1967). *Bug Jack Barron* (1969) transplanted the same combative spirit into a near-future account of corrupt media manipulation—a theme that remained one of Spinrad's continuing preoccupations. *The Iron Dream* (1972) is an ingenious item of **metafiction** presenting a novel that Adolf Hitler might have written had he immigrated to the United States after World War I and become a **pulp sf** writer instead of guiding the Nazi party to power, **transfiguring** the history of Germany in the 1930s into a paranoid **postholocaust fantasy** in which Aryan chauvinism ultimately wins a Pyrrhic victory. *A World Between* (1979) is an ingenious **Utopian** novel in which media manipulation by two parties of potential oppressors is subverted, while *Songs from the Stars* (1980) carefully assesses New Age opposition to "black technology." *The Void Captain's Tale* (1983) is an allegorical space opera about the difficulties of piloting an erotic drive, whose sequel *Child of Fortune* (1985), imports similar analogies into a quirky bildungsroman. Spinrad's subsequent novels were mostly naturalistic, including the futuristic political fantasy *Russian Spring*

(1991), but his novellas, including those collected in *Other Americas* (1988), "Journals of the Plague Years" (1988), and *Deus X* (1992) were more imaginatively extravagant. *Greenhouse Summer* (1999) returned to a slightly more distant future, once again foregrounding the use of broadcasting media as a political instrument. Spinrad's short sf is eclectically sampled in *The Star-Spangled Future* (1979).

**STABLEFORD, BRIAN (1948– ).** British writer who began publishing **sf** in 1965. His early fiction includes numerous **space operas** and **planetary romances.** *The Mind-Riders* (1976) is an early representation of **virtual reality.** *The Realms of Tartarus* (1977) is an **Orphean fantasy.** *The Walking Shadow* (1979) is a far-ranging **evolutionary fantasy**. The hybrid **alternative history** *The Empire of Fear* (1988) was followed by a more extravagant **metaphysical fantasy** of similar ilk, comprising *The Werewolves of London* (1990), *The Angel of Pain* (1991), and *The Carnival of Destruction* (1993). Much of his later work was set in the context of a **future history** developed in *The Third Millennium: A History of the World AD 2000–3000* (1985, with **David Langford**), in which sophisticated **biotechnology** facilitates a **Utopian** transformation of global society. Numerous short stories—including those collected in *Sexual Chemistry: Sardonic Tales of the Genetic Revolution* (1991)—elaborated and explored alternatives to the scenario before it was reconfigured in a **series** of novels comprising *Inherit the Earth* (1998), *Architects of Emortality* (1999), *The Fountains of Youth* (2000), *The Cassandra Complex* (2001), *Dark Ararat* (2002), and *The Omega Expedition* (2002). Unrelated short fiction is sampled in *Complications and Other Stories* (2003). Stableford's critical work includes a definitive history of *Scientific Romance in Britain 1890–1950* (1985) and many of the thematic articles in the **Clute/Nicholls** *Encyclopedia* (1979, rev. 1993).

**STAPLEDON, OLAF (1886–1950).** British writer active as a poet and philosopher before publishing his first novel, *Last and First Men* (1930), a **future history** of humankind extending over two billion years. It was one of the key works of the 1930s revival of British **scientific romance**, establishing Stapledon as the most important writer in that genre between the world wars. The sequel, *Last Men in London* (1932), employs one of humankind's ultimate descendants as a viewpoint for an exhaustive critical examination of contemporary society. *Odd John: A Story between Jest and Earnest* (1935) revisits the theme of **J. D. Beresford's** *The Hampdenshire Wonder*, but allows its atavistic **superman** to grow up and discover others of his kind. The **visionary fantasy** *Star Maker* (1937) sets the history told in *Last and First Men* in a galactic context, tracking the evolutionary history of the universe and evaluating it critically as an imperfect exercise in creationism; the opening phase of a discarded first draft was published as *Nebula Maker* (1976).

*Sirius: A Fantasy of Love and Discord* (1944) is an account of the relationship between a dog with **artificially enhanced intelligence** and his creator's daughter. In the novella *The Flames* (1947) a representative of a sun-dwelling **alien** species requests asylum on Earth. *Darkness and the Light* (1942) is an essay in **speculative nonfiction** offering two alternative future histories. *Old Man in New World* (1944) is a **Utopian** sketch. *Death into Life* (1946) is a visionary fantasy anticipating the future evolution of a collective spiritual entity not unlike the one imagined in Teilhard de Chardin's **Omega Point** theory. The protagonist of *A Man Divided* (1950) has superhuman interludes, but his inability to sustain them drives him crazy. Stapledon's short fiction and some exercises in speculative nonfiction were assembled in *Far Future Calling* (1980), edited by **Sam Moskowitz.**

Stapledon's influence is very obvious in subsequent scientific romance and postwar British **science fiction**, most notably the **far-futuristic fantasies** of **Brian Aldiss** and **Arthur Clarke**; he also provided suggestive pointers to such U.S. **pulp** writers as **Laurence Manning** and **John W. Campbell Jr.** It was not only the imagery of his work that became a significant consultation point for future writers but his experiments in literary method; the extreme narrative distance of the "Stapledonian voice" of *Last and First Men* and *Star Maker* was starkly opposed to the intimacy and informality of reader-friendly fiction, but its elevation to scarecrow status in writing manuals could not set aside the particular utility that far-reaching exposition has in **sf**.

***STARTLING STORIES.*** U.S. **pulp magazine** (1939–55) founded by Leo Margulies as a companion to *Thrilling Wonder Stories*. It was distinctive in featuring a novel in every issue; the niche was initially colonized by conventional action-adventure fiction, but later editors **Sam Merwin** (1945–1951) and Sam Mines (1951–1954) allowed its scope to be exploited in a more experimental spirit, with the result that it became the primary venue for the **decadent science-fantasy** of **C. L. Moore** and **Jack Vance**—whose romantic inclinations had been prefigured in the novel occupying the slot in the first issue, **Stanley G. Weinbaum's** *The Black Flame*. **Arthur Clarke's** *Against the Fall of Night* and **Charles Harness's** *Flight into Yesterday* began the sophistication of the decadent element of such fiction, and **Philip José Farmer's** *The Lovers* added a further dimension to it.

**STEAMPUNK.** A term coined in the late 1980s, by analogy with **cyberpunk**, to describe stories that imported a mischievously irreverent sensibility into **metafictional** tales set in the past—usually in **alternative** versions of the 19th century. Such stories manifest a keen awareness of the traditions of popular fiction, including (but by no means restricted to) **Vernian** romance and **Wellsian scientific romance**. The U.S. writer whose work demanded the invention of the new label was **Howard Waldrop**; key exemplars included two stories he wrote with **Stephen Utley**, "Custer's Last Jump" (1976) and "Black as the Pit, from Pole to Pole" (1977). **Michael Moorcock's** *The Warlord of the Air* (1971), **Harry Harrison's** *Tunnel through the Deeps* (1972), and **Manly Wade Wellman's** *Sherlock Holmes's War of the Worlds* (1975) might have been the subgenre's foundation stones had they not been slightly lacking in the "punkish" or "gonzo" sensibility that was more lavishly displayed in **K. W. Jeter's** *Morlock Night* (1979), **Tim Powers's** *The Anubis Gates* (1983), **James Blaylock's** *Homunculus* (1986), and Waldrop's "The Night of the Cooters" (1987). Most of these were labeled retrospectively; works consciously written as bravura exercises in steampunk include *The Difference Engine* (1990) by **William Gibson** and **Bruce Sterling**, **Rudy Rucker's** *The Hollow Earth* (1990), and **Paul di Filippo's** *The Steampunk Trilogy* (1995).

**STEELE, ALLEN (1958– ).** U.S. writer who began publishing **sf** in 1988, much of his early work consisting of meticulously detailed space program thrillers, including *Orbital Decay* (1989), its sequels *Lunar Descent* (1991) and *Labyrinth of Night* (1992), and numerous short stories reprinted in *Rude Astronauts* (1992) and *Sex and Violence in Zero-G* (1999), notably the novella *The Weight* (1995). *Clarke County, Space* (1990) uses a similar background for a comedy thriller. *The Jericho Iteration* (1994) and *Oceanspace* (2000) are **technothrillers**, the former deriving suspense from seismological investigations and the latter from undersea exploration. *The Tranquility Alternative* (1996) is an **alternative history** set on the **moon**. *A King of Infinite Space* (1997) launched a new space **series**. In *Chronospace* (2001) a timeship sent to investigate the Hindenburg disaster accidentally creates an alternative world. *Coyote: A Novel of Interstellar Exploration* (2002) is a **mosaic** account of difficult colonization. More short fiction is collected in *All-American Alien Boy* (1996) and *American Beauty* (2003).

**STEPHENSEN-PAYNE, PHILIP (1952– ).** British **bibliographer** whose Galactic Central **series** of "Bibliographies for the Avid Reader," launched in 1985—compiled in collaboration with Gordon Benson Jr.—extended to 58 volumes by 2003. It includes most of the major writers in the genre, offering comprehensive accounts of their work and relevant secondary sources.

**STEPHENSON, ANDREW M. (1946– ).** Venezuelan-born British writer who began publishing **sf** in 1971. *Nightwatch* (1977) is a **first contact** story. *The Wall of Years* (1979) is an intricate **timeslip fantasy** focused on a crucial moment in British history, involving Alfred the Great.

**STEPHENSON, NEAL (1959– ).** U.S. writer who produced two near-future thrillers, *The Big U* (1984) and *Zodiac: The Eco-Thriller* (1988) before importing **cyberpunk** elements lavishly into the far more adventurous *Snow Crash* (1993). *Interface* (1994) and *The Cobweb* (1996), written in **collaboration** with his uncle George Jewsbury and bylined Stephen Bury, also concentrate, though more narrowly, on the impact of information technology on political culture. *The Diamond Age; or, Young Lady's Illustrated Primer* (1995) moved on to a distinctive post-cyberpunk sensibility, employing a **nanotechological** educational device as an instrument of social evolution. The intricate conspiracies featured in several of these novels were vastly recomplicated in *Cryptonomicon* (1999) and its sequel *Quicksilver* (2003), where they are extrapolated back into the historical past in order to analyze their dynamic involvement with the emergent future.

**STERLING, BRUCE (1954– ).** U.S. writer who began publishing **sf** in 1976. His first novel, *Involution Ocean* (1977) is a picaresque **planetary romance.** Similar picaresque elements were carried into a very different milieu in *The Artificial Kid* (1980), whose protagonist's street-fighting exploits are recorded by cameras that turn his supposedly anarchic life into a glossy docu-soap, until he finds a mission in life. The ambience of the novel became fundamental to the notion of **cyberpunk**, which Sterling defined and promoted in the pages of his fanzine *Cheap Truth* (1984–1986) before publishing its showcase **anthology** *Mirrorshades* (1986). His own accounts of the future development of information technology are artfully recomplicated by parallel developments in **biotechnology.** In the Shaper/Mechanist **series** culminating in *Schismatrix* (1985)—whose shorter elements, including "Spider Rose" (1982), "Swarm" (1982), and "Cicada Queen" (1983), were first collected, with other materials in *Crystal Express* (1989) before being restored to their proper context in *Schismatrix Plus* (1996)—the competition between these two strands of technological evolution generates a complex pattern of cults and movements following different trajectories of posthuman evolution, which are forced to take their projects into space when Earth is devastated by a machine revolt.

*Islands in the Net* (1988) is a near-future political thriller. *The Difference Engine* (1990, with **William Gibson**) is a **steampunk** novel tracking the results of a computer revolution in 19th-century England. *Heavy Weather* (1994) is a **technothriller** about chasing tornadoes. *Holy Fire* (1996) offers a painstaking but thoughtfully ambitious description of existential transition to the posthuman condition. *Distraction* (1998) is a political **satire** set in a fragmented near-future United States afflicted by climatic change. "Hollywood Kremlin" (1998) launched a satirical picaresque series starring Leggy Starlitz, the exemplary protagonist of *Zeitgeist* (2000). Sterling's later short fiction is collected in *Globalhead* (1992) and *A Good Old-Fashioned Future* (1999). *Tomorrow Now: Envisioning the Next Fifty Years* (2002) is an enterprising exercise in **speculative nonfiction**.

**STERNBERG, JACQUES (1923– ).** Belgian writer whose surreal **satirical** fiction of the 1950s often used **sf** motifs, sometimes in ways that anticipated **new wave** sf; **alien** interference with human affairs is usually treated in a blackly comic manner. Notable translated works include a satirical account of future moral relaxation, *Sexualis '95* (1959, tr. 1967), and the **dystopian** title story of *Future without Future* (1974).

**STEVENSON, ROBERT LOUIS (1850–1894).** Scottish writer in various genres whose *Strange Case of Dr. Jekyll and Mr. Hyde* (1886) was a seminal work of **horror-sf.**

**STEWART, GEORGE R. (1895–1980).** U.S. writer whose only **sf** novel, *Earth Abides* (1949) is a meticulous account of the difficult reconstitution of society in the wake of a great plague.

**STEWART, IAN (1945– ).** British writer and popularizer of science who began publishing **sf** in 1979, most of his ***contes philosophiques*** appearing in ***Analog***. The novella "Displaced Person" (1987) is a study in exotic cultural evolution. *Flatterland: Like Flatland, Only More So* (2001) is a **dimensional fantasy** in which A Square's descendant Victoria Line undertakes an educational voyage through the **multiverse.** Stewart's **collaborations** with biologist Jack Cohen include *The Collapse of Chaos* (1994), a work of **speculative nonfiction** including some exemplary **fabulations**, and *Wheelers* (2000), an ambitious **hard sf** novel featuring exotic **alien** life. The latter dramatizes ideas further explored in *Evolving the Alien: The Science of Extraterrestrial Life* (2002).

**STIEGLER, MARC (1954– ).** U.S. writer who began publishing **sf** in 1980. The 1989 title story of his collection *The Gentle Seduction* (1990) is a careful account of the advent of a technological **singularity.** *Valentina: Soul in Sapphire* (1984), written with Joseph H. Delaney (1932–1999), is an **existentialist fantasy** about an **artificial intelligence.** *David's Sling* (1988) is a **political fantasy** about the impact of information technology. *Earthweb* (1999) describes the defense of Earth against the latest in a series of **alien** killing machines.

**STIRLING, S. M. (1953– ).** French-born **Canadian** writer whose first venture into **sf** was *Marching through Georgia* (1988), an **alternative**

**history** in which a state established in South Africa begins a violent takeover of the world described with some relish in *Under the Yoke* (1989) and *The Stone Dogs* (1990); supplements to the **series** include *Drakon* (1995) and the **shared-world anthology** *Drakas!* (2000). The trilogy comprising *Island in the Sea of Time* (1997), *Against the Tide of Years* (1999), and *On the Oceans of Eternity* (2000) is a detailed **timeslip robinsonade.** *Peshawar Lancers* (2001) is an alternative history in which the British Empire reigns supreme in the 21st century; *Conquistador* (2003) is a similarly provocative alternative history of the Americas.

**STITH, JOHN E. (1947– ).** U.S. writer who began publishing **sf** in 1979. *Scapescope* (1984) describes life in a future defense complex. *Memory Blank* (1986) is an amnesiac fantasy set in a **Lagrange colony**. *Death Tolls* (1987), *Deep Quarry* (1989), and *Redshift Rendezvous* (1990) are crime thrillers set in extraterrestrial locations, the last featuring a **hyperspace** in which the velocity of light is only 22 miles per hour. In *Manhattan Transfer* (1993) the island is kidnapped by **aliens.** *Reunion on Neverend* (1994) is a convoluted thriller. *Reckoning Infinity* (1997) is an account of a mysterious **alien** artifact. Stith's short fiction is collected in *The Early Stith* (2001) and *All for Naught* (2001).

**STOCKTON, FRANK R. (1834–1902).** U.S. writer, principally of comedies, including many fantasies. His short fiction includes a few humorous **Edisonades**, notably "A Tale of Negative Gravity" (1884). The **future war** novel *The Great War Syndicate* (1889) and the futuristic **Vernian** romance *The Great Stone of Sardis* (1898) are notable examples of early American **sf**.

**STOVER, LEON E. (1929– ).** U.S. anthropologist and **critic**; much of his work in the latter vein offers an unfashionably hostile account of the ideas of **H. G. Wells**, as represented in the fictional dialogues between Wells and Lenin contained in *The Shaving of Karl Marx* (1982). He also published a combative study of *Robert A. Heinlein* (1987) and a more sympathetic one of his friend *Harry Harrison* (1990), with whom he edited an **sf anthology**, *Apeman, Spaceman* (1968). *Science Fiction from Wells to Heinlein* (2002) suggests that the genre's history came to an effective end in the 1970s.

**STROSS, CHARLES (1964– ).** British writer who began publishing **sf** in 1987. His work is extraordinarily innovative. "The Atrocity Archive" (2002) is a novel humorously blending Lovecraftiana and higher mathematics, and **H. P. Lovecraft's** influence is also manifest in the collection *Toast and Other Rusted Futures* (2002). *Singularity Sky* (2003; aka *Festival of Fools*) is a post-**cyberpunk space opera** featuring a not-very-godlike **Omega Point.** The Accelerando sequence of stories begun with "Lobsters" (2001) constructs a hectic **future history** that sweeps through a technological **singularity** and surges on. Stross has worked in **collaboration** with **Simon Ings** and **Cory Doctorow.**

**STRUGATSKY, ARKADY (1925–1991) and BORIS (1931– ). Russian** brothers who began writing **sf** in 1959. An early novella was used as the title story of the showcase **anthology** *Destination: Amaltheia* (1962); other early material is featured in the collection *Noon: 22nd Century* (1962, exp. 1967; tr. 1978) and the **mosaic** *Space Apprentice* (1962, tr. 1982). The conventional optimism of this work was, however, firmly set aside in the exotic catastrophe story *Far Rainbow* (1963, tr. 1967), *Hard to Be a God* (1964, tr. 1973)—in which an agent of Earth finds it impossible to instill a progressive spirit in a quasi-feudal society suspiciously reminiscent of prerevolutionary Russia—and the **dystopian** *The Final Circle of Paradise* (1965; tr. 1976).

A better translation of *Far Rainbow* was issued in 1979 in an omnibus with the 1968 **satire** *The Second Invasion from Mars*, whose blackly comedic spirit also pervades the **chimerical** *Monday Begins on Saturday* (1965, tr. 1977) and *The Tale of the Troika* (1968). The latter appeared in an omnibus with an even bleaker tale of confrontation with the incomprehensible, *Roadside Picnic*, in 1977 before the latter item was reprinted independently. The still-ironic suspicion expressed by *The Snail on the Slope* (1966–1968, tr. 1980) that scientific progress is an uphill struggle in continual danger of stalling was converted into dark pessimism in the trilogy comprising *Prisoners of Power* (1969–1971, tr. 1978), *Beetle in the Anthill* (1979–1980, tr. 1980), and *The Time Wanderers* (1985–1986, tr. 1987). *The Ugly Swans* (1966–1967, tr. 1979) offers vague hopes of a new order to come but *Definitely Maybe* (1976–1977, tr. 1978) refuses to reiterate it. The brothers' subsequent work, which became much sparser, remained untranslated.

**STURGEON, THEODORE (1918–1985).** U.S. writer born Edward Hamilton Waldo, who adopted his stepfather's surname in childhood, choosing a new forename to accompany it. He began publishing **sf** in 1939, when he became a member of **John Campbell's** stable. He was more comfortable in ***Unknown*** than ***Astounding***, and never understood why readers admired "Microcosmic God" (1941), whose plot was fed to him by Campbell. The final story of his first creative phase, the novella "Killdozer!" (1944)—in which an earth-moving machine is infested with a malign alien intelligence—was far more typical of his outlook. His later work—mostly published in ***Galaxy***, save for the pattern-setting "Maturity" (1947)—sought solutions for human problems in mental evolution, never in technology, and his exaggerated awareness of the lives of quiet desperation that most people seemed to live gave his accounts of quasi-magical redemption an unusual depth of feeling.

*The Dreaming Jewels* (1950, aka *The Synthetic Man*), the **mosaic** *More Than Human* (1953), and *The Cosmic Rape* (1958) are all redemptive fantasies of a remarkably fervent stripe, and similar stories are scattered through the many collections whose contents were chronologically reordered in a definitive set of *The Complete Stories of Theodore Sturgeon* begun with *Volume I: The Ultimate Egoist* (1994), *Volume II: Microcosmic God* (1995), *Volume III: Killdozer!* (1996), *Volume IV: Thunder and Roses* (1997), *Volume V: The Perfect Host* (1998), *Volume VI: Baby Is Three* (1999), *Volume VII: A Saucer of Loneliness* (2000), and *Volume VIII: Bright Segment* (2002), with more to come. His productivity dwindled drastically after the publication of the thoughtful **Utopian** fantasy *Venus Plus X* (1960), which addresses fundamental questions of sexual politics; several of his subsequent publications were aborted novels rough-hewn to pass muster as shorter pieces. Sturgeon's work was as conspicuously **soft** and sentimental as **Ray Bradbury's**, most of it being **ambiguous science-fantasy**, but its remarkable intensity of feeling and sense of style established him as the most interesting of all the writers who were pressed into the genre because they could find no other hospitable market.

**SUDDABY, DONALD (1900–1964).** British writer who used the pseudonym Alan Griff on a number of fantasies published in the 1930s and the romance of **miniaturization** *Lost Men in the Grass* (1940). The third novella in the **mosaic** *Masterless Swords* (1947) is a futuristic fantasy, but Suddaby was more successful commercially when he adapted his work for the **children's sf** market. The **space operas** *The Star Raiders* (1950) and *Prisoners of Saturn* (1957) fit comfortably enough into that milieu, but the **disaster story** *The Death of Metal* (1952) and the extrapolation of one of his early Alan Griff stories as *Village Fanfare; or, The Man from the Future* (1954) are firmly set in the dourly meditative tradition of **scientific romance.**

**SULLIVAN, TIM (1948– ).** U.S. writer who first ventured into **sf** in 1977. *Destiny's End* (1988) is a complex **far-futuristic fantasy.** *The Parasite War* (1989) describes an exotic **alien** invasion. *The Martian Viking* is a psychotropic fantasy (1991). In *Lords of Creation* (1992) a paleontologist discovers dinosaur eggs on the eve of an alien invasion.

**SULLIVAN, TRICIA (1968– ).** U.S. writer whose first **sf** thriller, *Lethe* (1995), is set in the aftermath of biological warfare. *Someone to Watch Over Me* (1997) is a love story enlivened by post-**cyberpunk** motifs. *Dreaming in Smoke* (1998) recapitulates the theme of **E. M. Forster's** "The Machine Stops" in an exotic context. *Maul* (2002) is a marginal sexual-political **satire**.

**SUPERHEROES.** A term commonly used in connection with the strand of **pulp** crime fiction that was driven by the pressure of **melodramatic inflation** to cultivate ever-more-powerful heroes in order to confront threats of ever-increasing magnitude posed by ever-more-exotic villains. The subgenre was displaced into **comic** books long before the pulps died out, but its extensions into the **sf** field, in such magazines as *Captain Future*, generated abundant progeny within the genre during the 1940s and 1950s, including **E. E. Smith's** Lensmen, the protagonists of most of **A. E. van Vogt's** novels, and **John Russell Fearn's** Golden Amazon. Superheroes continued to recur in subsequent sf in such **psi-powered** figures as **Ian Wallace's** Croyd and numerous **Roger Zelazny** protagonists, and such deceptive geniuses as **Lois McMaster Bujold's** Miles Vorkosigan.

**SUPERMAN.** A term that first achieved prominence as a translation of Friedrich Nietzsche's *Übermensch*, which had earlier been rendered "overman" in the parlance of such British Nietzscheans of the 1890s as John Davidson and **M. P. Shiel.** It was soon conflated—syncretically, although few of its users realized how different the notions were—with the idea that *Homo sapiens* was bound to be replaced one day by a "fitter" species, usually designated *Homo superior*, whose advent was anticipated in such **scientific romances** as **H. G. Wells's** *The Food of the Gods* and **J. D. Beresford's** *The Hampdenshire Wonder*. Supermen were used as figures of menace in a good deal of early **pulp sf**, which routinely assumed that *Homo superior* would have put away such childish things as emotion and morality, facilitating a relentless and methodical pursuit of absolute power. Such assumptions were decisively challenged in 1939–1940 by **Stanley G. Weinbaum's** *The New Adam*, **A. E. van Vogt's** *Slan*, and **Jack Williamson's** *Darker Than You Think*, thus opening up a productive ideological battleground whose terrain was fiercely disputed through the 1950s **psi** boom. The co-option of the term for the name of a paradigmatic comic-book **superhero** helped erase its last pejorative undertones. The motif generated numerous thoughtful **existentialist fantasies** in the 1960s and 1970s and benefited from further complication thereafter by inexorable increases in the deployment of **genetic engineering** and **cyborgization**.

**SURVIVALIST FICTION.** A subgenre of futuristic fantasy closely connected with an actual movement whose members—often inspired by fundamentalist religious beliefs—believe that a nuclear holocaust is not merely inevitable but desirable, as a means of sorting out the wheat of humankind from the chaff and putting a decisive end to the liberal laxity of the modern world. Foreshadowed in **sf** by such works as **Robert A. Heinlein's** *Farnham's Freehold* and novels by **Dean Ing**, it became a separate genre in the 1980s, when such specialist writers as Jerry Ahern, James Barton, and "James Axler" (Laurence James) began to develop it as an avid pornography of violence devoid of any substantial speculative content. **Postholocaust fantasies** continued to host a survivalist strand into the 21st century, but such genre sf works as **David Brin's** *The Postman* usually depicted survivalists as dangerous lunatics.

**SUVIN, DARKO (1930– ).** Croatian-born academic, resident in **Canada** from 1968–2001, who wrote two important books about **sf**: the theoretically inclined *Metamorphoses of Science Fiction: On the Poetics and History of a Literary Genre* (1977 in French, rev. 1979 in English) and the detailed historical and sociological study *Victorian Science Fiction in the U.K.: The Discourses of Knowledge and of Power* (1983), which includes an invaluable annotated **bibliography** of its subject matter. The former is a conscientious attempt to define how sf achieves its effects, and how it differs from "fantasy," in terms of its use of **novums** to generate **cognitive estrangement**; *Positions and Presuppositions in Science Fiction* (1988) amplified its arguments.

**SWANWICK, MICHAEL J. (1950– ).** U.S. writer who began publishing **sf** in 1980, early examples of his remarkably varied and elegantly polished short fiction being collected in *Gravity's Angels* (1991). His earliest long works—the **mosaic postholocaust fantasy** *In the Drift* (1984), the **cyberpunk** thriller *Vacuum Flowers* (1987), and the **hard sf** novella *Griffin's Egg* (1991)—all refer back to mythical symbols and tend toward transcendental conclusions without embracing **hybridization**, but his subsequent works adopted a more cavalier attitude to genre boundaries. *Stations of the Tide* (1991) dispatches a quasi-angelic agent with a briefcase full of godlike power to a world trembling on the brink of **apocalyptic** ecological metamorphosis. *Jack Faust* (1997) is an ingeniously forceful **transfiguration** of the legend, in which scientifically advanced **aliens** make Faust a gift of absolutely everything he wants to know, correctly anticipating that the corrupting power will lead him to destroy the world in spite of his good intentions. In *Bones of the Earth* (2002) a **time-traveling** paleontologist struggles to avoid awkward paradoxes, making deft use of a rigorously scientific attitude. Further collections are *A Geography of Unknown Lands* (1997), *Moon Dogs* (2000), and *Tales of Old Earth* (2000).

**SWIFT, JONATHAN (1667–1745).** Irish **satirist**. The third part of his **mosaic robinsonade** *Travels into Several Remote Nations of the World in Four Parts . . . by Lemuel Gulliver* (1726, aka *Gulliver's Travels*) involves a tour of the flying island of Laputa and various associated domains, where scientific inquiry is a top priority and its technological spin-off has transformed human lives in various ways, most aptly symbolized by the immortal but senile Struldbruggs of Luggnagg. Antiscientific polemics of this kind are as easily assimilated into the prehistory of **sf** as celebrations of scientific progress, and the **chimerical** quality that their presence lends to the genre—in stark contrast to **Gernsbackian** and **Campbellian** attitudes—results in a certain strength-building dynamic tension. Unlike most sf, Swiftian anti-sf makes abundant use of **mad scientists**, because it holds that the quest for scientific understanding is itself a form of insanity. The fourth book of *Gulliver's Travels*, in which human Yahoos are regarded with utter contempt by horselike Houyhnhnms, is also echoed in a great deal of modern sf and the fundamental method of the mosaic recurs frequently in sf series. The term "Gulliveriana" is sometimes used as a category description of antique satirical **imaginary voyages**, as well as such belated sequels to Swift's original as Barry Pain's "The New Gulliver" (1913), **Frigyes Karinthy's** *Capillaria,* and Varoujan Kazanjian's *Gulliver in Cloneland* (2000, bylined Ariazad).

## – T –

**TAINE, JOHN (1883–1960).** Pseudonym used for **sf** by Scottish-born U.S. mathematician Eric Temple Bell. His **technothrillers** *The Gold Tooth* (1927) and *Quayle's Invention* (1927) were conventional enough for book publication, creating market space for *Green Fire* (1928, written 1919), inspired by Frederick Soddy's popularization of the properties of radium, and the spectacular mutational romances *The Greatest Adventure* (1929) and *The Iron Star* (1930). The **Gernsback pulps** provided belated homes for the phantasmagoric **alien** infestation story *The Crystal Horde* (1930 as "White Lily"; book 1952), the **mutant superman** story *Seeds of Life* (1931, book 1951), and the groundbreaking **time-travel** story *The Time Stream* (1932, but written 1921; book 1946). His later pulp fiction—including the novels "Twelve Eighty-Seven" (1935) and "Tomorrow" (1939)—was less enterprising. **Small presses** issued the autobiographical **transfiguration** *The Forbidden Garden* (1947) and the novellas making up the unfortunately mispackaged *The Cosmic Geoids and One Other* (1949; it was supposed to be "geodes"). *G.O.G. 666* (1954) is a garish thriller.

**TECHNOLOGICAL DETERMINISM.** The hypothesis that social change is largely a response to technological innovation. Philosophers of history were initially inclined to view social progress as intellectual progress: a matter of increasing knowledge and changing ideas leading to the Age of Reason and the Age of Enlightenment. Archaeologists, by contrast, saw prehistory in terms of evolving technology, as the Stone Age was succeeded by the Bronze Age and the Iron Age. The two modes of thought came together in the 19th century when Karl Marx, objecting to the idealist history of G. W. F. Hegel, proposed that historical change was fundamentally material—a matter of technologies of production and the dynamic tension between social classes defined by their relationship to those means—and that ideas were "superstructural" by-products. Marx's obsession with "correcting" the political ideas generated by the contemporary material reality, however, left the technological determinist aspects of his theory to be developed and varied by others. His successors in this respect included William Ogburn, who proposed that all social change can be seen as a series of adjustments to new technological opportunities; Lewis Mumford, who inverted Ogburn's perspective in order to ask what social imperatives had selectively generated rapid technological progress in the Western world (he concluded that war and political oppression had been the principal engines of innovation); and Harold Innis, who proposed that communication technologies, rather than technologies of material production, are the chief determinants of social and political institutions.

When **Isaac Asimov** defined the significant fraction of **sf** as "social **science fiction**," he was tacitly assuming an Ogburnian view of social change, although a good deal of **Campbellian** sf takes a tacitly Mumfordian view, focusing on spurs to technological progress rather than its consequences, and on interesting feedback effects. The Innis thesis came into its own in sf of the 1980s, when it became a tacit assumption of **cyberpunk** sf (assisted by the propagandizing of Innis's chief disciple, Marshall McLuhan), but it had been tacitly fundamental to considerations of the politics of interplanetary relations, especially in **galactic empires.**

**TECHNOTHRILLER.** A term coined by reviewers to describe books following the standard plot formula of thriller fiction—in which a heroic protagonist enters into a contest of wits and strength with a malevolent antagonist, ultimately averting the threat posed by his or her evil machinations—which employ **science-fictional** devices to heighten the threat in question. **Melodramatic inflation** exerts an obvious pressure on the thriller genre, to which such writers as Ian Fleming, Robin Cook, Ken Follett, Tom Clancy, and **Michael Crichton** have responded in various ways, but an opposed counterpressure arises if the imaginative devices become too ambitious, because the plots are then endangered by the absurdities of the **Frankenstein syndrome.** Given that the formula requires a normalizing ending, in which the threat is comprehensively defused, it is inconvenient to invoke science-fictional motifs that have obvious potential to change the world. Technothriller writers who become so entranced with their inventions that they stray into genre sf, therefore—examples include **Martin Caidin** and **D. F. Jones**—may find their work falling between two stools, unable to satisfy either population of habitual readers. Sf writers who produce technothrillers in order to bid for the greater economic rewards available in the thriller genre may have useful skills to bring to the work, but the necessity of providing psychopathic antagonists and normalizing endings tends to prey on their science-fictional conscience.

**TELEVISION.** Even after the advent of radio, **sf** writers often assumed that a technology of visual reproduction and transmission would be more widely used as an adjunct to the telephone than as a medium of broadcast entertainment. When the potential of the medium was finally recognized, that prospect was initially viewed with utter horror, broadcast TV playing a central role in such vivid **dystopian** fantasies as **George Orwell's** *Nineteen Eighty-Four* and **Ray Bradbury's** *Fahrenheit 451*. (Ironically, Bradbury had more of his literary work adapted for TV than any other sf writer, and the 1955 BBC-TV production of *1984* was one of the medium's early artistic highlights). Subsequent treatments of TV's social instrumentality—even relatively sympathetic ones, such as **Norman Spinrad's** *A World Between*—assume that its evil potential is vast, and that its employment for good is likely to require heroic effort.

This antipathy has not made the slightest difference to the near-universal avidity with which TV broadcasts are consumed, but it has had a slight coloring effect on attitudes to the fact that TV displaced **paperback** books as the primary medium of genre sf during the 1990s. This shift was significant because TV's dependence on regular scheduling makes it much more dependent on genres than **theater** or **cinema**; making shows in batches—usually of 13 or 26 to comprise "seasons"—strongly favors the use of segmental **series** whose units employ normalizing endings. TV **sci-fi** has enormous difficulty in accommodating the extrapolative ambitions and explanatory imperatives of **hard sf**, preferring **technothrillers** and shows featuring futuristic cops, secret agents, vigilantes, and heroic outlaws, all conspicuously softened—often to the texture of soap opera—no matter how many gadgets are deployed in the plots. TV sf is virtually defined by its inability to make progress, and that fraction of the genre displaced into the medium is effectively lifeless. Hopes that TV sf might serve as a portal disposing its audience to an interest in more serious material were soon disappointed; instead, TV **tie-ins** and clones began a gradual displacement of hard sf from the paperback medium.

**TEMPLE, WILLIAM F. (1914–1989).** British writer who began publishing **sf** in 1938, having earlier been an ardent fan and—along with his housemate **Arthur C. Clarke**—a pillar of the British Interplanetary Society. Among his works, however, only *The True Book about Space Travel* (1954) and his **children's sf** trilogy featuring Martin Magnus (1954–1956) show any sign of subscription to the myth of the **space age.** *Four Sided Triangle* (1939, exp. 1949) is an ironic tale in which a **science-fictional** device fails to solve the problem of unrequited love; "Immortal's Playthings" (1953; exp. as *Battle on Venus*, 1963) and the **mosaic** *The Automated Goliath* (1962) are gaudy melodramas, and "A Trek to Na-Abiza" (1961; exp. as *The Three Suns of Amara*, 1962) is a colorfully **satirical Odyssean fantasy.** *Shoot at the Moon* (1966) goes so far as to travesty conventional space age hero-myths, and *The Fleshpots of Sansato* (1968) is a **Swiftian dystopia.**

**TENN, WILLIAM (1920– ).** Pseudonym of U.S. writer Philip Klass, who began publishing **sf** in 1946. He became one of the key "satirists" of the 1950s, although **satire** is only one element of his ***contes philosophiques***, central to the sharp **political fantasies** "The

Liberation of Earth" (1953), "Null-P" (1951), and "The Masculinist Revolt" (1965), but muted in more extended and more thoughtful comedies like "Time in Advance" (1956) and "Time Waits for Winthrop" (1957, aka "Winthrop was Stubborn"). Almost all his work was assembled in a six-volume **paperback** set in 1968, which supplemented reprints of *The Human Angle* (1956) and *Time in Advance* (1958) with the novel *Of Men and Monsters* and the collections *The Seven Sexes*, *The Square Root of Man*, and *The Wooden Star*. The omissions were restored to the two-volume **NESFA Press** edition of his collected works issued as *Immodest Proposals* and *Here Comes Civilization* (both 2001). Tenn abandoned writing for an academic career in the mid-1960s; he is not the Philip J. Klass who built a reputation in the 1980s as a debunker of **UFOlogical** delusions.

**TEPPER, SHERI S. (1929– ).** U.S. writer in several genres, who first appeared in an **sf magazine** in 1963 as Sheri S. Eberhart, although her career began in earnest with the ecopolitical fantasy *The Awakeners* (1987, initially in two volumes). Much of her subsequent sf—including *After Long Silence* (1987, aka *The Enigma Score*); the **postholocaust** fantasy *The Gate to Women's Country* (1988); the loosely knit **series** comprising *Grass* (1989), *Raising the Stone* (1990), and *Sideshow* (1992); and *Shadow's End* (1994)—is in a similar vein, the **political fantasy** elements routinely featuring religious autocracies and foregrounding sexual-political issues. *Beauty* (1991) is a **hybrid** text **transfiguring** folkloristic material into **dystopian** fantasy, and some of her subsequent works are careful hybrids whose sf qualifications are carefully hoarded behind a genre fantasy facade, becoming effective only in the climactic phases; examples include *Six Moon Dance* (1998), *Singer from the Sea* (1999), and *The Visitor* (2002). *The Family Tree* (1997) is a surreal account of an enigmatic **ecocatastrophe.** *The Fresco* (2000) is an enterprising **first contact** thriller. *The Companions* (2003) is an ecological fantasy set in an overpopulated future.

**TERRAFORMING.** A term coined by **Jack Williamson** in his Seetee series to describe the adaptation of planetary biospheres to render them habitable by human beings—a subcategory of the kind of ecological engineering sometimes called "ecopoeisis." As **sf** writers reluctantly took aboard astronomical revelations regarding the utter inhospitability of the other planets in the solar system, terraforming projects became increasingly common, the scale of the imagined task growing considerably between **Arthur Clarke's** *The Sands of Mars* (1951) and **Kim Stanley Robinson's Mars** trilogy (1992–1996). By the end of the 20th century, the optimistic hope that the galaxy might be full of ready-made Earth clones had declined to the point at which terraforming was a common feature of accounts of interstellar colonization. The notion has also been taken seriously as a basis for conceivable projects, in such books as Martin J. Fogg's *Terraforming: Engineering Planetary Environments* (1995).

**TEVIS, WALTER S. (1928–1984).** U.S. writer in various genres whose first venture into **sf** was in 1957. *The Man Who Fell to Earth* (1963) is a heartfelt account of frustrated **alien** supplication. *Mockingbird* (1980) is a parable of social and personal mechanization. *The Steps of the Sun* (1983) is a tale of extraterrestrial redemption. His short sf is collected in *Far From Home* (1981).

**THEATER.** The theater does not easily lend itself to the kind of set dressing that much **sf** would require; the frailty of its artifice is neatly summarized in the metaphorical connotations of deus ex machina, a legacy from the days when gods were lowered onto the set from a conspicuously un-Olympian scaffold. Some sf cast in dramatic form would be very difficult to stage; **George Bernard Shaw's** *Back to Methuselah* is a cardinal example. The ease with which human actors can pretend to be machines is, however, reflected in a history that began long before **Karel Čapek's** *R.U.R.* introduced the term **robot**, ranging from the anonymous skit *Mechanical Jane* (1910) through *The Perfect Woman* (1948) by Wallace Geoffrey and Basil Mitchell to Alan Ayckbourn's *Henceforward* (1988). Similar convenience facilitated stage adaptations of *Frankenstein* and *Dr. Jekyll and Mr. Hyde*, although the notorious Grand Guignol theater in Paris had to work harder on its adaptation of **H. G. Wells's** *The Island of Dr. Moreau*. **Timeslips** are relatively easy to arrange, as in J. B. Priestley's several time plays, most notably *Dangerous Corner* (1932) and *Time and the Conways* (1937), as well as J. M. Barrie's *Mary Rose* (1924) and Ayckbourn's *Communicating Doors* (1994). Plays in which the cast is hiding out from a relatively nebulous threat, as in **Upton Sinclair's** *A Giant's Strength* (1948) and Marghanita Laski's *The Offshore Island* (1954, book 1959), also present few problems.

The examples set by Čapek and Shaw inspired other specialist playwrights to dabble in philosophical sf, including Lionel Britton (1887–1971), author of *Brain* (1930)—one of the first representations of a giant computer—and *Spacetime Inn* (1932), and Charles Duff, author of *Mind Products Limited: A Melodrama of the Future* (1932). **Fritz Leiber**, whose father ran a Shakespearean company, wrote several short plays, and set his novel *The Big Time* (1958) in a single location requiring minimal special effects, inviting dramatization. U.S. theater companies that have been interested in sf include **Stuart Gordon's** Organic Theater in Chicago, which produced Gordon's own *Warp!* (1971) and an adaptation of **Joe Haldeman's** *The Forever War* (1974), and Michael Blake's Moebius Theater company, founded in 1976, whose adaptations include *The Island of Dr. Moreau* (1999) and **Ray Bradbury's** *Martian Chronicles* (2000). The British comic actor Ken Campbell formed the Science Fiction Theatre of Liverpool in the 1970s to dramatize the Illuminatus trilogy by Robert Shea and **Robert Anton Wilson**, following it with Neil Oram's *The Warp* (1979); a similar spirit was inherent in Richard O'Brien's cult classic *The Rocky Horror Show* (1974) and has been effectively carried forward by Chris and Tim Britton's Forkbeard Fantasy company, whose calculatedly **chimerical** productions include *The Fall of the House of Usherettes* (1995), *The Barbers of Surreal* (1998), and *Frankenstein: The True Story* (2001). Ralph Willingham's *Science Fiction and the Theatre* (1993) is a useful study.

**THOMAS, THEODORE L. (1920– ).** U.S. writer who began publishing **sf** in 1952. He sometimes used the pseudonym Leonard Lockhard, most notably on a **series** of **humorous** articles, some of which were co-written with his fellow lawyer **Charles L. Harness.** He **collaborated** with **Kate Wilhelm** on two ironic **disaster stories**, *The Clone* (1965) and *The Year of the Cloud* (1970), but his shorter work—which includes the novella "The Weather Man" (1962), about meteorological control—was never collected.

**THOMAS, THOMAS T. (1948– ).** U.S. writer whose first **sf** novel, *The Doomsday Effect* (1986)—in which a black hole goes into orbit around the Earth—was bylined Thomas Wren; *Flare* (1992, with **Roger Zelazny**) is also a **hard sf disaster story.** *First Citizen* (1987) is a **political fantasy** in which a fragmented United States is reunited. *Me: A Novel of Self-Discovery* (1991) is an **existentialist fantasy** about an **artificial intelligence.** *Crygender* (1992) is an account of **future biotechnology** in an **ecocatastrophic** context.

**THURSTON, ROBERT (1936– ).** U.S. writer who began publishing **sf** in 1971. Much of his work is **existentialist fantasy** touching on issues of sexual politics; *Alicia II* (1978), *A Set of Wheels* (1983), and *Q Colony* (1985) approach such subject matter from different directions.

**TIE-IN.** A book associated with a **cinema** film, **TV** series, or **game.** Novelizations of successful silent movies first appeared in the 1920s but such spin-offs did not become commonplace until the 1960s. Tie-ins are particularly significant in the field of TV sf because the literary medium is not bound by the same limitations of special effects as TV production, so the hypothetical universe of a TV series can be more extravagantly decorated in supplementary books. Game tie-ins began as dramatizations of role-playing games like Dungeons and Dragons, which was itself an extension of conventional literary fantasy, but soon expanded to take in computer games, war games, and even board games, whose literary spin-off has to add far more material. Because TV series are heavily dependent on normalizing endings, and games entirely so, tie-ins are invariably formularized and tie-in **series** are necessarily segmental.

**TIME MACHINE.** A mechanical device for traveling in time, whose popularization by **H. G. Wells** was a great leap forward for **sf. Visionary fantasy** had previously been the favorite medium for encapsulating glimpses of the future, but its obvious limitations were compounded when the method of achieving narrative closure by having a protagonist wake up became a tired cliché. Sleeping for a long time had the greater disadvantage of only providing one-way tickets. Charles Dickens employed ghosts to move Scrooge back and forth in time in *A Christmas Carol* (1843), and various magical agents provided similar services in didactic children's fantasy, but such devices were intrinsically ill fitted to sf. The Wellsian time machine was, in consequence, an extremely useful facilitating device, rapidly borrowed by "A Disciple" for use in *The Coming Era; or, Leeds Beatified* (1900) and **William Wallace Cook** for *A Round Trip to the Year 2000* (1903) and imported into the **pulps** by such writers as **Ray Cummings**, **Jack Williamson**, and Ralph Milne Farley, giving them and their characters the freedom to roam through time at will. A Wellsian time machine is, of course, no more rationally plausible than a Dickensian ghost or a helpful fairy, but the apologetic jargon that Wells borrowed from **C. H. Hinton** made it seem psychologically plausible.

**TIME PARADOX.** A paradox arising as a result of **time travel** into the past. The classic example involves murdering an ancestor, so that one could never have been born to carry out the deed. Time paradoxes were adopted into comic fantasy in the 19th century, F. Anstey's *The Time Bargain* (1891, aka *Tourmalin's Time Cheques*) being an exceptionally convoluted example. The paradoxicality might seem to exclude the subgenre's incorporation into **sf**, but the notion of **alternative histories**, especially if they are arrayed in **parallel worlds**, provides a convenient escape clause. In much the same way that there are self-fulfilling **prophecies** as well as self-negating ones, there are time paradoxes that bend causal sequences into loops instead of breaking them, and the aesthetics of such causal loops have fascinated sf writers sufficiently to generate a whole subgenre of ingenious paradox-avoidance stories, notable early examples being **Ross Rocklynne's** "Time Wants a Skeleton" and **Robert Heinlein's** "By His Bootstraps" (both 1941). Simple loops can be twisted into more convoluted knots with sufficient ingenuity, as in Heinlein's sarcastic **existentialist fantasy** "All You Zombies . . ." (1959).

**TIME POLICE.** An agency designed to protect history against changes introduced by rogue **time-travelers**, who are often eager to exploit ignorance of future technologies. Such organizations usually consist of secret police rather than uniformed officers; U.S. examples are often tacitly or explicitly modeled on the CIA, as in **Kage Baker's** Company **series**. The variant in which agents protect a unique historical sequence from perversion by outlaw time-travelers, as in **Isaac Asimov's** *The End of Eternity* or **Diana Wynne Jones's** *A Tale of Time City*, tends to seem claustrophobic by comparison with the **multiversal** variants, and is less amenable to **extrapolation** into series. Notable examples of time police series can be found in the work of **Sam Merwin**, **Poul Anderson**, **H. Beam Piper**, and **John Brunner.** The variant in which vast armies are engaged in eternal open conflict—as in **Fritz Leiber's** Change War series or **Barrington J. Bayley's** *The Fall of Chronopolis*—makes up in melodramatic brio what it sacrifices in subtle ingenuity.

**TIMESLIP ROMANCE.** A story whose protagonist suffers a sudden unexplained dislocation in time, usually but not invariably "falling" into the past. The paradigm example within genre **sf** is **L. Sprague de Camp's** *Lest Darkness Fall*, although its original appearance in ***Unknown*** serves as a reminder that the formula was well established in other fantasy genres. The second element of the term emphasizes its frequent use in love stories, to the extent that it eventually became a recognized category of genre romance publishing, whose appeal is neatly encapsulated by such omnibuses as *Timeswept Brides* (Jove, 1996). Sf variants usually focus on the impact of the displaced person's scientific and technical knowledge on the society into which he (male protagonists dominate in sf to the same extent as female ones in love stories) is delivered; **Mark Twain's** *A Connecticut Yankee in King Arthur's Court* (1889) provided a prototype. As the subgenre developed within sf, it became increasingly common for groups of protagonists—sometimes gathered in timeslipped vehicles—to be displaced, and timeslips became increasingly likely to engulf entire towns. Timeslips occasionally bring visitors from other eras into the present, as in **E. V. Odle's** *The Clockwork Man*. Another variant—which extends into the margins of sf because it touches on philosophical issues of determinism and free will—involves protagonists slipping back to an earlier point in their own personal history, as in Louis Marlow's *The Devil in Crystal* (1944).

**TIME TRAVEL.** See TIME MACHINE and TIMESLIP ROMANCE.

**TIPTREE, JAMES JR. (1915–1987).** Pseudonym of U.S. writer Alice Hastings Bradley Sheldon, who used her experience in the CIA to establish Tiptree as a coherent false identity before "he" made his debut in 1967, but gave herself away in 1977 by revealing too many authentic biographical details. Tiptree's reputation was primarily based on elegant and affectively powerful short fiction, much of which is collected in *Ten Thousand Light Years from Home* (1973), *Warm Worlds and Otherwise* (1975), *Star Songs of an Old Primate* (1978), *Out of the Everywhere and Other Extraordinary Visions* (1981), and *Crown of Stars* (1988). A few more short stories were combined with nonfiction pieces in *Meet Me at Infinity* (2000). The fact that Tiptree had been so widely accepted as a male writer lent an extra edge to such deft **feminist** parables as "The Girl Who Was Plugged In" (1973) and "The Women Men Don't See" (1973), although "The Screwfly Solution" (1977, as Raccoona Sheldon) and the novella "Houston, Houston, Do You Read?" (1977) demonstrated that the author was also capable of brutal unsubtlety; it is entirely appropriate that an award for **sf** that challenges gender assumptions—founded in 1992—was named the Tiptree Award. Her two novels—the **first contact** story *Up the Walls of the World* (1978) and the **transfiguration** of the movie *Key Largo*, *Brightness Falls from the Air* (1985)—are flamboyant melodramas; the loosely knit **mosaics** *The Starry Rift* (1986) and *Tales of the Quintana Roo* (1986) contrive bigger pictures of a slightly more restrained kind.

**TODAY & TOMORROW SERIES.** A **series** of essays in **speculative nonfiction** extrapolated by Kegan Paul, Trench, and Trubner from their 1924 editions of **J. B. S. Haldane's** *Daedalus; or, Science and the Future* and **Bertrand Russell's** ideological riposte *Icarus; or, the Future of Science*. Another 106 appeared before the series was terminated in 1930; many of the contributors—including **John Gloag**, **Gerald Heard**, **J. Leslie Mitchell**, and A. M. Low—went on to write **scientific romances**; some (including **Muriel Jaeger** and Winifred Holtby) had already done so. **André Maurois** contributed an **sf** story, **J. D. Bernal** the most extravagant item of **futurology.** The series provided an important stimulus to discussion of future possibilities among the British intelligentsia, and laid important intellectual groundwork for the renaissance of scientific romance that began as it ended.

**TOLSTOY, ALEXEI (1882–1910).** Russian writer in several genres. His ventures into **sf** are *Aelita* (1922, rev. 1937; tr. 1957), which features a socialist revolution on **Mars**, and *The Garin Death Ray* (1926, tr. as *The Death Box*, 1936; rev. tr. 1955), a fantasy of temporary conquest.

**TRACY, LOUIS (1863–1928).** British journalist, a colleague of **M. P. Shiel** (who wrote a few chapters of Tracy's **sf** serial, *An American Emperor*, 1897, while he was ill). *The Final War* (1896) is the most jingoistic of all the **future war** novels of its period and helped to popularize the myth of a "war to end war." *The Lost Provinces* (1898) and *The Invaders* (1901) are more conventional. Some of Tracy's later thrillers have marginal sf elements, most notably *Karl Grier* (1906).

**TRAIN, OSWALD (1915–1988).** British-born U.S. **small press** publisher. He was a cofounder in 1947 of Prime Press, which reprinted **pulp sf** by **George O. Smith**, **Lester del Rey**, and **Theodore Sturgeon**, among others. In a later era, he published **Sam Moskowitz's** collections of material by **A. Merritt** and **Olaf Stapledon** under his own imprint, although it was mainly devoted to detective fiction.

**TRANSFIGURATION.** The absence from **sf** of any standard plot formula, and the impossibility of improvising one, posed awkward difficulties for writers of **pulp** sf, who often moved the basic plot formula of crime fiction—especially its thriller and western variants—into a futuristic or extraterrestrial setting. Another favorite ploy was to produce sf versions of myths, folktales, historical episodes, and literary classics, and it is these that warrant description as "transfigurations." Transfiguration is also a favorite device of writers in other fantasy genres, who often recast old stories in more recent settings or transplant them into different cultures—a practice that was presumably routine in the days of oral transmission, given the large numbers of variants of popular folktales recorded at different times in different places. Frequently transfigured stories often give rise to useful subgenres, including **Odyssean**, **Orphean**, and **Promethean** fantasies, as well as such embarrassments as **shaggy god stories.** Genre sf pioneers fond of employing transfiguration as a method of plot generation included **Nelson Bond**, **Edmond Hamilton**, **Isaac Asimov**, **Alfred Bester**, and **Robert A. Heinlein** (whose transfigurations of *The Prisoner of Zenda* and *The Count of Monte Cristo* must have been written in the knowledge that the former had already been transfigured by Hamilton and the latter by Bester). Straightforward transfigurations usually seem absurdly contrived, but writers who use the originals as springboards for work that diverges into more profitable imaginative territory—like Heinlein's transfiguration of **Kipling's** *Kim* into *Citizen of the Galaxy*—often gain valuable imaginative impetus from their parasitic phases. Identifying nonobvious transfigurations—as Gary K. Wolfe spotted Faulknerian transfigurations in the work of **Gregory Benford**—is an interesting critical game; even obvious ones—like **Robert Silverberg's** transfigurations of **Joseph Conrad**—provide useful grist for academic mill-workers.

**TREMAINE, F. ORLIN (1899–1956).** U.S. editor who took over ***Astounding*** in 1933, remaining at the helm for 50 issues before handing control to his protégé **John Campbell**, whose Don A. Stuart stories came close to his ideal of what **sf** ought to be, for which he coined the term "thought variant." Tremaine guaranteed to publish at least one thought-variant story per issue alongside more conventional **pulp** adventure fiction; the notion is an early version of what **Kingsley Amis** was to call an "idea-as-hero" story foregrounding what **Darko Suvin** called a **novum.** Tremaine subsequently edited the sf pulp *Comet* and published a number of undistinguished sf stories, including at least one as "Warner van Lorne."

**TSIOLKOVSKY, KONSTANTIN (1857–1935).** Russian scientist who was the first person to popularize the notion that space flight would be possible using the principle of jet propulsion, in his monograph *Free Space* (1883). All his **sf** is didactic, intended for the instruction and inspiration of **children**; it is translated, along with nonfiction, in the omnibus *The Call of the Cosmos* (1963). The novella "On the Moon" (1893) and the collection "Dreams of Earth and Sky" (1895) are weak imitations of **Camille Flammarion** but the novel "Outside the Earth" (1916, rev. 1920; previously published in a different translation as *Beyond the Planet Earth*, 1960) describes the first stages in the colonization of the solar system, entitling Tsiolkovsky to be retrospectively recognized as the originator of the myth of the **space age.**

**TUBB, E. C. (1919– ).** British writer who began publishing **sf** in 1951 and became remarkably prolific. He began multiplying pseudonyms while participating in the postwar British **paperback** boom, publishing under various house names as well as his own. The most notable of his early works were the account of the colonization of **Mars** assembled in the **mosaic** *Alien Dust* (1952–1953, book 1955), the thriller *The Resurrected Man* (1954), the **planetary romance** *City of No Return* (1954), and the hectic adventure story *Enterprise 2115* (1954, as by Charles Grey; aka *The Mechanical Monarch*). His production slowed when the paperback boom ended, but picked up again when he began working for **Donald A. Wollheim**, first at Ace and later at **DAW.** *The Winds of Gath* (1967) launched a 32-volume **Odyssean fantasy** series of planetary romances, whose concluding volume, *The Return* (1997), appeared 12 years after its immediate predecessor from **small press** publisher Gryphon Books. Tubb also wrote a series of juvenile **space operas** bylined Gregory Kern, modeled on **Edmond Hamilton's** Captain Future stories. His more ambitious works, including *Death Is a Dream* (1967) and *Death Wears a White Face* (1979), were few and far between, but the repetitious plotting of the Dumarest **series** was offset by the **decadent** exoticism of its backcloth, which eventually built an intriguing mosaic image of ecological and social profusion. His short sf is sampled in *The Best Science Fiction of E. C. Tubb* (2003).

**TUCK, DONALD H. (1922– ). Australian bibliographer** who compiled and published *A Handbook of Science Fiction* in 1954, issuing an updated version in two volumes in 1959 before expanding its coverage considerably for publication by **Advent** as *The Encyclopedia of Science Fiction and Fantasy through 1968* (3 vols., 1974, 1978, 1982). Attempts to construct further updates were frustrated by the rapidity with which new data piled up. The groundwork laid by the project was valuable to the compilers of the first edition of the **Clute/Nicholls** *Encyclopedia*, even though the second volume of its final version (dealing with authors whose names began with the letters M–Z) arrived too late to lend them much assistance.

**TUCKER, WILSON (1914– ).** U.S. writer who was active in **sf fandom** from 1930, publishing several important **fanzines**; he endeared himself to his fellow fans by routinely attaching their names to characters in the fiction he began publishing in 1941, which included detective stories as well as sf. *The City in the Sea* (1951) is a **postholocaust fantasy** whose themes were revisited in the **Fortean** fantasy *Ice and Iron* (1974, rev. 1975) and the suspended animation story *Resurrection Days* (1991). *The Long Loud Silence* (1952, rev. 1970) is a grim account of a holocaust in progress. *The Time Masters* (1953, rev. 1971) and its sequel *Time Bomb* (1955, aka *Tomorrow Plus X*) are mysteries featuring an immortal hero. *Wild Talent* (1954, aka *The Man from Tomorrow*) is a stereotypical **psi** story. *The Lincoln Hunters* (1958) and *The Year of the Quiet Sun* (1970) employ **time travel** to illuminate aspects of American politics. His short sf is sampled in *The Best of Wilson Tucker* (1982).

**TURNER, GEORGE (1916–1997). Australian** writer and critic who wrote several novels before his first venture into **sf**, the **postholocaust fantasy** *Beloved Son* (1978); *Vaneglory* (1981) and *Yesterday's Men* (1983) are set in the same **future history.** *The Sea and Summer* (1987; aka *Drowning Towers*) introduced a different postholocaust scenario inset with similar political and technological themes connected with potential uses of **biotechnology**; these were carried forward in *Brain Child* (1991), featuring **artificially enhanced intelligence**, *The Destiny Makers* (1993), and *Genetic Soldier* (1994). *Down There in Darkness* (1999), which features a future Earth "cleansed" of industrial civilization, links the two **series**. His short fiction is collected in *Pursuit of Miracles* (1990).

**TURNER, JAMES (1945–1999).** U.S. publisher who was in charge of the Arkham House program from 1973–1996. He issued numerous collections by **sf** writers under the Arkham imprint—beginning with **Michael Bishop** in 1982—before setting up his own company, Golden Gryphon Press, to continue the series. Significant collections by **Greg Bear**, **John Kessel**, **Alexander Jablokov**, and others were issued under the former label, while **James Patrick Kelly**, **R. Garcia y Robertson**, and **Robert Reed** were featured under the latter. Golden Gryphon was taken over after his death by his brother Gary, who continued its work. These volumes plugged a significant gap, commercial publishers having given up on story collections by all but the most successful brand-name authors.

**TURTLEDOVE, HARRY (1949– ).** U.S. writer who began working in various fantasy genres in the late 1980s, initially as Eric Iverson, finding his métier as a leading exponent of **alternative history** fiction. *Agent of Byzantium* (1987) drew on his academic specialty, as did many of his early fantasies. The **mosaic** *A Different Flesh* (1988) describes a United States in which *Homo sapiens* is not the only thriving hominid species, while *A World of Difference* (1990) is an alternative interplanetary novel, but *The Guns of the South* (1992) set the pattern for much of his future work in providing a meticulous account of a crucial conflict reaching a different resolution. The Worldwar **series** comprising *In the Balance* (1994), *Tilting the Balance* (1995), *Upsetting the Balance* (1996), and *Striking the Balance* (1996), is similar. The Great War series, comprising *How Few Remain* (1997), *American Front* (1998), *Walk in Hell* (1999), and *Breakthroughs* (2000) extends into the American Empire series comprising *Blood and Iron* (2001), *The Center Cannot Hold* (2002), and *The Victorious Opposition* (2003). The Darkness series comprises *Into the Darkness* (1999), *Darkness Descending* (2000), *Through the Darkness* (2001), *Rulers of the Darkness* (2002), and *Jaws of the Darkness* (2003). The War between Provinces series comprises *Sentry Peak* (2000), *Marching through Peachtree* (2001), and *Advance and Retreat* (2002). *The Two Georges* (1995) is a **collaboration** with actor Richard Dreyfuss. *Ruled Britannia* (2002) features a Britain conquered by the Spanish Armada. Turtledove's other sf—including the stories collected in *Kaleidoscope* (1990) and *Counting Up, Counting Down* (2002); the mosaics *Noninterference* (1988) and *Earthgrip* (1991); and the Colonization series comprising *Second Contact* (1999), *Down to Earth* (2000), and *Aftershocks* (2001)—mostly consists of thoughtful accounts of constructive human/**alien** interaction.

**TWAIN, MARK (1835–1910).** Pseudonym of U.S. writer Samuel Langhorne Clemens. *A Connecticut Yankee in King Arthur's Court* (1889) is a significant prototype of **sf timeslip romances**, studying the impact of a 20th-century handyman on sixth-century England. Twain published numerous comic fantasies, but other stories with sf elements that he began were never completed. These include the fantasies of **miniaturization** "The Great Dark" (written 1898, published 1972) and "Three Thousand Years among the Microbes" (written 1905, published 1967). *The Science Fiction of Mark Twain* (1984, aka *Tales of Wonder*), edited by **David Ketterer**, collects 20 stories.

## – U –

**UFOLOGY.** When UFO—an acronym signifying unidentified flying object—was adopted as a description to avoid the pejorative implications of **flying saucer**, people investigating such sightings began to style themselves UFOlogists, but both terms quickly fell into the same disrepute as their predecessor. Different schools of UFOlogy employ markedly different theoretical assumptions in attempting to interpret sightings; some regard them as evidence of **alien** visitation, while others regard them as psychological phenomena, and a third party is dedicated to explaining all mysteries away by identifying the objects concerned as aircraft, planets that appear to be moving because they are being viewed from moving vehicles, and so forth. The first school attracts the most publicity, many of its adherents having moved on from mere sightings to investigate accounts of abductions by aliens, mostly recalled under hypnosis and usually involving various kinds of intimate investigative probing (which the psychological school tends to interpret in symbolic terms). Although the produce of UFOlogy is treated with some respect in **cinema** and **TV sci-fi**, the great majority of **sf** writers are skeptical; credulous UFOlogists are treated with scathing contempt when they appear as characters in accounts of alien contact, although the psychological school and its Jung-endorsed theories are sometimes treated seriously, as in **Ian Watson's** *Miracle Visitors*.

***UNKNOWN.*** U.S. **magazine** founded as a companion to ***Astounding*** in 1939. It folded in 1943 as a result of wartime paper shortages, not long after expanding its name to *Unknown Worlds*. It was designed to complement *Astounding* by publishing various kinds of fantasy that were excluded, by definition, from **sf** (while also avoiding trespassing on ***Weird Tales*'s** territory), but rapidly developed a highly distinctive character by virtue of its mobilization of the narrative energy derivable from contentedly absurd confrontations of skeptical, rational, and technologically skilled protagonists with magical intrusions or entire magical worlds. This kind of fiction, foreshadowed in the comedies of Thorne Smith, was taken to a new level of sophistication and considerably broadened in scope by **L. Sprague de Camp** (often in **collaboration** with **Fletcher Pratt**), with assistance from **L. Ron Hubbard**.

Both writers also employed the method in more seriously inclined experimental ***contes philosophiques***, as did **Robert A. Heinlein** in "The Devil Makes the Law" (1940, aka "Magic, Inc."), **Jack Williamson** in *Darker Than You Think* (1940, book 1949), and **Fritz Leiber** in *Conjure Wife* (1943, book 1953), unorthodox ghost stories, and sword-and-sorcery adventures. **Chimerical** texts were not new, but *Unknown* provided an invaluable laboratory for the investigation of the potential of chimerical fantasies, paving the way for a great deal of subsequent work published on the margins of the genre sf marketplace.

**UTLEY, STEVEN (1948– ).** U.S. writer who began publishing **sf** in 1973. He pioneered **steampunk** with **Howard Waldrop** in "Custer's Last Jump" (1976) and "Black as the Pit, from Pole to Pole" (1977). Much of his later work involved **time-trips** to the distant past, as in a **series** of stories about a timegate to the Paleozoic era launched on the SciFiction website in 2000. His short fiction is sampled in *Ghost Seas* (1997).

**UTOPIA.** An Anglicization of the Greek *outopos* ("no place"), whose employment by Thomas More in a 1516 political **satire** including an **imaginary voyage** to the eponymous island state gave its name to a genre of imaginative fiction. Although More's Utopia is not an example of an ideal state (as Plato's *Republic* had appeared to be), it was routinely mistaken for one and the term was soon being widely construed as if it were derived from *eutopos* ("good place"), eventually generating the contrary term **dystopia** ("hard place"). Some modern scholars, notably Frank Manuel, attempt to dispel the confusion by using eutopia as a description for accounts of better societies, also arguing that a decisive shift in such representations took place at the end of the 18th century—pioneered by **Louis-Sebastien Mercier**—when many visions of ideal societies were displaced into the future rather than being placed on remote islands, thus becoming "euchronias" rather than eutopias. A further shift took place in the 20th century, displacing much attention from euchronian images of the future to "eupsychian" ideas in which ideal states of mind replace ideal states as the key goals of social evolution. As defined by Abraham Maslow in 1954, a eupsychia is a society designed to ensure psychological health and the maximization of opportunities for self-fulfillment.

**Sf** is replete with images of nonexistent places, but only those that are consciously "eutopian" tend to be categorized as Utopian fantasies by the majority of critics; Manuel's more scrupulous and potentially more useful terminology never caught on. Dystopian imagery far outweighs eutopian imagery even in sf that is firmly committed to the cause of progress. This is only partly explicable by the greater utility of dystopian imagery in melodramatic plotting; literary sf favors dystopian imagery to an even greater extent than genre sf. The sources of dystopian pessimism are various. Writers of **Swiftian** antiscience fiction and some writers of **soft sf** are alarmed by technological progress itself, either because they feel that it is intrinsically bad, or because they subscribe to the argument of **Bertrand Russell's** *Icarus; or, the Future of Science*, which holds that human beings are incapable of using technology wisely. **Hard sf** writers, on the other hand, are often alarmed by the suspicion that the golden opportunities offered by technological progress are being wasted or frustrated by obsolete political institutions and social attitudes.

## – V –

**VANCE, JACK (1916– ).** U.S. writer who began publishing **sf** in 1945; he used his full name (John Holbrook Vance) on detective stories. Some of his early work, including the picaresque adventures collected as *The Many Worlds of Magnus Ridolph* (1948–1950, book 1996; exp. *The Complete Magnus Ridolph*, 1984), was wantonly **humorous** but his wit soon became subtly muted, manifest as an idiosyncratic dry irony. The stories assembled into the **mosaic** *The Dying Earth* (1950) were pivotal exercises in **far-futuristic fantasy**; later works set in the same milieu include the mosaics *The Eyes of the Overworld* (1966) and *Cugel's Saga* (1983), the novella *Morreion* (1973, book 1979), and the novel *Rhialto the Marvelous* (1984). *The Last Castle* (1967) offers a more carefully **hybridized** image of the far future. Vance deployed a similar wry romanticism in such **space operas** as *The Five Gold Bands* (1950, book 1953 as *The Space Pirate*) and "Planet of the Damned" (1952, book 1958 as *Slaves of the Klau*; rev. as *Gold and Iron*, 1982) and such exotic **planetary romances** as *Son of the Tree* (1951, book 1964), *Big Planet* (1952, book

1957; restored text 1978), and *The Houses of Iszm* (1954, book 1964), which were far more hospitable to it.

Most of Vance's subsequent work involved the establishment of exotic societies on colony worlds, usually involving complex processes of manipulative social control, as in *To Live Forever* (1956), *The Languages of Pao* (1958), "The Moon Moth" (1961), and *The Dragon Masters* (1963). Vance's planetary romances often feature makeshift societies improvised by castaways, refugees, and outcasts, like those distributed across *Big Planet*—further explored in *Showboat World* (1975)—the floating culture of *The Blue World* (1966), and the patchworks featured in the Planet of Adventure quartet (1968–70), the Durdane trilogy (1973–1974), and the Alastor Cluster **series** (1973–1978). Such societies often have strong artistic interests, as in *Space Opera* (1965) and *Emphyrio* (1969), and idiosyncratic sports. Vance gradually developed a **future history** to contain and coordinate his sf, whose most detailed segment deals with the Gaean Reach, featured in *The Gray Prince* (1974), *Maske: Thaery* (1976), *Night Lamp* (1996), *Ports of Call* (1998), and *Lurulu* (2001). His further adventures in space opera, including the extended revenge fantasy contained in the Demon Princes sequence (1964–1981) are calculatedly nostalgic exercises in **pulp** fiction. In the 1980s, as genre fantasy took off, Vance began to deemphasize the sf elements of his work, but maintained the planetary romance format in the epic Cadwal Chronicles, comprising *Araminta Station* (1987), *Ecce and Old Earth* (1991), and *Throy* (1992). David G. Mead's *An Encyclopedia of Jack Vance* (2002) is a comprehensive guide to his fictional universe.

**VANDERMEER, JEFF (1968– ).** U.S. writer and **small press** publisher. He founded the Ministry of Whimsy Press in 1984, but sold it to Prime Books in 2001. He began publishing **fabulations**, some with **sf** elements, in 1985; many are **metafictions** set in the **decadent** city of Ambergris, collected in *City of Saints and Madmen: The Book of Ambergris* (2001, exp. 2002). *Veniss Underground* (2003) is an **Orphean fantasy** featuring a **biotechnologically** supplied underworld. With Mark Roberts, VanderMeer edited the elaborately bizarre *The Thackeray T. Lambshead Pocket Guide to Eccentric and Discredited Diseases* (2003).

**VAN GREENAWAY, PETER (1929–1988).** British writer whose first novels were the **postholocaust** fantasy *The Crucified City* (1962) and the ambiguous **Utopian** fantasy *The Evening Fool* (1964). Many of his subsequent thrillers deploy **sf** motifs in more enterprisingly **satirical** fashion than is common in that genre; the most notable are *The Medusa Touch* (1973); *graffiti* (183), another postholocaust fantasy; *Manrissa Man* (1982), featuring intelligent apes; and *Mutants* (1986), in which the spin-off from a **biotechnological** experiment runs out of control.

**VAN SCYOC, SYDNEY J. (1939– ).** U.S. writer who began publishing **sf** in 1962. Most of her work deals with intimate human/**alien** relationships that hold out the promise of a transcendence of human limitations, or at least a route to greater empathy. *Saltflower* (1971); *Assignment Nor'Dyren* (1973); *StarMother* (1976); *Cloudcry* (1977); *Sunwaifs* (1981); the trilogy comprising *Darkchild* (1981), *Bluesong* (1983), and *Starsilk* (1984); *Drowntide* (1987); *Feather Stroke* (1989); and *Deepwater Dreams* (1991) all sing from the same hymn sheet.

**VAN VOGT, A. E. (1912–2000). Canadian**-born writer resident in the United States after 1944. His first **sf** story, "Black Destroyer" (1939), made a considerable impact and he became a key member of the ***Astounding*** stable, although the ideas on which he drew—including Alfred Korzybski's theory of "General Semantics"—seemed suspiciously **pseudoscientific** to some readers and the "intensive recomplication" of his plots with material drawn more or less at random from his unconscious, usually via the dreams that he painstakingly recorded on awakening, often rendered them nonsensical. His crucial role in the **Campbellian** crusade was to import a quasi-mystical sense of human destiny, which looked forward eagerly to the replacement of *Homo sapiens* by **psi**-powered **supermen.** *Slan* (1940, book 1946; rev. 1951) was so successful in seducing readers to take the side of its beleaguered child protagonist against the resentful prejudices of soon-to-be superseded common humans that "fans are slans" became a fashionable slogan in **fandom.**

The couplet comprising the **mosaic** *The Weapon Shops of Isher* (1941–1949, book 1951) and *The Weapon Makers* (1943, book 1946) pitted its superhuman hero (who establishes the quasi-magical weapon shops to protect the right to bear arms against all oppression) against a decadent Earthly empire, and rewarded his success with an enigmatic promise of galactic fame and fortune. The convoluted novella "Recruiting Station" (1942; reprinted with "The Changeling" in *Masters of Time*, 1950, and separately as *Earth's Last Fortress*) is similar. *The Winged Man* (1944, book 1966), a novel he wrote in **collaboration** with his wife, Edna Mayne Hull (1905–1975)—who also wrote sf of her own—was more straightforward. The Korzybskian couplet comprising *The World of Null-A* (1945, book 1948; rev. 1970) and *The Player of Null-A* (1948–1949, book 1956 as *The Pawns of Null-A*; rev. 1966) features a far more flexible superman whose promised destiny, though equally enigmatic, is even more grandiose. The author wrote *Null-A Three* (1984 in French; 1985) much later, without adding anything substantial. A third couplet, comprising the mosaic *Empire of the Atom* (1946–1947, book 1957) and *The Wizard of Linn* (1950, book 1962) seems to have begun as a **transfiguration** of Robert Graves's *I, Claudius*.

Van Vogt seemed to lose his way after publishing *The House That Stood Still* (1950) and "The Shadow Men" (1950, book 1953 as *The Universe Maker*), although most of his short fiction had yet to be reprinted, in the collections *Destination: Universe* (1952) and *Away and Beyond* (1952)—extensively sampled in *Transfinite: The Essential A. E. van Vogt* (2003)—and the mosaics *The Voyage of the Space Beagle* (1950), *The Mixed Men* (1952), and *The War against the Rull* (1959). These mosaics—unlike earlier ones—had to be extended to book length by the addition of new material, some of which linked short series to initially unrelated material, and it was these that van Vogt dubbed **fix-ups**. He produced several more, including *The Silkie* (1969) and *Quest for the Future* (1970), before returning to the production of novels; the most notable he wrote thereafter are *Children of Tomorrow* (1970); the phantasmagoric *The Battle of Forever* (1971); the eccentric **political fantasies** *Future Glitter* (1973) and *The Anarchistic Colossus* (1977); and the **time-travel** fantasy *Cosmic Encounter* (1980).

Van Vogt's work had sufficient power to generate a subgenre of van Vogtian fantasy, whose chief practitioners included **Charles L. Harness**, **Ian Wallace**, and **Barrington J. Bayley**; many such works are more elegantly organized than his paradigm examples, but that does not work entirely to their advantage. Like **Jack Williamson**, van Vogt learned much about the craft of popular fiction from John Gallishaw's writing manuals (although his attempts to pass on what he had learned were sometimes misunderstood) but he also believed that every popular genre has a typical form of "fictional sentence." What characterizes sf, he asserted, is that every such sentence has to leave something carefully unspecified for the reader's inquisitive imagination to work upon; this was a policy he followed to extremes that no other writer has yet been willing to attempt.

**VARLEY, JOHN (1947– ).** U.S. writer who began publishing **sf** in 1974, rapidly establishing a reputation as a writer of stylish and highly imaginative short fiction; his early works are collected in *The Persistence of Vision* (1978, aka *In the Hall of the Martian Kings*) and *The Barbie Murders* (1980, aka *Picnic on Nearside*). A loosely defined **future history** formulated in these stories—the first to feature elaborate uses of **biotechnology**—also formed the backcloth to his first novel, *The Ophiuchi Hotline* (1977), in which information transmitted from the stars brings unwelcome news regarding the fate of humankind. In the trilogy comprising *Titan* (1979), *Wizard* (1980), and *Demon* (1984), the Saturnian moon Titan turns out to be an exotically surprising **alien** artifact. *Millennium* (1983) features a very different future whose citizens employ **time travel** to kidnap humans from the past in the hope of repopulating a devastated planet; its final revelation exhibits a keen awareness of the pressure of **melodramatic inflation**, which contributed to the difficulty Varley had in following it up—although the even deeper pessimism of *Steel Beach* (1992) suggests that his awareness of the inevitability of **ecocatastrophe** was also a factor. Later short fiction, including the novella "PRESS ENTER []" (1984), is collected in *Blue Champagne* (1986). In *The Golden Globe* (1998) an actor tours the solar system with a Shakespearean troupe. *Red Thunder* (2003) is a calculatedly old-fashioned adventure story modeled on **Robert Heinlein's** *Rocket Ship Galileo*.

**VERNE, JULES (1828–1905). French** writer who came to be seen as one of the founding fathers of the **sf** genre, although he kept the speculative elements of his work under a relatively tight rein during the greater part of his career, on the advice of his publisher, P.-J. Hetzel. The effect of this restraint was to turn the majority of his *voyages extraordinaires* into modest exercises in imaginary tourism, but when he did allow his imagination greater scope he brought an unprecedented verisimilitude to the description of bold exploratory ventures. He might have been far more inventive had Hetzel agreed to publish an early exercise in futuristic fiction, but he was persuaded to shelve that aspect of his ambition; if the text published as *Paris au XXe siècle* (1994; tr. as *Paris in the 20th Century*, 1996) is genuine, it offers a glimpse of the writer that Verne might have become had he followed the prospectus laid down by Félix Bodin.

Verne's first significant venture into sf was *Voyage au centre de la terre* (1863, tr. as *Journey to the Center of the Earth*), an exemplary account of an expedition in which scientific observations are continually made as a matter of course, until melodrama overtakes method in a subterranean world where species from remote prehistory still survive, having followed their own pattern of evolution. Other **imaginary voyages** that laid important foundation stones for sf were *De la terre à la lune* (1865, tr. as *From the Earth to the Moon*) and its sequel *Autour de la lune* (1870, tr. as *Around the Moon*), and *Vingt mille lieues sous les mers* (1870, tr. as *Twenty Thousand Leagues under the Sea*; unabridged ed. 1992). Although he ventured into space again in *Hector Servadac* (1877) and reproduced the pattern of *Twenty Thousand Leagues under the Sea* with an airship in place of a submarine in *Robur le conquérant* (1886, tr. as *the Clipper of the Clouds*) and its sequel *Maître de la monde* (1904, tr. as *Master of the World*), the imaginative impact of the earlier works was irreproducible.

Verne did, however, produce other significant works of **speculative fiction** less typical of his output, including the title story of *Une fantaisie du Docteur Ox* (1872, tr. as "Dr. Ox's Experiment"), a comic proto-**Edisonade**; *Les cinq cents millions de la bégum* (1879, tr. as *The Begum's Fortune*), based on a manuscript by **André Laurie**, which contrasts **Utopian** and **dystopian** experimental cities; *L'île à hélice* (1895, tr. as *Propellor Island*), in which the world's richest men construct a movable island as a tax-avoidance measure; *Face au drapeau* (1896, tr. as *For the Flag*), about the development of an unprecedentedly powerful explosive; and *Le village aérien* (1901, tr. as *The Village in the Tree Tops*), about the discovery of a new primate species. Some of his later works—including *L'invasion de la mer* (1905, tr. as *The Invasion of the Sea*), about a project to flood the Sahara Desert—were rewritten by his son Michel (1861–1925), who published a few works of his own under his father's name; the most important of these **collaborations** is an elegiac novella published in *Hier et demain* (1910, tr. as *Yesterday and Tomorrow*), known in translation as "The Eternal Adam."

Verne's *voyages extraordinaires* were the inspiration of a significant genre of "Vernian romances,"—launched by George Sand's *Laura: Voyage dans le cristal* (1864, tr. as *Journey within the Crystal*) as soon as she had read *Voyage au centre de la terre* in manuscript—which became an important element of juvenile fiction. The editing of translations of Verne's work for the children's market in Britain and the United States often made them seem more primitive than the originals by cutting the passages detailing scientific equipment and observation; most imitations of Verne produced in those nations are devoid of speculative acumen and literary elegance, but the widening network of influences was a vital factor in preparing the ground for the development of a genre in which those aspects might one day be restored. In 1958, I. O. Evans set out to prepare a comprehensive English edition of Verne's works, some of which he translated for the first time; unfortunately, many were split in two in order to be accommodated within a standardized format and the translations were often abridged. The collection was trailed by extracts in *Jules Verne—Master of Science Fiction* (1956) and Evans also wrote one of several biographies of the author, *Jules Verne and His Work* (1965).

**VERSINS, PIERRE (1923–2001).** Pseudonym of **French** writer and scholar Jacques Chamson, long resident in Switzerland. He began publishing **sf** in 1951, producing several sf novels and numerous short stories as well as editing a notable **fanzine**, *Ailleurs* (1957–1962), but his primary contribution to the genre was the compilation of the *Encyclopédie de l'Utopie, des voyages extraordiarires et de la science fiction* (1972), which summarized his extensive research into the history of the genre. Although no such work carried out by a single individual could be entirely comprehensive, it was an amazingly assiduous enterprise. The Versins encyclopedia was the model for the original version of the **Clute/Nicholls** *Encyclopedia*, although it remains invaluable in its own right because of its extensive coverage of continental European sf; it provided a basis for a more comprehensive study of *French Science Fiction, Fantasy, Horror and Pulp Fiction* (2000) by Jean-Marc and Randy Lofficier. The research collection on which the encyclopedia was based was donated to the town in which Versins lived in 1975, thus creating the **Maison d'Ailleurs.**

**VIDAL, GORE (1925– ).** U.S. writer of literary fiction who often used **sf** devices in his **satirical** fictions. *Messiah* (1954) is a futuristic fantasy in which a charismatic cult leader reconciles the American masses to the prospect of death. *Visit to a Small Planet* (1956, book 1960) originated as a 1955 **TV** play (broadcast live) and was produced on Broadway before publication. *Kalki* (1978) is a sarcastic **apocalyptic fantasy.** *Live from Golgotha* (1992) features a competition between TV producers armed with a time-viewer to obtain exclusive documentary rights to the crucifixion. *The Smithsonian Institute* (1998) is a nostalgic **time-travel** fantasy.

**VILLIERS DE L'ISLE, ADAM (Jean-Marie-Mathias-Philippe-Auguste, Comte de) (1840–1889). French** writer whose extreme suspicion of the idea of progress and hatred of technological innovation led him to feature **sf** devices in several of his **satires**, including the **hybrid** occult fantasy *Claire Lenoir* (1867, rev. 1887) and a few stories in the classic collection *Contes cruels* (1883, tr. as *Sardonic Tales* and *Cruel Tales*), most notably "Celestial Publicity," about the future of advertising; later works in the same vein include those translated as "Etna in Your Own Home" and "The Love of the Natural" in *Claire Lenoir and Other Stories* (2004). In *L'Ève future* (1886, tr. as *The Eve of the Future* and *Tomorrow's Eve*) a nobleman disillusioned with actual women commissions Thomas Edison to build him a perfect bride; the story thus became a significant anticipator of 20th-century tales of **robots** and **androids.**

**VINGE, JOAN D. (1948– ).** U.S. writer who began publishing **sf** in 1974 (while married to **Vernor Vinge**) with "Tin Soldier," a **transfiguration** of a story by Hans Christian Andersen. Andersen also supplied the basic imagery of *The Snow Queen* (1980), a **hybrid science-fantasy** whose sequels are *World's End* (1984), *The Summer Queen*

(1991), and *Tangled Up in Blue* (2000). *The Outcasts of Heaven Belt* (1978, reprinted with a related novella as *Heaven Chronicles*) is about sexual politics in the asteroid belt. *Psion* (1982) and its sequel *Catspaw* (1988)—the latter issued as a juvenile—are more relaxed space adventures. Her short sf, much of it dealing with human/**alien** communication, is collected in *Fireship* (1978), *Eyes of Amber and Other Stories* (1979), and *Phoenix in the Ashes* (1985).

**VINGE, VERNOR (1944– ).** U.S. writer who began publishing **sf** in 1965. *Grimm's World* (1969; exp. as *Tatja Grimm's World*, 1987) is a **mosaic planetary romance**; *The Witling* (1976) features **psi powers** in a space colony setting. After publishing the novella *True Names* (1981)—a groundbreaking work anticipating the central themes of **cyberpunk** fiction, including **virtual reality**—Vinge made rapid progress to become a leading writer of **hard sf**. The couplet comprising *The Peace War* (1984) and *Marooned in Realtime* (1986) is an impressive exercise in unbridled **extrapolation**, using the development of "stasis-fields" as a **portal** to the near and remote future, allowing the near-future development of human civilization and the eventual evolution of humankind to be panoramically displayed. *A Fire upon the Deep* (1992) and its prequel *A Deepness in the Sky* (1999) are wide-ranging sophisticated **space operas**, similarly making ingenious use of time dilatation to lay out an expansive **future history** on a galactic scale. Vinge's short sf is collected in *True Names and Other Dangers* (1987) and *Threats . . . and Other Promises* (1988), recombined in *The Collected Stories of Vernor Vinge* (2001). His highly influential popularization of the notion of a technological **singularity** was only peripherally reflected in his own fiction.

**VIRTUAL REALITY.** A term that became fashionable in **sf** in the 1980s, describing artificially generated scenarios into which computer users can "project themselves," usually by using eyepieces that allow them to look into a synthesized "world" and gloves that allow them to control their movements therein and manipulate its native objects. More intimate engagement is permitted by the kind of "jacking" connections envisaged in such **cyberpunk** fictions as **William Gibson's** *Neuromancer*, or the direct sensory feeds envisaged in such pioneering works as **E. M. Forster's** "The Machine Stops" (1909) and **Lau-**

**rence Manning** and **Fletcher Pratt's** "City of the Living Dead" (1932). Other kinds of "virtual reality" featured in sf before the advent of personal computers involved synthesized dreams, but the advent of computer games gave sudden impetus to the notion that enhanced interactivity with gaming scenarios was not merely possible but inevitable and imminent. The term was quickly taken up by computer engineers, who had introduced the concept of "virtuality" in 1980, perhaps influencing such early sf uses of "virtual reality" as **Damien Broderick's** in *The Judas Mandala* (1982); it was rapidly popularized by such books as Howard Rheingold's *Virtual Reality* (1991).

**VISIONARY FANTASY.** A subgenre in which fantastic materials are presented as dreams in order to conserve rational plausibility—as writers oppressed by the naturalistic conventions of 19th-century fiction often felt obliged to do. It is convenient to make some distinction between the overlapping categories of quasi-oracular visionary fantasy, **hallucinatory fantasy** (in which the fictitiousness of the experience is acknowledged) and delusional fantasy (in which the focus tends to be on the psychology of the dreamer as reflected in the content of the dream). The use made of visionary fantasy within the field of **religious fantasy** often demands that visions be taken seriously as revelations of future destiny, overriding the contingent nature of useful **prophecy** in a manner that serious **sf** cannot easily tolerate, although **Olaf Stapledon's** *Star Maker* provided a shining example. The essential lameness of the closing move that ends a story by having its protagonist wake up from a dream assisted the search for such replacement-facilitating devices as **portals** and **time machines**, and also encouraged the development of surreal fantasies, which resemble dreams but refuse to conclude with a bathetic awakening, like various works by **R. A. Lafferty** and **Michael Kandel's** *Panda Ray*.

**VOLTAIRE (1694–1778).** Pseudonym used by **French** philosopher François-Marie Arouet, whose importance as a precursor of the **sf** genre lay in his development of the fantastic ***conte philosophique*** as a means of making seriously discomfiting argumentative points in a playful manner. In *Micromégas* (1952) a giant from a planet orbiting Sirius visits Earth, accompanied by a Saturnian of slightly less spectacular dimensions, in order to comment on the utter folly of human delusions of grandeur. *Candide* (1759), which lays waste to the optimistic philosophy of Gottfried Wilhelm Leibniz, provided a model for many subsequent **satires**, including numerous sf novels.

**VONARBURG, ÉLISABETH (1947– ).** French-born **Canadian** writer who began publishing **sf** in 1978. Several of her early stories are set within a **future history** in which a **decadent** civilization completes a gradual collapse initiated by a nuclear war in spite of its mastery of new **biotechnologies**, while a new and more malleable species of *métames* emerges as a candidate successor of humankind; the **series** culminated in an earnest redemptive fantasy translated as *The Silent City* (1981, tr. 1988). *In the Mother's Land* (1992, tr. 1992; aka *The Mareland Chronicles*) is similarly set in a postcatastrophe scenario, where mutation has led to a dramatic imbalance in the make-up of the population, females far outnumbering males. *Reluctant Voyagers* (1994; tr. 1995) features a future **dystopia** in which Francophone Canadians respond to the problem of being confined to a dwindling enclave. She was literary editor of the Québeçois sf magazine *Solaris* from 1979–1990. Her short fiction is sampled in *The Slow Engines of Time* (2001).

**VONNEGUT, KURT JR. (1922– ).** U.S. writer who began publishing **sf** in 1950 but tried with all his might to avoid categorization as an sf writer after being advised by **Robert Scholes** that sf was the most critically despised of all the commercial genres. His novels are ironic Jeremiads rather than **satires**, combining dark humor with unashamed sentimentality in lamenting the apparent inability of the vast majority of human beings to behave humanely. *Player Piano* (1952) is a **dystopia** about the soul-destroying effects of automation. *The Sirens of Titan* (1959) is an extended ***conte philosophique*** featuring a Tralfamadorian **alien**, whose species reappears (in a slightly different form) in *Slaughterhouse-Five; or, The Children's Crusade* (1969), which casts its protagonist adrift in time in order that he might begin reconciling himself to having been—as Vonnegut had—one of the very few survivors of the fire-storming of Dresden during World War II.

*Cat's Cradle* (1963), *Galapagos* (1985), and *Hocus Pocus* (1990) are sarcastic **apocalyptic fantasies.** Some works with sf inclusions, such as *Breakfast of Champions* (1973), the play *Happy Birthday, Wanda June* (1973), and *Slapstick* (1976), reprocessed ideas from earlier books in a conspicuously dispirited manner; the first-named, like the fragmentary *Timequake* (1997), features Vonnegut's parody of a despised sf writer, Kilgore Trout (the name sardonically echoes **Theodore Sturgeon**), who had a brief phantom career of his own when Vonnegut allowed **Philip José Farmer** to publish a novel under that pseudonym—a decision he subsequently regretted. There are some items of sf among the short stories collected in *Welcome to the Monkey House* (1968), most notably the satirical account of an egalitarian future "Harrison Bergeron" (1961).

**VON NEUMANN MACHINE.** A machine able to build a working copy of itself, whose name derives from John von Neumann's 1966 paper exploring the theory of self-replicating machines. The notion had been anticipated in **sf** by **Philip K. Dick's** "Autofac" (1955) and "von Neumann probes" became a key element in many **space-age** scenarios attempting to identify the means by which interstellar space might best be explored and exploited.

## – W –

**WALDROP, HOWARD (1946– ).** U.S. writer who began publishing **sf** in 1973. *The Texas-Israeli War: 1999* (1976, with Jake Saunders), is a futuristic comedy. He found his métier writing **fabulations** set in transfigured pasts, in which history and myth (including literary myth) are **chimerically** mingled. His early ventures in this vein included pioneering **steampunk** stories written in **collaboration** with **Steven Utley** and others—collected in *Custer's Last Jump and Other Collaborations* (2003)—and solo efforts assembled in *Howard Who?* (1986) and *All About Strange Monsters of the Recent Past* (1987). These two items were combined in the omnibus *Strange Things in Close-up* (1989) and the latter was combined with a **transfiguration** of the legend of Hercules, *A Dozen Tough Jobs* (1989), as *Strange Monsters of the Recent Past* (1991). His third collection, *Night of the Cooters* (1990), was also issued an omnibus with *A Dozen Tough Jobs* in 1991. *Them Bones* (1984) is a more earnest and convoluted exercise in twisting time and technology. *You Could Go Home Again* (1993), a novella reprinted in the collection *Going Home Again* (1998), is an **alternative history** in which Thomas Wolfe struggles to recover lost memories in a world in which World War II never happened. The novella *A Better World's in Birth!* (2003) features an alternative history in which socialism was victorious throughout Europe after the revolutions of 1848.

**WALLACE, IAN (1912–1998).** Pseudonym of U.S. educational psychologist John Wallace Pritchard, who was active as a writer in other genres before publishing the breezy **van Vogtian space opera** *Croyd* (1967); its eponymous superhuman protagonist reappeared in *Dr. Orpheus* (1968), which makes extravagant and ingenious use of his ability to move back and forth in time. *Pan Sagittarius* (1973) continued the **series** with a different incarnation of the hero, further emphasizing the **hybridization** of Greek myth deployed in the previous volume, but Croyd reclaimed center stage from his alter ego in the more orthodox melodrama *A Voyage to Dari* (1974). In *Z-Sting* (1979) a malfunction in the fully mature Croyd's peace-enforcing technology threatens to destroy the world, while *Megalomania* (1989) further escalates the space-operatic scale in accordance with the principle of **melodramatic inflation.** The **apocalyptic fantasy** *The World Asunder* (1976)—largely set in 1952, when it might have been written—and the hybrid **Promethean fantasy** *The Lucifer Comet* (1980) are related to the series, although Croyd is not their hero. The **future history** mapped out in these volumes (whose order of publication does not correspond to their internal chronological sequence) also served as background to a series of neatly wrought mysteries comprising *Deathstar Voyage* (1969), *The Purloined Prince* (1971), *The Sign of the Mute Medusa* (1977), and *Heller's Leap* (1979); Croyd lends a hand in the last-named. *The Rape of the Sun* (1982), which features multiple echoes of Shakespeare's plays and derives its bizarre plot from a literal reading of one of the bard's more colorful metaphors, is a distinct enterprise.

**WALLIS, GEORGE C. (1871–1956).** British writer in various genres, who wrote prolifically for the popular **magazines** in the late 1890s, contributing **Vernian** romances and **future war** stories to the boys' papers and introducing a **pulpish** verve into such **scientific romances** as the **Flammarionesque** "The Last Days of Earth" (1901) and "The Great Sacrifice" (1903). His enthusiasm for **sf** attracted him to the **Gernsback** pulps, to which he contributed "The World at Bay" (1928, bylined B. and G. C. Wallis, the former being his cousin). He published more stories in the British pulp *Tales of Wonder* in 1938–1941 and one sf novel, *The Call of Peter Gaskell* (1947), during the post–World War II **paperback** boom.

**WANDREI, DONALD (1908–1987).** U.S. writer associated with **H. P. Lovecraft's** circle, who cofounded Arkham House with **August Derleth.** His first **sf** publication was the striking **far-futuristic fantasy** "The Red Brain" (1927), whose **apocalyptic** sequel, "On the Threshold of Eternity" (1937) was appended to it in the collection *The Eye and the Finger* (1944). His work for the sf **pulps** was exceptional for its cavalier extravagance, which treated all imaginative limits with calculated disrespect; "Colossus" (1934), which casually inverts the premise of **microcosmic romance**, is typical. Much of it was reprinted in *Strange Harvest* (1965) before the definitive *Colossus: The Collected Science Fiction of Donald Wandrei* (1989) was compiled. *Frost* (2000) collects 1930s pulp stories featuring the eponymous scientific detective. His **Cthulhu Mythos** novel *The Web of Easter Island* (1948) emphasizes the sf aspects of the framework.

**WATERLOO, STANLEY (1846–1913).** U.S. writer whose prehistoric romance *The Story of Ab* (1897) and story of serial reincarnation *A Son of the Ages* (1914) influenced similar works by **Jack London** strongly enough to prompt talk of plagiarism, although—like Waterloo's relatively mild **future war** story *Armageddon* (1898)—they are themselves derivative of British models.

**WATKINS, WILLIAM JON (1942– ).** U.S. writer whose first venture into **sf**, written with Gene Snyder, was the **ecocatastrophe** story *Ecodeath* (1972); the pair subsequently **collaborated** on the **political fantasy** *The Litany of Sh'reev* (1976). *Clickwhistle* (1973) is about communication between humans and dolphins. *The God Machine* (1973) is an eccentric **miniaturization** fantasy. *What Rough Beast* (1980) is a messianic fantasy that anticipates the advent of **cyberpunk.**

*The Centrifugal Rickshaw Dancer* (1985) and its sequel *Going to See the End of the Sky* (1986) are hectic futuristic thrillers. *The Last Deathship off Antares* (1989) introduces elements of political fantasy into a story about a rebellion on a prison ship. In *Cosmic Thunder* (1996) transparent **aliens** ameliorate Earth's millenarian panic.

**WATSON, IAN (1943– ).** British writer who began publishing **sf** in 1969. His first novel, *The Embedding* (1973), was a sophisticated application of linguistic science and the philosophy of language to issues of communication between different human cultures and **alien** visitors. *The Jonah Kit* (1975) extrapolated the theme to take aboard communication with whales and cosmological speculations. *Orgasmachine* (1976 in French), an account of a factory producing customized female **androids**, never found an English-language publisher. *The Martian Inca* (1977) was the first of several novels in which the evolution of the human mind obtains an artificial boost; *Alien Embassy* (1977), *Miracle Visitors* (1978), *God's World* (1979), and *The Gardens of Delight* (1980) carried the theme forward in increasingly phantasmagoric fashion. In *Under Heaven's Bridge* (1981), written with **Michael Bishop**, the latter's anthropological interests serve as a calming influence. The **hybrid metaphysical fantasy** *Deathhunter* (1981) demonstrated Watson's increasing willingness to trifle with bizarre ideas for their own sake—a tendency already demonstrated by the inventive short fiction collected in *The Very Slow Time Machine* (1979) and *Sunstroke* (1982).

The challenging qualities of Watson's work were moderated as the 1980s progressed, although *Chekhov's Journey* (1983), a thriller about the Tunguska explosion, and the trilogy of **planetary romances** comprising *The Book of the River* (1984), *The Book of the Stars* (1984), and *The Book of Being* (1985) retain a buoyant exoticism. *Converts* (1984) and *Queenmagic, Kingmagic* (1986) are ineffectually quirky, but the **virtual reality** story *Whores of Babylon* (1988) and the folkloristic **transfiguration** *The Fire Worm* (1988) are more robust and *The Flies of Memory* (1990) is an enterprising philosophical fantasy. He dabbled in supernatural **horror** fiction and published two **technothrillers**—*Hard Questions* (1996) and *Oracle* (1997)—but retained a more ambitious sf element in a hybrid transfiguration of the *Kalevala* issued in two volumes as *Lucky's Harvest*

(1993) and *The Fallen Moon* (1994). Watson's later short story collections—*Slow Birds* (1985), *Evil Water* (1987), *Salvage Rites* (1989), *Stalin's Teardrops* (1991), *The Coming of Vertumnus* (1994), and *The Great Escape* (2002)—continued to feature sf stories alongside more varied **fabulations**.

**WATTS, PETER (1958– ). Canadian** writer who began publishing **sf** in 1990 with an intense psychological drama set in a seabed habitat, subsequently expanded into the novel *Starfish* (1999); the sequel *Maelstrom* (2001) tracks the aftermath of its climactic disaster. *Ten Monkeys, Ten Minutes* (2001) collects his short fiction.

**WEAVER, MICHAEL D. (1961–1998).** U.S. writer who began publishing **sf** with the **cyberpunk** thriller *Mercedes Nights* (1987), in which the eponymous clones of a movie star are retailed as sex slaves. *My Father Immortal* (1989) is a meditative study of an exodus from a devastated Earth. *A Second Infinity* (1996) complements that theme by returning its protagonist from a **far-future Utopia** to the same **apocalyptic** scenario.

**WEBB, SHARON (1936– ).** U.S. writer who began publishing **sf** in 1964, initially signing herself Ron Webb. She drew on personal experience in a **series** of stories about a starfaring nurse collected as *The Adventures of Terra Tarkington* (1985). The trilogy comprising the **mosaic** *Earthchild* (1982), *Earth Song* (1983), and *Ram Song* (1984) describes difficult social and psychological adjustments to the advent of problematic technologies of longevity. There is a fugitive sf element in one of her medical **technothrillers**, *The Halflife* (1989).

**WEBER, DAVID (1952– ).** U.S. writer whose first venture into **military space opera** was a **collaboration** with Steve White, *Insurrection* (1990). After publishing the first of the trilogy comprising *Mutineers' Moon* (1991), *The Armageddon Inheritance* (1993), and *Heirs of Empire* (1996), he launched a long **series** of **transfigurations** of C. S. Forester's Hornblower novels, featuring Honor Harrington, with *On Basilisk Station* (1993); it continued with *The Honor of the Queen* (1993), *The Short Victorious War* (1994), *Fields of Dishonor* (1994), *Flag in Exile* (1995), *Honor among Enemies* (1996), *In Enemy Hands*

(1997), *Echoes of Honor* (1998), *Ashes of Victory* (1999), and *War of Honor* (2000). His other collaborations with White include *Crusade* (1992), *In Death Ground* (1977), and *The Shiva Option* (2002); his other solo sf novels include *Path of the Fury* (1992) and *Empire from the Ashes* (2003).

**WEINBAUM, STANLEY G. (1902–1935).** U.S. writer who dabbled in other genres before publishing the groundbreaking "A Martian Odyssey" (1934). He rapidly established a reputation for inventive work, many of his stories bringing a new ecological sensibility to such depictions of **alien** life as "The Lotus Eaters," "The Mad Moon," "Flight on Titan," and "Parasite Planet" (all 1935). He had already written a Jekyll-and-Hyde **horror-sf** story that had not sold—it eventually appeared as *The Dark Other* (1950)—and he made two similarly unsuccessful attempts to write a futuristic love story, whose two posthumously published (1936 and 1939) versions were eventually **fixed up** as *The Black Flame* (1948; restored text of second version only, 1995). Nor did his third and best novel—a painstaking account of a **superman** growing up as a "feral child" in human society, *The New Adam* (1939)—sell before his premature death. **Sam Moskowitz** assembled all his short fiction in *A Martian Odyssey and Other Science Fiction Tales* (1975).

***WEIRD TALES.*** U.S. **pulp magazine** founded in 1923, which folded a year later but was swiftly resuscitated under the editorship of Farnsworth Wright and the pervasive influence of **H. P. Lovecraft**, whose circle of correspondents adopted the magazine as the principal vehicle for their literary experiments. *Weird Tales* published a good deal of **sf** in the late 1920s, including early **space operas** by **Edmond Hamilton**, but surrendered the field thereafter to the specialist magazines, with the exception of the sf elements embedded in Lovecraftian fiction. The magazine also provided a home to the sword-and-sorcery fiction of Robert E. Howard, which remained a significant annex to pulp sf until its market situation was spectacularly transformed in the 1970s. Several sf writers, including **Jack Williamson** and **David Keller** as well as Hamilton, found *Weird Tales* a congenial secondary market, and some of the more enterprising writers who started off in its pages—including **Fritz Leiber** and **C. L. Moore**—found that ***Un-***

***known*** and the sf pulps offered more scope to their talents; it retained a sufficiently close association with pulp sf to be included in the interests and activities of the sf community. *Weird Tales* became markedly less innovative after 1937, when both Howard and Lovecraft died, **Clark Ashton Smith** having already completed his prolific phase; Dorothy McIlwraith—who succeeded Farnsworth Wright in 1939—presided over a long and gradual twilight until it folded in 1954. Such affection was attached to the name in the fan community, however, that *Weird Tales* was resurrected continually in the 1970s, 1980s, and 1990s before the publishers of its sixth incarnation, George Scithers and Darrell Schweitzer, resuscitated it yet again under the aegis of **DNA Publications** in 1998.

**WELLMAN, MANLY WADE (1903–1986).** Angola-born U.S. writer in several genres, most notable for his **horror** fiction and supernatural Americana. He first ventured into the **sf pulps** in 1931, his most notable contributions being the **alien** invasion story "Nuisance Value" (1938, book 1959 as *The Dark Destroyers*); *Giants from Eternity* (1939, book 1959), in which geniuses from various eras are recruited to confront an **apocalyptic** threat; and the **timeslip romance** *Twice in Time* (1940, book 1957). His later work included a proto-**steampunk mosaic** account of *Sherlock Holmes's War of the Worlds* (1975) written in **collaboration** with his son Wade.

**WELLS, H. G. (1866–1946).** British writer who published "The Chronic Argonauts" (1988) in his own *Science Schools Journal* while working as a teacher, extrapolating ideas about future evolution he had absorbed from Charles Darwin's popularizer Thomas Henry Huxley. He published **speculative nonfiction** in the popular magazines that burst forth in some profusion in the early 1890s, including a classic essay on "The Man of the Year Million" (1893), and soon began reembodying his ideas in fiction, producing two more serial versions of "The Chronic Argonauts" before it appeared in book form as *The Time Machine: An Invention* (1895), becoming a paradigm example of **scientific romance**—which was and still is describable as "Wellsian fiction."

Wells was inevitably compared with **Jules Verne** on the one hand, and **George Griffith** on the other, but the exploratory fervor of his imagination was far greater than either, as he demonstrated in a remarkable sequence of works extrapolating premises drawn from his speculative nonfiction with unprecedented boldness and skill. *The Island of Dr. Moreau* (1896) is an allegorical **satire** featuring animals surgically gifted with human form, partly inspired by Victor Hugo's *L'homme qui rit*. *The Invisible Man: A Grotesque Romance* (1897) is a satirical thriller. *The War of the Worlds* (1898), which introduced **alien** beings as competitors in a universal struggle for existence, determined to take possession of Earth when the exhausted biosphere of **Mars** can no longer support them, set a precedent that was to loom large over 20th-century Anglo-American **sf**. *When the Sleeper Wakes* (1899; rev. *The Sleeper Awakes*, 1910) is a messianic fantasy of future revolution against oppressive capitalism. Alongside these works he published many shorter scientific romances, collected with a few items in other genres in *The Stolen Bacillus, and Other Incidents* (1895), *The Plattner Story, and Others* (1897), and *Tales of Space and Time* (1900).

Unfortunately, Wells's output of innovative work did not long survive the turn of the century. *Anticipations of the Reaction of Mechanical and Human Progress upon Human Life and Thought* (1901) pioneered the genre of speculative nonfiction nowadays called **futurology**, while *The First Men in the Moon* (1901) employs **antigravity** as a facilitating device complementary to the **time machine**, which could have opened up all of space as well as all of time had Wells cared to make further use of them. Instead, he decided to submit his imaginative power to the yoke of politically guided **prophecy** after writing an essay on *The Discovery of the Future* (1902) and persuading himself, fatally, that the future was indeed "discoverable." He was also moved by the knowledge that he would only acquire literary respectability by writing books whose didacticism was more muted and that paid more attention to characterization—which he determinedly set out to do, although he continued to dispute with Henry James as to whether the literary world was large enough to admit "novels of ideas" as well as "novels of character." Wells conceded the point by desertion, but he was probably right to judge that he had no chance of winning, and that **speculative fiction** was doomed to suffer the contempt of literary snobs no matter what it might achieve in its own terms. With a convert's zeal, he insisted on subsuming his own scientific romances within the broader category of "Fantastic and Imaginative Romances" when he listed his publications, and when he eventually condescended to publish an omnibus of *The Scientific Romances of H. G. Wells* (1933) his introduction was vitriolically dismissive of his earlier ambitions.

*The Food of the Gods and How It Came to Earth* (1904) begins as scientific romance but turns into propaganda for **Utopian** socialism. *A Modern Utopia* (1905) and *In the Days of the Comet* (1906) deploy their facilitating devices with apologetic contempt, abandoning all the devices of plausibility so carefully invoked in the scientific romances. "The Land Ironclads" (1903), *The War in the Air* (1908), and *The World Set Free* (1914) all made innovative contributions to the **future war** subgenre, although the atypical horrific attitude adopted by the earlier examples gave way to greater enthusiasm as Wells decided that socialist reconstruction would not begin in earnest until the old order had been obliterated—a prospect he revisited with increasing relish in his subsequent Utopian exercises, most notably *Men Like Gods* (1923) and *The Shape of Things to Come* (1933). He wrote a number of "sarcastic fantasies" in the latter part of his career, but the objects of their sarcasm include the methods of exploratory speculation that he had pioneered, and the ideative produce thereof, which are perversely parodied in *The Autocracy of Mr. Parham* (1930), *The Croquet Player* (1936), *The Camford Visitation* (1937), and *Star Begotten: A Biological Fantasia* (1937). Even so, Wells remained the idol of 20th-century scientific romance and sf—and rightly so, given the measure of his achievements in the first seven years of his career. No other writer was ever so spectacularly innovative or so ingenious in providing innovations with a fine gloss of plausibility.

**WESTERFELD, SCOTT (?– ).** U.S. writer whose first **sf** publication was *Polymorph* (1997), a near-future thriller featuring shape-shifters. *Fine Prey* (1998) is a similar thriller in which humans adopt **alien** ways. *Evolution's Darling* (2000) is an **existentialist fantasy** about love and art appreciation featuring liberated **artificial intelligences** in new bodies. In the couplet comprising *The Risen Empire* and *The Killing of Worlds* (both 2003), a **galactic empire** under threat from religiously inclined **cyborgs** explodes into hectic violence.

**WHITE, JAMES (1928–1999).** British writer born and resident in Ulster, who began publishing **sf** in 1953. After producing the subtle invasion story "Tourist Planet" (1956)—to whose book version, *The Secret Visitors* (1957), he added a violent ending at the insistence of the publisher—he devoted much of his effort to ingenious accounts of activities at Sector General, a hospital catering to a wide variety of species with radically different life-support needs. The medical problems soon broadened out to encompass the activities of the military corps responsible for making new **first contacts** and settling interspecific disputes; their responsibility to go to extreme lengths in order to avoid and ameliorate violence generated the first explicitly pacifist **space opera series**, whose later volumes staunchly maintain that ideological stance, in stark contrast to the parallel tradition of American **military sf.** The series comprises the **mosaics** *Hospital Station* (1962), *Star Surgeon* (1963), *Major Operation* (1971), *Ambulance Ship* (1979), and *Sector General* (1983), and the novels *Star Healer* (1985), *Code Blue—Emergency* (1987), *The Genocidal Healer* (1992), *The Galactic Gourmet* (1996), *Final Diagnosis* (1997), *Mind Changer* (1998), and *Double Contact* (1999).

Although it is very varied, much of White's other sf is similarly distinguished by a strict adherence to the Hippocratic principle that one should do one's utmost to ensure that one's actions do no harm. *Second Ending* (1962) is an elegiac **far-futuristic fantasy.** *Open Prison* (1965) is a stirring drama of near-impossible escape. *The Watch Below* (1966) is a meticulous comparison of two cultures enduring stressful imprisonment. *All Judgment Fled* (1968) and *Federation World* (1988) are accounts of problematic first contacts. *Tomorrow Is Too Far* (1971) is a thriller embodying a **conceptual breakthrough.** *The Dream Millennium* (1974) is a thoughtful **visionary fantasy** about an Exodus from a war-ruined Earth. The uncharacteristically **dystopian** *Underkill* (1979) conscientiously confronts possibilities set aside by the Sector General stories. *The Silent Stars Go By* (1991) is a remarkable **alternative history** in which technological progress moves more rapidly than it did in our world. White's short fiction is sampled in *Deadly Litter* (1964), *The Aliens among Us* (1969), and *Future Past* (1982).

**WHITE, TED (1938– ).** U.S. writer and editor who began publishing **sf** in 1963 with a story written in **collaboration** with **Marion Zimmer Bradley**, which became part of the **mosaic** *Phoenix Prime*

(1966), the first of a **series** of **Burroughsian planetary romances.** White also wrote in collaboration with **Terry Carr**, with whom he produced *Invasion from 2500* (1964) as Norman Edwards; Dave van Arnam, with whom he produced the **parallel worlds** story *Sideslip* (1968); and **David Bischoff**, with whom he wrote *Forbidden World* (1978). His most notable solo efforts are the **dimensional fantasy** *The Jewels of Elsewhen* (1967) and *By Furies Possessed* (1980), an ideological riposte to the paranoid aspects of **Robert A. Heinlein's** *The Puppet Masters*. White was assistant editor of ***The Magazine of Fantasy & Science Fiction*** (1963–1968) before taking over ***Amazing Stories*** and *Fantastic* from 1969–1978, gradually restoring them as significant and enterprising vehicles for new work after some years of cannibalizing their own heritage.

**WILDER, CHERRY (1930–2002).** Pseudonym of New Zealand-born writer Cherry Barbara Lockett Grimm, who wrote **poetry** and other kinds of fiction before her first venture into **sf** in 1974. Most of her work tracks the unfolding of problematic human/**alien** relationships, as in the juvenile trilogy comprising *The Luck of Brin's Five* (1977), *The Nearest Fire* (1980), and *The Tapestry Warriors* (1983) and the **planetary romance** couplet comprising *Second Nature* (1982) and *Signs of Life* (1996). Her carefully wrought short fiction, much of it **hybridizing** sf and mythical fantasy, is sampled in *Dealers in Light and Darkness* (1995).

**WILHELM, KATE (1928– ).** U.S. writer who began publishing **sf** in 1957. Her early work is collected in *The Mile-Long Spaceship* (1963, aka *Andover and the Android*). She became increasingly adventurous as her participation in the **Milford Writers' Conference** (where she met her second husband, **Damon Knight**) fuelled her stylistic ambitions. Her subsequent **fabulations** made ingeniously subtle use of sf motifs, as displayed in the collections *The Downstairs Room and Other Speculative Fiction* (1968), *Abyss: Two Novellas* (1971), *The Infinity Box* (1971), *Somerset Dreams* (1978), *Listen, Listen* (1981), *Children of the Wind* (1989), and *And the Angels Sing* (1992). Many of her novels are mysteries, but she used sf motifs in *The Clone* (1965, with **Theodore L. Thomas**), *The Killer Thing* (1967, aka *The Killing Thing*), *The Nevermore Affair* (1966), *Let the Fire Fall* (1969) and *The Year of the Cloud* (1970, with Thomas). The exuberant **existentialist fantasy** *Margaret and I* (1971) and the tense futuristic thriller *City of Cain* (1974) are marginal. *The Clewiston Test* (1976) is one of the genre's most compelling descriptions of scientists at work. The **mosaic** *Where Late the Sweet Birds Sang* (1976) is a **postholocaust fantasy** in which the future of humankind rests precariously on the fortunes of several groups of clones. *Juniper Time* (1979) is a painstaking **ecocatastrophic** fantasy. Wilhelm's subsequent sf novels describe the fallout from various unorthodox experiments; *A Sense of Shadow* and *Welcome, Chaos* (1983) are primarily existentialist fantasies, whereas *Huysman's Pets* (1986) and *Crazy Time* (1988) are comedies.

**WILLIAMS, LIZ (1965– ).** British writer who began publishing **sf** in 1997. *The Ghost Sister* (2001) tracks the exploits of an emissary on a world whose ecosphere is precariously balanced. *Empire of Bones* (2002) is a **political fantasy** set in India in the wake of the discovery that Earth was seeded with human life from a world called Rasasatra. *The Poison Master* (2003) is a **hybrid science-fantasy** in which an alchemist on the planet Latent Emanation sets out to liberate humankind from the Lord of the Night. *Nine Layers of Sky* (2003) is a **metaphysical fantasy** set in the 21st-century remnants of the Soviet Union.

**WILLIAMS, PAUL (1948– ).** U.S. editor and writer most notable as the founder of the groundbreaking rock music magazine *Crawdaddy*. His contributions to **sf** began when he was appointed **Philip K. Dick's** literary executor; he wrote *Only Apparently Real: The World of Philip K. Dick* (1986) and skillfully annotated the five-volume set of Dick's complete short fiction. He then performed the same useful service for the more extensive set of volumes collecting **Theodore Sturgeon's** short fiction.

**WILLIAMS, SEAN (1967– ). Australian** writer who began publishing **sf** in 1991; three early stories were collected in *Doorway to Eternity* (1995). *Metal Fatigue* (1996) is a thriller set in a beleaguered city in a war-torn United States. *The Resurrected Man* (1998) is a murder mystery in which **matter transmitters** function as duplicators. With Shane Dix he wrote the Evergence trilogy of **space operas** comprising *The Prodigal Sun* (1999; based on *The Unknown Soldier*, 1995), *The Dying Light* (2000), and *A Dark Imbalance* (2001). In the **series** begun with *Echoes of Earth* (2002) and *Orphans of Earth* (2003) the starship *Frank Tipler*, crewed by "engrams," encounters various exotic **alien** species.

**WILLIAMS, TAD (1957– ).** U.S. writer of best-selling fantasies. The four-volume **hybrid** epic *Otherland*, comprising *City of Golden Shadow* (1996), *River of Blue Fire* (1998), *Mountain of Black Glass* (1999), and *Sea of Silver Light* (2001), is about a "private **multiverse**" constructed in **virtual reality.**

**WILLIAMS, WALTER JON (1953– ).** U.S. writer who worked in other genres before venturing into **sf** with *Ambassador of Progress* (1984), an account of cultural resurgence. Williams's admiration for the works of **Roger Zelazny** is very evident in *Knight Moves* (1985) and *Hardwired* (1986), the latter novel's homage to *Damnation Alley* continuing in the sequels *Voice of the Whirlwind* (1987) and *Solip:system* (1989), whose **cyberpunk** inclusions were isolated for **extrapolation** in a very different setting in *Angel Station* (1989). The last-named also continues trends initiated in the picaresque space adventures *The Crown Jewels* (1987) and *House of Shards* (1988). *Days of Atonement* (1991) is a near-future thriller. *Elegy for Angels and Dogs* (1990) is a sequel to Zelazny's "The Graveyard Heart," and *Aristoi* (1992) similarly returns to a more distant Zelaznyesque future. *Metropolitan* (1995) is a **hybrid** account of a world-city whose technology is powered by geomancy; *City on Fire* (1997) is a sequel. *Rock of Ages* (1995) is another picaresque fantasy. *The Praxis* (2002) launched a **far-futuristic space opera series**. Williams's short fiction is sampled in *Facets* (1990) and *Frankensteins and Foreign Devils* (1998).

**WILLIAMSON, JACK (1908– ).** U.S. writer who began publishing **sf** in 1928 and became the only writer of that vintage to continue his career into the 21st century. His early work, including the novellas "The Alien Intelligence" (1929) and "The Moon Era" (1932), shows the strong influence of **A. Merritt.** He **collaborated** occasionally with **Miles J. Breuer.** The **series** comprising *The Legion of Space* (1934; rev. book, 1947), "The Cometeers" (1936; combined with

"One against the Legion," 1939 in *The Cometeers*, 1950)—were significant early **space operas**, whose second element introduced the term **android** to genre sf. "The Legion of Time" (1938) pioneered the kind of **alternative history** story in which potential futures fight for the privilege of actuality.

Williamson adapted his work to **John Campbell's** requirements by producing the **hybrid** *Darker Than You Think* (1940) for ***Unknown*** and the series comprising the **mosaic** *Seetee Ship* (1942–1943, rev. book 1951) and the novel *Seetee Shock* (1949, book 1950), bylined Will Stewart—which introduced the concept of **terraforming** and spawned the **comic** strip *Beyond Mars*—for ***Astounding.*** The classic ***conte philosophique*** "With Folded Hands" (1947), a skeptical response to **Isaac Asimov's robot** stories, was fused with its sequel ". . . And Searching Mind" (1948)—not entirely to their advantage—as *The Humanoids* (1950). "The Equalizer" (1947) is another sophisticated *conte philosophique*. *Dragon's Island* (1951), which introduced the term **genetic engineering** to genre sf, was probably the first sf story in which spaceships grow on trees.

Much of Williamson's work in the 1950s—when he completed a B.A. in English and an M.A. thesis on "A Study of the Sense of Prophecy in Modern Science Fiction"—was done in collaboration, including the space opera *Star Bridge* (1955 with **James Gunn).** He struck up a productive relationship with **Frederik Pohl**, with whom he wrote the juvenile trilogy comprising *Undersea Quest* (1954), *Undersea Fleet* (1956), and *Undersea City* (1958); they went on to write the Starchild trilogy (1964–1969), the Cuckoo series (1975–1983), the **disaster novel** *Land's End* (1988), and the cosmological fantasy *The Singers of Time* (1991). His solo works of the period included the mosaics *The Trial of Terra* (1962), *The Power of Blackness* (1976), and *Brother to Demons, Brother to Gods* (1979) and the novels *Bright New Universe* (1967) and *The Moon Children* (1972).

Williamson rested on past laurels in producing the belated sequels *The Humanoid Touch* (1980) and *The Queen of the Legion* (1983) but found new impetus when he followed the **genetic engineering** fantasy *Manseed* (1983) with the sophisticated space opera *Lifeburst* (1984) and the **conceptual breakthrough** thriller *Firechild* (1986). *Beachhead* (1992) describes an expedition to **Mars.** *Demon Moon* (1994) is a cleverly constructed hybrid. In *The Black Sun* (1997) space colonists visit a dead star. *The Silicon Dagger* (1999) is a near-futuristic thriller. *Terraforming Earth* (2001) is an elegiac fantasy. A multivolume edition of Williamson's complete short fiction commenced with *The Metal Man and Others* (1999), *Wolves of Darkness* (1999), *Wizard's Isle* (2000), and *Spider Island* (2002).

**WILLIS, CONNIE (1945– ).** U.S. writer who published an **sf** story in 1971 but returned to the field in 1978 to produce the fervent short fiction collected in *Fire Watch* (1985)—whose 1982 title story, describing a **time-traveling** historian's educational field trip to the London Blitz, set a pattern reiterated in *Doomsday Book* (1992), where the object of the enquiry is the Black Death. Her first novel, *Water Witch* (1982), written in **collaboration** with **Cynthia Felice**, was a lighthearted **planetary romance** whose playfulness was reproduced in the further collaborations *Light Raid* (1989) and *Promised Land* (1997). *Lincoln's Dreams* (1987) is another intense historical fantasy, focusing on the American Civil War. *Uncharted Territory* (1994) is a relatively slight account of problematic relationships and **alien** encounters. *Remake* (1994) follows the conscience-stricken exploits of a computer technician hired to eliminate all trace of smoking from archived movies. *Bellwether* (1996) is a comedy about **prediction** and chaos theory. *To Say Nothing of the Dog* (1998) is a comedy in which strayed time-travelers end up in Victorian London. *Passage* (2001) is about near-death experiences. More short sf is collected in *Impossible Things* (1993). *Miracle and Other Christmas Stories* (1999) includes two sf stories.

**WILSON, F. PAUL (1946– ).** U.S. writer who began publishing **sf** in 1971. His principal work in the genre is a **series** of **existentialist fantasies** cast as futuristic thrillers, whose superhuman hero repeatedly saves the solar system; its book versions are *Healer* (1976), *Wheels within Wheels* (1978), *An Enemy of the State* (1980), and the collection *The Tery* (1990). His subsequent works were mostly thrillers and supernatural **horror** stories, but *Mirage* (1996) and *Masque* (1998), both cowritten with Matthew J. Costello, have elements of existentialist fantasy and the **mosaic** *Sims* (2003) is a near-future thriller in which **genetically engineered** chimpanzees are used as cheap labor.

**WILSON, RICHARD (1920–1987).** U.S. writer who was a member of the **Futurians** in the 1930s and began publishing **sf** in 1940. Like other members of the group he published mildly **satirical** comedies in the 1950s magazines, the best of his work being collected in *Those Idiots from Earth* (1957) and *Time out for Tomorrow* (1962). His three novels, *The Girls from Planet 5* (1955), *And Then the Town Took Off* (1960), and *30-Day Wonder* (1960) offer wryly laid-back accounts of eccentric **alien** invasions. His output became sparse thereafter; his later short fiction, including "Mother to the World" (1968) and *The Kid from Ozone Park & Other Stories* (1987), is more sentimentally inclined.

**WILSON, ROBERT ANTON (1932– ).** U.S. writer who made a considerable impact with *Illuminatus!* a three-decker conspiracy fantasy—comprising *The Eye in the Pyramid*, *The Golden Apple*, and *Leviathan* (1975; omnibus 1984)—written with Robert Shea, which moves slowly toward a threatened near-future **apocalypse.** Wilson wrote several solo sequels in various genres, whose **sf** elements—save for the co-option of the **Cthulhu Mythos**—are muted, although they all participate in the author's mission to promote various **pseudoscientific** theses by means of "guerrilla ontology." The expansion of *The Sex Magician* (1974) into the *Schrödinger's Cat* trilogy—comprising *The Universe Next Door* (1979), *The Trick Top Hat* (1980), and *The Homing Pigeons* (1981)—makes much of analogies between the sense-defying movements of its plot and the transactions of subatomic particles. *Reality Is What You Can Get Away With: A Screenplay* (1992) **satirizes** the orthodoxies of sf.

**WILSON, ROBERT CHARLES (1953– ).** U.S.-born writer resident in **Canada** since 1962, who began publishing **sf** in 1974. His novels, most of which are **portal fantasies**, are remarkably various and ingenious in designing and connecting exotic **parallel worlds.** *A Hidden Place* (1986) is a dexterous **hybridization** of sf and fairy mythology. In *Memory Wire* (1987) contact with a displaced fragment of a **cyberpunk** near future is maintained by means of "oneiroliths." *Gypsies* (1989) is a **multiversal Odyssean fantasy.** In *The Divide* (1990) different personalities develop in disconnected brain hemispheres. *A Bridge of Years* (1991) moves back and forth between 1991 and 1961 in the context of shifting **alternative histories.** *The Harvest* (1993) is an extended Faustian ***conte philosophique*** in which **aliens** offer to fulfill human ambitions. In *Mysterium* (1994) a small town is catapulted into a dark alternative history. *Darwinia* (1998) repeats the motif on a continental scale, exploring more distant reaches of alternativity. *Bios* (1999) describes the problematic exploration of a seemingly idyllic world whose biochemistry is toxic to humans. In *The Chronoliths* (2001) a limited technology of **time travel** becomes the basis of a bold experiment in self-fulfilling **prophecy**. In *Blind Lake* (2003) a distant and possibly nonexistent alien culture is observed through an intelligent telescope. Wilson's short sf is sampled in *The Perseids and Other Stories* (2000).

**WILSON, ROBIN SCOTT (1928– ).** U.S. scholar who published a few **sf** stories as Robin Scott, beginning in 1970, but made a more significant contribution to the genre as the founder of the **Clarion** workshop in 1968. He edited three **anthologies** (1971–1973) featuring its early graduates and two anthologies-cum-writing-guides: *Those Who Can: A Science Fiction Reader* (1973) and *Paragons: Twelve Science Fiction Writers Ply Their Craft* (1996).

**WILSON, WILLIAM (?–?).** Scottish **poet** who coined the term "**science-fiction**" in *A Little Earnest Book upon a Great Old Subject* (1851), which devotes two chapters to "The Poetry of Science," as defined by **Robert Hunt.** The only example of "science-fiction" he cites is *The Poor Artist* (1850) by Richard Henry Horne, a romantic fantasy in which an impoverished artist impresses the object of his love with a series of sketches of a coin as viewed through the eyes of seven very various observers.

**WINGROVE, DAVID (1954– ).** British writer whose editorial ventures included 11 issues of the BSFA journal *Vector* and the eccentrically designed reference work *The Science Fiction Source Book* (1984). He assisted **Brian Aldiss** in updating his history *Billion Year Spree* for reissue as *Trillion Year Spree* (1986). His own **sf** mostly consists of an eight-volume epic, *Chung Kuo*, set in a future dominated by a globalized and sclerotized Chinese culture, comprising *The Middle Kingdom* (1989), *The Broken Wheel* (1990), *The White Mountain*

(1991), *The Stone Within* (1992), *Beneath the Tree of Heaven* (1993), *White Moon, Red Dragon* (1994), *Days of Bitter Strength* (1995), and *The Marriage of the Living Dark* (1997).

**WOLFE, GENE (1931– ).** U.S. writer in several genres who began publishing **fabulations** employing **sf** motifs in 1967. His early work, most of which appeared in **Damon Knight's** *Orbit*, was variously **ambiguous**, **hybrid**, and **chimerical**, establishing an unusually flexible and innately unsettled literary terrain whose experience some readers find exhilarating and others merely confusing, though none doubts its originality and significance. The multilayered and stubbornly cryptic **mosaic planetary romance** *The Fifth Head of Cerberus* (1972) and the four stories gathered into *The Wolfe Archipelago* (1983)—including "The Island of Doctor Death and Other Stories" (1970), which also featured in *The Island of Doctor Death and Other Stories and Other Stories*, 1980)—illustrate the thematic games to which he seems addicted. *Operation ARES* (1970), his only narrowly defined sf novel, was apprentice work; the **Odyssean time-travel** fantasy *Free Live Free* (1984) and the elaborate **portal fantasy** *There Are Doors* (1989) are more typical of his alchemical method. Wolfe began an extensive **series** of sophisticated **far-futuristic fantasies**—which became the most prominent modern landmark of that subgenre—with the Book of the New Sun, comprising *The Shadow of the Torturer* (1980), *The Claw of the Conciliator* (1981), *The Sword of the Lictor* (1982), and *The Citadel of the Autarch* (1983), subsequently adding several short stories, mock explanatory essays, and a sequel, *The Urth of the New Sun* (1987), before extrapolating its themes in two further multivolume novels, one comprising *Nightside the Long Sun* (1993), *Lake of the Long Sun* (1994), *Caldé of the Long Sun* (1994), and *Exodus from the Long Sun* (1996), and the other *On Blue's Waters* (1999), *In Green's Jungles* (2000), and *Return to the Whorl* (2001). His other short story collections include *Gene Wolfe's Book of Days* (1981) and *Endangered Species* (1989).

**WOLLHEIM, DONALD A. (1914–1990).** U.S. editor who became a very active participant in 1930s **fandom** and a key member of the **Futurians.** He produced numerous **fanzines** and founded a Fantasy Amateur Press Association (FAPA). He began publishing **sf** professionally in 1934 but his production was always sparse, his principal ambition being to work as an editor. In 1941 he persuaded a **pulp** publisher to produce *Cosmic Stories* and *Stirring Science Stories*, promising to edit them without a supportive budget, although they soon folded. He produced the first **paperback** showcase **anthology**, *The Pocket Book of Science Fiction* (1943), and went to work after World War II for the pulp-descended paperback company Avon, persuading them to produce two anthology **series**, the *Avon Fantasy Reader* and the *Avon Science Fiction Reader*, as well as two short-lived pulp magazines. He moved to Ace Books in 1952, initially taking charge of several genre lines in order to have the privilege of developing the sf line, which became a central element of the new marketplace.

Although Wollheim strongly favored action-adventure sf, especially series of **space operas** and **planetary romances**, his editorial policy was sufficiently flexible to accommodate experimental work by such writers as **Philip K. Dick**, **Samuel R. Delany**, and **Ursula K. le Guin**, and he became a vital conduit into the U.S. market for many British writers, including **John Brunner** and **Barrington J. Bayley.** He also reprinted a great deal of pulp sf, making the history of the genre clearly manifest to readers of the 1960s and 1970s. Wollheim never had the kind of formative vision that made **John Campbell** so important as an editor—when Wollheim founded an up-market line of "Ace Specials," he handed editorial responsibility to **Terry Carr**—but he did have a profound affection for the genre and a missionary zeal that made him a similarly important force in its promotion. His nebulous vision of the genre was summarized in *The Universe Makers* (1971); in 1972 he founded **DAW Books** to continue his mission.

Much of Wollheim's own sf was pseudonymous, most of his novels for adults—most notably *Across Time* (1957), *Edge of Time* (1958), and *Destiny's Orbit* (1962)—being bylined David Grinnell. He used his own name on numerous juveniles, including the Mike Mars series (8 vols., 1961–1964) and collections of his short work, most notably *Two Dozen Dragon Eggs* (1969).

**WOLVERTON, DAVE (1957– ).** U.S. writer who began publishing **sf** in 1985. A 1987 novella was expanded into *On My Way to Paradise*

(1989), in which mercenaries are hired to defend an extraterrestrial colony. The couplet comprising *Serpent Catch* (1991) and *Path of the Hero* (1993) describes the collapse of a patchwork experiment in **terraforming** and prehistoric reconstruction. A trilogy of **space operas** featuring insectile **aliens** comprises *The Golden Queen* (1994), *Beyond the Gate* (1995), and *Lords of the Seventh Swarm* (1997).

**WOMACK, JACK (1956– ).** U.S. writer whose loosely linked novels, launched with *Ambient* (1987), became prototype post-**cyberpunk** thrillers, their **sf** elements integrated into an ornately **decadent** backcloth that serves as a setting for fervent **political fantasies** and psychodramas. *Terraplane* (1988) complicates the scenario with an **alternative history.** *Heathern* (1990) introduces an enigmatic messiah to an earlier point in the **future history** (which was soon overtaken by actual history). *Elvissey* (1993) further complicates the **time-twisting** element of the **series**. *Random Acts of Senseless Violence* (1993) fills in a chronological gap between *Heathern* and *Ambient*. In the 1968-set *Going, Going, Gone* (2000) a psychotropic drugs tester saves New York.

***WONDER STORIES*.** The central element in a group of **pulp magazines** founded by **Hugo Gernsback** after he lost control of ***Amazing Stories***. Initially launched in 1929 as two monthly magazines, *Air Wonder Stories* and *Science Wonder Stories*, *Wonder Stories* was the result of their amalgamation in 1930, by which time it already had a companion *Wonder Stories Quarterly*. The quarterly died with the Stellar Publishing Company Gernsback had established to contain the group in 1933, but *Wonder Stories* continued under the imprint of Continental Publications until 1936, when Gernsback sold it as a going concern to Better Publications—who changed its title to *Thrilling Wonder Stories* before adding new companions, including ***Startling Stories*.** The actual editorial work for Stellar was done by David Lasser, who was replaced at Continental by **Charles Hornig**. Desperate to outcompete his old brainchild, Gernsback tried to cultivate **fandom** by founding the Science Fiction League, but the more powerful competition provided by ***Astounding***—which paid far more for contributions, although it would not entertain the didactic aspirations of Gernsbackian **sf**—reduced his editors' options considerably. Even so, the *Wonder* group became an important vehicle for offbeat pulp fiction by **Clark Ashton Smith** and **Laurence Manning**, and published a good deal of translated European material. Significant authors who made their debuts there included **Stanley G. Weinbaum** and John Beynon Harris (**John Wyndham**). *Thrilling Wonder*, which endured until 1955, reverted to conventional action-adventure fiction.

**WORLD-BUILDING.** A term that became popular in **sf** writers' workshops in the 1970s, describing a central element of the sf writer's task; it is a dual process, embracing the work that goes on "behind the scenes" in developing a coherent imaginary world with its own ecology, geography, history, and so forth, and the work that goes into introducing readers to that world in such a way that their knowledge of it grows in an orderly, manageable, and engaging fashion. Initially used to describe projects involving worlds whose physical circumstances are radically different from Earth's, as widely featured in the works of **Hal Clement** and **Poul Anderson**, the term was eventually also applied to Earth-clones in various fantasy genres. The two component words are separated in such pioneering guides as Anderson's "The Creation of Imaginary Worlds: The World Builder's Handbook and Pocket Companion" (1974, in **Reginald Bretnor's** *Science Fiction Today and Tomorrow*) but the portmanteau version became more common after 1980.

**WORLD SF.** An international association of professionals established in 1976 at the first World Science Fiction Writers' Conference in Dublin. One of its purposes was to lend organizational status to invitations issued to writers from communist countries, who could not otherwise obtain exit visas—the decision was taken that its annual conference was always to be held somewhere other than the United States or the USSR—and the organization faded away once Eastern European communism collapsed in the late 1980s. The conference held in Chengdu, China, in 1991 proved to be the last (the next conference was scheduled to take place in Yugoslavia, but that nation did not last long enough to host it). While it was active, the organization published an occasional newsletter, and it lent its name to two showcase **anthologies** of international **sf** published in 1986.

**WORMHOLE.** The extensive theoretical development of the concept of black holes in the 1970s threw up the notion that they might serve as entrances to "metaspatial tunnels" giving access to distant parts of the cosmos or to **parallel worlds**, which were immediately nicknamed "wormholes." One version of the notion, proposing that black holes might be connected to "white holes" from which the energy drawn into them was expelled, was popularized by **John Gribbin's** *White Holes: Cosmic Gushers in the Universe* (1977). Wormholes were rapidly adopted as a convenient facilitating device for faster-than-light travel, adding a useful theoretical gloss to the "stargates" that had long been familiar in **sf portal fantasies.**

**WRIGHT, JOHN C. (1961– ).** U.S. writer who began publishing **sf** in 1994. "The Farthest Man from Earth" (1995) is a **Promethean fantasy** whose manner and theme anticipate the "Romance of the Far Future" trilogy begun with *The Golden Age* (2002) and *The Phoenix Exultant* (2003)—to be completed by *The Golden Transcendence*—which is a **far-futuristic fantasy** set in an opulent problematically **Utopian** solar system.

**WRIGHT, S. FOWLER (1874–1965).** British writer and publisher, whose primary interest was **poetry**; he founded the Empire Poetry League, which grew out of the competitions he used to finance his **small press** activities, and released the trade edition of his first **scientific romance**, *The Amphibians: A Romance of 500,000 Years Hence* (1924) through the League's Merton Press. His second, *Deluge* (1928), initially released under his own imprint, was boosted to best-seller status in the United States by William Randolph Hearst's Cosmopolitan Publishing Company (in anticipation of a movie that did not materialize until 1933) and Wright—whose accountancy business had recently gone bankrupt—launched himself into a new career as a professional writer in several genres. His first two novels had been extracted from much longer manuscripts written several years earlier; he reissued the first with further text as *The World Below* (1929) and published further extracts from the second as *Dawn* (1929) but never completed either project. The **hybrid robinsonade** *The Island of Captain Sparrow* (1928) stands alone, but the prehistoric fantasy *Dream, or the Simian Maid* (1931) launched another **series** which similarly came apart as the second volume, shorn of its connecting material, had to be issued by another publisher as

*Vengeance of Gwa* (1935), bylined Anthony Wingrave; the third appeared very belatedly as *Spiders' War* (1953).

Wright's short **sf**, collected in *The New Gods Lead* (1932; exp. as *The Throne of Saturn*, 1949; further exp. as *S. Fowler Wright's Short Stories*, 1996) is a remarkably graphic multifaceted assault on the notion of a "**Utopia** of comforts." The polemical quality of his work—extolling a Rousseauesque **libertarianism**—sometimes offended readers who mistook its import. The struggle to produce work at a rapid pace to support his 10 children soon took its toll on his imaginative vitality, however, and Wright's later work became increasingly slapdash. The world-blackmail story *Power* (1933) deteriorates into a routine thriller, as does the **future war** trilogy comprising *Prelude in Prague: The War of 1938* (1935; the U.S. edition *The War of 1938*, has a different ending), *Four Days War* (1936), and *Megiddo's Ridge* (1937) and the striking futuristic fantasy *The Adventure of Wyndham Smith* (1938). Some of the mysteries he bylined Sydney Fowler also have sf elements, notably *The Bell Street Murders* (1931) and *The Adventure of the Blue Room* (1945).

**WYLIE, PHILIP (1902–1971).** U.S. writer in several genres whose first venture into **sf** was the **superman** story *Gladiator* (1930). He followed it with *The Murderer Invisible* (1931), which won him the opportunity to work on the script of the Hollywood movie based on **H. G. Wells's** *The Invisible Man*. *When Worlds Collide* (1933) and *After Worlds Collide* (1934), written with Edwin Balmer, **transfigure** the story of Noah in a definitive **cosmic breakout** story. Two **fabulations** with sf elements are included in the text of his fervent quasi-confessional bildungsroman *Finnley Wren* (1934).

Wylie was interrogated by the FBI on first submitting the atomic bomb story "Paradise Crater" (1945) but was allowed to publish it after Hiroshima and went on to write two variant accounts of nuclear attacks on the United States, *Tomorrow* (1954) and *Triumph* (1962), as well as a thriller about the terrorist threat posed by *The Smuggled Atom Bomb* (1951). Accusations of misogyny occasioned by his feverish polemic *Generation of Vipers* led him to write *The Disappearance* (1951), tracking two **alternative** worlds in which human males and females find themselves abruptly isolated from their counterparts. Late in life, his anxieties about nuclear holocaust were transferred to the prospect of **ecocatastrophe**, dramatized in *Los Angeles: A.D. 2017* (1971, novelized from a **TV** script) and *The End of the Dream* (1972).

**WYNDHAM, JOHN (1903–1969).** The best-known byline of British writer John Wyndham Parkes Lucas Beynon Harris, who began publishing **sf** in the **pulp magazines** in 1931 as John Beynon Harris, some of that work being collected under the Wyndham byline in *Wanderers of Time* (1973) and *Exiles on Asperus* (1979). He published two sf novels as John Beynon, the **lost world** story *The Secret People* (1935) and the interplanetary fantasy *Planet Plane* (1936; aka *Stowaway to Mars*), whose 1938 sequel eventually became the title story of *Sleepers of Mars* (1973).

The Wyndham byline made a spectacular debut in the futuristic thriller *The Day of the Triffids* (1951), in which the people of England, almost all of whom have been fortuitously blinded, are harassed by ambulant plants. Carefully avoiding the **science fiction** label in the United Kingdom, he followed it up with a **series** of exotic **disaster stories**, all marketed domestically as thrillers. In *The Kraken Wakes* (1953, aka *Out of the Deeps*) the continents are inundated by sea-dwelling **aliens**. *The Chrysalids* (1955) is a **postholocaust fantasy.** In *The Midwich Cuckoos* (1957, aka *Village of the Damned*) the inhabitants of an English village are inseminated with superhuman children by aliens. *Trouble with Lichen* (1960) tracks an ecological disaster. In the meantime, Wyndham continued to write short fiction for sf and other magazines, much of which was reprinted in *Jizzle* (1954), *The Seeds of Time* (1956), and *Consider Her Ways and Others* (1961), although the orthodox **space-age series** assembled in the **mosaic** *The Outward Urge* (1959; exp. 1961) was credited as a **collaboration** with the imaginary "Lucas Parkes" to avoid prejudice to his reputation. *No Place Like Earth* (2003) is an eclectic sampler.

Although he completed an expansion of a 1963 short story into the **children's sf** novel *Chocky* (1968), Wyndham never finished the novel about giant spiders published posthumously as *Web* (1979). His success was significant, opening up domestic space for writers like **John Christopher**, **Charles Eric Maine**, and **John Lymington** to publish similarly science-fictionalized thrillers, but the conservative tenor of his most popular works—which portray heroic struggles to reconstitute British decency in direly inhospitable circumstances, mirroring the xenophobic and technophobic attitudes many of his readers applied to the actuality of 1950s Britain—was diametrically opposed to the progressive attitudes manifest in such works as *The Outward Urge*.

## – Y –

**YARBRO, CHELSEA QUINN (1942– ).** U.S. writer in several genres, who began publishing **sf** in 1969. Almost all of her sf is alarmist, including the bleak futuristic novels *Time of the Fourth Horseman* (1976), *False Dawn* (1978), and *Hyacinths* (1983), and many of the short stories in *Cautionary Tales* (1978) and *Signs & Portents* (1984). Her subsequent work includes a long **series** of lightly **hybridized** historical fantasies employing the vampire Comte Saint-Germain as a sympathetic but disillusioned observer in a panoramic survey of man's inhumanity to man throughout the ages.

**YEFREMOV, IVAN (1907–1972). Russian** writer, a leading figure in the revival of interest in Soviet **sf** in the 1950s. His tentative early work is translated in *Meeting over Tuscarora* (1946, bylined Efremov), but *Stories* (1954) added two ambitious novellas to material reproduced therefrom: "Shadow of the Past" (1947) and "Stellar Ships." More adventurous still was the 1959 novella "Cor Sepentis," framed as an ideological reply to **Murray Leinster's** "First Contact," which it considers to be corrupted by Western paranoia. A version of it was used as the title story of the showcase collection *The Heart of the Serpent* (1961). Yefremov's novel *Andromeda* (1958, tr. 1959) is a bold attempt to envisage a future communist **Utopia**, but a less optimistic sequel was suppressed. G. V. Grebens's *Ivan Efremov's Theory of Soviet Science Fiction* (1978) evaluates his pivotal contribution to Soviet sf.

**YERMAKOV, NICHOLAS (1951– ).** U.S. writer who began publishing **sf** in 1981. The trilogy of **planetary romances** comprising *Last Communion* (1981), *Epiphany* (1982), and *Jehad* (1984) is an extended investigation of the quest to commandeer an **alien** biology that facilitates a kind of life after death. The action-adventure fantasies

*Journey from Flesh* (1981) and *Fall into Darkness* (1982) and the early **virtual reality** thriller *Clique* (1982) were less esoteric, but Yermakov nevertheless ran into a newly emergent problem associated with computerized stock control that led publishers to discard writers when their sales began to fall. He responded by marketing subsequent works under other names, most notably a lighthearted **series** of jokily **metafictional time-police** stories bylined Simon Hawke, launched with *The Ivanhoe Gambit* (1984), which proved so successful that he eventually junked his old identity and changed his name.

**YOUNG, ROBERT F. (1915–1986).** U.S. writer who began publishing **sf** in 1953 and produced a steady stream of delicately polished **fabulations** in various fantasy genres for two decades, moving between extremes of heartfelt sentimentality and slapstick **satirical** comedy. Two samplers, *The Worlds of Robert F. Young* (1965) and *A Glass of Stars* (1968), concentrated on shorter works, although many of his best stories were novelettes. A few were belatedly expanded to novel length, but "To Fell a Tree" (1959) is far more effective than *The Last Yggdrasil* (1982), and "Jonathan and the Space Whale" (1962) gained little in being built up into the **mosaic** *Starfinder* (1980). *Eridahn* (1983), expanded from "When Time Was New" (1964), is a juvenile prehistoric fantasy.

## – Z –

**ZAGAT, ARTHUR LEO (1895–1949).** U.S. writer in various **pulp** genres who first ventured into **sf** in collaboration with **Nat Schachner** in 1930. His subsequent work included the **hybrid** submarine fantasy *Drink We Deep* (1937); a **series** of stories in which young guerrillas fight back against conquerors of the United States, launched with "Tomorrow" (1939); *Seven Out of Time* (1939), in which a sample of contemporary humans are subjected to clinical study by an emotionless descendant species; and "Slaves of the Lamp" (1946), a **political fantasy** featuring technologically enforced pacifism.

**ZAHN, TIMOTHY (1951– ).** U.S. writer who began publishing **sf** in 1979, quickly establishing himself as an ***Analog*** regular. In the couplet comprising *The Blackcollar* (1983) and *Blackcollar: The Backlash Mission* (1986) guerrilla fighters resist an **alien** occupation of Earth. The trilogy comprising *Cobra* (1985), *Cobra Strike* (1986), and *Cobra Bargain* (1988) and the **mosaic** *Warhorse* (1982–1984, rev. 1990) are standardized **military sf.** *A Coming of Age* (1985), about a world where **psi-powered** children lose their talents at puberty, displayed a versatility given further scope in novels set against a complex **galactic empire** background, including *Spinneret* (1985), *Triplet* (1987), and *Deadman Switch* (1988). The trilogy comprising *Conqueror's Pride* (1994), *Conqueror's Heritage* (1995), and *Conqueror's Legacy* (1996) is about an alien invasion of an interstellar commonwealth. *The Icarus Hunt* (1999) is a hyperspatial chase thriller. *Angelmass* (2001) is a **far-futuristic fantasy.** *Manta's Gift* (2002) features dolphin-like aliens. *Dragon and Thief* (2003) began a juvenile series featuring alien dragons. Zahn's short fiction is collected in *Cascade Point* (1986), *Time Bomb and Zahndry Others* (1988), *Distant Friends and Others* (1992), and *Star Song and Other Stories* (2003).

**ZAMIATIN, YEGEVNY (1884–1937). Russian** writer in various genres, whose significance to the **sf** genre is the extremism of the **dystopia** published in translation as *We* (1924), whose painstaking description of the utter annihilation of individuality by a technologically assisted autocracy, allegedly in the cause of social equality, set an important precedent for such works as **Ayn Rand's** *Anthem* and **George Orwell's** *Nineteen Eighty-Four*.

**ZARONOVITCH, PRINCESS VERA.** Pseudonym used as a byline on *Mizora: A Prophecy* (1880–1881; book 1890), an enterprising **Utopian satire** describing an advanced society whose **biotechnological** sophistication has done away with the need for the male of the species (and brunettes). The book version was copyrighted in the name of Mary E. Bradley, whose byline is extended to Mary E. Bradley Lane in modern editions, but the chain of evidence is too weak to sustain a confident attribution, just as the book is too tongue-in-cheek to sustain its **feminist** credentials.

**ZEBROWSKI, GEORGE (1945– ).** Polish-descended, Austrian-born writer resident in the United States since 1951, who began publishing

**sf** in 1970. A fascination with vast panoramic surveys of space and time, first displayed in *The Omega Point* (1972)—which was subsequently integrated with *Ashes of Stars* (1977) into *The Omega Point Trilogy* (1983)—was further developed in the **Stapledonian** *Macrolife* (1979) and its sequel *Cave of Stars* (1999). The juveniles *Sunspacer* (1984) and *The Stars Will Speak* (1985), supplemented with a third part in *The Sunspacer Trilogy* (1996), and the sprawling *Stranger Suns* (1991), which cannibalized *The Star Web* (1975), are similarly inclined. The languid cynicism of these attempted epics is more concentrated in *Brute Orbits* (1998), in which social undesirables are exported from Earth in hollowed-out asteroids. *The Killing Star* (1995, with **Charles Pellegrino**) is a **disaster story.** Zebrowski's short fiction is sampled in *The Monadic Universe* (1977, exp. 1985), *Swift Thoughts* (2002), and *In the Distance, and Ahead in Time* (2003). He edited several **anthologies**, some in **collaboration**, of which the most notable were the four volumes of *Synergy* (1987–1989).

**ZELAZNY, ROGER (1937–1995).** U.S. writer who began publishing **sf** in 1962, making an immediate impact with his exceptionally vivid short fiction, the best of which was collected in *Four for Tomorrow* (1967, aka *A Rose for Ecclesiastes*) and *The Doors of His Face, the Lamps of His Mouth, and Other Stories* (1971). Much of his work **hybridized** sf and mythological fantasy, often drawing on anthropological and psychoanalytical interpretations, after the fashion of his first novels *This Immortal* (1966) and *The Dream Master* (1966). In order to describe the psychodramas of humans whose technologies have gifted them with godlike power, he employed wholesale **transfiguration** in the **Promethean fantasy** *Lord of Light* (1967), in which a reconstituted Hindu pantheon is undermined by an inventively subversive Buddha in the context of an extraterrestrial colony. The similar *Isle of the Dead* (1967) and *Creatures of Light and Darkness* (1969) exhausted the potential of the formula.

*Damnation Alley* (1969) is a down-to-earth action-adventure. *Jack of Shadows* (1971) anticipated Zelazny's digression into unalloyed magical fantasy in the Amber **series**. The hero of *Isle of the Dead* reappeared in the fragmented thrillers *Today We Choose Faces* (1973) and *To Die in Italbar* (1973); *Bridge of Ashes* (1976) and *Roadmarks* (1979) are similarly fragmented tales of **time-twisting**. *Doorways in the Sand* (1976) and the secret agent stories in *My Name Is Legion*

(1976) were more effective as thrillers, but *Deus Irae* (1976), written in **collaboration** with **Philip K. Dick**, and *Eye of Cat* (1982) were unable to recapture the energy of earlier mythological hybrids. *Coils* (1980, with **Fred Saberhagen**) and *Flare* (1992, with **Thomas T. Thomas**) are highly atypical excursions into **hard sf**, but the majority of the books Zelazny wrote in his later years, alone or in collaboration, were formulaic exercises in other fantasy genres. *Frost and Fire* (1989) is the most interesting of his later collections, in terms of sf content.

**ZIESING, MARK V. (1953– ).** U.S. book dealer and **small press** publisher. With his brother Michael he published a supplement to **Gene Wolfe's** New Sun **series**, *The Castle of the Otter* (1982) and *The Wolfe Archipelago* (1983), then assumed sole responsibility for collections and offbeat items by a variety of writers, including **Bruce Sterling**, **James P. Blaylock**, **Howard Waldrop**, **Ian Watson**, and **Kim Stanley Robinson.** Like **James Turner**, Ziesing made an important contribution to the promotion of short **sf** when the commercial publishers largely abandoned single-author collections, but his list was considerably more varied.

**ZINDELL, DAVID (1952– ).** U.S. writer who began publishing **sf** in 1985. *Neverness* (1988) is a sprawling epic **hybrid** of **space opera** and other kinds of fantasy, which established an important exemplar for attempts made by commercial publishers in the 1990s to "repackage" sf in a manner that would recommend it to the genre fantasy audience. Its sequel, the Requiem for *Homo Sapiens* trilogy comprising *The Broken God* (1993), *The Wild* (1996), and *War in Heaven* (1998), adopted the standard format of the emergent genre.

**ZIVKOVIC, ZORAN (1948– ).** Serbian scholar and writer who frequently used **sf** motifs in his **fabulations**, as in the **mosaics** *Time-Gifts* (1998), in which a **time-traveler** offers redemptive opportunities to various dying individuals; the reality-defying *Impossible Encounters* (2000); the whimsical *Seven Touches of Music* (2001), in which music becomes a trickster bringing welcome disruptions to the lives of Albert Einstein and other exemplary individuals; and a group of stories about imaginary libraries in the **anthology** *Leviathan 3*, edited by Forrest Aguirre and **Jeff VanderMeer.** *The Writer* (1999) is a surreal **satire** whose protagonist is an sf writer.

# Bibliography

## GENERAL REFERENCE WORKS

Barron, Neil, ed. *Anatomy of Wonder: A Critical Guide to Science Fiction*. 4th ed. New Providence, N.J.: Bowker, 1995.

Clute, John, and Peter Nicholls. *The Encyclopedia of Science Fiction*. 2nd ed. London: Orbit, 1993.

Gunn, James E., ed. *The New Encyclopedia of Science Fiction*. New York: Viking, 1988.

James, Edward, and Farah Mendlesohn, eds. *The Cambridge Companion to Science Fiction*. Cambridge: Cambridge University Press, 2003.

Magill, Frank N., ed. *Survey of Science Fiction Literature*. 5 vols. Englewood Cliffs, N.J.: Salem, 1979. Rev. in combination with *Survey of Modern Fantasy Literature*, 1983 as *Magill's Guide to Science Fiction and Fantasy Literature*, ed. the Editors of Salem Press, 1996; abridged as *Classics of Science Fiction and Fantasy Literature*, ed. Fiona Kelleghan, 2002.

Tuck, Donald H. *The Encyclopedia of Science Fiction and Fantasy through 1968: A Bibliographic Survey of the Fields of Science Fiction, Fantasy, and Weird Fiction through 1968*. 3 vols. Chicago: Advent, 1974, 1978, and 1982.

Tymn, Marshall, and Mike Ashley, eds. *Science Fiction, Fantasy, and Weird Fiction Magazines*. Westport, Conn.: Greenwood, 1985.

Versins, Pierre. *L'Encyclopédie de l'utopie, des voyages extraordinaire et de la science-fiction*. Lausanne, Switzerland: L'Age d'Homme, 1972.

## HISTORICAL STUDIES

Aldiss, Brian W. *Billion Year Spree*, London: Gollancz, 1973. Rev., with David Wingrove, as *Trillion Year Spree*. London: Gollancz, 1986.

Alkon, Paul K. *Science Fiction before 1900: Imagination Discovers Technology*. Studies in Literary Themes and Genres, no. 3. Boston: Twayne, 1994.

———. *Origins of Futuristic Fiction*. Athens: University of Georgia Press, 1987.

Armytage, W. H. G. *Yesterday's Tomorrows: A Historical Survey of Future Societies*. London: Routledge & Kegan Paul, 1968.

Ashley, Michael. *The History of the Science Fiction Magazines*. 4 vols. London: New English Library, 1974–78.

——. *The Time Machines: The Story of the Science-Fiction Pulp Magazines from the Beginning to 1950*. Liverpool, U.K.: Liverpool University Press, 2001.

Carter, Paul A. *The Creation of Tomorrow: Fifty Years of Magazine Science Fiction*. New York: Columbia University Press, 1977.

Chalker, Jack L., and Mark Owings. *The Science-Fantasy Publishers: A Critical and Bibliographic History*. Westminster, Md.: Mirage Press, 1991; revised ed. 1992.

Cioffi, Frank. *Formula Fiction? An Anatomy of American Science Fiction, 1930–1940*. Westport, Conn.: Greenwood Press, 1982.

Clareson, Thomas. *Some Kind of Paradise: The Emergence of American Science Fiction*. Westport, Conn.: Greenwood Press, 1985.

——. *Understanding Contemporary American Science Fiction: The Formative Period (1926–1970)*. Columbia: University of South Carolina Press, 1990.

Clarke, I. F. *The Pattern of Expectation: 1644–2001*. London: Cape, 1979.

del Rey, Lester. *The World of Science Fiction, 1926–1976: The History of a Subculture*. New York: Garland, 1976.

Gunn, James E. *Alternate Worlds: The Illustrated History of Science Fiction*. Englewood Cliffs, N.J.: Prentice-Hall, 1975.

Guthke, Karl S. *The Last Frontier: Imagining Other Worlds from the Copernican Revolution to Modern Science Fiction*. Ithaca, N. Y.: Cornell University Press, 1990.

Harbottle, Philip, and Steven Holland. *Vultures of the Void: A History of British Science Fiction Publishing, 1946–1956*. San Bernardino, Calif.: Borgo Press, 1993.

James, Edward. *Science Fiction in the Twentieth Century*. Oxford, U.K.: Oxford University Press, 1994.

Knight, Damon. *The Futurians: The Story of the Great Science Fiction "Family" of the 30s that Produced Today's Top SF Writers and Editors*. New York: John Day, 1977.

Landon, Brooks. *Science Fiction after 1900: From the Steam Man to the Stars*. Studies in Literary Themes and Genres, no. 12. Boston: Twayne, 1997.

Lundwall, Sam J. *Science Fiction: What It's All About*. New York: Ace, 1971.

Manfredo, Stéphane. *La science fiction aux frontières de l'Homme*. Paris: Gallimard, 2000.

Moore, Patrick. *Science and Fiction*. London: Harrap, 1957.

Moskowitz, Sam. *The Immortal Storm: A History of Science Fiction Fandom*. Atlanta, Ga.: Atlanta Science Fiction Organization, 1954.

——. *Under the Moons of Mars: A History and Anthology of "Scientific Romance" in the Munsey Magazines, 1912–1920*. New York: Holt, 1970.

——. *Science Fiction in Old San Francisco*. Vol. 1, *History of the Movement from 1854-1890*. Kingston, R.I.: Grant, 1980.

Panshin, Alexei, and Cory Panshin. *The World beyond the Hill: Science Fiction and the Quest for Transcendence*. Los Angeles: Tarcher, 1989.

Philmus, Robert M. *Into the Unknown: Science Fiction from Francis Godwin to H. G. Wells*. Berkeley: University of California Press, 1970.

Pohl, Frederik. *The Way the Future Was: A Memoir*. New York: Ballantine, 1979.

Polak, Fred. *The Image of the Future*. Amsterdam, Netherlands: Elsevier, 1973.

Sadoul, Jacques. *Histoire de la science-fiction moderne*. 2 vols. Paris: Albin Michel, 1973.

Schenkel, Elmar, and Stefan Welz, eds. *Lost Worlds and Mad Elephants: Literature, Science, and Technology, 1700–1900*. Leipzig, Germany: Galda + Witch Verlag, 1999.

Seed, David, ed. *Anticipations: Essays on Early Science Fiction and Its Precursors*. Liverpool, U.K.: Liverpool University Press, 1995.

Stableford, Brian. *Scientific Romance in Britain, 1890–1950*. London: Fourth Estate, 1985.

Stover, Leon. *Science Fiction from Wells to Heinlein*. Jefferson, N.C.: McFarland, 2002.

Suvin, Darko. *Victorian Science Fiction in the U.K.: The Discourses of Knowledge and Power*. Boston: G. K. Hall, 1983.

Warner, Harry Jr. *All Our Yesterdays: An Informal History of Science Fiction Fandom in the Forties*. Chicago: Advent, 1969.

——. *A Wealth of Fable: The History of Science Fiction Fandom in the 1950s*. New York: Fanhistorica, 1976.

Willingham, Ralph. *Science Fiction and the Theater*. Westport, Conn.: Greenwood Press, 1993.

Wollheim, Donald A. *The Universe Makers: Science Fiction Today*. New York: Harper, 1971.

## AESTHETIC AND THEORETICAL STUDIES

Amis, Kingsley. *New Maps of Hell: A Survey of Science Fiction*. London: Gollancz, 1960.

Armitt, Lucy. *Theorizing the Fantastic*. New York: Arnold, 1996.

Asimov, Isaac. Social Science Fiction. In *Modern Science Fiction: Its Meaning and Its Future*, ed. Reginald Bretnor, 157–96. New York: Coward-McCann, 1953.

Bacon-Smith, Camille. *Science Fiction Culture*. Philadelphia: University of Pennsylvania Press, 2000.

Ben-Tov, Sharona. *The Artificial Paradise: Science Fiction and American Reality*. Ann Arbor: University of Michigan Press, 1995.

Booker, Keith. *Monsters, Mushroom Clouds, and the Cold War: American Science Fiction and the Roots of Postmodernism, 1946–1964*. Westport, Conn.: Greenwood Press, 2001.

Botting, Fred. *Sex, Machines, and Navels: Fiction, Fantasy, and History in the Future Present*. Manchester, U.K.: Manchester University Press, 1999.

Brigg, Peter. *The Span of Mainstream and Science Fiction*. Jefferson, N.C.: McFarland, 2002.

Broderick, Damien. *Reading by Starlight: Postmodern Science Fiction*. New York: Routledge, 1995.

——. *Transrealist Fiction: Writing in the Slipstream of Science*. Westport, Conn.: Greenwood Press, 2000.

Bukataman, Scott. *Terminal Identity: The Virtual Subject in Postmodern Science Fiction*. Durham, N.C.: Duke University Press, 1993.

Butor, Michel. The Crisis in the Growth of Science Fiction. In *Inventory: Essays*, 224–32. London: Jonathan Cape, 1970.

Campbell, John W. Jr. Concerning Science Fiction. In *The Best of Science Fiction*, ed. Groff Conklin, v–xi. New York: Crown, 1946.

Conklin, Groff. Introduction. In *The Best of Science Fiction*, xv–xxviii. New York: Crown, 1946.

de Camp, L. Sprague. Imaginative Fiction and Creative Imagination. In *Modern Science Fiction: Its Meaning and Its Future*, ed. Reginald Bretnor, 119–54. New York: Coward-McCann, 1953.

Elkin, Deborah. Hugo Gernsback's Ideas of Science Fiction, 1915–26. *Fantasy Commentator* 40 (Winter 1989–90):246–58.

Freedman, Carl. *Critical Theory and Science Fiction*. Hanover, N.H.: Wesleyan University Press, 2000.

Grenier, Christian. *La science-fiction, lectures de l'avenir*. Nancy, France: Presses Universitaires de Nancy, 1994.

Hartwell, David J. *Age of Wonders: Exploring the World of Science Fiction*. 2nd ed. New York: Tor, 1996.

Huntington, John. *Rationalizing Genius: Ideological Strategies in the Classical American Short Story*. New Brunswick, N.J.: Rutgers University Press, 1989.

Knight, Damon. *In Search of Wonder*. Chicago: Advent, 1956. Rev. ed. 1967.

——. *Turning Points: Essays on the Art of Science Fiction*. New York: Harper and Row, 1977.

Lawler, Donald L. *Approaches to Science Fiction*. Boston: Houghton Mifflin, 1978.

Lerner, Frederick Andrew. *Modern Science Fiction and the American Literary Community*. Metuchen, N.J.: Scarecrow Press, 1985.

Malmgren, Carl. *Worlds Apart: Narratology of Science Fiction*. Bloomington: Indiana University Press, 1991.

Martin, Graham Dunstan. *An Inquiry into the Purposes of Speculative Fiction—Fantasy and Truth*. Lewiston, N.Y.: Edwin Mellen, 2003.

Mendlesohn, Farah. Towards a Taxonomy of Fantasy. *Journal of the Fantastic in the Arts* 13, no. 2 (2002):173–87.

Moorcock, Michael. A New Literature for the Space Age. *New Worlds* 142 (May–June 1964):2–3.

Panshin, Alexei, and Cory Panshin. *SF in Dimension: A Book of Explorations*. Chicago: Advent, 1976.

Parrinder, Patrick. *Science Fiction: A Critical Guide*. London: Longmans, 1979.

———. *Science Fiction: Its Criticism and Teaching*. London: Methuen, 1980.

———, ed. *Learning from Other Worlds: Estrangement, Cognition, and the Politics of Science Fiction*. Liverpool, U.K.: Liverpool University Press, 2000.

Pierce, John J. *Foundations of Science Fiction: A Study in Imagination and Evolution*. Westport, Conn.: Greenwood Press, 1987.

———. *Great Themes of Science Fiction: A Study in Imagination and Evolution*. Westport, Conn.: Greenwood Press, 1987.

———. *Odd Genre: A Study in Imagination and Evolution*. Westport, Conn.: Greenwood Press, 1994.

———. *When World Views Collide: A Study in Imagination and Evolution*. Westport, Conn.: Greenwood Press, 1989.

Puschmann-Nalenz, Barbara. *Science Fiction and Postmodern Fiction: A Genre Study*. New York: Peter Lang, 1992.

Rabkin, Eric. The Composite Novel in Science Fiction. *Foundation* 66 (Spring 1966):93–100.

Roberts, Adam. *Science Fiction*. New Critical Idiom Series. London: Routledge, 2000.

Rose, Mark. *Alien Encounters: Anatomy of Science Fiction*. Cambridge, Mass.: Harvard University Press, 1981.

Scholes, Robert. *The Fabulators*. New York: Oxford University Press, 1967. Rev. as *Fabulation and Metafiction*. Urbana: University of Illinois Press, 1979.

———. *Structural Fabulation: An Essay on Fiction of the Future*. Notre Dame, Ind.: University of Notre Dame Press, 1975.

Scholes, Robert, and Robert Kellogg. *The Nature of Narrative*. New York: Oxford University Press, 1966.

Scholes, Robert, and Eric Rabkin. *Science Fiction: History/Science/Vision*. New York: Oxford University Press, 1977.

Sherman, Delia. An Introduction to Interstitial Arts: Life on the Border. *Interstitial Arts* at www.endicott-studio.com/IA/IA-intro.html, 2003 (accessed 15 September 2003).

Slusser, George E., and Eric S. Rabkin, eds. *Styles of Creation: Aesthetic Technique and the Creation of Fictional Worlds*. Athens: University of Georgia Press, 1993.

Spinrad, Norman. *Science Fiction in the Real World*. Carbondale: Southern Illinois University Press, 1990.

Stableford, Brian. *The Sociology of Science Fiction*. San Bernardino, Calif.: Borgo Press, 1987.

Stockwell, Peter. *The Poetics of Science Fiction*. London: Longman, 2000.

Suvin, Darko. *Metamorphoses of Science Fiction: On the Poetics and History of a Literary Genre*. New Haven, Conn.: Yale University Press, 1979.

——. *Positions and Presuppositions in Science Fiction*. Kent, Ohio: Kent State University Press, 1988.

Webb, Janeen, and Andrew Enstice, eds. *The Fantastic Self: Essays on the Subject of the Self*. Perth, Australia: Eidolon, 1999.

Wendland, Albert. *Science, Myth, and the Fictional Creation of Alien Worlds*. Ann Arbor, Mich.: UMI Research Press, 1984.

Westfahl, Gary. *The Mechanics of Wonder: The Creation of the Idea of Science Fiction*. Liverpool, U.K.: Liverpool University Press, 1998.

Williamson, Jack. The Logic of Fantasy. In *Of Worlds Beyond: The Science of Science Fiction Writing*, ed. Lloyd Arthur Eshbach, 39–49. Reading, Pa.: Fantasy Press, 1947.

Wolfe, Gary K. *The Known and the Unknown: The Iconography of Science Fiction*. Kent, Ohio: Kent State University Press, 1979.

——. *Critical Terms for Science Fiction and Fantasy: A Glossary and Guide to Scholarship*. Westport, Conn.: Greenwood, 1986.

## MISCELLANEOUS ANTHOLOGIES AND ESSAY COLLECTIONS

Aldiss, Brian W. *This World and Nearer Ones: Essays Exploring the Familiar*. London: Weidenfeld & Nicholson, 1979.

——. *The Detached Retina: Aspects of Sf and Fantasy*. Liverpool, U.K.: Liverpool University Press, 1995.

Atheling, William, Jr. [James Blish]. *The Issue at Hand: Studies in Contemporary Magazine Science Fiction*. Chicago: Advent, 1964.

——. *More Issues at Hand: Critical Studies in Contemporary Science Fiction*. Chicago: Advent, 1970.

Blish, James. *The Tale That Wags the God*. Ed. Cy Chauvin. Chicago: Advent, 1987.

Bould, Mark, ed. *Strange Attractors: Papers from the Second Annual AFFN Conference*. Plymouth, U.K.: AFFN, 1995.

Bretnor, Reginald, ed. *Modern Science Fiction: Its Meaning and Its Future*. New York: Coward-McCann, 1953; rev. ed. Chicago: Advent, 1979.

——, ed. *Science Fiction: Today and Tomorrow*. New York: Harper, 1974.

Clareson, Thomas D., ed. *Many Futures, Many Worlds: Theme and Form in Science Fiction*. Kent, Ohio: Kent State University Press, 1977.

——, ed. *SF: The Other Side of Realism: Essays on Modern Fantasy and Science Fiction*. Bowling Green, Ohio: Bowling Green State University Popular Press, 1971.

——, ed. *Voices of the Future*. Bowling Green, Ohio: Bowling Green State University Popular Press, 3 vols. (3rd coedited with Thomas L. Wymer), 1976–83.

Clute, John. *Look at the Evidence: Essays and Reviews*. New York: Serconia, 1995.

——. *Scores: Reviews 1993–2003*. Harold Wood, Essex, U.K.: Beccon Publications, 2003.

——. *Strokes: Essays and Reviews, 1966–1986*. Seattle, Wash.: Serconia, 1988.

Delany, Samuel R. *The Jewel-Hinged Jaw: Notes on the Language of Science Fiction*. Elizabethtown, N.Y.: Dragon Press, 1977.

——. *Starboard Wine: More Notes on the Language of Science Fiction*. Pleasantville, N.Y.: Dragon Press, 1984.

——. *Silent Interviews: On Language, Race, Sex, Science Fiction, and Some Comics*. Hanover, N.H.: Wesleyan University Press, 1994.

De Vos, Luk, ed. *Just the Other Day: Essays on the Suture of the Future*. Antwerp, Belgium: Restant, 1985.

Emelina, Jean, and Denise Terrel. *Actes du Premier Colloque International de Science-Fiction de Nice: Images de l'ailleurs-espace interieur*. Nice, France: Centre d'étude de la métaphore, 1984.

Franklin, H. Bruce. *Future Perfect: American Science Fiction of the Nineteenth Century—An Anthology*. New York: Oxford University Press, 1966; revised 1970; revised as *Future Perfect: American Science Fiction in the Nineteenth Century—An Anthology*, New Brunswick, N.J.: Rutgers University Press, 1995.

Garnett, Rhys, and R. J. Ellis, eds. *Science Fiction Roots and Branches: Contemporary Critical Approaches*. New York: St. Martin's Press, 1990.

Gunn, James E. *Inside Science Fiction: Essays on Fantastic Literature*. San Bernardino, Calif.: Borgo, 1992.

Hollinger, Veronica, and Joan Gordon, eds. *Edging into the Future: Science Fiction and Contemporary Cultural Transformation*. Philadelphia: University of Pennsylvania Press, 2002.

Jones, Gwyneth. *Deconstructing the Starships: Science, Fiction and Reality*. Liverpool, U.K.: Liverpool University Press, 1999.

Langford, David. *The Complete Critical Assembly: The Collected White Dwarf (and GM and GMI) SF Review Columns*. Holicong, Pa.: Cosmos, 2002.

——. *Up through an Empty House of Stars: Reviews and Essays 1980–2002*. Holicong, Pa.: Cosmos, 2003.

Le Guin, Ursula K. *Dancing at the Edge of the World: Thoughts on Words, Women, Places*. New York: Grove, 1989.

——. *The Language of the Night: Essays on Fantasy and Science Fiction*. New York: Putnam, 1979. Rev. ed. New York: HarperCollins, 1992.

Lem, Stanislaw. *Microworlds: Writings on Science Fiction and Fantasy*. Ed. Franz Rottensteiner. New York: Harcourt, 1985.

McCaffery, Larry, ed. *Storming the Reality Studio: A Casebook of Cyberpunk and Postmodern Science Fiction*. Durham, N.C.: Duke University Press, 1991.

Malik, Rex, ed. *Future Imperfect: Science Fact and Science Fiction*. London: Francis Pinter, 1980.

Malzberg, Barry N. *The Engines of the Night: Science Fiction in the Eighties*. New York: Doubleday, 1982.

Manlove, Colin. *Science Fiction: Ten Explorations*. Kent, Ohio: Kent State University Press, 1986.

Moskowitz, Sam. *Strange Horizons: The Spectrum of Science Fiction*. New York: Scribner, 1976.

Nicholls, Peter, ed. *Science Fiction at Large*. London: Victor Gollancz, 1976.

Riley, Dick, ed. *Critical Encounters: Writers and Themes in Science Fiction*. New York: Ungar, 1978.

Rose, Mark, ed. *Science Fiction: A Collection of Critical Essays*. Englewood Cliffs, N. J.: Prentice Hall, 1976.

Rucker, Rudy. *Seek! Selected Nonfiction*. New York: Four Walls Eight Windows, 1999.

Samuelson, David. *Visions of Tomorrow: Six Journeys from Outer to Inner Space*. New York: Arno Press, 1975.

Sandison, Alan, and Robert Dingley, eds. *Histories of the Future: Studies in Fact, Fantasy, and Science Fiction*. New York: Palgrave, 2001.

Sawyer, Andy, and David Seed, eds. *Speaking Science Fiction: Dialogues and Interpretations*. Liverpool, U.K.: Liverpool University Press, 2000.

Sayer, Karen, and John Moore, eds. *Science Fiction, Critical Frontiers*. New York: St. Martin's Press, 2000.

——. *The Science Fiction Novel: Imagination and Social Criticism*. Chicago: Advent, 1959.

Shippey, Tom, ed. *Fictional Space: Essays on Contemporary Science Fiction*. Oxford: Blackwell, 1991.

Slusser, George E., Colin Greenland, and Eric S. Rabkin, eds. *Storm Warnings: Science Fiction Confronts the Future*. Carbondale: Southern Illinois University Press, 1987.

Slusser, George E., George R. Guffey, and Mark Rose, eds. *Bridges to Science Fiction*. Carbondale: Southern Illinois University Press, 1980.

Slusser, George E., Eric S. Rabkin, and Robert Scholes, eds. *Coordinates: Placing Science Fiction and Fantasy*. Carbondale: Southern Illinois University Press, 1983.

Tymn, Marshall B., ed. *The Science Fiction Reference Book*. Washington, D.C.: Starmont House, 1981.

Westfahl, Gary, and George Slusser, eds. *Science Fiction, Canonization, Marginalization, and the Academy*. Westport, Conn.: Greenwood Press, 2002.

Williamson, Jack, ed. *Teaching Science Fiction: Education for Tomorrow*. Philadelphia, Pa.: Owlswick, 1980.

## BIBLIOGRAPHIES

Bleiler, Everett F. *The Checklist of Fantastic Literature: A Bibliography of Fantasy, Weird and Science Fiction Books Published in the English Language*. Chicago: Shasta, 1948. Rev. ed. *The Checklist of Science-Fiction and Supernatural Fiction*. Glen Rock, N.J.: Firebell, 1978.

———. *Science-Fiction, the Early Years: A Full Description of More Than 3,000 Science-Fiction Stories from Earliest Times to the Appearance of the Genre Magazines in 1930, with Author, Title, and Motif Indexes*. Kent, Ohio: Kent State University Press, 1990.

Bleiler, Everett, F., and Richard Bleiler. *Science-Fiction: The Gernsback Years*. Kent, Ohio: Kent State University Press, 1998.

Briney, R. E., and Edward Wood. *SF Bibliographies: An Annotated Bibliography of Bibliographic Works on Science Fiction and Fantastic Fiction*. Chicago: Advent, 1972.

Brown, Charles N., and William G. Contento. *The Locus Index to Science Fiction (1984–1998)*, combined with William G. Contento, *Index to Science Fiction Anthologies and Collections*. Oakland, Calif.: Locus Press, 1999 [CD-ROM].

Burgess, Michael, and Lisa R. Bartle. *Reference Guide to Science Fiction, Fantasy, and Horror: Second Edition*. Westport, Conn.: Greenwood, 2003.

Clareson, Thomas. *Science Fiction in America, 1870s–1930s: An Annotated Bibliography*, Westport, Conn.: Greenwood, 1984.

Clarke, I. F. *The Tale of the Future from the Beginning to the Present Day: An Annotated Bibliography*. 3rd ed. London: London Library, 1978.

Currey, Lloyd W. *Science Fiction and Fantasy Authors: A Bibliography of First Printings of Their Fiction and Selected Nonfiction*. Boston: G. K. Hall, 1979.

Day, Donald B. *Index to the Science Fiction Magazines, 1926–1950*. Portland, Ore.: Perri Press, 1952.

Green, Scott E. *Contemporary Science Fiction, Fantasy, and Horror Poetry: A Resource Guide and Bibliographical Dictionary*. Westport, Conn.: Greenwood Press, 1989.

Hall, H. W. *Science Fiction and Fantasy Reference Index 1879-1985: An International Author and Subject Index to History and Criticism*. 2 vols. Detroit, Mich.: Gale, 1987.

———. *Science Fiction Book Review Index 1923–73; 1974–79; 1980–84*. 3 vols. Detroit, Mich.: Gale, 1975–85.

Locke, George W. *Voyages in Space: A Bibliography of Interplanetary Fiction 1801–1914*. London: Ferret Fantasy, 1975.

Miller, Stephen T., and William G. Contento. *Science Fiction, Fantasy, & Weird Fiction Magazine Index (1890–1998)*. Oakland, Calif.: Locus Press, 1999 [CD-ROM].

Reginald, Robert. *Science Fiction and Fantasy Literature: A Checklist, 1700–1974*. 2 vols. Detroit, Mich.: Gale, 1979.

Sargent, Lyman Tower. *British and American Utopian Literature 1516–1986*. 2nd ed. New York: Garland, 1988.

Stephensen-Payne, Philip, and Gordon Benson Jr. *Galactic Central Bibliographies for the Avid Reader*. Leeds, Yorkshire, U.K.: Galactic Central Publications, 1985–2003. 58 vols.: 1. Poul Anderson; 2. Gordon R. Dickson; 3. A. Bertram Chandler; 4. Hal Clement; 5. Edgar Pangborn; 6. H. Beam Piper; 7. William Teen; 8. Wilson Tucker; 9. Harry Harrison; 10. Jack Williamson; 11. John Brunner; 12. James White; 13. Anne McCaffrey; 14. Bob Shaw; 15. Margaret St. Clair; 16. John Wyndham; 17. Manly Wade Wellman; 18. Philip K. Dick; 19. Gene Wolfe; 20. Leigh Brackett and Edmond Hamilton; 21. C. L. Moore and Henry Kuttner; 22. Fritz Leiber; 23. Philip José Farmer; 24. Eric Frank Russell; 25. John Christopher; 26. Brian W. Aldiss; 27. George R. R. Martin; 28. Jack Vance; 29. Cyril M. Kornbluth; 30. Keith Laumer; 31. James Tiptree Jr.; 32. Theodore Sturgeon; 33. Michael Bishop; 34. Frederik Pohl; 35. Piers Anthony; 36. Frank Herbert; 37. Fred Saberhagen; 38. Roger Zelazny; 39. Clifford D. Simak; 40. Marion Zimmer Bradley; 41. Andre Norton; 42. Robert A. Heinlein; 43. C. J. Cherryh; 44. Charles L. Harness; 45. Keith Roberts; 46. James Bish; 47. A. E. van Vogt; 48. Brian Stableford; 49. John T. Sladek; 50. Ray Cummings; 51. Stanton A. Coblentz; 52. Grant Allen; 53. Lloyd Biggle Jr.; 54. George Allan England; 55. Perley Poore

Sheehan; 56. Michael G. Coney; 57. Daniel F. Galouye; 58. Barry N. Malzberg.

Strauss, Erwin S. *Index to the Science Fiction Magazines, 1951–65*. Cambridge, Mass.: MIT Science Fiction Society, 1966.

Tymn, Marshall B., and Roger C. Schlobin. *The Year's Scholarship in Science Fiction and Fantasy 1972–1975*. Kent, Ohio: Kent State University Press, 1979. Supplements: 1976–1979 (1983); 1980 (1983); 1981 (1984); 1982 (1985). (Further supplements for 1983–88 in *Extrapolation* and for 1989 in *The Journal of the Fantastic in the Arts*)

## THEMATIC STUDIES

### General

Bailey, J. O. *Pilgrims through Space and Time: Trends and Patterns in Scientific and Utopian Fiction*. New York: Argus, 1947.

Bainbridge, William Sims. *Dimensions of Science Fiction*. Cambridge, Mass.: Harvard University Press, 1986.

Disch, Thomas M. *The Dreams Our Stuff Is Made Of: How Science Fiction Conquered the World*. New York: Free Press, 1998.

### Aliens

Slusser, George E., and Eric S. Rabkin, eds. *Aliens: The Anthropology of Science Fiction*. Carbondale: Southern Illinois University Press, 1987.

### Alternative History

Chapman, Edgar L., and Carl B. Yoke, eds. *Classic and Iconoclastic Alternate History Science Fiction*. Lewiston, N.Y.: Edwin Mellen, 2003.

Hellekson, Karen. *The Alternate History: Refiguring Historical Time*. Kent, Ohio: Kent State University Press, 2001.

### Apocalyptic Fantasy

Bull, Malcolm, ed. *Apocalypse Theory and the Ends of the World*. Oxford, U.K.: Blackwell, 1995.

Clute, John. *The Book of End Times: Grappling with the Millennium*. New York: Harper Prism, 1999.

Dubanski, Ryszard. The Last Man Theme in Modern Fantasy and SF. *Foundation* 16 (May 1979):26–30.

Ketterer, David. *New Worlds for Old: The Apocalyptic Imagination, Science Fiction, and American Literature*. Bloomington: Indiana University Press, 1974.

Kreuziger, Frederick A. *Apocalypse and Science Fiction: A Dialectic of Religious and Secular Soteriologies*. Chico, Calif.: Scholars Press, 1982.

Rabkin, Eric S., Martin H. Greenberg, and Joseph D. Olander, eds. *The End of the World*. Carbondale: Southern Illinois University Press, 1983.

Seed, David, ed. *Imagining Apocalypse: Studies in Cultural Crisis*. London: Macmillan, 2000.

Wagar, W. Warren. *Terminal Visions: The Literature of Last Things*. Bloomington: Indiana University Press, 1982.

## Biotechnology

Pastourmatzi, Domna, ed. *Biotechnological and Medical Themes in Science Fiction*. Thessaloniki, Greece: Aristotle University, 2003.

## Children's Science Fiction

Reid, Susan Elizabeth. *Presenting Young Adult Science Fiction*. Boston: Twayne, 1998.

Sands, Karen, and Marietta Frank. *Back in the Spaceship Again: Juvenile Science Fiction Series since 1945*. Westport, Conn.: Greenwood Press, 1999.

Sullivan, C. W. III, ed. *Young Adult Science Fiction*. Westport, Conn.: Greenwood Press, 1999.

## Cybernetics

Hayles, N. Katherine. *How We Became Posthuman: Virtual Bodies in Cybernetics, Literature and Informatics*. Chicago: University of Chicago Press, 1999.

Porush, David. *The Soft Machine: Cybernetic Fiction*. New York: Methuen, 1985.

Warrick, Patricia S. *The Cybernetic Imagination in Science Fiction*. Cambridge, Mass: MIT Press, 1980.

## Cyberpunk

Butler, Andrew M. *Cyberpunk*. Harpenden, U.K.: Pocket Essentials, 2000.

Featherstone, Mike, and Roger Burrows. *Cyberspace/Cyberbodies/Cyberpunk: Cultures of Technological Embodiment*. Thousand Oaks, Calif.: Sage, 1995.

Heuser, Sabine. *Virtual Geographies: Cyberpunk at the Intersection of the Postmodern and Science Fiction*. Amsterdam: Rodolpi, 2002.
Slusser, George E., and Tom Shippey, eds. *Fiction 2000: Cyberpunk and the Future of Narrative*. Athens: University of Georgia Press, 1992.
Sterling, Bruce. Preface. In *Mirrorshades: The Cyberpunk Anthology*, vii-xiv. New York: Arbor House, 1986.

## Ecology

Yanarella, Ernest J. *The Cross, the Plow and, the Skyline: Contemporary Science Fiction and the Ecological Imagination*. Parkland, Fla.: Brown Walker Press, 2001.

## The Far Future

Broderick, Damien, ed. *Earth Is but a Star: Excursions through Science Fiction to the Far Future*. Crawley, Australia: University of Western Australia Press, 2001.

## Feminism and Sexuality

Armitt, Lucie, ed. *Where No Man Has Gone Before: Women and Science Fiction*. London: Routledge, 1991.
Attebery, Brian. *Decoding Gender in Science Fiction*. London: Routledge, 2002.
Balsamo, Anne. *Technologies of the Gendered Body: Reading Cyborg Women*. Durham, N.C.: Duke University Press, 1996.
Bammer, Angelika. *Partial Visions: Feminism and Utopianism in the 1970s*. New York: Routledge, 1991.
Barr, Marleen S. *Alien to Femininity: Speculative Fiction and Feminist Theory*. Westport, Conn.: Greenwood Press, 1987.
———. *Feminist Fabulation: Space/Postmodern Fiction*. Iowa City: University of Iowa Press, 1992.
———, ed. *Future Females: A Critical Anthology*. Bowling Green, Ohio: Bowling Green State University Popular Press, 1981.
———, ed. *Future Females, the Next Generation: New Voices and Velocities in Feminist Science Fiction Criticism*. Lanham, Md.: Rowman and Littlefield, 2000.
———. *Lost in Space: Probing Feminist Science Fiction and Beyond*. Chapel Hill: University of North Carolina Press, 1993.
Barr, Marleen, and Nicholas Smith, eds. *Women and Utopia: Critical Interpretations*. Lanham, Md.: University Press of America, 1983.

Bartkowski, Frances. *Feminist Utopias*. Lincoln: University of Nebraska Press, 1989.

Burwell, Jennifer. *Notes on Nowhere: Feminism, Utopian Logic, and Social Transformation*. Minneapolis: University of Minnesota Press, 1997.

Davin, Eric Leif, and Norman Metcalf. Presumption of Prejudice: Women Writers of the 1929–49 Science Fiction Magazines and Their Lost Legacy. *Fantasy Commentator* 53/54 (Winter 2001–02):24–74.

———. Hidden From History: The Female Counterculture of the 1950–1960 Science-Fiction Magazines. *Fantasy Commentator* 55/56 (Spring 2003):138–91.

Donawerth, Jane L. *Frankenstein's Daughters: Women Writing Science Fiction*. Syracuse, N.Y.: Syracuse University Press, 1997.

Donawerth, Jane L., and Carol A. Kolmerten, eds. *Utopian and Science Fiction by Women: Worlds of Difference*. Syracuse, N.Y.: Syracuse University Press, 1994.

Garber, Eric, and Lin Paleo. *Uranian Worlds: A Reader's Guide to Alternative Sexuality in Science Fiction and Fantasy*. 2nd. ed. Boston: G. K. Hall, 1990.

Haraway, Donna J. A Cyborg Manifesto: Science, Technology, and Socialist-Feminism in the Late Twentieth Century. In *Simians, Cyborgs, and Women: The Reinvention of Nature*, 149–81. New York: Routledge, 1991 [first published 1985].

King, Betty. *Women of the Future: The Female Main Character in Science Fiction*. Metuchen, N.J.: Scarecrow Press, 1984.

Larbalestier, Justine. *The Battle of the Sexes in Science Fiction*. Middletown, Conn.: Wesleyan University Press, 2001.

Lefanu, Sarah. *In the Chinks of the World Machine: Feminism and Science Fiction*. London: Women's Press, 1988.

Merrick, Helen, and Tess Williams, eds. *Women of Other Worlds: Excursions through Science Fiction and Fantasy*. Perth, Australia: University of Western Australia Press, 1999.

Notkin, Debbie, and the Secret Feminist Cabal, eds. *Flying Cups and Saucers: Gender Explorations in Science Fiction and Fantasy*. Cambridge, Mass.: Edgewood Press, 1998.

Palumbo, Donald, ed. *Erotic Universe: Sexuality and Fantastic Literature*. New York: Greenwood Press, 1986.

Roberts, Robin. *A New Species: Gender and Science in Science Fiction*. Urbana: University of Illinois Press, 1993.

Rosinsky, Natalie M. *Feminist Futures: Contemporary Women's Speculative Fiction*. Ann Arbor, Mich.: UMI Research Press, 1984.

Russ, Joanna. *To Write Like a Woman: Essays in Feminism and Science Fiction*. Bloomington: Indiana University Press, 1995.

Shaw, Debra Benita. *Women, Science and Fiction: The Frankenstein Inheritance*. New York: Palgrave, 2001.

Shinn, Thelma J. *Worlds within Women: Myth and Mythmaking in Fantastic Literature by Women*. Westport, Conn: Greenwood Press, 1986.
Staicar, Tom, ed. *The Feminine Eye: Science Fiction and the Women Who Write It*. New York: Ungar, 1982.
Testenko, Tatiana. *Feminist Utopian Novels of the 1970s: Joanna Russ and Dorothy Bryant*. London: Routledge, 2003.
Weedman, Jane, ed. *Women Worldwalkers: New Dimensions of Science Fiction and Fantasy*. Lubbock: Texas Tech Press, 1985.
Wolmark, Jenny. *Aliens and Others: Science Fiction, Feminism, and Postmodernism*. Iowa City: University of Iowa Press, 1994.
——, ed. *Cybersexualities: A Reader on Feminist Theory, Cyborgs, and Cyberspace*. Edinburgh, U.K.: Edinburgh University Press, 1999.

## Hard SF

Slusser, George E., and Eric S. Rabkin, eds. *Hard Science Fiction*. Carbondale: Southern Illinois University Press, 1986.
Westfahl, Gary. *Cosmic Engineers: A Study of Hard Science Fiction*. Westport, Conn.: Greenwood Press, 1996.

## Humor

Hassler, Donald M. *Comic Tones in Science Fiction: The Art of Compromise with Nature*. Westport, Conn.: Greenwood Press, 1982.

## Imaginary Voyages

Gove, Philip Babcock. *The Imaginary Voyage in Prose Fiction*. New York: Columbia University Press, 1941.

## Linguistics

Meyers, Walter E. *Aliens and Linguists: Language Study and Science Fiction*. Athens: University of Georgia Press, 1980.

## Longevity

Yoek, Carl B., and Donald M. Hassler, eds. *Death and the Serpent: Immortality in Science Fiction and Fantasy*. Westport, Conn.: Greenwood Press, 1985.

## Medicine

Westfahl, Gary, and George Slusser, eds. *No Cure for the Future: Disease and Medicine in Science Fiction and Fantasy*. Westport, Conn.: Greenwood Press, 2002.

## Mythology

Fredericks, Casey. *The Future of Eternity: Mythologies of Science Fiction and Fantasy*. Bloomington: Indiana University Press, 1982.

## New Wave SF

Ballard, J. G. Which Way to Inner Space? *New Worlds* 118 (May 1962):2–3, 116–18.

Greenland, Colin. *The Entropy Exhibition: Michael Moorcock and the British "New Wave" in Science Fiction*. London: Routledge, 1983.

## Philosophy

Clark, Stephen R. L. *How to Live Forever: Science Fiction and Philosophy*. London: Routledge, 1995.

Miller, Fred D., Jr., and Nicholas D. Smith, eds. *Thought Probes: Philosophy through Science Fiction*. Englewood Cliffs, N.J.: Prentice Hall, 1981.

Myers, Robert E., ed. *The Intersection of Science Fiction and Philosophy: Critical Studies*. Westport, Conn.: Greenwood Press, 1983.

Phillips, Michael, ed. *Philosophy and Science Fiction*. Buffalo, N.Y.: Prometheus, 1984.

Smith, Nicholas D., ed. *Philosophers Look at Science Fiction*. Chicago: Nelson Hall, 1982.

## Politics

Hassler, Donald M., and Clyde Wilcox, eds. *Political Science Fiction*. Columbia: University of South Carolina Press, 1997.

## Postholocaust Fantasy

Yoke, Carl B., and Donald M. Hassler, eds. *Phoenix from the Ashes: The Literature of the Remade World*. Westport, Conn: Greenwood Press, 1987.

## Race and Ethnicity

Leonard, Elizabeth Anne, ed. *Into Darkness Peering: Race and Color in the Fantastic*. Westport, Conn.: Greenwood, 1997.

## Religion

Reilly, Robert, ed. *The Transcendent Adventure: Studies of Religion in Science Fiction/Fantasy*. Westport, Conn.: Greenwood Press, 1984.

## Science

Goswami, Amit, and Maggie Goswami. *The Cosmic Dancers: Exploring the Physics of Science Fiction*. New York: Harper, 1983.
Nicholls, Peter, David Langford, and Brian Stableford. *The Science in Science Fiction*. London: Michael Joseph, 1982.
Stocker, Jack H., ed. *Chemistry and Science Fiction*. Washington, D.C.: American Chemical Society, 1998.

## Slipstream

Sterling, Bruce. Slipstream. *Science Fiction Eye* 1, no. 5 (July 1989):77–80.

## Space Travel and Extraterrestrial Colonization

Baxter, Stephen. Martian Chronicles: Narratives of Mars in Science and SF. *Foundation* 68 (Autumn 1996):5–15.
Clarke, Arthur C. Science Fiction: Preparation for the Age of Space. In *Modern Science Fiction: Its Meaning and Its Future*. Ed. Reginald Bretnor, 197–220. New York: Coward-McCann, 1953.
Emme, Eugene E., ed. *Science Fiction and Space Futures Past and Present*. San Diego, Calif.: American Astronautical Society, 1982.
Flammarion, Camille. *Les Mondes imaginaires et les mondes réels: voyage pittoresque dans le ciel et revue critique des théories humaines, scientifiques et romanesques, anciennes et modernes sur les habitants des astres*. Paris: Didier et cie, 1864; exp. Paris: Marpon et Flammarion, 1892.
Green, Roger Lancelyn. *Into Other Worlds: Space Flight in Fiction from Lucian to Lewis*. New York: Abelard-Schumann, 1958.
Mogen, David. *Wilderness Visions: Science Fiction Westerns*. Vol. 1 San Barnardino, Calif.: Borgo Press, 1982; exp. 1994.

Nicolson, Marjorie Hope. *Voyages to the Moon*. New York: Macmillan, 1948.

Ordway, Frederick I., and Randy Liebermann, eds. *Blueprint for Space: Science Fiction to Science Fact*. Washington, D.C.: Smithsonian Institution, 1992.

Wachhorst, Wyn. *The Dream of Spaceflight: Essays on the Near Edge of Infinity*. New York: Basic Books, 2000.

Westfahl, Gary, ed. *Space and Beyond: The Frontier Theme in Science Fiction*. Westport, Conn.: Greenwood Press, 2000.

## Technology

Berger, Albert I. *The Magic That Works: John W. Campbell and the American Response to Technology*. San Bernardino, Calif.: Borgo, 1993.

Dunn, Thomas P., and Richard D. Erlich, eds. *The Mechanical God: Machines in Science Fiction*. Westport, Conn.: Greenwood Press, 1982.

Erlich, Richard D., and Thomas P. Dunn, eds. *Clockwork Worlds: Mechanical Environments in SF*. Westport, Conn.: Greenwood Press, 1983.

## Time Travel

Foote, Bud. *The Connecticut Yankee in the Twentieth Century: Travels to the Past in Science Fiction*. Westport, Conn.: Greenwood Press, 1990.

Nahin, Paul J. *Time Machines: Time Travel in Physics, Metaphysics, and Science Fiction*. New York: Springer-Verlag (American Institute of Physics Press), 1999.

Westfahl, Gary, George Slusser, and David Leiby. *Worlds Enough and Time: Explorations of Time in Science Fiction and Fantasy*. Westport, Conn.: Greenwood Press, 2002.

## Utopian and Anti-Utopian Studies

Albinski, N. B. *Women's Utopias in British and American Fiction*. London: Routledge, 1988.

Berger, Harold. *Science Fiction and the New Dark Age*. Bowling Green, Ohio: Bowling Green University Press, 1976.

Bloomfield, P. *Imaginary Worlds or the Evolution of Utopia*. London: Hamish Hamilton, 1932.

Brown, E. B. *Brave New World, 1984, and We: Essays on Anti-Utopia*. Ann Arbor, Mich.: Ardis, 1976.

Elliott, Robert C. *The Shape of Utopia: Studies in a Literary Genre*. Chicago: University of Chicago Press, 1970.

Ferns, Chris. *Narrating Utopia: Ideology, Gender, Form in Utopian Literature*. Liverpool, U.K.: Liverpool University Press, 1999.

Fortunati, Vita, and Raymond Trousson, eds. *Dictionary of Literary Utopias*. Paris: Honoré Champion, 2000.

Gerber, Richard. *Utopian Fantasy: A Study of English Utopian Fiction since the End of the Nineteenth Century*. London: Routledge, 1955.

Goodwin, Barbara, ed. *The Philosophy of Utopia*. London: Frank Cass, 2001.

Gottlieb, Erika. *Dystopian Fiction East and West: Universe of Terror and Trial*. Montreal: McGill-Queens University Press, 2001.

Greven-Borde, Hélène. *Formes du roman utopique en Grande-Bretagne (1918–1970)*. Paris: Presses Universitaires de France, 1984.

Hillegas, Mark R. *The Future as Nightmare: H. G. Wells and the Anti-Utopians*. Oxford, U.K.: Oxford University Press, 1967.

Kilgore, De Witt Douglas. *Astrofuturism: Science, Race, and Visions of Utopia in Space*. Philadelphia: University of Pennsylvania Press, 2003.

Klaic, Dragan. *The Plot of the Future: Utopia and Dystopia in Modern Drama*. Ann Arbor: University of Michigan Press, 1992.

Kumar, Krishan. *Utopia and Anti-Utopia in Modern Times*. Oxford, U.K.: Blackwell, 1987.

Manuel, Frank E., and Fritzie P. Manuel, eds. *Utopian Thought in the Western World*. Cambridge, Mass.: Belknap Press, 1980.

Moylan, Tom. *Demand the Impossible: Science Fiction and the Utopian Imagination*. New York: Methuen, 1986.

———. *Scraps of the Untainted Sky: Science Fiction, Utopia, Dystopia*. Boulder, Colo.: Westview Press, 2000.

Moylan, Tom, and Raffaella Baccolini, eds. *Dark Horizons: Science Fiction and the Utopian Imagination*. London: Routledge, 2003.

Pordzick, Ralph. *The Quest for Postcolonial Utopia: A Comprehensive Introduction to the Utopian Novel in New English Literature*. New York: Peter Lang, 2001.

Rabkin, Eric S., Martin H. Greenberg, and Joseph D. Olander, eds. *No Place Else: Explorations in Utopian and Dystopian Fiction*. Carbondale: Southern Illinois University Press, 1983.

Roemer, Kenneth, ed. *America as Utopia*. New York: Burt Franklin, 1981.

Schaer, Roland, Gregory Claes, and Lyman Tower Sargent, eds. *Utopia: The Search for the Ideal Society in the Western World*. New York: Oxford University Press, 2000.

Sibley, Mulford Q. *Technology and Utopian Thought*. Minneapolis: Burgess, 1973.

Spinozzi, Paola, ed. *Utopianism/Literary Utopias and National Cultural Identities: A Comparative Perspective*. Bologna, Italy: Cotepra, 2001.

Walsh, Chad. *From Utopia to Nightmare*. London: Bles, 1962.

Zaki, Hoda M. *Phoenix Renewed: The Survival and Mutation of Utopian Thought in North American Science Fiction 1965–1982*. Mercer Island, Wash.: Starmont House, 1988. Rev. ed. San Bernardino, Calif.: Borgo Press, 1993.

## War

Anisfield, Nancy, ed. *The Nightmare Considered: Critical Essays on Nuclear War Literature*. Bowling Green, Ohio: Bowling Green University Press, 1991.

Bartter, Martha J. *The Way to Ground Zero: The Atomic Bomb in American Science Fiction*. Westport, Conn.: Greenwood, 1988.

Booker, M. Keith. *Monsters, Mushroom Clouds, and the Cold War: American Science Fiction and the Roots of Postmodernism, 1946–1964*. Westport, Conn.: Greenwood, 2001.

Brians, Paul. *Nuclear Holocausts: Atomic War in Fiction, 1895–1984*. Kent, Ohio: Kent State University Press. 1987.

Carpenter, Charles A. *Dramatists and the Bomb: American and British Playwrights Confront the Nuclear Age, 1945–1964*. Westport, Conn.: Greenwood Press, 1999.

Clarke, I. F. *Voices Prophesying War: Future Wars 1763–3749*. Oxford, U.K.: Oxford University Press, 1966; 2nd ed., 1992.

Davies, Philip John, ed. *Science Fiction, Social Conflict and War*. Manchester, U.K.: Manchester University Press, 1990.

Dowling, David. *Fictions of Nuclear Disaster*. Iowa City: University of Iowa Press, 1987.

Franklin, H. Bruce. *War Stars: The Superweapon and the American Imagination*. New York: Oxford University Press, 1988.

Newman, John, and Michael Unsworth. *Future War Novels: An Annotated Bibliography of Works in English Published since 1946*. Phoenix, Ariz.: Oryx Press, 1984.

Seed, David. *American Science Fiction and the Cold War: Literature and Film*. London: Fitzroy Dearborn, 1999.

Slusser, George, and Eric S. Rabkin. *Fights of Fancy: Armed Conflict in Science Fiction and Fantasy*. Athens: University of Georgia Press, 1993.

# NATIONS AND REGIONS

## Comparative Studies

Bozzetto, Roger. Intercultural Interplay: Science Fiction in France and the United States (as Viewed from the French Shore). *Science-Fiction Studies* 17, no. 1 (1990):1–24.

Griffiths, John. *Three Tomorrows: American, British, and Soviet Science Fiction*. New York: Barnes and Noble, 1980.

## Australia

Blackford, Russell, Van Ikin, and Sean McMullen. *Strange Constellations: A History of Australian Science Fiction*. Westport, Conn.: Greenwood, 1999.

Collins, Paul, Steven Paulsen, and Sean McMullen, eds. *The MUP Encyclopedia of Australian Science Fiction and Fantasy*. Melbourne, Australia: Melbourne University Press, 1998.

Stone, Graham. *Australian Science Fiction Index 1925–1967*. Canberra, Australia: Australian Science Fiction Association, 1968; *Supplement 1968–1975*. Sydney, Australia: Australian Science Fiction Association, 1976.

———. *Notes on Australian Science Fiction*. Sydney, Australia: Author, 2001.

## British Isles

Aldiss, Brian W. British Science Fiction Now. *SF Horizons* 2 (1965):13–37.

Bailey, K. V., Gregory Benford, Cy Chauvin, Vladimir Gopman, Péter Kuckza, Josef Nesvadba, Franz Rottensteiner, and Koichi Yamano. British SF as Seen from Abroad. *Foundation* 30 (March 1984):5–50.

Kincaid, Paul. *A Very British Genre: A Short History of British Fantasy and Science Fiction*. Folkestone, U.K.: British Science Fiction Association, 1995.

Ruddick, Nicholas. *Ultimate Island: On the Nature of British Science Fiction*. Westport, Conn.: Greenwood, 1993.

## Canada

Ketterer, David. *Canadian Science Fiction and Fantasy*. Bloomington: Indiana University Press, 1992.

Ransom, Amy J. (Un)common Ground: National Sovereignty and Individual Identity in Contemporary Sf from Québec. *Science Fiction Studies* 27, no. 3 (2000):439–60.

## China

Huss, Mikhael. Journey to the West: SF's Changing Fortunes in Mainland China. *Science Fiction Studies* 27, no. 1 (2000):92–104.

Lu Yingzhong and Wu Yan. *An Introductory Course on SF Literature*. Taipei, China: Wu Nan Book Publishing, 2001.

## Czechoslovakia

Adamovi, Ivan. Czech SF in the Last Forty Years. *Science-Fiction Studies* 17, no. 1 (1990):50–59.

## Eastern Europe

Kasack, Wolfgang. *Science-Fiction in Osteuropa*. Berlin: Arno Spitz, 1984.

## France

Gouanvic, Jean-Marc. *La Science-fiction française au XXe siècle (1900–1968)*. Atlanta, Ga.: Rodopi, 1994.

Lofficier, Jean-Marc, and Randy Lofficier. *French Science Fiction, Fantasy, Horror and Pulp Fiction: A Guide to Cinema, Television, Radio, Animation, Comic Books, and Literature from the Middle Ages to the Present*. Jefferson, N.C.: McFarland, 2000.

Nicot, Stéphane, ed. *Les Univers de la Science-Fiction: Essais*. Nancy, France: Galaxies, 1998.

Torres, Anita. *La science-fiction française*. Paris: L'Harmattan, 1998.

## Germany

Fischer, William B. *The Empire Strikes Out: Kurd Lasswitz, Hans Dominik and the Development of German Science Fiction*. Bowling Green, Ohio: Popular Press, 1984.

Fisher, Peter S. *Fantasy and Politics: Visions of the Future in the Weimar Republic*. Madison: University of Wisconsin Press, 1991.

Heidtmann, Horst. *Utopisch-phantastische Literatur in der DDR: Untersuchungen zur Entwicklung eines unterhaltungliterarischen Genres von 1945–1979*. Munich, Germany: Wilhelm Fink Verlag, 1982.

Innerhofer, Roland. *Deutsche Science Fiction 1870–1914: Rekonstruktion und Analyse der Anfange einer Gattung*. Vienna: Bohlau, 1996.

Kruschel, Karsten. *Spielwelten zwischen Wunschbild und Warnbild: Eutopisches und Dystopisches in der SF-Literatur der DDR in den achtziger Jahren* Passau, Germany: Erster Deutscher Fantasy Club, 1995.

## Greece

Pastourmatzi, Domna. Hellenic Magazines of Science Fiction. *Science Fiction Studies* 26, no. 3 (1999):412–30.

———. Space Flight and Space Conflict in Hellenic Science Fiction. *Foundation* 77 (Autumn 1999):59–83.

## Italy

Calabrese, Fabio. Italian Sf: Trends and Authors. *Foundation* 34 (Autumn 1985):49–56.

## Japan

Matthew, Robert. *Japanese Science Fiction: A View of a Changing Society*. London: Routledge, 1989.

Takayuki, Tatsumi, Christopher Bolton, and Istvan Csisery-Tonay, eds. Japanese Science Fiction. *Science Fiction Studies* 29, no. 3 (2002):321–484.

## Latin America

Bell, Andrea L., and Yolanda Molina-Gavilán. *Cosmos Latinos: An Anthology of Science Fiction from Latin America and Spain*. Middletown, Conn.: Wesleyan University Press, 2003.

Causo, Roberto S. *Ficção Cientifica, Fantasia e Horror no Brasil: 1875–1950*. Brasõpolis, Minas Gerais, Brazil: Edouard Guimaraes, 2003.

Dziubinskyj, Aaron. The Birth of Science Fiction in Spanish America. *Science Fiction Studies* 30, no. 1 (2003):21–32.

Lockhart, Darrell B. *Latin American Science Fiction Writers: An A-to-Z Guide*. Westport, Conn.: Greenwood Press, 2004.

Molina-Gavilán, Yolanda. *Ciencia Ficcion en español: Una mitalogia moderna ante el cambio*. Lewiston, N.Y.: Edwin Mellen, 2002.

Tavares, Braulio. *Fantastic, Fantasy and Science Fiction Literature Catalog*. Rio de Janeiro: Biblioteca Nacional, 1993.

## Portugal

Holstein, Alvaro de Sousa, and José Manuel Morais. *Bibliografia da Ficção Cientifica e Fantasia Portuguesa*. Lisbon: Black Sun, 1993.

## Romania

Robu, Cornel. Milestones of Postwar Romanian Science Fiction. *Foundation* 49 (Summer 1990):5–22.

## Russia

Banerjee, Anindita. Electricity: Science Fiction and Modernity in Early Twentieth-Century Russia. *Science Fiction Studies* 30, no. 1 (2003):49–71.

Glad, John. *Extrapolations from Dystopia: A Critical Study of Soviet Science Fiction*. Kingston, N.J.: Kingston Press, 1982.

Heller, Leonid. *De la science-fiction soviétique: par delà le dogme, un univers*. Lausanne, Switzerland: L'Age d'Homme, 1979.

Lahana, Jacqueline. *Les mondes parallèles de la science-fiction soviétique*. Lausanne, Switzerland: L'Age d'Homme, 1979.

McGuire, Patrick L. *Red Stars: Political Aspects of Soviet Science Fiction*. Ann Arbor, Mich.: UMI Research Press, 1985.

Suvin, Darko. *Russian Science Fiction 1956–1974: A Bibliography*. Elizabethtown, N.Y.: Dragon Press, 1976.

## Spain

Núñez Ladeveze, Luis, ed. *Utopia y realidad: La ciencia ficción en España*. Madrid: Editions del Centro, n.d. (c1976).

Santiáñez-Tió, Nil. Nuevos mapas del universo: Modernidad y ciencia ficción en la literatura española del siglo XIX (1804–1905). *Revista Hispánica Moderna* 47, no. 2 (1994):269–88.

# STUDIES OF INDIVIDUAL AUTHORS

## Collections

Aldiss, Brian W., and Harry Harrison, eds. *Hell's Cartographers: Some Personal Histories of Science Fiction Writers*. London: Weidenfeld and Nicolson, 1975.

Bleiler, Everett F., and Richard Bleiler. *Science Fiction Writers: Critical Studies of the Major Authors from the Early Nineteenth Century to the Present Day*. 2nd ed. New York: Scribner, 1999.

Cowart, David, and Thomas J. Wymer, eds. *Dictionary of Literary Biography*. Vol. 8, *Twentieth-Century American Science-Fiction Writers*. 2 vols. Farmington Hills, Mich.: Gale, 1981.

Davin, Eric Leif. *Pioneers of Wonder: Conversations with the Founders of Science Fiction*. Buffalo, N.Y.: Prometheus, 1999.

Greenberg, Martin H., ed. *Fantastic Lives: Autobiographical Essays by Notable Science Fiction Writers*. Carbondale: Southern Illinois University Press, 1981.

Harris-Fain, Darren, ed. *Dictionary of Literary Biography*. Vol. 255, *British Fantasy and Science-Fiction Writers, 1918–1960*. Farmington Hills, Mich.: Gale, 2003.

——, ed. *Dictionary of Literary Biography*. Vol. 261, *British Fantasy and Science-Fiction Writers since 1960*. Farmington Hills, Mich.: Gale, 2003.

Jakubowski, Maxim, and Edward James, eds. *The Profession of Science Fiction: Writers on Their Craft and Ideas*. London: Macmillan, 1991.

Jarvis, Sharon, ed. *Inside Outer Space: Science Fiction Professionals Look at Their Craft*. New York: Ungar, 1985.

McCaffery, Larry, ed. *Across the Wounded Galaxies: Interviews with Contemporary American Science Fiction Writers*. Urbana: University of Illinois Press, 1990.

Moskowitz, Sam. *Explorers of the Infinite: Shapers of Science Fiction*. Cleveland, Ohio: World, 1963.

——. *Seekers of Tomorrow: Masters of Modern Science Fiction*. Cleveland, Ohio: World, 1966.

Platt, Charles. *Dream Makers: The Uncommon People Who Write Science Fiction*. 2 vols. New York: Berkley, 1980–83. Rev. as *Dream Makers: Science Fiction and Fantasy Writers at Work* . New York: Ungar, 1987.

Schweitzer, Darrell, and Jefrey M. Elliot, eds. *Science Fiction Voices*. 4 vols. San Bernardino, Calif.: Borgo Press, 1979–82.

Stableford, Brian. *Algebraic Fantasies and Realistic Romances: More Masters of Science Fiction*. San Bernardino, Calif.: Borgo Press, 1995.

——. *Outside the Human Aquarium: Masters of Science Fiction*. San Bernardino, Calif.: Borgo Press, 1995.

Tolley, Michael J., and Kirpal Singh, eds. *The Stellar Gauge: Essays on Science Fiction Authors*. Melbourne, Australia: Norstilia Press, 1980.

Van Belkom, Edo. *Northern Dreamers: Interviews with Famous Science Fiction, Fantasy, and Horror Writers*. Kingston, Ontario, Canada: Quarry, 1998.

Walker, Paul. *Speaking of Science Fiction*. Oradell, N.J.: Luna 1978.

## Brian W. Aldiss

Aldiss, Brian W. *Bury My Heart at W. H. Smith's: A Writing Life*. London: Hodder & Stoughton, 1990.

Collings, Michael. *Brian W. Aldiss*. Mercer Island, Wash: Starmont, 1986.

Griffin, Brian, and David Wingrove. *Apertures: A Study of the Writings of Brian Aldiss*. Westport, Conn.: Greenwood Press, 1984.

Mathews, Richard. *Aldiss Unbound: The Science Fiction of Brian W. Aldiss*. San Bernardino, Calif.: Borgo Press, 1977.

## Poul Anderson

Miesel, Sandra. *Against Time's Arrow: The High Crusade of Poul Anderson*. San Bernardino, Calif.: Borgo Press, 1978.

## Piers Anthony

Collings, Michael R. *Piers Anthony*. Mercer Island, Wash.: Starmont House, 1983.

## Isaac Asimov

Asimov, Isaac. *I, Asimov: A Memoir*. New York: Doubleday, 1994.
Fiedler, Jean, and Jim Mele. *Isaac Asimov*. New York: Ungar, 1982.
Goble, Neil. *Asimov Analyzed*. Baltimore, Md.: Mirage Press, 1972.
Gunn, James E. *Isaac Asimov: The Foundations of Science Fiction*. New York: Oxford University Press, 1982.
Hassler, Donald M. *Isaac Asimov*. Mercer Island, Wash: Starmont, 1991.
Olander, Joseph D., and Martin H. Greenberg, eds. *Isaac Asimov*. New York: Taplinger, 1977.
Palumbo, Donald. *Chaos Theory, Asimov's Foundations and Robots, and Herbert's Dune: The Fractal Aesthetics of Epic Science Fiction*. Westport, Conn.: Greenwood Press, 2002.
Patrouch. Joseph F. Jr. *The Science Fiction of Isaac Asimov*. Garden City, N.Y.: Doubleday, 1974.
Slusser, George Edgar. *Asimov: The Foundations of His Science Fiction*. San Bernardino, Calif.: Borgo Press, 1980.
Touponce, William F. *Isaac Asimov*. Boston: Twayne, 1991.

## J. G. Ballard

Brigg, Peter. *J. G. Ballard*. San Bernardino, Calif.: Borgo Press, 1985.
Delville, Michael. *J. G. Ballard*. Plymouth, U.K.: Northcote House, 1998.
Goddard, James, and David Pringle, eds. *J. G. Ballard: The First Twenty Years*. Hayes, U.K.: Bran's Head, 1976.
Pringle, David. *Earth Is the Alien Planet: J. G. Ballard's Four-Dimensional Nightmare*. San Bernardino, Calif.: Borgo Press, 1979.
Stephenson, Gregory. *Out of the Night and Into the Dream: A Thematic Study of the Fiction of J. G. Ballard*. Westport, Conn.: Greenwood Press, 1991.

## Iain M. Banks

Middleton, Tim. The Worlds of Iain M. Banks: A Critical Introduction. *Foundation* 76 (Summer 1999):5–16.

## Alfred Bester

Wendell, Carolyn. *Alfred Bester*. Mercer Island, Wash: Starmont House, 1982.

## James Blish

Ketterer, David. *Imprisoned in a Tesseract: The Life and Work of James Blish*. Kent, Ohio: Kent State University Press, 1987.

Stableford, Brian. *A Clash of Symbols: The Triumph of James Blish*. San Bernardino, Calif.: Borgo Press, 1979.

## Leigh Brackett

Carr, John L. *Leigh Brackett; American Writer*. Polk City, Iowa: Drumm, 1986.

## Ray Bradbury

De Koster, Katie, ed., *Readings on "Fahrenheit 451."* San Diego, Calif.: Greenhaven Press, 2000.

Johnson, Wayne L. *Ray Bradbury*. New York: Ungar, 1980.

Mogen, David. *Ray Bradbury*. Boston: Twayne, 1986.

Olander, Joseph P., and Martin H. Greenberg, eds. *Ray Bradbury*. New York: Taplinger, 1980.

Reid, Robin Anne. *Ray Bradbury: A Critical Companion*. Westport, Conn.: Greenwood Press, 2000.

Slusser, George Edgar. *The Bradbury Chronicles*. San Bernardino, Calif.: Borgo Press, 1977.

Touponce, William F. *Ray Bradbury*. Mercer Island, Wash: Starmont House, 1989.

———. *Ray Bradbury and the Poetics of Reverie: Fantasy, Science Fiction, and the Reader*. Ann Arbor, Mich.: UMI Research Press, 1984.

## John Brunner

De Bolt, Joseph W., ed. *The Happening Worlds of John Brunner*. Port Washington, N.Y.: Kennikat Press, 1975.

## Edgar Rice Burroughs

Holtsmark, Erling B. *Edgar Rice Burroughs*. Boston: Twayne, 1986.
Kudlay, Robert R., and Joan Leiby. *Burroughs' Science Fiction*. Geneseo, N.Y.: School of Library and Information Science, 1973.
Lupoff, Richard A. *Barsoom: Edgar Rice Burroughs and the Martian Vision*. Baltimore, Md.: Mirage Press, 1976.
Mullen Richard D. Edgar Rice Burroughs and the Fate Worse Than Death. *Riverside Quarterly* 4, no. 3 (1970):186–91.
Roy, John Flint. *A Guide to Barsoom*. New York: Ballantine, 1976.

## John W. Campbell Jr.

Bangsund, John. *John W. Campbell: An Australian Tribute*. Canberra, Australia: Parergon Books, 1974.
Campbell, John W. *The John W. Campbell Letters, Volume 1*. Ed. Perry A. Chapdelaine Sr., Tony Chapdelaine, and George Hay. Franklin, Tenn.: AC Project, 1985.
———. *The John W. Campbell Letters, Volume 2: Isaac Asimov and A. E. van Vogt*. Ed. Perry A. Chapdelaine Sr., Tony Chapdelaine, and George Hay. Franklin, Tenn.: AC Project, 1993.

## Card, Orson Scott

Collings, Michael R. *In the Image of God: Theme, Characterization, and Landscape in the Fiction of Orson Scott Card*. Westport, Conn.: Greenwood Press, 1990.

## Arthur C. Clarke

Clarke, Arthur C. *Astounding Days: A Science Fictional Autobiography*. New York: Bantam, 1990.
Hollow, John. *Against the Night, the Stars: The Science Fiction of Arthur C. Clarke*. New York: Harcourt Brace, 1983. Rev. ed., Athens: Ohio University Press, 1987.
Olander, Joseph P., and Martin H. Greenberg, eds. *Arthur C. Clarke*. New York: Taplinger, 1977.
Rabkin, Eric S. *Arthur C. Clarke*. West Linn, Ore.: Starmont House, 1979. Rev. ed. 1980.
Slusser, George Edgar. *The Space Odysseys of Arthur C. Clarke*. San Bernardino, Calif.: Borgo Press, 1978.

## Hal Clement

Hassler, Donald M. *Hal Clement*. Mercer Island, Wash.: Starmont House, 1982.

## Samuel R. Delany

Barbour, Douglas. *Worlds Out of Words: The SF Novels of Samuel R. Delany*. Frome, Somerset, U.K.: Bran's Head, 1979.
McEvoy, Seth. *Samuel R. Delany*. New York: Ungar, 1983.
Slusser, George Edgar. *The Delany Intersection*. San Bernardino, Calif.: Borgo Press, 1977.
Weedman, Jane Branhan. *Samuel R. Delany*. Mercer Island, Wash.: Starmont House, 1982.

## Philip K. Dick

Butler, Andrew. *Philip K. Dick*. Harpenden, U.K.: Pocket Essentials, 2000.
Carrere, Emmanuel. *I Am Alive and You Are Dead: The Strange Life and Times of Philip K. Dick*. New York: Holt/Metropolitan, 2003.
Gillespie, Bruce, ed. *Philip K. Dick: Electric Shepherd*. Melbourne, Australia: Norstrilia Press, 1975.
Greenberg, Martin H., and Joseph P. Olander, eds. *Philip K. Dick*. New York: Taplinger, 1983.
Mackey, Douglas A. *Philip K. Dick*. Boston: Twayne, 1988.
Mullen, R. D., Istvan Csisery-Ronay, Jr., and Arthur B. Evans, eds. *On Philip K. Dick: 40 Articles from Science-Fiction Studies*. Terre Haute, Ind.: SF-TH, 1992.
Palmer, Christopher. *Philip K. Dick: Exhilaration and Terror of the Postmodern*. Liverpool, U.K.: Liverpool University Press, 2003.
Pierce, Hazel. *Philip K. Dick*. Mercer Island, Wash.: Starmont House, 1982.
Rickman, Gregg. *To the High Castle: Philip K. Dick, a Life*. Long Beach, Calif.: Fragments West/Valentine Press, 1989.
Robinson, Kim Stanley. *The Novels of Philip K. Dick*. Ann Arbor, Mich.: UMI Research Press, 1984.
Sutin, Lawrence. *Divine Invasions: A Life of Philip K. Dick*. New York: Harmony, 1989.
Taylor, Angus. *Philip K. Dick and the Umbrella of Light*. Baltimore, Md.: T-K Graphics, 1975.
Warrick, Patricia S. *Mind in Motion: The Fiction of Philip K. Dick*. Carbondale: Southern Illinois University Press, 1987.

## Thomas M. Disch

Delany, Samuel R. *The American Shore: Meditations on a Tale of Science Fiction by Thomas M. Disch—Angouleme*. Elizabethtown, N.Y.: Dragon Press, 1978.

## Gardner Dozois

Swanwick, Michael. *Being Gardner Dozois*. Baltimore, Md.: Old Earth Books, 2001.

## Harlan Ellison

Slusser, George Edgar. *Harlan Ellison: Unrepentant Harlequin*. San Bernardino, Calif.: Borgo Press, 1977.

Weil, Ellen, and Gary K. Wolfe. *Harlan Ellison: The Edge of Forever*. Columbus: Ohio State University Press, 2002.

## Philip José Farmer

Brizzi, Mary T. *Philip José Farmer: A Reader's Guide*. West Linn, Ore.: Starmont House, 1980.

Chapman, Edgar L. *The Magic Labyrinth of Philip José Farmer*. San Bernardino, Calif.: Borgo Press, 1985.

## John Russell Fearn

Harbottle, Philip J. *The Multi-Man: A Biographic and Bibliographic Study of John Russell Fearn*. Wallsend, Northumberland, U.K.: Author, 1968.

## William Gibson

Cavallaro, Dani. *Cyberpunk and Cyberculture: Science Fiction and the Work of William Gibson*. London: Athlone Press, 2000.

Olsen, Lance. *William Gibson*. Mercer Island, Wash.: Starmont House, 1992.

## Charlotte Perkins Gilman

Gough, Val, and Jill Rudd, eds. *A Very Different Story: Studies on the Fiction of Charlotte Perkins Gilman*. Liverpool, U.K.: Liverpool University Press, 1998.

## Joe Haldeman

Gordon, Joan. *Joe Haldeman*. Mercer Island, Wash.: Starmont House, 1980.

## Harry Harrison

Stover, Leon. *Harry Harrison*. Boston: Twayne, 1990.

## Robert A. Heinlein

Franklin, H. Bruce. *Robert A. Heinlein: America as Science Fiction*. New York: Oxford University Press, 1980.

Gifford, James. *Robert A. Heinlein: A Reader's Companion*. Citrus Heights, Calif.: Nitrosyncretic Press, 2000.

Greenberg, Martin H., and Joseph P. Olander, eds. *Robert A. Heinlein*. New York: Taplinger, 1978.

Heinlein, Robert A. *Grumbles from the Grave*. Ed. Virginia Heinlein. New York: Ballantine, 1989.

Panshin, Alexei. *Heinlein in Dimension: A Critical Analysis*. Chicago: Advent, 1968.

Patterson, William H., Jr., and Andrew Thornton. *The Martian Named Smith: Critical Perspectives on Robert A. Heinlein's Stranger in a Strange Land*. Citrus Heights, Calif.: Nitrosyncretic Press, 2001.

Slusser, George Edgar. *Robert A. Heinlein: Stranger in His Own Land*. San Bernardino, Calif.: Borgo Press, 1976.

———. *The Classic Years of Robert A. Heinlein*. San Bernardino, Calif.: Borgo Press, 1977.

Stover, Leon. *Robert A. Heinlein*. Boston: Twayne, 1987.

## Frank Herbert

Miller, David M. *Frank Herbert*. Mercer Island, Wash.: Starmont House, 1980.

O'Reilly, Timothy. *Frank Herbert*. New York: Ungar, 1981.

## Robert Hunt

Stableford, Brian. Resisting Panthea's Siren Song: Robert Hunt and the Poetry of Science. *Foundation* 85 (Summer 2002):45–65.

## Kurd Lasswitz

Rottensteiner, Franz. Kurd Lasswitz: A German Pioneer of S.F. *Riverside Quarterly* 4, no. 1 (1969):4–18.

## Ursula K. le Guin

Bittner, James. *Approaches to the Fiction of Ursula K. le Guin*. Ann Arbor, Mich.: UMI Research Press, 1984.
Bucknall, Barbara J. *Ursula K. le Guin*. New York: Ungar, 1981.
Cummins, Elizabeth. *Understanding Ursula K. le Guin*. Columbia: University of South Carolina Press, 1990.
DeBolt, Joseph W., ed. *Ursula K. le Guin: Voyager to Inner Lands and Outer Space*. Port Washington, N.Y.: Kennikat Press, 1979.
Olander, Joseph P., and Martin H. Greenberg. *Ursula K. le Guin*. New York: Taplinger, 1979.
Rochelle, Warren G. *Communities of the Heart: The Rhetoric of Myth in the Fiction of Ursula K. le Guin*. Liverpool, U.K.: Liverpool University Press, 2001.
Slusser, George Edgar. *The Farthest Shores of Ursula K. le Guin*. San Bernardino, Calif.: Borgo Press, 1976.
Spivack, Charlotte. *Ursula K. le Guin*. Boston: Twayne, 1984.

## Fritz Leiber

Byfield, Bruce. *Witches of the Mind: A Critical Study of Fritz Leiber*. West Warwick, R.I.: Necronomicon Press, 1991.
Frane, Jeff. *Fritz Leiber*. San Bernardino, Calif.: Borgo Press, 1980.
Staicar, Tom. *Fritz Leiber*. New York: Ungar, 1983.

## Lem, Stanislaw

Davis, Marion J. *Stanislaw Lem*. Mercer Island, Wash.: Starmont House, 1990.
Ziegfeld, Richard E. *Stanislaw Lem*. New York: Ungar, 1985.

## H. P. Lovecraft

Carter, Lin. *Lovecraft: A Look behind the Cthulhu Mythos*. New York: Ballantine, 1972.
Gatto, John Taylor. *The Major Works of H. P. Lovecraft*. New York: Monarch Press, 1977.
Joshi, S. T. *H. P. Lovecraft*. Mercer Island, Wash.: Starmont House, 1982.

——. *A Subtler Magick: The Writings and Philosophy of H. P. Lovecraft*. Gillette, N.J.: Wildside Press, 1999.

Joshi, S. T., and David E. Schultz, eds. *An H. P. Lovecraft Encyclopedia*. Westport, Conn.: Greenwood Press, 2001.

Schweitzer, Darrell, ed. *Discovering H. P. Lovecraft, Revised and Expanded*. Holicong, Penn.: Wildside Press, 2001.

——. *The Dream Quest of H. P. Lovecraft*. San Bernardino, Calif.: Borgo Press, 1978.

## Anne McCaffrey

Brizzi, Mary T. *Anne McCaffrey*. Mercer Island, Wash.: Starmont House, 1986.

## Ken MacLeod

Butler, Andrew M., and Farah Mendlesohn. *The True Knowledge of Ken MacLeod*. Reading, U.K.: SF Foundation, 2003.

## Louis-Sebastien Mercier

Forsström, Riikka. *Possible Worlds: The Idea of Happiness in the Utopian Vision of Louis-Sébastien Mercier*. Helsinki: Suomalisen Kirjallisuuden Seura, 2002.

## Walter M. Miller Jr.

Secrest, Rose. *Glorificemus: A Study of the Fiction of Walter M. Miller, Jr.* Lanham, Md.: University Press of America, 2002.

## Michael Moorcock

Greenland, Colin. *Michael Moorcock: Death Is No Obstacle*. Manchester: Savoy, 1992.

## Frederik Pohl

Clareson, Thomas D. *Frederik Pohl*. Mercer Island, Wash.: Starmont House, 1987.

## Christopher Priest

Ruddick, Nicholas. *Christopher Priest*. Mercer Island, Wash.: Starmont House, 1989.

### Keith Roberts

Roberts, Keith. *Lemady: Episodes of a Writer's Life*. Gillette, N.J.: Wildside Press, 1999.

### J. H. Rosny aîné

Vernier, J.-H. The SF of J. H. Rosny the Elder. *Science Fiction Studies* 2, no. 2 (1975):156–63.

### Joanna Russ

Cortiel, Jeanne. *Demand My Writing: Joanna Russ, Feminism, Science Fiction*. Liverpool, U.K.: Liverpool University Press, 1999.

### Nat Schachner

Moskowitz, Sam. The Science Fiction of Nat Schachner (3 parts). *Fantasy Commentator* 43–46 (Spring 1992; Fall 1992; Winter 1993–94):160–79; 292–303; 52–73.

### Melissa Scott

Chernaik, Laura. Difference, the Social and the Spatial: the Fictions of Melissa Scott. *Foundation* 82 (Summer 2001):25–43.

### Robert Silverberg

Chapman, Edgar L. *The Road to Castle Mount: The Science Fiction of Robert Silverberg*. Westport, Conn.: Greenwood Press, 1999.

Clareson, Thomas D. *Robert Silverberg*. Mercer Island, Wash: Starmont House, 1983.

Elkins, Charles L., and Martin H. Greenberg, eds. *Robert Silverberg's Many Trapdoors: Critical Essays on His Science Fiction*. Westport, Conn.: Greenwood Press, 1992.

### Cordwainer Smith

Hellekson, Karen. *The Science Fiction of Cordwainer Smith*. Jefferson, N.C.: McFarland, 2001.

Lewis, Anthony R. *A Concordance to Cordwainer Smith*. 2nd ed. Framingham,

Mass.: NESFA Press, 2000
McGuirk, Carol. The Rediscovery of Cordwainer Smith. *Science Fiction Studies* 28, no. 2 (2001):161–200.
Porter, Andrew, ed. *Exploring Cordwainer Smith*. New York: Algol Press, 1975.

## E. E. Smith

Sanders, Joe. *E. E. "Doc" Smith*. Mercer Island, Wash.: Starmont House, 1986.

## Olaf Stapledon

Crossley, Robert. *Olaf Stapledon: Speaking for the Future*. Liverpool, U.K.: Liverpool University Press, 1994.
Fiedler, Leslie A. *Olaf Stapledon: A Man Divided*. New York: Oxford University Press, 1983.
Kinnaird, Jon. *Olaf Stapledon*. Mercer Island, Wash.: Starmont House, 1986.
McCarthy, Patrick A. *Olaf Stapledon*. Boston: Twayne, 1982.
McCarthy, Patrick A., Martin H. Greenberg, and Charles Elkins, eds. *The Legacy of Olaf Stapledon: Critical Essays and an Unpublished Manuscript*. Westport, Conn.: Greenwood Press, 1989.

## Arkady and Boris Strugatsky

Potts, Stephen W. *The Second Marxian Invasion: The Fiction of the Strugatsky Brothers*. San Bernardino, Calif.: Borgo Press, 1991.

## Theodore Sturgeon

Diskin, Lahna F. *Theodore Sturgeon*. Mercer Island, Wash.: Starmont House, 1981.
Menger, Lucy. *Theodore Sturgeon*. New York: Ungar, 1981.

## William F. Temple

Ashley, Mike. Tell Them I Meant Well: A Tribute to William F. Temple. *Foundation* 55 (Summer 1992):5–24.

## James Tiptree Jr.

Boulter, Amanda. Alice James Raccoona Tiptree Sheldon Jr.: Textual Personas in the Short Fiction of Alice Sheldon. *Foundation* 63 (Spring 1995):5–31.

Dozois, Gardner. *The Fiction of James Tiptree, Jr.* New York: Algol Press, 1977.
Siegel, Mark. *James Tiptree, Jr.* Mercer Island, Wash.: Starmont House, 1985.
Van der Spek, Inez. *Alien Plots: Female Subjectivity and the Divine in the Light of James Tiptree's "A Momentary Taste of Being."* Liverpool, U.K.: Liverpool University Press, 2000.

## Jack Vance

Cunningham, A. E., ed. *Jack Vance: Critical Appreciations and a Bibliography*. Boston Spa, Yorkshire, U.K.: British Library, 2000.
Mead, David G. *An Encyclopedia of Jack Vance, 20th-Century Science Fiction Writer*. 3 vols. Studies in American Literature no. 50. Lewiston, N.Y.: Mellen, 2002.
Rawlins, Jack. *Demon Prince: The Dissonant Worlds of Jack Vance*. San Bernardino, Calif.: Borgo Press, 1986.
Tiedman, Richard. *Jack Vance: Science Fiction Stylist*. Wabash, Ind.: Coulson, 1965.
Underwood, Tim, and Chuck Miller, eds. *Jack Vance*. New York: Taplinger, 1980.

## A. E. van Vogt

Drake, H. L. *A. E. van Vogt: Science Fantasy's Icon*. N.p.: Author, 2001.

## Jules Verne

Butcher, William. *Verne's Journey to the Centre of the Self: Space and Time in the Voyages Extraordinaires*. London: Macmillan, 1990.
Butor, Michel. The Golden Age in Jules Verne. In *Inventory: Essays*, 114–45. London: Jonathan Cape, 1970.
Compère, Daniel. *Jules Verne, Écrivain*. Genève: Droz, 1991.
Compère, Daniel, and Jean-Michel Margot. *Entretiens avec Jules Verne, 1873–1905*. Genève, Switzerland: Slatkine, 1998.
Evans, Arthur B. *Jules Verne Rediscovered: Didacticism and the Scientific Novel*. Westport, Conn.: Greenwood Press, 1988.
Evans, I. O. *Jules Verne and His Work*. London: Arco, 1965.
Lynch, Lawrence W. *Jules Verne*. Boston: Twayne, 1992.
Martin, Andrew. *The Mask of the Prophet: The Extraordinary Fictions of Jules Verne*. New York: Oxford University Press, 1990.
Smyth, Edmund J., ed. *Jules Verne: Narratives of Modernity*. Liverpool, U.K.: Liverpool University Press, 2000.

Taves, Brian, and Stephen Michaluk Jr. *The Jules Verne Encyclopedia*. Lanham, Md.: Scarecrow Press, 1996.

## Kurt Vonnegut Jr.

Boon, Kevin Alexander, ed. *At Millennium's End: New Essays on the Work of Kurt Vonnegut*. Albany: State University of New York Press, 2001.

Goldsmith, David H. *Kurt Vonnegut: Fantasist of Fire and Ice*. Bowling Green, Ohio: Popular Press, 1972.

Klinkowitz, Jerome. *Kurt Vonnegut*. London: Methuen, 1982.

Klinkowitz, Jerome, and John Somer, eds. *The Vonnegut Statement*. New York: Delacorte, 1973.

Leeds, Marc. *The Vonnegut Encyclopedia: An Authorized Compendium*. Westport, Conn.: Greenwood Press, 1995.

Leeds, Marc, and Peter J. Reed, eds. *Kurt Vonnegut: Images and Representations*. Westport, Conn.: Greenwood Press, 2000.

Lundquist, James. *Kurt Vonnegut*. New York: Ungar, 1977.

Mayo, Clark. *Kurt Vonnegut: The Gospel from Outer Space*. San Bernardino, Calif.: Borgo Press, 1977.

Merrill, Robert, ed. *Critical Essays on Kurt Vonnegut*. Boston: G. K. Hall, 1990.

Morse, Donald E. *The Novels of Kurt Vonnegut: Imagining Being an American*. Westport, Conn.: Greenwood Press, 2003.

Mustazza, Leonard. *Forever Pursuing Genesis: The Myth of Eden in the Novels of Kurt Vonnegut*. Lewisburg, Pa: Bucknell University Press, 1990.

——, ed. *The Critical Response to Kurt Vonnegut*. Westport, Conn.: Greenwood Press, 1994.

Rackstraw, Loree, ed. *Draftings in Vonnegut: The Paradox of Hope*. Cedar Falls: University of Northern Iowa, 1988.

Reed, Peter J. *Kurt Vonnegut, Jr.* New York: Warner, 1972.

Reed, Peter J., and Marc Leeds, eds. *The Vonnegut Chronicles: Interviews and Essays*. Westport, Conn.: Greenwood Press, 1996.

Schatt, Stanley. *Kurt Vonnegut, Jr.* Boston: Twayne, 1976.

## H. G. Wells

Beresford, J. D. *H. G. Wells*. London: Nisbet, 1915.

Bergonzi, Bernard. *The Early H. G. Wells: A Study of the Scientific Romances*. Toronto, Ontario: University of Toronto Press, 1961.

——, ed. *H. G. Wells: A Collection of Critical Essays*. New York: Prentice-Hall, 1976.

Costa, Richard Hauer. *H. G. Wells*. Boston: Twayne, 1985.
Crossley, Robert. *H. G. Wells*. Mercer Island, Wash.: Starmont House, 1986.
Gill, Stephen. *The Scientific Romances of H. G. Wells*. Cornwall, Ontario, Canada: Vesta, 1975.
Hammond, John R. *H. G. Wells and the Short Story*. New York: St. Martin's Press, 1992.
Haynes, Roslynn D. *H. G. Wells, Discoverer of the Future: The Influence of Science on His Thought*. London, Macmillan, 1980.
Huntington, John. *The Logic of Fantasy: H. G. Wells and Science Fiction*. New York: Columbia University Press, 1982.
Kemp, Peter. *H. G. Wells and the Culminating Ape: Biological Themes and Imaginative Obsessions*. London: Macmillan, 1982.
McConnell, Frank. *The Science Fiction of H. G. Wells*. New York: Oxford University Press, 1981.
Niles, P. H. *The Science Fiction of H. G. Wells: A Concise Guide*. Clifton Park, N.Y.: Auriga, 1980.
Parrinder, Patrick. *Shadows of the Future: H. G. Wells, Science Fiction and Prophecy*. Liverpool, U.K.: Liverpool University Press, 1996.
Partington, John. *Building Cosmopolis: The Political Thought of H. G. Wells*. Aldershot, U.K.: Ashgate, 2003.
Slusser, George, Patrick Parrinder, and Danièle Chatelain, eds. *H. G. Wells's Perennial Time Machine: Selected Essays from the Centenary Conference: "The Time Machine: Past, Present and Future," Imperial College, London, July 26–29, 1995*. Athens: University of Georgia Press, 2001.
Suvin, Darko, and Robert M. Philmus, eds. *H. G. Wells and Modern Science Fiction*. Lewisburg, Pa.: Bucknell University Press, 1977.
Wells, H. G. Preface. In *The Scientific Romances of H. G. Wells*. London: Gollancz, 1933.
Williamson, Jack. *H. G. Wells: Critic of Progress*. Baltimore, Md.: Mirage Press, 1973.

## Jack Williamson

Williamson, Jack. *Wonder's Child: My Life in Science Fiction*. New York: Bluejay, 1984.

## Gene Wolfe

Andre-Driussi, Michael. *Lexicon Urthus: A Dictionary for the Urth Cycle*. San Francisco, Calif.: Sirius, 1994.
Gordon, Joan. *Gene Wolfe*. Mercer Island, Wash.: Starmont House, 1986.

### Womack, Jack

Barbour, Douglas. The Violent Logic of Late Capitalism: Jack Womack's Sf. *Foundation* 72 (Spring 1998):20–33.

### S. Fowler Wright

Stableford, Brian. Against the New Gods: The Speculative Fiction of S. Fowler Wright. *Foundation* 29 (November 1983):10–51.

### John Wyndham

Ketterer, David. ed. [My Brother] John Wyndham, A Memoir by Vivian Beynon Harris. *Foundation* 75 (Spring 1999):5–50.

### Ivan Yefremov

Grebens, G. V. *Ivan Efremov's Theory of Soviet Science Fiction*. New York: Vantage Press, 1978.

### Roger Zelazny

Krulik, Theodore. *Roger Zelazny*. New York: Ungar, 1986.

Yoke, Carl B. *Roger Zelazny*. West Linn, Ore.: Starmont House, 1979.

## WRITING GUIDES AND MANUALS

Bova, Ben. *Notes to a Science Fiction Writer*. New York: Scribner, 1975. Rev. ed. Boston: Houghton Mifflin, 1981.

Bretnor, Reginald, ed. *The Craft of Science Fiction*. New York: Harper, 1976.

Budrys, Algis. *Writing Science Fiction and Fantasy*. Eugene, Ore.: Pulphouse, 1990.

Card, Orson Scott. *How to Write Science Fiction and Fantasy*. Cincinnati, Ohio: Writer's Digest, 1990.

de Camp, L. Sprague. *Science Fiction Handbook: The Writing of Imaginative Fiction*. New York: Hermitage House, 1953. Rev. ed. with Catherine C. de Camp, as *Science Fiction Handbook—Revised: A Guide to Writing Imaginative Literature*. New York: McGraw-Hill, 1975.

Eshbach, Lloyd Arthur, ed. *Of Worlds Beyond: The Science of Science Fiction Writing*. Reading, Pa.: Fantasy Press, 1947.

Evans, Christopher. *Writing Science Fiction*. London: A & C Black, 1988.
Gunn, James. *The Science of Science-Fiction Writing*. Lanham, Md.: Scarecrow Press, 2000.
Heinlein, Robert A. On the Writing of Speculative Fiction. *Of Worlds Beyond: The Science of Science Fiction Writing*. Ed. Lloyd Arthur Eshbach, 11–19. Reading, Pa.: Fantasy Press, 1947.
Rusch, Kristine Kathryn, and Dean Wesley Smith. *Science Fiction Writers of America Handbook: The Professional Writer's Guide to Writing Professionally*. Eugene, Ore.: Writers Notebook Press, 1990.
Shaw, Bob. *How to Write Science Fiction*. London: Allison and Busby, 1993.
Stableford, Brian. How Should a Science Fiction Story End? *The New York Review of Science Fiction* 78 (February 1995):1, 8–15.
———. *Writing Fantasy & Science Fiction*. London: Teach Yourself Books, 1997.
Tuttle, Lisa. *Writing Fantasy and Science Fiction*. London: A & C Black, 2001.
Wilson, Robin Scott, ed. *Those Who Can: A Science Fiction Reader*. New York: Mentor, 1973.

## SPECULATIVE NONFICTION

Achenbach, Joel. *Captured by Aliens: The Search for Life and Truth in a Very Large Universe*. New York: Simon & Schuster, 1999.
Benford, Gregory. *Deep Time: How Humanity Communicates across Millennia*. New York: Avon/Bard, 1999.
Bernal, J. D. *The World, the Flesh, and the Devil: An Enquiry into the Future of the Three Enemies of the Rational Soul*. London: Kegan Paul, Trench and Trubner, 1929.
Clarke, Arthur C. *The Challenge of the Spaceship*. New York, Harper, 1959.
———. *The Coming of the Space Age*. New York: Meredith, 1967.
———. *The Exploration of Space*. London: Temple, 1951.
———. *Profiles of the Future*. London: Gollancz, 1962.
———. *Voices from the Sky*. New York: Harper and Row, 1965.
Cowley, Robert, ed. *What If? Eminent Historians Imagine What Might Have Been*. 2 vols. New York: Putnam, 1999–2001.
Ehrlich, Paul R. Ecocatasrophe. *Ramparts* 8 (1969):24–28.
Haldane, J. B. S. *Daedalus; or, Science and the Future*. London: Kegan Paul, Trench & Trubner, 1923.
———. *The Inequality of Man and Other Essays*. London: Chatto & Windus, 1932.
———. *Possible Worlds and Other Essays*. London: Chatto & Windus, 1927.
Dyson, Freeman. Time without End: Physics and Biology in an Open Universe. *Reviews of Modern Physics* 51 (1979):452–54.

Hardin, Garrett. The Tragedy of the Commons. *Science* 162 (1968):1243–48.
Hoyle, Fred. *The Intelligent Universe: A New View of Creation and Evolution*. London: Michael Joseph, 1983.
Hoyle, Fred, and Chandra Wickramasinghe. *Lifecloud: The Origin of Life in the Universe*. London: Dent, 1978.
——. *Evolution from Space*. London: Dent, 1981.
Langford, David. *War in 2080: The Future of Military Technology*. Newton Abbot, U.K.: Westbridge, 1979.
Lasser, David. *The Conquest of Space*. New York: Penguin, 1931.
Ley, Willy. *The Conquest of Space*. New York: Viking, 1949.
Lovelock, James. *Gaia: A New Look at Life on Earth*. Oxford, U.K.: Oxford University Press, 1973.
——. *The Ages of Gaia; A Biography of Our Living Earth*. Oxford, U.K.: Oxford University Press, 1988.
Moravec, Hans. *Mind Children: The Future of Robot and Human Intelligence*. Cambridge, Mass.: Harvard University Press, 1988.
Sheffield, Charles. *Borderlands of Science*. New York: Baen, 1999.
Squire, J.C., ed. *If, or History Rewritten*. Viking: New York, 1931.
Stableford, Brian, and David Langford. *The Third Millennium: A History of the World, AD 2000–3000*. London: Sidgwick & Jackson, 1985.
Sterling, Bruce. *Tomorrow Now: Envisioning the Next Fifty Years*. New York: Random House, 2002.
Teilhard de Chardin, Pierre. *The Future of Man*. London: Collins, 1964.
——. *The Phenomenon of Man*. London: Collins, 1959.
Tipler, Frank. *The Physics of Immortality: Modern Cosmology, God and the Resurrection of the Dead*. New York: Doubleday, 1994.
Toffler, Alvin. *Ecospasm*. New York: Bantam, 1975.
Wells, H. G. *Anticipations of the Reaction of Mechanical and Scientific Progress upon Human Life and Thought*. London: Chapman and Hall, 1901.
——. *The Discovery of the Future*. London: Unwin, 1902.
——. *Early Writings in Science and Science Fiction*. Ed. Robert M. Philmus and David Y. Hughes. Berkeley: University of California Press, 1975.
——. *H. G. Wells: Journalism and Prophecy, 1893–1946*. Ed. W. Warren Wagar. New York: Houghton Mifflin, 1964.

## JOURNALS

*Extrapolation*. Brownsville: University of Texas at Brownsville and Texas Southernmost College.

*Foundation: The International Review of Science Fiction*. Reading, U.K.: SF Foundation.
*Journal of the Fantastic in the Arts*. Boca Raton: College of Arts and Letters, Florida Atlantic University.
*New York Review of Science Fiction*. Pleasantville, N.Y.: Dragon Press.
*Science Fiction Studies*. Greencastle, Ind.: SF-TH Inc. at DePauw University.
*SFRA Review*. Eau Claire, Wis.: Science Fiction Research Association.

## FANZINES

*Ansible*. Ed. David Langford, 94 London Road, Reading RG1 5AU, U.K.
*Chronicle* (formerly *Science Fiction Chronicle*). DNA Publications, P. O, Box 2988, Radford, VA 24142-2988.
*Fantasy Commentator*. Ed. A. Langley Searles, 48 Highland Circle, Bronxville, New York 10708-5909.
*The Fix: The Review of Short Fiction*. TTA Press, 5 Martins Lane, Witcham, Ely, Cambs. CB6 2LB, U.K.
*Locus: The Magazine of the Science Fiction & Fantasy Field*. Locus Publications, P. O. Box 13305, Oakland, CA 94661.
*Matrix*. British Science Fiction Association, 1 Long Row Close, Everdon, Daventry NN11 3BE, U.K.
*Nova Express*. Ed. Lawrence Person, P. O. Box 27231, Austin, Texas 78755-2231.
*PulpDom*. Ed. C. E. Cazedessus II, P. O. Box 2340, Pagosa Springs, CO 81147.
*Vector*. British Science Fiction Association, 1 Long Row Close, Everdon, Daventry NN11 3BE, U.K.
*The Wellsian*. H. G. Wells Society, 49 Beckingthorpe Drive, Bottesford, Nottingham NG13 0DN, U.K.

## WEBSITES

*The Alien Online* (news): www.thealienonline.net
*The Alternate Historian's Notebook*: www.marmotgraphics.com/althistory
*Analog*: www.analogsf.com
*Asimov's Science Fiction*: www.asimovs.com
*Asociación Española de Fantasia y Ciencia Ficción* (Spanish SF): www.aefcf.es
*Australian Sf Online*: www.eidolon.net
*British Science Fiction Association* (BSFA): www.bsfa.co.uk

*Center for the Study of Science Fiction* (University of Kansas): www.ku.edu/~sfcenter
*Definitions of Science Fiction*: www.panix.com/~gokce/sf_defn.html
*Emerald City* (reviewzine): ww.emcit.com
*Encyclopédie francophone de la science-fiction* (French SF): www.noosfere.com
*Fantastic Fiction* (author bibliographies): www.fantasticfiction.co.uk
*The Infinite Matrix* (news, articles, and fiction): www.infinitematrix.net
*Infinity Plus* (news, articles, and fiction): www.infinityplus.co.uk
*International SF Database*: www.isfdb.org
*Locus On-Line*: www.locusmag.com
*The New England Science Fiction Association* (including NESFA Press): nesfa.org
*Pages Française de la science-fiction* (French SF): http://sf.emse.fr
*Página Portuguesa de Ficção Cientfica e Fantasia* (Portuguese SF): www.geocities.com/Area51.Vault/1077
*Quadrant Science Fiction Search Engine:* www.fantascienza.com/quadrant
*Science Fiction and Fantasy Research Database* (bibliography of secondary sources): http://library.tamu.edu/cushing/sffrd
*Science Fiction and Fantasy Writers of America*: www.sfwa.org
*Science Fiction Foundation Collection*: www.liv.ac.uk/~asawyer/sffc1.html
*Science Fiction Research Bibliography* (bibliography of secondary sources): www.wsu.edu/#brians/sciencefiction/sf_research.html
*Science Fiction and Fantasy Writers of Japan*: ww.sfwj.or.jp
*SciFan* (bibliographies and web links): www.scifan.com
*Sci-Fi Channel* (includes Sci Fiction fiction site and Science Fiction Weekly news site): www.scifi.com
*Sci-Fi List* (database of paperbacks and pulp magazines): scifilist.com
*SFF Net* (incorporates numerous author sites): www.sff.net
*SF-Lovers* (information; incorporates Science Fiction Research Guide): www.sflovers.org
*SF Reviews*: www.sfreviews.net and www.sfreviews.com
*SFRevu* (interviews, articles, and reviews): www.sfrevu.com
*SF Site* (includes numerous subsidiary sites, including those of *The Magazine of Fantasy & Science Fiction* and *Interzone*): www.sfsite.com
*SpecFicWorld* (resources for writers and sf fans): www.specficworld.com
*Uchronia: The Alternate History List*: www.uchronia.net
*The Ultimate Science Fiction Web Guide* (links; incorporates SF Timeline): www.magicdragon.com/Ultimate SF
*University of Michigan Fantasy and Science Fiction Website* (includes an electronic library and a symbolism dictionary): ww.umich.edu/~umfandsf

## About the Author

**Brian Stableford** (B.A., University of York; D.Phil., University of York) is a part-time lecturer in creative writing at King Alfred's College, Winchester. He has been a professional writer since 1965, publishing more than 50 novels and 200 short stories, as well as several nonfiction books, thousands of articles for periodicals and reference books, several translations from the French, and a number of anthologies. His novels include *The Empire of Fear* (1988), *Young Blood* (1992), and a future history series comprising *Inherit the Earth* (1998), *Architects of Emortality* (1999), *The Fountains of Youth* (2000), *The Cassandra Complex* (2001), *Dark Ararat* (2002), and *The Omega Expedition* (2002). His nonfiction includes *Masters of Science Fiction: Essays on Six Science Fiction Writers* (1981; revised and expanded as *Outside the Human Aquarium: Masters of Science Fiction*, 1995), *The Science in Science Fiction* (in collaboration with Peter Nicholls and David Langford, 1982), *Scientific Romance in Britain* (1985), *The Sociology of Science Fiction* (1987), *Algebraic Fantasies and Realistic Romances: More Masters of Science Fiction* (1995), *Opening Minds: Essays on Fantastic Literature* (1995), *Teach Yourself Writing Fantasy and Science Fiction* (1997), *Yesterday's Bestsellers* (1998), and *Glorious Perversity: The Decline and Fall of Literary Decadence* (1998). Reference books to which he has made major contributions include the Clute/Nicholls *Encyclopedia of Science Fiction* (1979; 2nd ed. 1993); Neil Barron's *Anatomy of Wonder* (2nd. ed. 1981; 3rd ed. 1987; 4th ed. 1995): Everett F. Bleiler's *Science Fiction Writers* (1982; 2nd edition ed. Richard Bleiler 1999), and *Supernatural Fiction Writers* (1985; supplementary vol. ed. Richard Beiler, 2003); and the *Cyclopedia of Literary Places* (2003).